Baseball's Most
Wanted

Also by Floyd Conner

Golf!
Fore!
This Date in Sports History
Day by Day in Cincinnati Reds History
Day by Day in Cincinnati Bengals History
Pretty Poison
Lupe Velez and Her Lovers

Baseball's Most **Wanted**

The Top 10 Book of
the National Pastime's
Outrageous Offenders,
Lucky Bounces,
and Other Oddities

Floyd Conner

Brassey's

WASHINGTON, D.C.

Copyright © 2000 Brassey's

Published in the United States by Brassey's. All rights reserved. No part of this book may be reproduced in any manner whatsoever without written permission from the publisher, except in the case of brief quotations embodied in critical articles and reviews.

Library of Congress Cataloging-in-Publication Data

Conner, Floyd, 1951–
  Baseball's most wanted : the top 10 book of the national pastime's outrageous offenders, lucky bounces, and other oddities / Floyd Conner.— 1st ed.
    p. cm.
  Includes index.
  ISBN 1-57488-229-5
    1. Baseball players—Miscellanea.   I. Title

GV865 .A1 C63 2000
796.357'092'273—dc21
[B]

99-086476

Printed in Canada

Brassey's
22841 Quicksilver Drive
Dulles, Virginia 20166

Designed by Pen & Palette Unlimited

First Edition

10 9 8 7 6 5 4 3

Contents

Introduction 1

On the Dotted Line 5
  Baseball's most unusual contracts

Memorable Memorabilia 11
  A gallery of costly collectibles

The Naturals 16
  The Hollywood connection

Running for Office 22
  Politics and baseball do mix

Out of Their League 27
  Ballplayers who excelled in other sports

Playing the Field 33
  Diamond Don Juans

The Fair Sex 39
  Women who have left their mark on the game

Clothes Encounters 44
  Less than uniform apparel

Smarter than the Average Berra 48
  Players with brain and brawn

Stengelese and Other Tongues   55
   Languages spoken only in ballparks

Notable Nicknames   63
   A roster of intriguing monickers

Hot Dogs   68
   Baseball's biggest show-offs

Worst Practical Jokers   74
   The sport's most notorious pranksters

Flakes   80
   They marched to their own drummers

The Bullpen   87
   Oddballs in the bullpen

Curses   93
   Baseball's twilight zone

Lucky Bounces   98
   They'd rather be lucky than good

The Meat of the Order   104
   They were what they ate

Fat Tubs of Goo   108
   Baseball's heavy hitters

Graybeards   112
   The oldest players on record

Playing Young   118
   Ten teenagers who played the game

Minor League Phenoms   123
   Major stars of the minors

False Promise   127
   Sometimes first impressions aren't the best

One Game Wonders   132
  Kings for a day

One Year Wonders   137
  They had their summer in the sun

Going Batty   142
  Their bats were hits

Having a Ball   147
  Sandpaper, spitters, and shineballs

Records that Aren't Meant to Be Broken   153
  The least known unbreakable records

The Mendoza Line   157
  The worst hitters of all time

Sultans of Swish   161
  Three strikes, you're out

The Worst Pitching Performances of All Time   165
  The most horrendous shellings in baseball history

I'm a Loser   169
  Some pitchers can't win

Gopher Balls   174
  Pitchers who gave up their share of homers

Wild Things   179
  Moundsmen who were out of control

Head Hunters   183
  They pitched high and tight

Beaned in Boston   188
  Baseball's marked men

Error of Their Ways   192
  Games slipped through their fingers

Mismanagement 196
   The least successful managers

Travelin' Men 201
   Have suitcase, will travel

Baseball's Worst Trades 205
   Baseball's biggest steals

Baseball's Weirdest Trades 211
   Some of baseball's strangest swaps

Outrageous Owners 215
   Notable and notorious owners

Worst Promotions 226
   Ten promotions that backfired

It's All in the Game 231
   Anything can happen at a baseball game

Baseball's Most Embarrassing Moments 236
   Moments they'd rather forget

Unlikely World Series Heroes 241
   Unexpected Mr. Octobers

Goats 246
   Baseball's most infamous blunders

Spoilers and Nemeses 254
   Yankee killers and other spoilers

What Might Have Been 258
   Promising careers cut short

Blackballed 264
   African American stars prior to Jackie Robinson

Racism in Baseball 269
   The dark side of the national pastime

Kill the Umpire — 274
  Umpires who were attacked on the field

Media Blitz — 278
  Strained relations between players and the press

Fanatics — 283
  When fans become fanatics

With Teammates like These — 288
  With teammates like these who needs enemies

Donnybrooks — 293
  These players put punch into the lineup

The Bases Are Loaded — 299
  The bases aren't the only thing that's loaded

Illegal Substances — 304
  Baseball's drug connection

You Can Bet on It — 309
  Baseball can be a gamble

Out of Their Heads — 315
  Mental blocks and mental breakdowns

Overcoming Handicaps — 321
  Physically handicapped players in the major leagues

Freak Injuries — 325
  Baseball's strangest injuries

The Big Hurt — 330
  Serious on-the-field injuries

Cheaters Sometimes Win — 335
  Rules are meant to be broken

Say It Ain't So, Joe — 340
  Ten banned from baseball

Grand Slammers 345
  For these players crime didn't pay

Suicide Squeeze 350
  Major leaguers who took their own lives

They Got Murdered 356
  Ballplayers who were homicide victims

Murderers' Row 360
  Players with the killer instinct

Baseball's Greatest Mysteries 365
  The game's unsolved mysteries

Bibliography 373

Index 376

Introduction

The 2000 season marks the 125th anniversary of major league baseball. During that time more than 15,000 players have appeared in the big leagues. Fewer than 200 of the game's immortals have been enshrined in the Baseball Hall of Fame. Their achievements are well known to any baseball fan. But what about all those other players?

Baseballs Most Wanted honors the game's most outrageous offenders. The book contains top ten lists of the worst hitters, wildest pitchers, and poorest fielders ever to play the game. The lists feature the unlikeliest heroes, most infamous goats, craziest fans, zaniest promotions, and the strangest things to occur during a game.

In today's market of high-priced free agents, pitcher Kevin Brown earns $15 million a year from the Los Angeles Dodgers. By contrast, Chicken Wolf, the lowest paid major leaguer ever under contract, was paid $9 a week to play for Louisville in 1882. Ten years later, Bumpus Jones pitched a no-hitter in his first major league game, and he wasn't even under contract. In 1899, a cigar store clerk, Eddie Kolb, actually gave the Cleveland Spiders a box of cigars for the privilege of pitching a major league game.

What do the following minor leaguers have in common? Joe Bauman set a professional baseball record by hitting seventy-two home runs in a season. Another slugger, Bob Crues, set another single season record by batting in 254 runs. Hector Espino set a minor league record with 484 career home runs. Bill Thomas won a record 383 games in his career. These minor league phenoms share one thing. None of them ever played in the major leagues.

In baseball almost anything can happen. The 1869 Cincinnati Red Stockings, baseball's first all professional team, had their 130-game undefeated streak snapped when an overzealous fan in Brooklyn jumped on the back of outfielder Cal McVey as he chased a fly ball. Another Cincinnati player, Edd Roush, was ejected from a game for falling asleep in the outfield. Dan Friend once played left field while dressed in a bathrobe. Manager Bobby Bragan entertained a crowd by performing a strip tease in the dugout.

Hall of Fame pitcher Jim Bunning, now a United States senator representing the commonwealth of

Kentucky, is not the only major league baseball player to go on to a successful career in politics. John Tener won twenty-five games in the majors and was later elected governor of Pennsylvania. Outfielder Fred Brown played in nine games with Boston at the turn of the century before turning to politics and serving terms as both governor and senator of the state of New Hampshire. After his playing days were over, pitcher Wilmer "Vinegar Bend" Mizell was a six-term congressman representing North Carolina. In his youth former New York Governor Mario Cuomo was an outstanding prospect in the Pittsburgh Pirates' organization. Future President Ronald Reagan was an announcer for the Chicago Cubs when he was discovered by Hollywood.

Some players just prefer carrying a big stick. Hack Miller, a .323 lifetime batter, used bats as heavy as sixty-five ounces. Another perennial .300 hitter, Bill "Little Eva" Lange, once brought a six-foot-long bat to the plate. On the other end of the scale, Eddie Gaedel, the smallest player in major league baseball history, also used the smallest bat, measuring a mere seventeen inches.

This book introduces you to nearly 700 of baseball's most wanted players. Their offenses range from inept play to outrageous behavior. Be on the lookout for these individuals.

On the Dotted Line

Since the era of free agency began in the 1920s, baseball salaries have escalated rapidly. In 1999, the Los Angeles Dodgers signed ace right-hander Kevin Brown to a contract that will pay him $105 million over a seven-year period. By contrast, the entire payroll of the 1997 Pittsburgh Pirates totaled only $9 million. Players haven't always been so fortunate. Both Babe Ruth and Joe DiMaggio earned less than $1 million in their entire careers. The lowest paid player in baseball history was rookie Chicken Wolf, who earned $9 a week in 1882. Here are some of the most outrageous contracts in baseball history.

1. **JOE BORDEN**

Pitcher Joe Borden called himself Josephus the Phenomenal because of his extraordinary pitching. When the National League was founded in 1876, Borden was the winning pitcher in the first game. He also pitched the first no-hitter. Boston owner Nathaniel Apollonio rewarded Borden with a three-year contract (multiyear contracts were unheard of at the time) at the then exorbitant salary of $2,000 per year. When Borden failed to live up to expectations, he was made the groundskeeper to help earn his salary. Dissatisfied with his work as a groundskeeper, Boston bought out his salary. Josephus the Phenomenal was out of baseball at age twenty-two.

2. BUMPUS JONES

On October 14, 1892, the final day of the season, twenty-two-year-old Xenia, Ohio, farmboy Bumpus Jones walked into the Cincinnati Reds clubhouse and told manager Charles Comiskey that he wanted to be a big league pitcher. Comiskey decided to give the brash youngster a chance. Bumpus shocked everyone by pitching a no-hitter against the Pittsburgh Pirates in his very first game. He played the game without a contract, making him the greatest bargain in baseball history. Unfortunately, Jones could never recreate the magic of his debut and won only one more game in the majors.

3. EDDIE KOLB

The 1899 Cleveland Spiders were, perhaps, the worst team in baseball history. Managed by an

Australian undertaker named Joe Quinn, the Spiders won only 20 games and lost 134. The team was so bad that Cleveland didn't even want them, and they were forced to play their last 35 games on the road. Not surprisingly, they lost 40 of their last 41 games. On the final day of the season, a clerk at a tobacco shop named Eddie Kolb was permitted to pitch the game in exchange for a box of cigars. True to form, the Spiders lost 19–3.

4. CHARLIE KERFELD

Houston Astros' reliever Charlie Kerfeld was very proud of his uniform number 37. When he signed his contract for the 1987 season, he insisted that he be paid $110,037.37 plus thirty-seven boxes of Jell-O. Weight problems forced the hefty hurler out of baseball at age twenty-three.

5. RUBE WADDELL

Catcher Ossee Schreckengost of the Philadelphia A's was upset when zany pitcher Rube Waddell became his roommate. Waddell had the annoying habit of eating in bed. His midnight snacks included limburger cheese sandwiches and animal crackers. They shared a double bed on the road, and Schreckengost refused to sign his 1903 contract unless the team ordered Waddell to stop eating animal crackers in bed. Schreckengost complained that the crumbs kept him awake.

6. BABE RUTH

Babe Ruth hit 45 home runs and batted in 154 runs in 1929. The next year Yankees' owner Jacob Ruppert offered The Babe a contract for $80,000, the highest in baseball history. When informed by reporters that he was being paid $5,000 more than President Herbert Hoover (who had the misfortune of being president when the stock market crashed), he replied, "I had a better year than he did."

7. THE CINCINNATI RED STOCKINGS

The 1869 Cincinnati Red Stockings were baseball's first all-professional team. The salaries ranged from $600 to $1,400 for star shortstop George Wright. The team toured the country, agreeing to play any team willing to pay them a third of the gate receipts. Over a two-year period, the Red Stockings won a record 130 games without a defeat. They won games by scores of 100–2 and 94–7. Despite the winning streak and minuscule salaries, the club showed a profit of only $1.39.

The 1869 Cincinnati Red Stockings

Despite a record 130-game undefeated streak, baseball's first all professional team, the 1869 Cincinnati Red Stockings, showed only a $1.39 profit.

8. HUGH DUFFY

In 1894, Boston outfielder Hugh Duffy set an all-time major league record when he batted .438. He also led the National League in hits, doubles, home runs, runs batted in, and slugging percentage. The club showed their appreciation by offering Duffy a $12.50 per month raise only if he agreed to become team captain. The captain was responsible for replacing lost equipment. As a result, Duffy actually received a salary cut.

9. KAL DANIELS

Kal Daniels was a hard-hitting outfielder with the Cincinnati Reds in the late 1980s. When contract negotiations stalled in 1989 with the controversial owner Marge Schott, Daniels proposed that they flip a coin to settle the salary dispute. Daniels won the toss and an additional $25,000.

10. JOE PAGE

Joe Page was a star relief pitcher for the championship New York Yankees teams of the late 1940s. Known as much for his late-night carousing, Page was offered one of the first contracts with incentive clauses. His pay varied by as much as $1,000 a month, depending on how well he behaved. Part of the reason for management's concern was that they were afraid Page would corrupt his roommate, superstar outfielder Joe DiMaggio.

Memorable Memorabilia

Not so many years ago, children collected baseball cards because they wanted to have their own reminders of their favorite players. Packs of cards cost a nickel and came with a rectangular pink stick that, if slowly moistened in your mouth, had a vague resemblance to chewing gum. You would tear through your pack hoping to find a Mickey Mantle or Ted Williams, but you mostly got Whammy Douglas or Rocky Bridges.

Today, baseball card packs often cost several dollars (even without gum). Star players like Ken Griffey Jr. or Roger Clemens are immediately placed in sheets to protect their value. Nobody would think of flipping cards or placing them in the spokes of a bicycle wheel. Baseball collectibles are big business as demonstrated by these examples of memorable memorabilia.

1. HONUS WAGNER

The Holy Grail of baseball collectibles is the Honus Wagner T-206 card. The cards were issued by cigarette companies between 1909 and 1911. Because Wagner objected to smoking, his card was soon withdrawn from circulation. As a result, only a few of the Wagner cards still exist. Hockey great Wayne Gretzky paid $451,000 for one, and it was later sold for more than $600,000.

2. EDDIE MURRAY

In 1996, Eddie Murray of the Baltimore Orioles hit his five hundredth career home run. Collectors were astonished when the fan who retrieved the ball was offered $500,000 for it by the owner of the Psychic Friends Network. The ball's value had been estimated to be no more than $5,000.

3. LOU GEHRIG

A partnership led by David Bowen considered themselves the luckiest men on the face of the earth in the 1990s when they paid $306,130 for the uniform worn by Lou Gehrig in his farewell to baseball on July 4, 1939.

Lou Gehrig
More than 50 years after he retired from baseball, Lou Gehrig's uniform sold for a record $306,130.

4. PETE ROSE

On September 11, 1985, Pete Rose collected hit number 4,192 to pass Ty Cobb and become baseball's all-time hit leader. Rose wore nine different uniforms during the game and sold every one of them. He also sold the bat that he used to tie the record for $129,000.

5. BILL BUCKNER

Boston Red Sox's first baseman Bill Buckner became a goat when he let a ground ball go through his legs during the sixth game of the 1986 World Series against the New York Mets. The ball was later purchased by actor Charlie Sheen at an auction for $93,000.

6. DAVID WELLS

New York pitcher David Wells purchased a cap worn by Babe Ruth for $35,000. On June 28, 1997, he wore the hat during the first inning of a game versus the Cleveland Indians. Wells pitched a shutout inning before putting on his own hat. After removing Ruth's cap, Wells was shelled for five runs in two innings.

7. SHOELESS JOE JACKSON

Shoeless Joe Jackson, a .356 lifetime hitter, was banned from baseball because of his involvement in the 1919 Black Sox scandal. In 1990, his signature was sold for $23,100, a record for a nineteenth- or twentieth-century autograph. Jackson was illiterate and copied the signature from one made by his wife.

8. DOUG RADER

Doug Rader played eleven years in the major leagues and managed the Rangers, White Sox, and Angels. Rader sometimes ate baseball cards during the game, saying he believed that he could absorb the statistical information of the opposing players.

9. ERNIE CAMACHO

Pitcher Ernie Camacho complained of a sore arm after an autograph session where he signed 100 photographs. It's hard to imagine that Camacho's signature was that much in demand, considering that he retired in 1988 with a lifetime record of seven wins and twenty losses.

10. GUS ZERNIAL

Everyone has his own favorite unusual baseball card. Some people like the Aurelio Rodriguez card that actually featured a photo of the team's batboy. Others appreciate the card in which Billy Martin extends his middle finger. My favorite is the 1952 Topps card of Philadelphia A's slugging outfielder Gus Zernial. Gus, wearing a pink undershirt and giving the high sign, holds a bat that has five baseballs stuck to it. The significance of the pose remains a mystery.

The Naturals

Over the years Hollywood has made many classic baseball movies, from *The Pride of the Yankees* to *The Natural*. Each of the following men had links with both baseball and the movie industry.

1. CHUCK CONNORS

Chuck Connors is best remembered for his role as Lucas McCain in the long-running television series, *The Rifleman*. Connors also starred in *Arrest and Trial, Branded, Cowboy in Africa,* and the immensely successful miniseries, Roots. Before turning to acting, Connors played professional basketball with the Boston Celtics (once shattering a backboard with a dunk) and from 1949 to 1951 played first base for the Brooklyn Dodgers and Chicago Cubs. He was discovered while playing minor league baseball in Hollywood

Joe DiMaggio
Joe DiMaggio's marriage to actress Marilyn Monroe lasted only nine months.

and given a small role in the film *Pat and Mike* starring Spencer Tracy and Katherine Hepburn.

2. JOHN BERARDINO

John Berardino was an infielder in the major leagues for eleven seasons. During his best season he batted in eighty-nine runs for the 1941 St. Louis Browns. After his career in baseball was over, Berardino began a successful acting career. Soap opera devotees will remember him as Dr. Steve Hardy on the popular *General Hospital*.

3. JOE DIMAGGIO

Many consider Joe DiMaggio the greatest all-around player in baseball history. The outfielder starred with the New York Yankees from 1936 to 1951. He married sex symbol Marilyn Monroe in 1954. Although the marriage lasted only nine months, DiMaggio and Monroe remained close until her death in 1962. Shortly after their wedding, Monroe entertained troops stationed in Korea. Marilyn was overwhelmed by the adulation she had received from the soldiers. "You can't imagine what it's like," she told Joe. "Yes, I can," he replied.

4. GENE AUTRY

Gene Autry, Hollywood's "Singing Cowboy," appeared in ninety-three films. An astute businessman, he became a multimillionaire. In 1960, he acquired the expansion California Angels and owned the ballclub for four decades.

5. BOB HOPE

For years, comedian Bob Hope was a minority owner of the Cleveland Indians. Hope had grown up in Cleveland. In 1968, he headed a syndicate prepared to buy the Washington Senators. The deal, however, fell through when Hope became ill.

6. BOB UECKER

Bob Uecker was a major league catcher from 1962 to 1967 with the Cardinals, Braves, and Phillies. A lifetime .200 hitter, he claimed that his biggest thrill was walking with the bases loaded. His self-deprecating humor landed him appearances on *The Tonight Show*. He also starred in the television series, *Mr. Belvedere,* and the film, *Major League.*

7. BEANS REARDON

John "Beans" Reardon was a major league umpire from 1926 to 1949. A friend of actress Mae West, he appeared in five of her films. Reardon got his nickname because of his problem with flatulence. Behind the plate he would often signal a strike by farting and belched when the pitch was a ball. The gas attacks were too much for some catchers, who had to call time out to catch their breath.

8. TURKEY MIKE DONLIN

Outfielder Mike Donlin was perhaps the most popular player of his day and retired in 1914 with a .333 career batting average. He missed several

Jim Bouton
Twenty game winner Jim Bouton wrote a best-selling tell-all baseball book, *Ball Four,* and appeared in a film directed by Robert Altman.

seasons in order to tour the vaudeville circuit with his wife, actress Mabel Hite. He earned the nickname "Turkey Mike" because of his arrogant strut. Donlin spent the last two decades of his life producing silent films in Hollywood.

9. BILL MURRAY

When Chicago Cubs' announcer Harry Caray suffered a stroke in the late 1980s, celebrity guest announcers filled in while he recuperated. One of the most memorable was comedian Bill Murray, a lifelong Cub fan. Murray brought his considerable comic skills to the booth. During Wrigley Field's first night game, the opposing leadoff batter hit a home run. Murray suggested that maybe the Cubs should return to all day games.

10. JIM BOUTON

Jim Bouton was a twenty-one-game winner with the New York Yankees in 1963. Seven years later, he authored the best-seller, *Ball Four*, the first tell-all book about baseball. In 1973, Bouton played a leading role in the Robert Altman detective film, *The Long Goodbye*.

Running for Office

Baseball and politics have been linked since April 14, 1910, when President William Howard Taft began a tradition by throwing out the first ball on opening day in Washington. That occasion was marred when Vice President James Sherman was knocked unconscious by a foul ball off the bat of Home Run Baker. Richard Nixon served as an arbiter during a 1985 salary dispute between umpires and management (he granted them a 40 percent salary increase). Each of these men had ties with both baseball and politics.

1. RONALD REAGAN

Ronald Reagan was a radio announcer for the Chicago Cubs before turning to acting. He was discovered in Los Angeles in 1937 when he accompanied the team west for spring training. Reagan got his big break in films when he replaced Ross Alexander, an actor who resembled him, who committed suicide. Reagan was a popular actor before turning to politics. He gained even greater fame when he became governor of California and in 1980 was elected president of the United States.

2. **JIM BUNNING**

Jim Bunning pitched a perfect game in 1964 and was elected to the Baseball Hall of Fame in 1996. After an unsuccessful campaign for governor of Kentucky in 1984, Bunning was elected to Congress in Kentucky's Fourth District. In 1998 he was elected to the United States Senate.

3. **MORGAN BULKELEY**

Morgan Bulkeley was the first president of the National League in 1876. After serving four terms as mayor of Hartford, Bulkeley was elected governor of Connecticut. In 1904 he was elected to the United States Senate.

4. **JOHN TENER**

Tener was a former major league pitcher (1885–90) who served a term in Congress representing Pennsylvania from 1909 to 1911. In 1912, he was elected governor of Pennsylvania, and the following year Tener was named president of the National League. For two years he served in both capacities.

5. FRED BROWN

Fred Brown saw limited action as an outfielder with Boston at the turn of the century. In 1923, Brown was elected governor of New Hampshire and a decade later served a term in the United States Senate.

6. WILMER "VINEGAR BEND" MIZELL

Vinegar Bend Mizell won ninety games in a baseball career that spanned a decade. He was born in Leakesville, Mississippi, but assumed the nickname of a nearby town, Vinegar Bend. (A wise choice, since "Leakesville" Mizell doesn't have the same ring). In 1962, Mizell gave up throwing baseballs to toss his hat into the political ring. He served six terms as a congressman representing a district in North Carolina.

7. DWIGHT EISENHOWER

Dwight Eisenhower was a star halfback at Army (West Point) and a promising baseball player. He batted .355 for Junction City of the Class D Central Kansas League before pursuing a military career. Eisenhower rose to be commander of the Allied forces in Europe during World War II and, in 1952, was elected president of the United States.

8. FIDEL CASTRO

Fidel Castro was a talented pitcher in Cuba with dreams of playing in the major leagues. He was so promising that he was given a tryout by the Washington Senators. Castro was not signed because of his lack of control. Instead of pitching for Washington, Castro became a revolutionary and overthrew the government of Cuba.

9. MARIO CUOMO

In 1951, Mario Cuomo was given a $2,000 bonus by the Pittsburgh Pirates. The next year the young outfielder was hitting over .350 when he injured his wrist crashing into a wall. Hot tempered, Mario once punched a catcher after he had made an ethnic slur. Unfortunately, the catcher was still wearing his mask, and Cuomo bruised his fingers. His promising career abruptly ended when he was beaned. Cuomo suffered a blood clot and was hospitalized for weeks. Doctors warned him that a similar beaning might be fatal. With his major league aspirations crushed, Cuomo embarked on a political career that culminated with his election as governor of New York.

10. HAPPY CHANDLER

A. B. "Happy" Chandler served two terms as governor of Kentucky and six years in the United

States Senate. His term as commissioner of baseball from 1945 to 1951 was noteworthy because of the elimination of the color barrier.

Out of Their League

Many professional baseball players have excelled in other sports. For example, Earle "Greasy" Neale played eight seasons as an outfielder with the Cincinnati Reds and later coached the Philadelphia Eagles to NFL championships in 1948 and 1949. In 1960, Pittsburgh shortstop Dick Groat was the National League Most Valuable Player. Before he played professional baseball, Groat was a two-time All-American basketball player at Duke and played a season with the Fort Wayne Pistons in the NBA. Here are some of the most accomplished two sport stars.

1. JIM THORPE

Jim Thorpe has often been called the world's greatest all-around athlete. He was the first athlete to win the gold medal in the decathlon, a feat that he accomplished at the 1912 Olympics.

Thorpe was forced to return the medal when it was learned he had briefly played professional baseball in the minor leagues in 1909. He played six years in the majors, hitting .327 in 1919. Thorpe had greater success in the NFL and was elected to the Pro Football Hall of Fame in 1963.

2. GEORGE HALAS

George Halas played in twelve games for the New York Yankees in 1919, batting an anemic .091. Halas was one of the founders of the National Football League and played eleven seasons on both defense and offense. He coached the Chicago Bears to six NFL championships, and his 325 wins set a record, which stood until 1993 when it was broken by Don Shula.

3. ERNIE NEVERS

Ernie Nevers's baseball career was undistinguished (a 6–12 record with the St. Louis Browns). On the gridiron, his play earned him induction into both the College and Pro Football Halls of Fame. His coach at Stanford, the legendary "Pop" Warner, called him "the greatest player I ever coached." Nevers set an NFL record when he scored forty points in a game against the Chicago Bears in 1929.

4. BO JACKSON

A commercial campaign by Nike suggested Bo Jackson knew how to play any sport. In football, the running back was good enough to win the Heisman Trophy. He announced that he intended to play both professional baseball and football, labeling his NFL career a "hobby." In 1989, he slugged 32 home runs and batted in 105 runs for the Kansas City Royals. His two-sport stardom ended when he suffered a devastating hip injury while playing for the Raiders. After hip replacement surgery, Jackson's football career was over, and his baseball skills declined.

5. DEION SANDERS

Deion Sanders was selected as one of the greatest cornerbacks on the 75th NFL anniversary team. "Neon Deion" played on Super Bowl champions in both San Francisco and Dallas. On the diamond, Sanders played outfield for the Yankees, Giants, and Reds. He played well enough to hit over .300 one season and was usually among the league leaders in stolen bases.

6. DAVE DEBUSSCHERE

Dave DeBusschere was a good enough pitcher with the Chicago White Sox to post a career 2.90

earned run average in his two seasons in the majors in 1962 and 1963. He gave up baseball to play professional basketball full time. During his twelve-season NBA career, DeBusschere scored over 14,000 points and played on championship teams with the New York Knicks. Other notable athletes who played in both major league baseball and the NBA include Ron Reed, Danny Ainge, and Gene Conley.

7. JACKIE JENSEN

Jackie Jensen was an All-American fullback at the University of California. A thousand-yard rusher, he ran sixty-seven yards for a touchdown in the Rose Bowl. He chose to play major league baseball instead of pro football. Brought up by the New York Yankees in 1950, he was groomed to be the replacement for Joe DiMaggio. Beaten out of the starting center field job by Mickey Mantle, Jensen later starred for the Boston Red Sox. He led the American League in runs batted in for three years and was the stolen base champion in 1954. He retired in 1961 at the peak of his career, partly due to an extreme fear of flying.

8. BILL SHARMAN

Bill Sharman teamed in the backcourt with Bob Cousy on several Boston Celtics' championship

Jackie Jensen
Before he became an All-Star outfielder for the Boston Red Sox, Jackie Jensen was an All-American running back for the University of California.

teams. One of the greatest free throw shooters in NBA history (88.3 percent), he was elected to the Pro Basketball Hall of Fame in 1975. He had one of the shortest and strangest careers in the major leagues. Called up to the major leagues by Brooklyn in late 1951, Sharman rode the bench as the Dodgers blew a huge lead in the final month. On September 27, umpire Frank Dascoli threw out every player in the Brooklyn dugout, including

Sharman. As a result, he became the only player in major league history to be thrown out of a game while never playing in one.

9. RANDY "MACHO MAN" SAVAGE

Randy Poffo was a minor league catcher in the Cardinals' and Reds' farm systems during the early 1970s. When he failed to reach the major leagues, he turned to professional wrestling. His father, Angelo Poffo, had been the United States wrestling champion. Billing himself as "Macho Man" Savage, Randy eventually won both the World Wrestling Federation and World Championship Wrestling titles.

10. MICHAEL JORDAN

Widely considered to be the greatest player in NBA history, Michael Jordan had led the Chicago Bulls to three championships when he decided to try professional baseball. With a batting average hovering around the .200 mark in the minors, Jordan never made it to the major leagues. Returning to basketball, he led the Bulls to three more NBA titles.

Playing the Field

Since major league baseball players spend so much time on the road, it's not surprising that some of them carry on highly active sex lives. Former Angels' general manager Dick "The Smiling Python" Walsh once threatened to tell a pitcher's wife about an adulterous affair if he didn't sign the contract offered. When Manager Leo Durocher was suspended from baseball for a year, one of the reasons was adultery. This section includes a rogues' gallery of baseball Casanovas.

1. BO BELINSKY

Baseball's undisputed Don Juan, Belinsky had a mediocre career as a pitcher (28–51 lifetime record), highlighted by a no-hitter against Baltimore in 1962. Off the field, he fashioned a Hall of Fame love life. Among the women Bo dated were Ann-Margret, Tina Louise, Connie Stevens,

Juliet Prowse, and the Shah of Iran's ex-wife, Queen Soraya. His most publicized romance was to blonde bombshell Mamie Van Doren. When they broke up, Bo lamented, "I needed her like Custer needed more Indians." Belinsky eventually married 1965 Playmate of the Year, Jo Collins.

Angels' publicity director Irv Kaze described Belinsky's appeal, "He's a handsome son of a bitch. You can almost feel the animal sex in him." Teammates recalled Belinsky stepping off a plane into the arms of three waiting women. On another occasion, Belinsky discovered a young lady hanging by her fingertips on the window sill outside his hotel room. "I had no choice but to let her in," Bo quipped. He claimed sex helped him relax. "No one ever died of it," Bo observed.

2. BABE RUTH

Babe Ruth was a man of large appetites. This carried over into his sex life. Author Fred Lieb noted, "One woman couldn't satisfy him. Frequently it took half a dozen." Ruth preferred the company of prostitutes and bragged that he had once had sex with every woman at a St. Louis brothel. Because the media in those days did not focus on the private lives of ballplayers, most of Ruth's fans were unaware of his sexual exploits.

3. JOE PEPITONE

Although Joe Pepitone hit 219 home runs, he never achieved the stardom that was expected of him. His downfall was a less than exemplary personal life. Pepitone was especially vain about his appearance, endlessly combing his hair. He was the first player to bring a hair dryer into the clubhouse and wore flashy clothes. Diane, his second wife, was said to have found slips of paper with the names of 150 women with whom Joe had sex. In 1974, Pepitone married a former Playboy bunny.

Joe Pepitone
Power-hitting first baseman Joe Pepitone was also a hit with the ladies.

4. STEVE GARVEY

For nineteen years, Steve Garvey was a star first baseman for the Los Angeles Dodgers and San Diego Padres. Six times he collected more than 200 hits and played in 1,207 consecutive games. For most of his career, he had an image of being baseball's "Mr. Clean." The clean-cut facade was shattered after a nasty divorce from his college sweetheart, Cyndi, in 1985. His sex life made headlines when it was revealed that he had impregnated two women just as he was about to marry a third.

5. PETE ROSE

Baseball's all-time hit leader, Pete Rose, had the reputation of being a womanizer. It was rumored that Rose had a mistress in each National League city. After his divorce from first wife Karolyn in 1984, he married Carol Woliung, a stunning blonde Playboy bunny and Philadelphia Eagles cheerleader. Rose joked that he got all the women because he always went in head first.

6. WADE BOGGS

The winner of five American League batting titles, Wade Boggs was considered the consummate hitter. In 1988, a story broke that the All-Star third baseman had been having an affair with an investment broker named Margo Adams. For four years, the two had traveled together on road trips while Boggs's wife, Debbie, remained home, unaware of the affair. Adams learned that Boggs was seeing other women and got revenge by having an affair with Steve Garvey. When Boggs attempted to end the relationship, Adams demanded $100,000 or she would reveal the affair to his wife. Boggs refused, and Margo filed a $11.5 million breach-of-contract suit, claiming she had performed various duties ranging from providing financial advice to washing his clothes. Adams received $100,000 for baring all in *Penthouse Magazine.* Boggs returned to his wife, stating that the revelations had made his marriage stronger.

7. VAN LINGLE MUNGO

The man with the lyrical name and the blazing fastball, Van Lingle Mungo was a somnambulist. When he wasn't walking in his sleep, he was sleeping with women. His most famous escapade occurred in Cuba where the Dodgers were training in 1941. According to Leo Durocher, Mungo was caught in bed with two women by one of their husbands. The Dodgers arranged to smuggle the pitcher out of the country. With the machete-wielding cuckold in close pursuit, Mungo was pulled inside an awaiting plane just in the nick of time, an escape worthy of Indiana Jones.

8. TILLIE SHAFER

Tillie Shafer was an infielder for the New York Giants between 1909 and 1913. He was known as the "Perfumed Note Man" because of the scented invitations he received from his many lady admirers.

9. FRITZ PETERSON AND MIKE KEKICH

New York Yankees' pitchers Fritz Peterson and Mike Kekich pulled off baseball's strangest trade in 1972. Peterson and Kekich swapped wives, children, pets, and even their station wagons. "It wasn't a wife swap; it was a life swap," Kekich concluded.

10. LOU SOCKALEXIS

John McGraw said that Lou Sockalexis was the greatest talent he had ever seen in baseball. The outfielder, a Penobscot Indian, destroyed a potentially great career through his excesses off the field. He was batting .338 during his rookie season in 1897 when he injured his foot jumping from the window of a whorehouse while celebrating the Fourth of July. Another time, he was so disoriented by a sexual marathon that he was barely able to stagger out on the field. He played in only ninety-four games, a career ruined by alcohol and women.

The Fair Sex

Although a woman has never played in a major league game, several women have had an impact on the game.

1. HELENE BRITTON

Long before Marge Schott was even born, Helene Britton became the first woman to own a major league team. She presided over the St. Louis Cardinals from 1911 to 1917. Although she met resistance from most of the male owners, she proved to be a capable executive and oversaw the day-to-day operations of the club.

2. JACKIE MITCHELL

Jackie Mitchell was the first woman to sign a professional baseball contract. In 1931, the left-handed pitcher signed to play for the minor league Chattanooga Lookouts. On April 2, 1931,

Mitchell pitched in an exhibition game against the mighty New York Yankees. The seventeen-year-old stunned the crowd by striking out Babe Ruth and Lou Gehrig. The next day Baseball Commissioner Kenesaw Mountain Landis barred women from playing professional baseball. His excuse was that baseball was "too strenuous for a woman to play."

3. BABE DIDRIKSON

Babe Didrikson is often called the greatest woman athlete of all time. She won two gold medals at the 1932 Summer Olympics and later became a champion golfer, winning thirty-one tournaments. In 1934, she pitched several games in spring training against major league opposition. Pitching for the Philadelphia A's, Didrikson pitched a shutout inning against Brooklyn.

4. ILA BORDERS

On May 31, 1997, Ila Borders became the first woman to play in a minor league game. Borders pitched for the St. Paul Saints against Sioux Falls. She gave up three runs without retiring a batter. The next day, Borders redeemed herself by striking out the side in a second relief appearance.

5. KITTY BURKE

Kitty Burke holds the distinction of being the only woman to come to the plate during a major league game. On July 31, 1935, Burke was one of the more than 30,000 spectators at Cincinnati's Crosley Field watching the Reds play the St. Louis Cardinals. The sellout crowd was so large that thousands of the spectators were permitted to stand on the field in foul territory. In the eighth inning, Babe Herman of the Reds stepped to the plate. Burke, who had been heckling batters all night, walked up and grabbed the bat from Herman. To everyone's amazement, pitcher Paul "Daffy" Dean threw her a pitch, which she grounded to an infielder. Frankie Frisch, the Cardinals' manager, argued that it should be the third out. The umpire disagreed, and Herman doubled as the Reds rallied for a 4–3 victory.

6. JOAN PAYSON

Joan Payson owned the New York Mets from 1962 to 1975. Under her ownership, the Mets were transformed from a hapless expansion team to world champions in 1969. Originally, Payson wanted to name the team the New York Meadowlarks.

7. MRS. CHARLEY JONES

Charley Jones was one of baseball's first sluggers. In 1879, he led the National League in home runs and runs batted in. A handsome grandstand idol, Jones was paid by a Cincinnati clothier for just walking around town wearing the tailor's latest styles. On one of these strolls, he was accompanied by another woman. His wife, not understanding the value of good advertising, threw cayenne pepper in his eyes, effectively ending his career.

8. HELEN DAUVRAY

Helen Dauvray was a popular actress in the late nineteenth century and the wife of New York Giants' shortstop John Montgomery Ward. At the time the National League and American Association, two established major leagues, played a World Series at the end of the season. Dauvray talked the owners into commissioning Tiffany's to design a silver cup that would be given to the first team to win three championship series. The Dauvray Cup was retired in 1891 when the American Association folded.

9. BEATRICE GERA

For years Beatrice Gera fought in court to have the opportunity to become the first woman professional umpire. Finally, on June 25, 1972, Gera was given her chance in a minor league game in Geneva, New York. When Auburn manager Nolan Campbell argued a close call, Gera burst into tears and resigned after one game. However, her efforts did clear the way for successful lady umps, such as Pam Postema, who umpired in the minor leagues for thirteen years.

10. MORGANNA, THE KISSING BANDIT

Morganna Roberts is an exotic dancer whose most noticeable asset is her sixty-inch bust. She has left her mark on the national pastime by running on the field and kissing players. Morganna has planted kisses on more than twenty-five players, including Pete Rose, Nolan Ryan, and Mike Schmidt. George Brett found the experience disconcerting. "After looking at her chest," he remembered, "it made the ball look like a pencil dot."

Clothes Encounters

On June 19, 1846, the first recorded baseball game was played between the New York Nine and the New York Knickerbockers. The Knickerbockers wore the first uniforms: blue trousers, white shirts, and straw hats. While players are required to wear their teams' uniforms, occasionally someone will come up with his own variation. Cleveland pitcher Johnny Allen wore a tattered sleeve on his uniform to distract batters. Big Ted Kluszewski, while playing for the Cincinnati Reds in the 1950s, wore no sleeves on his uniform to show off his massive arms. Here are some players whose uniforms were anything but uniform. As Yogi Berra once said, "I have every color of sweater except navy brown."

1. BOBBY BRAGAN

Bobby Bragan managed the Pirates, Indians, and Braves between 1956 and 1966. Bragan was notorious for his disputes with umpires. He was catching for the minor league Hollywood Stars when he argued a call at home plate. In disgust, he removed his chest protector, shin guards, mask, and cap. He continued the striptease in the dugout, throwing his uniform, shoes, and undershirt onto the field.

2. GERMANY SCHAEFER

Second baseman Germany Schaefer played in the major leagues from 1901 until 1918. Schaefer is best remembered for his outrageous antics on the field. During one rainy game he came to the plate wearing a raincoat and boots.

3. DAN FRIEND

On August 30, 1897, the Chicago Cubs were playing the New York Giants. The game was in the ninth inning, and the Cub pitcher had already showered when he was ordered to go in and play left field to replace a player who had been ejected. Friend trotted to his position wearing a bathrobe and his baseball cap.

4. WILLIE WELLS

Willie "the Devil" Wells was one of the best shortstops in the Negro League. In 1926, he suffered a serious beaning. The next time he came to bat, Wells was wearing a miner's hat to protect his head. The pitcher drilled him in the side, injuring his ribs.

5. JOHN COLEMAN

Philadelphia pitcher John Coleman was unexpectedly called in to replace an injured rightfielder in the sixth inning of a game on May 10, 1885. Coleman was so unprepared that he played the rest of the game in street clothes.

6. CONNIE MACK

Connie Mack managed the Philadelphia A's for fifty years. Rather than wear a uniform, Mack sat on the bench dressed in a suit and tie. During the 1890s, Baltimore manager Ned Hanlon frequently wore a silk top hat and spats.

7. THE 1882 NATIONAL LEAGUE UNIFORMS

In 1882, the National League experimented with color-coded uniforms. Each position had a different color uniform: first base (scarlet and white), second base (orange and black), shortstop (maroon), third base (gray and white), right field (gray), center field (red and black), left field (white), catcher (scarlet), and pitcher (blue). Since the uniforms did not yet have numbers, it was hoped that the color-coded uniforms would make it easier for the fans to identify the players. The experiment proved unpopular and was soon dropped.

8. FRANK LACORTE

On May 26, 1982, Houston pitcher Frank LaCorte walked the bases loaded in a game against the Montreal Expos. He was so angry with his performance that he burned his uniform in the clubhouse.

9. FRANK COGGINS

Frank Coggins was a utility player with the Washington Senators in the late 1960s. Coggins is remembered as one of the flashiest dressers in baseball history. A typical outfit would be a pink suit, knickers, and a straw hat. After his playing days were over, Coggins was employed by the FBI.

10. THE 1976 CHICAGO WHITE SOX UNIFORMS

One of owner Bill Veeck's least appreciated innovations was the uniform he unveiled for the 1976 Chicago White Sox. The players were forced to wear shorts—and endure the snickers of fans and opposing players.

Smarter than the Average Berra

On the whole, baseball players are not known for their intellectual endeavors. When asked if he knew of any literate players, the author W. P. Kinsella replied, "Tom Seaver is the only one who comes to mind. I do know that Steve Boros reads." Actually, some players have exhibited brain as well as brawn.

1. MOE BERG

Catcher Moe Berg was undoubtedly one of the most intelligent players to ever play professional baseball. A magna cum laude graduate of Princeton, he received a law degree from Columbia and studied philosophy at the Sorbonne in Paris. He declined an offer to teach in the romance language department at Princeton in order to play professional baseball.

John Montgomery Ward
Hall of Famer John Montgomery Ward was a successful attorney, author, agent, and labor leader.

Unfortunately, his baseball skills did not compare with his mental gifts. Brooklyn scout Mike Gonzalez coined the phrase, "good field, no hit" after watching Berg play. Pitcher Ted Lyons joked, "He can speak ten languages and can't hit in any of them." In fifteen seasons, Berg hit only six home runs. As a backup catcher, he spent most of his time in the bullpen. Each morning he bought at least a dozen foreign newspapers, which he would read during the game. He was the only player who kept a tuxedo hung in his locker.

As World War II approached, Berg used his linguistic abilities to serve his country. During a tour of American All-Stars in Japan before the war, Berg took espionage photos of Tokyo. After the war started, Berg posed as a Swiss businessman and German officer in order to attempt to obtain German atomic secrets.

Years later, Berg was offered a $35,000 advance to write an autobiography. He declined the offer when his editor mistook him for Moe Howard of the Three Stooges.

2. JOHN MONTGOMERY WARD

John Montgomery Ward was one of the most remarkable figures in baseball history. As a nineteen-year-old pitcher, he won forty-seven games, and the next season pitched a perfect game. His 2.10 career earned run average is the fourth lowest in baseball history. When he injured his pitching arm, Ward became a shortstop and collected over 2,000 hits. He was elected to the Baseball Hall of Fame in 1964.

Ward attended Penn State University and received his law degree from Columbia. He founded the first players' union, the Brotherhood, in 1885.

Five years later, he led the players to form their own league that competed with the established National League for a year. Ward wrote articles in the leading publications of the day on subjects ranging from psychology to human rights. He became a successful attorney, was the first player's agent, and was nearly elected president of the National League.

3. **TED LEWIS**

A twenty-game winner with Boston in 1897 and 1898, Ted Lewis retired at age twenty-nine to coach baseball at Harvard. He later taught English at Columbia University and was president of Massachusetts State College. The final nine years of his life, Lewis served as president of the University of New Hampshire. He sometimes discussed poetry and played catch in his backyard with the poet Robert Frost.

4. **JAY HOOK**

One of the original New York Mets, Jay Hook had a miserable 29–62 career record. He pitched the Mets to their first victory and was responsible for giving first baseman Marv Throneberry his nickname, "Marvelous." Hook earned a master's degree in mechanical engineering from Northwestern University. He wrote an article in the *New*

York Times explaining why a breaking ball curved. Apparently, the batters in the National League must have read the article before they faced Hook. A loser on the field, Hook became a big winner in the business world. He became a vice president at MASCO, a Detroit conglomerate, where he was in charge of making multimillion dollar deals.

5. DAVE BALDWIN

Dave Baldwin was a solid reliever who had a terrific 1.70 earned run average as a rookie with Washington in 1967. During his playing days Baldwin was an anthropologist in the off-season. In 1979, he earned a Ph.D. in genetics and four years later received his M.S. in systems engineering. Baldwin also published numerous scientific articles, children's stories, and humor pieces.

6. GEORGE DAVIS

On September 9, 1914, George Davis, a Harvard law student, pitched a no-hitter for the Boston Braves against Philadelphia. The next season the promising young pitcher retired to practice law.

7. JIM BROSNAN

Reliever Jim Brosnan was nicknamed "The Professor" because of his scholarly demeanor. Brosnan helped lead Cincinnati to the pennant in

1961, finishing with a 10–4 record. His journal of the pennant race, *The Long Season,* became a baseball classic. He wrote a second book, *Pennant Race,* as well as articles for *Sports Illustrated* and other publications. His writing was not appreciated by the baseball establishment because of its honest depiction of what took place behind clubhouse doors, and the Chicago White Sox sent Brosnan a contract in 1964 that forbade him to publish. Brosnan placed an ad in *The Sporting News* that read, "Free agent. Negotiable terms available. Respectfully request permission to pursue harmless avocation of professional writer." Forced to choose between baseball and writing, Brosnan chose the pen over the bullpen.

8. BOBBY BROWN

Bobby Brown was a third baseman for the New York Yankees from 1946 to 1954. His greatest moments came in four World Series in which he hit a combined .439. Brown attended Stanford, UCLA, and Tulane University School of Medicine. After retiring from baseball, he practiced cardiology in Fort Worth, Texas. From 1984 to 1994 he served as American League president.

9. BEN OGLIVIE

Ben Oglivie was a power-hitting outfielder from Panama who led the American League in home

Bobby Brown
Bobby Brown played in four World Series with the Yankees and later became a successful cardiologist and President of the American League.

runs (41) in 1980. Oglivie was more than just a smart hitter. He had wide intellectual interests and could finish a *New York Times* crossword puzzle in fifteen minutes. Teammates would find him engrossed in reading Jean-Jacques Rousseau or some other brainy material.

10. KEN HOLTZMAN

Lefthander Ken Holtzman won twenty-one games in 1973 and was one of the aces on the Oakland A's championship teams. Nicknamed "the Thinker," he read Marcel Proust's seven-volume masterpiece, *Remembrance of Things Past* in the original French.

Stengelese and Other Tongues

Baseball players have a language that is all their own. It makes perfect sense to them, but something is lost in the translation for the rest of us. Here are some of the leading purveyors of baseball speak.

1. YOGI BERRA

Yogi Berra was a Hall of Fame catcher and a pennant-winning manager, but his most lasting contribution to American culture may be his unique use of language. Describing the creeping shadows in left field, Yogi commented, "It gets late early out there." Yogi on the shrinking dollar: "A nickel ain't worth a dime anymore." When the Yankees held a Yogi Berra Night in his honor, Yogi quipped, "Thank you for making this night necessary." Two classic Yogiisms, "It was déjà vu all over again" and "It ain't over till it's over," have become catch phrases (no pun intended).

Casey Stengel
Fired after leading the New York Yankees to their tenth pennant in twelve years, manager Casey Stengel remarked, "I'll never make the mistake of being 70 again."

When Yogi's wife Carmen told him she had just seen *Dr. Zhivago,* a concerned Yogi asked, "Oh, what's the matter with you, now?" On watching Steve McQueen in *The Magnificent Seven,* Berra observed, "He made that movie before he died." With these remarkable perceptions, it was only natural that Berra be asked to review films on television. Yogi referred to the star of *Dirty Harry* as Cliff Eastwick. While reviewing Neil

Simon's *Biloxi Blues,* he informed viewers, "It reminded me of being in the army, even though I was in the navy." Berra denied that he was responsible for all the quotes attributed to him, "I didn't say everything I said."

2. CASEY STENGEL

Casey Stengel managed the New York Yankees to ten pennants between 1947 and 1960. The "Old Perfesser" once told his players, "Now all you fellers line up alphabetically by height." In July 1958, Stengel appeared before the U. S. Senate subcommittee antitrust hearings and befuddled politicians used to doubletalk with an hour of Stengelese. When an aging Casey was fired after the 1960 season, despite winning the pennant, he lamented, "I'll never make the mistake of being seventy again." Casey's epitaph says it all: "There comes a time in every man's life, at least once, and I've had plenty of them."

3. JERRY COLEMAN

Jerry Coleman played second base for the New York Yankees from 1949 to 1957. His most memorable moments have come as an announcer for the San Diego Padres. Coleman's propensity for the verbal miscue has his listeners hanging on every word. Coleman's "sun-blown pop-ups" and players "sliding into second base with a stand-up double" may confuse the uninitiated but delight the devotees. Who could ever forget Coleman's line, "Rich Folkers is throwing up in the bullpen"? Undoubtedly, Jerry's finest moment came when he described Padres' outfielder Dave Winfield chasing a long fly: "Winfield is going back. He hits his head against the wall. It's rolling back toward second base."

Choo Choo Coleman
One of the original New York Mets, catcher Choo Choo Coleman had such trouble giving signals to the pitcher that it was suggested that he color code his fingers.

4. PHIL RIZZUTO

Phil Rizzuto played shortstop on the Yankee team with Casey Stengel, Yogi Berra, and Jerry Coleman. One can only imagine the conversations this foursome would have during a game of bridge. The Scooter was a better player than his double play partner, Jerry Coleman, and almost his equal as an announcer. Rizzuto's specialties are inattention to detail, occasional lapses of memory, and meaningless anecdotes that he forgets to finish. Rizzuto once expressed amazement that Johnny Neun had managed the Yankees even though he had played while he was manager. Another time, he was worried that star pitcher Ron Guidry might have been struck by a line drive hit into the Yankees dugout. Rizzuto had failed to notice that Guidry was on the mound.

5. CHOO CHOO COLEMAN

Clarence "Choo Choo" Coleman was a catcher with the original New York Mets, perhaps the worst baseball team of the century. Coleman had dubious defensive skills, a .197 career batting average, and a way with words only his manager Casey Stengel could appreciate. Choo Choo had such a problem giving signals to the pitcher that the Mets considered painting his fingers blue for fast ball, red for curve, green for change-up. At the end of the season, teammate Charlie Neal confronted Choo Choo, "I bet you don't know who I am." Coleman replied, "You're number 4." Ralph Kiner asked him his wife's name and what she was like. Choo Choo answered, "Her name is Mrs. Coleman, and she likes me."

6. **DIZZY DEAN**

Dizzy Dean was the last National League pitcher to win thirty games in a season (1934), and his mangling of the English language as an announcer paved the way for ex-players such as Jerry Coleman to enter the booth. When Dizzy was knocked unconscious during a game, the headlines the next day read: "Dean's Head Examined: X-Rays Reveal Nothing." Dean described players being "purply [purposely] passed," "returning to their respectable bases," and "sludding into third." Dizzy, who admitted to flunking out of the second grade, was assailed by English teachers because of his prolific use of the word "ain't." Diz silenced his critics by saying, "A lot of people who don't say ain't ain't eatin."

7. **RALPH KINER**

Ralph Kiner led the National League in home runs for seven consecutive years and probably leads National League announcers in messing up players' names. The Mets star catcher, Gary Carter, became "Gary Cooper." Kiner called third baseman Tim Wallach "Eli Wallach" so many times that his teammates nicknamed him Eli. Two of Kiner's most hilarious misnomers were calling Dan Driessen "Diana Driessen" and referring to Don Bilardello as "Don Bordello."

8. DANNY OZARK

Danny Ozark managed the Philadelphia Phillies to three consecutive divisional titles from 1976 to 1978. Ozark earned the reputation as the Master of the Malaprop. After his club had blown a huge lead, Ozark lamented, "Even Napoleon had his Watergate." When his team was mathematically eliminated from the pennant race, an upbeat Ozark vowed, "We're not out of it yet."

9. HARRY CARAY

The voice of the Chicago Cubs for two decades, colorful Harry Caray was a bigger celebrity than most of the team's players. Harry's distinctive play-by-play style included reading the names of most anyone who was attending or watching the game. Fans were well aware of his much-expressed love of alcohol. He once referred to outfielder Dave Collins as Tom Collins. During a promo for Budweiser, he said, "I'm a Gub fan and a Bud man." Doctors advised Caray to give up drinking in 1994. They said he could take another drink when the Cubs won their next pennant. They won their last in 1945.

10. **MICKEY RIVERS**

Outfielder Mickey Rivers was known as "Mick the Quick" because of his extraordinary speed. During his playing days from 1970 to 1984, he exhibited verbal skills not heard in New York since the retirement of Yogi Berra. "What is the name of the dog on *Rin Tin Tin?*" Rivers asked. He stated that his goals were to "hit .300, score 100 runs, and stay injury-prone." Comparing the weather in New York and his native Florida, Rivers remarked, "The climax is about the same." Asked if he got along with owner George Steinbrenner and manager Billy Martin, Mickey replied, "Me and George and Billy, we're two of a kind."

Notable Nicknames

Many baseball players have nicknames. Babe Ruth was the "Sultan of Swat." Ted Williams was known as the "Splendid Splinter." Not every nickname is as well known. Jimmy Bannon's nickname was "Foxy Grandpa." Bris Lord was the "Human Eyeball." Pearce "What's the Use" Chiles's nickname says all you need to know about his career. For some players their nicknames are their main claim to fame: John "Pretzels" Pezzullo, Clarence "Cupid" Childs, Joe "Horse Belly" Sargent, Harry "Stinky" Davis, Walter "Cuckoo" Christenson, and George "White Wings" Tebeau. ESPN's Chris Berman gained notoriety for giving players whimsical nicknames (e.g., Oddibe "Young Again" McDowell). This section features baseball's most intriguing nicknames.

1. DEATH TO FLYING THINGS

Bob Ferguson earned the sobriquet "Death to Flying Things" because of his uncanny ability as a fielder. Baseball's first switch hitter, he scored the winning run for the Brooklyn Atlantics in 1870 to end the Cincinnati Red Stockings' record-winning streak. A no-nonsense competitor, Ferguson later became an umpire and broke a batter's arm with a bat during an argument.

2. THE FRESHEST MAN ON EARTH

Arlie Latham was one of the fastest players of his day. In 1887, while playing for St. Louis, the third baseman stole 129 bases and scored 163 runs. Latham was known as the "Freshest Man on Earth" because of his ebullient personality. After retirement, Latham spent sixteen years in England where he was a personal friend to King George V and taught the monarch the fine points of baseball.

3. TOMATO FACE

Outfielder Nick Cullop was given the nickname "Tomato Face" because his face turned bright red every time he became angry. In 1931, his final season, Cullop was frequently red-faced as he led the National League in striking out.

4. WAGON TONGUE

Bill "Wagon Tongue" Keister had a .312 lifetime batting average. Keister got his nickname because he rarely stopped talking. Unfortunately he was one of the worst fielding shortstops in baseball history. In 1901, he set the all-time record for the lowest single season fielding percentage (.861). Because he was such a liability in the field, "Wagon Tongue" played for a different team in each of his seven seasons.

5. THE NERVOUS GREEK

Lou Skizas got his nickname "The Nervous Greek" because of the strange ritual he performed every time he came to the plate. The outfielder played for the Yankees, A's, Tigers, and White Sox between 1956 and 1959. Before he stepped into the batter's box Skizas walked between the catcher and the umpire, rubbed the bat between his legs, and reached into his back pocket to touch a lucky Greek coin he kept there. He hit .314 as a rookie but his luck soon ran out, and by 1959 his average had nose-dived to .077.

6. THE APOLLO OF THE BOX

Pitcher Tony Mullane was known as the "Apollo of the Box" because of his good looks. The handsome righthander from Cork, Ireland, was so popular with female fans that the Cincinnati Red Stockings initiated Ladies Day every Monday when he pitched. Mullane won thirty games his first five full seasons and had 285 victories during his career, which lasted from 1881 to 1894. He also has the distinction of being the first ambidextrous pitcher.

7. **LADY**

In 1886, Charles Baldwin set a National League record for lefthanders when he won forty-two games. Baldwin employed an unusual hop-skip-and-jump delivery similar to a cricket player. When the delivery was outlawed the following season, Baldwin's effectiveness declined. He was nicknamed "Lady" by his teammates because he didn't drink, smoke, or curse. Ironically, his middle name was Busted.

8. **THE HUMAN RAIN DELAY**

Mike Hargrove is best known for managing the Cleveland Indians to their first pennant in forty years. As a player, the first baseman batted over .300 five times during his career from 1974 until 1985. He was known as "The Human Rain Delay" because of his deliberate ritual in the batter's box. The stalling tactic was so unnerving to pitchers that Hargrove twice led the league in walks.

9. THE MAD MONK

Russ Meyer won ninety-four games during his thirteen-year major-league career that ended in 1959. Nicknamed the "Mad Monk" because of his temper, he was a notorious bench jockey. After one bad outing, he threw his spikes into the shower, where they stuck in the ceiling.

10. BLIMP

In 1936, Babe Phelps set an all-time record for catchers when he batted .367 for the Brooklyn Dodgers. He might have done even better, but he had the bizarre habit of staying awake all night to listen to his heartbeat. Phelps was convinced that if his heart skipped four beats he would die. Babe was given the nickname "Blimp" because of his shape. Despite his nickname, he had an intense fear of flying and retired in 1940 when teams began traveling by air. From that time on he was referred to as the "Grounded Blimp."

Hot Dogs

Fans consume thousands of hot dogs a year while watching baseball games. The term has also been used to describe players with a tendency to show off. Enjoy the following line-up of hot dogs.

1. REGGIE JACKSON

Pitcher Darold Knowles said of Reggie Jackson, "There's not enough mustard in the world to cover that hot dog." Jackson personified "hot dog" during his flamboyant twenty-one-year career. He hit 563 home runs (sixth on the all-time list), but he also struck out a record 2,597 times. Reggie often would stand at home plate to admire his tape-measure home runs. He received the attention he coveted when he was traded to the New York Yankees in 1977. "I didn't come to New York to become a star," he modestly declared. "I brought my own star." Referring to himself as the "straw that stirs the drink," he was considered the "straw that broke the camel's back" by some teammates. When they came out with a candy bar named Reggie in his honor, sportswriter Dave Anderson said, "It's the only candy bar that tastes like a hot dog."

2. MIKE "KING" KELLY

King Kelly was one of the most popular and accomplished players of the nineteenth century. Playing every position during his career, he led his teams to nine pennants. He twice led the National League in hitting and batted .388 in 1886. More than any other player, Kelly enjoyed the spotlight. In his book, *Play Ball,* he wrote, "Every baseball club must have a star, just as a dramatic company must have a leading man." Kelly perfected the "Kelly Spread," an early version of the hook slide. The cry of "slide, Kelly, slide" was heard at ballparks throughout the National League. His most famous exploit occurred while he was managing Boston. An opposing player hit a pop fly near the dugout. The quick-witted manager announced, "Kelly now catching for Boston," and caught the ball for an out.

3. DIZZY DEAN

Jay "Dizzy" Dean was a Hall of Fame pitcher and a world-class hot dog. He constantly bragged about his pitching prowess and was usually able to back up his boasts. Prior to the 1934 season, Dizzy predicted that he and his brother "Daffy" would win at least forty-five games for the Cardinals. The Deans exceeded Dizzy's expectations by winning a combined forty-nine games. In September of that year, Dizzy pitched a three-hit shutout in the first game of a doubleheader versus Brooklyn. After brother "Daffy" no-hit the Dodgers in the nightcap, Dizzy remarked, "If I'd known Paul was going to pitch a no-hitter, I'd pitched one too."

4. SATCHEL PAIGE

It is estimated that Satchel Paige won more than 2,000 games and pitched more than 100 no-hitters during his long career. Unable to play in the major leagues until 1948 when he was forty-two, Paige once struck out twenty-two major leaguers in an exhibition game and defeated Dizzy Dean four times. Satchel used a wide arsenal of pitches that he gave names like "Long Tom," the bee ball, the trouble ball, and the celebrated hesitation pitch. Paige was a master storyteller and enhanced his legend with tales of his remarkable pitching feats. When he was finally permitted to play in the major leagues in 1948, he demonstrated his control by throwing strikes over a gum wrapper.

5. JOHN "THE COUNT" MONTEFUSCO

John "The Count" Montefusco never lacked confidence. The San Francisco Giants' righthander was National League Rookie of the Year in 1975 and no-hit the Atlanta Braves on September 29, 1976. Once, he guaranteed that he would shut out the Braves and made good his promise. Against the Big Red Machine, the brash rookie boasted that he would shut out Cincinnati and hit a home run. The Count pitched a shutout, hit a home run, and fanned Johnny Bench three times. On July 31, 1975, Montefusco predicted he'd throw another shutout against the Reds and strike out Johnny Bench four times. This time he was shelled for seven runs in two innings, the crushing blow a three-run home run by Bench. Unfazed, the Count revealed that his ultimate fantasy was to be brought to the park in a Rolls Royce and walk to the mound wearing a top hat, cape, and white gloves.

6. JEFFREY LEONARD

Jeffrey Leonard had a knack for irritating the opposition. The outfielder, known as "Penitentiary Face" because of his scowl, showed up pitchers when he hit a home run with his "one flap down" home-run trot (he held one arm against his side). During the 1987 National League Championship series he hit four home runs, taking nearly a minute to round the bases on one homer. Leonard sometimes carried his "nasty" bat to the plate. Obscene words were written on the label, which he waved in the catcher's face.

7. DEION SANDERS

"Neon" Deion Sanders knew how to showboat even as a rookie. He strode to the plate wearing ropes of gold jewelry around his neck. When he hit his first home run, he bent over to tie his shoe when he reached the plate, pointing his rear at the pitcher. Opposing pitchers frequently complained about his baserunning antics.

8. BROADWAY BILL SCHUSTER

Infielder Broadway Bill Schuster would yell at the top of his lungs whenever he got a hit or made a great play. These occurrences were not that frequent, as Broadway Bill only had sixty-one hits in his five-year career, which ended in 1945.

9. GEORGE "SHOWBOAT" FISHER

George Fisher batted .374 in 254 at bats as a rookie outfielder with the St. Louis Cardinals in 1930. The Gas House Gang was one of the most colorful teams in major league history, but Fisher was such a hot dog that he was given the nickname "Showboat." Despite having one of the highest batting averages in the National League, Fisher was not invited back to play with the Cardinals in 1931. The next season he batted only .182 with the St. Louis Browns and never played in the majors again.

10. **JAKE BECKLEY**

During his Hall of Fame career, from 1888 to 1907, first baseman Jake Beckley collected nearly 3,000 hits and batted over .300 thirteen times. He intimidated pitchers by pointing his bat at them and letting out a blood-curdling yell, "Chickazoola."

Worst Practical Jokers

For some players, the practical joke has been raised to an art form. From a simple hot foot to elaborate schemes, these pranksters made life miserable for their teammates.

1. MOE DRABOWSKI

Born in Ozanna, Poland, Moe Drabowski pitched in the major leagues for seventeen years. The high point of his career occurred in the first game of the 1966 World Series when the Oriole hurler struck out eleven Dodgers in relief. Drabowski's true claim to fame was his arsenal of practical jokes. While sitting in the bullpen, he might call for fast food or make long-distance calls to check on the weather in foreign cities. While playing Kansas City, he once called the A's bullpen and, while imitating manager Alvin Dark, told someone to start throwing. Starter Jim Nash, who was pitching a shutout, was so unnerved that he lost the game. While pitching for Kansas City, he imitated Charlie Finley and carried on bogus contract negotiations with players.

Drabowski put sneezing powder in the Orioles' air-conditioning system and a goldfish in the water cooler. On another occasion, he sent Chico Salmon a box with a boa constrictor in it. Other teammates found snakes in their locker. At a sports banquet, Brooks Robinson nearly had a heart attack when he discovered a king snake in a basket of dinner rolls.

Many of Moe's teammates were victims of the old hot foot tricks. He would let out the air in their tires or put limburger cheese in their cars. Drabowski was especially fond of throwing smoke bombs in showers and placing firecrackers in inappropriate places. His most outrageous moment came when he gave Baseball Commissioner Bowie Kuhn a hotfoot.

2. DANNY GARDELLA

Danny "Tarzan" Gardella was a power-hitting outfielder with the New York Giants during World War II. He successfully challenged baseball's reserve clause after being suspended for five years after jumping to the Mexican League. Gardella was notorious for his sometimes cruel practical jokes.

On V-E Day he dressed up like Hitler and convinced some that the Fuhrer was not dead. He told teammate Nap Reyes that he was considering suicide. Reyes heard a scream from his hotel room and rushed in to see the window open. Reyes, believing that Gardella had jumped twenty stories to his death, rushed to the window only to find him huddled on the ledge.

3. **RABBIT MARANVILLE**

One of baseball's biggest clowns, Hall of Fame shortstop Rabbit Maranville played in the major leagues from 1912 to 1935. Maranville like to put a pair of glasses on an umpire after a bad call. His idea of a good joke was to dangle teammates out of the hotel room windows. One night teammates heard Maranville shout that someone was trying to kill him, followed by a gunshot. Frantically, they broke the door down only to be greeted by a smiling Rabbit.

4. **JAY JOHNSTONE**

Jay Johnstone played twenty seasons in the majors, mainly as a part-time player. In 1980, the Los Angeles Dodgers acquired him because manager Tommy Lasorda believed the outfielder would help keep the team loose. Lasorda became the main target for his hijinks. During spring training,

Johnstone disconnected Lasorda's phone and tied the door of his room to a palm tree so he couldn't get out. With the help of his accomplice, pitcher Jerry Reuss, Johnstone removed the manager's prized photographs of his celebrity friends and replaced them with photos of Johnstone and Reuss. Players were also targets of Johnstone's chicanery. He put a melted brownie in Steve Garvey's glove and made it appear that Reuss had been the culprit.

5. ROGER MCDOWELL

During the late 1980s, Roger McDowell was the ace of the New York Mets' bullpen. He was also among the league leaders in practical jokes. McDowell placed firecrackers in the bat rack and shaving cream on the bullpen phone. Players routinely received the hot foot treatment courtesy of McDowell. Roger accumulated an extensive collection of masks—each to mimic another player or coach.

6. RICK DEMPSEY

Catcher Rick Dempsey played twenty seasons in the major leagues. A clutch hitter, his best moments came in the World Series in which he batted .324. Dempsey's practical jokes usually bordered on the dangerous. Once, when a group of his teammates were playing poker, Dempsey turned out the lights and imitated a robber who threatened to kill them if they didn't give him all their money. Dempsey's lasting contribution to the game may have been his headfirst slides on the tarp during rain delays while imitating Babe Ruth.

7. JOE PAGE

Yankees' reliever Joe Page devised one of the most famous practical jokes at the expense of teammate Snuffy Stirnweiss. Page propped a bear carcass on an outhouse toilet seat. Unsuspectingly, Snuffy opened the door only to have the bear fall over and pin him to the ground.

8. BO BELINSKY

Next to women, practical jokes were Bo Belinsky's favorite pastime. Bo promised to line up a teammate with a beautiful woman. The date turned out to be a drag queen. He gave another player the phone number of what he promised would be a dream date. The number actually belonged to crusty manager Bill Rigney. In the minors Bo and fellow hellraiser Steve Dalkowski learned that Miss Universe was staying in the adjoining suite. To get a better look, they drilled holes in the hotel wall.

9. ARLIE LATHAM

No one was safe when Arlie Latham was around. He tormented fans, teammates, rivals, and even owners with his shenanigans. He put on a bulbous nose and did a devastating impression of owner Chris Von der Ahe. John McGraw selected him to be the first third base coach. A gifted acrobat, Latham once somersaulted over manager Cap Anson and occasionally cartwheeled down the third base line when he sent a runner home.

10. BERT BLYLEVEN

Bert Blyleven won 287 games and struck out 3,701 batters during his outstanding career, which ended in 1992. Blyleven had a puckish sense of humor and was the undisputed king of the hotfoot. He attributed the secret to his outstanding curve ball to his long fingers. Born in Holland, Blyleven said the length of his fingers were the results of sticking them in dikes as a child.

Flakes

In baseball, a flake is someone whose behavior deviates from the norm. Meet some of baseball's biggest oddballs.

1. RUBE WADDELL

Blessed with a blazing fastball and sharp breaking curve, Rube Waddell led the league in strikeouts seven times between 1900 and 1907. The childlike pitcher would sometimes hold up the start of a game in order to play marbles with kids in the street. He was known to bolt off the mound and chase fire engines (at the age of three he had run away from home and was found sleeping in a firehouse). Opposing players could distract him by waving stuffed animals from the dugout.

Rube once jumped out a second-story window because he believed he could fly. Despite being one of the best pitchers in baseball, he never

Jackie Brandt
It is believed that the term flake was coined to describe the behavior of outfielder Jackie Brandt.

earned more than $2,800 in a season. The A's paid him in dollar bills because they believed it would help Rube make it last longer. During the off-season he earned extra money by wrestling alligators in Florida. Waddell died on April Fools' Day, 1914, at the age of thirty-seven.

2. BILL "SPACEMAN" LEE

Bill Lee was a good enough pitcher to win seventeen games for three consecutive seasons from 1973 to 1975. Nicknamed "Spaceman," the zany southpaw claimed he was normal, and it was the "northpaw" outlook on life that was strange. Lee admitted to sprinkling marijuana on his organic buckwheat pancakes. When he was fined $250 for the remark, he donated the money to an Eskimo charity. In Boston he wore the number 37 (which had been Jimmy Piersall's number) and asked if he could change it to 337 because the numbers would spell Lee upside down.

It was Lee who dubbed manager Don Zimmer the "Gerbil." He formed a group of players called the Loyal Order of the Buffalo Heads that mocked Zimmer. Boston City Councilor Albert O'Neil wrote Lee an angry letter with some misspelled words after Lee had called Boston a racist city. Lee wrote back a nice letter warning the city official that some idiot was using his stationery. The Spaceman read books by mystics and believed that the perfect pitcher would be a Tibetan priest who could make the ball disappear and reappear in the catcher's mitt. Lee authored an autobiography entitled *The Wrong Stuff* and ran for president on the Rhinoceros Party ticket.

3. **MARK "THE BIRD" FIDRYCH**

Mark Fidrych was working at a gas station when he was signed by the Detroit Tigers. The twenty-one-year-old pitcher surprised everyone by being called up to the majors in 1976. He celebrated his promotion by making love to his girlfriend on the pitching mound.

Fidrych was an immediate sensation, pitching a two-hitter in his first start. He won nineteen games as a rookie and led the American League in earned run average. Baseball had never seen anything like him. Fidrych got down on his hands and knees to manicure the mound. He talked to the ball and shook hands with his infielders. If a batter got a base hit, he refused to use the same ball again. After he got a batter out he would walk around the mound like a bird and occasionally flap his arms.

For a season "The Bird" was the word in Detroit. After a win, Fidrych would do a lap of the field waving to fans. One game he was warming up when he realized he had forgot to wear his protective cup. Totally uninhibited, he pulled down his pants and put on his cup. With his long blonde curls, he was a favorite of female fans. When he went to the barber shop, groupies would rush in and sweep up the golden locks. Sadly, "The Bird" injured his wing the following season and won only ten more major league games.

4. SUPER JOE CHARBONEAU

Like Fidrych, Joe Charboneau was a one-year wonder. In 1980, Charboneau was Rookie of the Year when he hit twenty-three home runs for the

Cleveland Indians. Super Joe seemed like someone out of *Animal House*. He dyed his hair different colors years before Dennis Rodman did. On a dare, he drank a bottle of beer through his nose. Charboneau frequently abused his body when doing stunts. He opened a bottle of beer with his eyesocket, cut away a tattoo, and even removed a tooth. He underwent two back operations and played in only seventy games after his rookie season.

5. FRENCHY BORDAGARAY

Frenchy Bordagaray was an outstanding pinch hitter during the 1930s and 1940s. Frenchy was a manager's nightmare. While chasing a fly ball, he lost his cap. Bordagaray went back and picked up his cap before renewing his quest for the ball. Another time he was chastised by manager Casey Stengel for not sliding. The next time he hit a home run, Frenchy slid into every base to show that he had learned his lesson.

6. JACKIE BRANDT

Some believe that the term "flake" derived from a teammate commenting on Jackie Brandt, "Things seem to flake off his mind and disappear." Brandt played outfield in the majors from 1956 to 1967. Questioned about his intensity before the 1962 season, Brandt promised, "This year I'm going to play with harder nonchalance." He blamed his inconsistent defensive play on the fact that when he ran hard, his eyeballs jumped up and down.

7. **JIM COLBORN**

Jim Colborn's best season was 1973, when he won twenty games for the Milwaukee Brewers. He also pitched a no-hitter against the Texas Rangers in 1977. A master of impersonation, he disguised himself as an umpire, groundskeeper, peanut vendor, batboy, and even as a mascot. If only he could have impersonated Jim Palmer.

8. **GEORGE STALLINGS**

If there was ever a manager (other than Casey Stengel) who was a flake, it was George Stallings. He managed the 1914 Boston Braves to one of the greatest comebacks in baseball history. In last place on the Fourth of July, the Miracle Braves rallied to win fifty-two of their sixty-six games to capture the pennant. Tremendously superstitious, he physically froze during a rally and would not move until the inning was over. He shook bats to "wake up" the lumber. Stallings believed loose paper or peanut shells on the floor of the dugout was bad luck, and opposing managers had players shred newspapers to annoy him. The manager was given the nickname "Bonehead" because that was what he frequently called his players.

9. RICK BOSETTI

Rick Bosetti was an outfielder of modest talent who played from 1976 to 1982. His legacy to the game was his ambition to urinate in the outfield of every stadium, a goal that he achieved.

10. KEITH RHOMBERG

Keith Rhomberg was an outfielder with the Cleveland Indians from 1982 to 1984. Despite a .383 lifetime batting average, he played in only forty-one games. One of his drawbacks was that for him, life was a game of tag. Whenever someone touched him, he insisted that he touch him back. A teammate tagged him with the ball and threw it over the outfield fence, prompting Rhomberg to frantically climb over the fence to retrieve the ball. Fans wrote taunting letters, to which he always replied because they had touched them last. Finally, opposing players began bumping against Rhomberg and were chased all over the field by the superstitious player. Thank God, he didn't play football.

The Bullpen

For some reason, relief pitchers have a tendency to be bigger flakes than players at other positions. Maybe it's because they have too much time on their hands in the bullpen.

1. BILL FAUL

Bill Faul attended the University of Cincinnati and broke Sandy Koufax's school record when he struck out nineteen batters in a game. He later set an NCAA record when he fanned twenty-four. Although no Koufax, Faul pitched in the majors from 1962 to 1970. After experiencing modest success as a starter, Faul was moved to the bullpen where he won only one more game. He held a degree as a doctor of divinity and had been a karate instructor in the Air Force. He practiced karate, and he also preached for the Universal

Christian Church. A licensed hypnotist, he hypnotized himself prior to each game. Before pitching to a batter, Faul waved his hand in front of his face. Considering his 12–16 lifetime record, he should have tried hypnotizing the batters.

2. JIM KERN

Jim Kern, despite control problems, had a sensational season with Texas in 1979, saving twenty-nine games and posting a 1.57 earned run average. Kern once told sportswriters he was working on a new pitch—a strike. The Texas bullpen was known as the "Cuckoo's Nest," and Kern was nicknamed "Emu" because he looked like a big bird. When fans in the stands asked for a ball, Kern not only obliged them, he tossed them his glove, cap, uniform, and socks. Another time Kern came out on the field wearing his uniform backwards.

3. AL HRABOSKY

Al "The Mad Hungarian" Hrabosky was a splendid reliever who compiled a 64–35 record during his career, which ended in 1982. The only thing better than his pitching was his act. Hrabosky would stomp in from the bullpen while the organist played "The Hungarian Rhapsody." The Mad Hungarian would psyche himself while rubbing up the ball. He was an intimidating sight with his Fu Manchu mustache and long hair. Hrabosky wore a Gypsy Rose of Death ring to ward off werewolves. Atlanta Braves' owner Ted Turner was so impressed that he signed him to an unprecedented thirty-year contract.

4. BRAD LESLEY

For a pitcher who won only one major league game, Brad "The Animal" Lesley left a lasting impression. Lesley pitched in the big leagues from 1982 to 1985. An imposing pitcher who stood 6 feet 6 inches and weighed 230 pounds, he would grunt and clench his fists every time he struck out a batter (which wasn't that often since he had forty-six career K's). The real strikeout king, Nolan Ryan, once imitated his act when he struck out a batter against Cincinnati.

5. TURK WENDELL

When Turk Wendell came up with the Chicago Cubs, he went through a series of rituals during each mound appearance. Turk waved to the centerfielder before each inning and insisted that the ball be rolled to him. Wendell made three crosses in the dirt. He always chewed licorice and wore two watches (one with the current time at his home in Massachusetts). When Turk walked to the dugout, he leaped over the foul line. Wendell wore uniform number 13, probably to prove that he wasn't superstitious.

6. **TUG MCGRAW**

Tug McGraw was an outstanding reliever who pitched with the Mets and Phillies between 1965 and 1984. Tom Seaver once said that McGraw only had forty-eight cards in his deck. Tug expressed a dislike for Astroturf because he didn't want to play on anything he couldn't smoke. McGraw gave his pitches names. He called his fastball Peggy Lee—Is That All There Is? Cutty Sark was a pitch that sailed. The Bo Derek was one "with a nice little tail on it." When asked what he did with a bonus, Tug replied, "I spent half of it on booze and broads. The other half I wasted."

7. **LARRY ANDERSEN**

Larry Andersen had a major league career that spanned three decades, from the 1970s to the 1990s. Andersen was the Steven Wright of baseball. He pondered such matters as why slim chance and fat chance meant the same thing, and how do you know when invisible ink is dry? While with the Phillies he sprayed on "instant hair" out of an aerosol can to significantly lower his hairline. Andersen will always be remembered as the man for whom the Red Sox traded Jeff Bagwell.

8. ROB DIBBLE

The nastiest of the "Nasty Boys" relievers that led the 1990 Cincinnati Reds to a world championship, Rob Dibble had more suspensions than Albert Belle. The man with the 100-mile per hour fastball was suspended for throwing at batter Eric Yelding, throwing at the legs of runner Doug Dascenzo, and hitting a fan with a ball he threw into the centerfield stands. Dibble refused to shake hands or sign more than a few autographs because he was afraid to hurt his arm. In 1994, he suffered a career-ending rotator cuff injury.

9. DON STANHOUSE

Don Stanhouse, a reliever in the major leagues from 1972 to 1982, earned the nickname "Stan the Man Unusual." Baltimore manager Earl Weaver called him "Full Pack" because he could smoke a pack of cigarettes by the time his reliever could finish the game. Stanhouse liked to hang upside down in the bullpen—a habit terminated when he fell on his head.

10. BILLY LOES

Billy Loes was one of the mainstays of the Brooklyn Dodgers' staff in the early 1950s. When he was a starter he declared that he didn't want to win twenty games because management would expect it every year. When he booted a ball hit back to the mound, the resourceful Loes explained that he had lost it in the sun.

Curses

You may not believe in them, but curses seemed to have had a major impact on baseball. You are about to enter baseball's twilight zone.

1. THE CURSE OF THE BAMBINO

Led by Babe Ruth, the best left-handed pitcher in the American League, the Boston Red Sox were the dominant team of the teens. Despite the team's success, Boston's owner Harry Frazee was strapped for cash to finance his new Broadway musical. He sold his star pitcher and part-time outfielder to the New York Yankees in 1920 for $100,000. With the Yankees, Ruth became the greatest slugger ever to play the game. The Red Sox, who had won five world championships and were baseball's dominant team, have never won another World Series. In contrast, the Yankees became the most successful franchise in sports history. By the way, the play Frazee produced with the money from the Yankees was "No, No, Nanette."

2. THE BILLY GOAT CURSE

For more than fifty years the Chicago Cubs have personified futility in major league baseball. In 1945, tavern owner William Sianis found a goat wandering the streets of Chicago. Apparently, the animal had fallen from a livestock truck. Sianis took the goat home and made it his pet. They were inseparable, and when he decided to take the goat with him to the fourth game of the 1945 World Series between the Cubs and the Detroit Tigers, the ushers at Wrigley Field refused to let Sianis enter the ballpark with his pet. Outraged, he shouted, "The Cubs will never win another pennant." And to this day, they haven't.

3. THE EX-CUB CURSE

The only thing worse than a Cub is an ex-Cub. Since 1945, the year the Cubs won their last pennant, only one team with three or more ex-Cubs has won a World Series. The only team to overcome the curse was the 1960 Pittsburgh Pirates, who somehow managed to win the series against the New York Yankees despite being outscored, 55–27. Teams with a surplus of ex-Cubs have a 1–13 record in the fall classic. The ex-Cub curse became well known in 1990 when Chicago columnist Mike Royko guaranteed that the heavily favored Oakland A's would lose to the Cincinnati Reds because they had the curse of having three ex-Cubs on their roster. The Reds swept the star-studded A's in four games.

4. PEDRO BORBON

Reliever Pedro Borbon was the wild man of the Big Red Machine teams in Cincinnati that dominated baseball in the 1970s. On one occasion an opposing player was forced to get a tetanus shot after Borbon bit him. When Pedro was traded to San Francisco in 1979, he placed a voodoo curse on the Reds, swearing that they would never win another pennant. Within a few years, the Reds had plummeted to the National League cellar. In 1990, Borbon agreed to lift the curse, and the Reds won their first pennant since he left.

5. THE CURSE OF THE ANGELS

Anaheim Stadium, home of the Anaheim Angels, was built in 1966 on the burial grounds of the Gabrieleño Indians. The Angels have experienced the worst luck of any team in baseball. While the ballpark was being built, pitcher Dick Wentz died of a brain tumor. In 1972, utility player Chico Ruiz was killed in an automobile accident. Five years later, promising shortstop Mike Miley met the same fate. The next season, star outfielder Lyman Bostock was shot to death in a case of mistaken identity. The Angels' luck appeared to be changing when they were on the verge of defeating the Boston Red Sox in the 1986 American League championship series when reliever Donnie Moore gave up a home run to Dave Henderson that turned the tide. The Angels lost the series and have never won a pennant. Three years later, Moore, despondent over surrendering the home run, took his own life.

6. FREDDY KAHAULUA

Pitcher Freddy Kahaulua had his own curse when he arrived in Angels' training camp in 1977. He was unable to lift his pitching arm. Kahaulua explained that his ex-girlfriend's mother in Hawaii had put a curse on him that prevented him from lifting his left arm. Desperate to find a solution, club officials contacted the woman, and she agreed to lift the curse. Immediately, Kahaulua was able to lift his arm and to pitch again.

7. BOB OJEDA

In July 1991, Los Angeles pitcher Bob Ojeda was shelled against the New York Mets, losing the game 9–4. He told reporters after the game that his poor performance was the result of voodoo. Ojeda explained that his ex-wife, with whom he was involved in a alimony dispute, had been sticking pins in a voodoo doll with Ojeda's face on it.

8. MIKE CUELLAR

Pitcher Mike Cuellar was a Cy Young winner who won 185 games in his career, which lasted from 1958 to 1977. In order to keep evil spirits out of his hotel room, the four-time twenty game winner stuffed paper in keyholes and under doors.

9. LEO CARDENAS

Leo Cardenas was a top shortstop during his major league career, which lasted from 1960 to 1975. A firm believer in the powers of voodoo, he had a collection of dolls dressed in other teams' uniforms. Cardenas prepared potions and went through a series of rituals before a game. Whenever he went into a hitting slump, he punished his bats by locking them in his car trunk.

10. JOSE RIJO

Cincinnati Reds pitcher Jose Rijo was the Most Valuable Player in the 1990 World Series. Rijo kept a voodoo doll in his locker, along with a picture of Pope John Paul II. When he pitched, he hung the photo of the Pope on the wall. He reasoned that he would lose only if the photo fell off the wall.

Lucky Bounces

Sometimes it's better to be lucky than good. Luck paid a pivotal role in the careers of these individuals.

1. CHARLES "VICTORY" FAUST

Pitcher Charlie Faust never won a game in the major leagues, but he helped the New York Giants win three pennants. In 1911, he approached manager John McGraw and said that a fortune teller had predicted that he would pitch for the Giants, and that they would win the pennant. Believing he might be good luck, McGraw let Faust suit up for the games.

Faust warmed up on the sidelines almost every game. It seemed as though every time he warmed up, the Giants had a big inning. Perhaps the players felt they needed insurance runs just in case Faust was ever brought into the game. McGraw did permit Faust to pitch two innings in which he gave up one run. As the fortune teller predicted, the Giants won the pennant in 1911. Faust became a popular attraction in vaudeville, telling audiences how he had clinched the pennant for New York. In both 1912 and 1913, the Giants experienced long losing streaks. McGraw summoned Faust, and the Giants went on to win the pennant both seasons. Faust's mental problems became more serious, and he was institutionalized. Without their good luck charm, the Giants finished ten games behind the Miracle Braves. On June 18, 1915, Faust's luck ran out, and he died at the age of thirty-four. The Giants finished last that season. A strange twist on the Faust legend.

2. JACK "LUCKY" LOHRKE

Jack Lohrke was an infielder in the major leagues from 1947 to 1953. The real story is that he survived long enough to play in the major leagues. During World War II he was part of the Normandy invasion and fought at the Battle of the Bulge. Four times, soldiers on both sides of him were killed, but Lohrke came through the war unscathed. When the war ended, Lohrke was scheduled to fly home in an army transport plane. He was bumped from the flight at the last minute, and the plane crashed, killing everyone on board. In 1946, Lohrke was playing minor league baseball with the Spokane Indians, when he was told to report to San Diego. He got off the team bus in Ellensburg, Washington. Fifteen minutes later the bus crashed into a ravine in the Cascade Mountains, killing nine players.

3. EDDIE BENNETT

Eddie Bennett was born with a deformed spine. He became a batboy for the 1919 Chicago White Sox. Outfielder Happy Felsch, who would become one of the players banned for life in the Black Sox scandal, would rub Bennett's hunchback for good luck. The White Sox won the pennant. The next season, Bennett became batboy for the Brooklyn Dodgers, and they, too, won the pennant. In 1921, Bennett moved to the Yankees, who won their first pennant. With Bennett in the dugout, the New York Yankees became a dynasty.

4. L'IL RASTUS

Rastus was a black youth discovered sleeping in a park by Ty Cobb. For some reason Cobb, an avid racist, believed the teenager was a good luck charm. For most of the 1908 season, the Tigers' players insisted on rubbing their fingers through Rastus's hair before going to the plate. When Detroit began losing late in the season, Rastus was let go by the Tigers. He turned up with

Chicago, and the Cubs defeated Detroit in the World Series, their last world championship. The next season Rastus returned to Detroit, and they won the pennant.

5. GOOSE GOSLIN

Rather than use a rabbit's foot as a good luck charm, Detroit outfielder Goose Goslin decided a live rabbit would be better. He kept a rabbit in the clubhouse during the 1935 World Series against the Chicago Cubs. Goslin's single in the ninth inning drove in the winning run in the sixth and deciding game.

6. BO BELINKSY

On the night before he threw his no-hitter against Baltimore, Angels pitcher Bo Belinsky stayed out until 4 A.M. with a comely blonde. Belinsky considered her to be his good luck charm, but no matter how hard he tried to locate her, he never saw her again.

7. VIDA BLUE

Three times during the 1970s, lefthander Vida Blue won twenty games for the Oakland A's. He insisted on wearing his lucky cap, which became discolored by sweat and dirt. On April 16, 1977, he was forced to discard the lucky hat because it

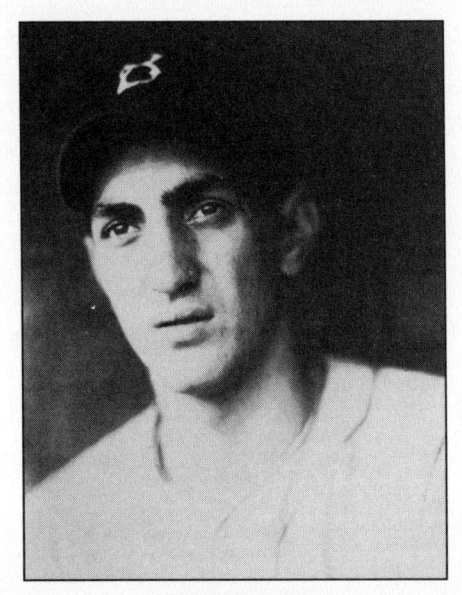

Ralph Branca
During the fateful 1951 season, Brooklyn
pitcher Ralph Branca wore number 13
on his uniform and won 13 games.

no longer conformed with the uniforms of his teammates. Blue led the American League in losses in 1977 and was traded to San Francisco.

8. DON STANHOUSE

Don Stanhouse was pitching for the Los Angeles Dodgers when he was given a stuffed monkey. Stanhouse brought the monkey to the clubhouse, and the Dodgers went on a winning streak. The monkey became Stanhouse's constant companion, even sharing beers to celebrate victories.

9. SUNSET JIMMY BURKE

Jimmy Burke played third base for five different teams between 1899 and 1905. He earned the nickname "Sunset" because he believed it was unlucky to eat dinner before the sun went down.

10. RALPH BRANCA

Brooklyn pitcher Ralph Branca seemed to be tempting fate when he posed for a photograph prior to the 1951 season. Branca, who wore number 13, posed with a black cat. He won thirteen games that season, then gave up Bobby Thomson's "Shot Heard Round the World" in the playoffs, which gave the Giants the pennant.

The Meat of the Order

Ballplayers sometimes use their meal money for strange things. Ron LeFlore was nicknamed the "Bosco Bear" because of his favorite beverage. Brett Butler was known to drink up to twenty cups of coffee before a game and was rarely caught napping on the basepaths. Denny McLain drank more than 100 bottles of Pepsi a week in his prime. Baltimore reliever Dick Hall once ate a seventeen-year cicada. See what's on the menu.

1. WADE BOGGS

Five-time batting champion Wade Boggs attributed much of his success to eating chicken. For nine years he ate nothing but chicken. Boggs chose from a thirteen-recipe rotation. Lemon chicken became a special favorite after Boggs rapped out seven hits in a doubleheader in 1982.

2. RUSTY STAUB

Rusty Staub retired in 1985 with 2,716 base hits. Nicknamed "Le Grand Orange" when he played in Montreal because of his red hair, the New Orleans native had the reputation of being a food and wine connoisseur. In August 1997, Staub served as a celebrity chef at the Trois Jean Bistro in New York. The menu included family recipes such as Soft Shell Crab Amandine and Shrimp Stuffed Eggplant.

3. PING BODIE

Ping Bodie was an outfielder in the American League from 1911 to 1921. During spring training in 1919, Bodie, who was playing for the Yankees, challenged an ostrich to a spaghetti eating contest. The epic encounter ended when the ostrich keeled over.

4. TOMMY LASORDA

In between diets, former Dodgers' manager Tommy Lasorda performed prodigious feats of eating. In one pregame meal in 1986, Lasorda won a bet by eating 100 oysters.

5. YOGI BERRA

When asked if he wanted his pizza sliced into four or eight pieces, Yogi replied, "Better make it four.

I don't think I can eat eight." The weight-conscious catcher once told a waitress, "I'll have some French fries, but no potatoes because I'm on a diet." Yogi once asked the clubhouse man to bring him a diet Tab.

6. BABE RUTH

Waite Hoyt said of Babe Ruth, "If you cut that big slop in half, most of the concessions of Yankees Stadium would come pouring out." For breakfast, Babe was known to eat chocolate ice cream washed down by beer, whiskey, and ginger ale.

7. JIMMIE FOXX

On July 3, 1940, slugger Jimmie Foxx was offered a dozen lobsters by a fan if he hit a home run. Foxx won the bet and ate all twelve lobsters in one sitting. Tragically, he choked to death on a piece of meat in 1967.

8. BEN MCDONALD

Louisiana native Ben McDonald swears that his favorite dish is squirrel head. He says that he finds the brain and tongue especially tasty.

9. MICKEY TETTLETON

Mickey Tettleton began his long and successful major league career with Oakland in 1984. In

1989, the catcher belted twenty-six home runs with Baltimore, fifteen more than he had ever hit in a season. He attributed his power surge to eating Fruit Loops cereal.

10. TOMMY BURNS

Tommy Burns played every position during his years in the majors from 1884 to 1895. A .301 career hitter, he was given the nickname "Oyster" because of the large number of oysters that he ate before each game. During the off-season, Burns made a living selling shellfish.

Fat Tubs of Goo

Baseball players come in all sizes. These players are of the extra large variety. Learn more about baseball's heavy hitters.

1. WALTER "JUMBO" BROWN

Jumbo Brown was the heaviest player in major league history, tipping the scales at nearly 300 pounds. The hefty hurler was good enough to lead the National League in saves in 1940 and 1941. Jumbo was so enormous that the Yankees billed him as the "man who swallowed a taxi cab."

2. TERRY FORSTER

Terry Forster pitched sixteen years in the majors and led the American League in saves in 1974. Unlike most relief pitchers, Forster was an excellent hitter, compiling a lifetime batting average of .397. In June 1985, he became immortalized when David Letterman described him as a "fat tub of goo." Forster, who weighted nearly 270 pounds, appeared on the program carrying seven hot dogs, a triple decker, two cans of Coke, and a candy bar. The reliever, capitalizing on his fame, made a music video entitled "Fat Is In." Forster joked, "A waist is a terrible thing to mind."

3. CHARLIE KERFELD

Twenty-two-year-old reliever Charlie Kerfeld was 11–2 with the Houston Astros in 1986. The only thing Kerfeld liked to do more than win was to eat. In July 1987, he was caught eating a plate of ribs in the bullpen during a game. As his weight ballooned past 250 pounds, he became less effective as a pitcher. Kerfeld didn't win another game and was out of baseball at age twenty-three. Charlie admitted that the only thing that intimidated him was a scale.

4. GARLAND BUCKEYE

Known as the "Pitching Pachyderm," Garland Buckeye had a 30–39 record in a career that ran from 1918 to 1928. The 260-pounder played guard for the NFL Cardinals from 1921 to 1924.

5. FATS FOTHERGILL

Bob "Fats" Fothergill batted over .300 his first eight seasons and retired in 1933 with a .326 batting average. Fothergill always seemed to hit .300

and weighed nearly as much. The overweight outfielder had a reputation for busting outfield fences while chasing fly balls. He once bit umpire Bill Dinneen during an argument. Fats, at the time in the midst of a crash diet, confessed, "That was the first bite of meat I had in a month."

6. DON ROBINSON

Don Robinson won fourteen games for Pittsburgh in 1978 and was voted the National League Rookie Pitcher of the Year. Concerned with Robinson's weight, management inserted an incentive clause that would pay him an extra $100,000 if he stayed below 225 pounds. Robinson renegotiated his contract to raise his weight limit to 235.

7. GATES BROWN

Pinch hitter extraordinaire Gates Brown batted .370 for the 1968 World Champion Detroit Tigers. On August 7, 1968, the Tigers were playing Cleveland when Brown was summoned to pinch hit. Caught by surprise, he was about to eat two hot dogs. Trying to conceal them from the manager, Brown stuffed them in his jersey. Brown hit a double and went into second head first. When he got up, Brown had mustard, catsup, and pieces of buns and wieners all over his uniform.

8. SHANTY HOGAN

James Hogan was a hard-hitting catcher who played from 1925 to 1937. The 240-pounder was nicknamed "Shanty" because he was shaped like a hut.

9. FAT FREDDIE GLADDING

Nicknamed the "Bear" and "Fat Freddie" because of his portly physique, Gladding was a solid reliever for thirteen seasons. He led the National League in saves while with Houston in 1969. Arguably the worst hitter in baseball history, he made only one hit in 450 games for a lifetime .016 average.

10. BOOG POWELL

Big Boog Powell slammed 339 home runs during his career, primarily with the Baltimore Orioles. He was the American League Most Valuable Player in 1970. Manager Frank Robinson once threatened to fine him $1,000 for every pound he weighed over 265. After an eating binge, his weight had soared to nearly 275. Today, Powell runs a successful barbecued ribs concession just beyond the right field stands in Baltimore's Camden Yards.

Graybeards

Life begins at forty for some players. Minnesota's Paul Molitor was forty years old when he led the American League with 225 hits in 1996. Phil Niekro of the Atlanta Braves led the National League with twenty-one wins in 1979 at the age of forty. Both Warren Spahn and Nolan Ryan pitched no-hitters after they turned forty. Impressive as these feats are, these players were in the prime compared to the players you are about to meet.

1. SATCHEL PAIGE

Satchel Paige was the oldest rookie in baseball history when he was signed by the Cleveland Indians in 1948. On September 25, 1965, the fifty-nine-year-old Paige pitched three scoreless innings for Kansas City against the Boston Red Sox to

Hoyt Wilhelm
Reliever Hoyt Wilhelm did not pitch in the major leagues until he was 28 years old and was 49 when he retired in 1972.

become the oldest player ever to appear in a major league game. Two years later, Satchel pitched an inning for Atlanta in an exhibition game versus AAA farm team Richmond and struck out two. His longevity secrets were revealed in his rules on how to stay young:

1. Avoid fried meats, which angry up the blood.
2. If your stomach disputes you, lie down and pacify it with cool thoughts.
3. Keep the juices flowing by jangling around gently as you move.

4. Go very light on the vices, such as carrying on in society. The social ramble ain't restful.

5. Avoid running at all times.

6. Don't look back. Something might be gaining on you.

Paige said, "Age is a matter of mind over matter. If you don't mind, it doesn't matter."

2. HUB KITTLE

The oldest man to play in a professional baseball game was Hub Kettle, who was sixty-three years old when he pitched an inning for a Class A team in Springfield, Illinois, in 1980.

3. MINNIE MINOSO

Minnie Minoso was nearly thirty when he broke into the major leagues in 1949. He made up for lost time, leading the league at various times in hits, doubles, triples, and stolen bases. On September 12, 1976, the fifty-three-year-old Minoso became the oldest player ever to get a base hit in a major league game. Four years later, he became the second player ever to appear in a major league game in five different decades. In 1990, the sixty-seven-year-old Minoso was scheduled to appear in a game for the Chicago White Sox, but Commissioner Fay Vincent refused to let him play because he felt it was just a ploy to increase attendance.

4. NICK ALTROCK

The other man to play in five different decades was Nick Altrock. He was a twenty-game winner for the Chicago White Stockings in 1905 and 1906. One of baseball's greatest clowns, Altrock appeared in his last game at the age of fifty-seven in 1933 with Washington.

5. PAT JORDAN

Pat Jordan was fifty-six years old when he pitched a scoreless inning for the Waterbury Spirits of the Northeast League on July 29, 1997. Jordan had last pitched professionally thirty-six years earlier for a Class D farm team of the Milwaukee Braves. In the years in between, he had been a successful writer, most notably for *Sports Illustrated.*

6. ORATOR JIM O'ROURKE

A graduate of the Yale Law School, Jim O'Rourke got his nickname because of his long-winded orations. A .310 lifetime hitter, he was elected to the Baseball Hall of Fame in 1945. In 1904, the fifty-two-year-old O'Rourke caught a game for the New York Giants and managed to hit a single and score a run. Eight years later, at the age of sixty, he caught an entire game for New Haven of the Connecticut League. O'Rourke was president of the league at the time.

7. JACK QUINN

Spitballer Jack Quinn won 247 games during his twenty-three-year career. He set a number of records for longevity. At age forty-six, he was the oldest pitcher to start a World Series game. When he was forty-seven, he became the oldest to hit a home run. Quinn was forty-nine years old when he became the oldest pitcher to win a major league game. Amazingly, he led the National League in saves with Brooklyn in 1932 when he was forty-nine years old.

8. HOYT WILHELM

Hoyt Wilhelm was the first relief pitcher to be inducted into the Baseball Hall of Fame. As a twenty-eight-year-old rookie in 1952, Wilhelm led the National League in earned run average, winning percentage, and games pitched. By the time he retired at age forty-nine in 1972, Wilhelm had pitched in a record 1,070 games.

9. CAP ANSON

Possibly the greatest player of the nineteenth century, Cap Anson played twenty-two seasons in

Chicago. In his final major league game on October 3, 1897, forty-five-year-old Anson belted two home runs.

10. CONNIE MACK

In 1950, fifty-six years after he managed his first major league game, Connie Mack, a few months shy of his eighty-eighth birthday, retired as manager of the Philadelphia Athletics.

Playing Young

Dwight Gooden won seventeen games for the Mets as a nineteen-year-old in 1984. All of the players in this chapter had major league experience before their eighteenth birthday.

1. JOE NUXHALL

Joe Nuxhall was a fifteen-year-old high school student in Hamilton, Ohio when he was signed to pitch for the Cincinnati Reds. On June 10, 1944, Nuxhall became the youngest player in major league history when he entered the game trailing 13–0 against the defending world champion St. Louis Cardinals. Nuxhall retired the first two batters, then gave up five runs on five walks and two hits. His earned run average for the game was an astronomical 67.50. Nuxhall recalled that he had been pitching to junior high students three weeks earlier and suddenly he's facing Stan Musial. He didn't pitch in the majors for another eight years, but eventually won 135 games.

2. CARL SCHEIB

Carl Scheib was another high school student pressed into major league action during World War II. On September 6, 1943, the sixteen-year-old became the youngest player in American League history when he pitched in a game for the Philadelphia Athletics. Although he pitched eleven years in the big leagues, Scheib was finished by the time he was twenty-seven.

3. JIM DERRINGTON

Sixteen-year-old Jim Derrington was the youngest player in the twentieth century to start a major league game. In 1956, he started for the Chicago White Sox, giving up five runs in six innings. Derrington never won a game and was out of the majors at the age of seventeen.

4. JOE RELFORD

Joe Relford, a twelve-year-old bat boy, was the youngest person ever to appear in a minor league baseball game. On July 19, 1952, Relford was put into a Class D game by Fitzgeralds' manager

Charlie Ridgeway as a lark in a hopelessly lost game. Relford grounded out but later made a great catch in the outfield. The manager and the umpire who permitted Relford to pinch hit were fired.

5. WILLIE MCGILL

Willie McGill was only sixteen years old when he won eleven games for Cleveland of the Players' League in 1890. McGill won twenty games as a seventeen-year-old, the youngest player ever to reach that milestone, but he was washed up by the age of twenty-two.

6. TOMMY BROWN

Tommy Brown was sixteen years old when he became the starting shortstop for the Brooklyn Dodgers in 1944. Nicknamed "Buckshot," he threw so erratically that the grounds crew sometimes placed the batting cage behind first base to protect the fans. At age seventeen, he became the youngest player to hit a home run in the majors.

7. ROGERS HORNSBY MCKEE

Rogers Hornsby McKee was sixteen years old when he pitched for the Philadelphia Phillies in 1943. McKee won only one game and was only seventeen years old when he pitched his last game in the majors.

8. BOB FELLER

Bob Feller was seventeen years old when he was brought up by Cleveland in 1936. In his major league debut, "Rapid Robert" struck out fifteen St. Louis Browns. Later that season he fanned seventeen Philadelphia A's in a game. Unlike many baseball prodigies, Feller went on to a long and successful career, winning 266 games.

9. MEL OTT

Another early bloomer, Mel Ott was only seventeen when he broke in with the New York Giants in 1926. In his first two seasons, Ott hit only one home run, but by the time he retired in 1947, he had set a National League record with 511 round trippers.

10. JAY DAHL

The Houston Astros made history when they started an all-rookie lineup in a game against the New York Mets on September 27, 1963. The team included future stars Joe Morgan, Rusty Staub, and Jimmy Wynn. The starting pitcher was seventeen-year-old Jay Dahl, who was knocked out of the box in the third inning of the 10–3 loss. Dahl never appeared in another major league game. On June 20, 1965, the nineteen-year-old was killed in an automobile accident, making him the youngest player with major league experience to die.

Minor League Phenoms

Minor league stardom doesn't always insure major league success. Each of these players were minor league sensations but had minor big league careers. Some never made it to the major leagues at all.

1. JOE BAUMAN

The unidentified flying objects over Roswell, New Mexico, in 1954 probably came off the bat of Joe Bauman. Playing for the Roswell Rockets in 1954, Bauman blasted 72 home runs and drove home 224 runs. His 72 homers and .916 slugging percentage are professional baseball records. Despite a .337 career batting average and 337 home runs, Bauman played only one game above Class A ball.

2. STEVE DALKOWSKI

Ted Williams, perhaps the greatest hitter of all time, proclaimed that Steve Dalkowski was the fastest pitcher he had ever seen. Unfortunately, he was also the wildest. During his nine-year career, Dalkowski walked 12.3 batters every nine innings. In 1957, he walked over two batters per inning. One of his high hard ones tore off a batter's ear lobe. Another fastball knocked the umpire twenty feet backwards. Not even the spectators were safe. A Dalkowski pitch was thrown so hard that it went through the screen behind home plate. He once pitched a one-hitter and lost 9–8. In 1959, he allowed forty-one hits in eighty-four innings and struck out 142 batters. The bad news is that he walked 190. He once fanned Joe Pepitone five times in one game. Just when it appeared that he had finally conquered his wildness and might reach the majors, he injured his arm.

3. RON NECCIAI

Ron Necciai pitched the most overpowering game in professional baseball history. On May 13, 1952, "Rocket" Ron struck out twenty-seven batters in a nine-inning no-hitter versus Welch. While pitching for Bristol in the Class C Appalachian League, he allowed only two hits and struck out seventy-seven in thirty-one innings. Rushed to the majors by the pitching-poor Pittsburgh Pirates, Necciai had a 1–6 record with a 7.08 earned run average in 1952. A sore arm and ulcer ended the Rocket's career before it ever really started.

4. HECTOR ESPINO

Hector Espino was the Babe Ruth of the minors. In a career that lasted from 1960 to 1984, he hit a minor league record 484 home runs. Espino spent most of his career in the Mexican Leagues because he claimed he was offended by the racial discrimination he had witnessed while playing for Jacksonville of the International League in 1964. Although the Cardinals, Mets, and Padres were interested in signing him, Espino turned down their offers because he did not want to play in the United States.

5. WALTER MALMQUIST

In 1913, Walter Malmquist set a professional baseball record when he batted .477 for York in the Nebraska State League. Despite his minor league heroics, Malmquist never reached the majors.

6. BOB RIESENER

Bob Riesener must have wondered what a guy had to do to make the majors. In 1957, pitching for Alexandria of the Class C Evangeline League, Riesener had a perfect 20–0 record. Buried in the talent-rich New York Yankees organization, he never played in the major leagues.

7. NIG CLARKE

Without a doubt the greatest power display in a professional game was an eight-home-run outburst by catcher Nig Clarke. He led his Corsicana team to a 51–3 rout of Texarkana in a game played on June 15, 1902. Clarke hit only six home runs in nine major league seasons.

8. **BILL THOMAS**

Bill Thomas pitched in more than 1,000 minor league games between 1926 and 1952. His 383 wins is a minor league record. Despite his success, Thomas toiled his entire career in the minors.

9. **BOB CRUES**

In 1948, Bob Crues hit sixty-nine home runs (including eight grand slams) and batted .404 for Amarillo of the West Texas-New Mexico League. His 254 runs batted in was a professional single season record. Like so many minor league record breakers, Crues never played in the major leagues.

10. **TOM LASORDA**

Lefthander Tom Lasorda struck out twenty-five batters while pitching for the Schnectady Blue Jays against the Amsterdam Rugmakers in 1948. In three major league seasons, two in Dodger blue, Lasorda had a 0–4 record and a 6.48 earned run average.

False Promise

It's always exciting when a young player breaks into the majors with a bang. More often than not, these players fail to live up to our expectations. Brooklyn outfielder Jack Dalton got five hits off Christy Mathewson in his second game but hit only .213 against the rest of the league. Frank Ernaga of the Chicago Cubs hit a home run and triple off Warren Spahn in his first two at-bats and had five extra base hits in his first eight at-bats. After the hot start, Ernaga had only two more extra base hits in the majors. All of the following players' best moments came at the very beginning of their careers.

1. BOBO HOLLOMAN

On May 6, 1953, Bobo Holloman of the St. Louis Browns pitched a no-hitter versus Philadelphia in his first major league start. The evening was so cold and rainy that owner Bill Veeck announced before the start of the game that rain checks would be provided for the 2,473 fans in attendance. Veeck was so impressed with the outing that he exercised a $25,000 option on the pitcher, instead of using the money to purchase the contract of minor league shortstop Ernie Banks. Holloman won only two more games in the majors while Banks had a Hall of Fame career in Chicago.

2. KARL SPOONER

In his major league debut on September 22, 1954, Brooklyn southpaw Karl Spooner struck out fifteen as he pitched a three-hit shutout against the pennant-winning New York Giants. Four days later, he fanned twelve in a four-hit whitewash of Pittsburgh. Spooner injured his arm the next spring and won only eight games. He was given the chance to start game six of the 1955 World Series against the New York Yankees. If he won, it would finally have ended the domination the Yanks had over the Dodgers in the fall classic. Spooner was shelled for five runs in the first inning, which proved to be his final appearance in the major leagues. The next day, another young lefthander, Johnny Podres, became a hero by shutting out the Yankees. Spooner's spot on the roster was filled by another promising southpaw. His name was Sandy Koufax.

3. CLINT HARTUNG

Perhaps the biggest bust in baseball history was Clint Hartung. Ballyhooed as the next Babe Ruth, Hartung had batted .567 and was 25–0 as a pitcher while playing for armed services teams during World War II. He showed promise as a rookie, batting .309 and compiling a 9–7 record as a pitcher with New York in 1947. The Giants couldn't decide if he should be a pitcher or play in the outfield. Soon it became apparent that he was a double threat: he couldn't pitch and he couldn't hit. On the mound his career earned run average was a dismal 5.02, and his batting average dipped to .238. Originally known as the "Hondo Hurricane," Hartung was later referred to as "Floppy."

4. BILL ROHR

In his major league debut on April 14, 1969, Boston lefthander Bob Rohr pitched eight innings of no-hit ball before New York's Elston Howard broke it up with a single. Rohr won only two more games and was through by the time he was twenty-two.

5. PAUL PETTIT

Paul Pettit was considered a can't-miss prospect. Pettit had pitched six no-hitters in high school and was brought to the majors at the age of nineteen by Pittsburgh in 1951. In his contract, the club promised to pay for an all-expenses paid honeymoon in Hawaii if he got married and called for a movie deal to film his life story if he became a star. The cameras never started rolling as Pettit won only one game in the major leagues.

6. JOE PATE

Joe Pate was 9–0 as a rookie pitcher with the Philadelphia A's in 1926. After the auspicious start, Pate never won another game in the major leagues.

7. RUSS VAN ATTA

Russ Van Atta may have had the greatest debut in major league history. On April 25, 1933, the Yankees' southpaw pitched a shutout against Washington, winning the game 16–0. He also had four hits in the game. After a 12–4 rookie season, Van Atta compiled a 21–37 record with a 5.60 career earned run average.

8. LEFTY RUSSELL

Philadelphia's Lefty Russell pitched a shutout in his major league debut on October 1, 1910. He lost his remaining five decisions in the majors, and his earned run average soared to 6.36.

9. BILL ROMAN

Detroit first baseman Bill Roman hit a home run in his first major league at-bat on September 30, 1964. Roman had only four more hits in the major leagues, and his lifetime batting average was an anemic .143.

10. JESSE STOVALL

Cleveland lefthander Jesse Stovall pitched an eleven-inning shutout in his major league debut on September 3, 1903. Stovall was out of baseball after a 3–13 record the next season.

One Game Wonders

One of the wonderful things about baseball is that anyone can become a hero for a day. These players had undistinguished careers interrupted by a game of a lifetime.

1. JOHN PACIOREK

John Paciorek was eighteen years old when he played his first game with the Houston Astros on September 29, 1963. He went three for three, walked twice, scored four runs, and batted in three. You could say he played the game of his life. You can say that because it was his only major league game. The next season Paciorek injured his back and batted only .135 in the minor leagues.

2. TOM CHENEY

Tom Cheney did something that Roger Clemens, Randy Johnson, Nolan Ryan, Steve Carlton, Tom

Seaver, and Sandy Koufax were never able to do. On September 12, 1962, Cheney, pitching for the Washington Senators, struck out twenty-one batters in a sixteen-inning game against Baltimore. The twenty-one strikeouts is a major league record for a pitcher in a single game. The record for a nine-inning game is twenty, shared by Roger Clemens and Kerry Wood. Cheney never had a winning season and finished his eight-year career with a 19–29 record.

3. CHARLIE ROBERTSON

In only his third major league game, Chicago White Sox pitcher Charlie Robertson pitched a perfect game against the Detroit Tigers on April 30, 1922. His stuff was so outstanding that Tiger players Ty Cobb and Harry Heilmann complained throughout the game that Robertson was doctoring the ball. In the ninth inning the umpire went to the mound and examined his uniform and glove but found no foreign substances. Robertson never recreated the magic of that day and had a dreadful 49–80 lifetime record.

4. CESAR GUTIERREZ

Light-hitting Detroit Tigers shortstop Cesar Gutierrez went seven for seven in a game on June 21, 1970. He tied the major league record for the most hits in a game without making an out. The seven hits matched his total for the entire 1971 season, his last in the majors.

5. RAY JANSEN

St. Louis Browns' third baseman Ray Jansen collected four hits in five at-bats in his big league debut on September 30, 1910. He never played another game, closing out his career with a .800 batting average.

6. MARK WHITEN

For most of his career, Mark Whiten has been a journeyman player, but on September 7, 1993, he tied two of baseball's most impressive single game records. The St. Louis outfielder hit four home runs and batted in twelve runs in the second game of a doubleheader against Cincinnati. Whiten is the only player to have both four homers and twelve RBIs in the same game. His final homer was a 440-foot shot to center field off Reds' flamethrowing reliever, Rob Dibble.

7. FLOYD GIEBELL

In the final days of the 1940 season, Detroit and Cleveland were locked in a close pennant race. On September 27 the Indians were scheduled to pitch their ace, Bob Feller. Unexpectedly, Detroit manager Del Baker handed the ball to rookie Floyd Giebell. The rookie shocked everyone by defeating Feller and the Indians 2–0 to clinch the pennant for Detroit. For Giebell, it was the third victory of his career, and his last.

8. KEN ASH

Ken Ash could be classified as a one-inning wonder. On July 27, 1930, the Cincinnati Reds reliever entered the game against Chicago in the sixth inning. With no outs and runners on first and second, Ash enticed Charlie Grimm to hit into a triple play on his first pitch. Ash had recorded three outs on just one pitch. The Reds rallied to win 6–5, and Ash was the winner, one of only six victories he was credited with in the majors.

9. GENE STEPHENS

Another one-inning wonder was Boston outfielder Gene Stephens. The Red Sox set an American League record when they scored seventeen runs in the seventh inning of a game against Detroit on June 11, 1953. Stephens set another record when he became the only modern player to collect three hits in an inning. Catcher Sammy White also set a record when he scored three runs. Groomed to be the replacement for Red Sox legend Ted Williams, Stephens never played regularly in the majors in twelve seasons.

10. **PHIL WEINTRAUB**

First baseman Phil Weintraub had played for the Giants, Reds, and Phillies between 1933 and 1938. After being out of the majors for six years, Weintraub was given another chance to play because many major leaguers were in the military during World War II. Weintraub made the most of his comeback with a career day on April 30, 1944. He batted in eleven runs, one short of the record, in a 26–8 Giants victory over Brooklyn. In seven major league seasons, Weintraub averaged fewer than thirty RBIs per season.

One Year Wonders

Superstars are players who are great every year. Some players only achieve greatness for one season. They are baseball's one-year wonders.

Zoilo "Zorro" Versalles
Minnesota shortstop Zoilo Versalles was the American League Most Valuable Player in 1965, a performance he never came close to duplicating.

1. ROSS BARNES

The National League's first star was Chicago second baseman Ross Barnes. He hit the first home run in National League history on May 2, 1876. That year he led the league in hits, runs, doubles, bases on balls, batting average, and slugging percentage. His .429 batting average was the result of his mastery of the fair-foul rule. Under the rules of the day, if any ball hit fair and kicked foul, it was in play. Barnes perfected the art of slapping balls that skipped foul and were almost impossible to defense. When the rule was changed the following season, his batting average plummeted 157 points. When Barnes missed some games due to a muscle injury, owner William Hulbert withheld $1,000 of his $2,500 salary.

2. FRED DUNLAP

The Union Association lasted only one year—1884. The unquestioned star of the league was second baseman Fred "Sureshot" Dunlap. Dunlap had signed with the new league for a record $3,400 per year. He led the Union Association in batting, hits, home runs, runs scored, and slugging percentage. When he returned to the National League in 1885, Dunlap's average dropped from .412 to .270.

3. JOCKO FLYNN

Jocko Flynn was the ultimate one-year wonder. In 1886, Flynn was 24–6 and led the National League in winning percentage while pitching for Chicago. For unknown reasons, he never pitched another game in the major leagues.

4. NED WILLIAMSON

Ned Williamson was light-hitting third baseman during the early years of the National League. Known primarily for his defensive skills, he became a slugger when the fences of Chicago's Lake Front Park were moved in to 196 feet in right field and 180 feet in left. Thanks to the short fences, Williamson hit a record twenty-seven home runs in 1884. He had never hit more than three in any of his first six seasons. When the fences were moved back the next year, Williamson's homer total fell to three. His record stood for thirty-five years until Babe Ruth hit twenty-nine in 1919.

5. EARL WEBB

In 1931, Boston outfielder Earl Webb set a single season record for doubles that still stands. His sixty-seven doubles were thirty-seven more than he had in any other season.

6. GEORGE WATKINS

Cardinals' outfielder George Watkins batted a sensational .373 in 119 games during his rookie season in 1930. After his fantastic rookie year, Watkins's average fell eighty-five points the next season.

7. ZOILO VERSALLES

Versalles was the runaway Most Valuable Player winner in 1965. The Twins' shortstop led the American League in at-bats, doubles, triples, and runs. His leadership helped Minnesota win their first pennant. Bothered by back problems, he never hit above .250 again.

8. BOB HAZLE

Brought up from the minors in July 1957, Bob "Hurricane" Hazle tore up the National League and was a major reason why the Milwaukee Braves won their first pennant. The next year Hurricane's average dipped from .403 to .179, and he was shipped to Detroit.

9. BILLY TAYLOR

In 1884 pitcher Billy Taylor won forty-three games while dividing his season between St. Louis of the Union Association and Philadelphia of the American Association. He won only seven games in six other seasons.

10. FRANK KNAUSS

As a rookie pitcher with Columbus of the American Association in 1890, Frank Knauss won seventeen games. He played four more seasons in the major leagues, but never won another game.

Going Batty

Bats can be the hitter's best friend and the pitcher's worst nightmare. Sluggers Josh Gibson and Darryl Strawberry were known to kiss their bats. Frankie Frisch hung bats in his barn to "cure" them. It was rumored that Joe Sewell, the hardest man in baseball history to strike out, used the same bat throughout his fourteen-year career. Ripper Collins collected broken bats that he used to build fences on his estate in Rochester, New York. Take a few swings with these sluggers.

1. PETE "THE GLADIATOR" BROWNING

One of the great students of hitting, Pete "The Gladiator" Browning is the man responsible for starting the customized bat industry. In 1884, Browning walked into the J. F. Hillerich's wood shop in his hometown of Louisville, Kentucky.

Browning was in a rare slump and ordered a bat made to his exact specifications. He immediately broke out of the slump and extolled the virtues of his personalized bat throughout the league. Overnight the small wood shop became Hillerich & Bradsby, the world's largest bat manufacturer and maker of the famed Louisville Slugger. Browning owned more than 700 bats, each of which he gave a name, often biblical in origin. The Gladiator won three batting titles and had a .343 lifetime batting average.

2. HACK MILLER

Hack Miller was the strong man of baseball. He performed amazing feats of strength, such as bending iron bars and pounding spikes into wood with his fist. Miller generally used a forty-seven-ounce bat, but once toted a sixty-five-ouncer to the plate. Between 1916 and 1925, the outfielder compiled a .323 lifetime batting average.

3. BILL "LITTLE EVA" LANGE

Bill "Little Eva" Lange was one of the best and most popular players of the 1890s. A great showman, Lange once went to the plate with a bat nearly six feet long, almost two-and-one-half feet longer than regulation. Little Eva hit a grounder and reached base on an error.

4. EDDIE GAEDEL

Only three feet seven inches tall, Eddie Gaedel was the smallest player ever to appear in a major league game. Sent up to pinch hit for the St. Louis Browns in a game against Detroit on August 19, 1951, Gaedel came to the plate carrying a toylike 17-inch bat, less than half the size of a normal bat. Instructed by owner Bill Veeck not to swing, Gaedel crouched at the plate, making it virtually impossible for Detroit pitcher Bob Cain to throw a strike. Gaedel was walked on four pitches.

5. TY COBB

Ty Cobb's .366 lifetime batting average is easily the best in baseball history. Cobb named his forty-two-ounce black bat "Magic." No one was permitted to touch it, and Cobb rarely let it out of his sight. The Georgia Peach once brought his bat to a wedding and frequently dined with it.

6. HEINIE GROH

Third baseman Heinie Groh played for the 1919 world champion Cincinnati Reds and was a mainstay with the New York Giants' championship teams of the early 1920s. Groh's trademark was his bottle bat, a specially designed bat with a thick barrel and tapered handle. Using his bottle bat, Groh twice led the league in doubles.

7. RICHIE ASHBURN

Hall of Fame outfielder Richie Ashburn was one of the game's great contact hitters. A .308 lifetime hitter, Ashburn was the National League batting champion in 1955 and 1958. Once, when Ashburn was mired in a rare slump, he took his bat to bed. "I wanted to know my bat a little better," he reasoned.

8. WEE WILLIE KEELER

Wee Willie Keeler stood only five feet four inches tall and used the smallest bat (with the exception of Eddie Gaedel) in professional baseball history. The bat was thirty inches long and only 2.5 inches in diameter. Keeler choked up halfway on the bat and mastered the Baltimore Chop in which he would hit down on the ball, allowing him to beat out infield hits. His .345 career batting average is fifth all-time, and his .432 average in 1897 is the best ever for a lefthanded batter.

9. JOHNNY MIZE

Slugger Johnny Mize used sixty bats, each one for a different pitcher. He used longer bats for lefthanders so he could reach pitches tailing away from him. Mize practiced his swing in the hotel room while puffing on a cigar. The "Big Cat" led the National League in home runs in 1939, 1940, 1947, and 1948.

10. **EDDIE COLLINS**

Eddie Collins played in the major leagues between 1906 and 1933 and was one of the greatest second basemen in baseball history. Collins sometimes buried his bats in shallow holes he called "graves" to "keep them lively." It must have worked because Collins wrapped out 3,311 hits in his long career.

Having a Ball

Baseballs used in major league games are uniform in size and weight. Each one weighs 5 to 5¼ ounces, measures 9 to 9¼ inches in circumference, and is 3 inches in diameter. The liveliness of the ball seems to vary from year to year. There have been dead ball eras as well as periods when juiced balls were in play. As evidenced by this chapter, some unusual things can be done to the horsehide during a game.

1. WILLIAM "BLONDIE" PURCELL

In the early days of baseball, umpires rarely removed a ball from play no matter how dirty or scuffed it was. On June 6, 1882, Buffalo pitcher Pud Galvin was having trouble throwing a curve because the ball was so soggy. Teammate Blondie Purcell cut the baseball in half so that the umpire would be forced to give Galvin a new one.

2. **ED WALSH**

Ed Walsh fashioned a 1.82 career earned run average, the lowest in the history of baseball. His secret to success was the nastiest spitter in the game. During Walsh's career, from 1904 to 1917, the spitball was a legal pitch. Sam Crawford complained that Walsh's wet one was so loaded up that all he could see was spit going by. Walsh licked the ball rather than spitting on it. The Philadelphia A's tried to break him of the unsanitary habit by rubbing horse manure on the horsehide. "I vomited all over the place," Walsh admitted. He retaliated by throwing beanballs at all the A's hitters.

3. **WHITEY FORD**

The New York Yankees won eleven pennants while Whitey Ford was their ace. The "Chairman of the Board" won 236 games and his .690 winning percentage is the third best in baseball history. Ford doctored the ball in more ways than any other pitcher. He cut the ball with a ring or sometimes had catcher Elston Howard slice it with a buckle on his shin guard. He perfected the "mud ball," which he loaded up while reaching for the resin bag. Ford's greatest creation was the "gunk" ball. The magic formula consisted of baby oil, turpentine, and resin. Whitey kept the concoction in a roll-on deodorant bottle. Unsuspecting,

Whitey Ford
Throwing illegal pitches such as the mud ball and gunk ball, Yankees' ace Whitey Ford won 236 games.

teammate Yogi Berra once used the deodorant after a shower and ran screaming from the locker room with his arms glued to his sides.

4. RUSS FORD

Not as well known as Whitey, Russ Ford nevertheless won twenty games three times between 1910 and 1914. Ford was the man credited with the discovery that if a pitcher scuffed the ball, it would dip in a manner that would make it extremely difficult to hit. He developed the emery ball, which he would scuff with emery paper concealed in his glove.

5. SMOKEY JOE WILLIAMS

Smokey Joe Williams pitched from 1905 to 1932 and was one of the greatest stars of the Negro Leagues. He once struck out twenty while no-hitting the New York Giants in 1917, and fanned twenty-seven in a Negro League game. Besides his blazing fastball, Smokey Joe had an arsenal of illegal pitches: sandpapered ball, emery ball, and his specialty, the goo ball on which he rubbed a black, tarlike substance.

6. RICK HONEYCUTT

Rick Honeycutt had a long and successful career as a pitcher, highlighted by an earned run average title in 1983. The low point of his career was in 1980 when he was discovered cutting a ball with a tack he had taped to his finger. Absentmindedly, he rubbed his finger across his face, cutting himself and narrowly missing taking his eye out.

7. BOBBY MATHEWS

The dubious distinction of being the inventor of the spitball belongs to Bobby Mathews. He won thirty games three consecutive seasons for Philadelphia from 1883 to 1885. Mathews was the first to realize that moisture placed on the ball causes it to drop dramatically just as it reaches the plate. Since the ball was blackened in those days, Mathews used the saliva to create a white spot, about the size of a quarter. The optical illusion also contributed to the effectiveness of the pitch.

8. HOD ELLER

Hod Eller was a twenty-game winner for the champion 1919 Cincinnati Reds and won two games during the World Series against the Chicago White Sox. Eller was the creator of the shineball, an erratically moving pitch that resulted from rubbing talcum powder on the baseball.

9. LARRY MACPHAIL

Larry MacPhail was the visionary executive who introduced night baseball. One of his innovations that failed, though, was yellow baseballs. MacPhail believed that the colored baseballs would be easier to see. They were used in four games during the 1938 season but were never adopted by the major leagues.

10. CHARLIE FINLEY

Oakland A's owner Charlie Finley, the man who brought the game white shoes and green and gold uniforms, tried to introduce orange baseballs to the national pastime. In 1973, he experimented with the orange-colored balls during spring training. Finley argued that the orange balls reduced the glare of the lights during night games. Like MacPhail's yellow balls, orange baseballs never gained acceptance.

Records that Aren't Meant to Be Broken

Records are meant to be broken. They said that Babe Ruth's career home run mark would never be broken, until Hank Aaron passed him in 1974. Ty Cobb's 4,191 career base hits seemed unassailable until Pete Rose came along. Joe DiMaggio's fifty-six-game hitting streak is often cited as the current record least likely to be broken. Here are some records even more unapproachable.

1. JACK TAYLOR

Perhaps the record least likely to be broken is Jack Taylor's mark of 188 consecutive complete games. Today's pitchers rarely finish what they start. From June 20, 1901 until August 9, 1906, Taylor was never knocked out of the box. His 1.33 earned run average in 1902 led the National League.

2. WILL WHITE

Almost totally forgotten today, pitcher Will White three times won forty or more games in a season. He set two single season records in 1879 while pitching for Cincinnati that will never be broken. White pitched seventy-five complete games and hurled 680 innings.

3. CY YOUNG

The great Cy Young won 511 games during his illustrious career that lasted from 1890 to 1911. To put the record in perspective, a player could win 20 games for twenty-five consecutive seasons and still fall 11 victories short.

4. OLD HOSS RADBOURNE

Today, twenty wins in a season is the standard of excellence for a pitcher. In 1884, Old Hoss Radbourne won sixty games pitching for Providence, a record that will almost certainly never be broken. Proving that figure was no fluke, he won forty-nine games the following season.

5. WAHOO SAM CRAWFORD

Hall of Fame outfielder Sam Crawford's career mark of 312 triples will never be challenged. He led the league in triples six times between 1902 and 1915. Crawford had the perfect combination of speed and power and played in the dead ball era when home runs were scarce.

6. OWEN WILSON

Another triple threat was Pittsburgh outfielder Owen Wilson. In 1912, he legged out thirty-six three baggers, a record not likely to be surpassed. Wilson never had more than fourteen triples in any other season.

7. MATCHES KILROY

When Nolan Ryan struck out 383 batters in 1973, he set the modern single season strikeout record. The Express still fell 130 strikeouts short of the record established by Matches Kilroy, who struck out 513 during his rookie season with Baltimore in 1886. Although Kilroy led the American Association with forty-six wins the next year, he never struck out more than 217 in a season for the remainder of his career.

8. HUGH DUFFY

It's been more than fifty years since Ted Williams was the last player to hit .400 in a season. Boston outfielder Hugh Duffy's record average of .438, which he achieved in the 1894 season, seems safe for at least another half-century.

9. BILLY HAMILTON

Sliding Billy Hamilton was one of the best players of the nineteenth century. In 1894, while playing with Philadelphia, he scored a record 196 runs. To put the achievement in perspective, when Ricky Henderson scored 146 runs in 1985 (the most in the majors since 1948), he still fell 50 runs short of Hamilton's record.

10. CLYDE BARNHART

Pittsburgh rookie third sacker Clyde Barnhart became the only major leaguer to hit safely in three games in one day. It occurred on October 2, 1920 in a rare tripleheader against Cincinnati.

The Mendoza Line

Bob Uecker has made a career joking about his poor hitting. Uecker's .200 career batting average undoubtedly gave him a lot of material. Mario Mendoza was a weak-hitting shortstop who played between 1974 and 1982. George Brett claimed that he always looked at the weekly listing of batting averages to see who was below the "Mendoza Line." The Mendoza Line has come to signify anyone hitting less than .200. Mendoza, a lifetime .215 hitter (who became a hitting instructor after he retired as a player), was Ty Cobb compared to the men included in this section.

1. BILL BERGEN

As a poor hitter, catcher Bill Bergen was in a class of his own. His .170 career batting average is 42 points lower than any other player with at least

2,500 at-bats. His .139 average in 1909 (he had only three extra base hits in 346 at-bats) is the lowest ever for a player with enough plate appearances to qualify for a batting title. Bergen finished 200 points behind batting champion Honus Wagner that season.

2. RON HERBEL

If Bill Bergen was the worst hitting nonpitcher, Ron Herbel may have been the worst hitter of all time. Herbel finished his major league career in 1971 with an all-time low .029 batting average, collecting only six hits in 206 at-bats. Only once in nine seasons did he have more than one hit.

3. BOB BUHL

Bob Buhl was a pretty good pitcher (166–132 lifetime record) who was a really bad hitter (.089 career batting average). In 1962, he set the standard for futility by going hitless in seventy at-bats.

4. JOHN VUKOVICH

John Vukovich was a utility player during the 1970s who was a futility player at the plate. Vukovich played all the infield positions and couldn't hit at any of them. In ten seasons, he compiled a horrible .161 batting average, averaging only nine hits per season.

5. RAY OYLER

Ray Oyler was such a bad hitter that the fans in Seattle formed a fan club. Members marveled at his sheer ineptitude with the bat. A .175 lifetime hitter, Oyler was replaced at shortstop by outfielder Mickey Stanley in the 1968 World Series after hitting a career low of .135 in 215 at-bats in 1968.

6. BILL HOLBERT

When catcher Bill Holbert came to the plate, there was an instant power outage. Over his twelve-year major league career, from 1876 to 1888, Holbert had 2,335 at-bats and never hit a home run. His career batting average was a dismal .208.

7. TOMMY THEVENOW

Shortstop Tommy Thevenow hit the only two regular season home runs of his career in 1926. For the next twelve seasons, Thevenow came to the plate a record 3,347 times without a homer.

8. DAL MAXVILL

Dal Maxvill personified the old adage "good field, no hit." In 1970, the Cardinals' shortstop set the record for the fewest number of hits (80) and fewest extra base hits (7) for a player appearing in 150 games. He proved it was no fluke by collecting only 80 hits again the following season.

9. BURLEIGH GRIMES

Burleigh Grimes was a Hall of Fame pitcher (270 wins) and a decent hitter (.248 batting average). However, in a 1925 game, he accounted for seven outs in only three at-bats. In consecutive at-bats "Ol' Stubblebeard" hit into two double plays and a triple play.

10. BUDDY BIANCALANA

Kansas City infielder Buddy Biancalana's hitting (or lack of it) was the butt of jokes made by David Letterman on his *Late Night* show. He kept a nightly countdown of how many hits Biancalana needed to pass Pete Rose as the all-time hit leader. Biancalana finished with 113, only 4,143 short of Rose. Not appreciating the comparisons, Buddy remarked, "I'm still a lot closer to Rose than he is in pursuit of Johnny Carson."

Sultans of Swish

Joe Sewell was the hardest man in major league history to strike out, fanning only once every 62.6 at-bats. By contrast, Dave Nicholson headed back to the dugout every 2.4 at-bats. The chapter is dedicated to the Kings of the K.

1. REGGIE JACKSON

The undisputed strikeout champion has to be Reggie Jackson. He fanned 2,597 times, 661 times more than his closest rival, Willie Stargell. Eighteen seasons Reggie whiffed more than 100 times, peaking at 171 in 1968. In essence, Jackson struck out the equivalent of four full seasons.

2. DAVE NICHOLSON

1940s slugger Bill Nicholson earned the nickname "Swish" because of his classic strikeout form. The nickname really should have belonged to Dave Nicholson, the 1960s outfielder who took the art of striking out to a new level. Dave struck out once every 2.48 at-bats, a record. His banner year was 1963 when he struck out what was then a record 175 times. He tied another record by fanning four times in a game on three separate occasions.

3. BOBBY BONDS

Bobby Bonds was not your typical leadoff hitter. He hit 332 home runs and struck out 1,757 times. In 1969, he set a major league record by striking out 187 times. The next season he upped the mark to 189. Ten times he fanned 120 or more times in a season.

4. JIMMIE FOXX

Ninety-seven of baseball's top one hundred career strikeout kings have played in the second half of the twentieth century. The only two old-timers to rank in the top fifty are Babe Ruth and Jimmie Foxx. "Double X" set a record by leading the American League in strikeouts seven times.

5. PETE INCAVIGLIA

Pete Incaviglia was the NCAA Player of the Year at Oklahoma State in 1985. In 1986, the rookie

Rangers' outfielder set an American League record with 185 strikeouts. He fanned 168 times the next season, thus proving it was no fluke.

6. ROB DEER

During his career from 1984 to 1993, outfielder Rob Deer struck out 1,379 times in only 3,831 at-bats. Deer fanned 186 times in 1987 and 179 the previous year.

7. GORMAN THOMAS

Milwaukee outfielder Gorman Thomas struck out 1,339 times in 4,677 at-bats. He led the American League with 175 strikeouts in 1979 and 170 the following season.

8. WOODIE HELD

An underappreciated strikeout artist, Woodie Held struck out nearly once every four times during his fourteen-year career, which ended in 1969. What made Woodie stand out were the frequent tantrums that followed his strikeouts.

9. WILLIE STARGELL

Willie Stargell is the all-time National League strikeout leader with 1,936. He struck out 100 or more times twelve consecutive years and led the league with 154 in 1971.

10. VINCE DIMAGGIO

The older brother of Joe DiMaggio, Vince led the National League in strikeouts a record six times. His 134 whiffs during the 1938 season set a record since eclipsed.

The Worst Pitching Performances of All Time

Batting practice usually occurs before the game, but in these instances the batters took batting practice after the National Anthem was sung. Here are the creme de la creme of badly pitched games.

1. JACK WADSWORTH

Perhaps the worst pitcher of all time, Jack Wadsworth also pitched the worst game in major league history. On August 17, 1894, Wadsworth, pitching for the Louisville Colonels, was mauled for twenty-nine runs and thirty-six hits by Philadelphia. Sam Thompson had six hits and hit for the cycle while three other teammates had five hits each. For his career, Wadsworth fashioned a 6–38 record with a 6.58 earned run average.

2. C. B. DEWITT

On June 15, 1902, the Corsicana Oilers walloped the Texarkana Tigers 51–3 in a Texas League game. Pitcher C. B. DeWitt (who also owned the team) was shellacked for fifty-one runs and fifty-three hits. He surrendered twenty-one home runs, eight of them to Nig Clarke.

3. DAVE ROWE

Cleveland outfielder Dave Rowe was asked to pitch a game against Chicago on July 24, 1882. Rowe was roughed up for twenty-nine hits and thirty-five runs in a 35–4 drubbing. Rowe pitched four games during his career, giving up fifty-four hits in twenty-three innings and compiling a 9.78 earned run average.

4. AL TRAVERS

In May 1912, Ty Cobb was suspended after beating a heckler senseless. His Tiger teammates went on strike to support Cobb. On May 18, Detroit faced the mighty Philadelphia Athletics with a team composed of amateurs and coaches. Seminary student Al Travers pitched a complete game, giving up twenty-four runs and twenty-six hits in a 24–2 loss. Cobb was soon reinstated, and Travers never pitched in another major league game.

5. DOC PARKER

Righthander Doc Parker gave up twenty-one runs and twenty-six hits against Brooklyn in his first game with Cincinnati in 1901. Batters were so eager to face Parker that they ran to the plate. "The next time I get in the box I hope to give a better account of myself," Parker vowed. For Parker, though, there would be no next time.

6. ED ROMMEL

Philadelphia A's owner Connie Mack decided to send only two pitchers on a one-day road trip to Cleveland. When starter Lew Krausse was knocked out in the first inning, reliever Ed Rommel entered the game. The game lasted eighteen innings with the A's prevailing 18–17. Rommel gave up twenty-nine hits, a record for a reliever, but still got the win. Cleveland's Johnny Burnett had a record nine hits in the game.

7. STUMP WEIDMAN

Stump Weidman led the National League in earned run average (1.80) in 1881. For most of his career, Stump was less successful. On September 6, 1883, Weidman gave up a record thirteen base hits in an inning while pitching for Detroit. In 1886, he led the National League in losses, with thirty-six.

8. WILLIAM REIDY

In 1901, Milwaukee pitcher William Reidy gave up a record ten consecutive hits in the ninth inning of a 13–2 loss to Boston. Reidy was a twenty-game loser that season.

9. JOE CLEARY

Making his major league debut on August 4, 1945, Joe Cleary of the Washington Senators was tagged for seven runs in one-third of an inning by the Boston Red Sox. His 189.00 career earned run average is the worst in major league history.

10. BIFF WYSONG

On August 10, 1930, lefthander Biff Wysong made his major league debut against Philadelphia. Wysong was honored in a special Appreciation Day by residents of his hometown, Clarksville, Ohio. Biff was knocked out of the box in the third inning as the Phillies routed the Reds 18–0. The Reds didn't appreciate Wysong's 19.29 earned run average and shipped him to the minors.

I'm a Loser

Some people just can't win. Although he had a respectable 3.62 earned run average, Steve Gerken went 0–12 with a Philadelphia A's club that won only fifty-two games in 1945. Happy Jack Townsend's 35–82 lifetime record left him with little to smile about. Dory Dean (4–26 career record) was never confused with Dizzy Dean. Other pitchers with a L next to their name in the box score were Buster Brown (48–105), Ike Pearson (13–50), Bill Bailey (34–78), and Kirtley Baker (9–38). If you think it can't get any worse than that, then read on.

1. **TERRY FELTON**

Terry Felton deserves special recognition as the pitcher who lost the most games without ever winning one. In 1980, he previewed things to come by going 0–3 with a 7.00 earned run average for the Minnesota Twins. The next season he made his one appearance memorable by giving up six runs in one inning. Felton ended his career with a flourish in 1982, losing all thirteen decisions. For his career Felton was a perfect 0–16.

2. ANTHONY YOUNG

Terry Felton would have had to lose a dozen more games to break the record of Anthony Young. From May 6, 1991 until July 24, 1993, Young lost an incredible twenty-seven straight decisions.

3. CLIFF CURTIS

On June 13, 1910, Boston righthander Cliff Curtis began a streak of twenty-three consecutive losses. A victim of nonsupport, Curtis had a career record of 28–61 in spite of a decent 3.31 earned run average.

4. JACK NABORS

Jack Nabors' career record of 1–25 is partly attributable to the fact that he played for the horrendous Philadelphia Athletics teams of 1915 and 1916. After a five-year championship run (1910–14), owner Connie Mack sold off his best players. Nabors was 0–5 as a rookie. Then he lost nineteen in a row during a 1–20 season for the 1916 A's (36–117), the worst record of any team of the twentieth century. Nabors was only the third losingest pitcher on the team.

5. JOHN COLEMAN

During his rookie season in 1883, Philadelphia pitcher John Coleman set records that will never be broken. Coleman lost forty-eight games and gave up 772 hits. Wisely, he played most of the rest of his career in the outfield. Coleman closed out his career in 1890 with twenty-three wins and seventy-two losses.

6. JOE HARRIS

Joe Harris was not the luckiest pitcher ever to play the game. Pitching for Boston between 1905 and 1907, Harris won three and lost thirty. In 1906, he led the American League in losses with twenty-one, including fourteen in a row. Even when he pitched a good game, he lost. He set an American League record by dueling with Philadelphia's Jack Coombs for twenty-four innings. Naturally, Harris lost, 4–1.

7. HUGH MULCAHY

Philadelphia's Hugh Mulcahy earned the nickname "Losing Pitcher" by leading the National League in losses in both 1938 and 1940. Phillies' fans thought their luck might be changing when

Mulcahy was the first major leaguer inducted into the service during World War II. How he fared during the war is a mystery, although Philadelphia fans may have suspected that any grenades he threw were probably lined back through his legs. Mulcahy did fight on the winning side in the war. Unfortunately, he was 45–89 lifetime, the worst winning percentage in the twentieth century for a hurler with more than 100 decisions.

8. **COLDWATER JIM HUGHEY**

Coldwater Jim Hughey was the ace of the remarkable 1899 Cleveland Spiders' pitching staff. The Spiders had the worst record in baseball history (20–134), and they owed much of it to Hughey, who was 4–30 and led the National League in losses. Coldwater Jim (who received his nickname, surprisingly, not because of all the early showers he took but because his hometown was Coldwater, Michigan) was 29–80 during his seven years in the majors, and his winning percentage is the lowest for any pitcher with at least 100 decisions. Other pitchers in the Spiders' rotation included "Crazy" Schmidt (2–17), Frank (no relation to Norman) Bates (1–18), "Still" Bill Hill (3–6), and Harry Colliflower (1–11).

9. BOB GROOM

Bob Groom lost nineteen consecutive games during his rookie season with Washington in 1909. He led the league in losses in 1909, 1914, and 1917. On the plus side, Groom won twenty-four games in 1912 and pitched a no-hitter in 1917.

10. MARK LEMONGELLO

Mark Lemongello was 22–38 during his career, which lasted from 1976 to 1979. Probably nobody ever took a loss harder than Lemongello. When taken out of a game he was known to beat his pitching hand and once bit his shoulder until it bled. In his final major league start, he threw the ball at the head of manager Roy Hartsfield before stomping off to the clubhouse. Lemongello's most spectacular tantrum occurred when he threw himself onto the banquet table in the clubhouse and lay in the mayonnaise and mustard for an hour.

Gopher Balls

A surprising statistic is that nine of the top twelve pitchers who have served up the most career home runs are in the Hall of Fame, and the other three will be someday. Twilight Ed Killian went almost four seasons without giving up a home run and won 102 games in his career. Robin Roberts threw over 500 gopher balls and won nearly 300 games.

1. ROBIN ROBERTS

Robin Roberts gave up a record 505 round trippers during his nineteen-year career. Many of them were solo shots he gave up in games in which he had a comfortable lead. Since he led the National League in wins four seasons in a row (1952–55) and won twenty games in six consecutive seasons (1950–55), he can be forgiven.

2. BERT BLYLEVEN

Bert Blyleven won 287 games, one more than Robin Roberts. In 1986, he set the single season record when he surrendered 50 home runs. His 384 career gopher balls places him in the all-time top ten.

3. FERGUSON JENKINS

Ferguson Jenkins's total of 284 wins is almost identical to that of Robin Roberts. Like Roberts he won twenty games six seasons in a row from 1967 to 1972, with a perennial doormat (the Chicago Cubs). Fittingly, his 484 gopher balls rank him second only to Roberts.

4. PHIL NIEKRO

Phil Niekro's knuckler was usually so difficult to hit that he won 318 games between 1964 and 1987 and was elected to the Hall of Fame. Conversely, he gave up 482 home runs (third on the all-time list).

5. PAUL FOYTACK

Paul Foytack of the Los Angeles Angels entered the record books on July 31, 1963 when he gave up four consecutive home runs to the Cleveland Indians. The hitters were not exactly Murderers'

Row: Woodie Held, pitcher Pedro Ramos, Tito Francona, and Larry Brown. An embarrassed Foytack admitted that his control was so bad that the last home run came on a knockdown pitch.

6. PEDRO RAMOS

Ramos, who hit one of the consecutive home runs off Foytack, was no slouch himself in giving them up. He gave up 315 in his career, one every seven innings he pitched. His nadir occurred in 1957 when he was tagged for 43 homers.

7. JACK FISHER

Jack Fisher led the National League in losses in 1965 and 1967 while with the lowly Mets. He deserves inclusion here because he gave up two memorable homers. He was on the mound in 1960 when Ted Williams hit a dramatic home run in his final career at-bat. The next season Roger Maris hit his sixtieth home run off Fisher to tie Babe Ruth's record.

8. TRACY STALLARD

Tracy Stallard has become a footnote in baseball history because he was the pitcher who allowed Roger Maris's record-breaking sixty-first home run in 1961. Stallard tried to remove the stigma by correctly pointing out that Maris had hit sixty

Jack Fisher

Pitcher Jack Fisher gave up Ted Williams's final home run in 1960 and Roger Maris's record-tying 60th homer the following season.

others. He also had the misfortune of being the opposing pitcher when Jim Bunning pitched his perfect game in 1964.

9. AL DOWNING

Al Downing was a fine pitcher who led the American League in strikeouts in 1964 and won twenty games for the Dodgers in 1971. Despite his accomplishments, he will always be remembered as the man who gave up Hank Aaron's historic 715th home run on April 8, 1974.

10. **TOM ZACHARY**

Almost no one remembers that Guy Bush gave up Babe Ruth's 714th and final home run. Many fans know that Tom Zachary allowed Ruth's 60th in 1927. Zachary, not appreciative of his everlasting fame, commented, "If you really want to know the truth. I'd rather thrown at his big, fat head." Zachary and Ruth became teammates the next season when the pitcher was traded from the Senators to the Yankees. Zachary won a game in the 1928 World Series and had a perfect 12–0 record in 1929.

Wild Things

Sportswriter Dick Young once wrote of Brooklyn pitcher Rex Barney, "He'd have been a great pitcher if home plate were high and outside." Red Ames threw a record 156 wild pitches in his career. Let yourself lose all control and take a walk on the wild side.

1. BILL STEMMEYER

Cannonball Bill Stemmeyer was the original Wild Thing. In 1886, while playing for Boston, Cannonball threw sixty-four wild pitches in only forty-one games. Despite his control problems, he managed to win twenty-two games that season.

2. AMOS RUSIE

Amos Rusie, the Hoosier Cannonball, had more than 200 walks five consecutive seasons. Rusie set the all-time record with 289 free passes in 1890.

3. DICK WEIK

Dick Weik must have been wild from birth. He walked 15 batters in his first minor league game in 1946. Of his twenty-six major league starts, he walked 10 or more four times. In 213 innings, Weik walked 237 batters. He finished his wild ride in the majors in 1954 with a record of six wins and twenty-two losses.

4. BILL GEORGE

Twenty-two-year-old rookie New York pitcher Bill George set a record by walking sixteen batters in a game against Chicago on May 30, 1887. On three other occasions, George walked thirteen.

5. GEORGE VAN HALTREN

As a rookie with Chicago in 1887, George Van Haltren walked sixteen men in a game. An adequate pitcher (40–31 career record), Van Haltren made the transition to the outfield where he became a star. Despite having his career shortened by a broken leg, Van Haltren batted .316, had 2,532 hits, scored 1,539 runs, and stole 583 bases.

6. BRUNO HAAS

On June 23, 1915, Philadelphia A's pitcher Bruno Haas walked sixteen batters in a game against

New York. After walking twenty-eight in fourteen innings, Haas was released and never pitched in the major leagues again.

7. DOLLY GRAY

In 1909, Washington pitcher Dolly Gray walked eight batters in an inning, including seven in a row. By the time the Senators told Dolly goodbye, he had won only fifteen games and lost fifty-one.

8. RYNE DUREN

Pitcher Ryne Duren wore Coke-bottle-thick glasses to correct the 20/200 vision in his left eye. He intentionally threw his first warm-up pitch to the backstop to intimidate the hitter. In the minors, he once hit a batter in the on-deck circle. Columnist Jack Murray wrote that Duren was the first guy in history to pitch in Braille. In 1958, Duren, pitching for the Yankees, led the American League in saves with twenty. Wildness and excessive drinking, however, cut short a potentially great career. For his career Duren walked six batters for every nine innings.

9. TOMMY BYRNE

Tommy Byrne led the league in hit batsmen five times. From 1949 to 1951, he led the American League in walks. In 1951, Byrne walked 150 in

143 innings. During his career he walked 1,037 in 1,362 innings, nearly seven per game.

10. **CHUCK STOBBS**

Washington lefty Chuck Stobbs uncorked the wildest pitch on record. On May 20, 1956, facing Bob Kennedy of the Tigers, Stobbs heaved a pitch seventeen rows into the stands. Once the loser of fifteen consecutive games, Stobbs had a flare for the spectacular. He was the victim of what is considered by many to be the longest home run in history. On April 17, 1953, Mickey Mantle hit a blast off Stobbs that was measured at 565 feet.

Chuck Stobbs
Lefty Chuck Stobbs gave up a 565 foot home run to Mickey Mantle and once uncorked a wild pitch that landed in the 17th row of the grandstand.

Head Hunters

The secret weapon of the pitcher is the beanball. The tradition of awarding first base to a hit batsman began after former minister Will White plunked several players. Brooklyn pitcher Joe Black threw at seven consecutive Reds after being taunted from the bench. Jim Kern called a no-hitter any game that he didn't hit anyone. Meet the maestros of chin music.

1. STAN WILLIAMS

From the time Stan Williams entered major league baseball in 1958 until he retired in 1972, he was the most feared man in baseball. He kept a list of players whom he intended to hit. If a player homered off him, his name was placed in his book. Batters rating four stars were in trouble. Home run king Hank Aaron had five stars next to his name. After beaning Aaron on the helmet,

Williams apologized, "I meant to hit you in the neck." Williams kept a photo of Aaron in the locker room, at which he practiced throwing. If a batter made the mistake of digging in at the plate, Williams would walk off the mound and suggest that he dig the hole six feet deep.

2. DON DRYSDALE

Stan Williams's Dodgers teammate Don Drysdale was twice the pitcher he was and his equal as a headhunter. Drysdale led the National League five times and set a modern record with 154 hit batsmen. Ironically, his record fifty-eight consecutive scoreless innings (since broken by Orel Hershiser) was made possible because of a nullified hit batsman. It appeared the streak was over when Giants' catcher Dick Dietz was hit with the bases loaded. However, the umpire ruled Dietz did not make an effort to get out of the way of the pitch.

3. PHIL KNELL

In 1891, Columbus pitcher Phil Knell set a single season record when he hit fifty-four batters. Knell won twenty-eight games that year and led the American Association in shutouts.

4. SAL "THE BARBER" MAGLIE

Sal Maglie earned the nickname "The Barber" because of the close shaves he gave hitters.

Don Drysdale
Dodgers' pitcher Don Drysdale set a modern record when he hit 154 batters during his career.

Maglie admitted that he threw at batters' heads because it was easier for them to move their heads than their bodies. Pittsburgh second baseman Danny Murtaugh wasn't able to get out of the way and suffered a fractured skull. Maglie confessed that his favorite target was Dodgers' catcher Roy Campanella because he was easily intimidated. The Barber retired in 1958 with a 119–62 record. Most hitters were relieved.

5. EARLY WYNN

Early Wynn, winner of 300 games, once boasted that he would knock down his own grandmother if she dug in on him. During batting practice, Wynn let his fifteen-year-old son take a few swings. After the youngster hit two balls hard, dad dusted him on the third pitch. Mickey Mantle once hit a ball up the middle, narrowly missing Wynn. Early motioned his first baseman behind Mantle and repeatedly threw at Mickey's legs.

6. BURLEIGH GRIMES

Burleigh Grimes was known as "Ol' Stubblebeard" because he didn't shave on the days he pitched. It was said that Grimes's idea of an intentional walk was four pitches aimed at the batter's head. He threw at Frankie Frisch almost every time he faced him and once tried to hit Goose Goslin while he was kneeling in the on-deck circle.

7. BOB GIBSON

Cardinals' ace Bob Gibson was total business when he was on the mound. He never became friendly with opposing players because in his words, "It doesn't make sense to make friends with a guy I plan to knock down or strike out." When friend Bill White was traded to Philadelphia, Gibson dusted him. Gibson hit San Francisco third baseman Jim Ray Hart in his second major league at-bat and broke his collarbone.

8. CHICK FRASER

Chick Fraser was a pitcher with spotty control who led the league in walks in 1896, 1901, and 1905 (National League in 1896 and 1905 and American League in 1901). Fraser hit a record 217 batters, one every fifteen innings. The man with the record for hit batsmen did throw a no-hitter in 1903.

9. PINK HAWLEY

Pink Hawley set the National League record with 195 hit batsmen in only nine seasons (1892–1900). In 1895, his best season, Hawley won thirty-two games for Pittsburgh.

10. LARRY SHERRY

From 1959 to 1962, pitcher Larry Sherry and catcher Norm Sherry formed a brother battery in Los Angeles. When Larry dusted his brother during an intersquad game, Norm yelled, "I'm going to tell mom."

Beaned in Boston

Players are hit by pitches for many reasons. Some hitters crowd the plate. Others are victims of pitchers' wildness. Often the player has hit one too many home runs off the pitcher. If a pitcher wants to hit a batter bad enough, there's little the hitter can do, although Browns' outfielder Willard Brown once dragged a mattress to the plate for protection. Take aim at some of baseball's favorite targets.

1. RON HUNT

Ron Hunt proudly proclaimed, "Some people give their bodies to science. I give mine to baseball." The second baseman set a major league record by being hit fifty times in 1971. He led the National League in that department seven times, and his career total of 243 is a league record. Hunt tied a record by getting plunked 3 times in a game.

2. DON BAYLOR

Don Baylor slugged 338 home runs in his career and paid for it by being hit a record 267 times. His 35 beanings in 1986 is an American League record.

3. MINNIE MINOSO

Minnie Minoso could do it all on the field, including getting hit by pitches. Minoso led the American League a record ten times in being hit. From 1951 to 1961, he led the league every year except 1955, when he missed some games after having his skull fractured by a Bob Grim pitch.

4. FRANK ROBINSON

Frank Robinson was the ideal candidate to be a target for pitches. He crowded the plate, and he was one of the greatest home run hitters (586, fourth all-time) in baseball history. As a result, Robinson was hit 198 times and led the league in that category seven times. The only thing that kept him from further punishment was that he seemed to hit better after he was knocked down.

5. FRANKIE CROSETTI

Frankie Crosetti was the Yankees' shortstop for seventeen seasons before the arrival of Phil Rizzuto. Crosetti led the American League in being hit by pitches eight times.

6. FRANK CHANCE

The Chicago first baseman had the dubious distinction of being hit a record five times in a double header on May 30, 1904. Chance once developed a blood clot on the brain and another time was beaned so severely that he lost his hearing.

7. DON ZIMMER

Don Zimmer suffered two of the most severe beanings in baseball history. A promising minor leaguer who was leading the American Association in homers, Zimmer was playing for St. Paul when he was beaned by pitcher Jim Kirk on July 7, 1953. He was unconscious for three weeks and couldn't speak for six. Four screws were inserted into his skull to help it mend. In July 1956, Zimmer was playing Brooklyn when he was hit in the head by Cincinnati pitcher Hal Jeffcoat and suffered a fractured cheekbone and was nearly blinded. Because Zimmer froze when a pitch sailed toward him, even Sal Maglie was afraid to throw at him.

8. STEVE EVANS

St. Louis outfielder Steve Evans set the major league mark for left-handed batters when he was hit thirty-one times during the 1910 season.

9. JOE ADCOCK

Milwaukee Braves' first baseman hit 336 home runs during his career. Adcock was the first player to hit a home run into the distant centerfield bleachers at the Polo Grounds, a blast of nearly 500 feet. On July 31, 1954, Adcock set a record with eighteen total bases (four homers and a double) in a game against Brooklyn. The next day Dodgers' pitcher Clem Labine beaned Adcock. A month later, Brooklyn pitcher Don Newcombe broke Adcock's hand with a fastball, ending his season. The next year Giants' pitcher Jim Hearn broke Adcock's arm. On July 17, 1956, Adcock was brushed back by Giants' hurler Ruben Gomez. When he charged the mound, Gomez threw the ball at his legs and ran for his life. The lumbering first baseman chased Gomez all over the field until the pitcher disappeared into the clubhouse where he huddled with a bat and an ice pick in case Adcock discovered where he was hiding.

10. WILLARD SCHMIDT

Cincinnati pitcher Willard Schmidt is the only player to ever be hit by a pitch twice in the same inning. It happened in a game played against Milwaukee on April 26, 1959. To make matters worse, Schmidt had to leave the game after being hit with a drive off the bat of shortstop Johnny Logan.

Error of Their Ways

Art Irwin is credited with being the first player to wear a glove. Considering his .856 fielding percentage, he was not the first to learn how to use one. Cincinnati second baseman Charles Smith made eighty-eight errors in only eighty games in 1880. Hall of Fame pitcher Tim Keefe made sixty-three errors in a season. Alexander Gardner once allowed twelve passed balls in a game. Dandelion Pfeffer made 828 errors in his career. When these players took the field, the defense rested.

1. ANDY LEONARD

On June 14, 1876, Boston second baseman Andy Leonard made nine errors in a 20–5 loss to Philadelphia. Leonard wisely moved to the outfield for most of the rest of his career.

2. HERMAN LONG

It was written that Herman Long played shortstop like "a man on a flying trapeze." Apparently he fell sometimes. Long made 1,037 errors, the most in major league history. In 1889 alone he made 117 miscues.

3. BILL SHINDLE

Bill Shindle, shortstop for the 1890 Philadelphia Quakers of the Players' League, set a single season record for futility when he made 122 errors.

4. MIKE GRADY

Incredibly, in 1899, third baseman Mike Grady of the New York Giants made four errors in one play. He began his comedy of errors by booting an easy grounder. Grady compounded his error by throwing wildly to first base. The runner rounded second and headed for third knowing Grady was there. Grady dropped the throw for error number three. The runner scored when Grady threw the ball into the grandstand for error number four.

5. PIANO LEGS HICKMAN

Charles "Piano Legs" Hickman of the New York Giants set a record for errors at third base with ninety-one in 1900. His fielding percentage was a dismal .842.

6. JOHN GOCHNAUR

Shortstop John Gochnaur was the original double threat man. His .185 batting average for both 1902 and 1903 were the two lowest for any player with over 400 at-bats. In 1903, his final season in the majors, he made ninety-eight errors, the twentieth-century single season record.

7. RABBIT GLAVIANO

On May 18, 1950, St. Louis Cardinals' third baseman Tommy "Rabbit" Glaviano made three consecutive errors in the ninth inning of a game against Brooklyn. His miscues, two wild throws and a boot, allowed the winning run to score in a 9–8 loss.

8. SHORTY FULLER

Washington shortstop Shorty Fuller made four errors in an inning in a game against Indianapolis on August 17, 1888. His errors allowed six runs to score, and he was removed from the game. His replacement, George Shoch, made two more errors that permitted the winning runs to score in a 11–7 loss.

9. DICK STUART

Dick Stuart was probably the worst fielding first baseman in baseball history. He led the league in errors at that position seven straight years from 1958 to 1964. As a rookie he made the most errors even though he played only sixty-four games. His ineptitude earned him the nickname "Dr. Strangeglove." When he was traded to Boston in 1963, Stuart belted forty-two home runs but also made twenty-nine errors. The fans in Boston once cheered when he picked up a piece of paper blowing across the field. Demoted to the minors in 1969, Stuart showed he hadn't lost his touch by leading the Pacific Coast League with 22 errors in less than half a season.

10. "BANANA NOSE" ZEKE BONURA

Perhaps the only man who could rival Dick Stuart as the worst defensive first baseman of all time was "Banana Nose" Zeke Bonura. Like Stuart, Banana Nose could hit the ball a mile and kick it even farther. Humorist Jean Shepherd recalled that Bonura had a range of "about six inches." Routine grounders would roll by as Bonura gave his "Mussolini Salute" with his glove. His specialty was calling the pitcher off a play and losing the race to the bag with the runner.

Mismanagement

It has often been said that managers are only as good as the players they have to work with. It can also be said that teams are only as good as their managers. On anyone's scorecard these managers must rank among the least successful in baseball history.

1. GUY HECKER

Guy Hecker was a spectacular player. In 1884 he won fifty-two games while pitching for Louisville of the American Association. Two years later Hecker batted .342 to become the only pitcher in baseball history to win a batting title. On August 15, 1886, he scored a record seven runs, hit three home runs, had six hits, and pitched a four-hitter. Hecker's gifts did not extend to managing. In 1890, he managed Pittsburgh to a 23–113 record.

2. JOE QUINN

A mortician in the off-season, Australian-born Joe Quinn usually had whatever team he managed buried in the cellar. He had a brief trial at the helm in St. Louis in 1895, winning thirteen and losing twenty-seven. Four years later, he managed the talent-depleted Cleveland Spiders to a 20–134 record, the worst in baseball history. Under Quinn's inspired guidance, the Spiders lost forty of their last forty-one games.

3. CHARLIE GOULD

In the National League's first season, 1876, Charlie Gould managed Cincinnati to a 9–56 record. Gould was fired as manager, although he did continue to play first base for Cincinnati for another season.

4. DOC PROTHRO

For sheer consistency, Doc Prothro deserves recognition in any discussion of bad managers. Doc piloted the Phillies to three consecutive last place finishes from 1939 to 1941. Never winning more than fifty games, his overall record was 138–320. When he wasn't losing games as a manager, Doc practiced dentistry in the off-season.

5. JACK AND DAVE ROWE

It's hard to decide which of the Rowe brothers, Jack or Dave, was the least successful manager. Jack Rowe managed Buffalo of the Players League to a 36–96 record in 1890. Brother Dave, who once gave up thirty-five runs in a game as a pitcher, had a career 44–126 record in two stints as manager of Kansas City in 1886 and 1888.

6. CHICKEN WOLF

The 1889 Louisville team was one of the worst of all time. Four managers guided the team to a 27–111 record, including twenty-six consecutive losses. During his stint, Chicken Wolf managed the team to a 15–51 mark. En route to Philadelphia, the team arrived in Johnstown, Pennsylvania, just in time for the legendary Johnstown Flood, which claimed 2,200 lives. It was thought that the team had perished, but fortunately for the rest of the league, they had found high ground and were unharmed.

7. HORACE FOGEL

Horace Fogel was a sportswriter who managed Indianapolis in 1887 to a 20–49 record. Fifteen years later, he managed the New York Giants for forty-one games before being replaced by Heinie Smith. While with the Giants, Fogel came up with the brilliant suggestion that pitcher Christy Mathewson be converted to a first baseman. His successor, Heinie Smith, lost twenty-seven of thirty-two games before being fired. Smith had the brainstorm to make Mathewson a shortstop. His replacement, John McGraw, put Matty on the mound, where he won 372 games in a Giants' uniform. McGraw, one of the greatest managers in major league history, guided the Giants to ten pennants.

8. **JIMMY DYKES**

Jimmy Dykes managed six different teams between 1934 and 1961. His twenty-one years of managing without winning a pennant or division title is a record. Dykes's teams never finished higher than third place.

9. **ROGERS HORNSBY**

A lifetime .358 hitter, Rogers Hornsby was arguably the greatest second baseman of all time. In 1926, his St. Louis Cardinals won the world championship while he served as a player-manager. However, nine of the thirteen years he managed, his teams finished in the second division. Hornsby had a less than ideal rapport with his players. Once, while managing in the minors, Hornsby went into the shower and urinated on a pitcher who had been knocked out of the box.

10. PONGO CANILLON

Joe "Pongo" Canillon managed Washington from 1907 to 1909. In two of the three seasons, his team finished in the cellar, and Pongo was fired after his team finished 42–110 in 1909. His career record as manager was 158 wins and 297 losses.

Travelin' Men

Some players just seem to be always passing through. Harry Simpson, an outfielder who played in the 1950s, was given the nickname "Suitcase" because he was traded so often. Pitcher Mike Ryba played in seventeen different minor leagues before he reached the majors in 1935.

1. BOBO NEWSOM

Between 1929 and 1953, Bobo Newsom changed uniforms seventeen different times. Three times Newsom was a twenty-game winner and three times he led the league in losses. He never played more than two full seasons with the same club. Newsom had five different stints with Washington because it was rumored that owner Clark Griffith enjoyed playing pinochle with him.

2. CHARLES "POP" SMITH

Infielder Charles "Pop" Smith played for eleven different teams in two leagues during his career, which lasted from 1880 to 1891. He saw action for Cincinnati, Cleveland, Worcester, Buffalo, and Boston of the National League, and Philadelphia, Baltimore, Louisville, Columbus, Pittsburgh, and Washington of the American Association.

3. TOMMY DAVIS

Tommy Davis won batting titles while playing for the Los Angeles Dodgers in 1962 and 1963. After spending his first eight seasons in Los Angeles, Davis played for the Mets, Astros, Cubs, White Sox, Pilots, A's, Orioles, Angels, and Royals.

4. DICK LITTLEFIELD

Pitcher Dick Littlefield was known as the "Marco Polo of Baseball." During his nine years in the majors (1950–58), Littlefield played for nine different clubs in ten different cities. In 1956, he was traded to the Dodgers for Jackie Robinson, but the trade was voided when Robinson retired. It's hard to understand why he was so much in demand, considering his 33–54 lifetime record.

5. MIKE MORGAN

At last count, pitcher Mike Morgan had played for eleven different major league clubs and a total of

Tommy Davis
Despite winning batting titles in 1962 and 1963, Tommy Davis played for ten different teams in the major leagues.

twenty professional teams. Morgan has made stops in Oakland, New York (Yankees), Toronto, Seattle, Baltimore, Los Angeles, Chicago (Cubs), St. Louis, Cincinnati, Minnesota, and Texas.

6. BOB MILLER

Pitcher Bob Miller played for ten different teams during his career, which lasted from 1957 to 1974. During a four-year period (1970–73), he played for seven different teams.

7. DIRTY JACK DOYLE

During his seventeen-year career (1889–1905), Dirty Jack Doyle played every position except pitcher. It seemed as though he played for almost every team. Doyle appeared in the uniforms of ten different teams.

8. KEN BRETT

Ken Brett, brother of superstar third baseman George Brett, pitched for ten different teams between 1971 and 1980. Brett was the youngest pitcher (age nineteen) to appear in a World Series and set another record for a pitcher by hitting home runs in four consecutive games.

9. GEORGE BRUNET

Lefty George Brunet played for nine different teams in his fifteen years (1956–71) in the majors. He led the American League in losses in 1967 and 1968 but was not traded either of those years.

10. TED GRAY

Pitcher Ted Gray would have qualified for frequent flier miles if they had existed in 1955. Despite only appearing in fourteen games that season, Gray played for four different teams: White Sox, Indians, Yankees, and Orioles.

Baseball's Worst Trades

A trade that is terrible for one team is great for another. The following transactions are the biggest steals in baseball history.

Milt Pappas
The Cincinnati Reds made one of the worst deals in baseball history in 1965 when they traded slugger Frank Robinson to Baltimore for pitcher Milt Pappas.

1. **BABE RUTH**

Babe Ruth was playing for Baltimore of the International League in 1914 when club owner Jack Dunn attempted to sell him to a major league team. Dunn offered Ruth, pitcher Ernie Shore (who later pitched a perfect game), and catcher Ben Egan to Connie Mack for $10,000. The financially strapped owner of the Philadelphia Athletics reluctantly declined. Cincinnati had an option to acquire two players from the Orioles. The Reds sent an inexperienced scout named Harry Stevens who passed over Ruth and Shore for outfielder George Twombly and shortstop Claude Derrick. Neither Twombly nor Derrick ever hit a home run for Cincinnati, while Ruth, of course, hit 714 in his illustrious career.

2. **CHRISTY MATHEWSON FOR AMOS RUSIE**

Amos Rusie was the hardest throwing pitcher of the nineteenth century. Five times the "Hoosier Thunderbolt" led the National League in strikeouts. Although the eight-time twenty-game winner had not pitched in two years, Cincinnati was glad to acquire him in exchange for an untested pitcher named Christy Mathewson. Washed up, Rusie only pitched three games for Cincinnati, giving up forty-four hits in twenty-three innings. Mathewson became the best pitcher in the

National League and won 372 games for the Giants.

3. FRANK ROBINSON FOR MILT PAPPAS

Cincinnati fans were devastated in 1965 when Reds owner Bill DeWitt traded slugger Frank Robinson to Baltimore for pitchers Milt Pappas and Jack Baldschun and outfielder Dick Simpson. DeWitt justified the trade by calling Robinson an "old thirty." In 1966, Robinson won the Triple Crown, and Baltimore won the world championship. Pappas won thirty games in Cincinnati in three seasons before being dealt to Atlanta.

4. NOLAN RYAN FOR JIM FREGOSI

In December 1971, the New York Mets acquired infielder Jim Fregosi from the California Angels. They sent the Angels four players: Don Rose, Leroy Stanton, Francisco Estrada, and Nolan Ryan. Fregosi played a little over a year in New York before being sent to Texas. Nolan Ryan won 324 games, pitched seven no-hitters and became baseball's all-time strikeout leader with 5,714.

5. JOE DIMAGGIO

Joe DiMaggio could have been the Cub Clipper. Chicago had the opportunity to purchase the talented outfielder but declined because they were wary of a knee injury that DiMaggio had suffered getting out of a car in 1934. DiMaggio joined the New York Yankees in 1936 and became an instant star.

6. LOU BROCK FOR ERNIE BROGLIO

In June 1964, the St. Louis Cardinals traded former twenty-game winners Ernie Broglio and Bobby Shantz along with Doug Clemens for Jack Spring, Paul Toth, and a young outfielder named Lou Brock. Shantz never won a game in Chicago, and Broglio had a miserable 14–31 record with the Cubs. Brock led the Cardinals to world championships in 1964 and 1967 and finished his Hall of Fame career with more than 3,000 base hits.

7. STEVE CARLTON FOR RICK WISE

The Cardinals were on the short end of the stick in 1972 when they traded lefthanded pitcher Steve Carlton to Philadelphia for righthander Rick Wise. Wise won thirty-two games over two years in St. Louis before being shipped to Boston. Carlton won four Cy Young Awards in Philadelphia and became the second winningest lefthander in baseball history with 329.

8. ROCKY COLAVITO FOR HARVEY KUENN

Cleveland fans were horrified in April 1960 when fan favorite Rocky Colavito was traded to Detroit for Harvey Kuenn. Colavito, who led the American League in home runs in 1959, smashed 139 home runs in four seasons in Detroit. Kuenn, the 1959 American League batting champion, played only one season in Cleveland. Many Tribe fans believe that the trade brought a curse on the team, which did not win another pennant for thirty-four years.

9. FERGUSON JENKINS FOR LARRY JACKSON

The Phillies thought they had acquired pitching help in 1966 when they received veteran right-handers Larry Jackson and Bob Buhl from the Cubs for rookie pitcher Ferguson Jenkins and

Larry Jackson
Larry Jackson had a losing season after being traded to the Philadelphia Phillies for pitcher Ferguson Jenkins who went on to have six 20-win seasons for the Chicago Cubs.

outfielders Adolfo Phillips and John Herrnstein. Jackson, who led the National League with twenty-four wins in 1964, had a losing record in Philadelphia. Buhl was 6–8 in 1966, then retired. Ferguson Jenkins won twenty games six seasons in a row for the Cubs.

10. RYNE SANDBERG FOR IVAN DE JESUS

The Cubs made another steal in 1982 when they traded shortstop Ivan De Jesus to Philadelphia for veteran shortstop Larry Bowa and rookie infielder Ryne Sandberg. Both De Jesus and Bowa played three full seasons for their respective teams, but Sandberg became a perennial All-Star second baseman.

Baseball's Weirdest Trades

Everybody hears about the blockbuster trades teams make, but for every big deal there are many lesser ones. You'll agree that these are some of the strangest trades ever made.

1. LINDY CHAPPOTEN

Minor league pitcher Lindy Chappoten was once traded in exchange for twenty uniforms. It proved to be a bargain as he went on to win twenty games.

2. TIM FORTUGNO

Tim Fortugno struck out twenty-four batters in a minor league game for El Paso. In 1989, the Reno Red Sox sold Fortugno to the Milwaukee Brewers for cash and twelve dozen baseballs. Fortugno never pitched a game in Milwaukee.

3. ERNIE HARWELL

In 1948, Brooklyn Dodgers' Branch Rickey wanted to secure the services of a minor league announcer named Ernie Harwell. He sent minor league catcher Cliff Dapper to the Atlanta Crackers in exchange for Harwell. The venerable Harwell became a fixture in the broadcasting booth, most notably spending over three decades announcing games in Detroit. Dapper is also an interesting story. Despite hitting .471 during a brief trial in Brooklyn in 1942, he was never given another chance to catch in the major leagues.

4. LOU BOUDREAU FOR CHARLIE GRIMM

On May 4, 1960, the Chicago Cubs traded manager Charlie Grimm for one of their announcers, Lou Boudreau, who had led the Cleveland Indians to the world championship in 1948 as a player-manager. After managing the Cubs to a 54–83 mark, Boudreau returned to broadcasting. Cubs owner Phil Wrigley replaced him with a college of coaches in which several coaches shared the responsibilities of managing.

5. CLIFF HEATHCOTE FOR MAX FLACK

The Chicago Cubs played a doubleheader against the St. Louis Cardinals on May 30, 1922. Between games, the Cardinals traded outfielder Cliff Heathcote to the Cubs for outfielder Max Flack. Both players were hitless in the first game, but each had hits in the nightcap for their new teams.

6. **HARRY CHITI**

On April 26, 1962, the Cleveland Indians traded catcher Harry Chiti to the New York Mets for a player to be named later. A few weeks later the Mets sent Chiti back to Cleveland as the player to be named later. In essence Harry Chiti was traded for himself.

7. **DICK COFFMAN FOR CARL FISCHER**

The St. Louis Browns traded pitcher Dick Coffman to the Washington Senators for pitcher Carl Fischer on June 9, 1932. Six months later, the Senators traded Coffman back to the Browns for Fischer. Coffman was 1–6 during his brief stay in Washington, and Fischer was 3–7 while playing for St. Louis.

8. **JOEL YOUNGBLOOD**

Joel Youngblood became the only major leaguer to get a base hit for two different teams in the same day. On August 4, 1982, Youngblood, playing for the New York Mets, singled off Chicago Cubs' pitcher Ferguson Jenkins. That afternoon he was traded to Montreal. He arrived in

Philadelphia in time to play an evening game against the Phillies and hit a pinch single off Steve Carlton. Youngblood had gotten base hits off two future Hall of Fame pitchers in the same day in different uniforms.

9. **MURRAY WALL FOR DICK HYDE**

In 1959, Boston pitcher Murray Wall was traded to Washington for reliever Dick Hyde. Wall appeared in a game for Washington before learning that the trade had been canceled because Hyde had a sore arm.

10. **"THREE FINGER" BROWN**

For two seasons the Federal League competed against the established National and American Leagues. The Federal League folded in 1916. In February of that year, the Chicago franchise of the Federal League traded Mordecai "Three Finger" Brown, Joe Tinker, Clem Clemens, Mickey Doolan, Bill Fischer, Max Flack, Claude Hendrix, Les Mann, Dykes Potter, Rollie Zeider, and George McConnell to the Chicago Cubs for cash.

Outrageous Owners

Until the era of free agency, the owners had the upper hand in dealings with players. Pittsburgh owner Barney Dreyfuss argued with Dick Bartell over the cost of a lobster dinner, eventually deducting $2.40 from the shortstop's paycheck. When a fan made off with rookie shortstop Phil Rizzuto's cap, the Yankees made him pay for it. Detroit owner Frank Nevin froze Ty Cobb's salary at $9,000 for three years even though he was winning the batting title every season. Let me introduce you to some of baseball's most outrageous owners.

1. BILL VEECK

Baseball's most imaginative owner, Bill Veeck, will be remembered for his amazing stunts. As a minor league owner in Milwaukee, he once had a new pitcher jump out of manager Charlie Grimm's birthday cake. In 1948, his Cleveland Indians won the world championship while drawing a record 2,620,627 fans. That year fans were outraged when word leaked out that Veeck was considering trading star shortstop Lou Boudreau to St. Louis. Veeck went from bar to bar to personally apologize to the fans.

Some of his most memorable moments came as owner of the financially strapped St. Louis Browns. In 1951, he sent midget Eddie Gaedel to the plate in a game against Detroit. A few days later, he staged Grandstand Manager's Night in which a thousand fans holding YES and NO placards decided the strategy for the game. As manager Zack Taylor sat idly in a rocking chair, the fans managed the hapless Browns to a 5–3 victory. What made Veeck's stunts even more effective is that he rarely announced them ahead of time. If a fan did not attend a game, he was always in danger of missing something unusual and entertaining.

Veeck owned the White Sox twice, and each time left his unique mark. When the "Go Go Sox" (so called because of their emphasis on speed) won the American League pennant in 1959, he once again hired Eddie Gaedel, this time to dress up like a Martian and "capture" the Sox double-play combination of Nellie Fox and Luis Aparicio. While in Chicago he also introduced the exploding scoreboard in 1960 and the infamous Disco Demolition Night in 1979, which resulted in a riot after fans built bonfires with disco records. To Veeck's credit, he tried to break baseball's color barrier in 1943 by buying the Philadelphia Phillies and signing the best Negro League players. When that plan was foiled, he later signed Larry Doby, who became the first African American to play in the American League.

2. CHARLIE O. FINLEY

Pitcher Mike Torrez called owner Charlie O. Finley the "Wizard of Odd." Finley's tenure as owner of the A's was always eventful. In Kansas City, he made a jackass, which he named Charlie O. after himself, the mascot. Fond of farmyard animals, he forced the players to enter the stadium on a mule team and had sheep grazing beyond the outfield fence. A mechanical rabbit delivered the baseballs to the umpire.

When the team moved to Oakland, Finley offered $300 to players who would grow handlebar mustaches. In their Kelly green and gold uniforms and white shoes, the "Swingin' A's" were instantly recognizable. Finley went too far when he asked pitcher Vida Blue to change his name to True Blue. Vida, whose name means life, was named after his father. Blue suggested, "Why doesn't he change his name to True Finley?"

A hatred of Finley was the uniting force for the players. During the 1973 World Series, Finley tried to put Mike Andrews on the disabled list after he made two costly errors. Despite the turmoil, the Oakland A's won three consecutive championships from 1972 to 1974.

3. **MARGE SCHOTT**

The controversial owner of the Cincinnati Reds has endured two suspensions for insensitive remarks concerning blacks, Jews, gays, and other minorities. She reportedly referred to outfielder Eric Davis as her "million dollar nigger." Marge warned her players not to accessorize because, in her words, "only fruits wear earrings." Her cost-cutting measures included selling the general manager's seat at Cinergy Field and briefly refusing to show scores from other games because it cost $200 a month. Classic Marge moments include giving year-old candy to employees at Christmas and presenting umpires with recycled flowers after the death of umpire John McSherry on Opening Day. Schott's pride and joy was her beloved St. Bernard Schottzie. She rubbed Schottzie hair on her players for good luck and printed a ticket calendar that featured twelve photos of the dog in various poses, such as Santa and Miss Liberty.

4. GEORGE STEINBRENNER

Johnny Carson joked, "There are close to eleven million unemployed, and half of them are Yankee managers." For the past quarter-century Steinbrenner has been in charge of the "Bronx Zoo." Over an eleven-year period, there were fourteen managerial changes. Billy Martin had five separate stints at the Yankee helm. Dick Howser was fired after winning 103 games in 1980. In 1982 alone the Yankees had five pitching coaches and three batting instructors.

Steinbrenner was suspended in 1974 after being convicted of making an illegal $100,000 contribution to the reelection committee for President Richard Nixon. The "Boss" was suspended indefinitely after it became known that he had paid gambler Howard Spira $40,000 to try to dig up dirt on outfielder Dave Winfield. For all his faults, Steinbrenner has presided over four world champion teams (1977, 1978, 1996, and 1998).

5. CHRIS VON DER AHE

Chris Von der Ahe was the nineteenth-century version of George Steinbrenner. "Der Boss," as the German-born owner of the St. Louis Browns was known, ordered thirty-two managerial changes in only seventeen years. Between 1895 and 1897, he changed managers twelve times. Like Marge Schott, he brought his dogs (greyhounds named Schnauzer and Snoozer) to the ballpark. Like Charlie Finley, his team wore multicolored silk uniforms. Baseball's first showman, he staged horse races and Wild West shows in the outfield.

Von der Ahe could attract a crowd on his own. He was a potbellied man with a nose that was described as looking like a "bunch of strawberries." He wore loud checkered suits, spats, and diamond stickpins. "Der Boss" owned a saloon near the ballpark and bought the team mainly to increase his bar profits. Von der Ahe sat in the dugout, viewing the game through a telescope. He encouraged players to get into fights and stomped on an umpire's feet until they were bloody. When it became too dark to play, Von der Ahe once placed candles in front of the dugout, starting a fire.

In 1898, Von der Ahe was ruined when the ballpark did burn down, and he went through a costly divorce. To make matters worse, Pittsburgh owner William Nimick had Von der Ahe kidnapped by private detectives and jailed because of an old debt. He died destitute, and former manager Charles Comiskey paid for his funeral. Despite the buffoonery, Von der Ahe's Browns won four consecutive American Association pennants between 1885 and 1888.

6. ANDREW FREEDMAN

Probably the most hated owner in baseball history, Andrew Freedman nearly destroyed the New York Giants' franchise during his reign of terror from 1895 to 1902. He took over a team that had finished forty-four games over .500 in 1894, and in one year the team sank from second to ninth place. Only once did his team finish above seventh place. The Giants had thirteen managers in seven years.

A politician in the infamous Tammany Hall, Freedman carried on feuds with everyone from sportswriters to owners. Backed by his own storm troopers, he beat up players, umpires, fans, and even owners. If umpires made calls that displeased him, he would not allow them into the Polo Grounds. He got involved in a bitter dispute with Amos Rusie that caused the star pitcher to sit out a season. The Giants finished last in 1902, Freedman's last as owner. The next season they finished second, and a year later they won the pennant.

7. JOHN TAYLOR

After inheriting the Boston Red Sox in 1904, John Taylor began dismantling the championship team. He traded batting champion George Stone to St. Louis and future home run king Gavvy

Cravath to Chicago. He dealt baseball's winningest pitcher Cy Young to Cleveland after Taylor had an all-night drinking session with owner Charles Somers. Although he knew almost nothing about baseball, he insisted on lecturing his players. Two years after winning the 1904 pennant, Boston lost 105 games and sank to last place.

8. **CHARLES COMISKEY**

If Chicago White Sox owner Charles Comiskey had not been such a tightwad, the Black Sox Scandal might never had occurred. In 1908, star pitcher Ed Walsh was paid $3,500 and became the last pitcher to win forty games in a season. Expecting a large raise, Walsh was pleased Comiskey handed him a check for $3,500 in appreciation of his brilliant season. Walsh assumed it was a bonus. He was stunned to receive a contract for the 1909 season for the same salary as the previous year. Only after he threatened to hold out, was he able to get a $1,500 bonus.

The 1919 White Sox were grossly underpaid. The Sox had won the 1917 World Series, but only second baseman Eddie Collins was fairly compensated. Pitcher Eddie Cicotte had led the American League in wins (28) and earned run average (1.53) in 1917, yet his salary for 1919 was only $3,500.

He had an incentive clause that would pay him $5,000 if he won thirty. Cicotte had twenty-nine wins with three weeks to go in the season when Comiskey ordered him not to pitch anymore. Comiskey said that he wanted Cicotte rested for the World Series, but Cicotte knew he was just trying to get out of paying the $1,500 bonus. So when gamblers offered Cicotte and the others $10,000 to throw the series, it's understandable why they accepted. Comiskey was so cheap that he let the team play in dirty uniforms until the players paid for the cleaning.

Perhaps Comiskey's most unforgivable act concerned pitcher Dickie Kerr. He had been one of the honest White Sox and won two games in the series. Kerr won twenty-one games in 1920 and nineteen games the next year. The miserly Comiskey offered Kerr $3,500. Kerr decided to accept an offer of $5,000 from a semipro team and was suspended from baseball. He met the same fate as his crooked teammates.

9. RAY KROC

Ray Kroc made his fortune creating the McDonald's hamburger chain. He bought the San Diego Padres in 1974. At their first home game on April 19, 1974, the Padres were being clobbered by Houston 9–2 in the eighth inning when Kroc grabbed the microphone and said, "I've never seen such stupid baseball playing in my life." Encouraged by his constructive criticism, the Padres lost 102 games that year. Kroc later admitted, "Baseball has brought me nothing but aggravation—it can go to hell." When asked about the future of the national pastime, Kroc said, "There's a lot more future in hamburgers than in baseball." Kroc died in January 1984. The Padres, free of Kroc's obtrusive ownership, went on to win their first pennant in 1984.

10. CALVIN GRIFFITH

Calvin Griffith made some comments that would even make Marge Schott blush. Griffith owned the Washington Senators and moved the franchise to Minnesota in 1964. Griffith explained that one of the reasons he made the move was that Washington, D. C. had too many African Americans and that they rarely attended games. He told the fans in Minnesota, "We came here because you've got good hard-working white people here." Griffith attributed a slump of catcher Butch Wynegar to his recent marriage. He suggested that one-night stands would have given him more time to concentrate on baseball. Pitcher Jim Kaat remarked that Griffith was so cheap that he "threw quarters around like manhole covers." Griffith may have best summed up his philosophy when he said, "I can't tell you what I intend to do. But I can tell you one thing: it won't be anything rational."

Worst Promotions

Since the days of Chris Von der Ahe, promotional gimmicks have been used by baseball to entice fans to the ballpark. Although many promotions have been successful, a few can only be described as disastrous.

1. TEN-CENT BEER NIGHT

On June 4, 1974, the Cleveland Indians staged a ten-cent beer night. After all, beer and baseball had been synonymous for a century. The lure of cheap beer brought a crowd of 25,134 thirsty fans to the game against the Texas Rangers. Over 65,000 glasses of dime beer were sold. As the evening progressed, the fans, saturated with beer, became rowdier. Drunken fans were pelting the bull pen with beer, firecrackers, and smoke bombs. The game was tied 5–5 in the ninth inning when a fan jumped out of the stands and tried to grab

Texas outfielder Jeff Burroughs's cap. Fans began pouring out into the field, attacking players and umpires. Pitcher Tom Hilgendorf and umpire Nestor Chylak were hit over the head with folding chairs, and several other players were injured. The game was forfeited to Texas.

2. DISCO DEMOLITION NIGHT

Chicago White Sox owner Bill Veeck decided to mark the end of the disco craze with Disco Demolition Night on July 12, 1979. While his intentions may have been noble, the result was nearly catastrophic. More than 50,000 fans paid the 98 cent admission for the opportunity to destroy the despised disco records. Overenthusiastic fans began tossing the discs onto the field like Frisbees. As a bonfire fueled by disco records commenced, over 5,000 fans ran onto the field. When they wouldn't return to their seats, the game was forfeited to Detroit.

3. ARMY DAY

On June 10, 1975, the Yankees (who were playing in Shea Stadium while Yankee Stadium was being renovated) held Army Day in honor of the armed services' two hundredth birthday. The highlight of the ceremony was an ear-splitting cannon barrage. When the smoke cleared, fans were stunned to see that the blast had shattered windows and blown away a section of the center-field fence.

4. SCRAP IRON DAY

During World War II, salvage drives at the ballpark were a common occurrence. On September 26, 1942, 11,000 youngsters were admitted free to the Polo Grounds for a game between the Giants and the Braves because they brought some metal for the war effort. With the Giants leading 5–2 in the eighth inning, the children began invading the field. Umpire Ziggy Sears, unable to restore order, forfeited the game to Boston.

5. GOOD OLD JOE EARLY NIGHT

Joe Early, a night watchman in Cleveland, wrote owner Bill Veeck in 1948 complaining that there were no nights to honor fans. Veeck responded by announcing a night in honor of Joe Early. At Good Old Joe Early night, the fan was presented with an outhouse, a backfiring model T, and some livestock. Besides the gag gifts, Early received a Ford convertible, appliances, and a watch.

6. THE SAN FRANCISCO CRAB

With the success of the San Diego Chicken, other teams attempted to develop their own mascots.

The San Francisco Giants conducted a poll to see what kind of mascot their fans preferred. Two-thirds of those who answered indicated they didn't want any at all. Undaunted, the Giants chose a crab. The mascot, introduced in 1984, looked as though it had just climbed from under a rock. It slithered across the field, threatening to give seafood a bad name. Fans responded by spitting on the monstrosity and pouring beer on it.

7. MR. RED

Cincinnati's answer to the San Francisco Crab was a mascot known as Mr. Red. Dressed in a Reds uniform, Mr. Red's head was a huge baseball. During a rally, he would stand atop the dugout attempting to whip the fans into a frenzy. Unfortunately, few of the fans could see what was happening because they were blocked by Mr. Red's enormous head. Eventually Mr. Red was retired, to the relief of box seat holders.

8. RANDY MYERS POSTER DAY

During the early 1990s, the Chicago Cubs had poster giveaway days honoring their best players. On Randy Myers Day, fans were given posters of the lefthanded reliever. Myers was not having his best day, and when he blew the lead, irate Cubs fans threw hundreds of Myers's posters onto the field.

9. HARMON KILLEBREW NIGHT

Harmon Killebrew belted 573 home runs, the most ever by a righthanded batter in the American League. After spending twenty-one years with the Washington Senators and Minnesota Twins, Killebrew was traded to Kansas City. When Kansas City visited Minnesota, Twins' owner Calvin Griffith decided to have Harmon Killebrew Night to honor the slugger. In a shameful display of indifference, fewer than 3,000 fans showed up to honor the team's greatest player.

10. BURYING THE PENNANT

In one of Bill Veeck's most bizarre promotions, the Cleveland Indians buried the 1948 pennant. During a pregame ceremony on September 23, 1949, the Indians, out of contention, formed a funeral procession. Veeck led the mourners, and manager Lou Boudreau served as a pallbearer. A cardboard tombstone marked the grave of the 1948 champs. Appropriately, the Indians were buried by the Tigers 5–0.

It's All in the Game

Anything can happen at a baseball game. Games have been called because of fog, hurricanes, and even a grasshopper invasion. In 1913, a St. Louis outfielder took a parasol onto the field after losing two fly balls in the sun. Pitcher John Clarkson once threw a lemon to demonstrate that it was too dark to continue play.

1. GROVER LAND

Keeping your eye on the ball was harder than usual at a 1915 Federal League game between the Brooklyn Tip Tops and the Baltimore Terrapins. Umpire Bill Brennan stacked the game balls in a pile behind the pitcher's mound. Brooklyn catcher Grover Land hit a ball up the middle that hit the pile of balls. They scattered all over the field like a rack of pool balls being broken. The infielders each picked up a ball and tagged the runner. Brennan, unable to determine which was the game ball, declared that Land was entitled to a home run.

2. **ABNER POWELL**

On August 22, 1886, the term "dogging it" took on a new meaning. Louisville and Cincinnati were tied 3–3 in the eleventh inning when the Colonels' Chicken Wolf hit a ball into the gap. As Cincinnati outfielder Abner Powell chased the ball, he awakened a dog that had been sleeping near the fence. The mutt grabbed Powell's trousers, and while he struggled to break free, Wolf circled the bases with the winning run.

3. **CAL MCVEY**

The Cincinnati Red Stockings, baseball's first all-professional team, brought a 130-game undefeated streak into a game against the Brooklyn Atlantics on June 14, 1870. The Red Stockings appeared to be on their way to another victory when they took a 7–5 lead in the eleventh inning. The Atlantics rallied for three runs in the bottom of the inning, thanks to an overzealous fan who jumped on the back of Cincinnati outfielder Cal McVey as he chased a fly ball.

4. CLARK GRIFFITH AND CONNIE MACK

On April 14, 1948, Clark Griffith, the seventy-eight-year-old owner of the Washington Senators, challenged Connie Mack, eighty-four-year-old owner of the Philadelphia A's, to a ninety-foot match race. The race ended in a flatfooted tie.

5. ICEBOX CHAMBERLAIN AND JOHN CLARKSON

Boston's John Clarkson and Cincinnati's Icebox Chamberlain were locked in a brilliant pitchers' duel on May 6, 1892. The game was scoreless in the fourteenth inning when play was halted by umpire Jack Sheridan because the setting sun was blinding the batters. When conditions didn't improve, Sheridan was forced to call the game on account of the sun.

6. RAINOUT AT THE ASTRODOME

Without even springing a leak, the Houston Astrodome was the site of a rainout on June 15, 1976. Seven inches of rain had flooded the streets, making it almost impossible to reach the ballpark. About twenty brave souls made it to the Astrodome. The game was canceled, and the intrepid fans were treated to a meal and given rain checks.

7. **FRANK CORRIDON**

New York Giants' pitcher Frank Corridon was the victim of his own fans on April 11, 1907. A freak snowstorm had hit the New York area. Corridon was pitching a shutout against Philadelphia in the eighth inning when fans began pelting the players with snowballs. The crowd was so uncontrollable that umpire Bill Klem forfeited the game to Philadelphia.

8. **EDD ROUSH**

Edd Roush once got ejected from a game without saying a word. On June 8, 1920, Roush was playing centerfield for Cincinnati in a game against the New York Giants at the Polo Grounds. Reds' skipper Pat Moran got into a heated argument with the umpires. As the debate raged, Roush laid down in the outfield and took a nap. Roush was so difficult to wake up that he was ejected for delaying the game.

9. **FRANK PETERS**

Portland manager Frank Peters took a lesson from volleyball in a Northwest League game against Tri-Cities on August 31, 1974. Peters rotated his players so that each one played a different position for an inning. The strategy worked—Portland won the game 8–7.

10. CHARLES CLANCY AND JACK CORBETT

Baseball is often criticized for the length of its games. However, Winston-Salem and Asheville once completed a North Carolina League game in thirty-one minutes. Managers Charles Clancy (Winston-Salem) and Jack Corbett (Asheville) agreed to play the August 30, 1916 game as quickly as possible so the teams could catch a train leaving at 3:00. At their managers' insistence, everyone swung at the first pitch. Once the Asheville pitcher made a pitch before his teammates had time to take the field. The transition was so confusing that the Winston-Salem centerfielder actually threw out his own teammate at second base. Winston-Salem won the game by the score of 2–1.

Baseball's Most Embarrassing Moments

Baseball can be an embarrassing game. Minor leaguer Ed Stewart once swung so hard that he knocked himself out. A hungover Pete Browning fell asleep after taking a long lead off from second base and was tagged out. Facing fireballer Walter Johnson in an exhibition game, Reds' outfielder George Harper went back to the dugout after only two strikes because he knew he couldn't hit the "Big Train's" fastball.

1. JIM ST. VRAIN

Pitcher Jim St. Vrain of the Chicago Cubs made an unbelievable baserunning blunder in a game against Pittsburgh in 1902. The weak-hitting pitcher, who normally batted righthanded, decided to try batting lefthanded to change his luck. St. Vrain hit a grounder to shortstop Honus Wagner and began running hard—down the third base line.

Babe Herman
Babe Herman's baserunning was so suspect that he once doubled into a double play.

2. WILBERT ROBINSON

Brooklyn manager Wilbert Robinson attempted to catch a ball dropped from an airplane. He didn't know that a grapefruit had been substituted for the baseball. When the grapefruit spattered in his glove, Robinson mistook the juice for blood. He lay on the ground moaning that he was mortally injured while the Dodgers laughed hysterically.

3. HACK WILSON

On July 4, 1934, Brooklyn manager Casey Stengel went to the mound to remove his pitcher, Boom Boom Beck, in a game at Philadelphia's Baker

Bowl. Beck, irate because he was being taken out of the game, fired the ball off the tin rightfield fence. Rightfielder Hack Wilson, who was badly hungover from a night of drinking, heard the sound of the ball hitting the wall and raced toward the fence. He retrieved the ball and made a perfect throw to second to nail the phantom runner.

4. JOSÉ CANSECO

Texas outfielder José Canseco used his head to turn a fly ball into a home run. On May 25, 1993, Canseco drifted back on a fly ball hit by Cleveland's Carlos Martinez. The ball bounced off Canseco's head and went over the fence for a home run. Four days later, Canseco tried his hand at pitching and required surgery after he blew out his right elbow.

5. LOU NOVIKOFF

Lou "the Mad Russian" Novikoff's entire career was an embarrassment. A four-time minor league batting champion, he never got the hang of major league fielding or playing the outfield in Chicago's Wrigley Field. Novikoff once stole third base with the bases loaded because, he explained, "I had such a good jump on the pitcher." His defense was even more atrocious. He claimed that he couldn't play Wrigley Field because the left field line was crooked. The Mad Russian also had a phobia about ivy and would get nowhere near the vines that covered the outfield walls at Wrigley.

6. BABE HERMAN

Babe Herman was a super hitter (.324 career batting average) who never quite got the hang of base running. His most infamous moment occurred on August 15, 1926 when Babe doubled into a double play. Herman, running with his head down, arrived at third base only to find two other Dodgers standing on the bag.

7. MARVELOUS MARV THRONEBERRY

First baseman Marv Throneberry personified the ineptitude of the original New York Mets. At manager Casey Stengel's birthday party, Throneberry asked why he wasn't given a piece of cake. Casey replied, "We'd given you a piece but we were afraid you'd drop it." Even when Marvelous Marv did something right, it turned out wrong. After hitting a triple, he was called out for missing first base. When Stengel went out to argue the call, a Mets' coach stopped him and said, "Don't bother, Casey, he missed second, too."

8. JOHNNY BENCH

During the third game of the 1972 World Series, Cincinnati catcher Johnny Bench came to bat against Oakland reliever Rollie Fingers with the Reds leading 1–0. Fingers indicated he was going to intentionally walk Bench on a 3–2 count. As Bench prepared to go to first base, Fingers threw a pitch on the outside corner to strike him out.

9. GEORGE FRAZIER

In the 1981 World Series, New York Yankees' George Frazier became the first pitcher to lose three games in a Fall Classic. On August 3, 1982, Frazier was on the mound with the Yankees trailing the White Sox 14–2. Owner George Steinbrenner ordered the public address announcer to apologize for the Yankees' performance and offer the fans a free ticket to a future game. Humiliated, Frazier hung his head on the mound.

10. JOE DIMAGGIO

Even the greats have their humbling moments. Toward the end of his career, the Yankees' Joe DiMaggio got involved in a feud with manager Casey Stengel. On July 8, 1951, DiMaggio made an error and was replaced in the second inning by rookie Jackie Jensen. DiMaggio retired at the end of the 1951 season.

Unlikely World Series Heroes

The World Series is a separate entity from the regular season. Everything is magnified; a clutch hit of an error has more significance than in a regular season game. One good play or a key hit can transform an ordinary player into a hero. Cleveland's Bill Wambsganss made an unassisted triple play in the 1920 World Series. Four years later, rookie Washington outfielder Earl McNeely became a hero when his ground ball hit a pebble and bounced over Fred Lindstrom's head for the series' winning hit. In 1983 light-hitting Baltimore catcher Rick Dempsey was named the World Series' Most Valuable Player after batting .385. Here are some of baseball's unexpected Mr. Octobers.

1. DON LARSEN

Pitcher Don Larsen had a 3–21 record with Baltimore in 1954. Larsen had the reputation of a man who enjoyed the nightlife. His manager in Baltimore, Jimmy Dykes, said, "The only thing he fears is sleep."

A month before the 1956 World Series, Larsen adopted his distinctive no-windup delivery. Larsen started Game two of the 1956 Series and was knocked out of the box in the third inning of a 13–8 loss to Brooklyn. Expectations weren't high three days later when Larsen started Game five. Larsen pitched the only perfect game in World Series history as the Yankees won 2–0.

2. BILL BEVENS

Pitcher Bill Bevens was only 7–13 for the Yankees in 1947. In Game four of the 1947 World Series, he was one out away from pitching a no-hitter when Dodgers' pinch hitter Cookie Lavagetto hit a double to drive in the winning runs as Brooklyn defeated New York 3–2. Neither Bevins nor Lavagetto played another game in the major leagues.

3. AL GIONFRIDDO

Al Gionfriddo batted only .175 and was used mainly as a defensive replacement by Brooklyn in 1947. During Game six of the 1947 World Series, Gionfriddo made a sensational catch of a 415-foot drive by New York's Joe DiMaggio, causing the Yankee Clipper to kick the dirt in disgust. Like

Bevins and Lavagetto, Gionfriddo never played in another major league game.

4. NIPPY JONES

First baseman Nippy Jones had not played in the major leagues for five seasons when he joined the Milwaukee Braves in 1957. Used sparingly, he was sent up as a pinch hitter in the fourth game of the 1957 World Series against New York. Jones insisted that he had been hit on the foot by a pitch thrown by Tommy Byrne. Braves' manager Fred Haney pointed out to umpire Augie Donatelli that there was shoe polish on the ball. Jones was awarded first base, and the Braves rallied to win the game and the series.

5. DUSTY RHODES

Dusty Rhodes, a .253 career hitter, outhit teammate Willie Mays in the 1954 World Series. Rhodes batted .667 with seven RBIs, including a game-winning three-run home run in Game one. Rhodes's heroics helped his New York Giants sweep the heavily favored Cleveland Indians, winners of a record 111 games, in four games.

6. SANDY AMOROS

Brooklyn outfielder Sandy Amoros entered Game seven of the 1956 World Series as a defensive replacement. The move paid off immediately as Amoros made a sensational running catch to rob the Yankees' Yogi Berra of an extra base hit. Amoros's game-saving catch propelled the Brooklyn Dodgers to a 2–0 victory and their only world championship.

7. BRIAN DOYLE

During his four-year career, second baseman Brian Doyle batted a feeble .161. The unlikely batting star of the 1978 World Series, Doyle batted .438 and scored four runs. His play helped the New York Yankees defeat the Los Angeles Dodgers in six games.

8. CHUCK ESSEGIAN

Rarely used outfielder Chuck Essegian hit two pinch hit home runs during the 1959 World Series. His homers in Game two and Game six helped the Los Angeles Dodgers defeat the Chicago White Sox in six games.

9. AL WEIS

Al Weis had a .219 career average, but his timely hitting was one of the main reasons the Miracle Mets upset the Baltimore Orioles in the 1969 World Series. Weis drove in the winning run in Game two, then hit a game-tying home run in Game five. For the series, Weis batted .455.

10. BILLY HATCHER

Cincinnati Reds' outfielder Billy Hatcher set a World Series record when he collected seven hits in his first seven at-bats during the 1990 Fall Classic against Oakland. Hatcher batted .750 as the Reds swept the heavily favored A's in four games.

Goats

A goat is a player who loses a big game because of a crucial mistake. It may be a baserunning blunder, a muffed fly ball, or an ill-timed gopher ball. More often than not, the goat is a star player. Oakland A's relief ace Dennis Eckersley gave up Kirk Gibson's dramatic home run in the 1988 World Series. Former Triple Crown winner Heinie Zimmerman chased Eddie Collins across home plate in the 1917 World Series. Many of these players had excellent careers marred by one boneheaded play.

1. **RALPH BRANCA**

From 1947 until 1951, Ralph Branca was one of the aces of the Brooklyn Dodgers staff. He won twenty-one games in 1947. Intelligent and personable, he didn't deserve the fate that awaited him.

Branca's Dodgers blew a thirteen-game lead in the final two months of the 1951 season and faced the New York Giants in a best-of-three playoff for the National League pennant. Branca had lost a game in the 1946 playoffs against St. Louis, but he was selected to start Game one against the Giants even though he had been beaten by New York six times during the season. He lost the first game 3–1 on a two-run home run by Bobby Thomson. The Dodgers easily won Game two, setting the stage for the deciding Game three. With twenty-game winner Don Newcombe on the mound for Brooklyn, the Dodgers led 4–2 in the ninth inning. There were two out and two runners on base when Ralph Branca was brought in to face Bobby Thomson. On a 0–1 pitch, Thomson hit a Branca high fastball over the left field fence for a game-winning home run. The "Shot Heard Round the World" gave the Giants the pennant and made Ralph Branca the goat. A photograph of Branca lying face down on the clubhouse steps symbolized his frustration.

2. BILL BUCKNER

Bill Buckner had over 2,700 hits during his career and won the National League batting crown in 1980. However, he will be forever remembered as the man who booted Mookie Wilson's grounder in the sixth game of the 1986 World Series. The Boston Red Sox had taken a 5–3 lead in the tenth inning and needed only one more out to clinch their first world championship in nearly seventy years. An improbable rally by the Mets tied the score. When Mookie Wilson's grounder went through Buckner's legs, the Mets tied the series. Two nights later, New York defeated Boston 8–5 to win the series. Buckner moved from Boston to Idaho and was traded the next season.

In Buckner's defense, his mobility was limited by bad ankles that had plagued him throughout the year. All season, manager John McNamara had been taking Buckner out in the late innings for a defensive replacement. Reliever Calvin Schiraldi deserves his share of blame. He was on the mound when the Mets rallied in Game six, and he was 0–2 in the series with a 13.50 earned run average.

3. **FRED MERKLE**

Fred "Bonehead" Merkle is that rare goat who made his historic blunder in the regular season. The New York Giants and Chicago Cubs were locked in a tight pennant race in 1908. On September 23, the Giants and Cubs were tied in the bottom of the ninth when Al Bridwell hit what appeared to be a game-winning single. Nineteen-year-old rookie Fred Merkle was the runner on first base. As the winning run scored, Merkle ran into the clubhouse without bothering to touch second. Chicago's Johnny Evers got the ball and stepped on second base, and the umpire called Merkle out. Since the game couldn't be resumed because the crowd had spilled out onto the field, National League president Harry Pulliam ruled that the game should be replayed only if necessary to decide the pennant. As it turned out, the teams ended up tied at the end of the regular season. When the Cubs won the playoff, Merkle's status as baseball's first great goat was ensured.

4. MITCH WILLIAMS

Mitch "Wild Thing" Williams saved forty-three games during the 1993 season for the Philadelphia Phillies. In Game four of the 1993 World Series against Toronto, the Phillies led 14–9 in the eighth inning and seemed certain to tie the series at two games apiece. The "Wild Thing" entered the game, and Toronto rallied for six runs and a 15–14 come-from-behind win. After the Phillies won Game five, Williams had a chance to redeem himself. The Phillies were leading 6–5 in the ninth inning when Williams surrendered a series-winning three-run homer to the Blue Jays' Joe Carter. Williams was 0–2 in the series with a 20.25 earned run average. After receiving numerous death threats from rabid Philadelphia fans, Williams was traded to Houston.

5. MICKEY OWEN

Mickey Owen was a solid defensive catcher who set a National League record by handling 476 chances without an error. In Game four of the 1941 World Series, Owen's Dodgers were leading the Yankees 4–3 in the ninth inning. With two out, pitcher Hugh Casey struck out Tommy Heinrich for the apparent game-winning out. Owen let the ball go to the backstop, allowing Heinrich to reach base. Owen's passed ball opened up the floodgates, and New York rallied for a 7–4 victory. The next day the Yankees won the series. It's probably unfair to single out Owen's miscue as the cause of the Dodgers' demise. He didn't give up the four runs in the ninth. It's also likely that Casey's pitch that got by Owen was a spitball, which is difficult to catch because of its sudden drop. Since the Yankees won the series in five games, they probably would have won anyway.

6. CHARLIE LEIBRANDT

For most of his career Charlie Leibrandt was a dependable lefthanded starter for Kansas City and Atlanta. In the sixth game of the 1991 World Series against Minnesota, his eleventh inning gopher ball to Kirby Puckett cost Atlanta the game in a series they went on to lose. A year later, Leibrandt gave up a two-run double to Toronto's Dave Winfield that helped clinch the world championship for the Blue Jays.

7. **TOM NIEDENFUER**

One of baseball's most underrated goats was Dodgers' pitcher Tom Niedenfuer. The hard-throwing reliever had fanned 102 in 106 innings during the 1985 season. In Game five of the 1985 National League championship series between Los Angeles and St. Louis, Niedenfuer gave up a game-winning home run to shortstop Ozzie Smith, his first ever from the left side of the plate. The next game Niedenfuer surrendered a towering game-winning home run to Jack Clark that sent St. Louis to the World Series.

8. **WILLIE DAVIS**

Willie Davis had over 2,500 base hits in his eighteen-year career and was a fleet outfielder. His difficulties during the 1966 World Series helped Baltimore sweep Los Angeles in four games. During the fifth inning of Game two, Davis made three errors as Jim Palmer defeated Sandy Koufax 6–0. Davis was in good company as the

Willie Davis
Los Angeles outfielder Willie Davis made three costly errors during Game two of the 1966 World Series.

Dodgers made six errors in the game. Los Angeles was shut out the final three games and hit only .142 for the series. Davis was even worse, with only one hit and a .063 batting average.

9. ROGER PECKINPAUGH

Washington shortstop Roger Peckinpaugh had been one of the heroes of the 1924 World Series, with a game-winning double in Game two and a .417 average. He was voted the American League Most Valuable Player in 1925, largely because of his defensive prowess. During the 1925 World

Series against Pittsburgh, his eight errors, including two costly miscues in the seventh and deciding game, doomed the Senators.

10. **FRED SNODGRASS**

Fred Snodgrass is almost as famous a goat as teammate Fred Merkel. His claim to shame occurred in the tenth inning of the eighth and final game of the 1912 World Series against Boston. Snodgrass dropped Clyde Engel's fly ball for a two-base error. Even though he made a sensational game-saving catch (which he called the best of his career) to rob Harry Hooper, Snodgrass received the blame when Boston rallied to win the game 3–2.

Spoilers and Nemeses

There are players whose notoriety comes at the expense of other players or teams. In 1908 Chicago pitcher Ed Reulbach defeated the Dodgers a record nine times. Ripper Collins called himself the "All-American Louse" because he broke up four no-hitters.

1. HUB "SCHUCKS" PRUETT

Hub Pruett had an undistinguished career, winning twenty-nine and losing forty-eight. It seemed that the only batter the screwball-throwing southpaw could get out consistently was Babe Ruth. During his rookie season in 1922, Shucks fanned Ruth thirteen times in sixteen at-bats.

2. LARRY JASTER

No pitcher has ever dominated a team in a year like Cardinals' lefthander Larry Jaster did the

Dodgers in 1966. In five starts, Jaster shut out the pennant winners five times. He held Los Angeles to twenty-four singles in those appearances.

3. FRANK LARY

Detroit pitcher Frank Lary won twenty-one games in 1956 and twenty-three in 1961. He was known as the "Yankee Killer" for good reason. Lary was 7–0 against the Bronx Bombers in 1958 and defeated them five times in a row in 1959. Overall, Lary was 27–13 against New York.

4. CESAR TOVAR

On September 22, 1968, Cesar Tovar of the Minnesota Twins played every position in a game against Oakland. The versatile Tovar led the American League at various times in hits, doubles, and triples. Tovar was the ultimate spoiler, breaking up five no-hitters during his career. The pitchers victimized by Tovar were Barry Moore (1967), Dave McNally (1969), Mike Cuellar (1969), Dick Bosman (1970), and Catfish Hunter (1975).

5. JIM BAGBY JR.

On July 17, 1941, pitcher Jim Bagby Jr. of the Cleveland Indians stopped Joe DiMaggio's fifty-six-game hitting streak when he induced him to hit into a double play in the eighth inning. Bagby was the son of Jim Bagby, a former thirty-game winner. In the minors DiMaggio had a sixty-one-game hitting streak stopped by Ed Walsh Jr., the son of Ed Walsh, baseball's last forty-game winner.

6. HAL GRIGGS

In 1957, Ted Williams set a record by reaching base sixteen consecutive times. He seemed like a cinch to extend the streak when he faced Washington's Hal Griggs. After all, Griggs would finish his career with a 6–26 record and a dreadful 5.50 earned run average. Somehow Griggs enticed Williams to ground out to end his streak.

7. HOWIE BEDELL

Don Drysdale's record 58⅔ consecutive shutout innings streak was broken in the fifth inning of a game against Philadelphia on June 8, 1968. The run was scored on a sacrifice fly by Howie Bedell. It was Bedell's only run batted in that season and one of only three in his career.

8. JIM QUALLS

Tom Seaver of the New York Mets was one out away from a perfect game against Chicago on July 9, 1969. The batter, Jim Qualls, was a rookie outfielder who finished his career with a .223 batting average. Qualls spoiled the perfect game with a single to left-center. Seaver did pitch a no-hitter with the Cincinnati Reds in 1978.

9. LARRY STAHL

Larry Stahl of the San Diego Padres, a .252 lifetime hitter, broke up a perfect game without even taking the bat off his shoulder. On September 2, 1972, Chicago's Milt Pappas retired twenty-six consecutive batters before he walked Stahl on a 3–2 count. Pappas always insisted that the pitch was a strike, and the umpire blew the call.

10. CHUCK CHURN

Pittsburgh's Elroy Face won his first seventeen decisions in 1959. Because of wins in his last five decisions in 1958, the forkballer's twenty-two consecutive victories placed him just two short of Carl Hubbell's major league record. On September 11, 1959, Face lost a 5–4 decision to the Los Angeles Dodgers. The winning pitcher was Chuck Churn, and the victory was one of only three in his career.

What Might Have Been

Baseball can be a cruel game. On September 15, 1971, Larry Yount, a promising pitcher for Houston, was making his major league debut. He injured his shoulder on his first warm-up pitch and never pitched in a major league game. His brother, Robin, would have a brilliant career and be one of the few players to make more than 3,000 hits. All of these players had potentially great careers shortened by injury or other circumstances.

1. HERB SCORE

Cleveland southpaw Herb Score led the American League in strikeouts his first two seasons and won twenty games in 1956. He was only twenty-three years old when he faced the New York Yankees on May 7, 1957. The Yankees' Gil McDougald lined a pitch that struck Score in the face. The pitcher fell to the ground, bleeding from his nose and mouth. He suffered a broken nose and a potential loss of vision in his right eye. Score missed the remainder of the season. When he returned the following year, he was not the same pitcher. Score's record before the injury was 38–20, but 17–26 after.

2. TONY CONIGLIARO

The tragic story of Tony Conigliaro is truly one of unrealized potential. Conigliaro was only twenty when he led the American League in home runs, the youngest ever to do so. Two years later, on August 18, 1967, the Red Sox outfielder was beaned by Angels' pitcher Jack Hamilton. The pitch fractured his cheekbone, dislocated his jaw, and damaged his eyesight. Conigliaro missed the rest of the season, as well as the following year, while his vision improved. He made an amazing comeback, and in 1970, Conigliaro belted thirty-six home runs, but deteriorating vision forced his retirement in 1975. Conigliaro suffered a debilitating heart attack in 1982 and died in 1990 at the age of forty-five.

3. PETE REISER

Leo Durocher observed that Pete Reiser may have been the best ball player he ever saw. "He had everything but luck," said Leo the Lip. In 1941, the twenty-two-year-old Brooklyn outfielder won the batting title and led the National League in doubles, triples, runs scored, and slugging percentage despite two serious beanings. Reiser was batting .383 on July 2, 1942, when he suffered a fractured skull from crashing into the outfield wall in St. Louis. After three years of relative safety in the military service during World War II, Reiser resumed his stay on the disabled list by breaking his ankle sliding into a base in 1946. The following year Reiser ran into the Ebbets Field wall with such force that he was given last rites. It was one of eleven times that Reiser was carried off the field. Seven times he either broke his collarbone or dislocated his shoulder. Other injuries included a broken neck, temporary paralysis, and a blood clot on the brain.

4. J. R. RICHARD

At 6 feet 8 inches, J. R. Richard intimidated hitters in much the same way that Randy Johnson does today. Richard struck out fifteen batters in his first major league game in 1971, but it would be another five years before he became a consistent winner. Richard won twenty games in 1976 and struck out over 300 batters in both 1978 and 1979. On July 30, 1980, Richard, who had been complaining of impaired vision and sluggishness, collapsed. A stroke had paralyzed his left side.

Although his condition did improve gradually, his comeback attempts were unsuccessful.

5. **RAY FOSSE**

Ray Fosse was the best young catcher in the American League when he was bowled over by Pete Rose in a home plate collision at the 1970 All-Star Game. The twenty-three-year-old catcher suffered a fractured shoulder and never displayed the potential he had exhibited prior to the injury. He had several stints on the disabled list. Fosse pinched a nerve in his neck trying to break up a fight in the clubhouse, and his foot was injured by a cherry bomb thrown by a fan. By 1975 his batting average had slipped to .140.

6. **AUSTIN MCHENRY**

St. Louis outfielder Austin McHenry was on his way to stardom in 1921 when he batted .350, with 201 hits and 102 runs batted in. Midway through the next season it was discovered that he had a brain tumor. McHenry died on November 27, 1922 at the age of twenty-seven.

7. **DAVE ORR**

Dave Orr was one of the great hitters of the 1880s. Never hitting below .300, Orr compiled a .342 career batting average. At 5 feet 11 inches,

250 pounds, he was an imposing sight. In 1893, he had his greatest season, batting .373 for Brooklyn. Orr was only thirty-one years old when a stroke ended his career.

8. BILL "LITTLE EVA" LANGE

Bill "Little Eva" Lange was such a great baserunner and hitter that he has been compared to Ty Cobb. Lange once held out in order that he could attend a heavyweight title fight featuring Gentleman Jim Corbett. A .330 lifetime hitter, he retired in 1899 at age twenty-eight to marry the daughter of a real estate magnate. His father-in-law disapproved of his daughter marrying a baseball player.

9. VON MCDANIEL

Eighteen-year-old Von McDaniel pitched a two-hit shutout against the Dodgers in his first major league start on June 4, 1957. A month later, the Cardinals' righthander threw a one-hitter against Pittsburgh. The next spring McDaniel injured his shoulder and pitched only two more innings in the majors. While Von McDaniel was finished at age nineteen, his brother Lindy pitched in the majors for twenty-one years.

10. WAYNE SIMPSON

Rookie pitcher Wayne Simpson was a principal reason that the 1970 Cincinnati Reds won 70 of their first 100 games. The twenty-one-year-old righthander won thirteen of his first fourteen decisions, including a one-hitter and a two-hitter. Selected to the All-Star Game, Simpson injured his shoulder and won only one more game that season. For the remainder of his career, Simpson had a record of 22–28.

Blackballed

On August 28, 1945, Jackie Robinson signed a contract to play professional baseball for the Montreal Royals, a farm club of the Brooklyn Dodgers. The signing was not announced publicly until October 23. Jackie Robinson broke baseball's color barrier with Brooklyn in 1947. In fact, many African Americans had paved the way for Robinson's breakthrough.

1. FLEET WALKER

Moses Fleetwood Walker actually played major league baseball sixty-three years before Jackie Robinson's first game. In 1884 Fleet Walker played in forty-two games for the Toledo Blue Stockings of the American Association, then considered a major league. Walker soon realized that he was a marked man. The catcher developed a primitive form of wooden shin guard to protect his legs from the well-aimed spikes of opposing baserunners. Even his teammates attempted to hurt Walker. Pitcher Tony Mullane threw the ball in the dirt, hoping to injure him. Mullane refused to take Walker's signals, but grudgingly admitted, "He was the best catcher I ever worked with." During the season Walker was attacked by a mob of abusive fans in Louisville. When blacks were banned from the major leagues, he played for several years in the minors.

An educated man, Walker attended Oberlin College and the University of Michigan. In 1891, he stabbed a man who had attacked him and was acquitted by an all-white jury. In 1908, Walker wrote a booklet on race in America entitled *Our Home Colony* in which he suggested that blacks could never achieve equality in America, and the best solution would be for them to return to Africa. During his last years Walker was editor of a newspaper, *The Steubenville Equator,* and owned several movie theaters.

2. **WELDAY WALKER**

Fleet Walker's younger brother, Welday, played five games in the outfield for Toledo in 1884. After African Americans were blacklisted from professional baseball, Welday filed a protest, reasoning that ability, not color, should determine whether a player be permitted to play on a team.

3. **SANDY NAVA**

Dark-skinned catcher Sandy Nava passed himself off as a Spaniard, Mexican, and even an Italian. Nava (whose real name was Irwin Sandy) carried off the ruse successfully enough to remain in the American Association until 1886. Nava has the distinction of being the first man of color to play in the National League, having played with Providence from 1882 to 1884.

4. **GEORGE TREADWAY**

Outfielder George Treadway claimed American Indian ancestry and was permitted to play in the major leagues until 1896. His best season was 1894 when he batted .328 and drove in 102 runs for Brooklyn.

5. **GEORGE STOVEY**

George Stovey, a light-skinned black from Canada, won a record thirty-five games for Newark of the Eastern League in 1887. That year, John Montgomery Ward, captain of the New York Giants, attempted to sign Stovey, but was blocked by the protests of Chicago's Cap Anson and others.

6. CHARLIE GRANT

In 1901, John McGraw, the manager of the American League Baltimore Orioles, was in Hot Springs, Arkansas, for spring training and there discovered a black bellhop named Charlie Grant. He was such a good second baseman that McGraw wanted to sign him. McGraw devised a plan in which he would attempt to pass off Grant as Chief Tokohoma, a full-blooded Cherokee. The plan was foiled by owner Charles Comiskey, who exposed Grant's true identity.

7. FRANK GRANT

Second baseman Frank Grant may have been the most talented African American player of the nineteenth century. Compared favorably to the white stars in the major leagues, Grant batted as high as .366 and won the International League batting title in 1877. His Buffalo teammates refused to sit with him for a team portrait, and Grant once had to grab a club to escape a beating. In Toronto, he endured chants of "Kill the nigger." Even more painful was the racism that kept him from playing in the major leagues.

8. RAMON HERRARA

Ramon Herrara, a Cuban infielder, played in the American League with Boston in 1925 and 1926.

Herrara holds the distinction of playing in both the major leagues and Negro Leagues.

9. BUD FOWLER

Bud Fowler broke professional baseball's color line when he played for New Castle in 1872. A superb pitcher and second baseman, Fowler played in numerous minor leagues, usually batting above .300. Had he not been black, he surely would have had the opportunity to play in the major leagues.

10. CHET BREWER

Chet Brewer nearly became the man who broke the color barrier. In 1943, Oakland owner Vince De Vicenzi wanted to give Brewer a tryout, but his manager, Johnny Vergez, refused. Two years later, Bakersfield, a farm team of the Cleveland Indians, wanted to give Brewer a tryout, but the plan was nixed by the parent team. Brewer, an outstanding pitcher, once won thirty games in the Negro League and pitched two no-hitters in the Mexican League.

Racism in Baseball

It seems almost unbelievable that blacks were not permitted to play in the major leagues until 1947. Since its beginnings, however, major league baseball has been plagued by racism. Ty Cobb refused to room with Babe Ruth because it was rumored he had African ancestry. Pitcher Kirby Higbe boasted that he had strengthened his arm by throwing rocks at blacks as a child in South Carolina. The following incidents represent the dark side of our national pastime.

1. CAP ANSON

Cap Anson was the dominant player of the nineteenth century. His tremendous influence on the game was instrumental in the establishment of the color barrier. In 1884, Chicago, managed by Anson, was scheduled to play an exhibition game against Toledo. When he saw their black catcher,

Fleet Walker, he yelled, "Get that nigger off the field." Toledo's manager insisted that Walker play, and Anson relented. Three years later, Anson again refused to play an exhibition game against a minor league team with black players. That same day, owners agreed to institute a color line. African Americans were not allowed to play in the major leagues for another sixty years.

2. KENESAW MOUNTAIN LANDIS

Considered the savior of baseball after he helped restore the game's integrity following the Black Sox scandal, baseball commissioner Kenesaw Mountain Landis must bear much of the responsibility for maintaining baseball's color barrier. Landis insisted that there was no formal rule that banned blacks from playing professional baseball. Despite his assurances, Landis blocked Washington and Pittsburgh from signing black players in the early 1940s. When Bill Veeck attempted to buy the Philadelphia Phillies in 1943 and stock the team with black players, Landis made sure another owner was found. A year after Landis's death, Branch Rickey signed Jackie Robinson.

3. JAKE POWELL

New York outfielder Jake Powell shocked radio audiences during an interview in Chicago on July 29, 1938. A policeman in the offseason, Powell told interviewer Bob Elson that he derived pleasure from "cracking niggers over the head." Commissioner Landis suspended Powell for ten days for the racist remark. He was forced to apologize only after leaders of the African American community threatened to organize a boycott of Yankees' owner Jacob Ruppert's brewery products. In 1948, Powell committed suicide in a Washington, D. C., police station after being questioned about a bad check charge.

4. BEN CHAPMAN

Another former Yankee outfielder, Ben Chapman reflected the racism that Jackie Robinson encountered when he joined the Brooklyn Dodgers in 1947. Chapman, the manager of the Philadelphia Phillies, baited Robinson with a steady stream of racial taunts. His insults compared blacks with monkeys and implied that they were thick-skulled and contracted venereal diseases. Chapman and some of his players would aim their bats at Robinson and make machine-gun sounds. Chapman was fired as Phillies' skipper in 1948.

5. DIXIE WALKER

Some of Jackie Robinson's worst opposition initially came from his Brooklyn teammates. Dixie Walker, the 1944 National League batting champion, circulated a petition objecting to Robinson's promotion to the big league club. The petition was ignored by manager Leo Durocher, and Walker demanded to be traded. The Georgia native came to accept playing with Robinson, but he was traded to Pittsburgh at season's end.

6. **CLAY HOPPER**

Jackie Robinson faced prejudice in the minors while playing for Montreal. His manager, the Mississippi-born Clay Hopper, reportedly asked Branch Rickey, "Do you really think a nigger is a human being?"

7. **GEORGE WEISS**

During his twenty-nine seasons (1932–60) with the New York Yankees, executive George Weiss oversaw teams that won nineteen pennants and fifteen world championships. Weiss expressed his reluctance to integrate the Yankees when he admitted, "I will never allow a black man to wear a Yankees uniform." Eight years after Jackie Robinson broke the color barrier, the Yankees finally brought up a black player, Elston Howard. Manager Casey Stengel marked the occasion by saying, "When I finally get a nigger, I get the only one who can't run."

8. **TOM YAWKEY**

The New York Yankees were positively progressive in race relations compared to the Boston Red Sox. The Red Sox, owned by Tom Yawkey, were the last major league team to integrate. The first black, Pumpsie Green, did not join the Red Sox until 1959.

9. **HANK AARON**

In 1974, Hank Aaron was about to surpass Babe Ruth's career home run record. What should have been one of the happiest moments of Aaron's life became a nightmare. During his quest for the record, the Atlanta Braves' outfielder received many racist threats. There was even a plot to kidnap his daughter, Gaile. He received police protection and took seriously the numerous death threats he received. "It was hell," Aaron remembered. It was no way to treat a hero.

10. **AL CAMPANIS**

While blacks had gained acceptance as players, progress in the positions of manager and executives has been slow. On April 6, 1987, Los Angeles Dodgers' General Manager Al Campanis appeared on *Nightline* on the occasion of the fortieth anniversary of Jackie Robinson's debut in the majors. Campanis outraged many when he suggested that African Americans "lacked some of the necessities" to become managers and hold front office positions. As the result of his remarks, Campanis was fired, and major league baseball hired more blacks in executive and managerial positions.

Kill the Umpire

"Kill the umpire" is more than just a baseball adage. Here are some frightening examples where the men in blue became black and blue.

1. SAMUEL WHITE

Minor league umpire Samuel White was hit over the head and killed during a game in Alabama in 1899.

2. ORA JENNINGS

In 1901, another minor league umpire, Ora Jennings, met the same fate during a game in Indiana.

3. HANK O'DAY

Hank O'Day was a National League umpire from 1893 until 1927. Early in his career, O'Day was badly beaten by irate St. Louis Cardinal fans after a disputed call. Armed police escorted the besieged umpire down the street, where he was pelted with rocks.

4. BILLY EVANS

Umpire Billy Evans had his skull fractured when he was struck in the head by a bottle thrown by a fan during a game at Sportsman's Park in 1907. In 1921, the umpire was attacked by Ty Cobb underneath the stadium in Washington, D. C. Cobb repeatedly smashed Evans's head into the concrete wall.

5. JACK WARNER

New York Giants' catcher Jack Warner was suspended five days for striking an umpire in 1903. Two days later, he was used as a substitute umpire when the men in blue didn't show up.

6. WILLIAM "LORD" BYRON

Baseball's original singing umpire, William "Lord" Byron, has the distinction of being punched out by both John McGraw and Ty Cobb. Byron, who sometimes sang out his calls, was an umpire in the major leagues from 1913 to 1919. On another occasion, he was chased from the field by a mob of angry rock-wielding fans.

7. SHERRY MAGEE

Sherry Magee was an outfielder who played between 1904 and 1910 and led the National League in runs batted in four times. While playing for Philadelphia, he broke the umpire's jaw after arguing a called third strike. Magee became an umpire himself in 1928.

8. BILLY MCLEAN

In 1906, Billy McLean was a twenty-two-year-old rookie umpire when he had his skull fractured by a flying bottle. Later in his career he was arrested after injuring a heckling fan by throwing a bat into the stands.

9. GEORGE MAGERKURTH

Before becoming an umpire, burly George Magerkurth had fought in seventy professional fights. His pugilistic training became useful in the minor leagues when he fought a promising first baseman named Ivy Griffin. Griffin took such a beating that it ended his career. In 1939, Giants' shortstop Billy Jurges got into a fight with Magerkurth after he claimed the umpire spit tobacco juice in his face. The following year a man out on parole attacked Magerkurth during a game at Ebbets Field. Magerkurth's lowest moment came in 1945 when he beat up a fan in Cincinnati who he thought was heckling him. The victim turned out to be a Dayton restaurant owner who was seated near the real culprit.

10. **TIM HURST**

Tim Hurst has the dubious honor of being the only umpire to be thrown out of both the National and American Leagues. Hurst kept players in line by hitting them over the head with his mask or by pinching them hard. In 1897, Hurst was barred from the National League for hitting a fan in Cincinnati with a beer stein. Twelve years later, he was given the heave-ho by the American League for spitting in the face of second baseman Eddie Collins.

Media Blitz

Infielder Rocky Bridges said, "I know what the word 'media' means. It's plural for mediocre." The relationship between ballplayers and the media has never been especially cordial. For years Steve Carlton refused to speak to the press. Albert Belle was accused of throwing a ball at a journalist. Here are examples of instances where the reporters made the headlines.

1. BILLY MARTIN

Billy Martin's unique rapport with players carried over to his relationships with the media. In 1978, Billy punched *Nevada State Journal* writer Ray Hager. Martin also called reporters Henry Hecht a "prick" and Deborah Herschel a "hooker."

2. PATSY TEBEAU

Henry Chadwick wrote that Cleveland manager Patsy Tebeau degraded the game of baseball more

Ted Williams
One of baseball's greatest hitters, Ted Williams had a less than cordial relationship with the media.

than any other player. Tebeau repeatedly assaulted umpires and once tore up a horseshoe wreath of flowers given to player Cupid Childs on a day honoring him. In 1896, Patsy beat up Cleveland reporter Elmer Pasco for negative remarks he made about Tebeau's Spiders.

3. **BRET SABERHAGEN**

In 1985, Kansas City's Bret Saberhagen became the youngest pitcher to win the Cy Young Award.

When Saberhagen was traded to the Mets, his relationship with the New York media was less than cordial. He sprayed a container of bleach on reporters, an offense that resulted in a five-game suspension. Earlier in the season Saberhagen tossed a firecracker into a crowd of reporters.

4. DAVE KINGMAN

Slugger Dave Kingman once showed his displeasure with a sportswriter by throwing a ten-gallon bucket of icewater over his head. He went too far when he sent a rat to a female reporter at the *Sacramento Bee*. Despite hitting thirty-five home runs for the Oakland A's in 1986, he was not offered a contract, costing him a chance to hit 500 home runs.

5. TED WILLIAMS

Ted Williams may have spit at fans in Boston, but he really hated the media. Teddy Ballgame was known to reply to interview requests by replying, "Go fuck off." If a writer approached him, the Splendid Splinter might remark, "Hey, what stinks? It was the shit you wrote last night." Thumper once lifted *Boston Globe* writer Hy Hurwitz up by his necktie, then cut the tie with scissors.

6. DEION SANDERS

In 1992, Deion Sanders attempted to become the first athlete to play in a professional baseball and football game on the same day. During the afternoon Deion played cornerback for the Atlanta Falcons. That night, he suited up to play outfield for the Atlanta Braves in the National League championship series against Pittsburgh. When he was criticized by CBS announcer Tim McCarver for risking injury by playing in an NFL game on the day of a crucial baseball playoff game, Sanders doused him three times with icewater in the clubhouse.

7. DENNY MCLAIN

Denny McLain won thirty-one games with the 1968 Detroit Tigers, but his world fell apart a few years later. In April 1970, he was suspended for his involvement in a bookmaking operation and in September of that same year for possession of a gun. In between, he dumped icewater on two Detroit sportswriters after a game.

8. GEORGE BRETT

Kansas City third baseman George Brett batted .390 in 1980 and was the American League's Most Valuable Player. Rather than reporting on his on-field achievements, Brett felt that the media concentrated too much on his problem with hemorrhoids. Brett reportedly once shoved a woman reporter and swung a crutch at another.

9. JIM KERN

Jim Kern pitched in the major leagues from 1974 to 1986. The flaky pitcher once ate the notes of a sportswriter after being told he might have to eat his words. On a airplane he once ate the pages of a book that a reporter was reading.

10. JOHN McGRAW

John McGraw battled umpires, players, and reporters. In 1905, Little Napoleon cursed at a reporter, then grabbed his nose and twisted it.

Fanatics

In the nineteenth century, spectators were called kranks. St. Louis owner Chris Von der Ahe referred to them as fanatics, which was shortened to fans. Throughout the history of baseball, some fans have acted like fanatics. In 1991, San Francisco pitcher Steve Decker sprained his left foot running from a horde of autograph hounds. The year before he broke Babe Ruth's single season home run record, Roger Maris was nearly struck by jagged pieces of grandstand seats thrown by Detroit fans. When fans cross the line, no one is safe.

1. EDDIE WAITKUS

Eddie Waitkus played first base for the Chicago Cubs in the late 1940s. While Waitkus was with the Cubs, a teenage girl named Ruth Ann Steinhagen became infatuated with him. She kept a shrine to him at the foot of her bed. Steinhagen was disconsolate when Waitkus was traded to Philadelphia after the 1948 season. She decided that if she couldn't have him, no one would. During a road trip to Chicago, Steinhagen arranged for a meeting in a room at the Edgewater Beach Hotel. Steinhagen told him, "I have a surprise for you." She pulled a rifle from the closet and shot Waitkus in the chest. Instead of finishing him off with a knife and killing herself, as she planned, Steinhagen briefly held his hand and then notified the front desk. Waitkus recovered and had his best season in 1950, helping the Whiz Kids to the pennant. Steinhagen spent three years in a mental hospital. She later claimed that the shooting had relieved her tension and that she had never felt so happy.

2. **1895 CLEVELAND SPIDERS**

The 1895 Temple Cup between the Baltimore Orioles and Cleveland Spiders was marred by several ugly incidents. During Game one in Cleveland, fans threw vegetables at the Baltimore players. When the Spiders defeated the Orioles in Baltimore, angry fans chased them from the field. The Spiders were paraded through the streets of Baltimore where they were stoned by irate fans.

3. **1908 CHICAGO CUBS**

The Chicago Cubs and New York Giants met in a one-game playoff to decide the National League champion of 1908. The Cubs, behind the pitching of Three Finger Brown, defeated the Giants and Christy Mathewson 4–2. Giants' fans knocked down the fence and drove the Chicago players from the field. The Cubs were trapped in the clubhouse for three hours before order was restored. Rioting after the game resulted in one death and extensive damage.

4. **BIRDIE TEBBETTS**

Cleveland fans were in an angry mood on September 27, 1940, when the Detroit Tigers clinched the pennant by defeating the Indians 2–0. Throughout the game the Tigers were pelted with eggs, fruits, and vegetables. The barrage culminated when Detroit bullpen catcher Birdie Tebbetts was hit with a crate of green tomatoes thrown from the stands. Umpire George Pipgras thought Tebbetts might be dead. After Tebbetts came to in the clubhouse, the police brought him the culprit. The fan was roughed up, and Tebbetts was later acquitted of assault charges.

5. WIN MERCER

Pitcher Win Mercer, a twenty-five-game winner in 1896, was the most popular player in Washington. In 1897, thousands of women came to the ballpark on Ladies Day to see their favorite. The ladies went crazy when umpire Bill Carpenter ejected Mercer during an argument. Hundreds of Mercer's female fans stormed the field and beat the beleaguered umpire to the ground. As he fled for his life, the rampaging women nearly laid waste to the ballpark before the police were summoned.

6. ROBERT JOYCE

On July 12, 1938, avid Brooklyn Dodgers' fan Robert Joyce shot and killed two men at Pat Diamond's Bar. The murders occurred following an argument with a New York Giants' fan over baseball.

7. 1984 DETROIT TIGERS

The celebration turned violent following the Detroit Tigers' victory over the San Diego Padres in Game five of the 1984 World Series. Fans rioted in the streets, torching police cars and throwing beer bottles. One person was killed, and scores were injured.

8. WALLY JOYNER

California first baseman Wally Joyner batted in 100 runs during his rookie season in 1986. That year he was nearly killed when he was grazed by a butcher knife thrown from the upper deck of New York's Yankee Stadium.

9. BOB WATSON

Houston outfielder Bob Watson was injured when he crashed into the wall at Cincinnati's Riverfront Stadium during a game against the Reds in 1974. As Watson lay bleeding on the warning track, fans showed their concern by pouring beer on the fallen player.

10. WHITEY WITT

On September 16, 1922, New York Yankees' centerfielder Whitey Witt was knocked unconscious by a bottle thrown from the stands at St. Louis' Sportsman's Park. The American League downplayed the incident, concocting a ludicrous scenario that Witt stepped on the bottle, which then flew up and conked him in the head.

With Teammates like These

Sometimes your teammates can be your worst enemies. Consider the following examples.

1. FRANK WARFIELD

Oliver "Ghost" Marcelle, the great Negro League third baseman, was playing winter ball in Cuba in 1928 when he got into a fight with teammate Frank Warfield. During the struggle, Warfield bit off Marcelle's nose. Marcelle wore a black patch over the hole but was so ashamed that he retired rather than show his face.

2. HEINIE ZIMMERMAN

Heinie Zimmerman won the Triple Crown in 1912 but was the goat of the 1917 World Series and was later banned from baseball for conspiring to throw games. Zimmerman nearly blinded Chicago teammate Jimmy Sheckard when he threw a bottle of ammonia at him. Manager Frank Chance grabbed Zimmerman and beat him senseless.

3. DUCKY MEDWICK

Joe "Ducky" Medwick personified the rowdy behavior of the Gas House Gang. The St. Louis outfielder terrorized opposing pitchers at the plate and his own pitchers on the field. In 1933, Cardinals' pitcher Tex Carleton was taking swings in batting practice when Medwick told him to get out of the cage and let the regulars hit. When Carleton took an extra swing, Ducky knocked him cold. Manager Gabby Street had to get another starter warmed up. Two years later, pitcher Ed Heusser made the mistake of accusing Medwick of not hustling in the outfield after a fly ball dropped in front of him. Ducky, never one to appreciate constructive criticism, flattened Heusser on the mound. A new pitcher had to be brought into the game.

4. LENNY RANDLE

On March 28, 1977, Texas Rangers' manager Frank Lucchesi was speaking with reporters behind the batting cage when he was brutally attacked by infielder Lenny Randle. Randle punched the fifty-year-old manager repeatedly until he was dragged off by teammates. His only explanation for the assault was that Lucchesi had called him a punk. Lucchesi suffered a broken jaw and required plastic surgery. To add insult to injury, Lucchesi was fired in June because management felt he had lost control of his players.

5. TY COBB

Ty Cobb was almost hated as much by his Detroit teammates as he was by the opposition. Cobb punched his roommate for having the audacity to take a bath before him. He decked pitcher Ed Siever on the final day of the 1906 season after he made a disparaging remark about Cobb's play in the outfield. Not satisfied, Cobb gave him another beating at the hotel that evening. His teammates despised Cobb to such an extent that they would do anything to make him look bad. When it appeared that Nap Lajoie had beaten Cobb out for the batting title, several Detroit players sent the popular second baseman a congratulatory telegram. Cobb was so fearful that his teammates would try to kill him that he kept a loaded gun under his pillow.

6. BUCK O'BRIEN

Buck O'Brien won twenty games for Boston in 1912, then lost Game three of the 1912 World Series to New York. When he gave up five runs in the first inning of Game six, his teammates beat him up after the game. Boston won the series four games to three, but O'Brien was traded to Chicago the next season.

7. **PHENOMENAL SMITH**

Pitcher John Smith nicknamed himself "Phenomenal" and claimed he was so good that he didn't even need his teammates behind him. His Brooklyn teammates took offense to Smith's remarks and decided to teach him a lesson. In his first start on June 17, 1885, the Dodgers intentionally made errors so that Smith would lose the game. The Dodgers made fourteen errors, half of them by shortstop Germany Smith in a 18–5 loss. The team fined each of the players $500, but Phenomenal was released to insure team harmony. Smith never had a winning season, and the only phenomenal thing about his eight-year career was that he managed to lose thirty games in 1887.

8. **ROBERT HIGGINS**

Robert Higgins was a black minor league pitcher in the 1880s. His inexcusable treatment by his Syracuse teammates typified the racism prevalent in the game. Whenever Higgins pitched, his teammates intentionally made errors, and they refused to allow him to be in the team photo.

9. OSSIE VITT

One of the most unpopular managers with his players was Cleveland skipper Ossie Vitt. He irritated the players by criticizing them in the press and chewing them out on the field when they made a bad play. Players demanded that they be traded or that Vitt be fired. They did what they could to undermine him, even if it meant losing a game. The team became known as the "Crybaby Indians" and were bombarded with baby bottles and jars of baby food. Cleveland lost the 1940 pennant by a game to Detroit, and Vitt was fired.

10. JOHNNY EVERS AND JOE TINKER

The Cubs' double play combination of Tinker to Evers to Chance was immortalized in a poem written by Franklin Adams. The men were so linked in the public mind that they were inducted together in the Hall of Fame in 1946. In fact, Tinker and Evers disliked each other intensely. The cause of the ill will was a seemingly insignificant dispute over a taxi in 1905. The two men didn't speak to one another for thirty-three years.

Donnybrooks

Jesse "The Crab" Burkett hit over .400 three times. He also was ejected in both games of a doubleheader after getting into three fights. Dour Frankie Crosetti once punched baseball clown Max Patkin. Here are some players who are guaranteed to add some punch to your lineup.

1. BILLY MARTIN

The undisputed King of the Sucker Punch, Billy Martin fought friend and foe alike. Martin was a good player and an excellent manager, but his enduring fame will be as a fighter. In 1952, he fought Boston outfielder Jimmy Piersall under the stands at Fenway Park. Two days later, Piersall was sent to the minors and suffered a nervous breakdown. Martin expressed some remorse for the incident. "I was only a jump away from the guys in the white suit myself," he admitted. That same year he decked catcher Clint "Scrap Iron" Courtney, whom Satchel Paige called "the meanest man I ever met."

Billy's most infamous fight as a player occurred in 1960. Martin, playing for Cincinnati, felt Chicago pitcher Jim Brewer had thrown at him. Martin flipped his bat at the pitcher. When Brewer tried to hand him the bat, Martin sucker punched him, breaking his cheekbone. Brewer underwent two eye operations and was out for the season. When Martin learned that Brewer had sued him for a million dollars, he smirked, "How does he want it, cash or check?"

Billy's boxing record as a manager was even more impressive. He beat up the traveling secretaries of the Minnesota Twins and Texas Rangers (the latter a sixty-year-old man). Martin flattened a reporter and, in his most famous bout, gave a fat lip to a marshmallow salesman named Joseph Cooper. Twice Martin fought his pitchers. In 1969, he knocked cold his twenty-game winner in Minnesota, Dave Boswell. The pitcher came out of the battle with a black eye, chipped tooth, and twenty stitches in his face. Billy fared less well in a 1987 encounter with Yankees' pitcher Ed Whitson. Billy's injuries included a broken right arm and bruised side. It was apparent that Billy was over the hill in 1988 when he was badly beaten in a Texas topless bar. First baseman Don Mattingly uttered his boxing epitaph, "That's like beating up your grandfather."

2. **ART "THE GREAT" SHIRES**

Art "The Great" Shires was a hard-hitting first baseman who batted over .300 three of his four major league seasons. In 1929, while captain of the White Sox, "Whattaman" Shires beat up his manager Lena Blackburne three times. One of the disputes concerned a red felt party hat Shires wore during batting practice. Shires decided to test his pugilistic skills as a professional. He knocked "Mysterious" Dan Daly cold in twenty-one seconds and won all of his fights except a decision loss to Chicago Bears' hulking center George Trafton. Baseball Commissioner Kenesaw Mountain Landis put a stop to his boxing career when he tried to arrange a bout with Cubs' outfielder Hack Wilson.

3. **JOHN MCGRAW**

By all accounts, John McGraw may not have been the best fighter in the world, but he was the most persistent. On May 16, 1894, McGraw got into a fight with Boston's Tommy Tucker, and while the two men battled, the ballpark burned down around them. Three years later, he and teammate Wee Willie Keeler fought nude on the clubhouse floor. One of McGraw's infrequent victories came in 1904 when he loosened the teeth of a young boy selling lemonade. He was less successful in 1913 when Philadelphia pitcher Ad Brennan decked him. The Giants' skipper was so hated that grateful fans sent Brennan a bouquet of flowers. McGraw had many encounters with umpires; the most famous came in 1917 when he belted Lord Byron, baseball's singing umpire. One of McGraw's most humiliating defeats came in 1920 when he received two black eyes in a scuffle with actor William Boyd, who later gained fame as Hopalong Cassidy.

4. BOSS SCHMIDT

Ty Cobb met his match when he challenged Detroit catcher Charley "Boss" Schmidt. Schmidt could hammer nails into wood with his bare hands and had once fought an exhibition against heavyweight champion Jack Johnson. Schmidt gave Cobb a merciless beating, breaking his nose and nearly closing both eyes.

5. DOLF CAMILLI

First baseman Dolf Camilli batted in more than 100 runs five times between 1936 and 1942. A no-nonsense type of player, Camilli came from a boxing family. His brother had died in the ring in a bout with Max Baer, the heavyweight champion. Dolf also had professional boxing experience that he put to use when necessary. He punched out Joe Medwick when he saw him bullying young shortstop Pee Wee Reese.

6. ASTYANAX DOUGLASS

Catcher Astyanax Douglass only played in eleven major league games, but he participated in one of baseball's greatest fights. On May 24, 1925, Douglass punched Philadelphia pitcher Jimmy Ring during a donnybrook on the field. The two men continued their fight in the clubhouse. Round three occurred at the train station that night.

7. JOHN L. SULLIVAN

John L. Sullivan was the heavyweight champion of the world from 1882 to 1892. A talented pitcher, he was offered a tryout by Cincinnati, but declined.

8. EDDIE MATHEWS

Eddie Mathews hit 512 home runs during his Hall of Fame career. The slugging third baseman also had the reputation of being one of the game's best boxers. He demonstrated his prowess in a 1960 game against Cincinnati. The Reds' Frank Robinson slid hard into third base. Mathews responded by flattening Frank, shutting his right eye. Robinson got his revenge by robbing Mathews of a home run later in the game.

9. BILL DICKEY

Yankees' catcher Bill Dickey threw one of baseball's most celebrated punches in a game against the Senators on July 4, 1932. Dickey broke the jaw of Washington outfielder Carl Reynolds after a close play at the plate. The fight precipitated one of the wildest brawls in baseball history. Dickey was suspended for thirty days.

10. NOLAN RYAN

Fans held their breath in 1993 when young Chicago third baseman Robin Ventura charged the mound to fight forty-six-year-old pitcher Nolan Ryan. Ryan grabbed Ventura in a headlock and planted six punches on his noggin.

The Bases Are Loaded

Many baseball greats were heavy drinkers: Grover Cleveland Alexander, Mickey Mantle, Hack Wilson, Ed Delahanty, King Kelly, and Rabbit Maranville, to name a few. In recent years, Dwight Gooden, Darryl Strawberry, and Bob Welch all sought treatment for their alcoholism. In 1989, reliever Mitch Williams was traded to Philadelphia. The Wild Thing wanted his old uniform number 28, which was being worn by John Kruk. Kruk agreed to relinquish his number in exchange for two cases of beer.

1. FLINT RHEM

St. Louis pitcher Flint Rhem led the National League with twenty wins in 1926. Rhem was scheduled to pitch a crucial game against Brooklyn in 1930 but failed to show up. Two days later, Rhem reappeared and claimed that he had been kidnapped by gamblers and forced to drink large amounts of whiskey to incapacitate him. Of course, Rhem had concocted the wild story after a drinking binge left him unable to pitch.

2. **BUGS RAYMOND**

Pitcher Bugs Raymond was such a chronic alcoholic that New York manager John McGraw hired a detective to keep tabs on him during his years with the Giants from 1909 to 1911. The surveillance ended when McGraw found Bugs and the detective in the midst of a drinking contest.

3. **RUBE WADDELL**

Rube Waddell had an ingenious ploy he used when he needed a drink. He had once outdueled the great Cy Young in a twenty-inning game. Waddell offered the game ball to a bartender for a drink. Bartenders all over the country proudly showcased the balls Waddell had given them.

Philadelphia owner Connie Mack devised a plan that he hoped would cure Rube of his drinking. Mack placed a worm in a glass of whiskey. As the worm wriggled and drowned, Mack asked Waddell if he understood the effects of drinking. Rube replied, "Yes, it means I won't get worms."

4. STEVE BILKO

Steve Bilko was a minor league sensation who never quite reached stardom in the majors, where he played from 1949 to 1962. Battling a weight problem, Bilko created a unique way to shed pounds. The first baseman had his bathtub filled with beer and ice. When hot water was poured on the mixture, Bilko had his own beer sauna. He sat on the toilet downing beers while sweating off the calories.

5. JOHNNY MIZE

Johnny Mize was known to enjoy a drink or two. In 1948, he finished a workout and went to take a shower. Giants' trainer Frank Bowman soaked his sweatshirt in alcohol. Bowman confronted Mize and asked if he had been drinking. When he denied it, Bowman lit the sweatshirt. Believing he had sweated alcohol during the workout, Mize swore he'd lay off the stuff.

6. RAY CALDWELL

New York manager Miller Huggins hired two detectives to tail alcoholic pitcher Ray Caldwell. When Caldwell joined the Indians, manager Tris Speaker had it written into his contract that he could only drink on the night after he pitched. The arrangement worked beautifully as Caldwell had his only twenty-game season in 1920.

7. **TOAD RAMSEY**

Toad Ramsey is credited with inventing the knuckleball. The pitch was so baffling that Ramsey won thirty-eight games in 1886 and struck out 499 batters. On July 25, 1888, Toad was arrested in Louisville for failing to pay a substantial overdue bar tab.

8. **TOM SEATS**

Tom Seats was a southpaw pitcher with great stuff but unsteady nerves. Brooklyn manager Leo Durocher discovered that if he gave Seats brandy before a game, he pitched well. Seats won ten games for the Dodgers in 1945, before General Manager Branch Rickey learned of the reason for his success and released the imbibing pitcher.

9. **PAUL WANER**

Pittsburgh outfielder Paul Waner had eight 200-hit seasons and a career batting average of .333. A hard drinker, Waner would sober up by doing from fifteen to twenty backflips before the game.

10. **PRESIDENT HERBERT HOOVER**

President Herbert Hoover attended Game three of the 1931 World Series between Philadelphia and

St. Louis. The country was in the depths of the Great Depression, and Hoover was not at the peak of his popularity. Baseball fans, unhappy after a decade of prohibition, chanted, "We want beer!" as the president left the ballpark.

Illegal Substances

The extent of the drug problem in baseball has become public in the last two decades. Dwight Gooden was on his way to becoming one of the greatest pitchers in baseball history until a problem with substance abuse derailed his career. Former Cy Young winner Vida Blue served three months in prison for possession of cocaine. Ex-Dodgers' outfielder Lou Johnson hocked his World Series ring to support his cocaine habit. Tim Raines kept a stash of cocaine in his hip pocket and slid headfirst to avoid damaging his drugs.

1. THE PITTSBURGH DRUG CONNECTION

The 1985 Pittsburgh drug trial exposed the widespread use of drugs by major league players. It became apparent that drug dealers had access to team clubhouses and that some players had been involved in not only the use of drugs but in their

Orlando Cepeda
Orlando Cepeda's election to the Hall of Fame may have been delayed because of a conviction for drug dealing.

distribution. Dave Parker, Keith Hernandez, Joaquin Andujar, Dale Berra, Jeff Leonard, Lonnie Smith, and Enos Cabell were suspended from baseball for one year by baseball commissioner Peter Ueberroth.

2. **STEVE HOWE**

Nobody has been given more second chances than pitcher Steve Howe. He was a talented young reliever for the Los Angeles Dodgers in the early 1980s when his problems with substance abuse began to surface. Howe was suspended for the entire 1984 season after testing positive for drugs. Between numerous drug rehabs, Howe has had stints with the Minnesota Twins, Texas Rangers, and New York Yankees.

3. **LAMARR HOYT**

LaMarr Hoyt led the American League in wins in 1982 and 1983. Hoyt started the All-Star Game in 1985, but the following year he won only eight games. Suspended for the 1987 season, Hoyt served forty-five days in jail for drug-related offenses. After a cache of cocaine and marijuana was discovered in his apartment, Hoyt was sentenced to a year in prison in 1988.

4. **DOCK ELLIS**

Dock Ellis was always controversial. In 1973, he showed up in a pregame workout wearing haircurlers. Dock admitted he was under the influence of LSD when he no-hit the San Diego Padres on June 12, 1970. Ellis remembered very little of the game. He was high on drugs during much of his twelve-year career. "I was using everything," Ellis admitted.

5. **ORLANDO CEPEDA**

Orlando Cepeda was the Most Valuable Player in 1967 and belted 379 home runs during his career.

His reputation suffered when he was sentenced to prison in his native Puerto Rico for drug dealing. The scandal undoubtedly delayed his entry into the Hall of Fame. After being passed over by the baseball writers, Cepeda was finally selected by the veterans' committee in 1999.

6. **PEDRO RAMOS**

Pedro Ramos led the American League in losses four consecutive seasons from 1958 to 1961. His bad luck continued in 1979 when he was charged with drug trafficking and possession of cocaine. Ramos was sentenced to three years in prison.

7. **PASCUAL PEREZ**

Pascual Perez was a flamboyant pitcher who was 14–8 with Atlanta in 1984. A recurring drug problem culminated that year when he spent three months in prison in the Dominican Republic for possession of cocaine. The drug problem showed the next season when his record slipped to 1–13.

8. **WILLIE AIKENS**

Willie Mays Aikens was on top of the baseball world when he hit four home runs for the Kansas City Royals during the 1980 World Series. Aikens batted .302 and hit a career high of twenty-three home runs in 1983. That year Aikens was involved in a drug scandal in Kansas City and spent nearly three months in a federal prison. The first baseman's batting average plummeted nearly 100 points the next season. "I began to plan my day around when I was going to get high," Aikens confessed.

9. BLUE MOON ODOM

Pitcher John "Blue Moon" Odom was one of the stars of the championship Oakland A's teams of the early 1970s. Odom retired in 1976 and a decade later was convicted of selling cocaine.

10. FERRIS FAIN

Ferris "Burrhead" Fain was the American League batting champion in 1951 and 1952. In March 1988, authorities raided Fain's farm in California and confiscated over a million dollars worth of marijuana. The sixty-six-year-old farmer swore that he never inhaled and that his prize crop was grown strictly for profit.

You Can Bet on It

In the early days of professional baseball, gamblers frequented the ballparks. Large sums of money were bet on the games, and players were sometimes offered bribes. The term "hippodroming" referred to the practice of fixing games. The 1919 World Series was fixed by gamblers and numerous players, and owners have gambled or had associations with gambling ventures. Willie Mays and Mickey Mantle were banished from baseball for a time because they worked for casinos. New York Yankees' owner Del Webb had holdings in several Las Vegas casinos. After retirement, Hall of Fame pitcher Rube Marquard worked for several racetracks, and outfielder Elmer Flick occasionally drove harness horses. Reliever Rob Murphy started his own computerized business that assisted owners to select thoroughbreds by pedigree.

1. **PETE ROSE**

Pete Rose, baseball's all-time leader in hits and games played, was banned from baseball in 1989 because of his alleged betting on baseball. Rose was known to bet heavily on racehorses and associated with people with gambling interests. For years Charlie Hustle had been investigated by major league baseball. Although the commissioner's office indicated they had substantial proof that Rose bet on baseball, he always denied it. Commissioner Bart Giamatti banned Rose from baseball for life. Rose accepted the ruling as long as it was stipulated that there be no official finding that he bet on baseball. Giamatti seemed to violate the agreement when he concluded at the press conference that Rose had bet on baseball. Giamatti died of a heart attack a week later.

2. **WILLIAM COX**

Philadelphia Phillies' owner William Cox was forced to sell his team and was banned in 1943 because he had bet on baseball. His offense was to make around twenty small bets ($25 to $100) on the Phillies to win. He claimed that most of the wagers involved buying dinners or cigars. Cox said he didn't know betting on baseball was against the rules. Considering that the Phillies were one of the worst teams in baseball, betting on them should have been punishment enough.

3. CHARLES STONEHAM

William Cox was a small-time gambler compared to New York Giants' owner Charles Stoneham. He acquired the club in 1919, the same year as the Black Sox scandal. One of Stoneham's partners in a business venture was Arnold Rothstein, the professional gambler who was the man behind the World Series fix. Stoneham owned a racetrack and casino in Havana and had numerous suspicious connections that made him a less than ideal major league owner.

4. LEN DYKSTRA

On the field Len Dykstra was known for his aggressive play. "Nails" helped lead the 1986 New York Mets to the world championship and hit four home runs in the 1993 World Series for Philadelphia. In 1991, Dykstra admitted to losing $78,000 in high-stakes poker games.

5. ROGERS HORNSBY

Rogers Hornsby may have been the greatest righthanded batter in baseball history. His .358 career batting average is second only to Ty Cobb. The Rajah didn't drink or smoke, but he gambled excessively on horses. In 1927, a Cincinnati bookmaker claimed that Hornsby owed him $92,000. The Kentucky Racing Commission notified Giants' owner Charles Stoneham that Hornsby owed them $70,000. Hornsby was never disciplined by the commissioner's office, although he was fired from a managerial position because of his betting.

6. **DICK ALLEN**

Dick Allen twice led the American League in home runs and was the Most Valuable Player in 1972. He admitted to losing large sums of money betting on and breeding thoroughbreds. Allen's brother, Hank, became a horse trainer after retiring from baseball. Dick Allen once said about Astroturf, "If horses can't eat it, I don't want to play on it."

7. **ALBERT BELLE**

Outfielder Albert Belle is one of baseball's most feared sluggers. On and off the field, Belle has been involved in numerous incidents, including allegedly trying to run over trick-or-treaters when they egged his house. Belle also admitted to losing as much as $40,000 betting on football, basketball, and golf matches. In 1997, he was interviewed in a federal investigation of bookmakers, although he was not the target of the probe.

8. BOB RHOADS

Bob Rhoads was a fine pitcher who won twenty-one games for Cleveland in 1906. One of baseball's great unsung heroes, he actually bailed out his team by gambling. The ballclub had run out of money on a preseason trip to Texas after two profitable weekend games in San Antonio were rained out. The owners needed $1,600 to pay hotel bills and purchase railroad tickets to Fort Worth where they were scheduled to play their next game. Bob Rhoads went to the Crystal Palace, a notorious gambling casino, and won $1,800 at the craps table. He gave the appreciative owners $1,600 and split the remaining $200 among the players.

9. BRIAN MCRAE

Friendly wagers are a part of any clubhouse. Cubs' outfielder Brian McRae bet weak-hitting pitcher Frank Castillo that he would never hit a home run in a game or batting practice. The stakes was a new Mercedes Benz. When Castillo connected for a homer in batting practice in 1997, McRae presented him with a $89,000 Mercedes Benz SL-320.

10. **DICK WAKEFIELD**

In one of baseball's dumbest wagers, Tigers' outfielder Dick Wakefield bet Boston's Ted Williams $100 that he would outhit him in 1946. Not surprisingly, Williams won the bet, .342 to .268.

Out of Their Heads

Outfielder Jim Eisenreich was bothered early in his career from the effects of Tourette's Syndrome, a neurological disorder. Even great players such as Mickey Cochrane and Josh Gibson experienced nervous breakdowns. Over the years professional baseball players have endured everything from mental blocks to bouts of insanity. Losing is a daily occurrence in baseball. However, some players have actually lost their minds.

1. ED DOHENY

Ed Doheny was 16–8 for the Pittsburgh Pirates in 1903. Just prior to the 1903 World Series, Doheny went berserk in Boston and beat several men over the head with a poker. Paranoid, he believed the men were detectives sent to spy on him. Committed to a mental institution in Danvers, Massachusetts, Doheny assaulted a doctor with a cast iron stove footrest. He never played another major league game.

2. JIMMY PIERSALL

Jimmy Piersall's battle with mental illness often took place on the field for everyone to see. He swung back and forth in the dugout like a monkey. In Detroit he took a can of bug spray to the outfield. Another time, he did a hula dance in the outfield. When he hit his one hundredth career home run in 1963, Piersall ran around the bases backwards. After a mental breakdown, Jimmy Piersall received electroconvulsive shock treatments and had an eight-month period that was a complete blank. Despite insensitive fans who called him "wacko" and threw things at him, Piersall played seventeen seasons in the majors.

3. FRED PERRINE

Fred Perrine suffered sunstroke while umpiring a game in Cleveland in 1911. Perrine had a nervous breakdown and was committed to the Napa Asylum for the Insane. Two years later he committed suicide in an Oakland asylum.

4. PETE "THE GLADIATOR" BROWNING

Pete Browning was one of the great hitters of the nineteenth century. He played for four teams between 1882 and 1894. Browning was affected by

Jim Piersall
To celebrate his 100th major league home run in 1963, Jim Piersall ran around the bases backwards.

a mastoid infection that left him deaf. An alcoholic, Browning received poor medical treatment that caused brain damage. The Gladiator was committed to an insane asylum.

5. RUBE FOSTER

Rube Foster was an outstanding pitcher and a founder of the Negro Baseball League. Honus Wagner, who faced Foster in exhibition games, called him "one of the greatest pitchers of all time." In 1926, Foster began to display strange symptoms. He chased imaginary fly balls in the street. One of his saddest delusions was that he was going to pitch in the World Series. Foster spent the last four years of his life in a mental institution in Kankakee, Illinois.

6. JOHNNY EVERS

A series of tragedies led to the nervous breakdown of Chicago Cubs' second baseman Johnny Evers. He was driving when he had an accident in which his best friend was killed. Shortly thereafter, his business partner squandered his life savings. Evers's breakdown caused him to miss most of the 1911 season.

7. TONY HORTON

Tony Horton hit twenty-seven home runs for Cleveland in 1969. The next season the first baseman began to show signs of mental illness. On May 24, 1970, he blasted three home runs but was disturbed because the Indians lost when he failed to hit his fourth. A month later, he crawled back to the dugout after striking out on a blooper pitch thrown by Steve Hamilton. After the final out of a game, Horton went out to his position at first base. Manager Alvin Dark led him back to the dugout. Following the breakdown, Horton was given psychiatric help, during which he was not allowed to watch a baseball game on television.

Only twenty-five years old, he never played another game in the majors.

8. ALEX JOHNSON

Alex Johnson won the American League batting title in 1970. Johnson's nonchalance in the outfield made him constant trade bait. On a hot afternoon the outfielder positioned himself in the shadow of the foul pole. He threw a pop bottle at pitcher Clyde Wright and was fined a record twenty-nine times in less than half a season. Johnson's psychiatrist successfully argued before an arbitration panel that he was suffering from mental distress and should be entitled to disability pay.

9. STEVE SAX

Numerous players have experienced mental blocks of some sort. Perhaps the best known happened to second baseman Steve Sax. Early in his career with the Los Angeles Dodgers, Sax developed a phobia about throwing to first base. As his number of errors mounted, his career was in jeopardy. He tried everything to correct the problem, even putting socks over his eyes and throwing blindly to first base. Finally, in 1985 he was able to correct the problem by visualizing successful throws.

10. DR. HERNDON HARDING

The Los Angeles Dodgers had one of their worst seasons in 1992, finishing the season with a 63–98 record. The team had psychiatrist Dr. Herndon Harding travel with them to deal with the players' mental distress over losing. Previously, the Dodgers had called in hypnotist Arthur Ellen to assist Maury Wills and Jerry Reuss with their performance. Ellen was able to help Reuss overcome his fear of pitching in Chicago's Wrigley Field.

Overcoming Handicaps

These players overcame extraordinary physical handicaps to play in the major leagues.

1. PETE GRAY

In 1945, the defending American League champion St. Louis Browns called up a one-armed outfielder named Pete Gray. He had lost part of his arm at age six when he jumped from a moving truck. Batting one-handed, Gray hit .381 to win the batting title with Three Rivers of the American Canadian League. In 1944, he was voted the Most Valuable Player in the Southern League and stole home ten times. Promoted to the big leagues, Gray batted .218, remarkable considering his handicap. Fielding presented even a bigger problem. Gray had to field the ball, put his glove under his stump right arm, remove the ball, and throw. Runners sometimes were able to take an extra base. After a tough loss, an angry teammate challenged Gray to a fight with one of his arms tied behind his back.

2. HUGH DAILY

Hugh "One Arm" Daily had lost his left hand in a gun accident. Daily won twenty-five games in 1883 with Philadelphia of the National League. The following season he led the Union Association with an incredible 483 strikeouts, including nineteen in one game. Daily pitched back-to-back one-hitters in July 1884.

3. JIM ABBOTT

Jim Abbott was born without a right hand. Abbott starred at the University of Michigan before beginning a successful major league career mainly with California. The highlight of his career was pitching a no-hitter for the Yankees against the Cleveland Indians on September 4, 1993.

4. BERT SHEPARD

Former minor league pitcher Bert Shepard lost a leg when he was shot down over Germany during World War II. On August 14, 1945, Shepard, equipped with a wooden leg, allowed only one run in five innings, pitching for Washington against Boston. It was his only major league appearance.

5. DUMMY HOY

Despite being hearing-impaired, William "Dummy" Hoy had more than 2,000 base hits, scored more than 100 runs eight times, and stole 597 bases. An outstanding outfielder, Hoy set a record by throwing out three runners at the plate in a game on June 19, 1889. In 1886 during a minor league game, Hoy jumped on the back of a horse and made a spectacular catch. He was ninety-nine years old in 1961 when he threw out the first pitch in Game three of the 1961 World Series.

6. DUMMY TAYLOR

Deaf-mute Luther "Dummy" Taylor won twenty-one games for the New York Giants in 1904. Umpire Tim Hurst once ejected Taylor for cursing him out in sign language.

7. THREE FINGER BROWN

Mordecai "Three Finger" Brown used his handicap to become a Hall of Fame pitcher. Brown won twenty games six seasons in a row for the Chicago Cubs, and his career 2.06 earned run average is the third best in baseball history. A childhood accident with a corn shredder cost him part of his right index finger. He broke two fingers in a separate accident, leaving them gnarled. His deformed hand allowed him to grip the ball in such a way that he released pitches with an unusual spin. Brown won 239 games and lost only 129 in his fourteen-year career.

8. DAVE KEEFE

Dave Keefe lost his middle finger in a childhood accident. Keefe pitched in the major leagues from 1917 until 1922. He invented the fork ball, which he gripped between his second and fourth fingers. The pitch was later perfected by Pittsburgh reliever Elroy Face, whose forkball was so effective that he once won twenty-two consecutive games.

9. RED RUFFING

Between 1936 and 1939, New York Yankees' pitcher Red Ruffing won 20 games four consecutive seasons. He pitched twenty-two years in the majors and won 273 games. The Hall of Famer accomplished all this despite losing four toes on his left foot in a mining accident as a youth.

10. TOM SUNKEL AND JACK FRANKLIN

During World War II several handicapped players saw action in the major leagues. The old adage 'an eye for an eye' took on new meaning in 1944 when Brooklyn sent down virtually blind pitcher Tom Sunkel and promoted Jack Franklin who was blind in one eye.

Freak Injuries

Players have injured themselves in the most bizarre ways. St. Louis outfielder Vince Coleman got his leg caught in a mechanical tarp roller during the World Series. Five-time batting champion Wade Boggs injured his ribs taking off a pair of cowboy boots. Pitcher Orel Hershiser pulled a back muscle lifting his year-old son. Pitching prospect Steve Sparks dislocated his left shoulder attempting to tear apart a phone book in spring training. Cubs' outfielder José Cardenal missed opening day when his eyelid stuck shut. California pitcher Don Aase tore cartilage in his rib cage sneezing. Believe it or not, the following things actually happened.

1. RAY CALDWELL

Ray Caldwell pitched a no-hitter in 1919 and won twenty games for Cleveland the next season. In 1919, he was pitching a game in Philadelphia when an electrical storm blew in. Since there were two out in the ninth inning, umpires let play continue. A bolt of lightning struck Caldwell on the mound and knocked him cold for five minutes. When Caldwell was revived, he insisted on finishing the game. He did so with a flourish, striking out the final batter. Ray Caldwell was not the first major leaguer to be struck by lightning during a game. Five years earlier, New York outfielder Red Murray was hit while running the bases.

2. **CREEPY CRESPI**

Frank "Creepy" Crespi was a promising second baseman with the St. Louis Cardinals from 1938 to 1942. He entered the military service during World War II. In 1943, Crespi broke his left leg playing an army baseball game. While recuperating, he broke it again when he crashed into a wall during a wheelchair race. Crespi never played again in the major leagues.

3. **BILLY MARTIN**

Joe DiMaggio retired from baseball after the 1951 season. The following spring training, DiMaggio was working as a television commentator. He asked former teammate Billy Martin to demonstrate his sliding technique. Martin executed a perfect headfirst and hook slide. DiMaggio asked Martin if he would do a break slide. Martin slid too hard into the bag and broke his ankle.

4. JOE SPRINZ

Catcher Joe Sprinz played briefly in the major leagues with Cleveland and St. Louis from 1930 to 1933. On August 3, 1939, the veteran catcher was playing for the minor league San Francisco Seals when, as a publicity stunt, he attempted to catch a baseball dropped from a dirigible flying 1,000 feet above Treasure Island in San Francisco Bay. It hit him in the face, shattering his jaw and knocking out four teeth.

5. STEVE FOSTER

Pitcher Steve Foster was notified that he was being called up to the Cincinnati Reds in 1992. As Foster prepared to drive to the airport, he injured his shoulder throwing a suitcase onto his truck.

6. KEN HUNT

Rookie outfielder Ken Hunt hit twenty-five home runs for the Los Angeles Angels in 1961. In April 1962, he was flexing his back in the on-deck circle when he broke his collarbone. Hunt never batted above .185 in the majors again.

Ken Hunt
Angel's outfielder Ken Hunt had a promising career curtailed when he broke his collarbone while flexing his back in the on deck circle.

7. CHARLIE HOUGH

Knuckleballer Charlie Hough is one of the few pitchers to play twenty-five years in the major leagues. In spite of his endurance, Hough once broke a finger shaking hands with a friend.

8. JOE DIMAGGIO

In his much-anticipated major league debut in 1936, Joe DiMaggio injured his foot. The injury was made worse when he burned it during heat therapy. DiMaggio went on to hit 29 home runs and knock in 125 runs as a rookie.

9. DAVE KINGMAN

Dave Kingman hit 442 home runs and would have hit many more if he hadn't spent so much time on the disabled list. Kingman spent eleven days on the DL after injuring his knee while arguing a call with an umpire.

10. HOOKS WILTSE

Hooks Wiltse was a twenty-game winner for the New York Giants in 1908 and 1909. On July 4, 1908, Wiltse pitched a ten-inning no-hitter against Philadelphia. His most embarrassing moment came in 1905 when he was removed from a game because he swallowed his chewing tobacco.

The Big Hurt

Baseball can be a dangerous game. Occasionally it can even be fatal. Hall of Famer Hughie Jennings was hit by pitches 260 times during his career and suffered three skull fractures. California pitcher Matt Keough underwent brain surgery in 1992 when he was hit by a line drive while sitting in the dugout. Wee Willie Keeler once dove head-first into a barbed wire fence making a catch and was left hanging there.

1. **RAY CHAPMAN**

Ray Chapman is the only major leaguer to be killed by a beaning. The Cleveland shortstop set a major league record with sixty-seven sacrifices in 1917 and the next year led the National League in runs scored. On August 17, 1920, he was facing Carl Mays of the New York Yankees. Chapman crowded the plate, and Mays had the reputation of throwing high and tight. The sidearmer threw a pitch that sailed into the side of Chapman's head. The impact was so loud it could be heard throughout the Polo Grounds. Mays thought the ball had hit Chapman's bat and threw the ball to first base. Chapman, assisted by teammates, attempted to walk to the clubhouse in centerfield but collapsed. He died on the operating table the next day.

2. **MIKE POWERS**

Mike Powers was known as Hall of Famer Eddie Plank's personal catcher. The veteran was behind the plate on April 12, 1909, the first game played in Philadelphia's Shibe Park. In the seventh inning, Powers crashed into the wall while chasing a pop fly. Although he suffered internal injuries, Powers remained in the game. Hospitalized, he underwent three operations before dying two weeks later of gangrene of the bowel.

3. **JOHNNY DODGE**

Third baseman Johnny Dodge played two seasons in the major leagues with Philadelphia and Cincinnati. On June 18, 1916, Dodge was playing for Mobile in the Southern Association when he was beaned by Nashville's Shotgun Rogers. Dodge's skull was fractured, and he passed away the next day.

4. JESSIE BATTERSON

Nineteen-year-old Springfield third baseman Jessie Batterson was hit by a pitch thrown by Omaha's Swede Carlson in a game played on July 4, 1933. Batterson was able to walk to the clubhouse before collapsing. Carlson was at his bedside when he died following surgery.

5. OTTIS JOHNSON

Ottis Johnson died after being hit by a pitch made by Jack Clifton in an Alabama-Florida League game on June 2, 1951. Seemingly unaffected by the tragedy, Clifton pitched a no-hitter in his next start.

6. JAMES CREIGHTON

Perhaps the greatest player before the advent of the major leagues, James Creighton revolutionized pitching by being the first pitcher to change speeds and snap his wrist on his pitches. His hitting was so phenomenal that he once made only four outs during a season. He was only twenty-one years old in October 1862 when, playing for the Brooklyn Excelsiors, he ruptured his bladder hitting a home run. The admirable Creighton died four days later.

7. DON BLACK

The highlight of pitcher Don Black's career was a no-hitter he pitched against the Philadelphia A's on July 10, 1947. The next season the Cleveland pitcher took a hard swing at a pitch during a game against St. Louis. Black staggered away and collapsed behind home plate. He had suffered a brain hemorrhage and never played baseball again. Indians' owner Bill Veeck staged a benefit that raised $40,000 for the fallen pitcher.

8. MOOSE SOLTERS

Julius "Moose" Solters batted in more than 100 runs three consecutive seasons from 1935 to 1937. During a pregame warmup, the White Sox's outfielder waved to his brother-in-law in the stands. While Solters was looking at the stands, a ball thrown by another player hit him in the head. The freak injury caused Solters gradually to go blind.

9. LARRY BROWN

One of the worst collisions in baseball history took place on May 4, 1966 between Cleveland shortstop Larry Brown and outfielder Leon Wagner. Brown suffered fractures of the skull, nose, and cheekbone while Wagner's nose was broken. Brown recovered and played eight more seasons in the majors.

10. **PAUL BLAIR**

Paul Blair won eight gold gloves as an outfielder for the Baltimore Orioles. His career was nearly ended in 1970 when he was beaned by California pitcher Ken Tatum. Blair lay motionless with blood trickling out of his nose, mouth, and ears. Umpire Ron Luciano thought Blair was dead. Luciano wrote that Blair was never the same hitter, and he was never the same umpire. Blair underwent two years of hypnotherapy to help him overcome fear at the plate.

Cheaters Sometimes Win

Over the years players and managers have found ways to cheat. Hall of Fame pitcher Whitey Ford doctored the ball in almost every way imaginable. Jake Beckley hid a ball under the first base bag, which he used to tag out unsuspecting runners.

1. JOHN MCGRAW

As a member of the notorious Baltimore Orioles of the 1890s, third baseman John McGraw used almost every trick in the book to win. With only one umpire, players could get away with almost anything. Outfielders hid balls in the high grass. McGraw was notorious for tripping and obstructing runners. One of his favorite tricks was to put his finger in the belt loop of runners tagging up at third to keep them from getting a good jump.

2. CONNIE MACK

Connie Mack was only thrown out of one game in sixty-one years, yet the respected Mr. Mack wasn't above cheating to gain an advantage. He froze baseballs in order to make them travel less far when hit and sneaked them into the game when his pitchers were on the mound. Mack had a spy hidden in the centerfield scoreboard to steal the opposing team's signals.

3. MORGAN MURPHY

On September 17, 1900, Cincinnati was playing Philadelphia when the Reds' third base coach Tommy Corcoran uncovered a sign-stealing scheme employed by the home team. Corcoran's spikes caught in a wire in the coaches' box. He pulled up the wire and discovered that it was connected to the Phillies' locker room where catcher Morgan Murphy sat by a window with a telegraph. He had been stealing signals and sending them to the Phillies' third base coach. One buzz meant a fastball, two buzzes a curve, and three a change-up.

4. GAYLORD PERRY

Baseball's most notorious spitball pitcher, Gaylord Perry, won 314 games in his career and Cy Young Awards in both leagues. Perry went through a series of motions on the mound, touching his

Gaylord Perry
The secret to 300-game winner Gaylord Perry's super sinker was the foreign substances he had in his cap, jersey, belt, and pants.

glove, uniform, face, and bill of his cap before delivering a pitch. He hid foreign substances on parts of his body, cap, jersey, belt, and pants. Perry chewed gum or sea moss to keep his saliva flowing. When he threw his "super sinker," it was almost impossible to hit.

5. ABNER DALRYMPLE

Chicago outfielder Abner Dalrymple led the National League in hits, home runs, and runs at various times in his career. Dalrymple kept a ball concealed in his uniform. In 1880, he took away a home run from Boston's Ezra Sutton when the umpire lost track of the flight of the ball.

6. EDDIE "THE BRAT" STANKY

Leo Durocher said of Eddie Stanky, "He can't hit, can't run, can't field. He's no nice guy, but all he does is win." Stanky threw dirt in the eyes of baserunners trying to steal second. "The Brat" was adept at kicking the ball out of fielders' gloves. In 1977, Stanky quit after managing the Texas Rangers for one day because he couldn't stand the attitude of modern players.

7. PREACHER ROE

Elwin "Preacher" Roe attributed his success to the development of a spitball. When Roe was traded to Brooklyn in 1948, he began throwing a spitball. Preacher was 34–47 without the spitter and 95–37 with it. "I didn't sin against God," Preacher said of his use of the illegal pitch.

8. NORM CASH

Norm Cash won the batting title in 1961 with a .361 average. It was the only time in his seventeen-year career that he batted above .286. The Detroit first baseman admitted that he had used a loaded bat during his career year.

9. HARRY STOVEY

Harry Stovey led the league in home runs five times between 1880 and 1889. Through no fault of his own, the gentlemanly Stovey was given credit for a batting crown he didn't win. Manipulations by an official scorer who kept the statistics credited Stovey with a .404 batting average in 1884. A century later, researchers discovered that his real average was .326.

10. **EDDIE AINSMITH**

Eddie Ainsmith caught for the Washington Senators from 1910 until 1918. On a dark afternoon he was behind the plate when fireballing Walter Johnson was on the mound. With a two-strike count, Ainsmith popped his glove, and the umpire called strike three without Johnson ever delivering the ball.

Say It Ain't So, Joe

The banishment of Pete Rose in 1989 is the latest instance of an individual being placed on the permanently ineligible list. More than thirty men have been banned from baseball for various offenses. Here are ten:

1. **THE CHICAGO EIGHT**

Eight members of the Chicago White Sox were banned from baseball for life for throwing the 1919 World Series against Cincinnati. The players, resentful of low salaries they were paid by White Sox owner Charles Comiskey, agreed to throw games in exchange for payments from gamblers betting on the Reds. The banished players included Shoeless Joe Jackson, a lifetime .356 hitter, and pitcher Eddie Cicotte, a 210-game winner. Others banned included infielders Chick Gandil, Buck Weaver, Swede Risberg, and Fred McMullin, outfielder Happy Felsch, and pitcher

Lefty Williams. Weaver claimed he did not participate in the fix nor did he receive any money, but he was banned by Commissioner Landis because he knew about it and didn't tell anyone.

2. JIM DEVLIN

Jim Devlin won thirty games in both of his major league seasons, and his 1.89 career earned run average is the third best in baseball history. During the first two years of the National League, he led pitchers in almost every significant category. His Louisville Grays looked as though they were on their way to the 1877 pennant when they lost several games suspiciously. After Louisville lost the pennant to Boston, rumors began circulating that the Grays had thrown games. Devlin, infielders Al Nichols and Bill Craver, and outfielder George Hall were banned for life. Players received as little as $10 for their involvement in the scandal. Devlin, who briefly was employed as a policeman, begged for reinstatement until his death at age thirty-four in 1883.

3. HAL CHASE

Slick-fielding first baseman Hal Chase won a batting title in 1916 and would probably be in the Hall of Fame if he hadn't been one of the most corrupt players ever to wear a uniform. Despite his obvious defensive skills, Prince Hal led the league in errors seven times. Although most of his managers suspected him of throwing games, he was so skillful that he managed to play fifteen years before he was unofficially blacklisted after the 1919 season. Reportedly, Chase won $40,000 betting on Cincinnati in the 1919 series. Following his banishment from the majors, Chase was also barred from the Pacific Coast League for involvement in a gambling ring and attempting to bribe an umpire.

4. RICHARD HIGHAM

Richard Higham has the dubious distinction of being the only major league umpire to be banished for life. In 1882, he was expelled for conspiring with gamblers to fix games.

5. HORACE FOGEL

The main reason that Philadelphia Phillies' owner Horace Fogel was banned for life was because he made unfounded charges that umpires made questionable calls to insure that the New York Giants won the 1912 pennant. Officially, he was banned for "undermining the integrity of the game."

6. HEINIE ZIMMERMAN

Heinie Zimmerman, the 1912 Triple Crown winner, was banished from baseball in 1919 for fixing games with his Giants' teammate Hal Chase.

7. BENNY KAUFF

Benny Kauff won the batting title in both years that the Federal League existed. In 1920, he was indicted for being part of an auto theft ring. Kauff owned a used car lot and was charged with receiving stolen property. Although he was acquitted in court, Commissioner Kenesaw Landis banned Kauff from baseball for life.

8. RAY FISHER

Ray Fisher won 100 games between 1910 and 1920 and pitched for Cincinnati in the 1919 World Series. He was banned from baseball in 1921 without a hearing or even an explanation. His offense was to accept the coaching position at the University of Michigan instead of signing a contract offered by the Cincinnati Reds. Fisher coached Michigan for thirty-eight years before being reinstated in the 1960s.

9. DUTCH LEONARD

Dutch Leonard threw two no-hitters, and his 1.01 earned run average in 1914 is the lowest in baseball history. He accused Ty Cobb and Tris Speaker, two of baseball's greatest stars, of fixing a game in 1919. Commissioner Landis dismissed the charges against Cobb and Speaker, but Leonard was banished for life for his involvement.

10. **JOE GEDEON**

Joe Gedeon is the least-known player banned because of the 1919 World Series. The St. Louis Browns' second baseman was banned for knowledge of the series fix. He was a close friend of Swede Risberg of the Black Sox.

Grand Slammers

Dozens of major leaguers have served time in jail or have had other run-ins with the law. Their crimes, or alleged crimes, have ranged from murders to misdemeanors.

1. LEN KOENECKE

Brooklyn outfielder Len Koenecke batted .320 in 1934, but he constantly broke curfews and ignored manager Casey Stengel's training rules. Stengel felt he was a bad influence on the team and sent Koenecke to the minors in September 1935. Koenecke got drunk and chartered a plane to Buffalo, where he had played in the minors. He attempted to take over the controls of the plane. During the struggle, pilot William Mulqueeny hit Koenecke over the head with a fire extinguisher. Mulqueeny was able to get the plane under control and made an emergency landing at a race track near Toronto. Len Koenecke, who had attempted history's first skyjacking, was dead.

2. **JOHN GLENN**

John Glenn played outfield and first base for Chicago in 1876 and 1877. In 1888, Glenn was accused of committing a robbery and raping a twelve-year-old girl. Glenn was accidentally shot and killed by a policeman who was trying to protect him from a mob.

3. **DENNY MCLAIN**

In 1985, former Tigers' pitcher Denny McLain was sentenced to twenty-three years in prison after being convicted on charges of racketeering, loan sharking, extortion, and possession of cocaine. After being released early, McLain was sentenced to eight years in prison for his involvement in a meatpackers' pension fund swindle.

4. **PETE ROSE**

In 1990, Pete Rose, baseball's all-time hit leader, pleaded guilty to two counts of filing false income tax returns. He failed to declare income of more than $354,000 on his 1985 and 1987 federal income tax returns. Rose spent five months in a federal prison in Marion, Illinois.

5. **TURKEY MIKE DONLIN**

The most popular player of his day, Turkey Mike Donlin batted .333 during his twelve-year career. In 1902, Donlin stalked Minnie Fields, an actress on whom he had a crush. Donlin assaulted her escort, Ernest Slayton, then hit the actress when she tried to intervene. Fields was knocked unconscious by the blow. For his crime, Donlin was sentenced to six months in jail and kicked out of the American League.

6. **RON LEFLORE**

Ron LeFlore was only twelve years old when he stole $1,500 from a grocery store. He spent a year in reform school when he was caught trying to crack a safe. He was nineteen years old in 1966 when he was arrested for armed robbery. LeFlore was sentenced to 5–15 years in prison. While serving his sentence at Jackson State Prison, he began playing baseball for the prison team. Inmates wrote Detroit manager Billy Martin raving about LeFlore's talent. In May 1973, Martin visited LeFlore in prison. A year after he was released, LeFlore made his major league debut. The outfielder played nine years in the majors and led both leagues in stolen bases.

7. JOE PEPITONE

Joe Pepitone was a colorful first baseman who played in the majors from 1962 until 1973. In 1985, Pepitone was pulled over by police officers in Brooklyn. Inside his automobile they discovered $70,000 worth of cocaine, heroin, and other illegal substances as well as a loaded gun. Pepitone served two months behind bars for the offenses.

8. KIRBY HIGBE

Brooklyn righthander Kirby Higbe led the National League with twenty-two wins in 1941. After his playing days were over, Higbe spent two months in jail in South Carolina for passing bad checks. He later worked as a prison guard.

9. BABE RUTH

On June 8, 1921, Babe Ruth was arrested for speeding in New York. Held in jail until midafternoon, he was permitted to change into his uniform in his cell. Given a police escort to Yankee Stadium, Ruth arrived in time to help the Yankees rally to a 4–3 victory.

10. DAVE WINFIELD

The New York Yankees were playing the Toronto Blue Jays on August 4, 1983, when outfielder Dave Winfield was arrested for a throw he made.

Between innings, he accidentally killed a seagull with a warm-up toss. Winfield killed two birds (the gull and the Jays) when he homered to give the Yankees a 3–1 victory. He was astonished to learn after the game that he was being arrested for cruelty to animals. The charges were dropped the next day.

Suicide Squeeze

Nearly 100 major league players and managers have committed suicide. They have killed themselves with guns, razors, strychnine, carbolic acid, carbon monoxide, and by hanging. Former outfielder Frank Bratchi ended his life in 1962 by drinking battery acid.

1. WILLARD HERSHBERGER

Cincinnati catcher Willard Hershberger is the only major leaguer to commit suicide during the season. In 1940 his Reds were contending for the National League pennant. Hershberger became despondent when he called for a pitch that the Giants' Harry Danning hit for a game-winning grand slam home run with two out in the ninth inning. Three days later, on August 3, Hershberger didn't come to the ballpark. When Hershberger's friend Dan Cohen was sent to check on him at the hotel, he found the catcher slumped in the bathtub. He had slashed his throat. Eleven years earlier, his father, ruined by the stock market crash, had sat on the rim of a bathtub and shot himself in the chest with a shotgun.

2. **DONNIE MOORE**

In 1985, Donnie Moore set an Angels' record with thirty-one saves and was voted the team's Most Valuable Player. The next season he saved twenty-one games despite pitching with a sore shoulder. More importantly, the Angels were in the playoffs. In Game five of the championship series against Boston, California led 5–2 going into the ninth inning. Leading three games to one, the Angels seemed on the verge of their first American League pennant. Moore was brought into the game with two outs in the ninth, a runner on first, and the Angels leading 5–4. Moore quietly got two strikes on batter Dave Henderson. He only needed one more strike. On a 2–2 pitch, Henderson hit a Moore delivery over the left-field fence to give the Red Sox the lead. The Angels tied the game in the bottom of the ninth, but Moore allowed the winning run in the eleventh inning. Boston won the next two games and the pennant. Moore said after the game, "I'll think about that until the day I die."

By 1988, arm miseries and a bone spur on his spine ended his career. On July 18, 1989, deeply in debt, with his marriage crumbling and his career over, Donnie Moore shot his wife, Tonya, three times. Rushed to the hospital by her daughter, she survived. With his ten-year-old son looking on, Moore, still haunted by the pitch that ruined his life, fatally shot himself.

3. **ART IRWIN**

Shortstop Art Irwin played thirteen seasons in the major leagues, finishing his career with Philadelphia in 1894. He is credited with being the first player to use a glove on a regular basis. On July 16, 1921, Irwin jumped overboard during a boat trip between New York and Boston. It was learned that he had been leading a double life. Irwin had one wife and family in Boston and another in Hartford.

4. **CHICK STAHL**

Outfielder Chick Stahl batted .358 as a rookie with Boston in 1897 and had a .307 career batting average. Late in the 1906 season, Stahl was named manager of a terrible Red Sox club that lost 105 games. He didn't want the responsibility and tried to resign in spring training the next year. Besides his doubts about being a manager, Stahl had plenty of problems off the field. His wife, Julia, was a drug addict and committed suicide a year after Stahl's death. In addition, another woman claimed she was pregnant with Stahl's child and threatened to make the news public if he didn't marry her. On March 29, 1907, Stahl committed suicide by drinking carbolic acid.

5. WIN MERCER

Chick Stahl was not the first newly appointed manager to take his own life. Five years earlier, Detroit skipper Win Mercer committed suicide by inhaling illuminating gas in a room at the Occidental Hotel in San Francisco on January 12, 1903. Mercer, who had lived up to his name by winning 131 games in the major leagues, left behind a suicide note warning of the evils of gambling and women. He was only twenty-eight years old.

6. HARRY PULLIAM

Pressure also contributed to the death of National League President Harry Pulliam in 1909. Pulliam had become league president in 1903 and led the senior circuit through an important transitional period, competing with the newly formed American League. His feud with Giants' manager John McGraw culminated with his ruling against New York in the celebrated Fred Merkle "bonehead" play. In February 1909, Pulliam had a nervous breakdown at the National League owners banquet. Five months later, on July 25, 1909, the thirty-nine-year-old Pulliam took off his clothes in his room in the New York Athletic Club and shot himself through the temple. Although the bullet had gone through his head and blown his right eye out, he was still conscious when help arrived, but he succumbed shortly thereafter. When McGraw learned of the tragedy, he joked, "I didn't think a bullet in the head could hurt him."

7. HUGH CASEY

Hugh Casey compiled a 75–42 record as a reliever with Brooklyn and three other teams between 1935 and 1949. He was notorious for his hard-drinking, womanizing lifestyle. Few players could drink as hard or fight as well. In July 1951, he called his estranged wife and threatened to blow his brains out if she didn't come back to him. When she refused, Casey kept his promise.

8. PEA RIDGE DAY

Clyde "Pea Ridge" Day would let out with a hog call when he struck out a batter. Unfortunately for him, it wasn't a common occurrence; he struck out forty-eight in four seasons in the majors. On March 21, 1934, Pea Ridge, Arkansas's most famous resident, depressed over an arm injury that curtailed his career, slit his throat with a hunting knife.

9. DANNY THOMAS

Outfielder Danny Thomas played two seasons with the Milwaukee Brewers. Devoutly religious, he refused to play ball on Sunday. On June 12, 1980, Thomas, accused of rape, committed suicide in a Mobile, Alabama, jail cell.

10. BRUCE GARDNER

Bruce Gardner was a pitching star in high school in the late 1950s. At age eighteen, he was offered a $66,000 bonus to sign with the Chicago White Sox. His coach advised him to complete his education at the University of Southern California. The advice proved unwise as Gardner received only a $12,000 bonus from the Dodgers upon graduation. A twenty-game winner in the minors, his dreams of a big league career were smashed by an arm injury. On June 7, 1971, he lay down on the pitching mound of the field where he played college ball. Clutching his college diploma, he fired a bullet through his head.

They Got Murdered

Since 1885, almost 40 major leaguers have been murdered. The players have been shot, stabbed, and even beaten to death with a baseball bat.

1. LYMAN BOSTOCK

Lyman Bostock was one of the finest young hitters of the late 1970s. The Twins' outfielder was second in the American League in batting in 1977 with a .336 average. The next year, Bostock went to the California Angels as a free agent. When he got off to a slow start, he asked owner Gene Autry to withhold his salary in April. By September, he was back near his usual .300. On September 23, he was riding in a car driven by his uncle in Gary, Indiana. Bostock was in the back seat with Barbara Turner, a woman he had just met. As the car stopped at an intersection, the woman's husband,

Leonard Turner, fired a shotgun blast through the back window. Bostock was hit in the head and died hours later.

2. ED MORRIS

Righthander Ed Morris won nineteen games as a rookie with the Boston Red Sox in 1928. On March 3, 1932, Morris was honored with a farewell fish fry in Century, Florida, on the eve of his departure for spring training. During the event, Morris got into an argument with a gas station owner, who then stabbed him to death.

3. LUKE EASTER

First baseman Luke Easter hit eighty-six home runs over a three-year period (1950–52) with the Cleveland Indians. He was employed as a bank messenger in Euclid, Ohio, in 1979 when he was the victim of a holdup. Easter was killed instantly by a blast from a shotgun.

4. EDDIE GAEDEL

Midget Eddie Gaedel gained baseball immortality in 1951 by coming to bat for the St. Louis Browns. Owner Bill Veeck took out a million dollar insurance policy on Gaedel to cover sudden death or sudden growth. While the latter never happened, the former did. In June 1961, Gaedel was mugged on a Chicago street. He managed to stagger home, where he died of a heart attack.

5. LARRY MCLEAN

At 6 feet 5 inches and 230 pounds, catcher Larry McLean was a huge man for his time. He played thirteen seasons in the big leagues. Known for his drunken brawls, he was cut by the Giants in 1915 when he challenged manager John McGraw to a fight outside a St. Louis hotel. Six years later, McLean was engaged in a barroom brawl in Boston with another former player, Jack McCarthy, when the bartender shot him dead.

6. BUGS RAYMOND

One of the game's most notorious drunks, pitcher Bugs Raymond, was out of major league baseball by the time he was twenty-nine. A year later, on September 7, 1912, he was dispatched by a blow to the head with a baseball bat during a barroom brawl in Chicago.

7. FLEURY SULLIVAN

Twenty-two year old Fleury Sullivan lost thirty-five games for Pittsburgh of the American Association in 1884. It was his only season in the major leagues. On February 15, 1897, Sullivan was murdered in the midst of a heated political argument in East St. Louis, Illinois.

8. ED IRVIN

Ed Irvin was one of the replacement players used for one game in 1912 when the Detroit Tigers went on strike in support of the suspended Ty Cobb. The third baseman hit two triples in three at-bats but was never given another chance to play in the majors. On February 18, 1916, Irvin died when he was thrown through a saloon window in Philadelphia.

9. PAT HYNES

Pat Hynes appeared as an outfielder and pitcher for St. Louis in 1903 and 1904. On March 12, 1907, he went out drinking to celebrate his thirty-third birthday. That night he was shot and killed by a bartender in an argument over the bar tab.

10. HI BITHORN

Cubs' pitcher Hi Bithorn won eighteen games and led the National League with seven shutouts in 1942. A sore arm ended his major league stay in 1947. Bithorn tried to resurrect his career pitching in the Mexican Leagues. On New Year's Day, 1952, Bithorn was shot and killed in El Mante, Mexico, while trying to flee from police.

Murderers' Row

Murderers' Row is a term associated with the dangerous line-up of the 1927 New York Yankees. The line-up in this section consists of major league baseball players who committed murder.

1. MARTY BERGEN

Catcher Marty Bergen was depressed by the sudden death of his son in 1899. His erratic behavior troubled his Boston teammates, and they informed owner Arthur Soden that they wouldn't return if Bergen remained with the team. On January 19, 1900, Bergen used an ax and razor to murder his wife, six-year-old daughter, and three-year-old son before committing suicide.

2. TERRY LARKIN

Terry Larkin was a good enough pitcher to win thirty-one games for Chicago in 1879. Strangely he never won another game. After his retirement in 1884, Larkin went berserk, shot his wife, and cut his own throat. He and his wife survived. However, he was institutionalized and unsuccessfully attempted suicide again. Released, Larkin murdered his father-in-law, and on September 16, 1894, committed suicide with a razor.

3. CHARLES SMITH AND FRANK HARRIS

Charles "Pacer" Smith was a pitcher with Cincinnati during the first two seasons of the National League. Nearly twenty years later, he shot and killed his five-year-old daughter and teenage sister-in-law. On November 28, 1895, Smith was hanged at the Decatur, Illinois, prison, becoming the only major leaguer ever to be executed. A former teammate, catcher Frank Harris, was scheduled to be executed that same day on an unrelated murder charge, but he received a reprieve.

4. CHARLIE SWEENEY

Twenty-one-year-old pitcher Charlie Sweeney set a major league record when he struck out nineteen batters in a game on June 7, 1884. The record would last more than 100 years until Roger Clemens broke it in 1986. Sweeney won forty-one games in 1884 but was banned from the National League for walking off the field during a game. Washed up at age twenty-four, Sweeney murdered a man in a San Francisco saloon in 1894. He died in prison eight years later.

5. **DANNY SHAY**

Danny Shay was a major league shortstop during the first decade of the twentieth century. In 1917, Shay was involved in an argument with a waiter over the amount of sugar in a bowl on his table at an Indianapolis hotel. Shay pulled a gun and shot the man to death. Shay claimed self-defense and was acquitted, possibly because the victim was black.

6. **HANK THOMPSON**

Hank Thompson was the third African American to reach the major leagues, making his debut with the St. Louis Browns in 1947. During spring training in 1948, Thompson shot and killed a man in a bar who had pulled a knife on him. The shooting was ruled self-defense, and Thompson went on to star for the New York Giants between 1949 and 1956.

7. **EDGAR MCNABB**

Edgar McNabb was a rookie pitcher with the 1893 Baltimore Orioles. His mistress was a striking blonde actress named Laura Kellogg. After an argument in a Pittsburgh hotel room, McNabb shot Kellogg twice in the neck. Paralyzed, Kellogg would later die from the wounds. On February 28, 1894, McNabb fatally shot himself in the mouth.

8. CESAR CEDENO

When Cesar Cedeno came up with Houston in 1970, he was touted as the "next Willie Mays." When he hit .320 in 1972 and 1973, he appeared to be fulfilling his promise. On December 11, 1973, Cedeno was spending the night with his nineteen-year-old mistress at a motel in Santo Domingo. During the night, the woman, Altragracia de la Cruz, was shot in the head and killed during an apparent struggle for Cedeno's gun. Cedeno claimed it was an accident and was found guilty of involuntary manslaughter. The punishment turned out to be a 100-peso fine. Cedeno played in the majors until 1986, but he never reached his Hall of Fame potential.

9. PINKY HIGGINS

Pinky Higgins was a hard-hitting third baseman who played in the majors from 1930 to 1946. In 1938, he set a major league record with twelve consecutive base hits. Higgins was convicted of vehicular homicide after he struck and killed a highway worker in 1968. Paroled after serving two months, he died of a heart attack the day after his release.

10. **ART SHIRES**

Art "The Great" Shires's four-year baseball career was overshadowed by his violent behavior. When he wasn't fighting professionally, he kept in shape by beating up players and managers. In 1928, he nearly killed a black fan in Waco, Texas, when he hit him with a baseball. Twenty years later, he was charged with murder during a fight with an old friend. Shires confessed, "I had to rough him up a good deal because he grabbed a knife and started whittling on my legs." At his trial he was acquitted because of testimony that death had been caused by cirrhosis of the liver, and the beating itself wouldn't have been fatal.

Baseball's Greatest Mysteries

Many fans wonder why the Cubs or Red Sox never win a championship. Let's conclude this book by contemplating some of baseball's unsolved mysteries.

1. WHO INVENTED BASEBALL?

The myth that Abner Doubleday invented baseball in Cooperstown, New York, in 1839, originated in 1907. A commission, headed by A. G. Spalding, had convened to determine the origins of the national pastime. An elderly man named Abner Graves claimed that he had been present at the first game in Cooperstown. When the Baseball Hall of Fame was built thirty years later, Cooperstown was selected as the site. Over the years, researchers have concluded that the Doubleday story is completely false. There is no evidence that Doubleday, who later gained fame as a union general in the Civil War, visited Cooperstown in 1839. Doubleday kept sixty-seven diaries in his lifetime, none of which even mentions baseball. More significantly, there are references to a game resembling baseball being played in America as early as the eighteenth century. In all likelihood, the game evolved from English games such as rounders and town ball. During the Cold War, the Russians even suggested that our national pastime had been copied from their game, lapta. A bizarre footnote occurred in 1924 when ninety-year-old Abner Graves, the man who concocted the Doubleday myth, murdered his wife and was committed to an institution for the criminally insane.

2. WHO INVENTED THE CURVE?

Candy Cummings won only twenty-one games, but he was one of the first inductees into the Baseball Hall of Fame because he claimed to have invented the curve ball. Cummings wrote that he got the inspiration for the pitch while throwing clam shells as a teenager in 1863. He threw his first curve in competition in 1867. A number of other pitchers claimed to be the pitch's originator. Alphonse Martin said he had been throwing the dropball since 1864. Fred Goldsmith claimed that he had invented the pitch in the mid-1860s. In

1870, he made headlines by demonstrating that the ball really curved. Previously, many thought the movement was just an optical illusion. Bitter over his lack of recognition, Goldsmith died in 1939 clutching the sixty-nine-year-old newspaper account of his demonstration. That same year Candy Cummings was inducted into the Hall of Fame.

3. **TY COBB AND TRIS SPEAKER**

Two legends of the game, Ty Cobb and Tris Speaker, probably fixed a game in September 1919. In 1926, Detroit pitcher Dutch Leonard revealed that he and Cobb met with Speaker and Smokey Joe Wood of the Indians to discuss fixing a game so that Detroit would finish third. The men also agreed to bet on the Tigers. Detroit won 9–5, but Cobb and Speaker were unable to get their bets down. Leonard revealed the fix in 1926, after Cobb demoted him to the minor leagues. As proof, he presented letters he had received from Cobb and Wood detailing the plot. Detroit owner Frank Nevin and American League President Ben Johnson, eager to keep the scandal out of the headlines, bought the letters for $20,000. When Commissioner Kenesaw Landis learned of the fix, he investigated the matter. Although he had banned numerous lesser players for similar offenses,

Landis allegedly decided it was not in the best interest of baseball to banish Cobb and Speaker. They did resign as managers, and both ended their careers as part-time players on the 1928 Philadelphia Athletics.

4. **PETE ROSE**

Pete Rose was banned from baseball in 1989 by Commissioner Bart Giamatti for allegedly betting on baseball. Rose has always denied the charge. However, there would appear to be substantial evidence that he not only bet on baseball, but that he wagered on games he was managing. At least nine of Rose's associates interviewed by the commissioner's office testified that he bet on baseball. They produced betting sheets in Rose's handwriting. Investigator John Dowd wrote a 225-page report that concluded that Rose bet thousands of dollars daily on baseball games and that he bet repeatedly on the Cincinnati Reds, the team he was managing. There is no evidence that he ever bet against the Reds, although Paul Janszen, one of Rose's cronies, claimed he would consider betting against them if the money was right. It must be noted the Giamatti appeared to already have his mind made up before all the evidence was in. It seemed more a battle of wills than a matter of principle. One of baseball's great players was banned from baseball and kept out of the Hall of Fame. Giamatti died of a heart attack a week after his ruling. Nobody really won.

5. **ED DELAHANTY**

Ed Delahanty's .346 lifetime batting average is the fifth best in baseball history. Big Ed was batting .333 in June 1903 when he was suspended for excessive drinking. On July 2, he was on a train bound for New York when he became rowdy. The conductor threw the drunken Delahanty off the train in Fort Erie, on the Canadian side of the Niagara River. Railroad workers testified that they had seen Delahanty chasing the train on foot across the railroad bridge. He apparently fell to his death, and his body was washed over Niagara Falls. Probably his death was accidental. However, some believe he committed suicide because he had recently taken out a large insurance policy with his daughter as his beneficiary. Others believe that because he was carrying valuable jewelry, and the diamonds were never found, that he might have been murdered.

6. **DON WILSON**

Houston pitcher Don Wilson threw no-hitters in 1967 and 1969. He was denied a chance at a third in September 1974, when manager Preston

Gomez removed him for a pinch-hitter in the ninth inning. On January 5, 1975, Wilson was found dead in his car, which was parked in the garage of his home. He had died from carbon monoxide poisoning. His five-year-old son, sleeping in his bedroom, also died. Although many believed Wilson committed suicide, his death was ruled accidental.

7. WHO WAS CASEY?

Ernest Thayer published his poem, "Casey at the Bat" in 1888. Although he insisted to his dying day that the mighty Casey was a completely fictional character, others have made claims that they were the inspiration for the character. Some think it was King Kelly, the most popular player of the time. Dan Casey and his brother Dennis, both active major leaguers in the 1880s, also laid claim, if for no other reason than because they shared the same name. It didn't seem to matter that Dan Casey was a pitcher. Why anyone would want to be the inspiration for a character who struck out and lost a game is an even greater mystery.

8. BILL THOMAS

Bill Thomas was a promising young pitcher in the Pacific Coast League. In April 1906, Thomas boarded a boat, the *Richard Peck,* headed for

New York. The night before the boat was to arrive in New York he instructed the porter to get him up early because he wanted to see the sunrise over the city. When the man entered Thomas's room, he found his bed empty. Thomas was never seen again. Whether he jumped or fell overboard or was the victim of foul play remains a mystery.

9. **RUBE WADDELL**

Before the 1905 World Series, gamblers offered Philadelphia ace Rube Waddell $17,000 not to play in the World Series. Waddell had led the American League with twenty-six victories, and his participation was essential if the A's were going to defeat the heavily favored New York Giants. Just prior to the series opener, Waddell claimed he hurt his pitching arm falling over a suitcase. Without Waddell, the A's won only one game in the series.

It was rumored that Waddell did make the deal with the gamblers, but he was cheated out of all but $500 of the bribe. Philadelphia owner Connie Mack insisted that Waddell was injured horsing around at the train station with teammate Andy Coakley. Whatever the truth, Waddell missed his only opportunity to pitch in the World Series. Another piece of evidence that would substantiate his claim of injury was that he never won twenty games again.

10. **STEVE BLASS**

One of the great mysteries of baseball is the sudden unexplained decline of Pittsburgh starter Steve Blass. From 1964 to 1972, Blass had won 100 games and lost 67. In 1972, he was 19–8 with a 2.49 earned run average. The next season he couldn't get the ball over the plate or anybody out. He walked eighty-four batters in eighty-eight innings. The previous season he had walked the same number of batters in 250 innings. His record slipped to 3–9, and his earned run average ballooned to 9.85. No advice from the pitching coach seemed to help. The trainers found nothing wrong with him physically. He tried everything: psychotherapy, hypnosis, visualization, and even meditation, but nothing worked. Perhaps Blass had experienced a mental block. The 1972 Pirates had lost the playoffs to Cincinnati in a heartbreaking ninth inning rally. Whatever the cause, no remedy was ever found, and Blass was out of baseball by 1974.

Bibliography

Berlage, Gai. *Women in Baseball.* New York: Praeger, 1994.

Blake, Mike. *Bad Hops and Lucky Bounces.* Cincinnati: Betterway Books, 1995.

Carter, Craig. *The Complete Baseball Record Book.* St. Louis: Sporting News, 1987.

Charlton, James. *The Baseball Chronology.* New York: Macmillan, 1991.

Conner, Floyd, and John Snyder. *Day By Day in Cincinnati Reds History.* New York: Leisure, 1983.

Dewey, Donald, and Nicholas Acocella. *The Biographical History of Baseball.* New York: Carroll & Graf, 1995.

Fusselle, Warner. *Baseball... A Laughing Matter.* St. Louis: Sporting News, 1987.

Gregorich, Barbara. *Women at Play.* New York: Harcourt Brace, 1993.

Gutman, Dan. *Baseball Babylon.* New York: Penguin, 1992.

Hoppel, Joe, and Craig Carter. *The Sporting News Baseball Trivia Book.* St. Louis: Sporting News, 1983.

James, Bill. *The Bill James Historical Abstract*. New York: Villard, 1986.

Kaufman, Alan, and James Kaufman. *The Worst Pitchers of All Time*. Jefferson (N. C.): McFarland, 1993.

Liss, Howard. *More Strange But True Sports Stories*. New York: Random House, 1981.

Marazzi, Rich, and Len Fiorito. *Aaron to Zipfel*. New York: Avon, 1985.

Nash, Bruce, and Allan Zullo. *The Baseball Hall of Shame*. New York: Pocket Books, 1985.

———. *The Baseball Hall of Shame II*. New York: Pocket Books, 1986.

———. *The Baseball Hall of Shame III*. New York: Pocket Books, 1987.

———. *The Baseball Hall of Shame IV*. New York: Pocket Books, 1990.

———. *Baseball Hall of Shame's Warped Record Book*. New York: Collier, 1991.

Nelson, Kevin. *Baseball's Greatest Insults*. New York: Fireside, 1984.

Nemec, David. *Great Baseball Feats, Facts, & Firsts*. New York: Plume, 1987.

Peary, Danny. *Cult Baseball Players*. New York: Fireside, 1990.

Porter, David. *Biographical Dictionary of American Sports: Baseball*. Westport (Ct.): Greenwood Press, 1987.

Reichler, Joseph. *The Baseball Encyclopedia*. New York: Macmillan, 1988.

Scheinen, Richard. *Field of Screams*. New York: Norton, 1994.

Shalin, Bruce. *Oddballs*. New York: Penguin, 1989.

Shatzin, Mike. *The Ballplayers*. New York: Arbor House, 1990.

Snyder, John. *Play Ball*. San Francisco: Chronicle, 1991.

———. *World Series*. San Francisco: Chronicle, 1995.

Thorn, John, and John Holway. *The Pitcher*. New York: Prentice Hall, 1987.

Thorn, John, and Pete Palmer. *Total Baseball*. New York: Warner, 1989.

Weiss, Peter. *Baseball's All Time Goats*. Holbrook (Mass.): Adams, 1992.

Index

Aaron, Hank, 153, 177, 183, 273
Aase, Don, 325
Abbott, Jim, 322
Adams, Margo, 36
Adcock, Joe, 191
Aikens, Willie, 307
Ainge, Danny, 30
Ainsmith, Eddie, 339
Alexander, Grover Cleveland, 299
Allen, Dick, 312
Allen, Hank, 312
Allen, Johnny, 44
Altrock, Nick, 115
Ames, Red, 179
Amoros, Sandy, 243
Andersen, Larry, 90
Anderson, Dave, 69
Andrews, Mike, 218
Andujar, Joaquin, 315
Ann-Margaret, 33
Anson, Cap, 79, 116, 266, 269
Aparicio, Luis, 216
Apollonio, Nathaniel, 6
Ash, Ken, 135
Ashburn, Richie, 145
Autry, Gene, 18, 356

Bagby, Jim, 256
Bagby, Jim, Jr., 255
Bagwell, Jeff, 90
Bailey, Bill, 169
Baker, Del, 135
Baker, Home Run, 22
Baker, Kirtley, 169
Baldschun, Jack, 207
Baldwin, Dave, 52
Banks, Ernie, 128
Bannon, Jimmy, 63
Barnes, Ross, 138
Barney, Rex, 179
Barnhart, Clyde, 156
Bartell, Dick, 215
Bates, Frank, 172
Batterson, Jessie, 332
Bauman, Joe, 2, 123
Baylor, Don, 189
Beck, Boom Boom, 237
Beckley, Jake, 73, 335
Bedell, Howie, 256
Belinksy, Bo, 33, 78, 101
Belle, Albert, 91, 278, 312
Bench, Johnny, 71, 240
Bennett, Eddie, 100
Berardino, John, 17
Berg, Moe, 48

Bergen, Bill, 157
Bergen, Marty, 360
Berman, Chris, 63
Berra, Dale, 305
Berra, Yogi, 44, 55, 59,62, 105, 149, 244
Bevens, Bill, 242, 243
Biacalana, Buddy, 160
Bilardello, Dan, 61
Bilko, Steve, 301
Bithorn, Hi, 359
Black, Don, 333
Black, Joe, 183
Blackburne, Lena, 295
Blair, Paul, 334
Blass, Steve, 372
Blue, Vida, 101, 217, 304
Blyleven, Bert, 79, 175
Bodie, Ping, 105
Boggs, Wade, 36, 104, 325
Bonds, Bobby, 162
Bonura, Zeke, 195
Borbon, Pedro, 95
Bordagaray, Frenchy, 84
Borden, Joe, 5
Borders, Ila, 40
Boros, Steve, 48
Bosetti, Rick, 86
Bosman, Dick, 255
Bostock, Lyman, 96, 356
Boswell, Dave, 294
Boudreau, Lou, 212, 216, 230
Bouton, Jim, 20, 21
Bowa, Larry, 210
Bowman, Frank, 301
Boyd, William, 296
Bragan, Bobby, 2, 44
Branca, Ralph, 102, 103, 246
Brandt, Jackie, 81, 84
Bratchi, Frank, 350
Brennan, Ad, 296
Brennan, Bill, 231
Brett, George, 43, 157, 204, 281

Brett, Ken, 204
Brewer, Chet, 268
Brewer, Jim, 294
Bridges, Rocky, 11, 278
Bridwell, Al, 248
Britton, Helene, 39
Brock, Lou, 208
Broglio, Ernie, 208
Brosnan, Jim, 52
Brown, Bobby, 53, 54
Brown, Buster, 169
Brown, Fred, 3, 24
Brown, Gates, 110, 333
Brown, Kevin, 1, 5
Brown, Larry, 176
Brown, Three Finger, 214, 285, 323
Brown, Tommy, 120
Brown, Walter, 108
Brown, Willard, 188
Browning, Pete, 142, 236, 316
Brunet, George, 204
Buckeye, Garland, 109
Buckner, Bill, 14, 247
Buhl, Bob, 158, 209
Bulkeley, Morgan, 23
Bunning, Jim, 2, 23, 177
Burke, Jimmy, 103
Burke, Kitty, 41
Burkett, Jesse, 293
Burnett, Johnny, 167
Burns, Tommy, 107
Burroughs, Jeff, 227
Bush, Guy, 178
Butler, Brett, 104
Byrne, Tommy, 181, 243
Byron, William, 275, 296

Cabell, Enos, 305
Cain, Bob, 144
Caldwell, Ray, 301, 325
Camacho, Ernie, 15
Camilli, Dolf, 296

Campanella, Ray, 185
Campanis, Al, 273
Campbell, Nolan, 43
Canillon, Joe, 200
Canseco, Jose, 238
Caray, Harry, 21, 61
Cardenal, Jose, 325
Cardenas, Leo, 97
Carleton, Tex, 289
Carlson, Swede, 332
Carlton, Steve, 132, 208, 214, 278
Carpenter, Bill, 286
Carson, Johnny, 160, 219
Carter, Gary, 61
Carter, Joe, 250
Casey, Dan, 370
Casey, Dennis, 370
Casey, Hugh, 250, 354
Cash, Norm, 338
Castillo, Frank, 313
Castro, Fidel, 25
Cedeno, Cesar, 363
Cepeda, Orlando, 305, 306
Chadwick, Henry, 278
Chamberlain, Icebox, 233
Chance, Frank, 190, 289, 292
Chandler, Happy, 25
Chapman, Ben, 271
Chapman, Ray, 330
Chappoten, Lindy, 211
Charboneau, Joe, 83
Chase, Hal, 341, 342
Cheney, Tom, 132
Childs, Cupid, 63, 279
Chiles, Pearce, 63
Chiti, Harry, 213
Christenson, Walter, 63
Churn, Chuck, 257
Chylack, Nestor, 227
Cicotte, Eddie, 222, 340
Clancy, Charles, 235
Clark, Jack, 251

Clark, Nig, 125
Clarkson, John, 231, 233
Cleary, Joe, 168
Clemens, Clem, 214
Clemens, Doug, 208
Clemens, Roger, 11, 132, 133, 361
Clifton, Jack, 332
Coakley, Andy, 371
Cobb, Ty, 13, 100, 133, 144, 153, 157, 166, 215, 262, 269, 275, 290, 296, 311, 343, 359, 367
Cochrane, Mickey, 315
Coffman, Dick, 213
Coggins, Frank, 47
Colavito, Rocky, 208
Colborn, Jim, 85
Coleman, Choo Choo, 58, 59
Coleman, Jerry, 57, 59, 60
Coleman, John, 46, 171
Coleman, Vince, 325
Colliflower, Harry, 172
Collins, Dave, 61
Collins, Eddie, 146, 222, 246, 277
Collins, Jo, 34
Collins, Ripper, 142, 254
Comiskey, Charles, 6, 220, 222, 267, 340
Conigliaro, Tony, 259
Conley, Gene, 30
Connors, Chuck, 16
Coombs, Jack, 171
Corbett, Jack, 235
Corcoran, Tommy, 336
Corridon, Frank, 234
Courtney, Clint, 294
Cousy, Bob, 30
Cox, William, 310, 311
Cravath, Gavvy, 222
Crawford, Sam, 148, 154
Creighton, James, 332

Crespi, Creepy, 326
Crosetti, Frank, 189, 293
Crues, Bob, 2, 126
Cuellar, Mike, 97, 255
Cullop, Nick, 64
Cummings, Candy, 366
Cuomo, Mario, 325
Curtis, Cliff, 170

Dahl, Jay, 121
Daily, Hugh, 322
Dalkowski, Steve, 78, 123
Dalrymple, Abner, 337
Dalton, Jack, 127
Daniels, Kal, 10
Danning, Harry, 350
Dapper, Cliff, 217
Dark, Alvin, 74, 318
Dascenzo, Doug, 91
Dascoli, Frank, 31
Dauvray, Helen, 42
Davis, Eric, 218
Davis, George, 52
Davis, Harry, 63
Davis, Tommy, 202, 203
Davis, Willie, 251
Day, Clyde, 354
De Jesus, Ivan, 210
Dean, Dizzy, 60, 69, 70, 169
Dean, Dory, 169
Dean, Paul, 41, 70
DeBusschere, Dave, 29
Decker, Steve, 283
Deer, Rob, 163
Delahanty, Ed, 299, 369
Dempsey, Rick, 77, 241
Derrick, Claude, 206
Derrington, Jim, 119
DeVicenzi, Vince, 268
Devlin, Jim, 341
DeWitt, Bill, 207
DeWitt, C.B., 165
Dibble, Rob, 91, 134

Dickey, Bill, 298
Didrikson, Babe, 40
Dietz, Dick, 184
DiMaggio, Joe, 5, 10, 17, 18, 30, 153, 164, 207, 240, 242, 255, 256, 326, 328
DiMaggio, Vince, 164
Dinneen, Bill, 110
Doby, Larry, 217
Dodge, Johnny, 331
Doheny, Ed, 315
Donatelli, Augie, 243
Donlin, Turkey Mike, 19, 347
Doolan, Mickey, 214
Doubleday, Abner, 365
Douglas, Whammy, 11
Douglass, Astynax, 297
Dowd, John, 368
Downing, Al, 177
Doyle, Brian, 244
Doyle, Jack, 203
Drabowski, Moe, 74
Dreyfuss, Barney, 215
Driessen, Dan, 61
Drysdale, Don, 184, 185, 256
Duffy, Hugh, 9, 155
Dunlap, Fred, 138
Dunn, Jack, 206
Duren, Ryne, 181
Durocher, Leo, 33, 37, 259, 272, 302, 338
Dykes, Jimmy, 199, 242
Dykstra, Len, 311

Early, Joe, 228
Easter, Luke, 357
Eckersley, Dennis, 246
Egan, Ben, 206
Eisenhower, Dwight, 24
Eisenreich, Jim, 315
Ellen, Arthur, 320
Eller, Hod, 151
Ellis, Dock, 306

Engel, Clyde, 253
Ernega, Frank, 127
Espino, Hector, 2, 125
Essegian, Chuck, 244
Estrada, Francisco, 207
Evans, Billy, 275
Evans, Steve, 190
Evers, Johnny, 249, 292, 318

Face, Elroy, 257, 324
Fain, Ferris, 308
Faul, Bill, 87
Faust, Charles, 98
Feller, Bob, 121, 135
Felsch, Happy, 100, 340
Felton, Terry, 169, 170
Ferguson, Bob, 64
Fidrych, Mark, 82
Fingers, Rollie, 240
Finley, Charlie, 75, 151, 217, 220
Fischer, Bill, 214
Fischer, Carl, 213
Fisher, George, 72
Fisher, Jack, 176, 177
Fisher, Ray, 343
Flack, Max, 212, 214
Flick, Elmer, 309
Flynn, Jocko, 139
Fogel, Horace, 198, 342
Folkers, Rich, 58
Ford, Russ, 149
Ford, Whitey, 148, 335
Forster, Terry, 108
Fortugno, Tim, 211
Fosse, Ray, 261
Foster, Rube, 317
Foster, Steve, 327
Fothergill, Fats, 109
Fowler, Bud, 268
Fox, Nellie, 216
Foxx, Jimmie, 106, 162
Foytack, Paul, 175

Francona, Tito, 176
Franklin, Jack, 324
Fraser, Chick, 187
Frazee, Harry, 93
Frazier, George, 240
Freedman, Andrew, 221
Fregosi, Jim, 207
Friend, Dan, 245
Frisch, Frankie, 41, 142, 186
Frost, Robert, 51
Fuller, Shorty, 194

Gaedel, Eddie, 3, 144, 216, 357
Galvin, Pud, 147
Gandil, Chick, 340
Gardella, Danny, 75
Gardenr, Bruce, 355
Gardner, Alexander, 192
Garvey, Steve, 36, 37, 77
Gedeon, Joe, 344
Gehrig, Lou, 12, 40
George, Bill, 180
Gera, Beatrice, 42
Gerkin, Steve, 169
Giamatti, Bart, 310, 368
Gibson, Bob, 186
Gibson, Josh, 142, 315
Gibson, Kirk, 246
Giebell, Floyd, 134
Gionfriddo, Al, 242
Gladding, Fred, 111
Glaviano, Rabbit, 194
Glenn, John, 346
Gochnaur, John, 194
Goldsmith, Fred, 366
Gomez, Ruben, 191
Gonzalez, Mike, 49
Gooden, Dwight, 118, 299, 304
Goslin, Goose, 101, 186
Gould, Charlie, 197
Grady, Mike, 193
Grant, Charlie, 267
Grant, Frank, 267

Graves, Abner, 365
Gray, Dolly, 181
Gray, Pete, 321
Gray, Ted, 204
Green, Pumpsie, 273
Gretzky, Wayne, 12
Griffey, Ken, Jr., 11
Griffin, Ivy, 276
Griffith, Calvin, 224, 230
Griffith, Clark, 201, 233
Griggs, Hal, 256
Grim, Bob, 189
Grimes, Burleigh, 160, 186
Grimm, Charlie, 135, 212, 216
Groat, Dick, 27
Groh, Heinie, 144
Groom, Bob, 59
Gutierrez, Cesar, 133

Haas, Bruno, 180
Halas, George, 28
Hall, Dick, 104
Hall, George, 341
Hamilton, Billy, 156
Hamilton, Jack, 259
Hamilton, Steve, 318
Haney, Fred, 243
Hanlon, Ned, 46
Harding, Herndon, 320
Hargrove, Mike, 66
Harper, George, 236
Harris, Frank, 361
Harris, Joe, 171
Hart, Jim Ray, 187
Hartsfield, Roy, 173
Hartung, Clint, 129
Harwell, Ernie, 212
Hatcher, Billy, 245
Hawley, Pink, 187
Hazle, Bob, 140
Hearn, Jim, 191
Heathcote, Cliff, 212
Hecker, Guy, 196

Heilmann, Harry, 133
Heinrich, Tommy, 250
Held, Woodie, 163, 176
Henderson, Dave, 96, 351
Henderson, Ricky, 156
Hendrix, Claude, 214
Herbel, Ron, 158
Herman, Babe, 41, 237, 239
Hernandez, Keith, 305
Herrara, Ramon, 267
Herrnstein, John, 210
Hershiser, Orel, 184, 325
Heusser, Ed, 289
Hickman, Piano Legs, 193
Higbe, Kirby, 269, 348
Higgins, Pinky, 363
Higgins, Robert, 291
Higham, Richard, 342
Hilgendorf, Tom, 227
Hill, Bill, 172
Hogan, Shanty, 111
Holbert, Bill, 159
Holloman, Bobo, 127
Holtzman, Ken, 54
Honeycutt, Rick, 150
Hook, Jay, 51
Hooper, Harry, 253
Hoover, Herbert, 302
Hope, Bob, 18
Hopper, Clay, 272
Hornsby, Rogers, 199, 311
Horton, Tony, 318
Hough, Charlie, 328
Howard, Elston, 129, 148, 272
Howe, Steve, 305
Howser, Dick, 219
Hoy, Dummy, 323
Hoyt, Lamarr, 306
Hoyt, Waite, 106
Hrabosky, Al, 88
Hubbell, Carl, 257
Huggins, Miller, 301
Hughey, Jim, 172

Hulbert, William, 138
Hunt, Ken, 327, 328
Hunt, Ron, 188
Hunter, Catfish, 255
Hurst, Tim, 277, 323
Hyde, Dick, 214
Hynes, Pat, 359

Incaviglia, Pete, 162
Irvin, Ed, 359
Irwin, Art, 192, 352

Jackson, Bo, 29
Jackson, Larry, 209
Jackson, Reggie, 68, 161
Jackson, Shoeless Joe, 14, 340
Jansen, Ray, 134
Jaster, Larry, 254
Jeffcoat, Hal, 190
Jenkins, Ferguson, 1, 75, 209, 213
Jennings, Hughie, 330
Jennings, Ora, 274
Jensen, Jackie, 30, 240
Johnson, Alex, 319
Johnson, Ban, 367
Johnson, Lou, 304
Johnson, Ottis, 332
Johnson, Randy, 132, 260
Johnson, Walter, 236, 339
Johnstone, Jay, 76
Jones, Bumpus, 2, 6
Jones, Charley, 42
Jones, Nippy, 243
Jordan, Michael, 32
Jordan, Pat, 115
Joyce, Robert, 286
Joyner, Wally, 287
Jurges, Billy, 276

Kahaulua, Freddy, 96
Kauff, Benny, 343
Kaze, Irv, 34

Keefe, David, 324
Keefe, Tim, 192
Keeler, Willie, 145, 296, 330
Keister, Bill, 65
Kekich, Mike, 38
Kelly, Mike, 69, 299, 370
Kennedy, Bob, 182
Keough, Matt, 330
Kerfeld, Charlie, 7, 109
Kern, Jim, 88, 183, 282
Kerr, Dickie, 223
Killebrew, Harmon, 230
Killian, Ed, 174
Kilroy, Matches, 155
Kiner, Ralph, 60
Kingman, Dave, 280, 329
Kinsella, W. P., 48
Kirk, Jim, 190
Kittle, Hub, 114
Klem, Bill, 234
Kluszewski, Ted, 44
Knauss, Frank, 141
Knell, Phil, 184
Knowles, Darold, 68
Koenecke, Len, 345
Kolb, Eddie, 2, 6
Koufax, Sandy, 87, 128, 133, 251
Krausse, Lew, 167
Kroc, Ray, 223
Kruk, John, 299
Kuenn, Harvey, 208
Kuhn, Bowie, 75

L'il Rastus, 100
Labine, Clem, 191
Lacorte, Frank, 47
Lajoie, Nap, 290
Land, Grover, 231
Landis, Kenesaw Mountain, 40, 270, 271, 295, 341, 343, 367
Lange, Bill, 3, 143, 262
Larkin, Terry, 360

Larsen, Don, 241
Lary, Frank, 255
Lasorda, Tom, 76, 105, 126
Latham, Arlie, 64, 79
Lavagetto, Cookie, 242, 243
Lee, Bill, 81
LeFlore, Ron, 104, 347
Leibrandt, Charlie, 250
Lemongello, Mark, 173
Leonard, Andy, 192
Leonard, Dutch, 343, 367
Leonard, Jeffrey, 71, 305
Lesley, Brad, 89
Letterman, David, 108, 160
Lewis, Ted, 51
Lieb, Fred, 34
Lindstrom, Fred, 241
Littlefield, Dick, 202
Loes, Billy, 91
Logan, Johnny, 191
Lohrke, Jack, 99
Long, Herman, 193
Lord, Bris, 63
Louise, Tina, 33
Lucchesi, Frank, 289
Luciano, Ron, 334
Lyons, Ted, 49

Mack, Connie, 46, 117, 167, 170, 206, 233, 300, 336, 371
MacPhail, Larry, 151
Magee, Sherry, 276
Magerkurth, George, 276
Malmquist, Walter, 125
Mann, Les, 214
Mantle, Mickey, 11, 30, 182, 186, 299, 309
Maranville, Rabbit, 76, 299
Marcelle, Oliver, 288
Maris, Roger, 176, 177, 283
Marquard, Rube, 309
Martin, Alphonse, 366

Martin, Billy, 15, 62, 219, 278, 293, 326, 347
Martinez, Carlos, 238
Mathews, Bobby, 150
Mathews, Eddie, 297
Mathewson, Christy, 127, 199, 206, 285
Mattingly, Don, 295
Maxvill, Dal, 159
Mays, Carl, 330
Mays, Willie, 243, 309, 363
McCarthy, Joe, 358
McCarver, Tim, 281
McConnell, George, 214
McDaniel, Lindy, 267
McDaniel, Von, 262
McDonald, Ben, 106
McDougald, Gil, 258
McDowell, Oddibe, 63
McDowell, Roger, 77
McGill, Willie, 120
McGraw, John, 38, 79, 98, 199, 267, 275, 282, 295, 300, 335, 353, 358
McGraw, Tug, 90
McHenry, Austin, 261
McKee, Rogers Hornsby, 120
McLain, Denny, 104, 281, 346
McLean, Billy, 276
McLean, Larry, 358
McMullin, Fred, 340
McNabb, Edgar, 362
McNally, Dave, 255
McNamara, John, 248
McNeely, Earl, 241
McRae, Brian, 313
McVey, Cal, 2, 232
Medwick, Joe, 289, 297
Mendoza, Mario, 157
Mercer, Win, 286, 353
Merkle, Fred, 248, 253, 353
Meyer, Russ, 67
Miley, Mike, 95

Miller, Bob, 203
Miller, Hack, 3, 143
Minoso, Minnie, 114, 189
Mitchell, Jackie, 39
Mize, Johnny, 145, 301
Mizell, Wilmer, 3, 24
Molitor, Paul, 112
Montefusco, John, 71
Moore, Barry, 255
Moore, Donnie, 96, 351
Moran, Pat, 234
Morgan, Joe, 121
Morgan, Mike, 202
Morris, Ed, 357
Mulcahy, Hugh, 171
Mullane, Tony, 65, 265
Mungo, Van Lingle, 37
Murphy, Morgan, 336
Murphy, Rob, 309
Murray, Bill, 21
Murray, Eddie, 12
Murray, Red, 326
Murtaugh, Danny, 185
Musial, Stan, 119
Myers, Randy, 229

Nabors, Jack, 170
Nash, Jim, 74
Nava, Sandy, 266
Neal, Charlie, 60
Neale, Earle, 27
Necciai, Ron, 124
Neun, Johnny, 59
Nevers, Ernie, 28
Nevin, Frank, 215, 367
Newcombe, Don, 191, 247
Newsom, Bobo, 201
Nichols, Al, 341
Nicholson, Bill, 161
Nicholson, Dave, 161
Niedenfuer, Tom, 251
Niekro, Phil, 112, 175
Nimick, William, 220
Nixon, Richard, 22, 219

Novikoff, Lou, 238
Nuxhall, Joe, 118

O'Brien, Buck, 290
O'Day, Hank, 274
O'Rourke, Jim, 115
Odom, Blue Moon, 308
Oglivie, Ben, 53
Ojeda, Bob, 96
Orr, Dave, 261
Ott, Mel, 121
Owen, Mickey, 250
Oyler, Ray, 159
Ozark, Danny, 61

Paciorek, John, 132
Page, Joe, 10, 78
Paige, Satchel, 70, 112, 294
Palmer, Jim, 85, 251
Pappas, Milt, 205, 207, 257
Parker, Dave, 305
Parker, Doc, 166
Pate, Joe, 130
Patkin, Max, 293
Payson, Joan, 41
Pearson, Ike, 169
Peckinpaugh, Roger, 252
Pepitone, Joe, 35, 124, 348
Perez, Pascual, 307
Perrine, Fred, 316
Perry, Gaylord, 336
Peters, Frank, 234
Peterson, Fritz, 38
Pettit, Paul1, 29
Pezullo, John, 63
Pfeffer, Dandelion, 192
Phelps, Babe, 67
Phillips, Adolfo, 210
Piersall, Jim, 82, 293, 316, 317
Pipgras, George, 285
Plank, Eddie, 331
Podres, Johnny, 128
Postema, Pam, 43
Potter, Dykes, 214

Index

Powell, Abner, 232
Powell, Boog, 111
Powell, Jake, 270
Powers, Mike, 331
Prothro, Doc, 197
Prowse, Juliet, 34
Pruett, Hub, 254
Puckett, Kirby, 251
Pulliam, Harry, 249, 353
Purcell, William, 147

Qualls, Jim, 256
Quinn, Jack, 116

Radbourne, Hoss, 154
Rader, Doug, 14
Raines, Tim, 304
Ramos, Pedro, 176, 307
Ramsey, Toad, 302
Randle, Lenny, 289
Raymond, Bugs, 300, 358
Reagan, Ronald, 3, 22
Reardon, Beans, 19
Reed, Ron, 30
Reese, Pee Wee, 297
Reidy, William, 167
Reiser, Pete, 259
Relford, Joe, 119
Reulbach, Ed, 254
Reuss, Jerry, 77, 320
Reyes, Nap, 76
Reynolds, Carl, 298
Rhem, Flint, 299
Rhoads, Bob, 313
Rhodes, Dusty, 293
Rhomberg, Keith, 86
Richard, J. R., 260
Rickey, Branch, 212, 270, 272, 302
Ridgeway, Charlie, 120
Rigney, Bill, 78
Rijo, Jose, 97
Ring, Jimmy, 297
Risberg, Swede, 340, 344

Rivers, Mickey, 62
Rizzuto, Phil, 59, 189, 215
Roberts, Morganna, 43
Roberts, Robin, 174, 175
Robertson, Charlie, 133
Robinson, Brooks, 75
Robinson, Don, 110
Robinson, Frank, 111, 189, 205, 207, 297
Robinson, Jackie, 202, 264, 270, 271, 272, 273
Robinson, Wilbert, 237
Rodriguez, Aurelio, 15
Roe, Preacher, 338
Rogers, Shotgun, 331
Rohr, Bill, 129
Roman, Bill, 131
Rommel, Ed, 167
Rose, Don, 207
Rose, Pete, 13, 36, 43, 153, 160, 261, 310, 340, 346, 368
Rothstein, Arnold, 311
Roush, Edd, 2, 234
Rowe, Dave, 166, 198
Rowe, Jack, 198
Royko, Mike, 95
Ruffing, Red, 324
Ruiz, Chico, 95
Ruppert, Jacob, 8, 271
Rusie, Amos, 179, 206, 221
Russell, Lefty, 130
Ruth, Babe, 5, 8, 14, 34, 40, 63, 78, 93, 106, 125, 129, 139, 153, 162, 176, 178, 206, 254, 269, 273, 283, 348
Ryan, Nolan, 43, 89, 112, 132, 155, 207, 298
Ryba, Mike, 201

Saberhagen, Bret, 279
Salmon, Chico, 75
Sandberg, Ryne, 210
Sanders, Deion, 29, 72, 281
Sargent, Joe, 63

Savage, Randy, 32
Sax, Steve, 319
Schaefer, Germany, 45
Scheib, Carl, 119
Schiraldi, Calvin, 248
Schmidt, Boss, 296
Schmidt, Crazy, 172
Schmidt, Mike, 43
Schmidt, Willard, 191
Schott, Marge, 10, 39, 218, 220, 224
Schreckengost, Ossee, 7
Schuster, Bill, 72
Score, Herb, 258
Sears, Ziggy, 228
Seats, Tom, 302
Seaver, Tom, 48, 90, 133, 256
Sewell, Joe, 142, 161
Shafer, Tillie, 38
Shantz, Bobby, 208
Sharman, Bill, 30
Shay, Danny, 362
Sheckard, Jimmy, 288
Sheen, Charlie, 14
Shepard, Bert, 322
Sheridan, Jack, 233
Sherman, James, 22
Sherry, Larry, 187
Sherry, Norm, 187
Shindle, Bill, 193
Shires, Art, 295, 364
Shoch, George, 194
Shore, Ernie, 206
Shula, Don, 28
Sianis, William, 94
Siever, Ed, 290
Simpson, Dick, 207
Simpson, Harry, 201
Simpson, Wayne, 263
Skizas, Lou, 65
Smith, Charles, 192, 202
Smith, Germany, 291

Smith, Heinie, 198
Smith, Lonnie, 305
Smith, Ozzie, 251
Smith, Pacer, 361
Smith, Phenomenal, 291
Snodgrass, Fred, 253
Sockalexis, Lou, 38
Soden, Arthur, 360
Solters, Moose, 333
Somers, Charles, 222
Spahn, Warren, 112, 127
Spalding, A. G., 365
Sparks, Steve, 325
Speaker, Tris, 301, 343, 366
Spira, Howard, 219
Spooner, Karl, 128
Spring, Jack, 208
Sprinz, Joe, 327
St. Vrain, Jim, 236
Stahl, Chick, 352, 353
Stahl, Larry, 257
Stallard, Tracy, 176
Stallings, George, 85
Stanhouse, Don, 91, 102
Stanky, Eddie, 338
Stanley, Mickey, 159
Stanton, Leroy, 207
Stargell, Willie, 161, 163
Staub, Rusty, 105, 121
Steinbrenner, George, 62, 219, 240
Stemmeyer, Bill, 179
Stengel, Casey, 56, 57, 59, 84, 85, 237, 239, 240, 272, 345
Stephens, Gene, 135
Stevens, Connie, 33
Stevens, Harry, 206
Stewart, Ed, 236
Stirnweiss, Snuffy, 78
Stobbs, Chuck, 182
Stone, George, 221

Index

Stoneham, Charles, 311, 312
Stovall, Jesse, 131
Stovey, George, 266
Strawberry, Darryl, 141, 299
Street, Gabby, 289
Stuart, Dick, 195
Sullivan, Fleury, 358
Sullivan, John L., 297
Sunkel, Tom, 324
Sutton, Ezra, 337
Sweeney, Charlie, 361

Taft, William Howard, 22
Tatum, Ken, 334
Taylor, Billy, 140
Taylor, Dummy, 323
Taylor, Jack, 153
Taylor, John, 221
Taylor, Zack, 216
Tebbetts, Birdie, 285
Tebeau, George, 63
Tebeau, Patsy, 278
Tener, John, 3, 23
Tettleton, Mickey, 106
Thayer, Ernest, 370
Thevenow, Tommy, 159
Thomas, Bill, 2, 126, 370
Thomas, Danny, 355
Thomas, Gorman, 163
Thompson, Hank, 362
Thompson, Sam, 165
Thomson, Bobby, 103, 247
Thorpe, Jim, 27
Throneberry, Marv, 51, 239
Tinker, Joe, 214, 292
Torrez, Mike, 217
Toth, Paul, 208
Tovar, Cesar, 255
Townsend, Jack, 169
Travers, Al, 166
Treadway, George, 266
Tucker, Tommy, 295

Turner, Ted, 89
Twombly, George, 206

Ueberroth, Peter, 305
Uecker, Bob, 14, 157

Van Atta, Russ, 130
Van Doren, Mamie, 34
Van Haltren, George, 180
Veeck, Bill, 47, 128, 144, 215, 227, 228, 230, 270, 333, 357
Ventura, Robin, 298
Vergez, Johnny, 268
Versalles, Zoilo, 137, 140
Vincent, Fay, 114
Vitt, Ossee, 292
Von der Ahe, Chris, 79, 219, 226, 283
Vukovich, John, 158

Waddell, Rube, 7, 80, 300, 371
Wadsworth, Jack, 165
Wagner, Honus, 12, 158, 236, 317
Wagner, Leon, 333
Waitkus, Eddie, 283
Wakefield, Dick, 314
Walker, Dixie, 271
Walker, Fleet, 264, 270
Walker, Welday, 265
Wall, Murray, 214
Wallach, Tim, 61
Walsh, Dick, 33
Walsh, Ed, 148, 222, 256
Walsh, Ed, Jr., 256
Wambsganss, Bill, 241
Waner, Paul, 302
Ward, John Montgomery, 42, 49, 50, 266
Warfield, Frank, 288
Warner, Jack, 275

Warner, Pop, 28
Watkins, George, 140
Watson, Bob, 287
Weaver, Buck, 340
Weaver, Earl, 91
Webb, Del, 309
Webb, Earl, 139
Weidman, Stump, 167
Weik, Dick, 180
Weintraub, Phil, 136
Weis, Al, 244
Weiss, George, 272
Welch, Bob, 299
Wells, David, 14
Wells, Willie, 45
Wendell, Turk, 89
Wentz, Dick, 95
West, Mae, 19
White, Bill, 186
White, Sammy, 135
White, Samuel, 274
White, Will, 154, 183
Whiten, Mark, 134
Whitson, Ed, 294
Wilhelm, Hoyt, 113
Williams, Lefty, 341
Williams, Smokey Joe, 150
Williams, Stan, 183
Williams, Ted, 11, 63, 123, 136, 155, 176, 177, 256, 279, 280, 314
Williamson, Ned, 139
Wills, Maury, 320
Wilson, Don, 369

Wilson, Hack, 237, 295, 299
Wilson, Mookie, 247, 248
Wilson, Owen, 155
Wiltse, Hooks, 329
Winfield, Dave, 58, 219, 251, 348
Wise, Rick, 208
Witt, Whitey, 287
Wolf, Chicken, 1, 5, 198, 232
Wood, Kerry, 133
Wood, Smokey Joe, 367
Wright, Clyde, 319
Wright, George, 8
Wrigley, Phil, 212
Wynegar, Butch, 224
Wynn, Early, 186
Wynn, Jimmy, 121
Wysong, Biff, 168

Yawkey, Tom, 272
Yelding, Eric, 91
Young, Anthony, 170
Young, Cy, 154, 222, 300
Young, Dick, 179
Youngblood, Joel, 213
Yount, Larry, 258
Yount, Robin, 258

Zachary, Tom, 178
Zeider, Rollie, 214
Zernial, Gus, 15
Zimmer, Don, 82, 190
Zimmerman, Heinie, 246, 288, 342

About the Author

Floyd Conner is a lifelong baseball fan and the author of ten books. His sports books include *Golf!*, *Fore!*, and *This Date in Sports History*. He also co-authored *Day By Day in Cincinnati Reds History* and the best-selling *365 Sports Facts a Year Calendar*. He lives in Cincinnati with his wife, Susan, and son, Travis.

The World Series' Most Wanted

Other sports titles from Brassey's, Inc.

Paths to Glory: How Baseball's Championship Teams Were Built by Mark L. Armour and Daniel R. Levitt

Bob Feller: Ace of the Greatest Generation by John Sickels

Throwbacks: Old-School Baseball Players in Today's Game by George Castle

Baseball's Most Wanted II: The Top 10 Book of More Bad Hops, Screwball Players, and Other Oddities by Floyd Conner

Mickey Mantle: America's Prodigal Son by Tony Castro

Weaver on Strategy: The Classic Work on the Art of Managing a Baseball Team by Earl Weaver with Terry Pluto

Baseball: The Writer's Game by Mike Shannon

Baseball's Most Wanted: The Top 10 Book of the National Pastime's Outrageous Offenders, Lucky Bounces, and Other Oddities by Floyd Conner

Boxing's Most Wanted: The Top 10 Book of Champs, Chumps, and Punch-Drunk Palookas by David L. Hudson Jr. and Mike Fitzgerald Jr.

The World Series' Most Wanted

The Top 10 Book of Championship Teams, Broken Dreams, and October Oddities

John Snyder

Brassey's, Inc.
WASHINGTON, D.C.

Copyright © 2004 by Brassey's, Inc.

Published in the United States by Brassey's, Inc. All rights reserved. No part of this book may be reproduced in any manner whatsoever without written permission from the publisher, except in the case of brief quotations embodied in critical articles and reviews.

Library of Congress Cataloging-in-Publication Data

Snyder, John, 1951–
    The World Series' most wanted : the top 10 book of championship teams, broken dreams, and October oddities / John Snyder.
       p. cm.
    Includes bibliographical references and index.
    ISBN 1-57488-728-9 (pbk. : alk. paper)
    1. World Series (Baseball)—Miscellanea. 2. Baseball teams—United States—Miscellanea. I. Title.
GV878.4.S685 2003
796.357'646—dc22   2003021545

Printed in Canada on acid-free paper

Brassey's, Inc.
22841 Quicksilver Drive
Dulles, Virginia 20166

First Edition

10 9 8 7 6 5 4 3 2 1

Contents

List of Photographs	xi
Introduction	xiii
In the Beginning Tales from the first World Series	1
The Bambino, and Other Curses Teams that haven't won a title in decades	6
A Plaque in Cooperstown, but No Ring Hall-of-Famers who never won a World Series ring	11
Snatching Defeat from the Jaws of Victory Six outs or fewer from a title—and lost	15
So Close, yet So Far They won three but couldn't win the fourth	24
Loser Takes Nothing Game Seven heartbreaks	31
Say It Ain't So, Joe The Black Sox controversy	37
Controversies More World Series scandals	42

Are You Blind? — 48
Questionable calls by the men in blue

Men and Women Behaving Badly — 54
Outlandish actions by players and fans

Butchery, Bobbles, and Boots — 60
Embarrassing errors in the field

Want to Get Away? — 65
Mistakes and boneheaded blunders

Brain Cramps — 69
Mental gaffes

Perfection and Near Perfection — 74
Top World Series pitching performances

Rack 'Em Up — 81
Top World Series strikeout performances

Winning Three — 87
Pitchers who won three games in a single Series

Surprise Packages — 93
Bad pitchers who pitched a great game

Losers in a Duel — 98
Pitchers on the wrong end of a 1–0 score

If I Didn't Have Bad Luck, I Wouldn't Have Any Luck at All — 104
More pitching heartbreakers

Mound Misadventures — 111
Records they'd rather not have

Not Again! — 116
Pitchers who gave up back-to-back homers

Contents

Helping His Own Cause — **121**
Home runs hit by pitchers

Surprising Power — **126**
World Series homers from unlikely sources

Stepping Up When It Matters Most — **131**
Big-time play from little-known players

Starting with a Bang — **137**
Leadoff home runs

There's Only One Chance to Make a First Impression — **142**
A home run in their first World Series at-bat

A Pinch of Homers — **147**
Pinch-hit homers

Sweeping the Bases — **154**
Grand Slams in World Series history

Back-to-Back — **158**
Home runs in two straight at-bats

Going Deep — **163**
Two homers in one game

Sweet Strokes — **169**
Batting records in World Series play

Hitting 'Em Where They Are — **176**
10 lowest career World Series batting averages

No-Hitters — **180**
Players who went hitless in an entire Series

Stop, Thief! — **184**
Stealing home plate

The Man-Eating Tarp — 188
  Bizarre and unusual injuries

X-Rays of Dizzy's Head Found Nothing — 193
  Star players on the DL

Put Me in, Coach, I'm Ready to Play — 197
  Backups who replaced an injured teammate and shined

DNP—Manager's Decision — 203
  World Series benchwarmers

Have Ring, Will Travel — 209
  Playing in multiple Series for multiple teams

Let Me See Some ID — 212
  Youngest World Series participants

Pitching Phenoms — 215
  Outstanding rookie pitchers

Hitting Phenoms — 220
  Outstanding rookie hitters

Fortysomethings — 225
  Oldest World Series participants

You Don't Have to Play the Game — 230
  Managers who never played

Do As I Say, Not As I Do — 236
  Managers who played, but not well

Boy Wonders — 241
  Youngest managers in the World Series

Wise Sages — 246
  Oldest managers in the World Series

Nothing to It — 251
  Rookie managers who led their teams to the Series

Get Out the Broom World Series sweeps	256
Blowouts Lopsided losses	261
Even the Browns and the Cubs The World Series during World War II	267
Commanders in Chief Presidential participation	271
As Seen on TV Television trivia	275
Other Sports Baseball wasn't their only game	281
Hi! I'm Felipe. This Is My Brother Matty. And This Is My Other Brother Jesus. Brothers who both saw World Series action	286
One and Only Hitters Unique hitting escapades	290
One and Only Pitchers Unique pitching escapades	294
The Case of the Three-Year-Old Batboy Odd occurrences	298
Cool Things That Didn't Fit in Any Other List More oddities from baseball's championship	303
World Series Lasts These will never happen again	308
Bibliography	313
Index	315
About the Author	325

Photographs

Bill Buckner	21
Jim Lonborg	76
Sandy Koufax	82
Orel Hershiser	119
Joe Garagiola	133
Kirk Gibson	153
Johnny Bench	166
Billy Hatcher	174
Eric Davis	190
Tim McCarver	205
Carlton Fisk	279

Introduction

The National League, established in 1876, and the upstart American League, which was created in 1901, endured two years of player raids and vicious hostility. The American League signed many of baseball's big-name stars off the National League rosters before a peace accord was reached in January 1903. The agreement didn't make provisions for a postseason series, but in August of that year the Pittsburgh Pirates and the Boston Americans (renamed the Red Sox in 1907) were comfortably in front of their respective leagues. Pirates owner Barney Dreyfuss issued a challenge to Americans owner Henry Killilea to play for baseball's championship. Killilea accepted, and a best-of-nine series was set up to begin October 1 in Boston. Although all 16 major league teams then in existence were located east of St. Louis and north of Washington, the two owners didn't hesitate to call the confrontation the World Series (or World's Series, as it was often referred to in print as late as the 1930s). There were many postseason play-offs in the 19th century, but this first meeting of the National and American League champions is recognized as the first modern World Series.

The 1903 event received scant attention in the media of the day outside of Boston and Pittsburgh, but by the time the Pirates reached the World Series again in 1909, the Fall Classic was a front-page story from coast to coast. Radio, much less television, was still science fiction at the beginning of the 20th century, but fans in large cities could still follow the game pitch by pitch. Many newspapers placed large electronic scoreboards on the outside of their office buildings, with each pitch relayed by telegraph, and thousands gathered to "watch" the game.

Television has brought an immediacy to the World Series that couldn't have been imagined 100 years ago. The first Fall Classic took place two months before the Wright Brothers' first flight. The games are now beamed by satellite into homes worldwide.

The World Series' Most Wanted is a collection of the greatest moments, fantastic finishes, and champions, as well as the worst defeats, outrageous characters, unlikely heroes, comebacks, bizarre injuries, rookie performances, outlandish stunts, strange occurrences, bad behavior, brain cramps, and plain old bad luck. The book also introduces the reader to many new and fascinating facts about baseball's premier event.

In the Beginning

The favored Pirates won three of the first four games in the first World Series in 1903, but the Americans rallied to win the final four contests to win the first world championship by a five-games-to-three margin. Although the Arizona Diamondbacks are credited with winning a world title more quickly than any other team in history by capturing the Series in 2001 in their fourth year of existence, this honor actually belongs to the Boston Red Sox, who won the world title in the third year of the franchise's existence.

1. HUNTINGTON AVENUE GROUNDS

The first World Series game was played in Boston on Huntington Avenue Grounds, located in the city's South End neighborhood. The ballpark's dimensions are estimated to be 350 feet to left field, 530 feet to center, and 280 feet to right field, but those distances were cut down considerably during the 1903 World Series because thousands of fans lined up behind ropes in the outfield. The small grandstand held only 9,000. The first game drew 16,242, and Game Three attracted 18,801. The contests in Pittsburgh were played at Exposition Park on the shore of the Allegheny River near the present-day site of PNC Park. Because of its location on the river's floodplain and notorious poor drainage, the outfield at Exposition Park could often be best described as a marsh. As in Boston, fans were lined up behind barriers against the outfield fences.

2. CY YOUNG

It's appropriate that the first pitch in the first World Series was thrown by Cy Young, baseball's all-time leading winner and the man for whom the annual award for the top pitcher in each league is named. He was also one of the top prizes in the American League player raids of National League rosters in 1901. Young bolted the St. Louis Cardinals to sign with Boston. He won an all-time record 511 major league games during his career, far ahead of Walter Johnson, who is second with 417. When he appeared in the 1903 World Series, Young had a career record of 379–200. He retired the first two batters to face him, but the next six hitters reached base and Pittsburgh scored four runs before Boston had a chance to bat. Pittsburgh won the game 7–3. Young made two more starts plus a seven-inning relief stint in the Series and finished the 1903 Series with a 2–1 record and a 1.85 earned run average in 34 innings.

3. GINGER BEAUMONT

Pittsburgh center fielder Ginger Beaumont was the first batter in the World Series. He flied out to Boston center fielder Chick Stahl. Beaumont was known for his speed despite his chunky five-foot-eight-inch, 190-pound build. He hit .311 in a 12-year career that began in 1899. Beaumont hit .341 and collected 209 base hits in 1903 and led the National League in hits in 1902, 1903, 1904, and 1907. His last big league appearance was in the 1910 World Series as a pinch-hitter for the Cubs against the Philadelphia Athletics.

4. CHICK STAHL

Chick Stahl, who recorded the first putout in World Series play, met a bad end. He was named Boston's manager in 1907 but committed suicide during spring training by swallowing carbolic acid. What drove Stahl to take his own life remains a mystery. It was obvious to observers at the time that he was under a great deal of stress, and many people attributed it to anxiety over taking the job as Red Sox manager, but it was more likely the result of excessive womanizing. Stahl had married the previous November, impregnated a second woman, and a third fired a gun at him twice for terminating their relationship.

5. DEACON PHILLIPPE

Deacon Phillippe was the winning pitcher in the first World Series game. Because of injuries and illnesses that decimated the Pittsburgh pitching staff, Phillippe was forced to start five of the eight games of the 1903 World Series. Each was a complete game. His five starts, five complete games, and 45 innings pitched remain records and will likely stand for an eternity. He made his second start with one day of rest, his third after two days off, and his fourth after three. He made his fifth start after two days' rest and the Pirates facing elimination. A weary Phillippe lost 3–0. He pitched admirably in the 1903 Classic, winning three and losing two with a 2.86 ERA. Phillippe finished his career in 1911 with a 189–109 record. He walked only 363 batters in 2,607 innings, the best walks-to-innings ratio in big league history by a pitcher throwing from the 60-foot-six-inch distance established in 1893.

6. ED DOHENY AND SAM LEEVER

One of the reasons that Deacon Phillippe had to start five games was the mental breakdown of Ed Doheny and an injury to Sam Leever just prior to the Series. A 16-game winner in 1903, Doheny went completely berserk in Boston and beat several men over the head with a poker because he believed that detectives were spying on him. Paranoid, he was committed to an insane asylum in Danvers, Massachusetts. There he assaulted a doctor with a cast-iron stove footrest. Doheny never pitched in another big league game and was still institutionalized when he died in 1916. Leever was not only an excellent pitcher, compiling a 25–7 mark in 1903, but also a championship trapshooter. Just before the World Series began, Leever injured his throwing shoulder in a shooting contest. He made two starts against Boston but was ineffective and lost both of them.

7. JIMMY SEBRING

Pittsburgh right fielder Jimmy Sebring collected the first home run in the World Series, a seventh-inning blast to center field in the first game off Cy Young. Sebring hit only four regular-season homers in 1903 and just six during his five-year big league career. Sebring quit major league baseball at the age of 27 while with the Cincinnati Reds in 1905 to return to his home in Williamsport, Pennsylvania, to care for his ailing wife. He continued to earn a living by playing for independent teams in the Williamsport area. Sebring returned to the majors in 1909 but lasted only 26 games.

8. TOMMY LEACH

Pirates third baseman Tommy Leach collected the first hit in World Series history and scored the first run. He remains the only player in World Series history to hit four triples in a single Series. He was helped by the ground rules, which stipulated that balls hit into the overflow crowds in the outfield were ground rule triples, in seven of the eight games. The two teams in 1903 combined to hit 25 triples and just 11 doubles during the Series. No other Series in history has had more than 11 triples. In the 1909 World Series, Leach was involved in a bizarre play while playing center field for the Pirates against the Detroit Tigers. The Pirates had moved to Forbes Field and placed temporary seats against the outfield wall behind a flimsy wooden fence with four horizontal planks. Retreating on a fly ball hit by Sam Crawford, Leach leaped against the fence, broke through the top two boards, and landed on his neck. The ball fell harmlessly for a home run.

9. BILL DINNEEN

The first pitching star of the first World Series was Boston's Bill Dinneen. He pitched not only the first shutout in the history of the Fall Classic, but the second as well. Dinneen shut out the Pirates in Game Two on three hits and fanned 11. In the eighth-game clincher in Boston, Dinneen outdueled Deacon Phillippe 3–0 on a four-hitter. Dinneen is one of only 10 pitchers who have thrown two shutouts in the World Series during a career, a list that includes five Hall-of-Famers. Dinneen won three of his four starts in the Series and had a 2.06 ERA. He struck out a total of 28 batters, which remained the record for a single Series until Bob Gibson broke it in 1964. Dinneen ended his playing career in 1909 with a record of 171–177. He was hired by the American League as an umpire and stayed on the job for 29 years. He umpired in 45 World Series games. He is also the only person to pitch a regular-season no-hitter and to umpire in one.

10. JIMMY COLLINS

Jimmy Collins was the manager of the championship Boston club in 1903. He was also the top third baseman of his era. Playing in all eight games, Collins batted .250 in the 1903 Series. Other player-managers who won a World Series include Fielder Jones (1906 White Sox), Frank Chance (1907–08 Cubs), Jake Stahl (1912 Red Sox), Tris Speaker (1920 Indians), Bucky Harris (1924 Senators), Rogers Hornsby (1926 Cardinals), Joe Cronin (1933 Senators), Frankie Frisch (1934 Cardinals), Mickey Cochrane (1935 Tigers), and Lou Boudreau (1948 Indians).

The Bambino, and Other Curses

The Cubs and the Red Sox continued to torture their fans during the 2003 post-season by blowing a golden opportunity to reach the World Series. Of the 24 big league franchises in existence in 1969, 10 have failed to win a World Series since the end of the Nixon administration.

1. **CHICAGO CUBS**

During the 1945 World Series, tavern owner William "Billy Goat" Sianis bought a box seat ticket for his pet goat, which he escorted to Wrigley Field. Club officials ordered Sianis to leave the premises and to take his goat with him. In retaliation, Sianis cast a "goat curse" on the Cubs, claiming the club would never play in the World Series again. Not only have the Cubs failed to appear in a World Series since 1945 but they haven't won a world championship since 1908, when Theodore Roosevelt was in the White House. That championship followed a similar triumph in 1907, which made the Cubs the first franchise to win back-to-back World Series. The last time the Cubs put together consecutive winning seasons was in 1971–72. The "goat curse" persists, although the Cubs tried to make amends by inviting William Sianis's nephew Sam Sianis to the 1984 National League Championship Series accompanied by a goat to parade on the field. Sam Sianis, who still owns the Billy Goat Tavern, was also the inspiration for a skit on *Saturday Night Live* featuring John Belushi, in which the late comedian hollered, "Cheeseburger! Cheeseburger! Cheeseburger! No Pepsi! Coke! No Fries! Chips!"

2. **CHICAGO WHITE SOX**

Defying almost all logic and statistical probability, neither of Chicago's major league baseball teams have captured a world championship since the White Sox won it all in 1917 or played in a World Series since 1959. The White Sox franchise fell on hard times after eight White Sox players conspired to throw the 1919 Series to the Cincinnati Reds and were barred from the sport for life. The White Sox didn't reach the World Series again for 40 years, when Chicago's American League entry lost to the Los Angeles Dodgers in six games in 1959. The current World Series drought has passed the 40-year mark, although the White Sox had the best record in the American League in both 1983 and 2000.

3. **BOSTON RED SOX**

The Red Sox won five of the first 15 World Series played, taking the championship in 1903, 1912, 1915, 1916, and 1918. Counting the Series won by the Braves in 1914, the city of Boston celebrated five world championships in seven seasons from 1912 through 1918. After the 1919 season ended with a sixth-place finish, the Red Sox sold pitcher-turned-outfielder Babe Ruth to the Yankees in the most infamous deal in baseball history. The "Curse of the Bambino" has cast a pall over Boston baseball ever since. The hated Yankees, who hadn't even played in the World Series before Ruth arrived, have been in 39 Fall Classics, winning it all 26 times. The Red Sox have been in the World Series four times (1946, 1967, 1975, and 1986) since 1918 and each time lost the seventh and deciding game, often in agonizing fashion.

4. **CLEVELAND INDIANS**

Cleveland hasn't celebrated a world championship since 1948, when player-manager Lou Boudreau led the club to a six-game win over the Boston Braves. The Indians had a 111–43 record in 1954, compiling an American League record .721 winning percentage, but were swept in the World Series by the New York Giants. Indians fans endured a long stretch during the 1960s, 1970s, 1980s, and early 1990s in which a winning record was rare and pennant contention was nonexistent. A move from cavernous Municipal Stadium to Jacobs Field in 1994 helped spark a revival in Cleveland baseball and World Series appearances in 1995 and 1997, but the Indians lost both times.

5. SAN FRANCISCO GIANTS

The Giants moved from New York to San Francisco in 1958 and have yet to win a World Series in California despite the presence of such players as Willie Mays, Barry Bonds, Willie McCovey, Juan Marichal, Gaylord Perry, and Orlando Cepeda. The last world championship for the franchise was in 1954, when the Giants upset the Indians in four games. In San Francisco, the Giants lost the World Series to the Yankees in 1962, to the Athletics in the earthquake-marred Series of 1989, and to the Angels in 2002.

6. TEXAS RANGERS

The Texas Rangers were born in 1961 as the Washington Senators, an expansion club that entered the American League in the same season as the Angels. The club moved to Texas in 1972 with Ted Williams as manager and has never reached the American League Championship Series, much less the World Series. The only postseason appearances by the Rangers were in the Division Series in 1996, 1998, and 1999, each time against the Yankees. After defeating the Yankees in the first game in 1996, the Rangers lost nine postseason games in a row while scoring a grand total of only 12 runs.

7. HOUSTON ASTROS

The state of Texas is still looking to host its first World Series. The Astros were established as an expansion club in 1962 in tandem with the Mets and reached the National League Championship Series in 1980 and 1986, only to lose. Since the play-off format was expanded to eight teams in 1995, Houston reached the Division Series in 1997, 1998, 1999, and 2001, but compiled only a 2–12 record. Together, the Rangers and the Astros dropped 23 of their last 26 postseason games since Houston's losses in the final two games of the 1986 NLCS.

8. MILWAUKEE BREWERS

Among the four 1969 expansion franchises, only the Kansas City Royals have won a world championship. The Brewers entered the American League with the Royals as the Seattle Pilots and moved to Milwaukee in 1970. The city was previously the home of the Braves from 1953 through 1965, and the club won the World Series in 1957 and appeared in another a year later. Since the Braves left for Atlanta, Milwaukee has hosted only one World Series, that in 1982, resulting in a seven-game Brewers loss to the Cardinals. Should the franchise ever reach the World Series again, it will become the first to represent both the American League and the National League in the Fall Classic. After 11 straight losing seasons, including a 56–106 debacle in 2002, it's unlikely to happen anytime soon.

9. SAN DIEGO PADRES

The Padres joined the National League in 1969 and didn't post a winning record for 15 years. During the early years, the club's most enduring legacy was owner Ray Kroc grabbing the public address microphone and claiming he'd never "seen such stupid ball playing in my life." "Every year it's predicted that the Padres are about to go somewhere," wrote sportswriter Tom Boswell in 1981. "And every year it turns out to be the beach." The Padres played in the World Series in 1984 against the Tigers and in 1998 against the Yankees but lost eight of the nine games. San Diego has had only eight winning seasons through 2002 and has never had more than two winning seasons in succession.

10. **MONTREAL EXPOS**

As the 2004 season opened, the future of the Expos in Canada was very much in doubt. Established in 1969, the Expos have never reached the World Series. The only League Championship Series appearance for the franchise was in 1981, when the club lost to the Dodgers. The Expos played 22 "home" games at Hiram Bithorn Stadium in San Juan, Puerto Rico, in 2003. Hiram Bithorn was a pitcher on the Chicago Cubs last World Series team in 1945.

A Plaque in Cooperstown, but No Ring

Dozens of players with careers that could be described as mediocre at best have played in more than one World Series, yet many of the game's greatest stars have reached the Hall of Fame without ever competing in a World Series.

1. **ERNIE BANKS**

Ernie Banks played 19 seasons in the majors between 1953 and 1971 as a shortstop and first baseman and clubbed 512 home runs, all with the Cubs, but never played in a postseason game. In fact, Banks played on only six teams that posted a winning record. The closest he came to the postseason was in 1969, when the Cubs held a $9^1/_2$-game lead over the Mets in the Eastern Division race, only to blow the advantage and finish second eight games out. Despite playing for a string of losing teams, Banks was known for his sunny disposition, his positive attitude, and the phrase "Let's play two." He won the Most Valuable Player award in both 1958 and 1959 with clubs that finished in fifth place.

2. **ROD CAREW**

Rod Carew spent 19 seasons in the majors, from 1967 through 1985, with the Twins and Angels and collected 3,053 hits. Carew came close to playing in the Series on several occasions. When he was a rookie in 1967, the Twins needed only to win one of the final two regular-season games against the Red Sox to win the American League pennant, but the Twins lost them both. Carew played in two League Championship Series with the Twins and two more with the Angels but was on the losing side all four times. Carew is the only player since 1900 to collect at least 3,000 hits without playing in the Series.

3. **GAYLORD PERRY**

As a rookie in 1962, Gaylord Perry pitched 13 games for the National League pennant–winning Giants but wasn't included on the World Series eligibility roster. Perry later played for the Indians, Rangers, Padres, Yankees, Braves, Mariners, and Royals through 1983 on the way to winning 314 big league games without experiencing the thrill of pitching in the World Series. Perry did pitch in the NLCS with the Giants against the Pirates in 1971, winning one start and losing another, as Pittsburgh won three of the four games. Gaylord's brother Jim won 215 big league games between 1959 and 1975 and made two relief appearances in the World Series with the Twins in 1965.

4. **FERGUSON JENKINS**

Ferguson Jenkins had seven seasons with 20 or more wins and posted a 284–226 lifetime record from 1965 through 1983. After breaking into the majors with eight games with the Phillies, Jenkins played for the Cubs, Rangers, and Red Sox. Not only did Jenkins not play for a league-pennant winner during his career but he never even played for a club that won a division title.

5. **GEORGE SISLER**

George Sisler batted .340 with 2,812 base hits as a first baseman with the St. Louis Browns, Washington Senators, and Boston Braves between 1915 and 1930 without playing in a World Series. He came close in 1922, when the Browns finished the season one game back of the first-place Yankees, but Sisler played on only four teams with a winning record in 16 seasons in the big leagues.

6. TED LYONS

Ted Lyons had a 260–230 record for a string of mediocre Chicago White Sox clubs between 1923 and 1946. He played on only six teams that had a winning record, and none of them ended the season fewer than eight games out of first place. The best finishes for a Chicago team during the Lyons era were third place in 1936, 1937, and 1941.

7. LUKE APPLING

Appling was a teammate of Lyons for more than a decade. He played his entire career with the White Sox, batting .310 with 2,749 hits, playing mostly as a shortstop. Like Lyons, Appling seldom played for a winning team, and none of his teams finished higher than third.

8. BILLY WILLIAMS

Billy Williams is yet another Chicago baseball player with a long Hall of Fame career who never played in a World Series. He was with the Cubs from 1959 through 1974. Williams went to the Oakland Athletics in 1975, a club that had won the world championship the previous three seasons. The Athletics couldn't make it four in a row, however, although they won the Western Division title. In the 1975 ALCS, Williams was hitless in eight at-bats as a designated hitter and the Red Sox swept the Athletics.

9. PHIL NIEKRO

Phil Niekro won 318 major league games in 24 seasons from 1964 through 1987, while with the Braves, Yankees, Indians, and Blue Jays, but he was never able to use his dancing knuckleball in the World Series. No player since 1900 has won more regular-season games without playing in the Fall Classic. Phil played in the NLCS with the Braves in 1969 and

1982 but had a loss and a no decision in two starts. He did throw out the first ball in a World Series, however, prior to Game Four between the Marlins and the Indians in Cleveland in 1997. Niekro stood on the mound amid snow flurries. The game-time temperature was 38 degrees, the coldest ever for a World Series game.

10. **HARRY HEILMANN**

Harry Heilmann won four batting titles with the Tigers and played in the outfield with Ty Cobb but never reached the World Series. He batted .342 during his major league career from 1914 through 1932. No one since 1900 has a higher lifetime batting average without playing in a World Series.

Snatching Defeat from the Jaws of Victory

Ten clubs have needed only seven outs or fewer to win a world championship but failed to close the deal.

1. **1912 NEW YORK GIANTS**

The 1912 World Series between the Giants and the Red Sox went to a deciding *eighth* game, because Game Two ended in a 6–6 tie, called after 11 innings due to darkness. The eighth game was played at Fenway Park, which had opened the previous April. The contest entered extra innings with the score 1–1. The Giants broke the deadlock by scoring in the 10th inning against reliever Smokey Joe Wood, on a double by Red Murray and a single by Fred Merkle. With Christy Mathewson on the mound for the Giants, the title appeared to be in the bag. Clyde Engle started the Boston 10th by lofting a towering fly to the outfield. New York center fielder Fred Snodgrass only had to move about 10 feet to make the play, but the ball bounced out of his glove. Harry Hooper followed with a low liner toward center, and Snodgrass made amends by making a remarkable running catch. After Steve Yerkes walked, Tris Speaker hit a harmless pop foul to the right side of the diamond. Mathewson, first baseman Fred Merkle, and catcher Chief Meyers all converged on the ball, but there was confusion over who would make the catch. Merkle had the best chance of making the play, but he stopped. Meyers made a desperate rush for the ball but couldn't reach it, and the pop-up fell harmlessly to earth in foul territory a few feet from first base. Given new life, Speaker singled to score Engle and send Yerkes to third. After Duffy Lewis was intentionally walked, Larry Gardner hit a sacrifice fly to give the Red Sox the championship. Snodgrass never lived down muffing the routine play in the 1912 Series. When he died nearly 62 years later in 1974, his obituary in *The New York Times* was headlined "Fred Snodgrass, 86, Dead, Ballplayer Muffed 1912 Fly." The Giants suffered a similar meltdown in 1924.

2. 1924 NEW YORK GIANTS

The Washington Senators reached the World Series for the first time in 1924, and faced the New York Giants, who won their 10th National League pennant in 21 years. The seventh game was played at Griffith Stadium in Washington, and the Giants led 3–1 going into the eighth inning. Pinch-hitter Nemo Leibold drilled a one-out double for the Senators off Giants pitcher Jesse Barnes, which brought Muddy Ruel to the plate. Ruel was hitless in his previous 18 at-bats in the Series but singled Leibold to third. Bennie Tate walked to load the bases. Earl McNeely hit a shallow fly ball to left field for the second out, with all the runners holding. Player-manager Bucky Harris hit a routine grounder toward third baseman Fred Lindstrom for what appeared to be the third out, but the ball took a wicked hop and careened over Lindstrom's head for a single that scored two runs to tie the score 3–3. It was still 3–3 in the 12th inning, with Jack Bentley on the mound for New York. With one out, Ruel lifted a pop foul behind home plate, but Giants catcher Hank Gowdy tripped over his mask and dropped the ball. Ruel promptly doubled. McNeely, a rookie with only 43 regular season games on his résumé, hit an easy grounder to third, but just as in the eighth inning, the ball inexplicably skipped over Lindstrom's glove and Ruel crossed the plate for the winning run.

3. **1925 WASHINGTON SENATORS**

The Senators were the victims of an incredible last-minute rally in the 1925 Series against the Pirates. The Senators took three of the first four games, but lost 6–3 in Washington and 3–2 in Pittsburgh to even the Series at three games apiece. The seventh game was delayed a day by rain, and it continued to rain throughout the deciding game, ranging from a drizzle to a downpour. The low rain clouds shrouded Pittsburgh's Forbes Field in darkness, and the playing field was a morass. Washington's starting pitcher was icon Walter Johnson, who opposed Vic Aldridge. The Senators blasted Aldridge for four runs in the first inning and led 6–4 heading into the seventh. Eddie Moore led off the Pittsburgh seventh and reached second base as Washington shortstop Roger Peckinpaugh muffed his pop-up in short left field. The gaffe led to two runs to tie the score at 6–6. Peckinpaugh broke the deadlock by smacking a solo homer in the eighth to put the Senators back on top, but there was more woe in store for him in the bottom half. Johnson retired the first two hitters and stopped the game briefly to call for the grounds crew to apply sawdust to the slippery mound. Earl Smith and Carson Bigbee both doubled to make the score 7–7. After Moore walked, Peckinpaugh fielded a Max Carey grounder and made a bad throw to second trying for the force. It was Peckinpaugh's eighth error of the Series, which set the all-time record. With the bases loaded, Kiki Cuyler hit a double, scoring two runs to give the Pirates a 9–7 win and the world championship. After the game, Cuyler was carried on the shoulders of grateful fans to his home a half mile from Forbes Field. Senators manager Bucky Harris was criticized by American League president Ban Johnson for leaving the 37-year-old pitcher in for the entire game, claiming the decision was made out of "mawkish sentiment." During the long afternoon, Johnson set single-game Series records for most hits allowed (15), most doubles allowed (eight), most extra base hits allowed (nine), and most total bases allowed (25).

The Pirates didn't win another world championship until 1960.

4. 1960 NEW YORK YANKEES

Entering the seventh game of the 1960 World Series at Forbes Field in Pittsburgh, the Yankees had outscored the Pirates 46–17. After losing the first game 6–4, the Yankees rebounded to win 16–3 and 10–0 before dropping 3–2 and 5–2 decisions. In Game Six, the Yankees stayed in contention by trouncing the Pirates again 12–0. Pittsburgh started the seventh game by taking a 4–0 lead with two runs in the first inning and two more in the second. The Yankees got on board with a run in the fifth and took a 5–4 lead with four in the sixth, the last three on Yogi Berra's homer into the right field stands. With two more tallies in the eighth, New York had a three-run lead and needed only six outs to win the Series. In the Pirates eighth, four singles netted two runs to cut the deficit to one run. With two on and two out, reserve catcher Hal Smith clubbed a three-run homer off Jim Coates to give Pittsburgh a 9–7 lead. It looked as though Smith was going to go down as one of the greatest heroes in Series history, but the Yankees came back to score twice to tie the game 9–9. Bill Mazeroski led off the Pirates ninth against Ralph Terry and, on a 1–0 pitch, ended the drama with a home run over the left field wall at the 402-foot sign to lift the Pirates to a 10–9 win and the world title. Mazeroski circled the bases waving his batting helmet in the air in a whirling motion amid fans enthusiastically pouring onto the field. It's the only time that a seventh game of a World Series ended with a home run. It's also the only game in World Series history in which no one struck out. It would be another 42 years before another *team* completed a World Series game without a batter striking out. It was accomplished by the Angels in Game Two in 2002 in an 11–10 win over the Giants.

5. 1975 BOSTON RED SOX

The Red Sox evened the 1975 World Series against the Reds with a thrilling victory in Game Six at Fenway Park. Trailing

6–3 in the eighth inning, Bernie Carbo hit a three-run homer to tie the score, and Carlton Fisk homered in the 12th over the left field foul pole to give the Sox a 7–6 victory. With Bill Lee on the mound, the Red Sox led 3–0 after five innings in the seventh game. With two out in the sixth, Lee threw a blooper pitch to Tony Perez that went sailing over the Green Monster for a two-run homer. A run-scoring single by Pete Rose with two out in the seventh off reliever Roger Moret tied the score 3–3. The Reds won it in the ninth on another two-out hit, a bloop single by Joe Morgan off Jim Burton. Will McEnaney retired Boston in order to seal the 4–3 victory. It was Cincinnati's first world championship since 1940.

6. **1985 ST. LOUIS CARDINALS**

The name Don Denkinger is not one to utter in polite company in the vicinity of St. Louis. The umpire's blown call in the sixth game of the 1985 World Series cost the Cardinals the world championship. The Cardinals had a three-games-to-two advantage and led the Royals 1–0 heading into the bottom of the ninth in Kansas City. Jorge Orta led off the ninth as a pinch-hitter and hit a bouncer to first baseman Jack Clark, who flipped the ball to pitcher Todd Worrell. Denkinger ruled that Orta was safe, and replays proved that Worrell beat Orta to the bag. The Cards were still in reasonably good shape, needing just three outs for the title, but Clark failed to catch a pop-up by Steve Balboni in foul territory. Balboni responded by stroking a single. A passed ball moved the Kansas City runners to second and third with one out, and Hal McRae was intentionally walked. With the bases loaded, pinch-hitter Dane Iorg singled to right field to give the Royals a 2–1 victory. There was still a Game Seven, and the Cardinals starting pitcher was John Tudor, who had won 23 of his last 25 decisions, counting the postseason. Tudor and the Cardinals came apart at the seams, however, and lost 11–0. Joaquin Andujar entered the game in relief in the fifth inning with the Cardinals trailing 9–0 and faced only two batters. He was ejected along with manager Whitey Herzog for arguing calls by Denkinger, who was umpiring behind the plate. Andujar had to be physically restrained from attacking Denkinger. Bret Saberhagen, who was just 21 years old and had become a father a day earlier, pitched the shutout.

7. **1986 BOSTON RED SOX**

The 1986 Red Sox are the only club in history to be one out away from a world championship only to lose. The Red Sox, in fact, were twice one strike away from sipping champagne, once while holding a two-run lead and once with a one-run advantage. In the sixth game against the Mets at Shea Stadium, the Red Sox scored two runs in the top of the 10th, the first on a homer by Dave Henderson, to take a 5–3 lead. Calvin Schiraldi retired the first two New York hitters in the bottom half before Gary Carter lined a 2–1 pitch to left for a single. Pinch-hitter Kevin Mitchell lined an 0–1 offering to center for another single, moving Carter to second. Schiraldi put Ray Knight in an 0–2 hole, and one strike away from Boston's first world championship since 1918, he allowed Knight to loop a single into center to score Carter. Bob Stanley replaced Schiraldi and ran Mookie Wilson to a 2–2 count. The Sox were again a strike away from winning when Stanley threw a wild pitch to allow Mitchell to score from third and Knight to move to second. Wilson grounded the next pitch over the first base bag and through Bill Buckner's legs for an error. Knight scored, and the Mets had an unbelievable 6–5 win. There was still a seventh game, but the ghosts of Red Sox past were still around to keep the "Curse of the Bambino" alive. Boston had a 3–0 lead in the sixth inning when the Mets scored three to tie. Knight broke the deadlock with a homer in the seventh, and the Mets won 8–5. It was also Knight's last game as a New York Met. The following February, he signed a free agent contract with the Orioles.

8. **1997 CLEVELAND INDIANS**

Cleveland hadn't celebrated a world champion baseball team since 1948. Heading into the ninth inning of Game

Snatching Defeat from the Jaws of Victory 21

Boston Red Sox

Bill Buckner's wide stance at the plate didn't translate well to playing defense in the 1986 World Series.

Seven in 1997 against the Marlins in Miami, the Indians were just two outs away. With Jose Mesa pitching and Cleveland leading 2–1, Moises Alou started the Florida ninth with a single. After Bobby Bonilla struck out, Charles Johnson singled to advance Alou to third. Craig Counsell put Alou across the plate with a sacrifice fly to tie the score 2–2 and send the contest into extra innings. The Marlins won the World Series in the 11th inning. With Charles Nagy pitching, Bonilla led off with a single, and Counsell reached base on an error by second baseman Tony Fernandez with one out. Jim Eisenreich was intentionally walked to load the bases, and after Bonilla was forced at the plate for the second out, Edgar Renteria whistled a single into center field for a 3–2 victory and the championship. By midseason in 1998, Marlins owner Wayne Huizenga sold, traded, or failed to offer a contract to all of his high-salaried players and Florida sank to a 54–108 record in 1998. It is easily the worst record by a defending world champion in history, shattering the previous mark by the 1991 Reds, who were 74–88.

9. 2001 NEW YORK YANKEES

There will never be another World Series like the one in 2001. It began just 46 days after the September 11 terrorist attacks. The third, fourth, and fifth games were played at Yankee Stadium, just 9½ miles (as the crow flies) from the World Trade Center. President George W. Bush threw out the first ball prior to Game Three. The attacks pushed the end of the regular season and the play-offs back a week, and for the first time, the World Series was played on Halloween and in November. The Yankees were gunning for their fourth consecutive world championship and were playing the Diamondbacks, who were in the Fall Classic for the first time in just the fourth year of their existence. Each team won three of the first six games, but Arizona outscored the Yankees 34–12. The Yankees won all three games in New York by one run, the final two in storybook fashion. Games Four and Five were both tied with two-run homers with two outs in the ninth and won in extra innings. The Yankees were just three outs away from their fourth straight title in the seventh game with a 2–1 lead heading into the ninth in Arizona and Mariano Rivera on the mound. At that point, Rivera had a phenomenal 0.69 ERA in 78$^{2}/_{3}$ postseason innings during his career and had recorded the final out of the 1998, 1999, and 2000 Series. He is the only pitcher to get the final out of a World Series three times in his career. He failed to make it four. A single by Mark Grace, an error by Rivera, and a one-out double by Tony Womack tied the score 2–2. Luis Gonzalez hit a single to bring Jay Bell across the plate with the championship run.

10. **2002 SAN FRANCISCO GIANTS**

The 2002 Giants had a 5–0 lead and were only eight outs away from hoisting their first world championship since moving to San Francisco in 1958 when disaster struck. Russ Ortiz shut out the Angels for six innings before giving up two one-out singles in the seventh. Giants manager Dusty Baker brought in Felix Rodriguez, and at the end of an eight-pitch at-bat, Scott Spezio homered off Rodriguez to close the gap to 5–3. Despite the Anaheim rally, San Francisco still needed just six outs for the title. Tim Worrell was on the mound for the Giants in the eighth and surrendered a leadoff homer to Darrin Erstad. After Tim Salmon and Garrett Anderson singled, Robb Nen was brought in to pitch to Troy Glaus, who doubled in two runs to put the Angels ahead 6–5. Troy Percival retired the Giants in order in the ninth. In Game Seven, the Giants went down 4–1.

So Close, yet So Far

Here are ten other clubs that have been on the verge of a world championship, only to fail to deliver in the clutch.

1. 1926 NEW YORK YANKEES

The St. Louis Cardinals reached the World Series for the first time in 1926 and trailed the vaunted Yankees three games to two heading into Yankee Stadium for the final two games. With Grover Cleveland Alexander on the mound, the Cardinals evened the Series with a 10–2 win in Game Six. (At 39, Alexander is the oldest pitcher to hurl a complete game in a World Series.) In the seventh game, the Cards led 3–2 in the seventh inning when the Yankees loaded the bases with two out off Jesse Haines, and manager Rogers Hornsby brought in Alexander in relief. Legend has it that Alexander spent the time after his Game Six victory celebrating into the wee hours of the night and was suffering from a hangover. On a 1–1 pitch, Tony Lazzeri lined a drive down the left field line that landed foul by only two feet. Alexander got the next pitch past Lazzeri for an inning-ending strikeout. Alexander retired the Yankees in order in the eighth and the first two batters in the ninth before he walked Babe Ruth. For reasons known only to himself, Ruth tried to steal second base and was thrown out. It is the only time that a World Series ended on a botched stolen base attempt.

2. **1934 DETROIT TIGERS**

Like the 1926 Yankees, the 1934 Tigers had a three-games-to-two lead over the Cardinals and needed just one win in their own ballpark to win a World Series. In the sixth game, the score was 3–3 in the seventh inning when Detroit pitcher Schoolboy Rowe allowed a double to eighth-place hitter Leo Durocher and a single to opposing pitcher Paul Dean to fall behind 4–3. The Tigers had their chances but failed to score. Pete Fox led off the seventh with a double but couldn't score. In the eighth, there were runners on second and third with one out, but Billy Rogell hit a shallow fly to center, with the runners holding, and Hank Greenberg fouled to first baseman Ripper Collins. In the seventh game, the Cardinals jumped all over the Tigers, winning 11–0, as Paul Dean's more famous brother Dizzy pitched the shutout. It set a record for the most lopsided Game Seven in Series history, tied by the Royals' 11–0 victory over the Cardinals in 1985.

3. **1946 BOSTON RED SOX**

The Red Sox suffered the first of their agonizing seventh-game defeats in 1946. Boston was in the World Series for the first time since 1918 and squared off against the Cardinals, who were in the Fall Classic for the ninth time since 1926. At Sportsman's Park in St. Louis, the Red Sox tied Game Seven 3–3 in the eighth on a two-run double by Dom DiMaggio, but he had to be removed from the game with a twisted ankle. Leon Culberson took DiMaggio's place in center field. With Bob Klinger pitching, Enos Slaughter led off the Cardinals eighth with a single. After the next two hitters were retired, Harry Walker lined a pitch over the head of shortstop Johnny Pesky. Culberson fielded the ball and relayed it back to Pesky, who was unaware that Slaughter hadn't slowed down and was rounding third. Pesky hesitated for just a split second before turning to throw home, but it was just long enough for Slaughter to score to give the Cards a 4–3 lead. Walker reached second and was credited with a double on the play. The Sox started the ninth with singles by Rudy York and Bobby Doerr, but Harry Brecheen retired the next three hitters to nail down the title.

4. 1952 BROOKLYN DODGERS

The Yankees won a record five consecutive World Series from 1949 through 1953, and only one of those was extended to seven games. That was against the Dodgers in 1952. The Dodgers won the first, third, and fifth games and needed just one win at Ebbets Field to claim Brooklyn's first world championship. The Yankees stayed alive in Game Six, winning 3–2. The Dodgers had the go-ahead run at the plate in the eighth and ninth inning but couldn't score. In the seventh game, Brooklyn was down 4–2 in the seventh inning but had the bases loaded with one out. Bob Kuzava was summoned from the bullpen and struck out Duke Snider. On a full count, Jackie Robinson lifted a pop-up to the right side of the infield. Kuzava stood transfixed, and first baseman Joe Collins lost sight of the ball in the sun. With two runners already across the plate and another rounding third, second baseman Billy Martin dashed forward at full speed and made a miraculous catch knee-high between the pitcher's mound and first base. The Dodgers didn't threaten in either the eighth or the ninth inning and went home disappointed again.

5. 1958 MILWAUKEE BRAVES

The 1957 Braves defeated the Yankees in seven games in the World Series. In 1958, it appeared as though they would win the world championship for the second year in a row over the Yankees after taking three of the first four games with two home games remaining. The Yankees captured the last three contests, however, beginning in Game Five in New York with a 7–0 victory behind Bob Turley. The sixth game in Milwaukee went to extra innings, and the Yankees scored two runs in the 10th, the first on a homer by Gil McDougald off Warren Spahn and the second on three two-out singles. The Braves rallied in their half but came up a run short. Hank Aaron drove in a run with a two-out single and went to third on another single by Joe Adcock. Casey Stengel replaced Ryne Duren with Turley, who saved the game by inducing pinch-hitter Frank Torre to line out to McDougald at second base. In the seventh game, the Yankees won 6–2, breaking a 2–2 deadlock with four runs in the eighth. Turley, pitching for the third game in a row, contributed $6^{2}/_{3}$ innings of relief, allowing just one run.

6. 1962 SAN FRANCISCO GIANTS

In the 1962 World Series, the Yankees won the first, third, fifth, and seventh games, while the Giants captured the even-numbered contests. The seventh game was played at Candlestick Park. The starting pitchers were Jack Sanford for the Giants and Ralph Terry for the Yankees. Just two years earlier, Terry had allowed the seventh-game, ninth-inning home run to Bill Mazeroski, which gave the Pirates the championship. Terry retired the first 17 batters to face him and still held a 1–0 advantage when the Giants went to bat in the ninth. Pinch-hitter Matty Alou opened the inning with a bunt single, only the third Giants hit of the game. After Matty's brother Felipe and Chuck Hiller both struck out, Willie Mays hit a drive toward the right field corner. Roger Maris made a great stop to prevent the ball from going to the wall but was suffering from a sore arm. Second baseman Bobby Richardson raced at full speed into the outfield to make Maris's throw as short as possible. Richardson made a perfect relay to hold Alou to third base. Willie McCovey ended the game by hitting a scorching line drive right at Richardson. Had the ball gone a foot to either the right or the left of Richardson, the Giants would have been world champions.

7. 1968 ST. LOUIS CARDINALS

The 1968 Cardinals put the Tigers in a 3–1 deficit in the 1968 World Series with two games left to be played in St. Louis. It looked as though the Cards would close out the Series in

Detroit in Game Five. Tigers starting pitcher Mickey Lolich gave up three runs in the first inning but shut out the Cards the rest of the way. St. Louis blew an opportunity to score in the fifth when Lou Brock elected to stand up instead of sliding on a play at the plate and was tagged out by Tigers catcher Bill Freehan. Detroit fought back with two runs in the fourth, but St. Louis was still eight outs away from the championship when Lolich hit a one-out single in the seventh. After Dick McAuliffe singled and Mickey Stanley walked to load the bases, Al Kaline hit a two-run single off Joe Hoerner to put the Tigers ahead 4–3. Another single by Norm Cash netted an insurance run, and the Tigers won 5–3. The Cardinals weren't even in the running in the sixth game, as Detroit took a 12–0 lead with a 10-run third inning and won 13–1. The Tigers won the seventh game 4–1, with the turning point coming when the score was 0–0 in the seventh inning. With two out, Cash and Willie Horton singled off Bob Gibson, and Jim Northrup lined a shot to center fielder Curt Flood, who won seven Gold Gloves during his career, including one in 1968. Flood misjudged the ball, however, and it sailed past him for a triple to score the first two runs of the game.

8. 1972 CINCINNATI REDS

The 1972 Reds were down three games to one and trailed Game Five against the Athletics in Oakland 4–2 after four innings but fought back with single runs in the fifth, eighth, and ninth innings to stave off elimination. Each of the first five games of the Series was settled by only one run, but in Cincinnati in Game Six, the Reds prolonged the Series with an 8–1 rout. In the seventh game, two misjudged fly balls by Reds center fielder Bobby Tolan helped stake the Athletics to a 3–1 lead. The Reds loaded the bases with one out in the eighth but could score only one run. Pete Rose lined out to Rollie Fingers to end the game with the tying run on first base, and the Athletics won their first World Series since

1930, when the club was located in Philadelphia. The six one-run games in 1972 is a World Series record.

9. **1973 NEW YORK METS**

The 1973 Mets reached the World Series with a 82–79 record, the worst of any postseason team in history. Managed by Yogi Berra, the Mets were in last place as late as August 31 but won 24 of their last 33 regular-season games and upset the Reds in the National League Championship Series. The Mets almost beat the defending champion Athletics in the World Series, taking three of the first five games, but lost the final two games 3–1 and 5–2 in Oakland. It was the second of three consecutive world championships for the Athletics. They won again in 1974, defeating the Dodgers in five games.

10. **1991 ATLANTA BRAVES**

The 1991 World Series matched the Braves and the Twins, two clubs that had finished in last place the previous season. The Twins won the Series in seven games in one of the most exciting Fall Classics ever staged. Five games were decided by one run, the winning run was scored in the last half inning of four contests, and a record three games went to extra innings, including the final two. Kirby Puckett was the hero of Game Six. He made an extraordinary leaping catch in the third inning and gave Minnesota a 4–3 win with a home run in the 11th. The Braves blew an opportunity to win Game Seven in the eighth inning. With the score 0–0, Lonnie Smith led off with a single to right field off Jack Morris and Terry Pendleton followed a drive off the left center field wall for a double. Smith lost sight of the ball, however, and hesitated rounding second base. He only reached third. Still, Atlanta had runners on second and third with none out. Morris bore down and induced Ron Gant to ground out to first baseman Kent Hrbek with the runners holding. After David Justice was intentionally walked to load the bases, Sid Bream hit into a double play, Hrbek to catcher Terry Harper and back to

Hrbek. The Twins won the title in the 10th. Dan Gladden started the inning with a double off Alejandro Pena and was sacrificed to third by Chuck Knoblauch. After intentional walks to Puckett and Hrbek, Gene Larkin drove a single to left center for a 1–0 Twins victory. Morris pitched all 10 innings for the shutout.

Loser Takes nothing

Here are ten more teams that have had the rug yanked out from under them in the seventh game of a World Series.

1. **1931 PHILADELPHIA ATHLETICS**

The Athletics in 1931 were gunning for their third consecutive world championship. They defeated the Cubs in 1929 and the Cardinals in 1930 and were facing the Cardinals again in 1931. In the deciding seventh game, Philadelphia was behind 4–0. St. Louis pitcher Burleigh Grimes pitched eight shutout innings, but was 38 years old and was suffering from a sore finger and a painful abdomen (he had an operation for appendicitis soon after the Series was over) and was running out of gas. While batting in the eighth, Grimes struck out intentionally to preserve his energy. While pitching in the ninth, Grimes walked Al Simmons and, after retiring two hitters, walked Jimmie Dykes. Dib Williams loaded the bases with a single, and pinch-hitter Doc Cramer drove a two-run single to center to make the score 4–2, and the Athletics had the winning run at the plate. Cardinals manager Gabby Street brought in Wild Bill Hallahan to replace Grimes, and Hallahan ended the threat by getting Max Bishop to fly out to center field.

2. 1940 DETROIT TIGERS

The 1940 Tigers took the lead three times in the World Series against the Reds, by winning the first, third, and fifth games, but couldn't close the deal. Bobo Newsom beat the Reds in the first and fifth contests and came back to pitch Game Seven after only one day of rest. He had a 1–0 lead heading into the seventh but allowed a two-run homer to Jimmy Ripple and lost 2–1.

3. 1947 BROOKLYN DODGERS

In a controversial selection, Dodgers manager Burt Shotton selected Hal Gregg, a pitcher with a 4–5 record and a 5.88 ERA that season, to start Game Seven against the Yankees in the World Series. Gregg stopped the Yankees in a seven-inning relief appearance in Game Four, allowing only one run in seven innings. In the first six games, Dodgers starters allowed 19 runs in $19^{2}/_{3}$ innings. Staked to a 2–0 lead, Gregg was sent to the showers in the fourth inning and lost 5–2. Yankees manager Bucky Harris wasn't exactly clairvoyant in his selection of a starting pitcher in the seventh game, going with rookie Spec Shea, who was knocked out in the second inning. But Harris was bailed out by the shutout relief work of Bill Bevens and Joe Page. Page was especially brilliant, allowing only one hit and no walks over five innings.

4. 1955 NEW YORK YANKEES

The Dodgers reached the World Series in 1916, 1920, 1941, 1947, 1949, 1952, and 1953 and lost them all, including the last five to the Yankees. The 1955 Series against the Yankees didn't start well for Brooklyn, as the Dodgers dropped the first two games at Yankee Stadium. The Dodgers rebounded to win the next three at Ebbets Field but dropped the sixth game 5–3. Dodgers manager Walter Alston, who used six different starting pitchers in the first six games of the Series, selected 23-year-old Johnny Podres to start Game Seven. Podres had a mediocre 9–10 record in 1955, although he beat the Yankees 8–3 in Game Three in his first complete game since June. Podres was magnificent in the seventh and deciding game, winning 2–0 to give Brooklyn its first world championship, ending decades of frustration for Dodgers fans. He needed some help from his defense in the sixth inning, however. With Gil McDougald on first base and Billy Martin on second and no one out, Yogi Berra lofted a fly ball down the left field line, which looked like an extra base hit that would score both runners. Brooklyn left fielder Sandy Amoros had been playing the left-handed Berra well into left center and had to sprint almost 150 feet across the Yankee Stadium outfield grass toward the point where the ball was dropping into the left field corner. Amoros lunged, caught it just a few inches into fair territory, and then spun quickly toward the infield and rifled the ball to shortstop Pee Wee Reese, who wheeled and threw to first baseman Gil Hodges to double up McDougald.

5. **1956 BROOKLYN DODGERS**

The Dodgers won the first two games of the 1956 World Series against the Yankees, scoring 19 runs, but ended up losing it in seven. The Yankees won four of the last five games as Whitey Ford, Tom Sturdivant, Don Larsen, Bob Turley, and Johnny Kucks each pitched complete games while allowing a total of only six runs. Larsen's Game Five win was a perfect game. While Dodgers fans were distraught over losing the World Series, they were most concerned about losing the team altogether. Owner Walter O'Malley was openly researching the possibility of moving his club to Los Angeles, and the transfer of the franchise to the West Coast became official in October 1957.

6. **1965 MINNESOTA TWINS**

The home team won each of the first six games of the 1965 World Series between the Dodgers and the Twins, and none of the contests was decided by fewer than four runs. The Twins won 8–2, 5–1, and 5–1 at Metropolitan Stadium, while the Dodgers took 4–0, 7–2, and 7–0 decisions in Los Angeles. In the seventh game in Minnesota, Sandy Koufax pitched his second consecutive shutout of the Series, winning 2–0. He struck out 10 batters in each of the whitewashings. Lou Johnson, a 32-year-old career minor league player who began the season at Spokane, hit a fourth-inning homer off the left field foul pole that broke a scoreless tie.

7. 1971 BALTIMORE ORIOLES

The Orioles reached the World Series for the third straight season in 1971. The Orioles lost to the Mets in five games in a shocking upset in 1969, dispatched the Reds in five games in 1970, and looked to earn back-to-back championships against the Pirates in 1971. The Orioles won the first two games in Baltimore, but the Pirates rebounded and extended the Series to seven games. Pittsburgh led Game Seven 2–0 heading into the eighth, when Elrod Hendricks and Mark Belanger led off the inning with singles off Steve Blass, but could score only one run and lost 2–1. Blass pitched two complete-game victories in the 1971 Series, allowing only two runs. He was 19–8 in 1972 with a 2.49 earned run average, but he suffered a mysterious collapse in 1973. That season, Blass was 3–9, had a 9.85 ERA, walked 84 batters in 89 innings, and added a new phrase to baseball's lexicon. Pitchers who have experienced a similar sudden and mysterious inability to control their pitches are said to suffer from "Steve Blass Disease."

8. 1979 BALTIMORE ORIOLES

The Orioles also lost the 1979 World Series in seven games in a rematch against the Pirates. Baltimore won three of the first four games and had two games remaining at Memorial Stadium, then dropped three decisions in a row by scores of 7–1, 2–0, and 4–1. The 1979 Pirates emphasized the team concept and togetherness by referring to themselves as a family and adopted the popular disco tune "We Are Family" by Sister Sledge. The group sang the National Anthem before one of the Series games. The patriarch of the "family" was 39-year-old Willie Stargell, nicknamed "Pops." In the seventh game, he had four hits, including two doubles and a homer. In the Series, Stargell set a record for the most extra base hits in a single Series (seven) and tied the mark for the most total bases (25). In 30 at-bats, he had 12 hits, including four doubles and three homers. He also scored seven runs and drove in another seven.

9. 1982 MILWAUKEE BREWERS

The 1982 World Series matched the Brewers against the Cardinals, a team owned by the Anheuser-Busch Brewery. The Brewers trounced the Cardinals 10–0 in the opener in St. Louis and won three of the first five games. The Cardinals evened the series with a 13–1 walloping of Milwaukee in a game halted twice by rain delays totaling $2\frac{1}{2}$ hours. The Brewers broke a 1–1 tie with two runs in the sixth inning of the seventh game, but the Cardinals rallied for three in their half. Two insurance runs in the eighth gave the Cardinals a 6–3 win and the club's ninth world championship, the most by any National League club and second only to the 26 won by the Yankees.

10. 1987 ST. LOUIS CARDINALS

The Cardinals failed to win their 10th world championship in the 1987 World Series against the Minnesota Twins. The Twins won the Western Division with an 85–77 record, only the fifth best in the American League in 1987, and were outscored 806 to 786. They are the only club in history to reach the World Series after giving up more runs than they scored during the regular season, and Minnesota's winning percentage of .525 is the worst of any world champion. But the Twins were tough at home in the Metrodome. During the regular season, they were 56–25 in the dome, the best home record of any team in the majors. Their mastery in the deafening atmosphere of the Metrodome continued in the postseason. The Twins won both games at home in a five-game victory over the Tigers in the ALCS and won all four in the dome against the Cardinals. In the seventh game, St. Louis scored two runs in the second inning to take a 2-0 lead but were shut down the rest of the way by Frank Viola and Jeff Reardon. The Twins won 4-2 with single runs in the second, fifth, sixth, and eighth innings. The Twins are the only team to win a World Series without winning a road game, and they accomplished it twice, in both 1987 and 1991. Counting the 1965 Series against the Dodgers, the Twins are 11-0 at home during the Fall Classic.

Say It Ain't So, Joe

The Cincinnati Reds defeated the Chicago White Sox in the 1919 World Series five games to three in a best-of-nine matchup. Rumors were swirling throughout the Series that many White Sox players failed to give their best in an attempt to lose after taking money from gamblers. The allegations were generated by a sudden change in the betting odds, which dramatically shifted from the White Sox as a 3–1 favorite to an 8–5 underdog. The erratic play of many of the Chicago players, especially pitchers Ed Cicotte and Lefty Williams, continued to fuel the reports. In September 1920, the eight conspirators were suspended, and the following August they were banned from organized baseball for life.

1. CHARLIE COMISKEY

If White Sox owner Charlie Comiskey hadn't been such a tightwad with his players, the Black Sox scandal might not have taken place. The White Sox won the World Series in 1917, yet Comiskey paid salaries that were among the lowest in baseball and also skimped on meal money and other amenities. The nickname "Black Sox" actually predates the 1919 Series. It was coined because the White Sox had the filthiest uniforms in baseball because Comiskey wanted to save money by cutting down on his laundry bill. His players were receptive to offers of cash from gamblers to "throw" the

Series in part as an act of revenge against Comiskey and his penurious policies.

2. CINCINNATI REDS

The White Sox' opponent in the 1919 World Series was the Cincinnati Reds, a club that has been unfairly characterized as an outfit that didn't belong on the same field with the White Sox. The 1919 Reds had a record of 96–44, compared to 88–52 for the White Sox. Cincinnati's winning percentage of .686 in 1919 was the highest in major league baseball for a single season between 1912 and 1927 and the best in the National League from 1912 until 1942. The image of the Reds as an overmatched club in the Series isn't just revisionist history. They were seen as an underdog by the leading baseball "experts" of the day, although the Cincinnati club were sentimental favorites. The headline over the article in *The Sporting News* previewing the 1919 Series read, "Joy If The Reds Win—Shock If They Do." One reason that the White Sox were heavily favored was that the American League had won eight of the previous nine World Series. Chicago was also the better-known team. The White Sox won the Series in 1917 and had been strong contenders for several years. They played in a major city and featured two great players in Eddie Collins and Joe Jackson. The Reds had never won a National League pennant before 1919 and had spent most of the 1910s in the second division. Cincinnati's only future Hall-of-Famer was center fielder Edd Roush. It's fruitless to speculate as to which team would have won if the 1919 Series had been played on the level, as the depth of the fix is unknown. The Series was thrown mainly on pitching and defense. Eddie Cicotte and Lefty Williams, both excellent control pitchers, had sudden lapses of wildness throughout the Series. The Black Sox who were in on the fix made a few glaring errors. The defensive omissions were mainly on throws that were just a little late or off line and on fly balls that were missed by a step.

3. CHICK GANDIL

First baseman Chick Gandil is considered to be the ringleader of the Black Sox. His contacts with gamblers Sport Sullivan, Abe Attell, and Billy Maharg paved the way for the scandal. Tired of salary squabbles with Comiskey, Gandil had already decided that 1919 would be his last season, and looked for a big payoff from gamblers as a stake for retirement. It was Gandil who contacted other players to join him in the conspiracy to throw the Series. Gandil reportedly received $35,000 of the estimated $80,000 to $100,000 put up by the gambling syndicate that bet on the Reds to win.

4. EDDIE CICOTTE

Eddie Cicotte might be in the Hall of Fame if he hadn't been banned as a result of losing the 1919 World Series. He had a 29–7 record in 1919 with a 1.82 ERA. Cicotte was named by White Sox manager Kid Gleason as the first-game starter. Cicotte hit Reds leadoff hitter Morrie Rath in the back with a pitch in the first inning as a sign to gamblers that the fix of the World Series was on. The Reds broke the game open with a five-run rally in the fourth. Cicotte repeatedly ignored the signals of catcher Ray Schalk and grooved pitches. Cincinnati won the game 9–1. Cicotte started the fourth game and lost 2–0, with both runs scored with the aid of two errors by the pitcher. He played to win the seventh game after the gamblers welched on promises of additional cash and emerged with a 4–1 victory. Cicotte had 21 wins in 1920 when he was banned from the sport. He finished his career with a 208–149 record and a 2.37 ERA.

5. LEFTY WILLIAMS

Lefty Williams started three games for the Sox in the 1919 Series and lost them all. Coming off a season in which he was 23–11, Williams lost the second game 4–2. He averaged 1.76 walks per nine innings during the regular season but walked six in the defeat. Catcher Ray Schalk was livid and pummeled Williams under the grandstand after the game. Kid Gleason and Chick Gandil also fought each other in the Chicago clubhouse. Williams was a 5–0 loser in the fifth game, which put the White Sox behind four games to one. In a normal year, that would have ended the Series, but in 1919 baseball's hierarchy decided on the best-of-nine format. After the White Sox won the sixth and seventh game, the gamblers began to get nervous and threatened Williams with physical harm if the White Sox won Game Eight. Williams wasted no time, surrendering four runs in the first inning as the Reds went on to win 10–5. He was 22–14 in 1920 when he was suspended.

6. **JOE JACKSON**

Outfielder "Shoeless" Joe Jackson was one of the greatest hitters the game has ever known. He had a .356 batting average during a 1,332-game career, the third highest average of all time, behind Ty Cobb and Rogers Hornsby. He hit .375 with six runs batted in during the 1919 Series, and his proponents use the statistics as proof that Jackson wasn't one of the conspirators in the fix. There is little doubt that Jackson accepted money from the gamblers, however. There is conjecture that the cash he received was far short of what was promised and that he went out and played as hard as possible.

7. **BUCK WEAVER**

Buck Weaver was asked to join in the conspiracy but refused. He hit .324 during the 1919 Series, with four doubles and a triple among his 11 hits. Even though he took no part in deliberately losing any of the games and took no money from gamblers, Weaver received a lifetime banishment because he had knowledge of the fix and failed to report it.

8. **THE OTHERS**

The other three players who were banned for their participation in throwing the Series besides Gandil, Cicotte, Williams,

Jackson, and Weaver were center fielder Happy Felsch, shortstop Swede Risberg, and reserve infielder Fred McMullin. The last was included because he learned of the fix and demanded a share of the money. It was feared that McMullin would make what he knew public, and he was paid off for his silence.

9. THE TRIAL

A grand jury in Chicago indicted the eight players involved in the scandal on September 28, 1920, on charges of conspiring to fix the 1919 World Series. Charlie Comiskey indefinitely suspended all eight, even though his White Sox still had a chance to win the American League pennant with five days remaining in the regular season. The Sox finished second to Cleveland, two games out. The trial began on July 18, 1921. The indictment was based largely on the confession of Eddie Cicotte and the accusations of Joe Jackson, but transcripts of the testimony of both men mysteriously disappeared. On August 2, the jury brought in a verdict of not guilty. The jurors lifted the players onto their shoulders and marched them around the courtroom. That night, the jurors and the eight Black Sox celebrated together in an Italian restaurant.

10. THE COMMISSIONER

Despite the verdict of not guilty, Commissioner Kenesaw Landis banned all eight players from baseball for life. The banishment has also continued into the "afterlife," as all eight players have been long since dead. Because of the edict of Landis and the refusal of subsequent commissioners to reverse his order, Joe Jackson remains ineligible for induction into the Hall of Fame.

Controversies

The Black Sox scandal hasn't been the only controversy in the history of the World Series.

1. JIMMY O'CONNELL AND COZY DOLAN

Five years after the Black Sox scandal, another gambling controversy marred the World Series. On October 1, 1924, three days before the start of the World Series between the Giants and the Senators, Commissioner Kenesaw Landis banned New York outfielder Jimmy O'Connell and coach Cozy Dolan after they admitted attempting to bribe Phillies shortstop Heinie Sand in order for the Philadelphia club to "go easy" on the Giants in their season-ending series. O'Connell implicated teammates Frankie Frisch, Ross Youngs, and George Kelly, who denied their involvement and were cleared by Landis. O'Connell was out of baseball at the age of 23. American League president Ban Johnson demanded that Frisch, Youngs, and Kelly be banned as well, and when Landis refused, Johnson boycotted the Series.

2. CHARLIE FINLEY AND MIKE ANDREWS

Controversy reigned supreme in the 1973 World Series, when mercurial Oakland owner Charlie Finley tried to release second baseman Mike Andrews after he made two critical errors. The Mets led the Athletics 7–6 in the 12th inning and had the bases loaded with two outs when Andrews allowed a grounder to dribble through his legs, which scored two runs. On the very next play, Andrews made another error on a high throw to first base, which scored another run. The Mets won the game 10–7. The following day, Finley claimed that Andrews was incapacitated by a shoulder injury and tried to replace him with another player on the roster. Commissioner Bowie Kuhn ordered that Andrews be reinstated and leveled a heavy fine on Finley for his attempts to "fire" Andrews by making false statements about the infielder's health. Andrews made a pinch-hitting appearance in the fourth game and received a standing ovation from the Shea Stadium crowd when he stepped up to the plate. Andrews grounded out in what proved to be his last plate appearance in the majors.

3. **BRAVES AND INDIANS**

The 1995 Series between the Atlanta Braves and the Cleveland Indians brought to the forefront the objections of many individuals who believe that the nicknames demean Native Americans. Protesters also disapproved of the tomahawk chop of Atlanta fans and of Cleveland's cartoonish logo of Chief Wahoo. Demonstrations were held at both Atlanta-Fulton County Stadium and Jacobs Field.

4. **DAVID JUSTICE**

On the travel day between the fifth and sixth games in 1995, Braves outfielder David Justice ripped Atlanta fans for being front-runners and too nonchalant. At the time, the Braves held a three-games-to-two lead over the Indians. Justice was booed in Atlanta when he batted in the second inning of the sixth game but was cheered wildly when he rocketed a Jim Poole pitch into the right field bleachers in the sixth inning with the game scoreless. The run held up for a 1–0 victory that gave the Braves their first world championship since 1957, when the franchise was located in Milwaukee. Pitchers Tom Glavine (eight innings) and Mark Wohlers (one inning) combined for a one-hitter. The only Cleveland hit was a single by Tony Pena in the sixth inning. On the negative side, Justice went on to set a World Series record by striking out eight consecutive times while with the Yankees against the Diamondbacks in 2001.

5. MICHAEL MUSMANNO

On the eve of the 1961 World Series between the Reds and the Yankees, Pennsylvania Supreme Court Justice Michael Musmanno, who was known as an ardent foe of communism, said that the Cincinnati Reds should change their nickname. Musmanno sent a 700-word letter to Reds manager Fred Hutchinson, in which he expressed fears that a headline like "Reds Murder Yanks" might cause some terrible scares in America. The publicity-seeking judge was not taken seriously.

6. JOHN LINDSAY AND BOWIE KUHN

New York mayor John Lindsay and baseball commissioner Bowie Kuhn battled over the placement of the American flag before the fourth game of the 1969 World Series. The game took place on October 15, a day on which millions of protesters against the Vietnam War were involved in a series of activities described by organizers as a moratorium to end the war. Lindsay, an outspoken critic of the war, had ordered the flags on all city-owned buildings flown at half-mast for a day of mourning in New York City. Shea Stadium, as a city-owned facility, was included in Lindsay's order. Kuhn, bowing to the protests of servicemen, countermanded Lindsay by restoring the flags to full-staff.

7. BILLY LOES

Before the 1952 World Series began, Dodgers pitcher Billy Loes was asked who would win. "I'd like to pick the Dodgers," said Loes, "but I have to go along with the Yankees in six games." Dodgers manager Charlie Dressen and Loes's teammates confronted the pitcher and asked him if what he said was true. Loes contended that he was misquoted and said he told the reporter that the Yankees would win in seven games. Loes started the sixth game of the Series with the Dodgers leading the Yankees three games to two and lost 3–2. During the game, he committed a balk by dropping a ball on the mound and had a grounder glance off his leg. After the game, Loes claimed that he dropped the ball because it contained "too much spit" and lost the ground ball "in the sun."

8. **1904**

Despite the success of the first World Series between champions of the National and American Leagues in 1903, there was no Series in 1904 because of the obstinance of New York Giants owner John Brush and manager John McGraw and their failure to recognize the new league. Brush and McGraw both had a long-standing feud with American League president Ban Johnson. The Giants brain trust was particularly angry that the American League placed a team in New York in 1903, then known as the Highlanders and in later years as the Yankees. The 1904 American League pennant race went down to the final weekend, with Boston nosing out New York for first place. The Giants refused to play Boston, which they deemed a champion "in a minor league"—in spite of the fact that the "minor league" Boston club had defeated National League champion Pittsburgh in the Series the previous fall. *The Sporting News* declared Boston the world champions by default, and Brush and McGraw were roasted in the press nationwide for months. To add to the bizarre twist to the story, Brush proposed by-laws in 1905 governing future World Series, which were passed by both leagues and became known as the "Brush Rules." Many of these rules are still in effect. Among them was a stipulation that a heavy fine be levied on any club that refused to play in the World Series. The only other World Series to be canceled was the one in 1994, because of the players' strike.

9. 1918 STRIKE THREAT

A federal government edict forced the 1918 regular season to end on Labor Day, and players had to either enlist in the military or take war-related jobs. A two-week extension was granted to the two participants in the World Series, which began on September 5. Prior to the fifth game of the 1918 Series between the Red Sox and Cubs in Boston, players from both teams threatened to strike because the winners' and losers' share of the gate receipts had been drastically reduced. The players' share in 1918 was less than one-third of what it had been in previous seasons for a variety of reasons. Attendance was lower at the games because the nation was embroiled in World War I, ticket prices were decreased, and baseball earmarked part of the gate money for wartime charities. Also, the second-, third-, and fourth-place clubs received part of the loot for the first time. Game Five was held up for an hour while negotiations were held between representatives of the players and the presidents of the American and National Leagues. Extra police were summoned to Fenway Park because of fears that there might be a riot should the contest be called off. The players backed off on their demands and threats to strike for fear of appearing greedy while the country was fighting a war, particularly in light of the fact that hundreds of wounded soldiers and sailors were seated in the grandstand. Because of a backlash against the players and their strike plans, only 15,238 fans showed up at Game Six. The Red Sox' winning share in 1918 was only $1,103 per player, compared to winning shares of $3,669 in 1917. In 1919, the winning players' share was a then-record $5,207.

10. JOSE FELICIANO

Jose Feliciano, a blind 23-year-old Puerto Rican soul singer, created a firestorm of controversy in 1968 when he sang the National Anthem on national television before the fifth game of the World Series in Detroit. Feliciano's interpretation was done to a slower beat in a blend of soul and folk styles to the accompaniment of an acoustic guitar, and it differed greatly from the usual formal rendition. Newspapers and radio and TV stations were flooded with protests by irate viewers, many of whom considered the performance to be unpatriotic. Feliciano was hired by the Tigers at the suggestion of play-by-play announcer Ernie Harwell. Two months earlier, Feliciano had reached number three on the *Billboard* chart with his single "Light My Fire," which in itself was an interpretation of a 1967 number one hit by the Doors. One of those who rushed to Feliciano's defense was NBC broadcaster Tony Kubek. "I feel the youth of America has to be served," said Kubek, "and this is the type of music they want." Today Feliciano's rendition would barely raise an eyebrow, as individual expressions of the "Star-Spangled Banner" have become commonplace and the lyrics have been sung in a wide variety of musical styles since his groundbreaking appearance.

In his first post-season performance since 1968, Feliciano sang the National Anthem before the fifth game of the National League Championship Series in 2003. He drew cheers from the crowd at Pro Player Stadium in Miami.

Are You Blind?

During the World Series, there are six umpires on the field instead of the usual complement of four, but the arbiters have made many controversial decisions.

1. BILL KLEM AND GEORGE HILDEBRAND

Bill Klem and George Hildebrand infuriated fans by calling the second game of the 1922 World Series between the Giants and Yankees at the Polo Grounds because of darkness. The Giants jumped out to a 3–0 lead in the first inning, only to see the Yankees chip away and send the game into extra innings with the score 3–3. After a scoreless 10th, Hildebrand and Klem called the game even though there was 45 minutes of sunlight remaining, enough to play at least one, and probably two, more innings. The game went into the books as a 3–3 tie. There was a near riot at the ballpark, as bottles and seat cushions were heaved onto the field after the announcement was made, and a group of furious fans, who assumed that the decision was made by Kenesaw Landis and not the umpires, charged the commissioner's box. Landis faced the swirling crowd calmly and bravely and raised his hand in an attempt to quiet them and explain the circumstances, but his voice was lost in the uproar. The police arrived to escort Landis to safety, but he waved his cane

Are You Blind?

at them as a gesture that he didn't need any protection and made his way across the field to the Giants club offices while trying to evade the officers. To placate the public, Landis donated the entire receipts of $120,000 to military hospitals for veterans disabled in World War I. Hildebrand and Klem defended their decision by stating that it was hazy and that the players were having difficulty seeing the ball in the final inning. The umpires feared that if the Giants had a long rally in their half of the 11th inning, it would have been too dark to finish the Yankees at-bat. The Giants went on to win the World Series with four victories and a tie.

2. **AUGIE DONATELLI**

Augie Donatelli awarded Milwaukee pinch-hitter Nippy Jones first base in 1957 after finding shoe polish on the baseball. The Yankees scored a run in the 10th in Game Four to take a 5–4 lead when Jones led off the Braves half of the inning batting for Warren Spahn against Tommy Byrne. Jones claimed that a low pitch by Byrne hit him on the foot, and he convinced skeptical home plate umpire Donatelli by showing him a shoe polish smudge on the ball. The Braves went on to score three runs in the inning, the final two on a home run by Eddie Mathews off Bob Grim, who relieved Byrne, to earn a 7–5 win. The victory evened the Series at two games apiece, and the Braves went on to take the world championship in seven. It proved to be Nippy's last appearance in a major league game. A nearly identical situation occurred with another batter named Jones during the 1969 World Series between the Mets and the Orioles. With Baltimore leading 3–0 in the fifth game, Cleon Jones was hit on the foot by a Dave McNally pitch. Umpire Lou DiMuro ruled that the ball missed Jones, then changed his mind when Mets manager Gil Hodges showed him the shoe polish stain on the ball. Jones was awarded first base, and Donn Clendenon followed with a home run. The Mets won the game 5–3 to take the world title.

3. LOU DiMURO AND SHAG CRAWFORD

Lou DiMuro, stationed at first base, was involved in another controversy in the fourth game of the 1969 World Series, along with home plate umpire Shag Crawford. With the score 1–1 in the 10th inning and Mets runners on first and second with none out, J. C. Martin bunted toward the first base line. Baltimore pitcher Pete Richert fielded it, but his throw to first base struck Martin on the wrist and the ball caromed into the outfield, allowing Rod Gaspar to score the winning run. Television replays and newspaper photos showed that Martin ran illegally inside the foul line, but both DiMuro and Crawford missed the infraction. Martin played 14 years in the majors and batted only .222. The controversial bunt came in the only World Series appearance of his career.

4. KEN BURKHARDT

In the sixth inning of Game One of the 1970 World Series in Cincinnati, Bernie Carbo of the Reds was a base runner on third when Ty Cline hit a chopper in front of the plate off a pitch by the Orioles' Jim Palmer. Neither the Orioles nor home plate umpire Ken Burkhardt expected Carbo to try to score. Burkhardt straddled the third base line to determine whether the ball was fair, unaware that Carbo was steaming down the line behind him. Burkhardt signaled a fair ball, and Orioles catcher Elrod Hendricks fielded it. Palmer hollered that Carbo was heading home, and Hendricks whirled to tag Carbo with his glove, but the ball was in his bare hand. Burkhardt, who had gotten in the way of both Hendricks and Carbo, had his back to the play after he was spun around in a collision with Carbo. On the seat of his pants, Burkhardt called Carbo out. Burkhardt wasn't in a proper position to make a call, Hendricks missed the tag, and Carbo didn't touch home plate until he stepped on it inadvertently while arguing the call. The score was 3–3 when the play took place. The Orioles scored a run in the seventh inning to win 4–3 and took the Series in five games.

5. **LARRY BARNETT**

Home plate at Riverfront Stadium in Cincinnati was the epicenter of another dispute during the 1975 World Series between the Reds and the Red Sox, when home plate umpire Larry Barnett refused to call interference on Reds pinch-hitter Ed Armbrister. With the Series even at a game apiece, the score 5–5 in the 10th inning of Game Three, and Cesar Geronimo as the Reds base runner on first, Armbrister bunted a ball a few feet in front of the plate. Boston catcher Carlton Fisk moved forward to field the ball, but he and Armbrister came together as Armbrister stepped toward first. After Fisk got to the ball, he threw it into center field in an attempt to force Geronimo. The bad throw allowed Geronimo to reach third and Armbrister to reach second. The Red Sox argued that Armbrister should be called out for interfering with Fisk, but Barnett disagreed. The Reds scored the winning run on Joe Morgan's single off Roger Moret and moved on to take the Series in seven games.

6. **GEORGE MORIARTY**

George Moriarty was an American League umpire from 1917 through 1926 and again from 1929 through 1940. During the two-year interval, he was the manager for the Detroit Tigers. He also played for the Tigers from 1908 through 1915. When he was selected as an umpire for the 1935 World Series between the Tigers and the Cubs, the contingent from Chicago questioned Moriarty's impartiality. Moriarty had enough of the Cubs verbal abuse in Game Three and ejected manager Charlie Grimm and players Woody English and Tuck Stainback.

7. **FRANK PULLI**

Frank Pulli earned the wrath of Tommy Lasorda and the Dodgers in the fourth game of the 1978 World Series at Yankee Stadium. The Dodgers led the Yankees 3–1 in the fifth inning with Yankees base runners Thurman Munson on second and Reggie Jackson on first with one out. Lou Piniella hit a perfect double play ball to shortstop Bill Russell, who stepped on second to force Jackson. Jackson froze in the base path a few feet off first base, and Russell's throw to first hit him on the hip and caromed toward right field. Munson scored, and Piniella was safe. The Dodgers claimed that Jackson deliberately swiveled his hip to get in the way of the throw and that Piniella should be called out, but Pulli ruled that Jackson wasn't guilty of obstruction. The Yankees tied the score in the eighth and won the contest 4–3 in the 10th. After dropping the first two games of the Series, the Yankees rallied to win the last four to defeat the Dodgers for the second year in a row.

8. **DREW COBLE**

Drew Coble was in the eye of the storm as the umpire at first base in the second game of the 1991 World Series between the Braves and the Twins. In the third inning with Minnesota up 2–1, Atlanta's Ron Gant tried to retreat to first base after hitting a single. Kent Hrbek, the Twins 250-pound first baseman, took a throw from pitcher Kevin Tapani. The 172-pound Gant stepped on the bag before Hrbek applied the tag, but Hrbek appeared to lean into Gant, lifting the runner off the base. Coble claimed that Gant's momentum carried him off the bag, and not Hrbek's tag, and called Gant out. The Twins won the game 3–2 on an eighth-inning home run by Scott Leius and won the Series in seven games.

9. **BOB DAVIDSON**

There has been only one triple play in the history of the World Series, pulled off unassisted by Indians second baseman Bill Wambsganss in 1920. There would have been a second one in 1992 if it weren't for a bad call by umpire Bob Davidson. It was in Game Three Toronto, the first ever World Series game in Canada, with the Blue Jays playing the Braves and a 0–0 score in the third inning. Deion Sanders on second and Terry Pendleton on first were the Atlanta base runners with none out. Dave Justice hit a drive to deep center over the head of center fielder Devon White. Racing to the wall, White leaped and made a sensational backhanded grab against the 400-foot sign. Pendleton passed Sanders on the base path for the second out, and in the judgment of Davidson, Sanders just avoided a tag by third baseman Kelly Gruber scrambling back to second during the subsequent rundown. Replays showed that Gruber grazed Sanders's foot with the tag, and Davidson admitted later that he blew the call. The Blue Jays eventually won the game 3–2 and took the Series in six games.

10. **BABE PINELLI**

After nearly 50 years, Babe Pinelli's called strike on the last pitch of Yankee Don Larsen's perfect game in the fifth game of the 1956 World Series against the Dodgers remains a source of debate. Some claim that the pitch was as much as a foot outside, but films show that it was probably a good call and certainly wasn't a bad one. Pinelli was a National League umpire from 1935 through 1956. Before the 1956 Series, he had announced his retirement, and this was his final game as an umpire behind the plate. After Larsen had retired 26 batters in a row, Brooklyn's Dale Mitchell was sent to the plate as a pinch-hitter. With the count 2–2, Pinelli called Mitchell out looking at a third strike. Films of the pitch don't show conclusively whether or not the pitch caught the corner of the plate, but if it missed, it certainly didn't miss by much. Catcher Yogi Berra snared the ball within the frame of his body, and Mitchell, who struck out only 119 times in 3,984 big league at-bats, started his swing before holding up.

Men and Women Behaving Badly

The World Series has often caused individuals to indulge in some out-of-the-ordinary behavior.

1. **FRANKIE CROSETTI**

The third game of the 1942 World Series between the Cardinals and the Yankees was interrupted by an argument over a call by umpire Ed Summers. Crosetti shoved Summers to the ground during the fracas and was suspended for the first 30 days of the 1943 regular season. Crosetti participated in 23 World Series in uniform, the all-time record. He was in eight Series as a player, between 1932 and 1943, and 15 as a coach, from 1947 through 1964, all with the Yankees. Crosetti was a part of 17 world championship teams, seven as a player and 10 as a coach.

2. **ROGER CLEMENS**

The 2000 World Series was marred by a bizarre incident involving Yankees pitcher Roger Clemens and Mets catcher Mike Piazza. During the regular season, Clemens hit Piazza in the head with a pitch. In the first inning of the second game of the World Series, Piazza hit a foul ball off a Clemens pitch that splintered his bat in three places. Not knowing the ball was foul, Piazza ran toward first base, and Clemens picked up the barrel of the bat and hurled it in Piazza's general direction. Piazza glared at Clemens, and the two exchanged words as both benches emptied, but there was no physical confrontation between Clemens and Piazza. Clemens pitched eight shutout innings, allowing only two hits, and gave the Yankees a 6–0 lead. The Mets scored five runs in the ninth, but it wasn't enough to forestall a 6–5 defeat. Clemens was fined $50,000 for the incident, which continues to have repercussions. The Yankees held Clemens out of the starting rotation during a Series in 2001 against the Mets at Shea Stadium. In 2002, during a game at Shea, Mets pitcher Shawn Estes was ejected after throwing a pitch behind Clemens. Clemens was ejected from an ALCS game in 1990, however, while pitching for the Red Sox against the Athletics. In the second inning of the fourth game, Clemens had a few choice words about the ball and strike calls of home plate umpire Terry Cooney and was sent to an early shower.

3. **MICHAEL SERGIO**

Skydiver Michael Sergio landed on the Shea Stadium infield during the first inning of the sixth game of the 1986 World Series. A 37-year-old from Manhattan, Sergio carried a banner hanging from his parachute that read, "Let's Go Mets." He was hustled off the field by New York City police and stadium security. On December 19, Sergio was sentenced to 100 hours of community service and levied with a $500 fine for criminal trespassing. Judge Phyllis Orljkoff Flug and her law secretary wrote a 16-line poem called "Ode to a Criminal Trespasser" for Sergio that was read at his sentencing. The poem began with the lines " 'Twas game six of the Series when out of the sky/Flew Sergio's parachute a Met banner held high" and concluded with "Community service and a fine you will pay/Happy holiday to all, and to all a good day."

4. **HUNTINGTON AVENUE GROUNDS**

The official attendance for the third game of the 1903 World Series is 18,801, but contemporary newspaper reports estimated that as many as 25,000 were inside the enclosure, which had only 9,000 seats. Attempts were made to contain the crowd behind ropes in the outfield, but the throng got away from police and surged all over the field. Others climbed over the outfield walls to enter the ballpark for free. Many rushed into the grandstand. Two women were seen struggling and only the quick work of Boston outfielder Chick Stahl and the police kept them from being trampled. The women were escorted under the grandstand until order was restored. The players and the police took baseball bats and tried to get the crowd back into the outfield. Their efforts were futile. As one group was forced back, another surged into the diamond. A fire hose was brought into the grounds to force the crowd off the playing field, but the hose was cut in several places. At last, police reinforcements arrived and swung their billy clubs wildly, which forced the uncontrollable mob off the diamond after several people were severely injured. The game began an hour late but with the crowd right behind home plate and about three feet from first and third bases. Players who were not in a defensive position or acting as a batter or a base runner had to stand in front of the crowd because it was impossible for them to get to their benches. It was agreed before the Series that balls hit into the overflow crowd would be ground rule triples, but for this contest only, the rule was amended. The crowd was so close to home plate that drives into the overflow were doubles. The Pirates won the game 4–2.

5. **ROYAL ROOTERS**

The Royal Rooters were a group of about 300 die-hard Red Sox fans who sat together at games in Boston and often followed the club on the road, including games in New York against the Giants during the 1912 Series. According to tradition, the group marched into Fenway Park about five minutes before the start of the game with a large banner headed by their band, which played the song "Tessie." The Royal Rooters then made their way to their seats, which had been reserved for them next to the Red Sox bench. Before the seventh game of the 1912 Series, the Royal Rooters found their usual seats occupied. The group broke onto the playing field just as the game started and made plans to raid the grandstand and forcibly remove those who had taken their seats. The Royal Rooters were stopped by a squad of mounted policemen and were kept behind a rope in the outfield, where they had to stand throughout the contest. The rest of the crowd at Fenway reacted angrily to the police's actions against the Royal Rooters. The episode delayed the start of the contest for 10 minutes. Red Sox ace pitcher Smokey Joe Wood allowed six runs in the first inning, and the Giants won 11–4, which evened the Series at three wins for each club with one tie. Boston mayor John Fitzgerald (grandfather of future president John F. Kennedy), urged a boycott of the eighth game because of the treatment of the Royal Rooters. Only 17,034 attended the eighth game, about half the capacity of Fenway.

6. HEINIE WAGNER

During the second game of the 1918 World Series, Red Sox third base coach Heinie Wagner took umbrage at remarks made by Otto Knabe from the Cubs bench. Wagner rushed the dugout, and the two exchanged punches. Knabe's teammates supported him by throwing Wagner out of the dugout. Wagner landed flat on his back and spent the rest of the afternoon with mud caked on the back of his uniform.

7. HEINIE MANUSH

Hall of Fame outfielder Heinie Manush appeared in only one World Series during his career, and it wasn't a pleasant experience. Playing for the Senators in 1933 against the Giants, Manush had only two singles in 18 at-bats, and his club lost the Series in five games. In the fourth game, Manush was ejected by umpire Charlie Moran in the bottom of the sixth inning for using offensive language. After Manush was ejected, he slapped Moran in the face. In the top of the seventh, Manush assumed his defensive position in left field and refused to leave. After a delay of several minutes, Manush was escorted off the playing field by second base umpire George Moriarty. As he returned to the dugout, Manush resumed his debate with Moran, which caused a further interruption in the action.

8. JIM GRAY

The lifetime ban on Pete Rose was lifted briefly in 1999 to allow him to participate in an organized baseball function for the first time in ten years. Rose was honored as a member of baseball's All-Century team in ceremonies before Game Two of the World Series between the Braves and the Yankees in Atlanta. Rose received a longer standing ovation than any other player introduced to the crowd, including hometown favorite Hank Aaron. NBC reporter Jim Gray leaped at the occasion to grill Rose in a tenacious interview, badgering him with questions aimed at eliciting an admission from Rose that he had bet on baseball. Network switchboards were jammed for hours with calls from angry viewers, forcing an on-air apology from Gray two nights later.

9. PETE ROSE

One of Jim Gray's questions to Pete Rose, asking him if he wasn't his "own worst enemy," was apt. Rose arrived late to the press conference preceding the All-Century team ceremonies because he was attending an autograph show at a casino in Atlantic City. Immediately following the Gray interview, Cincinnati's NBC affiliate, WLWT, ran a commercial for radio station WEBN that featured Rose urinating in a men's room.

10. MARGE SCHOTT

Reds owner Marge Schott managed to upstage the first lady and an impending war before the second game of the World Series in 1990 in Cincinnati. The commissioner's office and CBS gave Schott permission to speak to the crowd 30 minutes prior to game time, before the network began its coverage of the event. Both Commissioner Fay Vincent and CBS feared that Schott would embarrass baseball on national television. War with Iraq was looming, and troops were being bivouacked in the Middle East for an invasion, which took place the following January. During her speech, Schott dedicated the game to the troops in "the Middle West." While First Lady Barbara Bush was throwing out the first ball, Schott pushed aside television officials to grab the microphone again to make an unscheduled speech, this time on live television. Schott staggered noticeably on her way onto the field. Slurring her words and leaning awkwardly, Schott dedicated the World Series to the troops in "the Far East."

Butchery, Bobbles, and Boots

Despite being good enough to play on a league pennant winner, several players have made embarrassing gaffes in the World Series.

1. BILL ABSTEIN

Pirates rookie first baseman Bill Abstein made five errors and struck out 10 times in the 1909 World Series against the Tigers. Four of Abstein's errors occurred when he dropped throws. Pittsburgh owner Barney Dreyfuss was unforgiving and released Abstein immediately after the Series. Abstein played 25 more games in the big leagues with the St. Louis Browns in 1910, but he batted only .149.

2. ENOS SLAUGHTER

Yankees pitcher Bob Turley performed brilliantly in the sixth game of the 1956 World Series against the Dodgers, allowing only four hits while striking out 11 batters, but lost 1–0 in 10 innings. Left fielder Enos Slaughter should have caught three of the four balls that fell for hits. In the third inning, Slaughter lost Jim Gilliam's drive in the sun and allowed it to drop for a single. In the eighth, Slaughter lost sight of Clem Labine's double in the shadows. In the 10th, with two out and a Dodgers runner on second base, Slaughter misjudged Jackie

Butchery, Bobbles, and Boots

Robinson's liner. Slaughter leaped for the ball, but it was too late, and it sailed over his head for the game-winning run.

3. ART WILSON

Giants catcher Art Wilson dropped a throw that cost his club a victory in the second game against the Red Sox in 1912. Wilson entered the game in the 10th inning after regular catcher Chief Meyers was lifted for a pinch-runner during a rally that gave the Giants a 6–5 lead. With one out in the bottom of the 10th and the Giants still leading 6–5, Tris Speaker of the Red Sox hit a long drive to deep center. Speaker reached third easily and headed for the plate to try for an inside-the-park homer. Shortstop Tilly Shafer received the relay from center fielder Beals Becker and fired it home in plenty of time to allow Wilson to take the throw and place a tag on Speaker. Wilson couldn't corral the ball, however, and Speaker scored on the error to tie the score 6–6. After one more inning, the game was called for darkness with the game still deadlocked 6–6.

4. BRIAN HUNTER

Brian Hunter entered the first game of the 1999 World Series in the eighth inning as a defensive replacement for Braves first baseman Ryan Klesko with his club holding a 1–0 lead over the Yankees. Hunter proceeded to make two errors that cost Atlanta the game. After the first two Yankees reached base in the eighth, Chuck Knoblauch sacrificed but was safe at first when Hunter dropped his bunt for an error. With the bases loaded, Derek Jeter hit a two-run single to give the Yankees a 2–1 lead. Hunter's wild throw on a hit by Paul O'Neill allowed two more runs to cross the plate, and the Yankees won 4–1.

5. WILLIE DAVIS

Dodgers center fielder Willie Davis is the only player in World Series history to commit three errors in a single inning. It happened in the fifth inning of Game Two in 1966 against the

Orioles in Los Angeles. The game was scoreless with Boog Powell as the Baltimore runner at first base when Paul Blair lifted a fly toward center. Davis lost the ball in the sun, then dropped it for an error. Blair reached second, and Powell moved to third. The next hitter was Andy Etchebarren, who lofted another fly ball to center. Davis again lost the ball, then dropped it as Powell scored and Blair went to third. Davis threw to third in an attempt to retire Blair, but the throw was wild and Blair scored. Davis was charged two errors on the play, giving him three in a span of just two batters. The Orioles went on to win 6–0. The next inning, Davis caught a ball during warm-ups and was given a standing ovation. The losing pitcher was Sandy Koufax in what proved to be his final big league appearance. Davis also had only one hit in 16 at-bats as the Dodgers lost four straight.

6. WILLIE MAYS

Great players should go out of the game in a blaze of glory. Unfortunately, that wasn't the case for Willie Mays. At the age of 42, Mays entered the second inning of the 1973 World Series for the Mets against the Athletics in Oakland as a pinch-runner in the top of the ninth inning and stayed in the game in center field. Fielders on both teams battled a blinding sun throughout the first two games of the Series. Every ball hit into the air was an adventure, and fielders approached them like men searching for a light switch in a dark room. In the bottom of the ninth, Mays lost sight of the fly ball by Deron Johnson and fell down on the warning track. Johnson reached base on a double, and the A's scored two runs to tie the score 6–6. The Mets scored four times in the 12th, the first driven by Mays on a single in what turned out to be his final major league hit. The Mets won the game 10–7. Mays played in only one more big league game, as a pinch-hitter in the third game of the Series.

7. CHARLIE PICK

Cubs outfielder Charlie Pick ended Game Three in 1918 against the Red Sox with an ill-advised attempt to score on a passed ball. The Red Sox led 2–1 with two out in the bottom of the ninth when Pick beat out an infield hit and stole second. With Turner Barber batting, Boston hurler Carl Mays shot a pitch past catcher Wally Schang, which rolled 20 feet behind the plate. Pick darted for third. Schang made a quick recovery but threw high to third baseman Fred Thomas, who got a glove on the ball and knocked it a few feet into foul territory. Pick tried for home but was out on a perfect throw from Thomas to Schang.

8. MAX FLACK

Max Flack was another 1918 Cubs outfielder who suffered through a difficult Series against the Red Sox, by becoming the only player in Series history to be picked off base twice in a game. Flack's embarrassing afternoon came during Game Four. Flack led off the game with a single but was picked off when catcher Sam Agnew threw to first baseman Stuffy McInnis for the putout. Flack was nailed again in the fourth inning while on second base when Red Sox pitcher Babe Ruth wheeled and fired to shortstop Everett Scott. The Cubs lost 3–2. Flack helped lose Game Six in the field. With two out in the Red Sox third inning and runners on second and third, Flack dropped a liner off the bat of George Whitehead, allowing both runners to score. The two runs held up for a 2–1 victory, which gave the Red Sox their last world championship.

9. HERB WASHINGTON

Herb Washington was one of the most unique experiments in baseball history. He was hired by Athletics owner Charlie Finley as a designated pinch-runner. Washington played in 104 games in 1974 and 1975, all as a pinch-runner, and he never had an at-bat or played a game in the field. In the two seasons, he stole 30 bases in 47 attempts. In the second game of the 1974 World Series against the Dodgers, Washington was inserted into the game as a pinch-runner for Joe Rudi in the ninth inning with one out and Oakland trailing

3–2. He was quickly picked off base, however, by Los Angeles pitcher Mike Marshall. The A's failed to score any more runs and lost 3–2.

10. **DENNY DOYLE**

If it weren't for a baserunning mistake by Red Sox second baseman Denny Doyle, Carlton Fisk's 12th-inning home run in Game Six of the 1975 World Series might never have happened. In the ninth inning with the score 6–6, Boston loaded the bases with none out on a walk to Doyle, a single by Carl Yastrzemski, and a walk to Fisk. Fred Lynn hit a fly ball to George Foster, who caught it in foul territory in short left field. Using questionable judgment, Doyle tried to score but was thrown out by Foster for a double play. Rico Petrocelli ended the inning by grounding out.

Want to Get Away?

The World Series is the goal of every player in baseball, but many have wished they were somewhere else after making a dreadful mistake.

1. **MARINE COLOR GUARD**

Baseball's first international World Series, between the Atlanta Braves and the Toronto Blue Jays in 1992, resulted in an international incident. Prior to Game Two in Atlanta, a Marine Corps color guard carried the Canadian flag upside down. Canadians were mortified, and at the third game in Toronto vendors outside the Skydome did a brisk business selling upside down American flags. A Marine Corps unit from Buffalo rectified the situation by requesting to carry the Canadian flag with the Maple Leaf right side up before Game Three. The Marines received a standing ovation.

2. **DAVID WEST**

Pitcher David West allowed the first 10 batters to face him in World Series play to reach base on a homer, three doubles, two singles, and four walks. Pitching for the Twins in the third game against the Braves in 1991, West faced two hitters and walked them both. In the fifth game, he allowed a home run, a single, and two bases on balls without recording an out. With the Phillies in Game One versus the Blue Jays in 1993,

West faced two hitters and gave up two doubles. In the fourth game, he entered the game in the sixth inning with the Phillies leading 12–7 and surrendered a double and a single before finally recording an out. West gave up two runs in the inning, however, and the Phillies lost the game 15–14 in the highest-scoring contest in Series history. West faced one batter in the sixth game and issued a walk. Overall, West pitched one official inning in the World Series over five games and allowed seven hits, five walks, and seven earned runs for an ERA of 63.00.

3. **FREDDIE PAYNE**

In the second game of the 1907 World Series, Tigers catcher Freddie Payne tried to throw out Jimmy Slagle of the Cubs on a stolen base attempt. Payne's throw never reached second base because it nailed pitcher George Mullin in the head. The Tigers lost the game 3–1. Mullin is the only pitcher to appear in the World Series in a season after losing 20 games. He had a 20–20 record in 1907 and was 0–2 in the World Series.

4. **FIRPO MARBERRY AND THE PIRATES**

Senators pitcher Firpo Marberry batted out of turn in the third game of the 1925 World Series against the Pirates. Marberry entered the game as a reliever in the eighth inning and was placed in the fifth spot in the batting order in a double switch. With the Senators leading 4–3 in the bottom of the eighth, Marberry batted in the ninth slot in the order instead of Earl McNeely, who entered the game as a defensive replacement in center field. Marberry laid down a perfect sacrifice bunt to move Muddy Ruel to second base. The Pirates didn't protest the move, because none of them noticed that Marberry was hitting out of turn. The Senators failed to score in the inning, but Marberry earned a save by nailing down the 4–3 victory.

5. **JIMMIE DYKES**

In the sixth inning of the first game of the 1931 World Series, Chick Hafey of the Cardinals stole third base on a close play.

Athletics third baseman Jimmie Dykes immediately argued with the call by umpire Bill McGowan but failed to call time. While Dykes was commiserating with the umpire, Pepper Martin stole second base.

6. WILD BILL DONOVAN

Tigers pitcher Wild Bill Donovan hit an apparent single down the right field line in the fourth game of the 1907 World Series against the Cubs and trotted down to first base. Chicago right fielder Wildfire Schulte was hustling on the play and scooped up the ball to throw out Donovan at first base. Schulte wasn't immune to baserunning errors of his own in the postseason, however. Wildfire burned up the base paths but was extinguished in a hurry, holding the all-time record for most times caught stealing in a career with nine while playing for the Cubs in 1906, 1907, 1908, and 1910. Schulte was successful on only three stolen base attempts.

7. TIMO PEREZ

Lack of hustle by Mets outfielder Timo Perez was crucial in his club's first game loss to the Yankees in Game One in 2000. With the game scoreless in the first inning, Perez led off with a single. With one out, Todd Zeile sent a drive to left field. Perez was certain it would clear the wall and jogged toward second base. After he saw the ball strike the top of the wall, Perez began to run full speed but was thrown out at the plate. The Mets lost the game 4–3 in 12 innings.

8. HENRY KILLILEA

Despite winning the first World Series in 1903, Boston Red Sox owner Henry Killilea was vilified in the newspapers for his absentee ownership and skinflint operation. Many accused Killilea of selling the best seats at Huntington Avenue Grounds directly to ticket scalpers in exchange for a portion of the profits. It didn't help his relationship with the media when Killilea charged admission to writers covering the event. He even made Pittsburgh owner Barney Dreyfuss pay for a ticket. The reserve players on the Boston club had to work to take tickets. Dreyfuss donated a larger share of the profits to his athletes than Killilea, and as a result, the Pirates received $1,316 for losing the World Series while the Red Sox garnered $1,186 for winning. The controversy forced Killilea to sell the club the following April.

9. BUCK HERZOG AND ART FLETCHER

The left side of the New York Giants infield combined for five errors during Game Three in 1911 against the Athletics. Herzog made three errors at third base and Fletcher made two at shortstop as the Giants lost 3-2 in 11 innings. Herzog and Fletcher each made an error in Philadelphia's game-winning rally in the 11th. Fletcher stumbled to a record for most career errors in World Series history with 12 in 25 games with the Giants in 1911, 1912, 1913, and 1917. The Giants lost all four Series. Fletcher wasn't much with the bat in the Fall Classic either, compiling only a .191 batting average.

10. RUBE MARQUARD

During the 1920 World Series, Dodgers pitcher Rube Marquard was arrested on a charge of ticket scalping before the seventh game in Marquard's hometown of Cleveland. He was scheduled to pitch the game, but Brooklyn manager Wilbert Robinson started Burleigh Grimes instead of giving him one day's rest. The Dodgers lost 3-0. Marquard paid a fine after a court appearance but maintained his innocence by claiming he had bought the tickets for a friend and was turning them over. The Dodgers traded Marquard to the Reds the following February.

Brain Cramps

There have been many severe lapses in the thought processes of individuals and teams during the World Series.

1. **GUS MANCUSO**

Giants catcher Gus Mancuso had a brain cramp in the first game of the 1937 World Series against the Yankees. In the sixth inning, Giants manager Bill Terry signaled for Dick Coffman to enter the game as a relief pitcher for Carl Hubbell. As Coffman strolled to the mound, Mancuso turned to home plate umpire Red Ormsby and said that Harry Gumbert was the replacement for Hubbell. Gumbert was announced over the loudspeaker at Yankee Stadium as the pitcher of record. As Coffman was set to pitch against Tony Lazzeri, the Yankees objected, pointing to the rule that states that the announced pitcher of record had to pitch to at least one batter. Gumbert was sitting idly in the corner of the dugout and had to face Lazzeri without warming up. Lazzeri reached base on an error, and Coffman went back to the mound. Coffman walked four of the first batters he faced, and the Yankees won the game 8–1.

2. **PITTSBURGH PIRATES**

The Pirates in 1938 had a seven-game lead over the Cubs with four weeks left on the schedule. Anticipating a berth in the World Series for the first time since 1927, the Pirates added 2,500 permanent seats to Forbes Field. The Cubs rallied to nose out the Pirates for the National League pennant, however. Pittsburgh didn't host another World Series until 1960.

3. JOHNNY BENCH

Reds catcher Johnny Bench was the victim of a ruse during the third game of the 1972 World Series against the Athletics. With the count 3–2, runners on second and third base, and one out in the eighth inning, Oakland manager Dick Williams walked to the mound to talk to pitcher Rollie Fingers and pointed toward first base, creating the impression that he wanted Fingers to walk Bench intentionally. Catcher Gene Tenace also signaled for a walk, but Fingers threw the ball down the middle of the plate for a called strike three.

4. JOHN McGRAW

John McGraw's New York Giants won the World Series in 1905. Wishing to rub it into the opposition, McGraw outfitted his club in uniforms in 1906 with the words "World Champions" emblazoned across the front in large letters. The uniforms became objects of derision late in the 1906 season, when the Giants were hopelessly out of the pennant race. The club finished the season in second place but were 20 games behind the pennant-winning Cubs.

5. BILL BUCKNER

Bill Buckner will always be remembered for letting Mookie Wilson's ground ball roll though his legs as the Red Sox first baseman in the sixth game of the 1986 World Series against the Mets, but his baserunning helped cost the Dodgers two games against the Athletics in 1974. Playing left field for Los Angeles, Buckner singled in the first inning of the first game but was picked off first base, and the Dodgers lost 3–2. In the fifth and final game, Buckner was tagged out trying to stretch a double into a triple leading off the eighth inning. The Dodgers lost again 3–2.

6. **1907 CUBS**

For unexplained reasons, the Cubs wore their traveling gray uniforms instead of their home whites during the first game of the 1907 World Series played in Chicago. The Tigers also wore gray, causing considerable confusion. The only difference in the uniforms was in the caps and stockings. The Cubs had gray caps and blue stockings while the Tigers had black caps and stockings. Curiously, the two clubs wearing the same color uniform scored the same number of runs. The game ended in a 3–3 tie, called for darkness after 12 innings.

7. **1932 CUBS**

The 1932 Cubs are infamous for their "tightwad" cut of the World Series shares. Rogers Hornsby managed the Cubs for the first 99 games of the season, before being replaced by Charlie Grimm, but the Cubs voted against giving Hornsby a share of the receipts. Shortstop Mark Koenig was instrumental in Chicago's pennant run, batting .353 in 33 games after being acquired in August from the Pacific Coast League. Despite his contributions, Koenig was voted only a one-half share. Koenig was an ex-Yankee, and during the World Series, the Yankees mercilessly lambasted the Cubs from the dugout. The Yankees swept the Cubs in four straight games. Chicago players apparently failed to learn their lesson. In 1938, Grimm was replaced by Gabby Hartnett as manager in early August, and Cubs players voted against granting Grimm a World Series share. Again the Yankees swept the Cubs in the World Series.

8. **JIMMIE WILSON**

A mistake by Cardinals catcher Jimmie Wilson nearly cost his club a victory in the second game of the 1931 World Series against the Athletics. The Cardinals led 2–0 with two outs in the ninth with Philadelphia base runners Jimmie Foxx on second and Jimmie Dykes on first. Pinch-hitter Jim Moore swung and missed at a third strike, but home plate umpire Dick Nallin ruled that Wilson trapped the ball. Wilson, believing that the game was over, threw the ball to third base. Moore alertly reached first base while most of the Cardinals were leaving the field, loading the bases. Wilson was bailed out when Max Bishop, the next hitter, fouled out to first baseman Jim Bottomley, who made a sensational catch diving headfirst over the Athletics bull pen bench.

9. RED FABER

In the second game of the 1917 World Series against the Giants, White Sox pitcher Red Faber singled with two outs and Buck Weaver as a base runner on first. Faber advanced to second when the Giants tried to throw Weaver out at third. On the next pitch, Faber tried to steal third, quickly forgetting that Weaver already occupied the bag. Faber was tagged out after a beautiful headfirst slide in which he collided with Weaver's feet as he arrived.

10. HEINIE ZIMMERMAN

In the sixth and final game of the 1917 Series, Giants third baseman Heinie Zimmerman chased a run across home plate. With the game scoreless in the fourth inning, Eddie Collins of the White Sox reached first base on Zimmerman's error and moved around to third on another error by right fielder Dave Robertson. Happy Felsch bounced back to pitcher Rube Benton. Collins broke for the plate, and Benton threw the ball to Zimmerman, who in turn relayed to catcher Bill Rariden. Rariden chased Collins back within 15 feet of third and threw the ball back to Zimmerman. Zimmerman tried to tag Collins and missed, and Collins headed back in the direction of home plate. Zimmerman chased Collins instead of throwing the ball back to Rariden, who had to leap out of the base line to avoid being called for interference. Zimmerman was unable to place the tag on Collins, who raced across the plate with the go-ahead run. The White Sox scored three runs in the inning and won the game and the world championship 4–2. It was debated in the sports pages around the country for weeks whether Zimmerman or Rariden was most responsible for the gaffe. Many writers who witnessed the play blamed Rariden, rather than Zimmerman, for running Collins back too close to third base, which made a return throw from the third baseman difficult. Others cited Benton and first baseman Walter Holke for failing to cover home plate. Zimmerman was expelled from organized baseball in 1919 for trying to induce his Giants teammates to throw the final game of the season.

Perfection and Near Perfection

Don Larsen's perfect game in 1956 heads the list of the greatest pitching performances in World Series history.

1. DON LARSEN

Don Larsen burst into the national spotlight on October 8, 1956, when he pitched a perfect game against the Dodgers at Yankee Stadium. It's the only no-hitter in World Series history. Larsen started the second game of the 1956 World Series, and with the Yankees holding a 6–0 lead, he was knocked out in the second inning of a game that was eventually won by the Dodgers 13–8. Yankees manager Casey Stengel brought Larsen back three days later, and the pitcher retired 27 batters in succession for a 2–0 win. Larsen made 97 pitches. The final batter was pinch-hitter Dale Mitchell, who looked at a called strike. The swing from bum to hero was typical of Larsen's erratic career. He came to the Yankees in November 1954 as part of an 18-player trade with the Orioles. With Baltimore in 1954, Larsen had a record of only 3–21 and had a casual regard for training rules. "There's no use trying to reform him," said Orioles manager Jimmy Dykes. "The only thing he fears is sleep." During spring training with the Yankees in 1956, Larsen wrapped his convertible around a telephone pole well after the midnight curfew. "He was out mailing a letter," explained Stengel, who tolerated Larsen's late-night escapades as long as he was ready to pitch. Larsen had an 11–5 record during the 1956 regular season, but that proved to be his single-season career high in victories. His 15-year big league career ended in 1967 with an 81–91 win-loss ledger. Larsen pitched in five World Series, four of them with the Yankees and another with the San Francisco Giants and had a 4–2 record and a 2.75 ERA in 36 innings.

2. **JIM LONBORG**

The Red Sox and the Twins were tied for first place when they met on the final day of the 1967 regular season at Fenway Park. Jim Lonborg pitched the Sox to a 5–3 win to cap Boston's "Impossible Dream" of an American League pennant. The previous two seasons, the Red Sox were in ninth place. Lonborg had a regular-season record of 22–9 in 1967 and won the Cy Young Award. The best game he pitched all year was in the second game of the World Series against the Cardinals. He had a no-hitter going with two outs in the eighth inning when Julian Javier pulled a pitch down the left field line for a double. Lonborg settled for a 5–0, one-hit victory. In the fifth game, he defeated the Cardinals 3–1 with a three-hitter to set a World Series record for fewest hits allowed in two consecutive complete game starts. Lonborg pitched the seventh game on only two days' rest but was routed in a 7–2 defeat. Two months later, on Christmas Eve, he tore knee ligaments while skiing at Lake Tahoe. Lonborg was 27–29 for Boston over the next four years before he was traded to the Brewers. He never appeared in another World Series, although he pitched in a losing cause in the NLCS with the Phillies in 1976 and 1977.

3. **CLAUDE PASSEAU**

Wearing uniform number 13, Claude Passeau pitched a one-hitter for the Cubs against the Tigers in the 1945 World Series. It happened in Game Three in Detroit, which the Cubs won 3–0. The only two Tigers to reach base were Rudy York

Boston Red Sox

Jim Lonborg won the game that clinched Boston's "Impossible Dream" of reaching the World Series in 1967, and then came within four outs of a no-hitter in the second game of the Series.

on a second-inning single and Bob Swift on a sixth-inning walk. Passeau was near the end of a career in which he posted a 162–150 regular-season record. Unfortunately, he's better known for an errant pitch during an All-Star Game than the one-hitter in the World Series. In the 1941 All-Star Game, also at Detroit, Passeau surrendered a game-ending three-run homer to Ted Williams that lifted the American League to a 7–5 win.

4. ED REULBACH

Ed Reulbach of the Cubs pitched a one-hitter to defeat the White Sox 7–1 in Game Two of the 1906 World Series as freezing winds whipped through the White Sox home field at South Side Park. The only White Sox hit was a single by Jiggs Donahue in the seventh inning. There were also sterling pitching performances in the following two games as the autumn cold continued to grip Chicago. In the third game, Ed Walsh of the White Sox pitched a two-hitter and struck 12 Cubs batters to win 3–0. In Game Four, Three Finger Brown of the Cubs allowed just two hits in defeating the White Sox 1–0. Both Walsh and Brown made it to the Hall of Fame, but Reulbach has received no consideration at all for a plaque at Cooperstown despite a 182–106 record and a 2.28 career ERA. Reulbach is also the only pitcher in baseball history to pitch two complete-game shutouts in a doubleheader, which he accomplished against the Dodgers in 1908. In 1916, near the end of his career, Reulbach was active in efforts to unionize major league players and in the Prohibition movement. That year he made a public plea to all players to either stop the consumption of alcoholic beverages or, at the very least, to limit it to one glass of beer or wine at mealtime.

5. WAITE HOYT

The Yankees played in the World Series for the first time in 1921, and pitcher Waite Hoyt hurled 27 innings and allowed only two New York Giants runs, both unearned. In the second game, Hoyt pitched a two-hitter to win 3–0. Four days later in Game Five, Hoyt beat the Giants again 3–1. The Series in 1921 was a best-of-nine affair, and the Yankees went into the eighth game trailing four games to three. Hoyt was called upon again to keep the Yankees alive but lost 1–0 to Art Nehf. The Giants scored their run in the first inning when a two-out grounder rolled through the legs of shortstop Roger Peckinpaugh. During his career, Hoyt pitched in six World Series with the Yankees and another for the Athletics and had a 6–4 record and a 1.83 ERA in $83^{2}/_{3}$ innings. During the regular season, he was 237–182 and was elected to the Hall of Fame in 1969. From 1942 through 1965, he did the play-by-play on the Cincinnati Reds radio broadcasts.

6. GEORGE EARNSHAW

In Game Four of the 1931 World Series, Athletics pitcher George Earnshaw shut down the Cardinals on a two-hitter to win 3–0 at Shibe Park in Philadelphia. Earnshaw answered 38-year-old St. Louis hurler Burleigh Grimes, who had tossed a two-hitter the previous day to beat Philadelphia 5–2. In that game, Grimes held the Athletics hitless until Bing Miller singled with one out in the eighth. Earnshaw had a 127–93 regular-season record in the majors and was 4–3 in World Series play with a sparkling 1.58 ERA in $62^{2}/_{3}$ innings. He is the last pitcher to start consecutive World Series games, doing it in both 1929 (in Games Two and Three two days apart) and 1930 (in Games Five and Six two days apart). Earnshaw was born into wealth to a family on New York's social register and didn't reach the majors until he was 28. He enlisted in the navy during World War II at the age of 41, and reached the rank of lieutenant commander.

7. MONTE PEARSON

In the second game of the 1939 World Series, Yankees pitcher Monte Pearson had a no-hitter against the Reds in New York until Ernie Lombardi singled with one out in the eighth inning. Pearson ended the game with a two-hitter and a 4–0 victory. He finished his career in 1941 with a record of

100–61. One of his regular-season victories was a no-hitter against the Indians in 1938.

8. WARREN SPAHN

Matched up against Whitey Ford, Warren Spahn pitched a two-hitter to give the Braves a 3–0 win over the Yankees in New York in Game Four of the 1958 World Series. He won 363 games during the regular season, the sixth most of any pitcher in history. It is also the most by a left-hander and the most of any pitcher whose career began after 1911. Spahn pitched in three World Series for the Braves, one in Boston and two in Milwaukee, and was 4–3 with a 3.05 ERA in 56 innings.

9. WHITEY FORD

Whitey Ford pitched a two-hitter to defeat the Reds 2–0 in the opening game of the 1961 World Series. It was in the midst of a record-breaking streak of 33 consecutive scoreless innings. Ford pitched two shutouts in the 1960 World Series, downing the Pirates 10–0 with a four-hitter in the third game and 12–0 on a seven-hitter in the sixth game. The first-game whitewash of the Reds extended his streak to 27 scoreless innings, putting him in position to break the record of 29 set by Babe Ruth. Ruth's streak occurred when he pitched for the Red Sox in the 1916 Series against the Dodgers and in 1918 versus the Cubs. Before his death in 1948, Ruth often said that the scoreless inning record was the one he cherished the most, but Ford broke Ruth's mark in the fourth game in 1961, when he shut out the Reds for five innings before departing with an ankle injury. It came just seven days after Roger Maris hit his 61st home run to break the Babe's single-season home run record. Ford started the first game of the 1962 Series and stopped the Giants without a run in the first inning before allowing a run in the second on singles by Willie Mays, Jim Davenport, and Jose Pagan. Ford still won the game 6–2.

10. NELSON BRILES

Nelson Briles of the Pirates allowed two hits to the Orioles to win 4-0 in Pittsburgh. The gem came in the middle of a 14-year career in which Briles compiled a 129-112 record. He previously played in the World Series with the Cardinals in 1967 and 1968. Briles appeared in one more Series after 1971, but it was in front of a microphone when he sang the National Anthem in Oakland before the fourth game of the 1972 Fall Classic. The only pitcher since 1971 to pitch a complete game in a World Series while allowing two hits or fewer is Greg Maddux in Game One in 1995, when he lifted the Braves to a 3-2 win over the Indians.

Rack 'Em Up

The best strikeout performances by a pitcher in a World series include:

1. **BOB GIBSON**

Bob Gibson holds World Series records for the most strikeouts in a game (17), the most strikeouts in a single Series (35 in 1968), and the most games with 10 strikeouts or more (five). Overall, he struck out 92 batters in 81 World Series innings, all with the Cardinals. Gibson had a 7–2 record in the Series and a 1.89 ERA. His astonishing 17-strikeout performance occurred in the first game of the 1968 Series against the Tigers in Detroit. Gibson started the game by fanning six of the first seven batters he faced and closed it by striking out Al Kaline, Willie Horton, and Norm Cash in the ninth inning. He allowed five hits and walked one to win 4–0. That game capped one of the most incredible seasons by a pitcher in baseball history. He posted a 22–9 record and a microscopic 1.12 ERA in $304^{2}/_{3}$ innings and recorded 13 shutouts. Gibson also struck out 13 batters in a 5–2, 10-inning win over the Yankees in Game Five of the 1964 Series at Yankee Stadium. He recorded 10 strikeouts twice versus the Red Sox in 1967, including a 7–2 win in the seventh game. Gibson reached double digits in strikeouts for the fifth time in the fourth game in 1968, a 10–1 victory.

2. SANDY KOUFAX

Bob Gibson's 17 strikeouts in 1968 broke the record of Sandy Koufax, who ranks second in World Series history in single-game strikeouts with 15 in the opening game in 1963. Coming off a season in which he was 25–5 with 11 shutouts and a 1.88 ERA, Koufax fanned 15 to lead the Dodgers to a 5–2 win over the Yankees in New York. He struck out the first

Los Angeles Dodgers

Sandy Koufax ranks second in strikeouts in a World Series game, with fifteen.

five batters he faced and had 11 strikeouts in the first five innings. Koufax struck out 10 batters in two different games in 1965, both shutouts, against the Twins. In the fifth game he beat Minnesota 7–0 on four hits in Los Angeles. In the seventh game, he allowed only three hits and won 2–0. Koufax had a 4–3 record as a World Series pitcher, but his ERA was 0.95 and he struck out 61 batters in 57 innings.

3. CARL ERSKINE

Sandy Koufax snapped the 10-year reign of Carl Erskine as the single-game record holder in strikeouts in a World Series game. Erskine struck out 14 for the Dodgers in a 3–2 win over the Yankees at Ebbets Field in Game Three in 1953. Roy Campanella broke a 2–2 tie with a homer in the eighth inning. In the ninth, Erskine struck out the side. Two days earlier, he had started the Series opener but had been sent to the showers after allowing four runs in the first inning. Three days after fanning 14, Erskine lasted only four innings in a 4–3 loss to the Yankees. In the fifth game in 1952, Erskine had one of the strangest outings of any pitcher in Series history. He allowed only one hit and no runs in the first four innings but was raked for five runs in the fifth inning to fall behind 5–4. Erskine then retired 19 batters in a row to win 6–5 in 11 innings.

4. HOWARD EHMKE

Carl Erskine broke the single-game strikeout record set by Howard Ehmke of the Athletics in 1929. Ehmke started the first game against the Cubs that fall, and in one of the greatest stories in World Series history, he struck out 13 batters and won the game 3–1 before 50,704 people at Wrigley Field. Ehmke was 35 years old in 1929 and pitched only $54^{2}/_{3}$ innings during the regular season with just 20 strikeouts. He was near the end of a mediocre career that finished with a 166–166 record. Athletics manager Connie Mack had a starting rotation of Lefty Grove, George Earnshaw, and Rube Walberg, three pitchers who combined for a 62–25 record in 1929, all healthy and available. But in a brilliant hunch, Mack believed that Ehmke, with his assortment of off-speed sidearm breaking pitches coming out of the white-shirted background of the center field bleachers at Wrigley, was just the man to beat the Cubs. Mack told Ehmke of his plans to have him start the Series opener and sent him to scout the club during the final two weeks of the season. The Athletics manager wanted Ehmke's start to remain a secret, but word leaked out. On the morning of the game, *The New York Times* reported that "the Mack camp radiated mystery in all directions. The front line pitchers, Grove, Walberg, Earnshaw and Quinn, all expect to be called upon to pitch the opener, while the innermost whispers around the lobby hint that Howard Ehmke of all people, will take the slab." The idea seemed so preposterous, however, that most people dismissed it as a smoke screen. Ehmke's stunning World Series victory proved to be his last in the major leagues. He started the fifth game of the 1929 Series but was knocked out in the fourth inning after allowing two runs, although the Athletics rallied to win 3–2. He pitched only three games in 1930 before he was released by the club.

5. ED WALSH

Using a spitball, Ed Walsh of the White Sox fanned 12 batters and allowed only two hits in defeating the Cubs 3–0 in Game Three in 1906. Although he was only 17–13 during the 1906 regular season, Walsh pitched 10 shutouts. He hit his stride in 1908 when he posted a 40–15 record for the White Sox and a 1.42 ERA. Walsh finished his career with a 195–126 record and enshrinement in the Hall of Fame.

6. WILD BILL DONOVAN

Wild Bill Donovan of the Tigers struck out 12 Cubs during the first game of the 1907 World Series played in Chicago, but the game ended in a 3–3 tie because one of the strikeouts resulted in a passed ball. Donovan had a 3–2 lead with two out in the ninth inning with Chicago runners on second and third. Cubs pinch-hitter Del Howard swung and missed at a two-strike pitch that should have ended the game, but the ball got past Detroit catcher Boss Schmidt, which allowed Harry Steinfeldt to score. The game went three more innings before it was called because of darkness with the score 3–3. To add to Schmidt's woes, he allowed seven stolen bases, a World Series record for a single game. The Cubs won the last four games of the Series, and Schmidt made the final out. The Cubs defeated the Tigers in five games in 1908, and once more, Schmidt made the final out of the Series. He is the only player in World Series history to make the final out twice in a career. Donovan finished his career as an active player in 1918 with a 185–139 record. He died in 1923 in a train wreck on his way to attend baseball's annual winter meetings.

7. WALTER JOHNSON

Walter Johnson is second all-time in career victories with 417, all with the Washington Senators. He was also the career strikeout leader from the time he passed Tim Keefe in 1919 until Nolan Ryan broke the record in 1983. Despite his success, Johnson was 36 years old before he pitched in the World Series for the first time, starting the opener of the 1924 Fall Classic against the Giants in Washington. Before the game, Johnson was presented with a green Lincoln limousine by the fans. With President Calvin Coolidge in attendance, Johnson struck out 12 batters in a 12-inning game. Johnson pitched six games for the Senators in the 1924 and 1925 Series and had a 3–3 record and a 2.16 ERA with 35 strikeouts in 50 innings. He is also the oldest pitcher in Series history to throw a shutout. Johnson was 37 years old when he blanked the Pirates 4–0 in Game Four in 1925.

8. MORT COOPER AND DENNY GALEHOUSE

Mort Cooper of the St. Louis Cardinals and Denny Galehouse of the St. Louis Browns are the only opposing pitchers to each strike out at least 10 batters in the same World Series game. It happened in the fifth game of the 1944 Series, won by the Cardinals 2–0. Cooper struck out 12 batters while Galehouse fanned 10.

9. **TOM SEAVER**

Like Wild Bill Donovan and Walter Johnson, Tom Seaver struck out 12 batters in a World Series game he failed to win. Pitching for the Mets, Seaver fanned an even dozen during an eight-inning stint at Shea Stadium in the third game of the 1973 Series against Oakland. Seaver received a no decision in a contest that the Athletics won 3–2 in 11 innings.

10. **MOE DRABOWSKY**

The record for most strikeouts by a relief pitcher in a game is held by Baltimore's Moe Drabowsky, who whiffed 11 Dodgers hitters while pitching $6^{2}/_{3}$ innings in the first game of the 1966 World Series in Los Angeles. He also allowed no runs and only one hit and was the winning pitcher in a 5–2 decision. In addition, Drabowsky tied a Series mark by striking out six batters in a row in the fifth and sixth innings. Born in Ozanna, Poland, Drabowsky had an otherwise undistinguished career, posting an 88–105 record.

Winning Three

Thirteen pitchers have won three games in a single World Series. Deacon Phillippe of Pittsburgh and Bill Dinneen of Boston each won three in the first Series in 1903. Babe Adams also won three as a rookie for the Pirates in 1909. The other 10 pitchers to win three times are:

1. **CHRISTY MATHEWSON**

Christy Mathewson is the only pitcher to throw three shutouts in a single World Series. He pulled off the incredible feat in 1905 while pitching for the New York Giants against the Philadelphia Athletics. It followed a regular season in which he had a 32–8 record and a 1.27 ERA. In the opener, Mathewson defeated the Athletics 3–0 with a four-hitter in Philadelphia. Three days later in Game Three, he pitched another four-hitter to win 4–0, again in Philadelphia. After just one day of rest, Mathewson allowed six hits in a 2–0 victory in the fifth and deciding game. Mathewson wasn't the only pitcher in 1905 to put a string of zeros on the scoreboard. All five games in the 1905 Series were won with shutouts. In the second game, Chief Bender of the Athletics defeated the Giants 3–0. In the fourth game, Joe McGinnity of New York downed Philadelphia 1–0. Mathewson's pitching career ended in 1916. During World War I, he came in contact with poison gas in France and developed tuberculosis. He died in

1925 on the day of that season's World Series opener between the Pirates and the Senators. Ceremonies were held in his honor prior to Game Two.

2. JACK COOMBS

Philadelphia Athletics manager Connie Mack beat the Cubs in the 1910 World Series using only two pitchers. Chief Bender started and completed the first and fourth games, while Jack Coombs won Games Two, Three, and Five. Coombs was coming off a regular season in which he was 31–9, pitched 13 shutouts, and had a 1.30 ERA. He won the second game of the Series 9–3 in Philadelphia. After a travel day, Mack sent Coombs to the mound in Game Three, and was rewarded with a 12–5 victory in Chicago. Three days later, Coombs closed out the Series by winning 7–2. Coombs not only won three games in 1910 but he also contributed five hits, including a double, in 13 at-bats for a .385 average. Coombs won 28 games in 1911 and earned another victory in the World Series. The Athletics won the American League pennant in 1913, but Coombs missed the Series while suffering from typhoid fever, an illness that nearly killed him. He made a comeback, however, and won another game in the Fall Classic for the Dodgers in 1916, extending his win-loss record in the Fall Classic to 6–0.

3. SMOKEY JOE WOOD

Smokey Joe Wood was 34–5, including a 16-game winning streak, for the Red Sox in 1912. He pitched 10 shutouts and had an ERA of 1.91. Wood defeated the Giants 4–3 in the opener of the 1912 World Series in New York, striking out 11 batters. In Game Four, he won again with a 3–1 victory and eight strikeouts. After six games, the Red Sox had three wins and the Giants two with one game ending in a tie. Wood started the seventh game but allowed six runs in the first inning, and the Red Sox lost 11–4. Wood came into the eighth and deciding game at Fenway Park as a reliever in the eighth inning with the score 1–1. He allowed a run in the 10th inning, but his teammates bailed him out with two runs in their half to win the game 3-2 and take the world title. Wood pitched 344 innings during the regular season and another 22 in the World Series in 1912, and the workload was too much for a pitcher who was only 22 years old. By 1916, his pitching days were over, although he ended with a 117-57 lifetime record. After being traded to the Indians, Wood was converted into an outfielder in 1918 and lasted in the big leagues until 1924. He played in four games for Cleveland as a right fielder and pinch-hitter in the 1920 World Series against the Dodgers.

4. **RED FABER**

Red Faber had a 3-1 record for the White Sox in a six-game win over the Giants in the 1917 World Series. He beat the Giants 7-2 by pitching a complete game in the second game in Chicago but lost Game Four in New York 5-0, allowing three runs in seven innings. Two days later, Faber earned a victory in Game Five as a reliever. He pitched the final two innings, retiring all six men he faced, as the White Sox rallied from a 5-2 deficit to win 8 5 on three runs in the seventh inning and three more in the eighth. After a travel day, Faber started Game Six at the Polo Grounds and went all the way for a 4-2 win. He never pitched in another World Series, missing the controversial 1919 Series because of a sore ankle. Faber lasted in the majors until 1933, when he was 45 years old. He won 254 big league games and was elected to the Hall of Fame in 1964.

5. **STAN COVELESKI**

Stan Coveleski worked 72 hours a week in the coal mines in his native Pennsylvania when he was only 12 years old. He escaped from the mines to post a 215-142 record as a big league pitcher and was inducted into the Hall of Fame in 1969. His big moment was in the 1920 World Series against the Dodgers. Pitching for the Indians, Coveleski won all three starts, allowing only two runs in 27 innings. He won the opener 3–1 in Brooklyn, Game Four in Cleveland, and the seventh game 3–0, also in Cleveland.

6. **HARRY BRECHEEN**

Harry Brecheen beat the Red Sox three times in 1946 while leading the Cardinals to the world championship. He started the second game and allowed four hits to defeat the Red Sox 3–0 in St. Louis. In Game Six, Brecheen defeated Boston 4–1 to even the Series at three wins for each club. He entered the seventh game as a reliever in the eighth inning with the Cardinals ahead 3–1, no one out, and runners on second and third. He retired the first two batters he faced but allowed a two-run double to Dom DiMaggio to tie the score. The Cards took a 4–3 lead in the eighth, however, and Brecheen survived a shaky ninth. After he allowed the first two batters to reach base, he retired three batters in a row to nail down the world title. He also pitched in the World Series for St. Louis in 1943 and 1944. Overall, he was 4–1 with an 0.85 ERA in $32^{2}/_{3}$ innings of Series play. Brecheen was also the pitching coach for the Orioles in 1966, a staff that allowed only two runs in a four-game sweep of the Dodgers.

7. **LEW BURDETTE**

Lew Burdette pitched three complete games for the Milwaukee Braves in the 1957 Fall Classic against the Yankees and surrendered just two runs in 27 innings. He closed out the Series with 24 consecutive scoreless innings. Burdette beat the Yankees 4–2 in New York in Game Two. In the fifth game, with Whitey Ford on the mound for the Yankees, Burdette pitched a seven-hitter to win 1–0 in Milwaukee. Warren Spahn was supposed to pitch the seventh game but came down with a case of the flu. Braves manager Fred Haney brought Burdette back on just two days' rest, and Lew hurled another seven-hitter to win 5–0. It was the first time the franchise won a world championship since 1914, when it was located in Boston. The only other pitchers with at least two shutouts in a single World Series are Christy Mathewson in

1905, Whitey Ford in 1960, and Sandy Koufax in 1965. Burdette pitched for the Braves in the 1958 Series but lost two of three decisions to the Yankees.

8. BOB GIBSON

Bob Gibson holds the World Series record for most consecutive victories with seven. Pitching for the Cardinals, he beat the Yankees twice in 1964, the Red Sox three times in 1967, and the Tigers twice in 1968. Each was a complete game, and one of them lasted 10 innings. He also won the seventh game of the 1964 and 1967 Series to become the only pitcher to win two Game Sevens in his career. In those seven consecutive victories, Gibson allowed 11 runs, nine of them earned, and 39 hits in 64 innings while striking out 75 batters.

9. MICKEY LOLICH

Denny McLain won 31 games for the Tigers in 1968 and was supposed to lead his club in the World Series against the Cardinals. The hero of the Series turned out to be number two starter Mickey Lolich, who won three games. After McLain lost to Bob Gibson in the opener, Lolich beat the Cards 8–1 in St. Louis to even the Series. The Tigers lost Games Three and Four, and Lolich came back to start the fifth game in Detroit. He allowed three runs in the first inning but shut out the Cardinals the rest of the way to win 5–3. Tigers manager Mayo Smith gambled by pitching both McLain and Lolich on two days' rest in the sixth and seventh games. McLain defeated the Cardinals 13–1 in the sixth game to even the Series, and Lolich faced Gibson in the seventh game. Not only was Gibson riding his seven-game World Series winning streak, but in his first two starts of the Series, he allowed the Tigers only one run while striking out 27. Lolich upstaged Gibson to win 4–1, however, to give Detroit its first world championship since 1945.

10. RANDY JOHNSON

The only pitcher to win three games in a World Series since 1968 is Randy Johnson for the Diamondbacks against the

Yankees in 2001. In Game Two, Johnson pitched a three-hit shutout with 11 strikeouts to defeat the Yankees 4–0 in Phoenix and put the Diamondbacks up two games to none. The Yankees came back to win all three games in New York, however, the last two with stunning rallies to win in extra innings. Johnson started Game Six and went seven innings as the D'backs recovered to rout the Yankees 15–2. He entered the seventh game in relief in the eighth with two out, a runner on first, and the Yankees leading 2–1. Johnson retired the final batter in the eighth and all three he faced in the ninth. He earned his third victory of the 2001 Series when the Diamondbacks scored two runs in the ninth to win 3–2.

Surprise Packages

The only no-hitter in World Series history was thrown by Don Larsen, who had a lifetime record of 81–91. Many other pitchers with short, ineffective, or mediocre careers spun shutouts in the World Series.

1. **BILL JAMES**

After posting a 6–10 record as a rookie in 1913, Bill James helped the Boston Braves to the 1914 National League pennant with 26 wins against just seven defeats. In the second game of the World Series, James pitched a two-hit shutout to defeat the Philadelphia Athletics 1–0. Two days later, he pitched two innings of scoreless relief in Boston's 5–4, 12-inning victory. James pitched $332 1/3$ innings during the regular season and another 11 in the World Series, and the workload proved to be too much for a right arm that was only 22 years old. After the 1914 Series, James pitched in only 14 more big league games due to a shoulder injury.

2. **DICKIE KERR**

Rookie pitcher Dickie Kerr started Game Three of the 1919 World Series for the White Sox. Chicago lost the first two games with Eddie Cicotte and Lefty Williams on the mound, a pair of twirlers in on the fix with gamblers that threw the Series to the Reds. Kerr stopped the Reds with a three-hitter to win 3–0 at Comiskey Park. After the White Sox lost two more games in the best-of-nine series, Kerr was the winning pitcher again in Game Six, traveling 10 innings for a 5–4 victory. Kerr had a 13–7 record in 1919 and won 40 games over the next two seasons but was offered only a token raise from tightfisted White Sox owner Charlie Comiskey and quit organized baseball to pitch for independent teams. As a minor league manager in Daytona Beach, Florida, in 1940, Kerr converted a sore-armed pitcher named Stan Musial into an outfielder. Musial named his firstborn son Dickie and later bought Kerr and his wife a home in Houston.

3. **JIMMY RING**

The only player named Ring in major league history, Jimmy Ring helped the Reds win a world championship ring in 1919. Ring's fingers flung a three-hitter at the White Sox in Game Four to win 2–0. The three Chicago hits were by Joe Jackson, Happy Felsch, and Chick Gandil, a trio later suspended from baseball for life after being implicated in the Black Sox gambling scandal. Ring had a 12-year big league career, mostly with the Reds and the Phillies, and posted a 118–149 record.

4. **HOD ELLER**

Cincinnati's Hod Eller was another pitcher who threw a shutout in the 1919 World Series, defeating the White Sox 5–0 in Game Five in Chicago. Like Ring in the previous contest, Eller pitched a three-hitter. He struck out a total of nine batters, including a World Series record six in succession in the second and third innings. Although the shutout is tainted by the Black Sox scandal, those not implicated in the gambling fix, including future Hall-of-Famers Eddie Collins and Ray Schalk, had one hit in 11 at-bats and struck out four times. Eller had a 20–9 record in 1919 and often rubbed the ball with talcum powder and paraffin to create a slick surface that caused the ball to dart over the plate. Nicknamed the "shine ball," the pitch was outlawed by major league baseball after the 1919 season. Without his best pitch, Eller lasted only two more seasons and finished his career with a 60–40 record.

5. DUSTER MAILS

Duster Mails was on the Brooklyn Dodgers World Series roster in 1916, but he sat on the bench throughout the five-game loss to the Red Sox. He spent the next three seasons in the minors, before returning to the majors with Cleveland in late August 1920. A native of San Quentin, California, Mails helped the Indians win their first American League pennant in a close race with the White Sox and the Yankees by posting a 7–0 record and a 1.85 ERA down the stretch. All seven of his wins came in September and October, one of which was a pennant-clinching shutout of the White Sox. In the 1920 World Series, the Indians faced off against the Dodgers, the club that had given up on Mails four years earlier. Mails made his first appearance in Game Three, pitching $6^2/_3$ innings of shutout relief, although the Indians lost 2–1. He started the sixth game and continued his shutout streak by tossing a three-hitter to defeat the Dodgers 1–0. The Indians won the world title by winning five of the seven games in the best-of-nine series. Mails won 14 games for Cleveland the next season but had no more success in baseball after 1921. His career ended in 1926 with a 32–25 record.

6. JACK SCOTT

The Reds traded future Hall of Fame pitcher Rube Marquard and starting shortstop Larry Kopf to the Braves in February 1922 to acquire Jack Scott, who reported to spring training with a torn shoulder muscle. Scott pitched only one game in Cincinnati before he was released. The Giants signed Scott, and after his arm recovered, he won eight of 10 decisions during the regular season. Scott started the third game of the 1922 World Series against the Yankees and delivered a four-hitter to win 3–0. He ended his career in 1929 with a record of 103–109.

7. ERNIE WHITE

As a rookie for the Cardinals in 1942, Ernie White was 17–7 with a 2.40 ERA during the regular season and defeated the Yankees 2–0 in the third game of the World Series. He was repeatedly saved by spectacular catches from outfielders Stan Musial, Enos Slaughter, and Terry Moore. Arm problems and two missed seasons due to World War II shortened White's career. His last big league victory was in 1943, and he finished his career with a 30–21 record. No one with fewer career wins has pitched a complete-game shutout in the World Series.

8. CLEM LABINE

Clem Labine spent most of his 13 seasons in the majors in the bull pen and didn't pitch shutouts very often, but when he did, he made them count. His only two career regular-season shutouts were as a rookie for the Dodgers in 1951, the second in the second game of the best-of-three tie-breaker against the Giants, which he won 10–0. Labine pitched in 13 games in the World Series with the Dodgers in 1953, 1955, 1956, and 1959 and as a Pirate in 1960. Just one of the 13 appearances was a starting assignment. Pitching the day after Don Larsen's perfect game, Labine responded with a 1–0, 10-inning victory over the Yankees in the sixth game of the 1956 Series. The only individuals besides Labine to pitch extra-inning shutouts in the World Series are Christy Mathewson (1913) and Jack Morris (1991). Labine is also the only player with fewer than five regular-season career shutouts to pitch one in the World Series.

9. JOHNNY KUCKS

Johnny Kucks was 18–9 with the 1956 Yankees as a second-year, 23-year-old pitcher. He drew the start in the seventh game of the 1956 World Series and helped the Yankees to the world championship by pitching a three-hitter to defeat the Dodgers 9–0. Kucks never won another World Series game and won relatively few during the regular season. His career ended in 1960 with a record of 54–56.

10. **WALLY BUNKER**

Wally Bunker burst onto the major league scene as a rookie with the Orioles in 1964, when he had a record of 19–5, including a pair of one-hitters, at the age of 19. An injured elbow wrecked a promising career, however, and Bunker pitched his last big league game in 1971 at the age of 26. He finished his career with a 60–52 record, but he had one more moment of glory when he pitched a six-hit shutout in the third game of the 1966 World Series to beat the Dodgers 1–0 in the first-ever World Series contest played in Baltimore. Only five games in World Series history have been won by a 1–0 score with a home run providing the lone run. Two of them occurred in consecutive games won by the Orioles in 1966. Paul Blair backed Bunker with a fifth-inning homer. The next day, Frank Robinson beat the Dodgers 1–0 with a homer in the sixth.

Losers in a Duel

Through the 2003 season, 23 World Series games have ended with a 1–0 score. The losers of the pitching duels include:

1. **EDDIE PLANK**

Eddie Plank reached the Hall of Fame by compiling a 326–194 record, mostly with the Philadelphia Athletics, but he had almost no luck at all in the World Series. Plank is the only pitcher in Series history to lose two 1–0 decisions and he is the only pitcher to be on the losing end of four shutouts. In his first World Series in 1905, Plank lost twice to Christy Mathewson and the Giants, 3–0 in the first game and 1–0 in the fourth. The next time the Athletics made the Series was in 1910, and manager Connie Mack elected to use only right-handed pitchers against the Cubs and benched the southpaw Plank. In 1911 against the Giants, Plank entered the fifth game in relief in the 10th inning and allowed a run that lost the contest 4–3. The Athletics played the Giants again in 1913, and Plank was matched with Mathewson again. The two were locked in a scoreless duel until Plank allowed three runs in the 10th inning to lose 3–0. In 1914 against the Braves, he lost again 1–0 to Bill James in Game Two. In all, Plank pitched 54$^{2}/_{3}$ innings in the World Series and posted an excellent earned run average of 1.32 but ended up with only two victories against five defeats. His teammates scored only six runs for him while he was on the mound.

2. NICK ALTROCK

White Sox pitcher Nick Altrock defeated Three Finger Brown of the Cubs in the opener of the 1906 World Series by a 2–1 score but lost a 1–0 duel to Brown in the fourth game. Altrock had an 83–75 record as a major leaguer and would be long-forgotten if it weren't for his sense of humor. He became a coach with the Washington Senators in 1912 and held the job until 1953, delighting fans with his slapstick antics in the coaching box and before games. Along with partner Al Schacht, who was known as "The Clown Prince of Baseball," Altrock performed his pantomime act before World Series games during the 1920s and 1930s and on the vaudeville circuit during the off-season. In 1924, 1925, and 1933, Altrock and Schacht pulled double duty. They performed their comedy act before the games and served as base coaches for the Senators during the contests, with Altrock on first and Schacht on third.

3. HIPPO VAUGHN

On May 2, 1917, while pitching for the Cubs, Hippo Vaughn was the losing pitcher in the only double no-hitter in major league history. Vaughn and Fred Toney of the Reds each pitched nine innings without allowing a hit before Vaughn lost the game 1–0 by allowing a run and two hits in the 10th inning. The Cubs reached the World Series in 1918 against the Red Sox, and Vaughn's ill luck continued. Cubs manager Fred Mitchell believed the lefties were the best way to beat the Red Sox and started Vaughn and Lefty Tyler in all six games. Vaughn pitched three complete games and allowed only three runs but lost two of the games. He lost the opener 1–0 to Babe Ruth and the third game 2–1 to Carl Mays. Hippo beat the Red Sox 3–0 in the fifth game, but it only forestalled the inevitable Chicago Cubs World Series defeat as the Sox won Game Six to capture their last world championship. The Red Sox scored only nine runs in the six games, the fewest by any World Series winner.

4. SAD SAM JONES

Jones was known as "Sad Sam" for his downcast demeanor, and the moniker was appropriate when he lost the third game of the 1923 World Series while pitching for the Yankees by a 1–0 score to the Giants. The only run of the game was scored on a home run into the right field bleachers by Giants Casey Stengel in the seventh inning. Stengel trotted slowly around the bases, and when he crossed the plate, thumbed his nose in the direction of the Yankees bench. It was Stengel's second game-winning homer of the Series. The first was in the ninth inning of the first game, which was the first postseason contest ever played at Yankee Stadium. With the score 4–4, Stengel drove a pitch into deep left center for an inside-the-park homer. Due to frequently injured legs, 32-year-old Stengel moved around the bases like a man running in a sand trap, but he easily beat the throw home from left fielder Bob Meusel to give the Giants a 5–4 win. Those were the only two wins of the Series for the Giants, however, as the Yankees won the world championship for the first time in franchise history. Stengel would later gain fame by managing the Yankees to seven world titles, including five in a row from 1949 through 1953. The winning pitcher in the duel with Jones in Game Three of the 1923 Series was Art Nehf, who is the only pitcher to win two 1–0 World Series games in a career. Nehf also beat the Yankees 1–0 in the final game of the 1921 Series.

5. BOB FELLER

Bob Feller earned a first-ballot election to the Hall of Fame by using a blazing fastball to lead the American League in strikeouts seven times, along with composing a record of 266–162 during his major league career. He never won a World Series game, however. Feller spent his entire career, which started in 1936 and ended in 1956, as a member of the Indians. Cleveland reached the Series twice during that span. In 1948, Feller started the opener against the Braves in Boston. He allowed only two hits but lost 1–0 to opposing pitcher Johnny Sain on a controversial call by second base umpire Bill Stewart. In the eighth inning, Bill Salkeld of the Braves walked, and Phil Masi was sent in as a pinch-runner. After moving to second on a sacrifice, Masi appeared to be picked off by Feller on a tag by shortstop Lou Boudreau, but Stewart called Masi safe on the play. Tommy Holmes drove in Masi with a single for the 1–0 Braves win. Feller started Game Five before a crowd of 86,288 in Cleveland, but he allowed seven runs, and the Braves won 11–5. Those were the only two games that Cleveland lost in the six-game Series. In 1954, the Indians reached the Fall Classic again but were swept by the Giants. Despite a 13–3 record during the regular season, Feller didn't pitch in any of the four games.

6. **DON NEWCOMBE**

As a rookie with the Dodgers in 1949, Don Newcombe became the first African-American pitcher to start a World Series game. He was brilliant in the opening game of the Series, but opposing pitcher Allie Reynolds was better, tossing a two-hit shutout. Newcombe struck out 11 Yankee batters and allowed only five hits but lost 1–0 on a home run by Tommy Henrich leading off the ninth. It was the only time in World Series history that a 1–0 game ended on a home run. Newcombe's bad luck was only beginning. He started five World Series games for the Dodgers in 1949, 1955, and 1956 and had an 0–4 record and an 8.59 ERA. In addition, Newcombe twice had a chance to pitch the Dodgers into the World Series but failed. In the last game of the 1950 regular season, the Dodgers trailed the Phillies in the pennant race by one game and Newcombe was selected as the starting pitcher. The Phillies won 4–1 when he allowed a three-run homer to Dick Sisler in the 10th inning. Newcombe was also the starter in the third game of the best-of-three tie-breaking pennant play-off with the Giants in 1951. He carried a 4–1 lead into the ninth inning but exited after allowing a run and leaving two runners on base. Ralph Branca was brought on in relief and surrendered a three-run homer to Bobby Thomson to give the Giants a 5–4 win and the National League title.

7. JIM KONSTANTY

When the 1950 season began, Jim Konstanty was a relatively unknown 33-year-old relief pitcher with the Phillies. By the time the season ended, Konstanty was the National League MVP. He pitched in 74 games, all in relief, and had a 16–7 record, a 2.66 ERA, and 22 saves. When the World Series began against the Yankees, the Phillies starting rotation was in disarray. Ace Robin Roberts pitched 10 innings in the pennant-clincher on the last game of the regular season and wasn't available for the Series opener. As a result of the Korean War, which began in June, Curt Simmons was inducted into the army in early September. Bob Miller had a sore arm, and Bubba Church had been hit in the face by a line drive three weeks earlier. Phils manager Eddie Sawyer turned to Konstanty to start the opener. It was Konstanty's first major league start since 1946, but he allowed only one run and four hits in eight innings, and the Phillies lost 1–0 in Philadelphia. Vic Raschi pitched the Yankees shutout, allowing only two hits. Konstanty played in the majors until 1956 but never came close to the kind of success he enjoyed in 1950.

8. JIM BOUTON

Jim Bouton is best known for his 1970 book *Ball Four*, a scathing and irreverent look at baseball from a player's point of view. Bouton was uniquely qualified to write such a book, because he knew the highs and lows that an athlete has to endure. In 1963, his second season in the big leagues, Bouton had a 21–7 record for the Yankees and pitched superbly in a third-game start in the World Series against the Dodgers, although he lost 1–0 to Don Drysdale. In 1964, Bouton was 18–13 during the regular season and 2–0 in the World Series with a 1.56 ERA against the Cardinals. After 1964 he won only 16 more big league games while losing 46. He wrote *Ball Four* in 1969 while playing for the expansion Seattle Pilots, the Vancouver Mounties in the Pacific Coast League, and the Houston Astros, while struggling to stay in baseball as a relief pitcher. In 2002, *Sports Illustrated* ranked *Ball Four* as the third-greatest sports book of all time. Contained is one of the best quotes on baseball ever printed: "You spend a good piece of your life gripping a baseball," wrote Bouton, "and in the end it turns out that it was the other way around all the time."

9. **BLUE MOON ODOM**

With Oakland in the 1972 World Series, Blue Moon Odom started Game Three and allowed only one run and three hits in seven innings while fanning 11 but lost 1–0 to Jack Billingham and the Reds. Odom also made the last out in Game Five as a pinch-runner. With one out and the Athletics trailing 5–4 in the ninth, Odom was on third base when Bert Campaneris lifted a foul pop in foul territory behind first base. Second baseman Joe Morgan fielded the ball while backpedaling, and Odom reasoned that he had a chance to score with Morgan off-balance. Morgan righted himself, however, and threw out Odom in a close play at the plate. Blue Moon started the seventh game but was removed in the fifth inning, although the Athletics won 3–2 to take the first of their three straight world titles. Billingham, who defeated Odom in the third game, has the lowest earned run average of any pitcher in World Series history with at least 25 innings pitched. With the Reds in 1972, 1975, and 1976, Billingham allowed only one earned run in $25^{1}/_{3}$ innings for an ERA of 0.36.

10. **JOHN SMOLTZ**

John Smoltz started two World Series games in which the Braves lost 1–0, one of them resulting in a no decision. In the seventh game against the Twins in 1991, Smoltz went $7^{1}/_{3}$ innings without allowing a run. Jack Morris pitched a 10-inning shutout for Minnesota to win 1–0. In the fifth game in 1996, Smoltz lost to Andy Pettitte and the Yankees 1–0.

If I Didn't Have Bad Luck, I Wouldn't Have Any Luck at All

Many other pitchers have been unlucky in the World Series.

1. **BILL BEVENS**

The only pitcher other than Don Larsen to carry a no-hitter into the ninth inning of a World Series contest is Bill Bevens of the Yankees, in the fourth game in 1947 against the Dodgers at Ebbets Field. The Yankees led 2–1, with the Dodgers scoring a run in the fifth on two walks, a sacrifice, and a fielder's choice. Bevens had problems with his control all day, walking a World Series record 10 batters, two of them in the fateful ninth. With one out, Bevens issued a base on balls to Carl Furillo, and Al Gionfriddo entered the game as a pinch-runner for Furillo. Gionfriddo stole second, and Pete Reiser was walked intentionally, as Yankees manager Bucky Harris went against baseball convention by putting the winning run on base. Cookie Lavagetto was sent in as a pinch-hitter for Eddie Stanky and laced a double off the right field wall to score two runs. Just one out from a no-hitter and a 2–1 victory, Bevens ended up losing 3–2. Gionfriddo was heard from again in the sixth game at Yankee Stadium. As a defensive replacement in left field, he robbed Joe DiMaggio of extra bases with a spectacular running catch 415 feet from home plate. Despite the heroics of Lavagetto and Gionfriddo, the Yankees won the Series in seven games. It was also the last moment of glory for the three principals of the historic fourth game. Neither Bevens, Lavagetto, nor Gionfriddo played a major league game after the 1947 World Series.

2. **SHERRY SMITH**

Dodgers pitcher Sherry Smith was the losing pitcher in the longest game in World Series history. Smith was opposed on the mound by Babe Ruth, pitching for the Red Sox in Game Two of the 1916 Series in Boston. Ruth allowed a run in the first inning on an inside-the-park homer to Hy Myers, then shut out the Dodgers for the final 13 innings. Smith allowed the Red Sox to tie the contest in the third and matched Ruth until losing 2–1 in the 14th inning when pinch-hitter Del Gainor drove in a tally with a single. Smith pitched again in the World Series for the Dodgers in 1920 and ran into more bad luck, losing a 1–0 decision to Duster Mails and the Indians in the sixth game in Cleveland.

3. **CHARLIE LEIBRANDT**

With the Royals in 1985 and the Braves in 1991 and 1992, Charlie Leibrandt had an 0–4 record in the World Series. He lost two games as a starter and two as a reliever, usually by failing in a clutch situation. In the second game in 1985 against the Cardinals in Kansas City, Leibrandt entered the ninth with a two-out shutout and a 2–0 lead. He proceeded to allow four runs to lose the contest 4–2. Leibrandt was the Game One starter for Atlanta in 1991 against the Twins and went in to a 5–2 defeat. In the sixth game, Leibrandt took the mound in the 11th inning with the score 3–3 and faced only one batter. Kirby Puckett lined a Leibrandt pitch into the left field stands at the Metrodome for a game-winning homer. Leibrandt made his only appearance of the 1992 Series against the Blue Jays in Atlanta with the score tied 2–2 in the 10th inning of the sixth game and Toronto holding a three-games-to-two lead. After pitching a scoreless inning,

Leibrandt allowed two runs in the 11th inning on a double by Dave Winfield. The Braves scored a run in their half, but it wasn't enough to prevent the Blue Jays from winning Canada's first world championship.

4. HUGH CASEY

Dodgers reliever Hugh Casey had a tough time during the 1941 World Series against the Yankees. In the third game, he allowed two runs in the eighth inning to lose the game 2–1. Casey contributed to the rally defensively when he was late covering first base on Tommy Henrich's grounder to the right side of the infield. Heading into the ninth inning of Game Four, the Dodgers led the Yankees 4–3 at Ebbets Field in the first World Series played at the Brooklyn ballpark since 1920. A Brooklyn win would even the Series at two wins apiece. Casey retired the first two Yankees in the inning. On a 3–2 pitch to Henrich, Casey snapped a low sharp-breaking curveball, and the Yankees batter swung and missed. The ball skidded out of catcher Mickey Owen's mitt and rolled toward the Brooklyn dugout as Henrich reached first base. The Yankees scored four runs before Casey could get the third out. Joe DiMaggio singled, and Charlie Keller put the Yankees in the lead with a double that scored both Henrich and DiMaggio. After Bill Dickey walked, Joe Gordon hit another two-run double, and the Yankees won 7–4. The next day, the Yanks took the world title with a 3–1 win. Owen was charged with a passed ball and has long been saddled with the tag as one of the all-time "goats" of the World Series, but Casey is equally culpable. Some claim that Owen called for a fastball and Casey crossed him up by throwing a spitter. In 1951, less than two years after his playing career ended, Casey committed suicide at the age of 37.

5. MITCH WILLIAMS

Bearing the nickname "Wild Thing," Mitch Williams saved 43 games during the regular season for the Phillies in 1993 and two more in the NLCS against the Braves but was a dismal failure in the World Series versus the Blue Jays. Wearing uniform number 99, Williams was the losing pitcher in Game Four, the highest-scoring contest in Series history. Playing at Veterans Stadium in Philadelphia, Toronto scored three runs in the first inning, but the Phillies countered with four in their half and two more in the second. The Blue Jays took a 7–6 lead with four runs in the third, but Philadelphia tied the score in the fourth and added five more runs in the fifth. After seven innings, the Phils still led 14–9. The Blue Jays scored a run in the eighth and had two runners on base with one out when Williams entered the game. He allowed two singles, a walk, and a triple, and the Jays scored six times in the inning to win 15–14. The big blow came in Game Six. Toronto had a three-games-to-two lead in the Series when Williams came into the contest with a 6–5 lead in the ninth. He allowed a walk to Rickey Henderson, a single to Paul Molitor, and a dramatic three-run homer to Joe Carter over the left field wall on a 2–2 pitch that ended the Series with Toronto's second consecutive world title. The only other home run that ended a World Series was struck by Bill Mazeroski in 1960. The pitch to Carter was the last that Williams threw for the Phillies, and he was never again an effective pitcher. He lasted three more seasons in the majors with three clubs and walked 52 batters in 37 1/3 innings for an ERA of 7.96.

6. **PAT MALONE**

The Athletics defeated the Cubs in three of the first four games in 1929. Pat Malone, who was 22–10 during the regular season that year, was designated by Cubs manager Joe McCarthy as the starting pitcher in Game Five in Philadelphia to keep his club alive. Malone took a 2–0 lead and a two-hitter into the ninth before coming apart. He struck out Walt French to start the inning but allowed a single to Max Bishop and a homer to Mule Haas to tie the score. After Mickey Cochrane grounded out, Al Simmons doubled, and after Jimmie Foxx was intentionally walked, Bing Miller slashed a two-bagger to score Simmons with the Series-winning run. Two days earlier, in Game Four, Malone gave up a hit that capped a record-setting 10-run inning by the Athletics. The Cubs led 8–0 when Philadelphia came to bat in the bottom of the seventh inning. Simmons started things off with a homer off Charlie Root. After five singles, one of which Chicago center fielder Hack Wilson lost in the sun, Root was replaced by Art Nehf. Wilson lost another ball in the sun off a drive by Haas that went for a three-run inside-the-park home run to make the score 8–7. After Nehf walked Cochrane, Sherriff Blake relieved and gave up two singles, the second of which tied the score 8–8. Malone replaced Blake, loaded the bases by hitting Bing Miller with a pitch, and then gave up a two-run double to Jimmie Dykes that gave the Athletics a 10–8 victory.

7. PAT DARCY

The sixth game of the 1975 World Series between Cincinnati and Boston at Fenway Park is often considered the most exciting in baseball history. The Reds needed only one victory to take the club's first world championship since 1940 against a Red Sox club that hadn't won it all since 1918. Fred Lynn opened the proceedings with a three-run homer off Gary Nolan in the first inning, but the Reds came back to tie the game 3–3 in the fifth when Ken Griffey Sr. hit a two-run triple and scored on a single by Johnny Bench. George Foster put the Reds ahead with a two-run double in the seventh, and Cesar Geronimo added an insurance run in the eighth with a homer to give the Reds a 6–3 lead, but the Red Sox tied the score 6–6 on a three-run homer by Bernie Carbo. Boston loaded the bases with none out in the ninth but couldn't score. A double play started by Red Sox right fielder Dwight Evans stopped a Reds rally in the 11th. Evans made a spectacular catch, reaching into the stands to rob Joe Morgan of a home run, and doubled up Griffey at first. Pat Darcy, the Reds' eighth pitcher, retired the Red Sox in order in both the 10th and 11th innings, but he couldn't get past Carlton Fisk leading off the 12th. Fisk blasted off the foul pole top of

If I Didn't Have Bad Luck . . .

Fenway's "Green Monster" in left field to lift the Red Sox to a 7–6 win. Darcy had an 11–5 record as a 25-year-old rookie for the Reds in 1975, but he lasted only one more season. He had a 2–3 record and a 6.23 ERA for the Reds in 1976 and never again pitched in the majors.

8. JEFF WEAVER

Yankees pitcher Jeff Weaver surrendered the home run which proved to be the turning point of the 2003 World Series against the Marlins. Heading into Game Four at ProPlayer Stadium in Miami, the Yankees held a two-games-to-one lead. The Marlins led 3–1 heading into the ninth inning of Game Four, when Ruben Sierra hit a two-run, two-out, two-strike triple off Urgeth Urbina to tie the score 3–3. It was still 3–3 in the 12th when Weaver gave up a homer to Alex Gonzalez to lift the Marlins to a 4–3 win. The Marlins won Games Five and Six to take the world championship. The only other World Series homer struck later than the 10th inning was Carlton Fisk's in Game Six in 1975.

9. BARNEY SCHULTZ

As a 38-year-old reliever with little previous success in the big leagues, Barney Schultz used his knuckleball to save 14 games and post a 1.64 ERA for the pennant-winning Cardinals in 1964. In Game Three of the World Series against the Yankees in New York, Schultz threw only one pitch, which resulted in a game-winning home run by Mickey Mantle in the 10th inning to give the Yanks a 2–1 win. Mantle's blast was one of the longest in Series history, landing in the third deck at Yankee Stadium. In the sixth game, Schultz gave up four runs in one-third of an inning in an 8–3 Cardinals loss in St. Louis.

10. BYUNG-HYUN KIM

In his only two appearances in the 2001 World Series, Diamondbacks reliever Byung-Hyun Kim gave up two-out, two-run homers in the ninth inning on back-to-back nights at

Yankee Stadium in Games Four and Five. The fourth game was played on Halloween, and Arizona had a 3–1 lead with two out in the ninth with a runner on first base when Tino Martinez tied it up with a clutch homer into the center field seats. In the 10th, Kim retired two batters before allowing a game-winning homer to Derek Jeter. The same situation occurred the following night in the first Series game ever played in the month of November. The Diamondbacks led 2–0 in the ninth when Jorge Posada led off the inning with a double off Kim. The next two batters were retired before Scott Brosius belted a home run into the left field seats. The Yankees won the game 3–2 in the 12th inning on a run-scoring single by Alfonso Soriano off Albie Lopez.

Mound Misadventures

Many pitchers have set World Series records they would just as soon forget.

1. **CHARLIE ROOT**

Cubs pitcher Charlie Root was the first of three pitchers to share the record for most home runs allowed in a game with four. The third of the four is one of the most famous home runs in baseball history. Three batters into Game Three against the Yankees at Wrigley Field, Root was already behind 3–0 after Babe Ruth sent a three-run homer into the right center field bleachers. Lou Gehrig led off the third with another homer. The Cubs battled back to tie the score 4–4 when Ruth batted in the fifth. Ruth took two strikes, seemed to point his bat toward the pitcher's mound, then boomed a homer into the center field bleachers. Gehrig followed Ruth with a homer of his own. The debate over whether or not Ruth "called his shot" by pointing his bat toward the outfield to indicate that he would drive a pitch for a home run is part of baseball legend. According to the description by longtime sportswriter John Drebinger in the following day's edition of *The New York Times*, "Ruth came up in the fifth and in no mistaken motions the Babe notified the crowd that the nature of his retaliation would be a wallop right out of the confines of the park. Root pitched two balls and two strikes while Ruth signaled with his fingers after each pitch to let the spectators know exactly how the situation stood. Then the mightiest blow of all fell." The Associated Press report added that as Ruth "trotted around the bases he held up four fingers, signifying a home run." It proved to be the last of the Babe's 15 career World Series home runs.

2. JUNIOR THOMPSON

The second of the three pitchers to surrender four homers in a game was Junior Thompson of the Reds in 1939. In Game Three of the 1939 World Series against the Yankees at Crosley Field in Cincinnati, Thompson gave up home runs to Charlie Keller in the first inning, Joe DiMaggio in the third, and Keller and Bill Dickey in the fifth. The Reds lost 7–3. Thompson also made an ineffective start against the Tigers in 1940. His World Series résumé includes 13 runs allowed in eight innings for a 14.63 ERA.

3. DICK HUGHES

Dick Hughes compiled a 16–6 record for the pennant-winning Cardinals in 1967 as a 29-year-old rookie. In the World Series against the Red Sox, he tied a record by allowing four homers in a game and set one by giving up three home runs in an inning. Pitching in the fifth game at Fenway Park, Hughes allowed a second-inning homer to Rico Petrocelli, but the Cardinals still led 2–1 in the fourth. Yastrzemski led off the inning with a home run, and with two out, Reggie Smith and Petrocelli hit back-to-back round-trippers. The Red Sox went on to win 8–4. Hughes pitched only one more season in the majors and won just two games.

4. GEORGE FRAZIER

Only two pitchers have lost three games in a World Series. The first was Lefty Williams with the 1919 White Sox, who was accused of intentionally losing all three and banished from baseball for life. The second was Yankees relief pitcher

Mound Misadventures

George Frazier in 1981. The Yankees won the first two games of the Series against the Dodgers before losing four in a row. In the third game, Frazier relieved Dave Righetti in the third inning with the Yankees leading 4–3, and gave up two runs in the fifth to account for a 5–4 defeat. In the fourth game, Frazier surrendered two runs in the seventh with the score tied 6–6, and the Yankees lost 8–7. In Game Six, Yankees manager Bob Lemon, in a controversial decision, pinch-hit for starting pitcher Tommy John in the fourth inning with the score 1–1. Frazier relieved John and gave up three runs in the fifth, and the Dodgers won the game and the world championship with a 9–2 decision. Frazier appeared in the World Series again for the Twins in 1987 and pitched two shutout innings in what proved to be his last big league appearance. He ended a 10-year career with a regular-season record of 35–43.

5. **BRUCE KISON**

The only pitcher in World Series history to hit three batters in a game is Bruce Kison of the Pirates against the Orioles in the fourth game in 1971, played at Three Rivers Stadium in Pittsburgh. Kison was a 21-year-old rookie who had earned a reputation for pitching inside and being unafraid to plunk a batter with a pitch while in the minor leagues. Despite hitting Andy Etchebarren, Frank Robinson, and Dave Johnson with pitches, Kison was otherwise brilliant, pitching $6^1/_3$ innings in relief, allowing no runs and just one hit. He didn't walk a single batter. The Pirates won the game 4–3 in a contest that was historically significant because it was the first night game in World Series history. Kison had planned to get married four days later, on October 17, and refused to change the date even though the seventh game of the World Series was scheduled that day. While his teammates were spraying champagne in the clubhouse celebrating a world championship, Kison took a helicopter to the Baltimore airport, where he boarded a private jet to Pittsburgh in time for the wedding.

6. BRICKYARD KENNEDY

Pitching for the Pirates in the fifth game of the 1903 World Series against Boston in Pittsburgh, Brickyard Kennedy set a record for most runs allowed in a game. He allowed 10 runs in seven innings, although only four were earned. Kennedy pitched five shutout innings before giving up six runs in the sixth inning and four in the seventh. Pittsburgh lost the contest 11–2. It was the last game of Kennedy's career, in which he had a 187–159 record over 12 seasons.

7. HOOKS WILTSE

Giants pitcher Hooks Wiltse set the record for the most runs allowed in an inning with seven during a 13–2 loss to the Athletics in Game Six in 1911. Wiltse was shelled during the seventh inning of a $2^{1}/_{3}$-inning relief appearance. In the second game of the 1913 World Series, Wiltse was a hero playing first base. Starting first baseman Fred Merkle was out with an ankle injury, and backup Fred Snodgrass hurt himself in the third inning. Wiltse had played first base three times during the regular season in emergencies and was pressed into service again. Playing with a fielder's glove instead of a first baseman's mitt, Wiltse saved the game in the ninth inning with the score 0–0. Twice in the inning, he made a brilliant stop of a ground ball and threw home to nail an Athletics runner trying to score from third base. The Giants won the game 3–0 in 10 innings.

8. CARL HUBBELL

Carl Hubbell tied Wiltse's record by allowing seven runs in the sixth inning of the first game in 1937 in an 8–1 Giants loss to the Yankees. Hubbell had retired 13 batters in a row before coming apart at the seams. It was one of the few bad outings for Hubbell during a career in which he posted a 253–154 record and earned a ticket to Cooperstown.

9. ED SUMMERS

Tigers pitcher Ed Summers had a 24–12 record as a rookie in 1908 but set a record by allowing six consecutive hits against the Cubs in the first game of the World Series. The Tigers led 6–5 in Detroit when Summers took the mound in the ninth inning. After retiring the first batter of the inning, Summers gave up six straight singles, two of which failed to leave the infield. The Cubs also added two stolen bases and scored five runs to win 10–6. Summers finished his career with an 0–4 record in World Series play and a 68–45 mark during the regular season.

10. JOHNNY MILJUS

Johnny Miljus of the Pirates earned two distinctions during the fourth and final game of the 1927 World Series against the Yankees. He tied a record for most wild pitches in an inning with two and became the only pitcher in history to end a Series with a wild pitch. With the score 3–3 in the ninth inning, Miljus walked Earle Combs on four pitches, gave up a bunt single to Mark Koenig, threw a wild pitch that moved Koenig to second and Combs to third, intentionally walked Babe Ruth, and threw a wild pitch that scored Combs to give the Yankees a four-game sweep.

Not Again!

Through the 2003 World Series, there have been 13 instances in which a pitcher has surrendered back-to-back homers, including:

1. **EMIL YDE**

The first pitcher to allow back-to-back homers in a World Series was Emil Yde of the Pirates in the third inning of the fourth game in 1925 against the Senators. Yde pitched with a submarine motion, but it didn't fool Goose Goslin, who smacked a three-run homer. Joe Harris followed with a solo shot. Those accounted for the only runs in a 4–0 Senators win at Washington.

2. **BILL SHERDEL**

Cardinals pitcher Bill Sherdel thought he caught Babe Ruth looking at a third strike on an 0–2 pitch in the seventh inning of Game Four in 1928, but home plate umpire Bill Pfirman ruled it was a quick pitch because Ruth wasn't in the batter's box. After looking at two balls to even the count, Ruth smacked Sherdel's offering over the right field pavilion in St. Louis. It was the second of three homers Ruth hit during the afternoon. Lou Gehrig followed Ruth with a homer of his own that cleared the pavilion roof. It was Gehrig's fourth homer of the Series. The Yankees won 7–3 to complete a four-game sweep. Ruth and Gehrig also teamed for consecutive homers off Charlie Root of the Cubs in the third game in 1932. They are the only teammates to hit consecutive homers twice in World Series play. Sherdel finished his career with an 0–4 World Series record, losing twice to the Yankees, in 1926 and again in 1928.

3. **CURT SIMMONS**

Another Yankees home run duo targeted the pavilion roof at old Busch Stadium in St. Louis (known as Sportsman's Park prior to 1953) in Game Six in 1964. Facing Curt Simmons with the score 1–1 in the sixth inning, Roger Maris hit a homer onto the roof. Mickey Mantle followed with a blast that struck the screen on the back of the roof. The Yankees went on to win the game 8–3. Simmons pitched well in the third game of the 1964 Series, allowing only one run in eight innings, but wound up with a no decision. It was a 14-year wait for Simmons to reach the Fall Classic. While with the National League champion Phillies in 1950, Simmons was the first player drafted by the military during the Korean War, which began in June of that year. The military commitment cost Simmons a chance to pitch in the Series.

4. **DON DRYSDALE**

Don Drysdale and Frank Robinson had a long-standing feud during their years together in the National League. The Reds traded Robinson to the Orioles after the 1965 season, and he won the American League MVP award in 1966, leading Baltimore to the World Series against the Dodgers. Don Drysdale started the first game for Los Angeles, and in the first inning, Robinson launched a two-run homer. Brooks Robinson followed with another home run, and the Orioles began the four-game sweep of the Dodgers with a 5–2 victory. In the fourth game of the 1966 Series, Robinson hit a homer off Drysdale in the sixth inning that accounted for the only run in a 1–0 decision.

5. RICK WISE

Rick Wise allowed consecutive homers to Dave Concepcion and Cesar Geronimo, the 7–8 hitters in the Reds lineup, during the fifth inning of the third game of the 1975 World Series, played at Riverfront Stadium in Cincinnati. Six homers were hit during the evening in a contest won by the Reds 6–5 in 10 innings. Wise had a much better outing against the Reds at Riverfront Stadium while with the Phillies in the 1971 regular season, when he became the only pitcher in major league history to pitch a no-hitter and hit two home runs in the same game.

6. RON GUIDRY

The Dodgers and the Yankees split the first four games in the 1981 World Series, and the Yanks led 1–0 in the seventh inning of the fifth game in Los Angeles. Through his first $6^{1}/_{3}$ innings, Yankees pitcher Ron Guidry had allowed only two hits and had struck out nine, but with one out in the seventh, Pedro Guerrero and Steve Yeager homered into the left center field bleachers to give the Dodgers a 2–1 victory. Los Angeles took the world title in Game Six with a 9–2 decision at Yankee Stadium.

7. RON DARLING

The Red Sox appeared to have recovered from their heart-rending Game Six loss to the Mets in 1986 when Dwight Evans and Rich Gedman hit consecutive homers off Ron Darling in the second inning of the seventh game to take a 3–0 lead. The advantage held up until the sixth inning, when the Mets began another comeback and won the world title with an 8–5 victory.

8. OREL HERSHISER

Orel Hershiser had many great moments in baseball's postseason, but the first game of the 1997 World Series wasn't one of them. Pitching for the Indians against the Marlins in

Los Angeles Dodgers

Orel Hershiser was unable to duplicate the World Series success he found with the Dodgers while a member of the Cleveland Indians.

Miami, Hershiser gave up seven runs in 4$^1/_3$ innings. In the fourth inning, Moises Alou and Charles Johnson hit back-to-back homers off Orel, and the Marlins went on to win 7–4.

9. DAVID WELLS

With the score tied 2–2 in the fifth inning of the first game of the 1998 World Series in New York, Yankees pitcher David Wells surrendered a two-homer to Tony Gwynn, followed by a solo homer off the bat of Greg Vaughn. The Yankees rallied to win 9–6, however, to begin a four-game sweep of San Diego.

10. KEVIN APPIER

Anaheim hurler Kevin Appier is the latest pitcher to allow consecutive homers in the World Series. In the second game of the 2002 Classic, the Angels staked Appier to a 5–0 lead over the Giants in the first inning, but he squandered most of it in the second by allowing four runs, including back-to-back homers to Reggie Sanders and David Bell. The Giants took a 9–7 lead with four runs in the fifth inning but ended up losing 11–10.

Helping His Own Cause

Pitchers have occasionally helped themselves by hitting a home run in a World Series. Through the 2003 season, 14 homers have been hit by pitchers in the Fall Classic, with Dave McNally and Bob Gibson the only ones to do it more than once.

1. **JIM BAGBY SR.**

The first home run by a pitcher in the World Series was struck by Jim Bagby Sr. of the Indians in the historic fifth game in 1920 against the Dodgers, played at League Park in Cleveland. Following a season in which he posted a win-loss record of 31–12, Bagby hit his homer with two runners on base in the fourth inning off Burleigh Grimes. On the mound, Bagby allowed 13 hits but won the game 8–1. Grimes also surrendered the first grand-slam home run in Series history in the first inning of the same game. It was hit by Cleveland right fielder Elmer Smith with no one out after Grimes loaded the bases on three singles. The most famous play in Game Five wasn't by Bagby or Smith, however. It was by Indians second baseman Bill Wambsganss, who pulled an unassisted triple play in the fifth inning. It's not just the only unassisted triple play in Series but the only triple play of any kind. Dodgers pitcher Clarence Mitchell, who replaced Grimes, hit into the triple killing. With Pete Kilduff on second base and

Otto Miller on first, Mitchell lined to Wambsganss, who made a leaping one-handed catch with both runners moving on a hit-and-run play. Wambsganss stepped on second to force Kilduff and tagged Miller, who was standing in the base line as stiff as a statue as if stunned by the catch. Mitchell grounded into a double play in his next at-bat to make five outs in back-to-back plate appearances. Otherwise, Mitchell was an excellent hitter who was often used as a pinch-hitter, outfielder, and first baseman during his 18-year career. He finished his stay in the majors with a .252 average, only seven points behind Wambsganss's .259, in 13 seasons.

2. JACK BENTLEY AND ROSY RYAN

New York Giants pitchers Jack Bentley and Rosy Ryan both homered in the 1924 Series against the Senators. Ryan hit his off Allan Russell in the fourth inning of the third game, played at the Polo Grounds and won by the Giants 6–4. Ryan hit only one homer in 268 at-bats in the regular season, during his major league career. Bentley homered off Walter Johnson in Game Five in New York. It was hit in the fifth inning with a runner on base and broke a 1–1 tie. The Giants went on to win 6–2. Bentley was an excellent hitter, batting .291 with seven homers in 584 regular-season at-bats. He led the National League in pinch-hits in both 1923 and 1925 and was five for 12 overall in the World Series. He had a 46–33 career record as a pitcher.

3. JESSE HAINES

In the third game of the 1926 World Series, played in St. Louis, Cardinals pitcher Jesse Haines hit a three-run homer in the fourth inning off Dutch Ruether and shut out the Yankees 4–0. He was the first of two pitchers to hit a home run and pitch a shutout in the same World Series game. Haines reached the Hall of Fame with a 210–158 record as a pitcher. He hit three regular-season homers in 1,124 at-bats.

4. BUCKY WALTERS

The only pitcher besides Haines to hurl a shutout and hit a homer in the same World Series game was Bucky Walters of the Reds, against the Tigers in 1940. Detroit led the Series three games to two when Walters kept the Reds alive with a 4–0 win at Crosley Field in Cincinnati. He hit his homer in the eighth inning off Fred Hutchinson, who later managed the Reds in the 1961 World Series. Walters came to the majors in 1931 as a third baseman with the Red Sox. He was converted into a pitcher in 1934 while with the Phillies. The manager of the Phillies that season was Jimmie Wilson, who was also the Reds catcher when Bucky pitched the Game Six shutout in the 1940 Series. Walters finished his career with a 198–160 win-loss mark as a pitcher and won the National League MVP award in 1939 on the basis of his 27–11 record. He hit .243 with 23 homers in 1,966 lifetime at-bats.

5. **LEW BURDETTE**

Lew Burdette capped a seven-run first inning by hitting a three-run homer off Duke Maas in the Braves' 13–5 victory over the Yankees in Game Two of the 1958 World Series at County Stadium in Milwaukee. It was the only time in Series history that a club scored as many as seven runs in the first inning. Leadoff hitter Bill Bruton accounted for the first of the seven runs with a homer off Bob Turley.

6. **MUDCAT GRANT**

Twins pitcher Mudcat Grant hit a three-run homer in the sixth inning of the sixth game of the 1965 World Series off Howie Reed of the Dodgers. Grant pitched a complete game to win 6–1 at Metropolitan Stadium in Bloomington, Minnesota. Mudcat was 21–7 for the Twins in 1965, the highlight of his 145–119 career. As a hitter, he had six homers in 759 regular-season at-bats.

7. **BOB GIBSON**

Bob Gibson was the first of two pitchers to hit two homers in World Series play. He is also the only pitcher to hit a homer in a Game Seven. It happened in 1967 off Jim Lonborg of the Red Sox at Fenway Park in the fifth inning to give the

Cardinals a 3–0 lead. Gibson allowed only three hits and struck out 10 batters to win 7–2. He hit his second Series home run in the fourth game in 1968, leading off the fourth inning against Tigers pitcher Joe Sparma. In addition, Gibson drew a bases-loaded walk in the eighth inning and won 10–1. He also fanned 10 batters in that game. No one else has had a home run and reached double figures in strikeouts in the World Series during his career. Gibson did it in both 1967 and 1968 in the same game. He is also the only pitcher to homer in a Series game and to give up a homer to another pitcher. In the first game of the 1967 World Series, Gibson surrendered a third-inning home run to opposing pitcher Jose Santiago but allowed no other runs and won 2–1 in Boston. It was Santiago's first World Series at-bat, and he is the only pitcher to hit a World Series homer in a losing cause. He hit just one regular-season homer in 162 at-bats. Santiago's lone regular-season homer was off Mickey Lolich, who made World Series history of his own.

8. MICKEY LOLICH

Mickey Lolich batted 821 times during the regular season over a 16-year big league career and had a .110 batting average without a single home run. But he hit a homer in the World Series while playing for the Tigers in the second game of the 1968 Series against the Cardinals. It was struck in the first World Series at-bat of his career and broke a scoreless tie in the second inning. The drive was no wall-skimmer, easily clearing the left field fence at Busch Stadium and settling into the seats. The pitching victim was Nelson Briles, who lost an 8–1 decision to Lolich. Lolich went on to earn World Series Most Valuable Player honors by defeating the Cardinals three times, including a Game Seven duel with Bob Gibson by a 4–1 score.

9. DAVE McNALLY

Dave McNally's two World Series homers tied the record for career home runs by a pitcher set by Bob Gibson. But Mc-

Nally has a claim to fame that Gibson can't match. McNally is the only pitcher in Series history to belt a grand slam. He hit it while playing for the Orioles against the Reds in the sixth inning of the third game of the 1970 Series in Baltimore. The slam was served up by Wayne Granger in a contest won by the Orioles 9–3. McNally also homered in the fifth game against the Mets in 1969 at Shea Stadium off Jerry Koosman. McNally's homer gave the Orioles a 2–0 lead in the third inning. Another homer by Frank Robinson later in the inning put Baltimore ahead 3–0. Koosman allowed no more runs, however, and McNally couldn't hold the lead as the Mets won the game and the world championship 5–3.

10. **KEN HOLTZMANN**

The last pitcher to homer in a World Series was Ken Holtzmann of the Athletics in the fourth game in 1974 against the Dodgers. It was hit off Andy Messersmith in a 5–2 win. It is also the only home run hit by a pitcher since the designated hitter rule was passed in 1973. Holtzmann didn't make a plate appearance during the 1974 regular season.

Surprising Power

Pitchers aren't the only ones who have shown surprising power in a World Series game.

1. **TOMMY THEVENOW**

Tommy Thevenow played 15 years in the major leagues and hit only two regular-season home runs, both inside the park, in 4,164 at-bats. He holds the big league record for most consecutive regular-season at-bats without a homer. From September 24, 1926, through the end of his career in 1938, Thevenow went 3,347 at-bats without a home run while playing for the Cardinals, Phillies, Pirates, Reds, and Braves. He did hit a homer during the 1926 World Series, however, as a shortstop for the Cardinals. In the ninth inning of the second game at Yankee Stadium, Thevenow hit a drive off Sad Sam Jones to right field, which Babe Ruth dropped while running full speed. Thevenow just beat Ruth's throw to the plate. The official scorer ruled it a home run, which capped a 6–2 St. Louis victory. A .247 career hitter, Thevenow batted .417 in the 1926 Series with 10 hits in 24 at-bats.

2. **TOM LAWLESS**

Tom Lawless was traded even up for Pete Rose in 1984 when Rose went from the Expos to the Reds to serve as player-manager. Any comparison to Rose ends there. Lawless had a .207 career batting average with only two homers and 24 runs batted in over 531 at-bats between 1982 and 1990. Playing on the pennant-winning Cardinals in 1987, Lawless batted just 25 times during the regular season and had only two hits for an .080 batting average with a big fat zero in the RBI column. Due to an injury to third baseman Terry Pendleton, Lawless played three games at the position during the 1987 World Series against the Twins in a platoon with Jose Oquendo. Lawless had only one hit in 10 at-bats in the Series, but the hit was a three-run homer off Frank Viola during Game Four in St. Louis. The blast broke a 1–1 tie in the fourth inning of a game won by the Cardinals 7–2. Doing his best Reggie Jackson impersonation, Lawless stood at the plate to watch his drive sail toward the outfield and flipped his bat into the air when the ball cleared the fence.

3. DAVY JONES

Davy Jones was the Tigers leadoff hitter and left fielder in the 1909 World Series against the Pirates, playing in the same outfield as Hall-of-Famers Ty Cobb and Sam Crawford. In Game Five in Pittsburgh, Jones led off the game with a homer off Babe Adams. The ball cleared the temporary fence built in center field to hold back the overflow crowd of 21,706. It was Jones's first homer since 1904, when he was playing for the Cubs. Jones didn't hit another major league homer until 1914, while a member of the Pittsburgh Rebels of the Federal League. He finished his career with only nine home runs in 3,772 at-bats.

4. CHICK FEWSTER

Chick Fewster played left field for the Yankees in the sixth game of the 1921 World Series against the Giants in place of Babe Ruth, who was suffering from an infected arm and a bad knee. Ruth finished his career with 714 career homers. Fewster had only six of them in 1,963 regular at-bats, but with the score tied 3–3, Chick smacked a two-run homer in the second inning off Jesse Barnes, although the Giants recovered to win 8–5.

5. **AL WEIS**

As a utility infielder with the White Sox and the Mets, Al Weis hit only seven homers with a .219 batting average in 1,578 at-bats between 1962 and 1971. In 1969, Weis hit .215 for the Mets, playing second base against left-handed pitchers in a platoon with Ken Boswell. But in the Mets' shocking upset win over the Orioles in the 1969 World Series, Weis starred with his bat, collecting five hits including a homer, in 11 at-bats for a .455 batting average. Things didn't start well for the Mets. In the opening game in Baltimore, Orioles leadoff hitter Don Buford homered off Tom Seaver's second pitch, and the Mets went down to defeat 4–1. In Game Two, Weis hit an RBI single in the ninth inning off Dave McNally to break a 1–1 deadlock and lift the Mets to a 2–1 win. Boswell started Game Three at second base, won by the Mets 5–0 in New York. Weis returned in the fourth game and had two hits in the Mets' 2–1, 10-inning victory. In the fifth game, with the Mets trailing 3–2 in the seventh inning, Weis tied the score with a home run off McNally. It was the only home run that Weis ever hit at Shea Stadium. The Mets went on to win 5–3 to take the championship.

6. **BILL BATHE**

As a reserve catcher, Bill Bathe hit just .213 with eight homers in 183 career at-bats. He didn't hit a home run during the 1989 regular season, but he belted one in a pinch-hit role for the Giants during the World Series that fall against the Athletics. It came in Game Three, which was delayed for 10 days by the earthquake that struck the San Francisco Bay area. It was also Bathe's first World Series at-bat. Bathe's homer was one of seven hit that night in San Francisco, a record for most home runs in a game by two teams. Five of them were hit by the Athletics, which tied the mark for one team set by the 1928 Yankees. Two of Oakland's homers were struck by Dave Henderson, along with one each by Tony Phillips, Jose Canseco, and Carney Lansford. Besides Bathe, Matt Williams homered for San Francisco.

7. JIM MASON

Jim Mason has the unique distinction of being the only player to hit a homer in his only World Series at-bat. It occurred when he was a New York Yankee in 1976 against the Reds. Mason went into the game as a defensive replacement at shortstop and lined a homer into the left field stands at Yankee Stadium in the seventh inning off Pat Zachry, although the Yankees lost 6–2. Mason played nine seasons in the majors and hit only .203 with 12 homers in 1,584 at-bats.

8. KURT BEVACQUA

Kurt Bevacqua spent 15 seasons in the majors, from 1971 through 1985, as a utility player with six clubs, performing at every position except pitcher and catcher. In 1984 with the Padres, Bevacqua hit just .200 with one homer in 80 at-bats, but San Diego manager Dick Williams played a hunch and started Bevacqua in all five games as designated hitter in the World Series against the Tigers, and he responded with two home runs. (At the time, the DH rule was used in every game in even-numbered years.) Bevacqua became the "goat" of the first game when he was thrown out in the seventh inning while trying to stretch a double into a triple with no one out in the seventh inning in a 3–2 Padres loss in San Diego. In Game Two, Bevacqua hit a three-run homer off Dan Petry in the fifth inning that put the Padres ahead 5–3. The edge held up as relievers Andy Hawkins and Craig Lefferts combined to allow no runs and two hits in $8^{1}/_{3}$ innings. Bevacqua homered again in the fifth game in Detroit, but the Tigers won 8–4 to clinch the Series.

9. EDDIE MOORE

Second baseman Eddie Moore keyed a sixth game World Series win for the Pirates at Forbes Field in Pittsburgh's world championship season of 1925. With the Senators leading 2–0, Moore led off the third inning by drawing a walk on a full count that started a two-run rally that tied the score. He led off the fifth with a home run that provided the winning tally in the Pirates' 3–2 win. Moore played 10 seasons in the majors and hit just 13 homers in 2,484 at-bats.

10. **MARTY CASTILLO**

A home run for the Tigers in the third game of the 1984 World Series against the Padres was the highlight of Marty Castillo's career. He played five years in the majors as a reserve third baseman and catcher and hit only eight regular-season homers in 352 at-bats over five seasons.

Stepping Up When It Matters Most

Many other little-known players have had big moments in the World Series.

1. JACK LAPP

The 1911 New York Giants stole a major league record 347 bases but were shut down by Athletics catchers Ira Thomas and Jack Lapp in the World Series. The Giants attempted to steal 17 times and were successful in only four attempts. In the third game, won by the Athletics 3–2 in 11 innings, five Giants tried to steal a base, and all five were nailed by Lapp, who was a backup catcher for most of his nine-year big league career.

2. OLAF HENRIKSEN

Olaf Henriksen was one of baseball's early pinch-hitting specialists. He played seven years with the Red Sox, from 1911 through 1917, and never had more than 100 at-bats in a season, but he delivered a huge pinch hit in the eighth and deciding game of the 1912 World Series against the Giants. With his team trailing 1–0 with two outs in the seventh inning, Henriksen drove in a run with a double off Christy Mathewson to tie the score. Boston went on to capture the world championship with a 3–2 victory with a pair of runs in the

10th inning. Henriksen was born in Kirkerup, Denmark, but his nickname was "Swede."

3. HANK GOWDY

Catcher Hank Gowdy had an unbelievable World Series in 1914 to key the Boston Braves upset sweep of the Philadelphia Athletics. A .243 hitter during the regular season, Gowdy had six hits, including three doubles, a triple, and a homer, in 11 at-bats for an average of .545. He also drew five walks to reach base 11 times in 16 plate appearances. When the United States became involved in World War I in 1917, Gowdy was the first major leaguer to enlist and saw combat in France. During World War II, while serving as a coach for the Reds, Gowdy reenlisted at the age of 52 and became a special services officer at Fort Benning, Georgia, with the rank of major.

4. JOE GARAGIOLA

During his long career in television, Joe Garagiola made light of his playing career, in which he batted .257 during a nine-year stint as a catcher. As a rookie with the Cardinals in the 1946 World Series, the opposing Red Sox weren't laughing as Garagiola had six hits in 19 at-bats for a .316 average. In Game Four, he had four hits, including a double in a 12–3 victory in Boston.

5. KIKO GARCIA

Kiko Garcia had a 10-year career as a utility infielder in which he batted only .239. During the 1979 World Series with the Orioles against the Pirates, Garcia was a .400 hitter, collecting eight hits in 20 at-bats. In the third game, Kiko had four hits, including a double and a triple, in four at-bats. He drove in four runs and scored two in Baltimore's 8–4 victory in Pittsburgh. In the same contest, left fielder Benny Ayala, who had only 86 at-bats during the regular season, hit a two-run homer for the Orioles. In 1983, Garcia was on the Phillies

Stepping Up When It Matters Most

St. Louis Cardinals

Joe Garagiola hit .316 as a rookie in the 1946 World Series—almost 60 points higher than his career batting average.

roster in the World Series against the Orioles but didn't appear in a game.

6. DANE IORG

As a National Leaguer, Dane Iorg had never served as a designated hitter until the 1982 World Series. Playing for the Cardinals against the Brewers, Iorg took to the DH assignment without hesitation, picking up nine hits, including four doubles, in 17 at-bats for a batting average of .529. Iorg played in one more Series, with the Royals against his former Cardinals teammates in 1985. He hit only .223 during the regular season and had only one hit in two pinch-hit at-bats in the World Series, but that one hit was perhaps the most important in Kansas City baseball history. In the sixth game, Iorg's single in the ninth inning drove in two runs to give the Royals a 2–1 victory. The next evening, the Royals captured the only world championship in the franchise's history. Dane's brother Garth played for the Blue Jays in the 1985 ALCS against the Royals.

7. BILLY BATES

Reds infielder Billy Bates became an unlikely World Series hero during the second game in 1990 against the Athletics in Cincinnati. Bates was acquired by the Reds in a trade with the Brewers the previous June and had only five at-bats, and no hits, with his new club. Bates entered the 1990 World Series with only six major league hits and a batting average of just .125. Despite Bates's lack of hitting credentials, Reds manager Lou Piniella used him as a pinch-hitter with one out in the 10th inning to face Athletics reliever Dennis Eckersley, who held the opposition to a .160 batting average during the regular season. Bates beat out an infield single, moved to second on a single by Chris Sabo, and scored on a double by Joe Oliver to lead the Reds to a 5–4 victory. It was Bates's only career postseason plate appearance. It was also his last plate appearance in the major leagues.

8. MARK LEMKE

Braves second baseman Mark Lemke is the only player in World Series history to collect three triples in consecutive games. Lemke first assumed the mantle of hero with a single in the 12th inning of the third game that drove in the winning run in Atlanta's 5–4 triumph. In the ninth inning of Game Four against the Twins in Atlanta, he tripled with one out and scored the winning run in the Braves' 3–2 win. The next evening, Lemke hit two triples in Atlanta's 14–5 win. Overall, he had 10 hits and batted .417 during the 1991 Series. During the regular season, he hit only .234 and had just two triples. Lemke wasn't the only surprise hero in the 1991 Series. He scored the winning run in the fourth game on a sacrifice fly by journeyman catcher Jerry Willard. Scott Leius, a reserve rookie infielder with the Twins, hit a home run in the eighth inning of Game Two to give Minnesota a 3–2 win. Gene Larkin, a substitute outfielder, drove in the lone run as a pinch-hitter in the Twins' 1–0, 10-inning victory in Game Seven.

9. CRAIG COUNSELL

Craig Counsell has only six hits in 46 at-bats in the World Series through 2003, but he has participated in two game-winning seventh-game rallies. In 1997, as a 27-year-old rookie with the Marlins, Counsell tied the score 2–2 against the Indians in Miami by hitting a sacrifice fly with two out in the ninth inning. In the 11th, he reached base on an error and scored the winning run on Edgar Renteria's single. The Marlins had acquired Counsell only three months earlier in a trade with the Rockies. While playing for Arizona in the 2001 Series versus the Yankees, Counsell was hit by a pitch with one out to keep alive a rally that scored two runs and gave the Diamondbacks a 3–2 victory and the world title.

10. JOSE VIZCAINO

Jose Vizcaino didn't start in any of the 2000 Division Series or League Championship Series games for the Yankees but was in the starting lineup at second base in Game One of the World Series against the Mets. Yankees manager Joe Torre took a hunch and played Vizcaino because he was 10 for 19 during his career against Mets starting pitcher Al Leiter. Vizcaino collected four hits in six at-bats. His fourth base hit drove in the winning run in the 12th inning to give the Yankees a 4–3 victory. It ended the longest game, by time, in World Series history at four hours and 51 minutes. Another unsung Yankees second baseman had a big hit in the fifth and final game of the 2000 Series. In the ninth inning with the score 2–2, Luis Sojo drove in a run with a single. The Yankees took the title with a 4–2 victory.

Starting with a Bang

Through the 2003 season, 16 players have led off the first inning of a World Series game with a homer, including:

1. **PATSY DOUGHERTY**

In the second game of the first World Series in 1903, Boston's Patsy Dougherty became the first player to hit a leadoff homer and the first to homer twice in a game. Dougherty led off the first inning with an inside-the-park to deep right-center off Pittsburgh's Sam Leever at Huntington Avenue Grounds in Boston. Dougherty homered again in the seventh over the left field fence off reliever Bucky Veil. Boston won the game 3–0. The outburst wasn't typical of Dougherty's career. He is the only player with fewer than 40 career homers to hit two in a Series game, and it was the only time that he hit more than one homer in a game. Dougherty hit only 17 regular-season homers in 4,558 at-bats.

2. **PHIL RIZZUTO**

In the fifth and final game of the 1942 World Series, Yankees shortstop Phil Rizzuto homered into the lower left field stands at Yankee Stadium off Johnny Beazley of the Cardinals. Beazley settled down, however, and won the game 4–2 to clinch the world championship for St. Louis. Whitey Kurowski broke a 2–2 tie with a two-run homer in the ninth off Red

Ruffing. Rizzuto played in nine World Series with the Yankees, seven of them on the winning side. He just missed playing on two other world championship clubs. In 1943 he was in the service while the Yankees defeated the Cardinals. In 1956, his last season in the majors, Rizzuto was on the roster in late August when the Yankees acquired Enos Slaughter from the Athletics. Manager Casey Stengel and general manager George Weiss decided that Rizzuto should be the one to be cut from the squad to make room for Slaughter. Stengel and Weiss brought Rizzuto into the club offices on the pretense of asking for his advice on whom should be released. They had hoped that Rizzuto would bow out gracefully and volunteer to retire, but he named half the players on the roster before Stengel and Weiss had to inform Rizzuto that he was the one being let go. The Yankees moved on to defeat the Dodgers in seven games in the Series. Rizzuto went directly from the playing field to the Yankees broadcast booth, a job he held for nearly 40 years. He was elected to the Hall of Fame in 1994.

3. **DALE MITCHELL**

Cleveland left fielder Dale Mitchell led off Game Five of the 1948 Series with a homer off Nelson Potter of the Braves. The Indians lost the game 11–5 but won the Series in six games. Mitchell hit .312 in 1,127 major league games, but is best known as the final batter in Don Larsen's perfect game in Game Five of the 1956 World Series. Pinch-hitting for Sal Maglie, Mitchell looked at a ball outside and a called strike, swung and missed at a pitch to make the count 1–2, fouled a ball into the left field stands, and took a pitch on the outside edge of the plate that home plate umpire Babe Pinelli called strike three. It was Mitchell's second-to-last major league at-bat. His final plate appearance came two days later in Game Seven, when he grounded out as a pinch-hitter.

4. **GENE WOODLING**

Gene Woodling led off Game Five in 1953 at Ebbets Field by homering into the left field stands off Johnny Podres. It was the first of six homers hit in the contest, which was won by the Yankees 11–7. Woodling is one of eight players who played in all five of the World Series won consecutively by the Yankees from 1949 through 1953. The others are Yogi Berra, Johnny Mize, Phil Rizzuto, Hank Bauer, Vic Raschi, Ed Lopat, and Allie Reynolds. Woodling closed his career in 1962 as a member of the New York Mets club that lost 120 games.

5. **AL SMITH**

Al Smith of the Indians hit the first pitch of Game Two in 1954 for a home run over the left field roof of the Polo Grounds off Giants pitcher Johnny Antonelli. It was the only run that Cleveland scored in the game, however, as the Giants rallied to win 3–1. Smith was involved in a bizarre incident in the 1959 World Series while playing left field for the White Sox. In Game Two at Comiskey Park, Charlie Neal of the Dodgers homered into the first row of the stands. A fan scrambling for the ball knocked a cup of beer off the top of the wall. Smith had backed up to the wall in an attempt to catch Neal's hit and was looking straight up when the sudsy contents came tumbling down and splashed him in the face.

6. **TOMMIE AGEE**

In the first World Series contest ever played at Shea Stadium, Tommie Agee started the Mets half of the first inning with a home run off Jim Palmer, setting the stage for a 5–0 win in Game Three in 1969. In addition to the leadoff home run, Agee saved at least five runs with two tremendous catches in center field. In the fourth inning with two out and two runners on base, Elrod Hendricks drove a Gary Gentry pitch into deep left center, where Agee made a backhanded fingertip catch at the base of the wall. In the seventh, Gentry walked with the bases loaded and two out. Mets manager Gil Hodges brought in Nolan Ryan to pitch to Paul Blair, and Agee saved the day again with a belly-sliding catch of Blair's liner in right center. Ryan earned a save by pitching $2^{1}/_{3}$ innings of shutout ball, striking out three, in what proved to be the only World Series appearance of his career.

7. **PETE ROSE**

Pete Rose started off Game Five in 1972 with a home run off Catfish Hunter in Oakland. The Reds' 1–0 lead didn't last long, though, as the Athletics scored three runs in the second inning and were still ahead 4–2 after four innings. The Reds fought back to tie the score with a run in the fourth and another in the eighth and won the contest 5–4 on Rose's RBI single. Hunter is the only pitcher to give up a leadoff homer more than once in the World Series. It happened to him three times. The second was to Wayne Garrett of the Mets in the third game of the 1973 Series in New York. The Athletics came back to win the game 3–2 in 11 innings. The third was to Dave Lopes of the Dodgers in Game Six of the 1978 Series when Hunter was pitching for the Yankees. Lopes led off the first with a homer into the left field bleachers at Dodger Stadium, but the Yankees recovered to win the game 7–2 and take the world title for the second year in a row.

8. **LENNY DYKSTRA**

The Mets lost the first two games of the 1986 World Series to the Red Sox at Shea Stadium. Lenny Dykstra put the Mets back on track in Game Three with a leadoff homer off Oil Can Boyd at Fenway Park. It was the first of his four hits of the evening as New York won the game 7–1. Dykstra hit two homers for the Mets in the 1986 Series and slugged four of them for the Phillies in 1993. In just 50 World Series at-bats, Dykstra hit six home runs. He scored 13 runs and drove in 11 in 13 games, in addition to having a batting average of .320 and a slugging percentage of .700. The only players with a higher slugging percentage in World Series history (with a minimum of 50 plate appearances) are Reggie Jackson (.755), Babe Ruth (.744), and Lou Gehrig (.731). Dykstra's regular-season lifetime slugging percentage was .419. His six Series homers is also a record for a batter hitting out of the leadoff position in the batting order. Dykstra also starred in the NLCS. In 1986 he hit a two-run homer in the bottom of the ninth inning of Game Three to give the Mets a 6–5 win over the Astros. His pinch-hit triple in the Mets pennant-clinching sixth game sparked a three-run rally that tied the game, and his RBI single in the 16th inning provided the winning run in the longest postseason game in history. In Game Five in 1993, his 10th-inning homer beat the Braves 4–3 in Atlanta. Counting the NLCS, Dykstra hit .321 with 10 homers in 112 at-bats in the postseason.

9. RICKEY HENDERSON

Through the 2003 season, Rickey Henderson holds the regular-season record for most leadoff home runs in a career with 80. He also hit one of them in the World Series, in the fourth and final game in 1989. Henderson started off the Athletics' 9–6 win over the Giants at Candlestick Park with a homer off Don Robinson.

10. DEREK JETER

During the 2000 World Series, Derek Jeter batted leadoff in Game Four and second in the other four contests during the Yankees' five-game win over the Mets. In the game he led off, Jeter homered in the first inning off Bobby Jones to lead the Yankees to a 3–2 win at Shea Stadium.

There's Only One Chance to Make a First Impression

Through the 2003 season, 27 players homered in their first World Series at-bat, including:

1. **JOE HARRIS**

The first player to homer in his first World Series at-bat was right fielder Joe Harris of the Senators against the Pirates in 1925. It was the start of a remarkable series for Harris, who collected 11 hits, including three homers and two doubles, in 25 at-bats for a .440 average. The Senators released Harris a year later, and the Pirates, impressed by his World Series performance against them, acquired him to play first base. Harris appeared for Pittsburgh in the 1927 Series against the Yankees, but he was only three for 15 as the Pirates lost four in a row.

2. **MEL OTT**

Mel Ott homered in his first and last at-bats in the 1933 World Series for the Giants against the Senators. In the first inning of the first game, Ott hit a two-run homer into the lower right field stands at the Polo Grounds. He also had three singles during the afternoon, leading the Giants to a 4–2 win. In the fifth and final game, played at Griffith Stadium in Washington, Ott hit a 10th-inning homer off Jack Russell to clinch the world championship with a 4–3 victory.

3. **GEORGE SELKIRK**

After the Yankees sold Babe Ruth to the Braves in 1935, the man to replace him in right field was George Selkirk. Nicknamed "Twinkletoes," Selkirk was even given Ruth's uniform number, 3. Selkirk couldn't begin to fill Ruth's shoes, but in his first World Series at-bat, in the first game of the 1936 World Series against the Giants, Selkirk homered off Carl Hubbell. George played in six Series for the Yankees, from 1936 through 1942.

4. **ELSTON HOWARD**

Elston Howard became the first African-American to play for the Yankees when he was brought up from the minor leagues in 1955, eight years after the major league debut of Jackie Robinson. In his first at-bat in the World Series played that fall, Howard homered off Brooklyn pitcher Don Newcombe in Game One. As a rookie in 1947, Robinson was the first African-American to play in a World Series. The first black player to homer in the Series was Larry Doby with the Indians in 1948. The first pitcher was Satchel Paige, also with the 1948 Indians. Newcombe was the first African-American starting pitcher as a Dodger in 1949. The first winning pitcher was Joe Black with Brooklyn in 1952. The first African-American umpire in the postseason was Emmett Ashford in 1970. Cito Gaston became the first African-American manager in the Series when he guided the Blue Jays to back-to-back world titles in 1992 and 1993.

5. **ROGER MARIS**

In his first season with the Yankees following a trade from the Kansas City Athletics, Roger Maris won the American League Most Valuable Player award in 1960 and played in his first World Series. He launched a homer into the upper deck in the right field at Forbes Field in his first Series at-bat in Game One against the Pirates. Maris was the AL MVP again in 1961 after hitting 61 regular-season homers. In the World Series that year, he hit a ninth-inning homer to defeat the Reds 3–2 at Crosley Field. Maris played in five straight World Series for the Yankees, from 1960 through 1964, and two more with the Cardinals, in 1967 and 1968. He hit six homers in 152 Series at-bats, although his batting average was only .217.

6. **BROOKS ROBINSON**

Brooks Robinson played in four World Series for the Orioles, starting off with a home run in his first at-bat in 1966 facing Don Drysdale at Dodger Stadium. Of course, Brooks is best known for his Gold Glove defense at third base, especially against the Reds in 1970. Robinson made a half-dozen heart-stopping plays in almost every conceivable manner during the Orioles' five-game victory. He brought a halt to Cincinnati rallies by ranging far to his right with backhand stabs, to his left with stops in the hole, by charging the ball and making bare-handed throws, and by leaping in the air to snare drives ticketed for extra bases. Robinson also contributed mightily with a bat in his hands in 1970, batting .429 with two home runs, one of them a game winner in the seventh inning of the first game, which broke a 3–3 tie with a solo homer over the left field fence at Riverfront Stadium.

7. **GENE TENACE**

Gene Tenace became the first of two players in World Series history to hit a home run in his first two World Series at-bats, for the Athletics against the Reds in 1972. Tenace was an unlikely source for the power surge. During the 1972 regular season, he hit just five homers and batted only .225 in 227 at-bats. His previous experience in the postseason was in the 1971 and 1972 ALCS, and Tenace had only one hit in 20 at-bats. He was in the starting lineup as a catcher in the opening game in Cincinnati and hit a two-run homer in the second inning and a solo homer in the fourth, both off Gary Nolan. It was the first multiple-home-run game of Tenace's career. The pair of homers provided all the runs the Athletics needed to win 3–2. Tenace wasn't done. He homered in the fifth inning of Game Four at Oakland, which gave the Athletics a 1–0 lead, and hit a single and scored the winning run in the Athletics' two-run rally in the ninth inning to win another 3–2 decision. Tenace hit a fourth homer in the fifth game and drove in two of his club's three runs in the deciding seventh game, won again by the A's with a 3–2 score. He played in the World Series again, with the Athletics in 1973 and 1974 and with the Cardinals in 1982, and never hit another home run. Those were also his only four homers in 114 postseason at-bats, making his postseason batting average only .158. The only other player with homers in his first two World Series at-bats is Andruw Jones with the Braves against the Yankees in 1996.

8. **AMOS OTIS**

Amos Otis made an impact in his first World Series by homering in his first at-bat with the Royals against the Phillies in 1980. Otis had 11 hits, including three homers and two doubles, in 23 at-bats for a .478 average, but his heroics received little notice because the Royals lost in six games and his teammate Willie Aikens hit four homers. It was typical of Otis's career, in which he went almost unnoticed. During the 1970s, Otis ranked fourth in the majors in runs scored, ninth in hits, sixth in doubles, and 10th in stolen bases.

9. **BOB WATSON**

Bob Watson homered in his first World Series at-bat, as a Yankee against the Dodgers in 1981. Watson became baseball's first African-American general manager when he was hired by the Astros at the end of 1993. Two years later, he moved into the Yankees front office and was the general manager when the club won the world championship in 1996.

10. **BARRY BONDS**

Barry Bonds knew nothing but frustration during his first five forays into baseball's postseason. In the NLCS with the Pirates in 1990, 1991, and 1992, and the Division Series with the Giants in 1997 and 2000, Bonds hit only .196 with just one homer and six runs batted in in 97 at-bats. Although a world championship still eluded him, Bonds had a spectacular postseason with San Francisco in 2002. In 17 games, he hit .356 with a .978 slugging percentage and a .581 on-base percentage. He hit eight homers in 45 at-bats, drew 27 walks, scored 18 runs, and drove in 16. Bonds hit a homer in his first World Series at-bat, connecting off Jarrod Washburn in a 4–3 Giants win in San Francisco. He also homered in the second and third games to become the first player in history to homer in his first three Series games. He added another homer in Game Six and finished the Series with a .471 batting average, a .700 on-base percentage, a 1.294 slugging percentage (the best of any player in a World Series lasting longer than four games), a record 13 walks, four homers in 17 at-bats, eight runs scored and six runs batted in. Two of Barry's home runs at Anaheim during the 2002 Series traveled an estimated 485 feet each. On one of them, an Angels fan tried to toss the ball back onto the playing field, but the ball had been hit so deep that his throw didn't make it out of the seats.

A Pinch of Homers

Through the 2002 season, there have been 17 pinch-hit home runs in World Series history by 15 different players, including:

1. YOGI BERRA

Yogi Berra accounted for the first pinch-hit home run in World Series history in Game Three in 1947, played at Ebbets Field. Berra homered while batting for Sherm Lollar against Dodgers pitcher Ralph Branca. The Yankees lost the game 9–8 but came back to win the Series in seven games. Berra holds World Series records for most Series played (14), most consecutive World Series played (five), most Series played on a winning club (10), most games in his career (75), most at-bats in his career (259), most hits in his career (71), most singles in his career (49), and most doubles in his career (10). Berra is also the only player with both a pinch-hit homer and a grand slam in the World Series. Berra hit a grand slam in Game Two in 1956 off Don Newcombe of the Dodgers.

2. JOHNNY MIZE

Johnny Mize hit 359 home runs during his career with the Cardinals, Giants, and Yankees from 1936 through 1953. He would have had a shot at 500 career homers if he hadn't missed three seasons while serving in the navy during World War II. By the time Mize was acquired by the Yankees in 1949, he was near the end of the line, serving as a part-time first baseman and pinch-hitter, but he played on five world champion teams during his last five years in the majors. Mize intended to retire after the 1952 World Series but changed his mind after collecting six hits, including three homers and a double, in 15 at-bats as the Yankees defeated the Dodgers in seven games. One of his homers was in a pinch-hit role in Game Three off Preacher Roe.

3. **DUSTY RHODES**

No pinch-hitter in baseball history has had a better World Series than Dusty Rhodes of the Giants in 1954 in a four-game sweep over the Indians. In the 10th inning of the first game at the Polo Grounds, Giants manager Leo Durocher called upon Rhodes to pinch-hit for Monte Irvin with one out and two runners on base, the score 2–2, and Bob Lemon pitching for Cleveland. Rhodes smacked Lemon's first pitch for a home run to give the Giants a 5–2 win. The right field line at the Polo Grounds was only 257 feet long, and Dusty's drive barely cleared the wall. In Game Two, Rhodes pinch-hit for Irvin again, this time in the fifth inning with the Indians leading 1–0 and runners on first and third. Rhodes singled to tie the score, and the Giants added another run later in the inning to take a 2–1 lead. He stayed in the game in left field and homered off Early Wynn in the seventh inning to add an insurance run in the Giants' 3–1 victory. In the third game in Cleveland, Rhodes pinch-hit for Irvin in the third inning and hit a two-run single. In his first four at-bats in the 1954 Series, Rhodes had two homers and two singles and drove in seven runs. He was hitless in his final two at-bats in the third game and didn't play at all in Game Four, but the Giants closed out the Series with 6–2 and 7–4 wins. Rhodes played seven years in the majors and showed occasional power with 54 homers in 1,172 at-bats and a .253 batting average, but he never batted more than 244 times in a season because of difficulties hitting left-handers and deficiencies on defense.

4. CHUCK ESSEGIAN

Chuck Essegian is one of two players to hit two pinch-hit home runs in the World Series. Both of Essegian's homers were struck while he was with the Los Angeles Dodgers against the White Sox in 1959. The first was in the seventh inning of the second game with the Dodgers trailing 2–1 in Chicago. Essegian homered off Bob Shaw to tie the score 2–2. Later in the inning, Charlie Neal hit his second homer of the game, and the Dodgers went on to win 4–3. Essegian's second pinch-hit homer of the Series was belted in the ninth inning of the sixth and final game, won by the Dodgers 9–3 at Comiskey Park. During the 1959 regular season, Essegian hit only one homer in 124 at-bats. He is also one of only two athletes to play in both the Rose Bowl and the World Series. He played linebacker for Stanford in the Rose Bowl in 1952. The other is Jackie Jensen, who scored a 67-yard touchdown in the 1949 Rose Bowl for California and appeared in the 1950 World Series with the Yankees.

5. BERNIE CARBO

The only player besides Chuck Essegian to hit two pinch-hit homers in the World Series is Bernie Carbo in 1975. Carbo and his Red Sox teammates were playing against the Reds, a club on which he had played in the World Series in 1970. In Game Three, Carbo homered in the seventh inning off Clay Carroll in Cincinnati, although the Red Sox lost the game 6–5 in 10 innings. Carbo's pinch-hit homer in Game Six led to a Boston extra-inning win at Fenway, however. He came to the plate with the Red Sox trailing 6–3, two out, and runners on first and second. Facing Rawly Eastwick, Carbo barely got a piece of a two-strike pitch that dribbled foul and kept the at-bat alive. Carbo drove Eastwick's next offering into the bleachers for a three-run homer that tied the score 6–6. Carlton Fisk's dramatic home run in the 12th sealed Boston's 7–6 victory.

6. **ED SPRAGUE JR.**

With the Blue Jays in 1992, Ed Sprague Jr. hit a game-winning pinch-hit home run in his first World Series at-bat. Toronto lost Game One to the Braves in Atlanta 3–1 and were trailing 4–3 in the ninth inning of the second game when Sprague stepped to the plate against Jeff Reardon with a runner on first base. Sprague smacked a homer over the left field fence to lift the Blue Jays to a 5–4 victory. Cheering him on in the stands was his wife, Kristin Babb-Sprague, who won a gold medal for the United States in synchronized swimming in a controversial decision over a Canadian swimmer. During the previous regular season, Sprague had batted only 47 times and hit just one homer. His father, Ed Sr. was on the Reds roster during the 1972 World Series but didn't appear in a game.

7. **JIM LEYRITZ**

In postseason play with the Yankees in 1995, 1996, and 1999 and the Padres in 1998, Jim Leyritz had only 13 hits in 61 at-bats for a .213 average. Eight of his 13 hits were home runs, however, many of them in key moments. In the 1995 Division Series against the Mariners, Leyritz hit a two-run 15th-inning homer off Randy Johnson to give the Yankees a 7–5 win. It was not only the latest home run in postseason history but also an act of revenge. The previous May, Johnson had hit Leyritz in the face with a pitch. In the fourth game of the 1996 Series against the Braves in Atlanta, Leyritz hit a three-run homer in the eighth to tie the score 6–6. The Yankees won 8–6 in 10 innings in a game in which the club had trailed 6–0 after five innings. Leyritz had entered the game in the sixth inning as a defensive replacement. While playing with the Padres in the 1998 Division Series, Leyritz hit three homers in four games against the Astros. One of them in Game Three broke a 1–1 tie in the seventh inning and gave

San Diego a 2–1 victory. Back with the Yankees in 1999, Leyritz hit a pinch-hit homer in the fourth game of the World Series in a 4–1 win over Atlanta. It was the last home run hit during the 20th century.

8. BOB CERV

The New York Yankees and the Kansas City Athletics participated in 17 trades between 1955 and 1960. Bob Cerv was one of many players who was shuttled back and forth between the two clubs. He was rarely in the starting lineup during his big league career but made the most of an opportunity as an everyday player while he was with the Athletics in 1958 by hitting 38 home runs with a .305 average despite having his mouth wired shut for six weeks because of a broken jaw. Cerv hit 12 pinch-hit home runs in the regular season during his career. In the World Series, he was three for three as a pinch-hitter, with a homer in 1955 and singles in 1956 and 1960. In 1961, Cerv lived with Mickey Mantle and Roger Maris in an apartment in Queens while his two roommates were pursuing Babe Ruth's single-season home run record. The relationship between Maris and Mantle was depicted in Billy Crystal's HBO movie *61**, and an actor playing Cerv was in several scenes in the film.

9. JAY JOHNSTONE

Jay Johnstone lasted 20 seasons in the majors with eight clubs, mostly as a pinch-hitter, spare outfielder, and first baseman. One of baseball's all-time flakes, Johnstone played in only one World Series with the Dodgers in 1981 and was caught by television cameras on the bench wearing giant sunglasses during a night game. He pinch-hit three times during the Series against the Yankees and collected a home run and a single. The homer was struck off Ron Davis in the sixth inning of Game Four with a man on and tied the score 6–6. The Dodgers went on to win 8–7 in a Series in which Los Angeles lost the first two games but won the last four to take the title.

10. KIRK GIBSON

The king of all World Series pinch-hit home runs was executed by Kirk Gibson with the Dodgers in the first game of the 1988 World Series against the Athletics. A former tight end with Michigan State's football team, Gibson reached the majors in 1979 with the Tigers. In the 1984 World Series against the Padres he hit two homers and drove in five runs in the fifth and final game in Detroit, won by the Tigers 8–4. He also helped the Tigers with his legs, scoring from third base on a fly ball caught by San Diego second baseman Alan Wiggins in shallow right field. Gibson went to the Dodgers in 1988 as a free agent and won the Most Valuable Player award in his first season with the club. He was available in the World Series only on an emergency basis, however, because of an injured leg. The Dodgers trailed 4–3 entering the ninth inning of Game One in 1988 in Los Angeles. Dennis Eckersley retired the first two batters in the inning before walking Mike Davis. Dodgers manager Tommy Lasorda sent Gibson to the plate to pinch-hit for Alejandro Pena in a situation that fit the dictionary definition of *emergency*. The prospects weren't encouraging. Gibson was in obvious pain, hobbling from the dugout to the plate, and was swinging with only one leg firmly planted. He was facing one of the best relievers in baseball history, and at that point in his career, Gibson had 58 career pinch-hit at-bats with only 11 hits and no home runs. Gibson worked the count to 3–2 before driving a pitch into the right-field bleachers for a 5–4 Dodgers victory. The only other walk-off home run in World Series history that brought a team from behind was hit by Joe Carter for the Blue Jays in Game Six in 1993 against the Phillies. In a 2002 fan poll, Gibson's homer was ranked as one of the ten greatest moments in baseball history. It was the last postseason plate appearance of his career. Gibson didn't bat again in 1988 as the Dodgers defeated Oakland in five games. None of the subsequent teams he played for reached the postseason before his career ended in 1995.

A Pinch of Homers 153

Los Angeles Dodgers

In perhaps the most clutch performance in any World Series, hobbled Kirk Gibson stroked a pinch-hit, walk-off home run against Oakland star reliever Dennis Eckersley in 1998's opening game.

Sweeping the Bases

Through the 2003 season, there have been 17 grand-slam home runs in the World Series, including:

1. TONY LAZZERI

Batting eighth in the potent Yankee lineup, Tony Lazzeri hit a third-inning grand slam in Game Two of the 1936 World Series against the Giants. The ball landed in the lower right field stands at the Polo Grounds, as New York's American League club routed New York's National League club 18–4, setting Series records for the most runs scored in a game and the largest margin of victory. Lazzeri's grand slam was the second in World Series history, following the one struck by Elmer Smith of the Indians in 1920. Lazzeri also made baseball history earlier in the 1936 season on May 24, when he became the first player in major league history to hit two grand slams in a game, a feat accomplished by only 11 players through 2002. He also hit a solo homer and a two-run triple in the contest to drive an American League record 11 runs in a 25–2 rout of the Philadelphia Athletics. Second basemen accounted for four of the first eight World Series grand slams. Following Lazzeri were Gil McDougald in 1951, Bobby Richardson in 1960, and Chuck Hiller in 1962. Lazzeri also hit two homers in the fourth and final game of the 1932

Series as the Yankees completed a sweep of the Cubs with a 13–6 victory.

2. JIM NORTHRUP

Jim Northrup of the Tigers hit two grand slams in a regular-season game and another in the World Series in the same year. In all, Northrup hit five grand slams in 1968, four in the regular season and one in the World Series. On June 24, he hit two slams in a 14–3 trouncing of the Indians. Northrup's World Series slam was hit off Larry Jaster during the Tigers 10-run third inning in a 13–1 sixth-game victory in St. Louis. The only other team to score as many as 10 runs in an inning during the Fall Classic was the 1929 Athletics.

3. CHUCK HILLER

Chuck Hiller of the Giants hit the first World Series grand slam by a National Leaguer. It happened in the seventh inning of the fourth game of the 1962 Series against the Yankees. Hiller's slam was struck with two out off Marshall Bridges and broke a 2–2 tie in a game won by the Giants 7–3 at Yankee Stadium. In his previous at-bat in the fifth inning, Hiller had struck out with the bases loaded. The winning pitcher was Don Larsen, who pitched one-third of an inning of relief for San Francisco against his former club six years to the day after his perfect game. Hiller hit only 20 regular-season home runs during his career, none of them grand slams, in 2,121 at-bats. He is the only player whose lone career grand slam came during a World Series.

4. LONNIE SMITH

Lonnie Smith is the only designated hitter to hit a World Series grand slam and the only player to hit one outside of the United States. Smith swept the bases with a home run off Jack Morris in the fifth inning of Game Five while playing for the Braves against the Blue Jays in Toronto in 1992. Atlanta won the game 7–3.

5. DAN GLADDEN

Twins left fielder Dan Gladden is the only leadoff hitter to connect for a grand slam in the World Series. Gladden's slam was struck against Cardinals pitcher Bob Forsch in Minnesota's seven-run fourth inning in the first game in 1987 and helped his club to a 10–1 victory at the Metrodome. The grand slam was Gladden's only homer in 104 postseason at-bats with the Twins in 1987 and 1991.

6. KENT HRBEK

Gladden wasn't the only Minnesota Twin to hit a grand slam during the 1987 World Series. First baseman Kent Hrbek also connected for a bases-clearing homer. The Cardinals won three of the first five games and held a 5–2 lead before the Twins took a 6–5 lead with four runs in the fourth. The Twins loaded the bases in the sixth, and as Hrbek came to bat, Cardinals manager Whitey Herzog brought Ken Dayley in from the bull pen to replace Bob Forsch. Hrbek hit Dayley's first pitch for a grand slam, and the Twins went on to win the game 11–5. The only other teammates to hit grand slams in the same World Series are Yogi Berra and Bill Skowron with the Yankees in 1956.

7. BILL SKOWRON

Yankees first baseman Bill Skowron is the only player to collect a grand slam in the seventh game of a World Series. It was hit off Roger Craig in the seventh inning of a 9–0 thrashing of the Dodgers in 1956 in the last World Series game ever played in Brooklyn.

8. MICKEY MANTLE

Mickey Mantle hit a World Series record 18 home runs during his career, one of them a grand slam in the third inning of Game Five against the Dodgers in 1953. The Yankees led 2–0 and loaded the bases against Johnny Podres. Dodgers manager Charlie Dressen brought in Russ Meyer to face

Mantle, and batting left-handed, Mickey drove Meyer's first pitch into the deep left center field stands at Ebbets Field.

9. JOE PEPITONE

Joe Pepitone played in the majors from 1962 through 1973, and with his erratic play, after-hours activities, long hair, and flamboyant devil-may-care attitude often clashed with his more tradition-bound managers. Pepitone played in the World Series with the Yankees in 1963 and 1964. The Yankees were swept by the Dodgers in 1963, and Pepitone made a critical error at first base in the seventh inning of the fourth game when he lost sight of a throw from third baseman Clete Boyer in the background of white shirts in the Dodger Stadium grandstand. The error led to the winning run. Pepitone hit a grand slam during the Yankees 8–3, sixth-game win over the Cardinals in St. Louis. Barney Schultz loaded the bases on a single and two walks, and Cardinals manager Johnny Keane brought Gordon Richardson in to face Pepitone, who greeted the reliever with a homer onto the Busch Stadium right field pavilion roof.

10. KEN BOYER

The opposing third basemen in the 1964 World Series were brothers. Ken Boyer played third for the Cardinals, while his younger brother Clete manned the position for the Yankees. Each hit a home run in the Series and rounded third and headed for home past his brother. Ken hit a grand slam off Al Downing in the sixth inning of the fourth game with the Cardinals trailing 3–0 in New York. The slam accounted for all four Cardinals runs in their 4–3 victory. Ken and Clete both homered in the seventh game. Ken's home run, which also came off a Downing pitch, gave the Cardinals a 6–0 lead in the fifth inning. Clete homered in the ninth off Bob Gibson, but it wasn't enough to prevent a 7–5 Yankee loss. The Boyers are the only brothers to homer in the same Series. Ken and Clete had an older brother named Cloyd, who played five seasons in the majors but never appeared in the World Series.

Back-to-Back

Through the 2003 season, there have been 25 instances in which a player hit at least two homers in succession in a World Series game, including:

1. **REGGIE JACKSON**

Reggie Jackson earned the nickname "Mr. October" by becoming the only player to hit home runs in three consecutive World Series plate appearances, the only one to connect for home runs in four consecutive at-bats, the only one to collect five homers in a single Series, the only one to hit seven homers in consecutive years, and the only one to hit four homers in consecutive games. Jackson's career slugging percentage of .755 in the Series is the best of all time (among players with minimum of 50 plate appearances). His most astounding achievement came with the Yankees in the 1977 World Series against the Dodgers, when he homered five times. He hit three in a row in Game Six at Yankee Stadium, each on the first pitch from three different pitchers. The Yankees won three of the first four games with Jackson hitting his first homer in Game Four off Rick Rhoden in a 4–2 New York victory. In Game Five, the Dodgers stayed alive by winning 10–4 in Los Angeles. Jackson homered in his final at-bat, a two-run blast off the foul pole in the eighth inning off Don Sutton. In his first at-bat in the sixth game, Jackson walked on four Burt Hooton pitches and crossed the plate on a homer by Chris Chambliss to tie the score 2–2. Facing Hooton again in the fourth, Jackson homered with a man on to put the Yankees ahead 4–3. The lead was widened to 6–3 in the fifth inning, when Reggie hit a two-run homer off Elias Sosa. Jackson hit his third homer in the eighth against Charlie Hough, and the Yankees clinched the title with an 8–4 triumph. Counting his home run in his final at-bat in the fifth game, Jackson hit homers on four consecutive swings. Overall, Jackson had a .357 batting average and 10 home runs and 24 RBIs in 98 at-bats in five World Series with the Athletics and Yankees.

2. **BABE RUTH**

The only player besides Reggie Jackson to homer three times in a game is Babe Ruth. The Babe went one better than Reggie, however, by hitting three in a game twice. Ruth also had four multiple-home-run games in the Series. No one else has more than two. Ruth became the first to hit back-to-back homers in the World Series in Game Two against the Giants in 1923. He broke a 1–1 tie by hitting a two-run homer in the fourth inning off Hugh McQuillan and added another in the fifth facing Jack Bentley to lead the Yankees to a 4–2 victory. Ruth's first three-home-run explosion occurred in the fourth game in 1926 against the Cardinals in St. Louis. He hit solo homers in the first and third innings off Flint Rhem and a two-run shot in the sixth facing Hi Bell, which landed in the center field bleachers 450 feet from home plate. Ruth also walked twice and set a World Series record (since tied) by scoring four runs as the Yankees won 10–5. He walked 11 times during the 1926 Series, a record that stood until Barry Bonds was given 13 passes by the Angels in 2002. Ruth's second three-home-run game also happened in St. Louis in the fourth and final game of the 1928 Fall Classic. He homered in the fourth and seventh innings off Bill Sherdel and in the eighth against Grover Cleveland Alexander. The Yankees won 7–3. His fourth multiple-home-run game was in the Yankees 7–5 win in Game Three in 1932 against the Cubs in Chicago, the second of which was his famous "called shot."

Ruth had 72 multiple-home-run games during the regular season but hit more than two only twice. He homered three times against the Athletics in 1930 and as a member of the Braves against the Pirates in 1935. The three homers in the 1935 game were the last of his career.

3. LOU GEHRIG

The third game of the 1932 World Series was the only one in which two players hit at least two home runs. Lou Gehrig and his Yankee teammate Babe Ruth both hit two balls out of Wrigley Field in the 7–5 decision over the Cubs. Gehrig's homers came in consecutive plate appearances in the third and fifth innings. He also hit back-to-back homers in the third game in 1928 against the Cardinals in St. Louis. The first was a booming homer that landed on top of the right field pavilion. The second was inside the park in the fourth inning as Cardinals center fielder Taylor Douthit missed a shoestring catch and let the ball sail behind him. Both were struck off Jesse Haines. Gehrig is also one of 13 players to hit an All-Star Game homer and a World Series homer in the same year. He did it in both 1936 and 1937. Others who have hit All-Star and World Series homers in the same year include Joe Medwick (1934), Joe DiMaggio (1939), Jackie Robinson (1952), Mickey Mantle (1955 and 1956), Ken Boyer (1964), Harmon Killebrew (1965), Roberto Clemente (1971), Frank Robinson (1971), Steve Garvey (1977), Sandy Alomar Jr. (1997), Derek Jeter (2001), Barry Bonds (2002) and Jason Giambi (2003).

4. DUKE SNIDER

Brooklyn Dodgers center fielder Duke Snider is the only player to hit four homers in two different World Series. He hit four in 1952 during a seven-game loss to the Yankees. Two were struck in consecutive at-bats in the sixth and eighth innings of Game Six at Ebbets Field off Vic Raschi, but they accounted for the Dodgers' only runs in a 3–2 defeat. In 1955, Snider clubbed four homers as the Dodgers beat the

Yanks in seven. He homered twice in Game Five, which was won by the Dodgers 5–3 in Brooklyn. They were hit in back-to-back plate appearances in the third and fifth innings off Bob Grim.

5. **JOE COLLINS**

Many players who were average performers at best have had the good fortune to play on a dynasty and reach the World Series repeatedly. Joe Collins is a case in point. As a first baseman for the Yankees, he played in seven World Series between 1950 and 1957. He hardly shined with a .163 average in 92 at-bats, but he had a big moment in the first game of the 1955 Series against the Dodgers when he homered in consecutive at-bats off Don Newcombe at Yankee Stadium in a Yankees 6–5 win.

6. **YOGI BERRA**

Yogi Berra hit homers in his first two at-bats in the seventh game of the 1956 Series leading the Yankees to a clinching 9–0 win over the Dodgers. Both were struck off Don Newcombe. Berra hit .360 with nine hits, including two doubles and three homers, in 25 at-bats in 1956 in addition to 10 runs batted in and five runs scored. He would have won the World Series MVP award if it weren't for Don Larsen's perfect game. Berra never won a World Series MVP award, but he was the American League MVP in 1951, 1954, and 1955. In addition, Berra finished third in the MVP voting in 1950, fourth in 1952, second in 1953, and second in 1956. No other player in history has finished in the top four in the MVP balloting seven years in a row.

7. **TONY PEREZ**

Reds first baseman Tony Perez was 0 for 15 with seven strikeouts when he stepped to the plate in the fourth inning of the fifth game of the 1975 World Series against Reggie Cleveland of the Red Sox. Perez broke out of his slump with a home run to tie the score 1–1, then hit a three-run shot off Cleveland in the sixth. The Reds won 6–2. In the seventh game, Perez started the Reds comeback to take the world title. With Cincinnati trailing 3-0 with a runner on base in the sixth, he pounced on a Bill Lee blooper pitch and drove it over Fenway Park's left field wall. The Reds won 4-3 with a run in the ninth.

8. EDDIE MURRAY

Eddie Murray yanked two home runs out of Veterans Stadium in Philadelphia in consecutive at-bats in the second and fourth innings off Charlie Hudson to lead the Orioles to a 5-0 win in Game Five in 1983 that clinched the world championship. Murray was elected to the Hall of Fame on the first ballot in 2003 and is one of three players in baseball history, along with Hank Aaron and Willie Mays, to hit at least 500 career homers and collect at least 3,000 hits. Overall, however, Murray didn't have many shining moments in the World Series. With the Orioles in 1979 and 1983 and the Indians in 1995, he hit only .169 with four home runs in 65 at-bats.

9. ALAN TRAMMELL

A native of San Diego, Tigers shortstop Alan Trammell beat his hometown team in Game Four in 1984. Trammell hit a pair of two-run homers in back-to-back plate appearances in the first and third innings off Eric Show to account for all four Tigers runs in a 4-2 win over the Padres in Detroit. Show was one of four San Diego starting pitchers who were abject failures during a five-game loss to the Tigers. Show, Mark Thurmond, Tim Lollar, and Ed Whitson combined to pitch only $10^{1}/_{3}$ innings and allowed 25 hits, eight walks, and 16 earned runs for an ERA of 13.94.

10. CHRIS SABO

In the only World Series of his career, Reds third baseman Chris Sabo had nine hits in 16 at-bats for a .563 batting average in the Reds' four-game sweep over the Athletics in 1990. Sabo homered twice off Mike Moore in consecutive at-bats in the second and third innings of Game Three in Oakland, which the Reds won 8-3.

Going Deep

Through the 2003 season, 36 players have hit two home runs in a game, including:

1. **HARRY HOOPER**

Harry Hooper reached the Hall of Fame because of his defense in right field and his ability to reach base as a leadoff hitter, not because he hit home runs. During his 1915 season with the Red Sox, Hooper hit only two homers in 566 at-bats, but he matched that total in one game during the World Series that fall. The Red Sox won three of the first four games against the Phillies and looked to close out the Series in Game Five at Baker Bowl in Philadelphia. Baker Bowl was a bandbox of a ballpark with a capacity of only 18,000. The right field line was only 272 feet long, the fence in the right center field power alley was just 300 feet from home plate, and dead center field was an even 400 feet. Those dimensions were lessened even further during the 1915 World Series with the addition of temporary seats. The Red Sox hit three homers into the extra-seating area in Game Five, two of them by Hooper. In the third inning with the score 1–1, Hooper bounced a drive into the temporary bleachers in center, which under the ground rules then in effect was a home run. The Phillies moved ahead 4–2, but the Sox tied the score 4–4 on a two-run homer by Duffy Lewis into the bleachers.

Hooper provided the winning run in the ninth by hitting another homer into the bleachers for a 5–4 victory and the world championship. It was the first multiple-home-run game of Hooper's career. He had only two multiple-home-run games during the regular season in 17 years in the big leagues, both with the White Sox in 1921.

2. **BENNY KAUFF**

Benny Kauff of the Giants was hitless in his first 13 at-bats of the 1917 World Series against the White Sox before hitting an inside-the-park homer in the fourth inning of the fourth game on a drive that sailed over the head of Chicago center fielder Happy Felsch and rolled into the deep outfield at the Polo Grounds. Kauff homered again into the lower tier of the right field stands in the eighth inning. He received $200 for his efforts, since stage star Al Jolson and film actress Clara Kimble Young each put up $50 for every home run hit during the 1917 Series. It was the only multiple-home-run game of Kauff's career, which ended under bizarre circumstances. He was implicated in several gambling scandals, although nothing was proven. In 1921, Kauff and his brother were arrested for stealing a car. A jury acquitted Kauff, but Commissioner Kenesaw Landis banned him from baseball for life. Kauff sued Landis for reinstatement but lost.

3. **BOB ELLIOTT**

The Pirates traded third baseman Bob Elliott to the Boston Braves for Billy Herman, who became the Pittsburgh manager. It proved to be one of the worst trades in Pirates history as Elliott won the National League MVP award in 1947 and helped the Braves into the World Series in 1948 against the Indians. In Game Five in Cleveland, he hit a three-run homer off Bob Feller in the first inning and added another in the eighth to lead Boston to an 11–5 victory.

4. **TED KLUSZEWSKI**

Ted Kluszewski hit 171 homers for the Reds during a four-year period from 1953 through 1956, but he was 35 years old and in his 13th season in the majors when he played in his first World Series, as a member of the White Sox in 1959. Wearing his trademark cutoff sleeves, Kluszewski drove in a run with a single in his first at-bat in the first game against Roger Craig of the Dodgers. In the third inning, Kluszewski homered into the right field bleachers with a man on base, again off Craig. In the fourth inning facing Chuck Churn, Kluszewski hit another two-run homer. In his first three at-bats, Kluszewski had three hits, including two homers, and drove in five runs. The White Sox won the game 11–0. For the Series, Kluszewski hit .391 with a double and three homers and 10 runs batted in in 23 at-bats, although the Dodgers won the title in six games. During the 1970s he guided one of the greatest offensive clubs ever assembled when he served as batting coach for the Reds in four World Series.

5. CARL YASTRZEMSKI

The last player to win the triple crown by leading the league in batting average, home runs, and runs batted in was Carl Yastrzemski in 1967. Yastrzemski carried the Red Sox to their "Impossible Dream" of a pennant with a .326 average, 44 homers, and 121 runs batted in. In the World Series, he hit .400 with ten hits, including two doubles and three homers, but it wasn't enough to bring Boston a world championship, as St. Louis won the championship in seven games. Two of his three homers were struck in Game Two at Fenway Park. Both landed in the right field bleachers and accounted for four runs batted in during a 5–0 Red Sox win.

6. JOHNNY BENCH

Johnny Bench suffered through a slump-ridden season in 1976 when he batted only .234 with 16 homers during the regular season. In the World Series that fall, he earned MVP honors, however, in leading the Reds to a four-game sweep of the Yankees. Bench hit .533 with eight hits, including a double, a triple, and two homers, in 15 at-bats. Both homers were struck in the championship-clinching fourth game, which was won by the Reds 7–2. Bench hit a two-run homer just inside the left field foul pole in the fourth inning off Ed

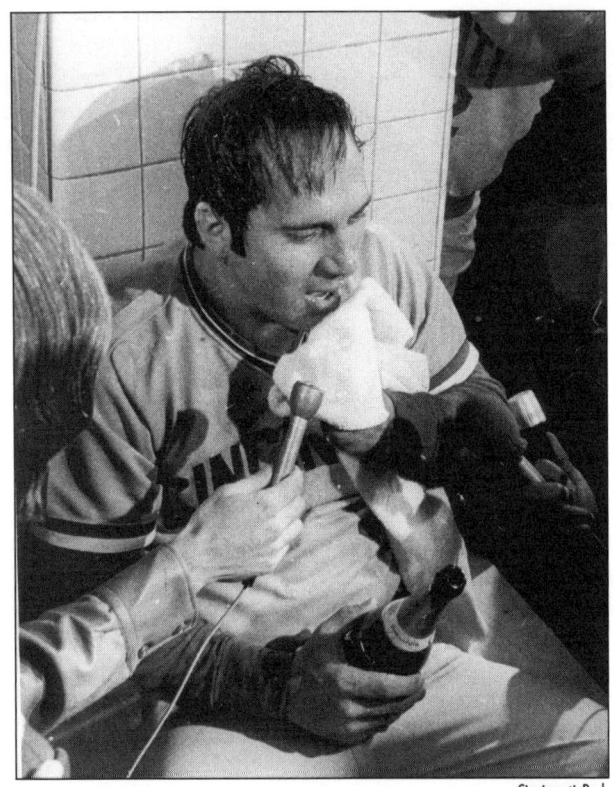

Cincinnati Reds

Johnny Bench earned MVP honors in the 1976 World Series, more than doubling his regular-season batting average and helping clinch the Series with a two-homer game.

Figueroa and a three-run shot into the left field seats in the ninth against Dick Tidrow. It was a great Series for catchers. Yankees backstop Thurman Munson hit .529 with nine hits in 17 at-bats.

7. **DAVE LOPES**

Dave Lopes hit two homers and drove in five runs in the first game of the 1978 World Series against the Yankees, leading the Dodgers to an 11–5 win in Los Angeles. The homers came only two days after Dodgers coach and Lopes's mentor Jim Gilliam died of a brain hemorrhage. The Dodgers won the first two games of the Series but lost the final four. The reverse occurred in 1981, when the Yankees opened with two wins before the Dodgers rebounded to win four in a row. Los Angeles won the world championship in 1981 in spite of Lopes, who committed six errors, a record for a second baseman in a single Series.

8. WILLIE AIKENS

Willie Aikens is the only player in history with two multiple-home-run games in the same World Series. Playing on his 26th birthday for the Royals against the Phillies in 1980, Aikens homered in the third and seventh innings in the first game, both off Bob Walk with a man on base, but the Royals lost 7–6 in Philadelphia. In a 5–3 Royals win in Game Four in Kansas City, Aikens hit a homer into the waterfall in the first inning off Larry Christenson and another in the second into the right field bull pen against Dickie Noles. Willie's full name was Willie Mays Aikens, and he was born in Seneca, South Carolina, just 15 days after his namesake's famous catch in the first game of the 1954 World Series. Willie Mays Aikens finished his career with four more World Series homers than Willie Mays. In 71 career at-bats in the Fall Classic with the Giants in 1951, 1954, and 1962 and with the Mets in 1973, Willie Mays failed to hit a single home run.

9. CHAD CURTIS

Chad Curtis hit only five homers for the Yankees in 1999, but he clubbed two in Game Three of the World Series against the Braves, including the game winner. The Braves had a 5–1 lead at Yankee Stadium when Curtis hit a solo homer in the fifth inning off Tom Glavine. The game went into extra innings after the Yankees added a run in the seventh and two more in the eighth. Curtis ended the game with a homer off

Mike Remlinger in the tenth to lift the Yankees to a 6–5 victory.

10. **TROY GLAUS**

In his first World Series game, Troy Glaus hit two home runs, one of them in his first at-bat. Glaus homered in the first and sixth innings off Jason Schmidt of the Giants in the 2002 opener, although the Angels lost 4–3 in San Francisco. Troy was a big part of Anaheim's comeback to take the Series in seven games. He hit .385 with 10 hits, including three doubles and three homers, seven runs scored, and eight RBIs to earn MVP honors. During the 2002 postseason, Glaus batted .344 and hit seven homers in 16 games. He was nearly the "goat" of the World Series, however. With none out and a Giants runner on first base in the fifth inning of Game Four, Kenny Lofton of the Giants hit a roller down the third base line. Glaus monitored the ball's progress, and when it veered foul by millimeters, Glaus bent down to pick it up, but by the time he could reach it, the ball angled back into fair territory. The Angels led 3–0 at the time, but Lofton's single sparked a three-run inning that tied the score. The Giants won 4–3 with a run in the seventh.

Sweet Strokes

Players with batting records in the World Series include:

1. **BOBBY RICHARDSON**

Bobby Richardson was a second baseman for the Yankees from 1955 through 1966 who hit .266 with just 34 homers in 1,412 regular-season games. Despite his lack of hitting credentials, Richardson holds World Series records for the most hits in a single Series (13), the most hits in a five-game Series (nine), the most runs batted in in a single Series (12), and the most runs batted in in a game (six). In 1960, Richardson drove in just 26 runs and had only one homer in 150 games. But in the World Series that fall against the Pirates, Richardson drove in 12 runs, including a record six in the third game in New York, which was won by the Yankees 10–0, by hitting a grand slam off Clem Labine in the first inning and a two-run single against George Witt in the third. Richardson played in 23 more World Series games during his career after 1960 and drove in only three more runs, but he had his share of moments. In 1961, he had nine hits in five games against the Reds. In 1962, Richardson caught a line drive off the bat of San Francisco's Willie McCovey to end the seventh game, stranding the potential winning run on second base. In 1964, he set a World Series record (since tied by two others) with 13 hits in 32 at-bats against the Cardinals. Overall, he hit .305 in 131 World Series at-bats. A devout Christian, Richardson delivered the benediction at the 1972 Republican National Convention that nominated Richard Nixon for a second term as president.

2. **LOU BROCK**

Lou Brock became the second of three players to collect 13 hits in a single Series in 1968 over 28 at-bats, although Brock's Cardinals lost the Series in seven games to the Tigers. Brock had had 12 hits in the Series the previous season when the Cardinals won in seven over the Red Sox. His 25 hits in consecutive World Series is also a record. In addition, Brock had nine hits in the Cardinals' seven-game victory against the Yankees in 1964. In the three Series combined, he had 34 hits in 87 at-bats for a .391 average, the all-time best by any player with at least 75 plate appearances. Brock set the record (since tied) with five extra base hits in consecutive games with three doubles, a triple, and a homer in Games Four and Five in 1968. In Game Four, he became the only player in Series history to hit a homer, a triple, and a double in a game. The homer was hit off Denny McLain and led off the first inning. Brock starred with his feet as well as his bat. He was the all-time leader in career stolen bases during the regular season until Rickey Henderson pushed him into second place in 1991, but Brock is still the theft leader in the World Series. He had a record 14 Series stolen bases during his career, which ties him with Eddie Collins. Brock is the undisputed leader in stolen bases in a single Series with seven in both 1967 and 1968. He also stole a record three bases in a single Series game twice, once in 1967 and the other in 1968. The only other two players to steal three bases in a Series game are Honus Wagner with the Pirates in 1909 and Willie Davis with the Dodgers in 1965.

3. **MARTY BARRETT**

In the only World Series of a 10-year career in which he batted .278, Marty Barrett became the third of three players to collect 13 hits in a Series while playing second base for the Red Sox in the 1986 seven-game loss to the Mets. (Strangely, all three players who had 13 hits in a Series played on the losing side.) Barrett also picked up 11 hits in the American League Championship Series that season against the Angels. He had 24 hits in 60 at-bats for a .400 batting average in the 1986 postseason. The success didn't carry over to Barrett's other two postseason appearances, in which he had only one hit in 15 at-bats in the 1988 and 1990 ALCS.

4. **PAUL MOLITOR**

Paul Molitor is the only player to collect five hits in a World Series game. He accomplished the feat in the very first Series game of his career, picking up five singles in six at-bats as the Brewers trounced the Cardinals 10–0 at St. Louis in the opener in 1982. Paul finished the Series with 11 hits in 31 at-bats, although the Brewers lost in seven games. Molitor picked up where he left off in the second and last Series of his career, with the Blue Jays in 1993. He had 12 hits in 24 at-bats in the Blue Jays' six-game victory over the Phillies. Molitor was a designated hitter for most of the regular season, and without the DH rule in effect for the three games in Philadelphia, he played first base in Game Three and third base in Games Four and Five. It was the first time he had played third base in a game in three years. In 1993, Molitor tied World Series records for the most hits in a six-game Series and the most runs scored (10) in a Series of any length.

5. **BILLY MARTIN**

Billy Martin set the record for the most hits in a six-game Series, since tied by Paul Molitor, Roberto Alomar, and Atlanta's Marquis Grissom in 1996. Martin helped the Yankees in 1953 to a fifth consecutive world championship with 12 hits in 24 at-bats against the Dodgers. His 12th hit ended the Series. In Game Six in New York with the Yankees holding a three-games-to-two lead, Carl Furillo of the Dodgers hit a two-run homer in the ninth inning to tie the score 3–3. In the bottom of the inning with Clem Labine pitching, Hank Bauer walked, Mickey Mantle reached base on a one-out infield single, and Martin added another single into center field to give the Yankees a 4–3 win and another championship. Martin managed the Yankees in the World Series twice. He lost to the Reds in four games in 1976 and won in six games over the Dodgers in 1977. Martin is one of only two managers in World Series history to be swept in the World Series one year and come back to win it the following year. The other is Bill McKechnie with the Reds in 1939 and 1940. Martin also managed the Yankees in 1978 but was fired on July 23 and replaced by Bob Lemon. In one of George Steinbrenner's more bizarre moves, the Yankees owner announced six days later, during ceremonies before an Old-Timers Game, that Martin would return in 1980. In all, Martin was hired and fired five times as Yankees manager by Steinbrenner. Lemon managed the Yankees to a World Series win against the Dodgers in 1978, was fired in 1979 (in favor of Martin), and was rehired in midseason in 1981 (replacing Dick Howser) and led the Yankees to another world championship.

6. **MARQUIS GRISSOM**

Lou Brock holds the World Series record for the highest batting average (among players with a minimum of 75 plate appearances) with a .391 mark. Marquis Grissom is right behind Brock with a .390 average. Thus far in his career, Grissom has had 30 hits in 77 at-bats while playing for the Braves in 1995 and 1996 and the Indians in 1997.

7. **BOBBY BROWN**

Bobby Brown of the 1947 Yankees set the record for most pinch-hits in a single World Series with three, since tied by Dusty Rhodes (1954 Giants), Carl Warwick (1964 Cardinals), Gonzalo Marquez (1972 Athletics), and Ken Boswell (1973 Mets). Brown pinch-hit four times in the 1947 Series against the Dodgers and hit two doubles and a single and drew a walk. He played again for the Yankees in the World Series in 1949, 1950, and 1951 and continued his outstanding hitting. He finished his career with 18 Series hits in 41 at-bats. Brown's .439 average is the best by any player with at least 40 at-bats. Strangely, Brown started only 10 of the 17 World Series games he appeared in and finished only four of those. Brown hit .279 in 548 regular-season games. He earned a medical degree in 1950 from Tulane University and quit as an active player in 1954 at the age of 29 to start his internship. Brown became a respected cardiologist but returned to baseball in 1984 as the president of the American League, a position he held for ten years.

8. GONZALO MARQUEZ

As a rookie for the Athletics in 1972, Gonzalo Marquez was almost unstoppable as a pinch-hitter. He was seven for 16 in the role during the regular season, two for three in the ALCS against the Tigers, and three for five in the World Series versus the Reds. In Game Four at Oakland, Marquez pinch-hit a single with one out, which started a two-run rally that won the game 3–2. It was the only time in Series history that a team collected three pinch-hits in an inning, as the Athletics' Dick Williams pushed all the right buttons. The other two pinch-hits were by Don Mincher and Angel Mangual, the latter driving in the winning run. Marquez played only two more seasons in the majors and hit just .186 in 102 at-bats.

9. FRANK ISBELL

Frank Isbell is the only player in World Series history with four extra base hits in a game. Playing second base for the White Sox in Game Five in 1906 against the Cubs, Isbell hit four doubles in an 8–6 victory. They were the only four extra base hits that he collected in the six-game Series, although he had three singles in the championship-clinching sixth game. The seven hits in consecutive games set a record since tied by Fred Lindstrom (1924 Giants), Monte Irvin

(1951 Giants), Thurman Munson (1976 Yankees), Paul Molitor (1982 Brewers), and Billy Hatcher (1990 Reds).

10. **BILLY HATCHER**

Billy Hatcher hit just .264 during his 12-year big league career, but he holds the record for the most hits in consecutive at-bats in a single Series with seven, which he accomplished with the Reds while playing center field against the Athletics in 1990. He accomplished this in the first seven World Series at-bats of his career. He also set a record by reaching base in nine consecutive plate appearances. In Game One in Cincinnati, Hatcher had two doubles, a single, and a walk in four plate appearances as the Reds won 7–0. In the second contest, he had a triple, two doubles, a single, and a walk in five plate appearances as the Reds won 5–4 in 10 innings. Hatcher's streak ended in the first inning of the third game when he grounded into a double play, but he went two for five with a pair of singles in an 8–3 win. In his first at-bat in

Billy Hatcher connects on one of his World Series–record seven consecutive hits in 1990.

the fourth game, Hatcher was hit in the hand by a pitch and had to leave the game, but Herm Winningham, his replacement in center field, had two hits in three at-bats as the Reds completed the sweep of the Athletics with a 2–1 win. Hatcher had nine hits in 12 at-bats during the 1990 Series to set the batting average record (among players with minimum of 10 at-bats) for a single Series at .750. He also tied records for the most bases reached in a game (five) and the most extra base hits in consecutive games (five). In addition, Hatcher hit the latest home run in either an LCS or a World Series, poking a 14th-inning homer as a member of the Astros in Game Six of the 1986 NLCS against the Mets. He finished his career with a .404 batting average and a .654 slugging percentage in 52 postseason at-bats.

Hitting 'Em Where They Are

The 10 lowest batting averages in World Series history (among players with a minimum of 45 at-bats, excluding pitchers) have been compiled by:

1. MARV OWEN

Playing third and first base for the Tigers in the 1934 and 1935 World Series, Marv Owen had only three hits, all singles, in 49 at-bats for an average of .063. Included was a streak of 31 consecutive at-bats without a hit, a World Series record. Owen finished his nine-year career in 1940 with a .275 regular-season average.

2. DAL MAXVILL

Dal Maxvill was a slick fielding shortstop who compiled a .217 batting average in 3,443 regular-season at-bats between 1963 and 1975. His is the lowest average by any player in history with at least 3,200 at-bats. Maxvill was even worse in the World Series with the Cardinals in 1964, 1967, and 1968, collecting only seven hits in 61 at-bats for an average of .115. Maxvill was on the Oakland Athletics roster during the 1972 Series but didn't play in a game.

3. TAYLOR DOUTHIT

Taylor Douthit hit .291 during his big league career but was better known for his speed and range in center field. With the Cardinals in the 1926, 1928, and 1930 World Series, Douthit was seven for 50 for an average of .140. He missed the final three games of the 1926 Series after colliding with left fielder Chick Hafey while pursuing a fly ball.

4. DICK GREEN

Dick Green was the starting second baseman for the Athletics on the 1972, 1973, and 1974 world championship teams. He had six hits in his first 15 World Series at-bats, but was only one for 32 after that to finish his career with a .149 Series average. Green scored just one run in Series play and drove in only two. He wasn't much better in the American League Championship Series, going six for 37. Green was in the starting lineup in 35 postseason games but was lifted for a pinch-hitter in 21 of them.

5. TRAVIS JACKSON

Travis Jackson reached the Hall of Fame on his .291 batting average as a shortstop for the Giants between 1922 and 1936, not his record in the World Series. He played in the Fall Classic in 1923, 1924, 1933, and 1936 and was just 10 for 67 for an average of .149, the lowest of any player with more than 50 at-bats. A double in 1933 was Jackson's only extra base hit.

6. JOSE CANSECO

In his first World Series game, Jose Canseco rocketed a grand-slam home run to give the Athletics a 4–2 lead over the Dodgers in the opening game in 1988. From then on, it was all downhill. Oakland lost the game 5–4 on Kirk Gibson's heroic walk-off homer in the ninth inning and eventually lost the Series in five games. The grand slam was Canseco's only hit of the Series, as he went one for 19. He finished his career with seven hits in 45 at-bats for a World Series average of .156.

7. EVERETT SCOTT

Before Cal Ripken Jr. and Lou Gehrig, there was Everett Scott. Scott played in 1,307 consecutive games from 1916 through 1925 as shortstop for the Red Sox and Yankees, which still ranks as the third-longest playing streak in major league history. The streak ended on May 6, 1925, when Scott was benched for poor hitting in favor of Pee Wee Wanninger. Less than a month later, Gehrig started his 2,130 consecutive-game streak as a pinch-hitter for Wanninger. In June 1925, the Yankees sent Scott to the Senators. He was on Washington's World Series roster in 1925 but didn't play in a game. Scott did play in the World Series for the Red Sox in 1915, 1916, and 1918 and the Yankees in 1922 and 1923 but collected only 14 hits in 90 at-bats for an average of .156. It's the lowest average of any Series participant with more than 70 at-bats.

8. JOHNNY ROSEBORO

Johnny Roseboro played in the majors from 1957 through 1970, and he is best known for being hit in the head with a bat in 1965 by Juan Marichal during a brawl involving the Dodgers and the Giants. Roseboro was the starting catcher for the Dodgers in the 1959, 1963, 1965, and 1966 World Series, but he had only 11 hits in 70 at-bats for an average of .157.

9. BRIS LORD

Bris Lord was a journeyman outfielder who hit .256 for three American League clubs between 1905 and 1913. He played for the Athletics in the World Series in 1905, 1910, and 1911 but batted just .159 on 11 hits in 69 at-bats.

10. **MULE HAAS**

Mule Haas, an outfielder with the Philadelphia Athletics in 1929, 1930 and 1931, collected only ten hits in 62 at-bats for a World Series batting average of .161. He had much more success in the regular season, batting .292 in 12 big league seasons.

No-Hitters

In baseball jargon, going hitless in a game is known as "wearing the collar." Many unfortunate players have worn the collar for an entire World Series.

1. DAL MAXVILL

Dal Maxvill holds the record for the most at-bats in a single Series without a hit. In the seven games with the Cardinals in 1968, Maxvill was 0 for 22. He played errorless ball at shortstop, but St. Louis lost the Series in seven games to the Tigers.

2. JIMMY SHECKARD

Jimmy Sheckard played in the majors as an outfielder from 1897 through 1913 and at one time or another led the National League in on-base percentage, slugging percentage, home runs, triples, runs scored, stolen bases, walks, sacrifice hits, and outfield assists. He was wildly inconsistent, however. From 1901 through 1904, his batting averages were .354, .265, .332, and .239. With the Cubs in the 1906 World Series, Sheckard was in one of his down cycles, going hitless in 21 at-bats against the White Sox. He hit only one ball out of the infield. Sheckard played in three more Series for the Cubs and finished his career with 14 hits in 77 at-bats in the Fall Classic for a .182 batting average.

3. **BILLY SULLIVAN SR.**

Playing as a catcher for the 1906 White Sox, an outfit known as the "Hitless Wonders," Billy Sullivan Sr. was hitless in 21 at-bats against the Cubs. He struck out nine times and never played in another Series. The only individual with more career at-bats in the World Series without a hit is Athletics pitcher George Earnshaw, who was 0 for 22 with 11 strikeouts in 1929, 1930, and 1931. Sullivan's son, Billy Jr., was a catcher for the Tigers in the 1940 Series and had just two hits in 13 at-bats.

4. **RED MURRAY**

Playing in his first World Series, Giants right fielder and cleanup hitter Red Murray not only went hitless in 21 at-bats in a six-game loss to the Athletics but also made three errors, which remains the record by an outfielder for a single Series. He was 0 for 12 with runners on base and 0 for six with runners in scoring position. Murray rebounded to go 10 for 31 in the Series against the Red Sox in 1912 and four for 16 versus the Athletics in 1913, but the Giants lost both of those Series as well.

5. **GIL HODGES**

Gil Hodges played in seven World Series as a first baseman for the Dodgers between 1947 and 1959 and played reasonably well, batting .267 with five homers in 131 at-bats. In a six-game loss to the Yankees, however, Hodges was hitless in 21 at-bats. After his playing career ended, Hodges became the manager of the New York Mets, and in 1969, he engineered one of the biggest upsets in World Series history. The Mets were 73–89 in 1968 and finished in ninth place in the 10-team National League. Prior to 1968, the Mets had never won more than 66 games in a season. Division play began in 1969, and the Mets leaped to first place, overcoming a 9½-game deficit to the Cubs. After disposing of the Braves in the first National League Championship Series, the

Mets met the Orioles in the World Series. Baltimore had a record of 109–53 in 1969 and was the overwhelming favorite in the Series, especially after winning the first game. The "Miracle Mets" rebounded, however, to win the final four games to win an improbable world title. The Mets failed to reach the postseason again under Hodges. He died of a heart attack just before the start of the 1972 season, two days before his 48th birthday.

6. LONNY FREY AND WALLY BERGER

Reds second baseman Lonny Frey was 0 for 17 in the 1939 World Series against the Yankees. Left fielder Wally Berger was hitless in 15 at-bats as the Yankees won all four games. Frey looked to redeem himself in the 1940 Series against the Tigers but was limited to two at-bats because of a freak injury. Five days before the Series began, the heavy metal cover on the dugout watercooler fell on Frey's right foot, which opened a deep gash and broke a bone in his big toe. Frey batted once for the Yankees in the 1947 Series and finished his career 0 for 20 in the postseason. The Reds released Berger early in the 1940 season. He also played for the Giants in the 1937 Series and was 0 for three. Berger finished his career with an 0 for 18 batting record in the World Series, and was 0 for eight in the All-Star Game while playing for the Braves in 1933, 1934, and 1935.

7. FLEA CLIFTON

Flea Clifton had only 195 at-bats as a major leaguer and batted only .200 as a utility infielder for the Tigers between 1934 and 1937. He was pressed into service in the 1935 World Series against the Cubs when first baseman Hank Greenberg broke his wrist. Marv Owen moved to first base, and Clifton was installed at third. Owen had one hit in 20 at-bats in the Series while Clifton was 0 for 16. Despite the holes in the bats of both players, the Tigers defeated the Cubs in six games.

8. MIKE EPSTEIN

Mike Epstein dubbed himself "Superjew" and was compared to Hank Greenberg early in his career, but there was nothing super about Epstein's performance in the 1972 World Series. Playing first base for the Athletics against the Reds, Epstein was hitless in 16 at-bats. It was the only World Series of his career. Combined with his record in the League Championship Series, Epstein hit .094 in 32 at-bats in the postseason.

9. **RAFAEL BELLIARD**

Rafael Belliard lasted 17 seasons in the majors despite a .221 batting average, a .259 slugging percentage, and only two home runs in 2,301 at-bats because of his defensive abilities at shortstop. He was the picture of futility playing for the Braves during the 1995 World Series against the Yankees, when he was hitless in 16 at-bats.

10. **BILL DAHLEN**

Bill Dahlen played 21 seasons in the majors from 1891 through 1911 and is one of the best players in baseball history without a plaque at Cooperstown. His only chance at playing in a World Series was in 1905 as a shortstop for the Giants. Dahlen went 0 for 15, although his club defeated the Athletics in five games. Despite the lack of a base hit, Dahlen accounted for the first theft of home plate in a World Series. In the fifth inning of the third game, Dahlen reached base on a force, stole second, moved to third on Art Devlin's single, and stole home on a double steal as Devlin swiped second.

Stop, Thief!

There have been 14 instances in which a player has stolen home plate in World Series play, including:

1. GEORGE DAVIS

White Sox shortstop George Davis stole home in the third inning of the fifth game of the 1906 World Series. It was part of a double steal in which Patsy Dougherty stole second. The run tied the score 3–3, and the Sox went on to win 8–6. Davis was elected to the Hall of Fame in 1998, 58 years after his death.

2. JIMMY SLAGLE

Cubs center fielder Jimmy Slagle missed the 1906 World Series with an injury but was off and running in 1907, stealing two bases in each of the first two games against the Tigers. One of the fastest players of his era and nicknamed "The Human Mosquito" for his small stature, Slagle finished the Series with six stolen bases, a record for a five-game Series. His steal of home occurred in the seventh inning of the fourth game. With two out, Slagle was on third and player-manager Frank Chance was on first with Wild Bill Donovan pitching. Chance intentionally got himself caught in a rundown and avoided the tag long enough for Slagle to steal home. The Cubs won the game 6–1 in Detroit.

3. TY COBB

Ty Cobb was the first in World Series history with a "clean" steal of home, one that was not part of a double steal. In the third inning of Game Two in Pittsburgh with the Tigers leading 4–2, Cobb was a runner on third base when Pirates manager Fred Clarke brought Howie Camnitz in from the bull pen to replace Vic Willis. The first batter to face Camnitz was George Moriarty, and before Camnitz could complete the at-bat, Cobb stole home. The Tigers won the game 7–2.

4. BUTCH SCHMIDT

The Boston Braves set the tone for their eventual sweep of the Philadelphia Athletics in the first game of the 1914 World Series with a 7–1 victory. One of the runs was scored in the eighth inning on a double steal. With Hank Gowdy as a runner on first and Butch Schmidt on third, Rabbit Maranville struck out on a Weldon Wyckoff pitch. Gowdy took off on a steal of second, and on catcher Jack Lapp's throw, Schmidt headed for home. Schmidt was safe on a return throw from Athletics second baseman Eddie Collins.

5. MIKE McNALLY

Mike McNally played 10 seasons in the majors as a utility infielder. He never played in more than 100 games in any one season, yet he played on six clubs that won an American League pennant. McNally was on the roster of the Red Sox in 1915 and 1916; the Yankees in 1921, 1922, and 1923; and the Senators in 1925. In addition, McNally was serving in the military in 1918 during World War I when the Red Sox captured the American League flag. In the fifth inning of the first game of the 1921 World Series against the Giants, McNally doubled, moved to third on a sacrifice, and stole home. The Yankees won 3–0.

6. BOB MEUSEL

The 1921 Yankees are the only club with two steals of home in a World Series. The day after McNally's theft of the plate,

Bob Meusel stole home during the Yankees' second consecutive 3–0 win over the Giants. Meusel is the only player with two steals of home in the Series. The second one was in the sixth inning of Game Three in 1928, which was won by the Yankees 7–3 in St. Louis. Meusel scored on a double steal with Tony Lazzeri swiping second.

7. MONTE IRVIN

Monte Irvin had a tremendous World Series for the Giants against the Yankees in 1951. Playing in the Series for the first time in his career, Irvin collected 11 hits in 24 at-bats for a .458 average. He had seven hits in his first nine at-bats. In the opener, played at Yankee Stadium, Irvin had four hits, including a triple, and stole home in the very first inning. After hitting a single, Irvin went to third on a Whitey Lockman ground-rule double and completed the circuit with a steal of home on a high pitch by Allie Reynolds, sliding under a tag by Yogi Berra.

8. JACKIE ROBINSON

Jackie Robinson stole home in a controversial play in the eighth inning of the first game of the 1955 World Series at Yankee Stadium. The Dodgers trailed the Yankees 6–3 when Carl Furillo led off the inning with a single off Whitey Ford. After Gil Hodges flied out, Robinson reached second on a two-base error by third baseman Gil McDougald that moved Furillo to third. Don Zimmer hit a sacrifice fly that scored Furillo and sent Robinson to third base. With Frank Kellert at bat, Robinson danced off third and broke for the plate. Berra's tag pushed Robinson's leg away from the plate, but umpire Bill Summers ruled that Robinson's foot had touched the edge of the plate before the tag and ruled Robinson safe. Berra protested vigorously but the call stood. The play didn't change the outcome of the game, however, as the Yankees won 6–5.

9. TIM McCARVER

Tim McCarver is the only catcher to steal home in a World Series game and the only one to do it in a Game Seven. It took place in 1964 when McCarver played for the Cardinals against the Yankees. McCarver scored on a double steal with Mike Shannon pilfering second in the fourth inning. The Cardinals scored three times in the inning to break a scoreless tie and went on to win 7–5. McCarver also hit a game-winning homer during the Series. In Game Five, he hit a three-run homer in the 10th inning off Pete Mikkelsen to give St. Louis a 5–2 win at Yankee Stadium.

10. **BRAD FULLMER**

For 38 years, Tim McCarver was the last player to steal home in a World Series. That distinction was removed by Angels designated hitter Brad Fullmer in Game Two of the 2002 World Series with McCarver in the broadcast booth serving as an analyst for the Fox television network. Fullmer swiped home in Anaheim's five-run first inning on a double steal with Scott Spezio, who took second. The Angels won the game 11–10.

The Man-Eating Tarp

Many players have been injured either during or just before the World Series under tragic, bizarre, or unusual circumstances.

1. VINCE COLEMAN

The Cardinals lost Vince Coleman for the final three games of the 1985 National League Championship Series and all of the World Series because of a freak accident. As a rookie, Coleman led the league with 110 stolen bases that season, but he wasn't fast enough to get out of the way of the Busch Stadium automatic tarp machine. While performing stretching exercises before Game Four of the NLCS, Coleman was pinned under the tarp as it rolled over his left leg. He was trapped for 30 seconds, had to be removed from the field on a stretcher, and was diagnosed with a bone chip in his foot. Coleman recovered from the injury and topped the National League in steals for the next five seasons.

2. FREDDIE FITZSIMMONS

Dodgers pitcher Freddie Fitzsimmons was knocked out of the box, literally, by opposing pitcher Marius Russo of the Yankees in Game Three of the 1941 World Series at Ebbets Field. Fitzsimmons and Russo were locked in a scoreless tie in the top of the seventh when Russo's line drive caromed

The Man-Eating Tarp

off Fitzsimmon's left knee to shortstop Pee Wee Reese, who caught the ball on the fly. Fitzsimmons had to be helped from the field with a broken kneecap. Reliever Hugh Casey gave up two runs in the eighth, and the Yankees won the game 2–1. Nicknamed "Fat Freddie" for his tendency to put on weight, Fitzsimmons was 39 years old when he broke his knee and won only three more games in his career but finished his sojourn in the majors with 217 victories. The knee injury was only the second-most bizarre injury of his career. During spring training in 1927, while playing for the Giants, Fitzsimmons fell asleep in a rocking chair and rocked over three of the fingers on his pitching hand.

3. TONY KUBEK

After his playing career was over, Tony Kubek used his throat to become a successful broadcaster. As a player, Kubek is best remembered for injuring his throat during the seventh game of the 1960 World Series. It happened when he was playing shortstop for the Yankees against the Pirates in Pittsburgh. The Yankees led 7–4 in the eighth inning with none out and Gino Cimoli as the Pirates runner on first. Bill Virdon hit a tailor-made double-play ball toward Kubek, but it took a crazy bounce off the rock-hard Forbes Field infield and struck him in the Adam's apple. Coughing up blood, Kubek was forced to leave the game. The Pirates went on to score five runs in the inning to take a 9–7 lead and won the world championship 10–9 in the ninth on Bill Mazeroski's homer. Kubek played in six World Series during his nine-year major league career, all with the Yankees. It would have been seven if he hadn't missed the entire World Series in 1964 with a sprained wrist.

4. ERIC DAVIS

In the first inning of Game Four of the 1990 World Series, Reds left fielder Eric Davis made a diving catch of Willie McGee's line drive but suffered a lacerated kidney on the remarkable defensive play. While his teammates were cele-

Eric Davis's 1990 World Series began with a home run in his first at-bat and ended in the hospital with a lacerated kidney after a defensive gem.

brating their sweep of the Athletics, Davis was in an Oakland hospital. This led to a dispute with cost-conscious Reds owner Marge Schott, who refused to pay for Davis's flight home until public pressure forced her to relent and open her wallet. Davis set the stage for the sweep by homering in the first World Series at-bat of his career, hit off Dave Stewart in the first inning of the Reds' 7–0 first-game win.

5. **GEORGE BRETT**

George Brett had the most famous case of hemorrhoids in baseball history when he was tortured by the malady during the 1980 World Series against the Phillies. The hemorrhoids made him the butt of jokes from coast to coast, but Brett was in his usual place in the lineup at third base for the Royals in the opening game. After going 0 for four, he had two hits in two at-bats in Game Two but left in the sixth inning in considerable pain. Brett used the travel day to undergo minor surgery. In his first at-bat just hours after leaving the hospital, Brett hit a home run into the right field seats at Royals Stadium on a 1–1 pitch by Dick Ruthven. Brett went on to collect nine hits, including two doubles, a triple, and a homer, in 24 at-bats in the Series, although the Royals lost in six games.

6. **JAKE FLOWERS**

Cardinals third baseman Jake Flowers was hit in the face by a ground ball during fielding practice before the fourth game of the 1931 World Series against the Athletics and was knocked unconscious. Flowers started the game but left in the second inning after suffering from a dizzy spell.

7. **DON BLACK**

The playing career of Indians pitcher Don Black came to an end just before his club went to the World Series in 1948. On September 13 in the bottom of the second inning versus the St. Louis Browns, Black swung hard at a pitch and fouled it back into the stands. He staggered as he finished the swing, then walked away from the plate in a small circle behind the plate umpire and collapsed as an aneurysm caused a brain hemorrhage. Black was in critical condition when Cleveland owner Bill Veeck staged a benefit that raised $40,000 for Black's care. Black recovered from the immediate effects of the hemorrhage but was only 42 when he died in 1959.

8. **RAY CHAPMAN**

The Indians were involved in a grueling three-team pennant race in 1920 with the White Sox and Yankees when shortstop

Ray Chapman was killed by a pitch. He is the only player in major league history to die as a direct result of being hit by a pitch. The incident happened on August 20, when he was struck in the temple by a pitch from Yankees hurler Carl Mays. Chapman was taken to a hospital, never regained consciousness, and died 12 hours later. The Indians went on to win the American League pennant and defeated the Dodgers in the best-of-nine World Series, five games to two.

9. TONY CONIGLIARO

Tony Conigliaro was another player felled by a pitched ball during a tight pennant race. Early in 1967, at the age of 22, he became the youngest player in major league history to hit 100 home runs. On August 18 that season, he was smashed in the face by a fastball thrown by Jack Hamilton of the Angels. The blow broke Conigliaro's cheekbone and damaged his eyesight. Tony missed not only the World Series, which the Red Sox lost to the Cardinals in seven games, but the entire 1968 season as well. He came back to play in 1969 and clubbed 36 homers and drove in 116 runs in 1970 but had to retire in midseason in 1971 when his eye problems returned. More tragedy came Conigliaro's way in 1982, when he suffered an incapacitating heart attack. He died in 1990 at the age of 45.

10. GEORGE STEINBRENNER

Even owners can be injured in bizarre fashion during the World Series. In 1981, Yankees principal owner George Steinbrenner was involved in a fistfight with a couple of Dodgers fans in the elevator of the Hyatt Wilshire Hotel in Los Angeles after a fifth-game loss and wound up with a broken hand when one of his punches hit the door. To add insult to injury, the Dodgers won the Series in six games.

X Rays of Dizzy's Head Showed Nothing

Star players, many destined for Cooperstown, have been unable to play during the World Series because of injuries or illnesses.

1. DIZZY DEAN

Following a season in which he won 30 games, Cardinals pitcher Dizzy Dean was skulled during the 1934 World Series against the Tigers in Detroit. Dean was used as a pinch-runner in the fourth inning of the fourth game, failed to slide running to second base, and caught shortstop Billy Rogell's throw right on the forehead. The ball caromed more than 100 feet away into right field. Dean was carried off the field on a stretcher and taken to a hospital where X rays showed no damage. Dean, who was hardly known as a Rhodes Scholar, proudly announced, "The doctors X-rayed my head and found nothing." A day later, Dean took the mound and pitched well but lost 3–1. On one day of rest, Dizzy returned to pitch the deciding Game Seven and defeated the Tigers 11–0.

2. REGGIE JACKSON

Reggie Jackson became known as "Mr. October" for his heroics in five World Series with the Athletics in 1973 and 1974 and the Yankees in 1977, 1978, and 1981. In 98 at-bats,

Jackson batted .357, hit 10 home runs, drove in 24, and scored 21. He missed the entire World Series in 1972, however, with a pulled hamstring he suffered while attempting to steal home plate in the fifth and deciding game of the American League Championship Series against the Tigers.

3. **MICKEY MANTLE**

Mickey Mantle played in 65 World Series games, second only to Yogi Berra, who had 75. Mantle might have passed Berra, but he missed 12 games with a variety of injuries. In 1951, as a 19-year-old rookie, Mantle stepped on the wooden cover of the drain outlet in the Yankee Stadium outfield while chasing a fly ball in Game Two against the Giants. He ripped up his right knee and missed the final four games of the six-game Series. In 1955, a torn thigh muscle kept Mantle out of four games. In 1957, he was plagued by shinsplints and a shoulder injury and missed the sixth game against the Braves. In 1961, Mantle played in only two of the five games because of an abscess on his hip that caused blood from the wound to seep through the bandages and soak his flannel uniform.

4. **ROGER MARIS**

Roger Maris, Mantle's outfield partner for many years, also had a career hampered by injuries. In Game Two of the 1963 World Series, Maris injured his left knee running into the railing in right field at Yankee Stadium while chasing down a triple hit by Tommy Davis of the Dodgers. Maris missed the remainder of the Series.

5. **HANK GREENBERG**

Coming off a season in which he drove in 170 runs for the Tigers, Hank Greenberg missed the last four games of the 1935 World Series with a broken wrist after he was hit in Game Two by a pitch from Fabian Kowalik of the Cubs. Greenberg stayed in the game, but on the train trip that night from Detroit to Chicago his wrist swelled and the pain became unbearable. Problems with his wrist continued into the next season, and Greenberg played in only 12 games in 1936.

6. LOU GEHRIG

Lou Gehrig played in seven World Series for the Yankees. He was in uniform during the 1939 Series against the Reds but wasn't playing because he was slowly dying from amyotrophic lateral sclerosis, known more commonly today as Lou Gehrig's disease. Gehrig played the first eight games of the regular season in 1939, stretching his streak of consecutive games played to 2,130, but took himself out of the lineup because he could no longer make even routine plays. He was diagnosed with the disease at the Mayo Clinic in June 1939 and died on June 2, 1941.

7. TOMMY JOHN

Lou Gehrig had a disease named after him. Tommy John had a surgery named after him. Playing for the Dodgers, John missed the 1974 World Series because of an operation in which a ligament from his right wrist was transplanted into his left pitching elbow. It was the first time such an operation was performed on a pitcher, and doctors had little hope that he would be able to play again. John's career appeared to be over at the age of 31. He missed the entire 1975 season but came back to win 164 more big league games before his career ended at the age of 46 in 1989. John pitched in the World Series for the Dodgers in 1977 and 1978 and the Yankees in 1981. The careers of many other pitchers have been saved with Tommy John surgery.

8. JOHNNY EVERS

The 1910 season was not kind to Cubs second baseman Johnny Evers. Late in the season, he was the driver in a car accident that killed his best friend. A few weeks later, he lost his life savings when his business partner invested in two shoe stores that went bankrupt. A week before the World Series against the Athletics, Evers broke his leg sliding into home plate in a game against the Reds. During the following off-season, Evers contracted pneumonia, his daughter died, and he suffered a nervous breakdown. He missed most of the 1911 season but recovered to hit .341 for the Cubs in 1912 and was a key ingredient in the Boston Braves' rise to the world championship in 1914.

9. RUBE WADDELL

Hall of Fame pitcher Rube Waddell wasn't available to pitch in the 1905 World Series for the Athletics against the Giants after a season in which he was 26–11 with a 1.48 ERA. As eccentric as anyone who has ever put on a big league uniform, Waddell was injured late in the season when he tried to remove the straw hat of teammate Andy Coakley on a train platform. Waddell tripped over some luggage and fell heavily on his pitching shoulder.

10. ROLLIE FINGERS

Rollie Fingers was one of the most effective relief pitchers in World Series history. With the Athletics in 1972, 1973, and 1974, he saved six games and had a 1.35 ERA in 33 1/3 innings. While with the Brewers in 1982, Fingers missed the World Series with a torn arm muscle. Milwaukee could have used him. The bull pen gave up 10 runs in 13 innings in a seven-game loss to the Cardinals.

Put Me in Coach, I'm Ready to Play

On many occasions, the replacements for injured players have had a brief moment in the spotlight by making an impact coming off the bench in the World Series.

1. GEORGE ROHE

The 1906 Chicago White Sox were known as the "Hitless Wonders" because the club won the pennant despite finishing the season with a .230 batting average, a .288 slugging percentage, and only seven home runs, all of which were the worst figures in the American League that season. They were underdogs in the World Series against the crosstown Cubs, the winners of a major league record 116 games. The White Sox were also missing future Hall-of-Famer George Davis, the club's shortstop, at the start of the Series since he was out with an injury. Regular third baseman Lee Tannehill moved to short, and utility infielder George Rohe was pressed into service at third. During the regular season, Rohe hit .258 with just six extra base hits in 225 at-bats. In the World Series, Rohe batted .333 with seven hits, including a double and two triples, in 21 at-bats. Both of his triples were significant. The first three-bagger led to the first run of the Series and paced the White Sox to a 2–1, Game One victory. Rohe's biggest moment came in Game Three at the Cubs' West Side Park when he tagged Jack Pfiester for a bases-loaded triple in the sixth inning, which accounted for all the runs in the White Sox' 3–0 victory. Davis came back to play the final three games of the Series, but Tannehill went to the bench and Rohe remained in the lineup. The Sox won a stunning upset by defeating the Cubs in six games. After the Series, White Sox owner Charlie Comiskey proclaimed, "Whatever George Rohe may do from now on, he's signed on for life with me!" Rohe was the Sox regular third baseman in 1907, but he hit only .213 and was released at the end of the season and never played in the majors again.

2. **LARRY McLEAN**

In warm-ups before the second game of the 1913 World Series, Giants catcher Chief Meyers broke a finger. Second-stringer Larry McLean filled in for Meyers and belted out six hits in 12 at-bats off Athletics pitchers. One of the biggest players of his era, McLean was six-foot-five and weighed 228 pounds. He played in the majors from 1901 through 1915 with five clubs and was considered one of the top catchers in the game, when he wasn't drinking. He had a constant battle with alcohol throughout his adult life. Normally an affable sort with a gentle disposition, McLean became mean and belligerent when he drank. Several times during his career, McLean disappeared for days while on a bender. His big league career ended in 1915 when he challenged Giants manager John McGraw and his coaches to a fight outside a St. Louis hotel. McLean died in 1921 at the age of 39 when he was shot and killed by a bartender who acted in self-defense, during a fight in Boston.

3. **JIMMIE WILSON**

The Reds lost both of their catchers in the weeks leading up to the 1940 World Series, one to an injury, the other to a tragic suicide. Backup catcher Willard Hershberger took his own life in a hotel room in Boston on August 3, and starter Ernie Lombardi suffered a severely sprained ankle on September 15. Substituting for Lombardi was problematic for manager Bill McKechnie as his alternatives were not appealing. He had to choose between little-used rookies Bill Baker and Dick West and 40-year-old coach Jimmie Wilson, who came out of retirement after the death of Hershberger. Wilson had caught 1,525 games during his major league career, but only 40 of them had come since 1936. Lombardi gamely volunteered to play, but he was the slowest player in baseball on two completely healthy legs. McKechnie went with Wilson and didn't regret it. Despite being the only individual to catch in a World Series after his 40th birthday, Wilson batted .353 and recorded the only stolen base of the Series as the Reds defeated the Tigers in seven games. They were the last big league games that Wilson ever played. From 1941 through 1944, he managed the Cubs but never experienced a winning season. He died of a heart attack in 1947 at the age of 46.

4. **MICKEY HATCHER**

Kirk Gibson's home run in the first game of the 1988 World Series was rated one of the top 10 moments in baseball history in a 2002 fan poll, but if it wasn't for left fielder Mickey Hatcher's play in place of the injured Gibson, the Dodgers may not have won the World Series against the Athletics. Hatcher played mostly in right field and at first base during the regular season, appeared in only eight games in left, and had just one homer in 191 at-bats. The fun-loving Hatcher had seven hits in the World Series, including two home runs and a double, in 19 at-bats. His first home run came in his first World Series at-bat in the first inning of Game One off Dave Stewart. Hatcher drove in five runs and scored another five.

5. **JOHNNY BLANCHARD AND HECTOR LOPEZ**

The Yankees were without Mickey Mantle and Yogi Berra for much of the 1961 World Series against the Reds, but super subs Johnny Blanchard and Hector Lopez picked up the slack. Blanchard had four hits, including two homers and a double, in 10 at-bats, while Lopez was three for nine with a homer, a triple, and seven runs batted in. In the third game, Blanchard rammed a pinch-hit homer off Bob Purkey into the Crosley Field bleachers to tie the score. Roger Maris won the game 3–2 with another home run in the ninth. In the Game Five clincher, which the Yankees won 13–5, Blanchard and Lopez combined were five for eight, scored five runs, drove in seven, and had a double, a triple, and two home runs. Blanchard and Lopez were two of the nine players to appear in five consecutive World Series from 1960 through 1964. The others were Clete Boyer, Whitey Ford, Elston Howard, Mickey Mantle, Roger Maris, Bobby Richardson, and Ralph Terry. Berra played for the Yankees in 1960, 1961, 1962, and 1963 and managed the club in 1964.

6. BRIAN DOYLE

With Willie Randolph on the shelf, Brian Doyle played second base for the Yankees in the 1978 World Series against the Dodgers. At the time, Doyle was a 23-year-old rookie who had just 52 career regular-season at-bats, a .192 batting average, and no extra base hits. Doyle hit .438 in the Series, including a double, in 16 at-bats. The Yankees lost the first two games of the Series but rallied to win the next four. Doyle had three hits in Game Five and another three-hit salvo in the clincher. Included was a streak of hits in five consecutive plate appearances. Doyle and shortstop Bucky Dent were the eighth and ninth hitters in the Yankees lineup in the final two games and combined for 12 hits in 19 at-bats, scoring six runs and driving in another six. Doyle played three more big league seasons with the Yankees and the Athletics and finished his career with just 32 base hits, a .161 batting average, and a .201 slugging percentage in 191 regular-season at-bats.

7. BILL CUNNINGHAM

Giants center fielder Casey Stengel went out with a leg injury after the second game of the 1922 World Series against the

Yankees, and Bill Cunningham took his place. Cunningham had only two hits in 10 at-bats but made two spectacular defensive plays in the first inning of Game Four. With Yankees on first and second and none out, Cunningham ran down a drive off the bat of Babe Ruth in the deepest part of center field at the Polo Grounds. The next hitter was Wally Pipp, who hit a drive to right center that fell safely, but Cunningham flagged it down and, with a tremendous throw, nailed Pipp at second as he was trying for a double. The Yankees scored twice, but Cunningham's defense prevented a big inning, and the Giants recovered to win the game 4–3 and clinch the world championship the next day.

8. TITO LANDRUM

Tito Landrum hit only .249 in a nine-year career in which he never had more than 205 at-bats in a season, but he shined in the postseason subbing for injured players. With the Orioles in the 1983 ALCS, he played right field after only 47 regular-season at-bats. Landrum hit a 10th-inning home run in Game Four against a stiff wind at Comiskey Park that broke a scoreless tie and led Baltimore to a pennant-clinching 3–0 win over the White Sox. In the 1985 postseason with the Cardinals, Landrum played left field for Vince Coleman after Coleman's leg was rolled up in the Busch Stadium automatic tarp. Landrum was six for 14 with four runs batted in the NLCS against the Dodgers and nine for 25 in the World Series, including two doubles and a homer, versus the Royals.

9. JIM LINDEMAN

Another Cardinals replacement starred in the 1987 postseason. Jim Lindeman batted only .208 in 207 at-bats that season, but had 28 at-bats in the NLCS against the Giants and the World Series against the Twins, filling in at first base and in right field. He collected nine hits in the two Series combined, including a double and a homer.

10. **RICKY LEDEE**

After a 79-at-bat rookie season in 1998 in which he hit only .241 for the Yankees, and going hitless in five at-bats in the Division Series and the ALCS, Ricky Ledee starred in the World Series against the Padres. Playing in place of Darryl Strawberry, who was suffering from colon cancer, Lee had six hits, including three doubles, in 10 at-bats for a batting average of .600.

DNP—Manager's Decision

Many players on the World Series eligibility roster have been glued to the bench without getting an opportunity to play.

1. **CHARLIE SILVERA**

Catcher Charlie Silvera was on the Yankees roster in the World Series in 1949, 1950, 1951, 1952, 1953, 1955, and 1956. But as a backup for Yogi Berra, Silvera appeared in only one of the 42 games played in those seven Series. Silvera started the second game of the 1949 Series against the Dodgers, went 0 for two, and was lifted for a pinch-hitter in the eighth inning. It wasn't much better during the regular season. In nine seasons with the Yankees, Silvera spent most of his time warming up pitchers in the bull pen. He played in only 201 games despite batting .291. Silvera could console himself with the fact that he collected $46,386.45 in World Series money for appearing in just one contest.

2. **ARNDT JORGENS**

At least Charlie Silvera got into a game. Arndt Jorgens was eligible to play for the Yankees in the 1932, 1936, 1937, 1938, and 1939 Series but couldn't crack the lineup. Born in Modum, Norway, Jorgens was the backup catcher for Bill

Dickey. In 11 seasons in New York, Jorgens played in only 307 regular-season games.

3. BOB UECKER

One of the funniest players ever to put on a major league baseball uniform, Bob Uecker parlayed his often self-deprecating humor into a successful career as a broadcaster, author, and actor. Uecker was in the majors for six seasons as a catcher, from 1962 through 1967, and batted just .200. He was on the Cardinals World Series eligibility roster in 1964 but didn't play in a game as Tim McCarver caught every inning. Uecker did find a new use for a tuba, however. During batting practice, he borrowed a tuba from a member of the band scheduled to play the National Anthem and tried to direct fly balls into the large opening in the musical instrument. Uecker was sent a bill for $200 for the dents he put in the tuba. In 2003, he was elected to the Hall of Fame as a broadcaster.

4. MOE BERG

Moe Berg was a reserve catcher on the 1933 Washington Senators when he failed to play in any of the five Series games against the Giants. He was undoubtedly one of the most intelligent men ever to play professional baseball. A magna cum laude graduate of Princeton, he received a law degree from Columbia and studied philosophy at the Sorbonne in Paris. Berg declined an offer to teach in the romance language department at Princeton in order to play baseball. Unfortunately, his baseball skills didn't compare with his mental gifts. Reportedly, scout Mike Gonzalez coined the phrase "good field, no hit" after watching Berg play. Pitcher Ted Lyons joked, "He can speak 10 languages and can't hit in any of them." In 15 seasons in the majors with five clubs, Berg hit only six home runs. In 1934, Berg used his linguistic abilities to serve his country. In Japan as a member of a team of American All-Stars that included Babe Ruth, Berg took espionage photos of Tokyo for use by

DNP—Manager's Decision

St. Louis Cardinals

Tim McCarver caught every single inning of the 1964 World Series, keeping funnyman Bob Uecker planted firmly on the bench.

the State Department. Eight years later, General Jimmy Doolittle used these photographs in making the American air attack on Japan during World War II. After the war started, Berg posed as a Swiss businessman and a German officer in order to obtain German atomic secrets.

5. CHUCK DRESSEN

On the other bench during the 1933 World Series was Chuck Dressen. The Giants picked up Dressen late in the 1933 season after a run of injuries to their infielders. He sat on the bench during the entire Series, but his advice helped his club beat the Senators in Game Four. The Giants led 2–1 in the 11th when Washington loaded the bases with one out and pinch-hitter Cliff Bolton batting against Carl Hubbell. The Giants had a skimpy scouting report on Bolton because he had batted only 39 times during the season, but Dressen had seen Bolton in the minors and suggested that the Giants pull in the infield for a potential double play because Bolton was slow and tended to hit the ball on the ground. That is precisely what happened, as Bolton's grounder resulted in a game-ending twin killing. The following July, Dressen was named manager of the Reds. He managed the Dodgers in 1951 when the club blew a $13^1/_2$-game lead to the Giants in the National League pennant race. The Dodgers recovered to play in the World Series in 1952 and 1953 under Dressen but lost both times to the Yankees. He was fired after the 1953 Series because he demanded a multiyear contract. Dodgers owner Walter O'Malley had a policy of giving only one-year deals and refused to yield to Dressen's demands.

6. JUMBO BROWN

Listed in *Total Baseball* at six-foot-four and 295 pounds, pitcher Jumbo Brown is perhaps the heaviest player in major league history. He played 12 seasons in the majors, mostly as a reliever, and was on the Yankees roster during the 1932 and 1936 World Series, but he didn't appear in a game. In one of life's bitter ironies, Jumbo hailed from the microstate of Rhode Island.

7. CHET TRAIL

Chet Trail is the only player in history to appear on a World Series eligibility roster without ever appearing in a major league game. Due to the bonus rule in effect in 1964, the Yankees had to carry Trail on their 25-man roster all season, including the Series, even though he played shortstop for Greensboro in the Class A Carolina League. Although he was eligible to play in the 1964 World Series against the Cardinals, Trail wasn't even in the ballpark in either New York or St. Louis.

8. JOHNNY BERARDINO

Johnny Berardino was on the bench as a reserve infielder for the Indians during the 1948 World Series. He got the acting bug as a child and appeared in many *Our Gang* comedies, as well as an occasional film during baseball's off-season. As a publicity stunt dreamed up by Cleveland owner Bill Veeck, Berardino had his face insured for $100,000 in 1948. When his baseball career ended in 1952, Berardino tried acting as a full-time living as Johnny Beradino, dropping the second "r" in his name. He found only bit parts, however, and had to pawn his 1948 World Series ring to make ends meet. He finally found success in the early 1960s as Dr. Steve Hardy on the long-running soap opera *General Hospital,* a role he played for four decades.

9. MARK BROUHARD

With left fielder Ben Oglivie out with a rib injury in Game Three of the American League Championship Series, the Brewers used reserve Mark Brouhard at the position. The Brewers trailed the Angels two games to none in the best-of-five series. It was the first game Brouhard had played in 28 days, but he shook off the rust and had three hits, including a home run and a double, in four at-bats, scored four runs (tying a postseason record), and drove in three as the Brewers stayed alive with a 9–5 victory in Milwaukee. It proved to be the only postseason game of Brouhard's career. He didn't play in either of the Brewers' final two ALCS games or in any of their seven World Series contests against the Cardinals.

10. KIKI CUYLER

As the 1927 season started, the Pirates had an outfield consisting of three future Hall-of-Famers with Paul Waner in left, his brother Lloyd in center, and Kiki Cuyler in right. Cuyler was dropped from the starting lineup in midseason because of a batting slump and an argument with manager Donie Bush, and the Pirates skipper petulantly kept Cuyler out of the World Series that fall against the Yankees. In the fourth game, Bush used 20-year-old Fred Brickell as a pinch-hitter with the crowd at Forbes Field chanting, "We want Cuyler, we want Cuyler." Bush also benched future Hall of Fame shortstop Joe Cronin during the 1927 Series.

Have Ring, Will Travel

Many players have appeared in the World Series with at least three different franchises.

1. **LONNIE SMITH**

Lonnie Smith is the only player to appear in the World Series with four different clubs. Smith played on the Phillies as a rookie in 1980, the Cardinals in 1982, the Royals in 1985, and the Braves in 1991 and 1992. He was on the winning side in Philadelphia, St. Louis, and Kansas City.

2. **DON BAYLOR**

Don Baylor is the only person to play on three different teams in the World Series in three consecutive seasons. He was on the Red Sox in 1986, the Twins in 1987, and the Athletics in 1988. In addition, Baylor appeared in the ALCS with the Orioles in 1973 and 1974 and the Angels in 1979 and 1982 to become the only individual to play on five different teams in the postseason.

3. **FRED MERKLE**

Fred Merkle is best known for a baserunning blunder that cost the Giants a chance to go to the World Series in 1908. Merkle did make it to the Series five times with three clubs, but he was on the losing team on all five occasions, with the

Giants in 1911, 1912, and 1913; the Dodgers in 1916; and the Cubs in 1918.

4. JACK MORRIS

Jack Morris was the starting pitcher in Game One of the World Series for three different teams including the 1984 Tigers, the 1991 Twins, and the 1992 Blue Jays. All three clubs won the world championship. He started seven games altogether and was 4–2 in World Series play with a 2.96 ERA. A native of St. Paul, Minnesota, Morris pitched the Twins to the title with a 10-inning shutout in Game Seven in 1991, defeating the Braves 1–0.

5. MATT WILLIAMS

Matt Williams is the only player to hit home runs in the World Series for three different teams. He homered for the Giants in 1989, the Indians in 1997, and the Diamondbacks in 2001.

6. LUIS POLONIA

Luis Polonia holds the World Series record for most times a player was used as a pinch-hitter with 12. He played for the Athletics in 1988, the Braves in 1995 and 1996, and the Yankees in 2000. In 1996, Polonia pinch-hit in all six Series games against the Yankees but was 0 for five with a walk.

7. DAVE STEWART

Dave Stewart appeared in the World Series as a struggling rookie with the Dodgers in 1981; as one of the top pitchers in the game with the Athletics in 1988, 1989, and 1990; and as a pitcher with diminishing skills near the end of his career as a Blue Jay in 1993. Stewart had a record of 8–0 in the League Championship Series but was only 2–4 in the World Series.

8. HEINIE GROH

Third baseman Heinie Groh played in the World Series with the Reds in 1919; the Giants in 1922, 1923, and 1924; and the Pirates in 1927. He hit .474 (nine for 19) for the Giants in the 1922 World Series against the Yankees, and for many years he drove an automobile with a license plate bearing the number 474.

9. **EARL SMITH**

Earl Smith is the only individual to play on a team that was swept in the World Series in two consecutive seasons. Smith was on the 1927 Pirates and the 1928 Cardinals, clubs that both lost four straight to the Yankees. Smith also played on the winning side three times, with the 1921 and 1922 Giants and the 1925 Pirates.

10. **JOE BUSH**

"Bullet Joe" Bush played in the World Series with the Athletics in 1913 and 1914, the Red Sox in 1918, and the Yankees in 1922 and 1923. Bush is the youngest player to pitch a complete game, which he accomplished at the age of 20 years 316 days when he defeated the Giants 8–2. He is also the only pitcher to lose five consecutive World Series games. Overall, Bush was 2–5 with a 2.87 ERA in World Series play.

Let Me See Some ID

Nine individuals have played in the World Series as teenagers. The 10 youngest players to appear in a Series game are:

1. **FRED LINDSTROM**

At 18 years, 10 months, and 13 days, Fred Lindstrom is the youngest player ever to appear in a World Series game. Lindstrom batted only 79 times and hit .253 for the Giants in 1924, but he started all seven Series games against the Senators that fall at third base because of an injury to Heinie Groh. Lindstrom also batted in the crucial leadoff spot and responded with 10 hits, including two doubles, in 30 at-bats for a .333 average. Lindstrom batted .311 during his 13-year career and was elected to the Hall of Fame in 1976.

2. **KEN BRETT**

Ken Brett is the youngest pitcher to appear in the World Series. Brett was less than a month past his 19th birthday and had pitched in only one big league game when he was called upon to pitch the eighth inning of Game Four for the Red Sox in 1967 against the Cardinals. Brett contributed a scoreless inning, but Boston lost 6–0. Ken played 14 seasons in the majors and spent time with 10 clubs. Following his term with the Red Sox, Brett played for the Brewers, Phillies, Pirates,

Yankees, White Sox, Angels, Twins, and Dodgers before finishing his career as a teammate of his brother George in Kansas City. After his big league career was over, Brett did a Miller Lite beer commercial in which he couldn't figure out what town he was in.

3. WILLIE CRAWFORD

A native of Los Angeles, Willie Crawford had just turned 19 when he pinch-hit twice for the Dodgers in the 1965 World Series against the Twins. Crawford also played in the Series with the Dodgers in 1974.

4. TOM CARROLL

Tom Carroll was 19 when he appeared in two games as a pinch-runner for the Yankees against the Dodgers in 1955. Carroll was used mostly as a pinch-hitter during his three-year career. He played in 64 regular-season games but batted only 30 times, although he had nine hits for a .300 batting average.

5. PHIL CAVARETTA

Phil Cavaretta won the starting first base job for the Chicago Cubs when he was just 18 years old. He was 19 when he played all six games of the 1935 World Series against the Tigers, although he batted only .125 (three for 24). He was much better in the 1938 Series versus the Yankees, batting .462 (six for 13) and against the Tigers in 1945, hitting .423 (11 for 26), although the Cubs lost all three times. Cavaretta was the National League MVP in 1945 and played 20 seasons for the Cubs. He was a player-manager of the Cubs from 1951 through 1953 but was fired during spring training in 1954 after predicting that his club would be lucky to post a winning record. Cavaretta played two more seasons with the White Sox, closing a 22-year major league career.

6. DON GULLETT

Don Gullett pitched in the World Series for the Reds in 1970, 1972, 1975, and 1976 and with the Yankees in 1977. He was

19 in 1970 against the Orioles. Gullett started the first game of the World Series in 1976 against the Yankees and again in 1977 while playing for the Yankees. Arm troubles ended Gullett's career when he was only 27 years old with a 109–50 lifetime record during the regular season and a 2–2 record in the World Series.

7. TRAVIS JACKSON

Travis Jackson was just 19 when he played one game as a pinch-hitter for the Giants in 1923 versus the Yankees. The following year, Jackson was the starting shortstop for the Giants in the Series against the Senators. Jackson also played in the World Series for the Giants in 1933 and 1936 and was elected to the Hall of Fame in 1982.

8. MICKEY MANTLE

Mantle played in 12 World Series for the Yankees in his first 14 seasons in the majors, the first in 1951 when he was 19. Mantle holds career World Series records for most home runs (18), most runs scored (42), most total bases (123), most extra base hits (26), most runs batted in (40), most bases on balls (43), and most strikeouts (54).

9. ANDRUW JONES

Two players in history have hit home runs in their first two World Series at-bats. The first was Gene Tenace of the Athletics in 1972. The second was Braves center fielder Andruw Jones in the first game of the 1996 World Series, leading his club to a 12–1 thrashing of the Yankees in New York. Jones's homers were hit off Andy Pettitte and Brian Boehringer. Only 19, Jones also became the only teenager to hit a homer in the World Series.

10. CLAUDELL WASHINGTON

Claudell Washington was a little more than a month past his 20th birthday when he had four hits in seven at-bats for the Athletics in the 1974 World Series against the Dodgers. Washington lasted in the majors until 1990 but never played in another World Series.

Pitching Phenoms

Throughout the 100-year history of the World Series, many rookie pitchers have made a tremendous impact on the outcome.

1. **JOHNNY BEAZLEY**

Johnny Beazley was a marvelous 21–6 with a 2.14 ERA for the National League champion Cardinals in 1942 and followed that performance by defeating the Yankees twice in the World Series. The second win was in the fifth game and clinched the championship for St. Louis. Beazley spent the next three seasons serving in the military during World War II and hurt his arm pitching for a service team. He returned to the majors in 1946 but won only 10 more games.

2. **GENE BEARDEN**

The Indians needed a tie-breaking play-off game against the Red Sox in 1948 to win the American League pennant and selected rookie Gene Bearden as the starting pitcher. Bearden had just one day of rest, but he pitched a five-hitter to defeat the Red Sox 8–3 and put Cleveland in its first World Series since 1920. He finished the regular season with a 20–7 record, and his 2.43 ERA led the league. During the World Series against the Boston Braves, Bearden started Game Three and pitched a shutout to win 2–0. He also had two hits, including a double, in three at-bats. In the sixth-game clincher, Bearden sealed the victory with 1 2/3 innings of scoreless ball. For Bearden, just reaching the majors was an ordeal. During World War II, a cruiser on which he was stationed was sunk by the Japanese, and because of wounds he sustained in the attack, he had to have aluminum plates placed in his head and knee. His rookie season was his last taste of success in baseball, however. After 1948, he had a 25–31 record and a 4.63 earned run average.

3. **WHITEY FORD**

Whitey Ford had a 9–1 record for the Yankees as a rookie in 1950, with his only defeat coming in a relief stint during the last week of the season. Ford started the fourth game of the World Series against the Phillies and pitched 8 2/3 innings to win 5–2 and nail down a four-game sweep for his club. Ford missed the next two seasons due to military commitments, but returned in 1953 and picked up where he left off. Between 1950 and 1953, the Yankees won Ford's first 22 major league starts. He was 16–0 with six no decisions. His first loss came on June 16, 1953, by a 3–1 score to the St. Louis Browns. Two other long streaks were broken in the unusual game. The Yankees entered the contest with an 18-game winning streak, while the Browns came into Yankee Stadium having lost 14 games in a row. Ford finished his career in 1967 with a 236–106 record and holds several career World Series records, with the most wins (10), most losses (eight), games pitched (22), games started (22), innings pitched (146), walks (34), strikeouts (94), and consecutive scoreless innings (33).

4. **RYNE DUREN**

Ryne Duren was 29 years old before he completed his first full season in the majors because of his inability to control a blazing fastball. During his rookie season with the Yankees in 1958, Duren walked 44 batters in 76 innings, but he had a 2.01 earned run average as a stopper out of the bull pen.

In the World Series that season against the Braves, Duren had a win and a save and a 1.93 ERA in 9$^{1}/_{3}$ innings as the Yankees took the championship in seven games. He never reached those heights again, finishing his career in 1965 with a 27–44 record, but he was near the top of the list of pitchers that hitters hated to face. Duren frightened hitters by peering toward the plate with thick glasses to correct his 20/70 and 20/100 vision and by throwing pitches against the backstop during warm-ups. For batters, it was like facing Mr. Magoo armed with a 98-miles-per-hour fastball. In addition, Duren seldom pitched when he was sober. In a candid autobiography written after his career ended, he detailed his battle with alcoholism.

5. **LARRY SHERRY**

Without rookie reliever Larry Sherry, the Los Angeles Dodgers wouldn't have reached the World Series, much less won it. Summoned from the minors in midseason, Sherry was 7–2 with a 2.19 ERA. The Dodgers were forced to play a tie-breaking, best-of-three play-off against the Milwaukee Braves to determine the National League champion, and Sherry pitched 7$^{1}/_{3}$ innings of scoreless relief in the first game to defeat the Braves 3–2. During the World Series, Sherry became a national celebrity by winning two games and saving two others, allowing only one run in 12$^{1}/_{3}$ innings as the Dodgers defeated the White Sox in six games. Sherry had only sporadic success for the remainder of his career, which ended in 1968 with a 53–45 record and a 3.67 earned run average.

6. **RON GUIDRY**

In Game Four of the 1977 World Series, rookie Ron Guidry pitched the Yankees to a 4–2 complete-game win over the Dodgers. It was the start of a pattern. Guidry also pitched a game against the Dodgers in the 1978 Series and two in 1981 and closed his career with a 3–1 record in the Fall Classic, along with a 1.93 ERA in 32 innings. When his career ended in 1988, Guidry had a regular-season record of 170–91. His best season was in 1978, when he was 25–3 with a 1.74 earned run average.

7. FERNANDO VALENZUELA

The 1981 baseball season will be remembered for two events. One was the strike that interrupted the season for eight weeks from mid-June through mid-August. The other was Fernandomania. Valenzuela won his first eight starts for the Dodgers with five shutouts and an astounding ERA of 0.50. He finished the season with a 13–7 record and the Cy Young Award. Valenzuela's only start in the World Series against the Yankees came in Game Three, with the Dodgers trailing two games to none. He allowed four runs in the first three innings but shut the Yankees down the rest of the way for a 5–4 win, despite surrendering nine hits and seven walks. The Dodgers swept the final four games to take the world title. Valenzuela ended his career in 1997 with a 173–153 record.

8. MIKE BODDICKER

In the only World Series game of his career, Mike Boddicker of the Orioles shut out the Phillies on only three hits to win 5–0 in the fifth and final game of the 1983 World Series. He also pitched a complete-game shutout in the ALCS that season, defeating the White Sox 4–0 on five hits in Game Two while striking out 14 batters. Boddicker was 16–8 with five shutouts during the 1983 regular season and followed that up with a 20–11 season in 1984, in which he led the AL in ERA. He struggled for most of the remainder of his career, however, and was finished in 1993 with a 134–116 record.

9. JOHN LACKEY

John Lackey of the 2002 Anaheim Angels became the first rookie starting pitcher to win a Game Seven of a World Series since Babe Adams in 1909. Lackey pitched the first five innings of the Angels' 4–1 clincher over the Giants. A midseason recall from the minors, Lackey was 9–4 during the regular season in 18 starts.

10. FRANCISCO RODRIGUEZ

Francisco Rodriguez had the most amazing postseason by any rookie pitcher in history. Entering the Division Series for the Angels against the Yankees in 2002, Rodriguez was just 20 years old and had pitched only five big league games, all in relief, hurling 5^2/$_3$ innings without allowing an earned run and without a decision. He became the first pitcher to win his first career game in the postseason when he was the winning pitcher in two of the Angels' three victories over the Yankees. In the American League Championship Series versus the Twins, Rodriguez was 2–0 again, pitching 4^1/$_3$ scoreless innings. In the World Series, Rodriguez won another game, allowing just a pair of earned runs in 8^2/$_3$ innings. No other pitcher in history has won a World Series game without first posting a win during the regular season. His five wins in the postseason also tied the record set by Randy Johnson in 2001. Altogether, Rodriguez pitched in 12 of Anaheim's 16 postseason games, allowing four earned runs in 18^2/$_3$ innings. And Rodriguez became the youngest pitcher ever to win a World Series game, at 20 years 285 days, breaking the record set by Jim Palmer of the Orioles, who was 20 years 356 days old when he defeated the Dodgers 6–0 in Game Two in 1966.

Hitting Phenoms

Rookie batters have also made their presence felt during the World Series, especially New York Yankees.

1. GEORGE WATKINS

Cardinals right fielder George Watkins homered in his first World Series at-bat as a rookie, a blast over the right field wall at Shibe Park in Philadelphia in the second game of the 1930 World Series. He also hit a two-run homer in the third inning of the seventh game of the 1931 Series, won by the Cardinals with a 4–2 score over the Athletics. Watkins holds the record for the highest batting average by a rookie (among players with a minimum of 100 games), stroking a .373 mark in 1930, along with 17 home runs. He was nearly 30 years old when he made his big league debut and failed to maintain the success of his initial season. Watkins finished his major league career in 1936 with a .288 lifetime batting average.

2. PEPPER MARTIN

Pepper Martin was a relatively unknown Cardinals center fielder at the start of the 1931 World Series, but he became a national hero by putting together one of the greatest individual performances in postseason history. Against the Athletics, he had 12 hits, including four doubles and a triple, in

24 at-bats. Martin also stole five bases. All 12 hits and all five stolen bases came in the first five games of the Series over 18 at-bats. The Cardinals took the championship in seven games. Nicknamed "The Wild Horse of the Osage" for his aggressive play, Martin starred again in the 1934 Series against the Tigers. Playing third base, he was 11 for 31, and hit three doubles and a triple in addition to swiping two more bases. His .418 career batting average in the World Series is tied for the all-time best by a player with at least 50 at-bats. Paul Molitor also hit .418 with 23 hits in 55 at-bats for the 1982 Brewers and 1993 Blue Jays.

3. **JOE DiMAGGIO**

Joe DiMaggio played in 10 World Series during his 13-year major league career. The first one came in 1936, when he was a 20-year-old rookie. Against the Giants, DiMaggio hit .346 with nine hits, three of them doubles. The Yankees won the Series in six games.

4. **JOE GORDON**

As a rookie second baseman with the Yankees in 1938, Joe Gordon had six hits, including two doubles and a homer, in 15 at-bats for a .400 batting average during a four-game sweep of the Cubs. Gordon played in six World Series with the Yankees and the Indians and experienced his share of ups and downs. In 1941 in a five-game win over the Dodgers, he was seven for 14 with a double, a triple, and a homer. A year later, Gordon won the American League Most Valuable Player award but flopped in the World Series. He had only two hits in 21 at-bats and struck out seven times.

5. **CHARLIE KELLER**

Charlie Keller was the third Yankees rookie during the 1930s to star in a World Series. In a four-game sweep of the Reds in 1939, Keller was seven for 16, hitting three home runs, a triple, and a double. He drove in six runs while scoring another six. Keller was also involved in one of the most famous plays in Series history. In the 10th inning of Game Four, Keller was a base runner on first base with Frankie Crosetti on third when Joe DiMaggio singled. Crosetti scored on the hit, and while Reds right fielder Ival Goodman kicked the ball around, Keller steamed toward home plate. Catcher Ernie Lombardi reached for Goodman's throw just as Keller slammed into him. Keller was safe, but Lombardi was out, having been hit in the groin. Rounding third, DiMaggio saw the catcher motionless on the ground with the ball only five feet away. DiMaggio kept running and slid across the plate. Those runs gave the Yankees a 7–4 win to clinch the Series.

6. BILLY JOHNSON

Yankees third baseman Billy Johnson had six hits in 20 at-bats for a .300 average in the 1943 World Series against the Cardinals. Among his hits was a bases-loaded triple. Johnson played again in the World Series in 1947, 1949, and 1950. He hit three more triples in those three Series. His four career triples ties him for the career World Series record with Tommy Leach and Tris Speaker.

7. GIL McDOUGALD

Gil McDougald is the only rookie to hit a grand-slam home run in a World Series. He did it with the Yankees in Game Five in 1951 during a 13–1 trouncing of the Giants at the Polo Grounds. McDougald played in eight World Series during his 10-year career, and as a result of Yankees manager Casey Stengel's complex platoon system, McDougald started Series games at third base, second base, and shortstop and hit in every position in the batting order except cleanup and ninth. His 53 World Series games played ranks him fourth all time, behind only Yogi Berra, Mickey Mantle, and Elston Howard.

8. TONY KUBEK

Tony Kubek made a splash as a 20-year-old rookie with the Yankees in 1957. Another of Casey Stengel's versatile players, Kubek started World Series games that season in left field, center field, and third base while batting in the first, second, sixth, seventh, and eighth spots in the batting order. He had eight hits in 28 at-bats for a .286 batting average. Kubek hit two homers in Game Three, played against the Braves in his hometown of Milwaukee in the first-ever World Series game played in that city. It followed a season in which he hit only three home runs, and it was the first multiple-home-run game of his career. Kubek had only two other multiple-home-run games during his career, both during the 1960 regular season. In 1958, Kubek moved to shortstop, where he was the Yankees starter until 1965. Kubek is one of five players who have played at four different positions in the World Series. The others are Babe Ruth (pitcher, left field, right field, and first base), Jackie Robinson (first base, second base, left field, and third base), Elston Howard (left field, right field, first base, and catcher), and Pete Rose (right field, left field, third base, and first base).

9. TOM TRESH

Tom Tresh was the American League Rookie of the Year in 1962, hitting 20 home runs for the Yankees. He began the season at shortstop while Tony Kubek was serving in the army and moved to left field when Kubek returned in August. Tresh starred in the World Series against the Giants with nine hits, including a double and a homer, in 28 at-bats. His homer broke a 2–2 tie in the eighth inning of the fifth game, lifting New York to a 5–3 win. In the seventh game, won by the Yankees 1–0, Tresh robbed Willie Mays of extra bases with a running one-handed catch that barely stuck in the fingertips of his glove. Tresh was proclaimed the next Mickey Mantle, but his .286 regular-season batting average and 93 RBI as a rookie were career highs. He finished his career in 1969 with a .245 average.

10. WILLIE McGEE

Cardinals rookie center fielder Willie McGee had a stunning Game Three in 1982 in a 6–2 win over the Brewers in Milwaukee. He hit two homers that drove in four runs and robbed both Paul Molitor and Gorman Thomas of extra base hits with outstanding leaping catches above the fence. McGee had had only four homers at that point in his career, and it was the first time he had ever hit two homers in one game. He had only one other multiple-home-run game in the majors, that one during the 1985 regular season.

Fortysomethings

The ten oldest players ever to appear in a World Series are:

1. **JACK QUINN**

Jack Quinn pitched in the World Series with the Yankees in 1921 and the Athletics in 1929 and 1930 and hardly distinguished himself with an 0–1 record and an 8.44 earned run average in $10^{2}/_{3}$ innings, but he became the oldest individual ever to play in a World Series. He was 47 years old during a relief appearance in 1930. Quinn is also the oldest starting pitcher in Series history, which he accomplished at 46 in 1929. He holds several other regular-season oldest records in the major leagues. Quinn is the oldest to hit a home run (at 45 with the Athletics in 1929), the oldest to collect an extra base hit (at 47 with the Dodgers in 1931), and the oldest to win a game (at 49 with the Dodgers in 1932). Quinn pitched his last major league game on July 7, 1934, with the Reds, two days after his 50th birthday. He is the oldest player in major league history who was not part of a publicity stunt.

2. **JIM KAAT**

Jim Kaat pitched in the majors from 1959 through 1983 and won 283 games. He pitched in the World Series with the Twins in 1965, posting a 1–2 record in three starts against the Dodgers, and in four appearances with the Cardinals at the age of 43 in 1982.

3. **DAZZY VANCE**

Dazzy Vance was elected to the Hall of Fame based on a career in which he had a record of 194–140. He was 43 years old and near the end of the line when he played in the World Series for the only time in his career, with the Cardinals in 1934 against the Tigers. Vance pitched 1 1/3 innings of relief in the fourth game, allowing an unearned run during a 10–4 St. Louis defeat.

4. **BABE ADAMS**

Babe Adams pitched in the second World Series of his career in 1925 as a member of the Pirates at the age of 43, mopping up a 4–0 Game Four loss to the Senators with a scoreless inning of relief. In his first World Series, as a rookie in 1909, Adams was the hero, defeating the Tigers three times in three complete-game starts. During the 1909 regular season, Adams was a spot starter and reliever who hurled only 130 innings, although with an impressive 12–3 record and a 1.11 ERA. Pittsburgh manager Fred Clarke surprised nearly everyone by starting Adams in the first game of the Series over veterans Howie Camnitz (with a 25–6 record in 1909), Vic Willis (22–11), and Lefty Leifeld (19–9). The Tigers scored a run off Adams in the first inning, but he shut them down the rest of the way and won 4–1. Adams also won Game Five 8–4. Clarke selected Adams again in the seventh game on two days' rest. Adams shut out Detroit in 40-degree weather for an 8–0 win. Adams is the only rookie to win three games in a single World Series. He had a 194–140 record during his major league career and was one of the best control pitchers of all time, walking only 430 batters in 2,995 1/3 innings.

5. **MIKE RYBA**

Mike Ryba's last major league game was in the 1946 World Series, when he pitched for the Red Sox against the Cardinals at the age of 43. Ryba pitched two-thirds of an inning in a 12–3 Boston defeat in the fourth game. He played 10 seasons in the major leagues, the first in 1935 when he was 32 years old. In addition to pitching in 250 games, he appeared in 10 games as a catcher.

6. **DOLF LUQUE**

Dolf Luque pitched in the major leagues from 1914 through 1935 with the Braves, Reds, Dodgers, and Giants. One of the first natives of Cuba to play in the major leagues and the first Latin-American to play in a World Series, he was 194–179 during his career, which included a 27–8 season in Cincinnati in 1923. He appeared in the 1919 World Series with the Reds and in 1933 with the Giants against the Senators. In a season in which he turned 43 in August, Luque was 8–2 with a 2.69 ERA and four saves for the Giants in 1933. He made only one appearance in the World Series, but it came at a crucial junction. The Giants had won three of the first four games and were looking to close out the Series in Game Five. Luque entered the contest with the score of 3–3 and two outs in the Washington sixth with runners on first and third. He retired Luke Sewell on a ground out and shut out the Senators the rest of the way on just two hits. Mel Ott won the game for the Giants with a 10th-inning homer off Jack Russell. Luque was the winning pitcher in the 4–3 decision and became the oldest pitcher ever to win a World Series game. He also hit a single in his only at-bat and became the oldest player to collect a base hit in the Series.

7. **SAM RICE**

Sam Rice had a single as a 43-year-old pinch-hitter for the Senators in his only at-bat in the 1933 World Series against the Giants. It was near the end of a Hall of Fame career in which Rice collected 2,987 base hits, but he is best remembered for a play in the third game of the 1925 Series. Rice's Senators were leading the Pirates 4–3 in the eighth inning in Washington when he moved from center field to right in a defensive switch. With two out, Earl Smith hit a drive off Firpo Marberry toward Rice and the temporary overflow bleachers in right field. Rice was moving at top speed toward the bleachers with his glove outstretched and his back to the plate when he leaped high in the air to make the catch. His momentum carried him forward, and Rice hit the four-foot-high railing in front of the seats. The collision knocked the wind out of him, and for a few seconds Rice was bent over the railing before he could regain his equilibrium. There was uncertainty over whether Rice retained the ball, but second base umpire Cy Rigler, who raced into the outfield to make the call, didn't hesitate to rule that Rice made the catch. The Pirates protested, claiming that Rice dropped the ball and that a fan stuffed it back into his glove. There was no more scoring in the game, although Pittsburgh won the Series in seven games. Rice avoided questions about the play for the rest of his life, saying only that the umpire ruled it a legal catch, but announced that he left a letter with the Hall of Fame to be opened only after his death. When Rice died in 1974, he put an end to nearly 50 years of suspense by declaring, "At no time did I lose possession of the ball."

8. JOE NIEKRO

Phil Niekro's younger brother, Joe Niekro, was 42 when he reached the World Series for the first time in 1987 with the Twins and pitched two scoreless innings in relief during a 7–2 loss to the Cardinals in the fourth game. Joe started two postseason games with the Astros. In 1980, he pitched 10 shutout innings in Game Three against the Phillies, won by Houston 1–0 in 11 innings. In the 1981 Division Series versus the Dodgers, he pitched eight scoreless innings in the second game, and again Houston won 1–0 in 11 innings. In both cases, the Astros eventually lost the best-of-five series in five games. In all, Niekro pitched 20 postseason innings without allowing a single run but wasn't able to earn a victory because his team failed to score for him while he was on the mound.

9. **PETE ROSE**

Pete Rose is the oldest player in World Series history to play a fielding position other than pitcher. At 42, Rose played first base for the Phillies in 1983 against the Orioles. He hit a double among his five hits in 16 at-bats and became the oldest player to collect an extra base hit in the Fall Classic. Rose appeared in six World Series with the Reds and the Phillies and batted .269 in 34 games.

10. **ENOS SLAUGHTER**

Enos Slaughter is the only player to compete in three World Series after turning 40. As a 40-year-old in 1956, he became the oldest player in World Series history to hit a home run while playing for the Yankees against the Dodgers. It was a three-run shot in the sixth inning of the third game, which gave the Yankees a 4–2 lead in a contest that New York won 5–3. Slaughter hit .350 in 20 at-bats during the Series but didn't play in the seventh game because of his defensive lapses while he was playing left field in Game Six. He also played for the Yankees in the Series in 1957 and 1958, the latter at the age of 42, when he was used as a pinch-hitter in four games against the Braves.

You Don't Have to Play the Game

Eleven managers have taken teams to the World Series without ever playing in a major league game, including Jack McKeon with the Marlins in 2003.

1. PANTS ROWLAND

Pants Rowland's playing experience was limited to a few seasons as a minor league catcher. He was named manager of the White Sox in 1915 and led the club to the world championship in 1917 with a six-game victory over the Giants. The White Sox fired Rowland after their sixth-place finish in 1918, a year before the Black Sox scandal. Rowland never managed in the majors again, but he was an American League umpire from 1923 through 1927, served as president of the Pacific Coast League from 1941 through 1954, and worked in the Cubs front office.

2. ED BARROW

Ed Barrow was 50 years old when he was named manager of the Red Sox in 1918. In his first season in Boston, he won the world championship. Barrow never played in even the minor leagues, much less the majors. Before becoming the manager of the Sox, Barrow worked as a baseball reporter, a concession operator, a minor league club owner, and a manager in both the majors (with the Tigers in 1903 and

1904) and the minors. Early in the 1918 season, Barrow converted pitcher Babe Ruth into a first baseman and an outfielder. The Red Sox had contemplated converting Ruth from one of the top pitchers in the game into a full-time hitter for years, but it was a risk the club had been unwilling to take. Barrow was also reluctant, stating during spring training, "I'd be the laughingstock of baseball if I turned the best left-hander in the game into an outfielder." Barrow made the conversion just after the season started, however, because World War I enlistments and inductions had cut sharply into the club's offensive production. The pitching staff was left relatively unscathed by the wartime military commitments. Barrow hedged his bets and continued to use Ruth as a pitcher, though mainly as a spot starter, through the 1918 season. Ruth was in the starting lineup in only two of the six World Series games against the Cubs in 1918, both as a pitcher. The Red Sox sold Ruth in 1919, but Barrow hooked up with the Babe a year later, when he was named general manager of the Yankees and helped build one of the greatest dynasties in the history of professional sports. Barrow held the job until 1945, a period that included 14 American League pennants and 10 world championships.

3. **JOE McCARTHY**

Joe McCarthy never played in the majors, but that didn't stop him from becoming one of the most successful managers in baseball history. In 24 seasons with the Cubs, the Yankees, and the Red Sox between 1926 and 1950, he led nine clubs into the World Series and won with seven of them. His seven world championships is the all-time record, which he shares with Casey Stengel. McCarthy's overall win-loss record in the Series was 30–13. His first World Series was with the Cubs in 1929, but he was fired near the end of the 1930 season after finishing a close second. Hired by the Yankees in midseason in 1931, McCarthy won American League pennants in 1932, 1936, 1937, 1938, 1939, 1941, 1942, and 1943, winning the World Series every one of those seasons except 1942. He resigned in May 1946 and became the manager of the Red Sox in 1948. He narrowly missed racking up two more pennants in Boston, finishing one game behind in the pennant race in both 1948 and 1949.

4. EDDIE SAWYER

Eddie Sawyer guided a young Phillies team nicknamed "The Whiz Kids" to the pennant in 1950. Although the club lost the World Series to the Yankees in the minimum four games, the Phillies' future looked bright with young stars like Robin Roberts, Richie Ashburn, Curt Simmons, Del Ennis, Granny Hamner, Andy Seminick, and Willie Jones. The club never came close to another pennant under Sawyer, however, who was fired in 1952. Sawyer returned to manage the Phillies in 1958 but finished in last place two years in a row and resigned after an opening-day loss in 1960. "I'm 49 years old," said Sawyer, explaining his decision, "and I want to live to be 50."

5. JOHNNY KEANE

Johnny Keane spent 31 years in the Cardinals organization as a minor league player and manager and major league coach before getting a shot at managing the parent club in 1961. His 1964 Cardinals were 7 1/2 games behind the Phillies with two weeks remaining in the season, but in an unbelievable turn of events, the Cardinals overcame the seemingly insurmountable lead by winning 10 of their last 13 games while Philadelphia couldn't buy a victory. The Cards beat out the Phillies for the National League pennant and defeated the Yankees in the World Series. When it seemed as though the Cardinals were out of pennant contention, owner August Busch decided to fire Keane once the season was over and had contacted Leo Durocher about managing the club in 1965. Busch had a change of heart and was willing to extend Keane's contract after he won the World Series, but Keane resigned. Meanwhile in New York on the very same day, the Yankees announced the firing of Yogi Berra, even though he had won the American League pennant in his first season as manager. The bizarre twists and turns continued as the Yankees hired Keane to manage the club four days later. Keane took over a franchise that had won 14 pennants in the previous 16 years, but the move to New York proved to be disastrous as age and injuries took their toll and Keane finished in sixth place in 1965, the Yankees' first losing season in 40 years. After a 4–16 start in 1966, Keane was fired by the Yankees. He died of a heart attack in January 1967 at the age of 55.

6. **EARL WEAVER**

As a player, Earl Weaver never got out of the minors, but he earned induction into the Hall of Fame as a manager. Weaver managed the Orioles from 1968 through 1982 and again in 1985 and 1986 and led Baltimore to World Series appearances in 1969, 1970, 1971, and 1979. His 1970 club won the world championship. Weaver's clubs always had great pitching. From 1968 through 1980, he managed eight different pitchers to seasons of 20 or more wins a total of 22 times, including Jim Palmer (nine times), Dave McNally (four), Mike Cuellar (four), Pat Dobson (one), Mike Torrez (one), Wayne Garland (one), Mike Flanagan (one), and Steve Stone (one). Weaver was known for his ability to get under the skin of umpires. "The best way to test a Timex watch," said umpire Marty Springstead, "would be to strap it to his tongue."

7. **JIM FREY**

Jim Frey took over as manager of the Royals in 1980 and led the club to the World Series in his first season, although Kansas City lost the Series in six games to the Phillies. Frey was fired during the second half of the 1981 strike-interrupted season after the club lost 40 of its first 70 games. Frey was named manager of the Cubs in 1984 and won the Eastern Division title with the best record in the National League in his first season. The Cubs won the first two games of the best-of-five NLCS against the Padres before losing three in a row. Like everyone else who has managed the Cubs since 1945, Frey was unable to get the club into the World Series and was fired in midseason in 1986. A year later, he became the general manager of the Cubs and helped the franchise to another division title in 1989, but again Chicago fell short of reaching the World Series.

8. PAUL OWENS

Phillies general manager Paul Owens fired Pat Corrales on July 18, 1983, and took the job himself. Owens's only previous managing experience in the majors was in 1972, when he took over the Phillies in midseason and failed to get the club out of last place. In 1983, the Phillies were 47–30 under Owens and won the Eastern Division title. After dispatching the Dodgers in the NLCS, the Phillies lost to the Orioles in five games in the World Series.

9. JOHN McNAMARA

John McNamara didn't possess enough talent to reach the majors as a catcher, but he found steady employment as a manager. From 1969 through 1996, he managed the Athletics, Padres, Reds, Angels, Red Sox, and Indians. McNamara guided only one team into the World Series, however. He was at the helm of the Red Sox in 1986 when the club was on the brink of the world championship in Game Six against the Mets, only to lose and continue the slow torture of all Red Sox fans who desire to witness a world championship in their lifetime. The image of the ball rolling through Bill Buckner's legs was burned into the psyche of Sox fans forever, and New Englanders will never forgive McNamara for leaving Buckner and his gimpy ankle in the game instead of replacing him with defensive specialist Dave Stapleton.

10. JIM LEYLAND

Jim Leyland was never more than a backup catcher in the minor leagues, but he led four clubs into the postseason as a major league manager and was praised for his abilities to handle baseball's disparate personalities. His Pirates lost the NLCS in 1990 to the Reds and in 1991 and 1992 to the Braves. Hampered by free-agent defections led by Barry Bonds and Bobby Bonilla, Leyland's last four Pittsburgh teams had losing records. He went to Florida in 1997 and directed the Marlins to a world championship in his first season. Again, budgetary restraints dismantled Leyland's club. A year later, after the Marlins' high-salaried players were traded, sold, or left in free agency, Florida finished with a 54–108 record.

Do As I Say, Not As I Do

Many other managers have led clubs into the World Series after brief and largely ineffective major league playing careers.

1. **WALTER ALSTON**

Walter Alston batted only one time in the major leagues, with the Cardinals in 1936, and struck out. He was almost completely unknown when he became the manager of the Brooklyn Dodgers in 1954, a high-profile franchise that had won the National League pennant four of the previous seven seasons and narrowly missed winning two others. The Dodgers finished second to the Giants in the National League pennant race in 1954, but Alston led the Dodgers to their first world championship in 1955. The Dodgers were in the World Series again in 1956, and after moving to Los Angeles, in 1959, 1963, 1965, 1966, and 1974. Alston won four world titles. He managed the Dodgers for 23 seasons, longer than anyone else managed a single team with the exceptions of Connie Mack and John McGraw. Alston was inducted into the Hall of Fame in 1983.

2. **TOMMY LASORDA**

The man who replaced Walter Alston as manager of the Dodgers was Tommy Lasorda. As a pitcher in the majors,

Lasorda had only an 0–4 record with the Dodgers and the Athletics between 1954 and 1956, but he excelled as a manager. His exuberant personality helped goad the Dodgers into the World Series in 1977 and 1978, his first two seasons as their manager. Although the Dodgers lost to the Yankees in the Series both times, they won the world championship under Lasorda in 1981 and 1988. Lasorda stayed on the job until 1996. For 43 seasons, Alston and Lasorda were the only individuals to manage the Dodgers.

3. GEORGE STALLINGS

George Stallings played in only 17 big league games and had an 879–896 record as a major league manager, but he earned a place in baseball history by guiding the Boston Braves to a miracle pennant in 1914. Stallings took over the Braves in 1913. The previous four seasons, the club had failed to get out of last place and had never lost fewer than 100 games. Stallings's Braves climbed to fifth in 1913 with a 69–82 record but were in last place in 1914 as late as July 19. A tough taskmaster, Stallings directed an amazing turnaround, as the Braves won 60 of their last 76 games to win the pennant by 10½, then walloped the Athletics in the World Series, winning all four games. The Braves finished second in 1915 and third in 1916 before resuming their losing ways. Stallings was fired after the 1920 season.

4. TOM KELLY

Tom Kelly's major league career consisted of 49 games with the 1975 Twins as a first baseman, in which he batted only .181 with just one home run. He was much more successful as a manager with the Twins, winning the world championship in 1987 and 1991. Kelly had an embarrassing moment during the third game of the 1991 Series against the Braves in Atlanta, however. Unused to managing without the designated hitter rule, Kelly had no position players left in the 12th inning to pinch-hit for pitcher Mark Guthrie with the bases loaded and two out. Relief pitcher Rick Aguilera was sent to the plate as a pinch-hitter and flied out. Aguilera gave up a run in the bottom of the inning to lose the game 5–4.

5. **JOE ALTOBELLI**

Joe Altobelli hit just .210 as a first baseman and outfielder in 166 games with the Indians and the Twins between 1955 and 1961 but had some success as a manager with the Orioles and the Giants during the 1970s and 1980s. In 1983, Altobelli replaced legend Earl Weaver as Baltimore skipper and carried the Orioles to a world championship in his first season.

6. **TONY LA RUSSA**

La Russa had a forgettable career as a player, hitting .199 as a utility infielder with the Athletics, the Braves, and the Cubs from 1963 through 1973, but through the 2003 season, he has won 2,009 regular-season games as a manager. The only individuals with more victories are Connie Mack (3,731), John McGraw (2,763), Sparky Anderson (2,194), Bucky Harris (2,157), Joe McCarthy (2,125), and Walter Alston (2,040). La Russa won the American League pennant with the Athletics in 1988, 1989, and 1990 and the world championship in 1989. He is also one of only five individuals to earn a law degree and manage a big league team. The other four—Monte Ward, Miller Huggins, Hughie Jennings, and Branch Rickey—are all in the Hall of Fame.

7. **MAYO SMITH**

If it weren't for World War II, Mayo Smith probably wouldn't have played in the major leagues. With hundreds of professional players serving in the military, Smith appeared in 73 games for the last-place Athletics in 1945 as an outfielder, batting only .212. He managed the Tigers to the American League pennant in 1968 and succeeded with one of the greatest gambles in World Series history. Throughout the regular season, Smith shuffled outfielders Al Kaline, Willie Horton, Jim Northrup, and Mickey Stanley in and out of the lineup and sought a way to play all four of them in the postseason against the Cardinals. The weak point in the batting order was at shortstop, where Ray Oyler, Dick Tracewski, and Tom Matchick combined to hit only .165 in 654 at-bats. Smith started Mickey Stanley at shortstop in all seven games in the Series, even though Stanley had never played the position professionally before the final week of the 1968 regular season. Stanley made two errors and hit just .214, but that didn't prevent the Tigers from winning the world championship.

8. **DARRELL JOHNSON**

Darrell Johnson hit only .234 as a catcher in the big leagues, but he did play in the World Series with the Reds in 1961. In 1975, Johnson was the manager of the Red Sox in the World Series against the Reds and became the third of four Boston managers, along with Joe Cronin, Dick Williams, and John McNamara, to lose a Game Seven since the end of World War II. Johnson was fired by the Red Sox in midseason in 1976.

9. **SPARKY ANDERSON**

Sparky Anderson's big league career consisted of one season as a second baseman with the Phillies in 1959. In 152 games, he batted only .218 without a single home run. His major league managerial career began in 1970 in Cincinnati, and as a prematurely gray 36-year-old, he led the Reds into the World Series with a club dubbed the Big Red Machine. Anderson managed the Reds for nine seasons and made it into the Series again in 1972, 1975, and 1976, taking the world title in 1975 and 1976. The Reds unceremoniously fired him following a second-place finish in 1978, and a year later he became manager of the Tigers. He had limited success in Detroit but won another world championship in 1984.

10. **EDDIE DYER**

After a 15–15 record as a pitcher in six seasons with the Cardinals during the 1920s, Eddie Dyer worked his way back through the vast Cardinals farm system as a minor league manager to reach the parent club in 1946. He won a world championship in his first season as manager but was unable to finish first in the National League again and was fired in 1950.

Boy Wonders

The 10 youngest managers in World Series history are:

1. JOE CRONIN
The youngest manager in World Series history was Joe Cronin, who was 26 when he guided the Senators into the postseason in 1933. Cronin was one of the top shortstops in the game when he was named the Senators' manager at the end of the 1932 season, replacing Walter Johnson. He won the American League pennant in his first season and hit .309 and drove in 118 runs. The Senators lost the World Series in five games to the Giants. It was the last time a Washington club would reach the Fall Classic. Cronin married the adopted daughter of Senators owner Clark Griffith, but it wasn't enough to keep him in Washington. After the 1934 season, Cronin was traded to the Red Sox for Lyn Lary and $250,000. Cronin was also the player-manager in Boston. His playing career ended in 1945, but he continued to manage on the field until 1947. In 1946, his Red Sox were in the World Series for the only time between 1918 and 1967 but lost in seven games to the Cardinals. Cronin became the club's general manager at the end of 1947 and held the job until 1959, when he became president of the American League.

2. BUCKY HARRIS

The youngest manager to win the World Series was Bucky Harris, who like Cronin was a player-manager with the Senators and won a pennant in his first year on the job. Harris was only 27 and the club's starting second baseman when he became the manager in 1924. The Senators had never won an American League pennant and had finished in fourth place the previous season, but Harris drove the club to first and into the World Series against the Giants. The two teams split the first six games. In Game Seven, Harris started right-handed pitcher Curly Ogden, who had only a 9–8 record during the regular season. Harris had left-hander George Mogridge warming up under the stands, however, and Mogridge entered the contest after Ogden had faced only two batters. It was the only postseason appearance of Ogden's career. Facing a lineup stocked with left-handed hitters, Mogridge wasn't particularly effective, but right-handed relievers Firpo Marberry and Walter Johnson combined for seven innings in which they allowed only one unearned run, and the Senators won the game 4–3 in 12 innings. It was Washington's only world championship. Harris also starred with his bat during the Series, collecting 11 hits, including two home runs. For leading Washington to the title, Harris was nicknamed "The Boy Wonder." The Senators won the pennant again in 1925 and lost the Series in seven games to the Pirates. Harris managed in the majors until 1956 but won only one more pennant. In 1947, in his first year as the manager of the Yankees, he won the World Series in seven games against the Dodgers. He was fired a year later after finishing in third place, only two games out of first, and was replaced by Casey Stengel.

3. FRANK CHANCE

Frank Chance was only 29 years old and one of the best first basemen in the game when he managed his club to the highest winning percentage in modern major league baseball history. Chance's 1906 Cubs had a 116–36 record for a .763 winning percentage. The Cubs lost the 1906 World Series in six games to the White Sox in an astonishing upset but rebounded to win the World Series in 1907 and 1908, and only world titles in the history of the franchise. Chance was also the first manager to win a World Series in consecutive seasons. He put Chicago back into the World Series in 1910, losing in five games to the Athletics.

4. **ROGERS HORNSBY**

Rogers Hornsby was one of the greatest hitters the game has ever known, finishing his career with a .358 batting average. Over the five-year period from 1921 through 1925, his batting average was .402. He hit 144 home runs during those five seasons and twice led the league in the category. Hornsby was named manager of the Cardinals in midseason in 1925, when he was 29. The Cardinals had never finished as high as second in the National League pennant race, but Hornsby drove them into the World Series in 1926, his first full season on the job. The Cardinals polished off the Yankees in seven games, but it wasn't enough for Hornsby to keep his job. Belligerent, nasty, and rude, he angered nearly everyone in the Cardinals organization, including owner Sam Breadon, who traded him to the Giants. Hornsby later managed the Braves, Cubs, Browns, and Reds without reaching the World Series again.

5. **FRED CLARKE**

The third game of the first World Series in 1903 was Fred Clarke's 31st birthday. Clarke's Pirates won the game 4–2 that day against the Red Sox but lost the Series. Clarke was only 24 years old when he received his first major league managing job, with Louisville in the National League in 1897. As a player-manager, he won pennants with the Pirates in 1901, 1902, 1903, and 1909. Clarke won the world championship in 1909, beating the Tigers in seven games. He set a record in the seventh contest of the 1909 Series by becoming the only player to walk four times in a game. As a player, he collected 2,678 career hits and batted .312. Clarke was elected to the Hall of Fame in 1945.

6. LOU BOUDREAU

Lou Boudreau was just 24 years old when his managing career began with the Indians in 1942. He was also an outstanding shortstop, both offensively and defensively. In 1948, he guided the Indians to the pennant and won the American League MVP award by hitting .355 with 18 homers and 106 runs batted in. Cleveland needed a victory over the Red Sox in a one-game play-off to secure the American League flag, and Boudreau had two homers and two singles in an 8–3 victory. The Indians won the World Series over the Boston Braves in six games. Boudreau never played or managed in the World Series again, but he was elected to the Hall of Fame in 1970.

7. MICKEY COCHRANE

Mickey Cochrane played in five World Series, two of them as a player-manager. Cochrane was a star catcher with the Athletics in the Series in 1929, 1930, and 1931. Owner and manager Connie Mack began dismantling the team in the 1932 season, unable to pay high salaries in a Depression economy. Cochrane was sold to the Tigers after the end of the 1933 season and was named player-manager. He was 31 years old when the 1934 season began. The Tigers finished fifth in 1933 and hadn't won a pennant since 1909, but Cochrane led them to the American League flag in both 1934 and 1935. The Tigers lost the World Series in seven games to the Cardinals in 1934 but won in 1935 in six over the Cubs to capture the club's first world championship. Cochrane's playing career ended in 1937, when he suffered a severe beaning that fractured his skull in three places. A year later, he left professional baseball for good. Cochrane was elected to the Hall of Fame in 1947.

8. BILL CARRIGAN

Bill Carrigan was 29 and near the end of a mediocre playing career when he was named manager of the Red Sox in 1913. He led the team to a world championship in both 1915 and 1916, then retired to become a banker in his hometown of Lewiston, Maine. Carrigan was lured back to managing in 1927, but the Red Sox finished dead last under his tutelage three years in a row, and Carrigan retired again.

9. TRIS SPEAKER

Tris Speaker hit .345 and collected 3,514 hits between 1907 and 1928 and was one of the best defensive center fielders in the game's history. He played on the 1912 and 1915 Red Sox World Series teams but was traded to Cleveland just before the start of the 1916 season. Speaker was named the Indians' player-manager in 1919, when he was 31 years old and won the world championship in 1920, defeating the Dodgers in the Series. After the final out was made, Speaker dashed from his center field position and vaulted into the stands, where he gave his mother a long embrace.

10. JOHN McGRAW

John McGraw managed the New York Giants in nine World Series, the first in 1905 when he was 32 years old. He is the youngest individual to manage in the World Series after his playing career ended. McGraw was on the losing end of six Series, the all-time record. He lost four Series in a seven-year span from 1911 through 1917. Bobby Cox ranks second to McGraw, with four World Series defeats.

Wise Sages

The 10 oldest managers in the World Series are:

1. **CASEY STENGEL**

When Yankees general manager George Weiss hired Casey Stengel as manager at the end of the 1948 season, many thought he'd lost his mind. Stengel had managed previously for nine seasons in the majors, with the Dodgers and the Braves between 1934 and 1943, to an unspectacular 581–742 record. None of his clubs had finished higher than fifth place, and he was known more for his clownish behavior than for any intellectual acumen. Weiss was proven correct when Stengel guided the Yankees to a record five consecutive world championships in his first five years as manager and 10 pennants and seven World Series titles in all in 12 seasons. In 1960, Stengel was 70 years old when his Yankees lost the Series in seven games to the Pirates. The loss cost Stengel not only a chance to become the first manager to win eight World Series but his job as well. He was fired four days later, along with Weiss, by Yankees co-owners Dan Topping and Del Webb. Topping and Webb wanted younger minds at the helm, and Ralph Houk was called upon to replace Stengel. Weiss went on to head up the front office of the expansion Mets and hired Stengel as manager. Stengel's sense of humor was sorely tested with the National League's new club in New York. He managed the team from its inception in 1962 until July 1965 to a record of only 174–404. Despite all of his success with the Yankees, Stengel was barely above .500 as a big league manager, with 1,905 wins and 1,852 losses.

2. **CONNIE MACK**

Connie Mack was the owner of the Philadelphia Athletics from the time the club was established in 1901 until the franchise moved to Kansas City at the end of the 1954 season. As owner, Mack kept himself as manager from 1901 through 1950, by far the longest tenure of any manager with one club. He was 87 years old when he stepped down as manager. Under Mack, the Athletics always seemed to be at the top or the bottom of the American League, depending upon the club's financial situation. Mack won the American League pennant nine times but finished dead last 17 seasons. He won a record 3,731 games as a manager, but he also set a record for losses with 3,948. Mack was 68 in 1931, the last time the Philadelphia Athletics played in the World Series.

3. **BURT SHOTTON**

Leo Durocher was the manager of the Dodgers in 1947 when he was suspended by Commissioner Happy Chandler for one year for "conduct detrimental to baseball." General manager Branch Rickey turned to his old friend Burt Shotton to replace Durocher. Shotton was 62 and hadn't managed in the majors since 1934. Led by rookie first baseman Jackie Robinson, Shotton directed the Dodgers to the World Series although he lost in seven games to the Yankees. Durocher returned as Dodgers manager in 1948 but was fired in July and replaced by Shotton once more. The Dodgers won the pennant again in 1949 under Shotton but lost the Series to the Yankees. Shotton was fired at the end of the 1950 season.

4. **WALTER ALSTON**

Walter Alston was 62 years old the last time he managed a club in the World Series, in 1974. His Dodgers lost in five games to the Oakland Athletics in baseball's first all-California World Series. Alston's fourth world championship wasn't enough to get him a multiyear contract. Adhering to Walter O'Malley's company policy, Alston signed 23 one-year deals during his long tenure as Dodgers manager.

5. **JOE TORRE**

When he was hired as manager of the Yankees at the end of the 1995 season, Joe Torre had played 18 seasons in the major leagues and managed another 14 seasons without appearing in a World Series. With George Steinbrenner's track record of hiring and firing managers on a whim, Torre didn't appear to be in a secure position, but he endeared himself to the boss by winning a world championship in his first season. Through the 2003 season, Torre has managed the Yankees in six World Series, winning four. On opening day in 2004, Torre will be 63 years old.

6. **PAUL OWENS**

Paul Owens was 59 years old when he managed the Phillies in the 1983 World Series but he fit in nicely with a veteran team nicknamed the "Wheeze Kids." The roster included Pete Rose (age 42), Tony Perez (41), Joe Morgan (40), Ron Reed (40), Steve Carlton (38), and Tug McGraw (38).

7. **ROGER CRAIG**

Roger Craig pitched for world championship teams with the Dodgers in 1955 and 1959 and the Cardinals in 1964. He was 59 years old when he managed the Giants to four straight losses in the earthquake-racked 1989 Bay Area World Series to the Athletics.

8. **FRED HANEY**

When 56-year-old Fred Haney was hired as manager of the Milwaukee Braves in June 1956, he had a horrible career record of 288–526 as a big league skipper with the Browns from 1939 through 1941 and the Pirates from 1953 through 1955. In spite of the fact that he never managed a club that came close to a winning record, Haney came within an eyelash of managing the Braves to four consecutive National League pennants. In 1956, the Braves finished second, one game behind the Dodgers. The next two years, they were in the World Series, winning in seven games in 1957 and losing in seven in 1958, both against the Yankees. In 1959, the Braves finished the 154-game schedule in a tie with the Dodgers before losing the play-off. Haney was fired after the 1959 season despite his success. The Braves didn't reach the World Series again until 1991, 25 years after the franchise relocated to Atlanta.

9. BOBBY COX

Bobby Cox turned 63 a month into the 2004 season. Through the 2003 season, he has a record of 1,906–1,465 in the regular season but success in the postseason has been more fleeting. In five World Series with the Braves in 1991, 1992, 1995, 1996, and 1999, his record is only 11–18 with his only world championship coming in 1995, when Atlanta defeated Cleveland in six games. Cox has a record of only 2–10 in World Series games decided by one run. He should have been in the Series more often, because his clubs have had the best regular-season record in the league ten times, including Toronto in 1985 and Atlanta in 1992, 1993, 1995, 1996, 1997, 1998, 1999, 2002 and 2003. Cox had the best regular-season win-loss record in the majors in 1992, 1993, 1997, 1999 and 2003. He has a record of 30–31 in the League Championship Series and 22–11 in the Division Series through 2003.

10. JACK McKEON

Jack McKeon, at 72, became the oldest manager in major league history to lead a team to the World Series when he won the world championship with the Marlins in 2003. Jeff

Torborg was Florida's manager at the start of the 2003 season, and was replaced by McKeon on May 11. The Marlins lost seven of their first ten games under McKeon, but were 72–42 after May 23 to finish the season with a 91–71 record and a wild card berth in the playoffs. The Marlins overcame a three-games-to-one deficit to beat the Cubs in the NLCS, and a two-games-to-one deficit to defeat the Yankees in six games in the World Series. Previously, he managed the Royals (1973–75), Athletics (1977–78), Padres (1988–90) and Reds (1997–2000) without reaching the fall classic, although McKeon was general manager of the Padres when they played in the World Series in 1984.

Nothing to It

Through the 2003 season, 18 managers have led teams into the World Series in their first season, including:

1. **HUGHIE JENNINGS**

Hughie Jennings was the shortstop on the Baltimore Orioles clubs that won the National League pennant in 1894, 1895, and 1896. At the end of the 1906 season, Jennings took over as the manager of the Tigers, an outfit that finished sixth that season. Led by a young outfielder named Ty Cobb, Jennings's team won the American League pennant his first three years as manager. He failed to win a world championship, however, as Detroit lost the Series in 1907 to the Cubs in five games (with one tie), in five games again in 1908, and in seven to the Pirates in 1909. Catching was a particular weak point. Only three clubs in World Series history have stolen more than a dozen bases in a single Series, and all three were against Jennings's Tigers. The Cubs stole 16 bases in 1907 and 15 in 1908, and the Pirates stole a record 18 in 1909. The 1909 Tigers also set a World Series record for the most errors, with 19. Jennings managed the Tigers until 1920 and never reached the postseason again as a manager, but he coached in the World Series with the Giants under John McGraw in 1921, 1922, 1923, and 1924. Jennings died in 1928 of tuberculosis and was inducted into the Hall of Fame in 1945.

2. **PAT MORAN**

The only manager to lead the Phillies to a National League pennant from the club's birth in 1883 until 1950 was Pat Moran. In 1915, his first season as a big league manager, Moran put the Phillies into the World Series, although he lost in five games to the Red Sox. The Phillies fired Moran after the 1918 season, but he wasn't unemployed for long. The Reds hired Moran, and as he had in Philadelphia, he won a pennant in his first season. It was Cincinnati's first National League pennant. The Reds won the controversial 1919 World Series over Chicago's Black Sox. Moran never won another pennant, however. He died of Bright's disease during spring training in 1924.

3. **KID GLEASON**

Pat Moran's managerial opponent in the 1919 World Series was Kid Gleason, who won the American League pennant in his first year as manager. He was betrayed by eight of his players, however, who were involved in the conspiracy with gamblers to throw the Series. Gleason and the White Sox were on the verge of winning the pennant again in 1920 in a three-way fight with the Indians and the Yankees. During the final week of the season, newly appointed commissioner Kenesaw Landis suspended the eight Black Sox, and the Sox finished in second place, two games behind Cleveland. Gleason managed the decimated White Sox until 1923.

4. **GABBY STREET**

Gabby Street is best known for catching a ball dropped from the Washington Monument when he was a catcher for the Senators in 1908. He was named manager of the Cardinals in 1930 and led the club into the World Series in his first two seasons, winning the world title in 1931. Street was fired after the 1933 season but remained in the organization by putting his loquaciousness to good use as a radio broadcaster. Street held the job until his death in 1951 and in his later years was teamed with Harry Caray.

5. **CHARLIE GRIMM**

Charlie Grimm was the starting first baseman for the Cubs when he was named manager of the club, replacing Rogers Hornsby, with 55 games left in the season. Using a relaxed hand in contrast to the abusive Hornsby, the Cubs were 37–18 under Grimm and moved from second place, five games behind the Pirates, into the World Series, where they lost in four straight to the Yankees. Grimm also managed the Cubs in the Series in another losing effort in 1935 and was fired in midseason in 1938. He was rehired in 1944 and has the distinction of being the last Cubs manager to guide the franchise in a World Series. In 1945, the Cubs lost in seven games to the Tigers. Grimm and Hughie Jennings are the only individuals to manage a club in at least three World Series without winning one.

6. **GABBY HARTNETT**

The man who replaced Charlie Grimm in July 1938 as manager of the Cubs was Gabby Hartnett, who was near the end of a Hall of Fame career as a catcher. The Cubs were seven games behind the Pirates on September 4 but won 21 of their next 24 decisions to take first place. The game that put the Cubs on top of the National League took place on September 28 against the Pirates. With darkness descending on Wrigley Field, Hartnett hit a home run in the ninth inning to lift the Cubs to a 6–5 victory. After a four-game loss to the Yankees in the World Series, Hartnett managed the Cubs only two more seasons without gaining a whiff of first place.

7. **RALPH HOUK**

Never more than a third-string catcher during a brief big league playing career, Ralph Houk had the unenviable task of replacing Casey Stengel as Yankees manager at the end of the 1960 season, but he won the American League pennant in his first three seasons as manager and the world title in his first two. He is the only manager to win world championships in his first two seasons. The Yankees beat the Reds in five games in 1961 and the Giants in seven in 1962 before being swept by the Dodgers in 1963. Houk moved into the front office after the end of the 1963 season but returned to the Yankees dugout in 1966 and held the job until 1973. Houk also managed the Tigers (1974–78) and the Red Sox (1981–84) but never came close to managing in the World Series again.

8. **DICK WILLIAMS**

Dick Williams was 38 years old when he took over a Red Sox team that finished in ninth place in 1966 and hadn't had a winning season since 1958. Williams instilled toughness into a moribund franchise and won the pennant in his first year as manager, in 1967. Four teams, including the Tigers, the Twins, and the White Sox, had a chance to win the flag entering the final week, but Williams's Red Sox came out on top. In the World Series, the Red Sox lost in seven games to the Cardinals. Williams lasted only three years in Boston as his brusque demeanor began to grate on the players. In 1971, he became the manager in Oakland and won the world championship in 1972 and 1973. Williams resigned after the 1973 season after a running dispute with Athletics owner Charlie Finley and went on to manage the Angels (1974–76), the Expos (1977–81), the Padres (1982–85), and the Mariners (1986–88). In 1984, he guided the Padres into San Diego's first World Series and became one of two individuals to manage three different franchises in the Fall Classic. The other was Bill McKechnie, who managed the Pirates (1925), the Cardinals (1928), and the Reds (1939–40).

9. **HARVEY KUENN**

Harvey Kuenn is the only person to manage the Brewers in the World Series. A native of Milwaukee, Kuenn took over from Bob Rodgers in June 1982, when the club had a record of 23–24. The Brewers were 72–43 the rest of the way and won the Eastern Division title on the final day of the regular season against the Orioles. The Brewers lost the first two games of the best-of-five ALCS to the Angels, then rallied to win the American League pennant with three straight wins before falling to the Cardinals in the World Series. Kuenn was fired after a fifth-place finish in 1983. He died of cancer in 1988.

10. **BOB BRENLY**

The Diamondbacks gambled by hiring Bob Brenly as manager in 2001, and it paid off big-time with a world championship in his first season. Brenly had no prior experience as a big league manager and was a broadcaster for ESPN when he was hired to run the Diamondbacks.

Get Out the Broom

Fifteen teams have suffered the indignity of losing the World Series in four straight games, eight of them at the hands of the Yankees.

1. **1914 PHILADELPHIA ATHLETICS**

The Philadelphia Athletics came into the 1914 World Series seeking their fourth world championship in five years, having defeated the Cubs in 1919 and the Giants in 1911 and 1913. Their opponents were the "Miracle Braves" of Boston. The Braves hadn't posted a winning season since 1902 and were in last place as late as July 19 in 1914. Behind manager George Stallings, Boston won 60 of its last 76 games to win the National League pennant by $10^1/_2$ games. The Athletics, with a proven track record, were overwhelming favorites, but the Braves continued their miraculous ways, winning 5–1 and 1–0 in Philadelphia and 5–4 in 12 innings and 3–1 in Boston to complete the sweep. Owner and manager Connie Mack dismantled the team during the following off-season, selling or trading all of his top stars. The Athletics skidded into last place in 1915 with a 43–109 record and were even worse in 1916, when the club was a horrid 36–117, the worst winning percentage (.235) of any team since 1900. The Braves were competitive for a few years but didn't win another pennant until 1948.

2. **1927 PITTSBURGH PIRATES**

Legend has it that the 1927 Pirates were psyched out watching the Yankees take batting practice before the first game of the World Series and therefore fell meekly in four games while being outscored 23–10. The fact is, the Pirates had won a world championship two years earlier while the Yankees hadn't contracted a world championship since 1923. Pittsburgh had a talented team, but the 1927 Yankees were arguably the greatest aggregation in baseball history, compiling a 110–44 record during the regular season. In the 1928 World Series, the Yankees swept the Cardinals by a cumulative score of 27–10. It was a Series of revenge, as the Cards defeated the Yankees in seven games in 1926. The Athletics won the American League pennant in 1929, 1930, and 1931, but the Yankees returned in 1932 and celebrated by sweeping the Cubs, highlighted by Babe Ruth's famous "called shot" in the third game. Ruth and Lou Gehrig keyed all three sweeps. In the 12 games, the two Yankees stalwarts combined for 41 hits in 88 at-bats, for a .466 batting average, in addition to eight doubles, two triples, 12 homers, 37 runs scored, and 38 runs batted in.

3. **1938 CHICAGO CUBS**

The 1938 Cubs won the National League pennant by coming back from a seven-game deficit to the Pirates on September 4 to reach first place 23 days later. In the World Series, Chicago ran into a buzz saw, losing four straight to the Yankees. The 1936–39 Yankees won four consecutive World Series, compiling a 409–201 record during the regular season and a 16–3 mark in the Fall Classic while outscoring the National League opposition 113–52. The Yankees also swept the Reds in 1939 and became the second of three clubs to sweep the Series in successive years. The other two are the Yankees of 1927–28 and of 1998–99. The Reds recovered from their 1939 drubbing by defeating the Tigers in seven games in the 1940 World Series.

4. 1950 PHILADELPHIA PHILLIES

The 1950 Phillies were known as the "Whiz Kids" for their youthful lineup, which included future Hall-of-Famers Robin Roberts and Richie Ashburn. Before winning the National League pennant, the Phillies had been awful for decades, posting only one winning season between 1918 and 1948, and that was a 78–76 mark in 1932. The 1950 Phillies seemed to have the pennant all locked up with a 7½-game lead with 11 days left in the season but needed to defeat the Dodgers 4–1 in 10 innings on the final day of the season to clinch first place. The Whiz Kids were dazed heading into the World Series and lost four straight to the Yankees. The Phillies didn't reach the World Series again until 1980, when they defeated the Royals in six games for the only world championship in the club's history.

5. 1954 CLEVELAND INDIANS

The 1954 Indians posted a 111–43 record in 1954 and dethroned the Yankees, a club that had won the world championship the five previous seasons. The Indians were overwhelming favorites to defeat the New York Giants, who topped the National League with a 98–56 mark. The Series opened at the bathtub-shaped Polo Grounds in New York, and the unusual dimensions of the ballpark played a huge part in the outcome of the first game. With the score 2–2 in the eighth inning, Cleveland had runners on first and second with none out. Giants manager Leo Durocher brought in reliever Don Liddle to face Vic Wertz, who hit a 460-foot drive to center field. It would have been over the fence at any other major league ballpark, but at the Polo Grounds, Willie Mays had room to make a fantastic over-the-shoulder catch. The score was still 2–2 when Giants pinch-hitter Dusty Rhodes lofted Bob Lemon's first pitch for a homer that barely cleared the right field wall just 260 feet from home plate. The Giants won the final three games 3–1, 6–2, and 7–4. It was the only time all year that the Indians lost four straight games. Cleveland's longest losing streak during the regular season was only three games. The manager of the Indians was Al Lopez, who always seemed to come up second best. He managed the White Sox in the World Series in 1959 but lost in six games to the Dodgers. In the American League pennant race, Lopez finished in second place in 1951, 1952, 1953, 1955, and 1956 in Cleveland and in 1957, 1958, 1963, 1964, and 1965 in Chicago. As a manager in the All-Star Game, Lopez was 0–5.

6. 1963 NEW YORK YANKEES

The Yankees won the American League pennant five straight seasons from 1960 through 1964 but lost the World Series three times. In 1960 against the Pirates and in 1964 versus the Cardinals, the Yankees lost in seven games. In 1963, the Yankees were pummeled by the Dodgers in four straight by scores of 5–2, 4–1, 1–0, and 2–1.

7. 1966 LOS ANGELES DODGERS

The Dodgers silenced the Yankees' bats in 1963. In 1966 against the Orioles, the Dodgers' bats were absolutely mute. The Los Angeles club set the World Series records for the fewest runs scored (two), the most consecutive innings without scoring a run (the last 33 innings of the Series), the fewest hits (17), the lowest batting average (.142), the lowest slugging average (.192), and the fewest singles (13). The Dodgers weren't much better at fielding the baseball, committing six errors in Game Two. The Orioles' 33-inning scoreless streak was started by reliever Moe Drabowsky in Game One over the final six innings. Jim Palmer, Wally Bunker, and Dave McNally followed with complete-game shutouts in the next three games.

8. 1976 NEW YORK YANKEES

The 1976 Cincinnati Reds are the only club in history to sweep both the League Championship Series and the World Series. Following their Series win over the Red Sox in 1975, the Reds defeated the Phillies three straight in the 1976 NLCS and won four in a row over the Yankees in the Fall Classic. The Reds are one of only three National League clubs to win the World Series two years in a row. The others are the 1907–08 Cubs and the 1921–22 Giants.

9. 1989 SAN FRANCISCO GIANTS

The 1989 World Series between the Giants and the Athletics is justifiably remembered most for the images of the earthquake that struck northern California just before the third game at Candlestick Park. When play resumed after a break of 10 days, the Giants were unceremoniously bounced in four games by their cross-bay rivals from Oakland. The Athletics won 10 consecutive postseason games, including the final two games of the 1989 World Series against the Blue Jays, the 1989 World Series, and all four encounters with the Red Sox in the 1990 ALCS. It all came apart in the 1990 World Series, when the Athletics lost four straight to the underdog Reds. The Athletics are the only team in baseball history to win a League Championship Series in a sweep and lose a World Series in the same manner in the same year.

10. 1998 SAN DIEGO PADRES

The Padres fell victim to another Yankees juggernaut. The 1998 edition of the Yankees had a 114–48 record during the regular season and was 11–1 in the postseason against the Rangers, the Indians, and the Padres. Joe Torre's Yankees completed two World Series sweeps in a row by routing the Braves in 1999 and won a third straight world championship by downing the Mets in five games in 2000. The only other club to achieve a 12–1 record in three consecutive World Series was the 1937–39 Yankees. The 1998–2000 Yankees were an incredible 33–8 in the postseason.

Blowouts

Several teams have suffered through one-sided losses in the World Series.

1. **1936 NEW YORK GIANTS**

The worst defeat in World Series history was inflicted on the New York Giants by the New York Yankees in Game Two in 1936 at the Polo Grounds with a score of 18–4. Giants pitchers Hal Schumacher, Al Smith, Dick Coffman, Frank Gabler, and Harry Gumbert gave up 17 hits and issued nine walks in the barrage. Coffman, Gumbert, and Smith were consistently awful throughout the six games of the 1936 Series. They combined to allow 17 runs, all earned, in only four innings. The Yankees clinched the championship with a 13–5 thrashing of the Giants in Game Six.

2. **1960 PITTSBURGH PIRATES**

There have been only eight games in World Series history in which a club lost by 12 or more runs. The 1960 Pirates not only were victims of two of them but lost three games by double digits. The Pirates opened the Series with a 6–4 victory, but the Yankees won a 16–3 laugher in Game Two in Pittsburgh and followed it with a 10–0 rout in the third game in New York. The Pirates recovered from the bashing to win the next two games at Yankee Stadium 3–2 and 5–2. The

Yankees staved off elimination with a 12–0 massacre in Game Six back in Pittsburgh. In one of the best Game Sevens in history, the Pirates took the title with a 10–9 victory on Bill Mazeroski's walk-off homer in the ninth inning. The Yankees lost the 1960 Series despite setting records for the most runs scored (55), the highest batting average (.338), the most hits (91), and the most total bases (142).

3. **2001 NEW YORK YANKEES**

The Yankees stayed alive in the 2001 World Series against the Diamondbacks by taking a three-games-to-two lead on a pair of incredible comebacks in Games Four and Five, which they trailed by two runs with two outs in the ninth. The Diamondbacks rebounded from the heartbreaking defeats by pounding the Yankees 15–2 in Game Six in Phoenix. The Diamondbacks set a single-game team record for hits in a World Series game with 22. An amazing 23 of the first 30 Arizona hitters reached base against Andy Pettitte, Jay Witasick, and Randy Choate to take a 15–0 lead after only four innings. In the first World Series game of his career, Witasick set World Series records for the most runs allowed (nine) and the most earned runs allowed (eight) in just $1^1/_3$ innings. Witasick wasn't much better in the 2002 World Series with the Giants, allowing two runs in one-third of an inning over two appearances. Oddly, Witasick struck out all five batters he retired in the three Series games he pitched. Counting the Division Series and the League Championship Series, Witasick has allowed 14 earned runs and 20 hits in $5^1/_3$ innings in the postseason through 2003. His postseason ERA is 23.63.

4. **1951 NEW YORK GIANTS**

The 1951 New York Giants stormed back from a $13^1/_2$-game deficit by the Brooklyn Dodgers in the National League pennant race by winning 37 of their last 44 games to finish the 154-game schedule in a tie for first. In the best-of-three tie-breaking play-off, the Giants won the third game over the Dodgers 5–4 at the Polo Grounds in dramatic fashion on a four-run ninth-inning rally capped by Bobby Thomson's three-run homer. The miracle appeared to continue into the World Series as the Giants won two of the first three games, but the bubble burst when the Yankees won three in a row to take the title. Game Five at the Polo Grounds was a 13–1 trouncing as Yankees batters flexed their muscles by pounding Giants pitchers Larry Jansen, Monte Kennedy, and George Spencer.

5. **1968 ST. LOUIS CARDINALS**

Two teams have allowed 10 runs in an inning during the World Series. The first was the 1929 Chicago Cubs to the Philadelphia Athletics. The second was the 1968 Cardinals against the Tigers in Game Six. Detroit scored two runs in the second before breaking the game wide open with a 10-run spree in the third. Cardinals pitcher Ray Washburn allowed a walk and two singles to give up the first run. Larry Jaster came in from the bull pen and surrendered a single, a walk, and a grand-slam homer to Jim Northrup. Ron Willis and Dick Hughes combined to allow five more runs on four singles, a walk, and a sacrifice. Hughes never pitched another big league game. The Tigers won 13–1.

6. **1982 MILWAUKEE BREWERS**

The 1982 Brewers won three of the first five games of the World Series against the Cardinals but had no chance in a rain-soaked 13–1 defeat in Game Six, with the Cardinals scoring all of their runs off Don Sutton and Doc Medich. It was the last major league appearance for Medich, who went into medical practice in Pittsburgh. There were two rain delays in the game. The first lasted 26 minutes in the fifth inning, followed by a two-hour 13-minute adjournment in the sixth. Despite the stops and starts, rookie John Stuper pitched a complete game for St. Louis. The Cardinals closed out the Series with a 6–3 victory in Game Seven.

7. **2002 ANAHEIM ANGELS**

The Angels appeared to be headed for extinction in the 2002 World Series when they lost 16–4 to the Giants in Anaheim in Game Five to fall behind three games to two. Jeff Kent homered in both the six and seventh innings. San Francisco scored their runs off Jarrod Washburn, Ben Weber, and Scot Shields. The Angels recovered quickly from the drubbing to take the final two games for the first world championship in the franchise's history.

8. 1911 NEW YORK GIANTS

The Athletics closed out a contentious six-game Series in 1911 with a 13–2 thrashing of the Giants. It was an odd Series in which the teams traveled between each game, as the first, third, and fifth games were played in New York and the even-numbered contests were held in Philadelphia. In Game Two, Athletics third baseman Frank Baker hit a two-run homer off Rube Marquard in the sixth inning to give his club a 3–2 win. The next day, Baker homered in the ninth facing Christy Mathewson to tie the score 1–1 in a contest that was won by the Athletics 3–2 in 11 innings. The newspapers of the day dubbed him "Home Run" Baker for his long-distance hitting in the Series, and he was known by the nickname forever after. Baker was an unwitting center of controversy when he was spiked twice by Giants center fielder Fred Snodgrass, once in the first game and again in Game Three. Baker suffered a nasty gash on his hand from the first collision and one on his arm from the second. There was a delay of seven days between the third and fourth games because of rain in Philadelphia, made worse because the tarpaulin at Shibe Park covered only the plate and the pitcher's mound. During the weeklong hiatus, Snodgrass received death threats from some angry Philadelphia fans and had to leave the team hotel and escape to New York for his safety. Adding to the weirdness of the Series, Larry Doyle of the Giants scored the winning run in Game Five without touching home plate. With the score 3–3 in the 10th inning, Doyle was on third with one out when Fred Merkle lifted a fly ball to right field. Doyle raced toward home, but in his slide, he missed the plate by nearly a foot. No one on the Athletics noticed the gaffe by Doyle, and both clubs left the field. Home plate umpire Bill Klem had no choice but to let the run stand for a 4–3 New York victory.

9. **1996 ATLANTA BRAVES**

Playing in the World Series for the first time in 15 years, the New York Yankees lost the opener in 1996 to the Braves by a score of 12–1. The Braves closed out the last three games of the NLCS against the Cardinals with victories of 14–0, 3–1, and 15–0 and beat the Yankees 4–0 in the second game of the World Series. Atlanta outscored the opposition 48–2 in five consecutive postseason games, but the momentum came to a screeching halt as the Yankees won four in a row to win the Series in six games. The Braves suffered from the "Curse of the First Game Blow Out." Four teams have won the Series opener by nine or more runs, and each failed to win the world title. In 1945, the Cubs won the first game 9–0 to the Tigers and lost in seven games. In 1959, the White Sox beat the Dodgers 11–0 in the opener and lost in six. The 1982 Brewers started off defeating the Cardinals 10–0 and went down in seven games.

10. **1934 DETROIT TIGERS**

The Cardinals of the 1930s were known as the "Gashouse Gang" for their rough tactics. Leading 9–0 in the sixth inning of the seventh game of the 1934 World Series played in Detroit, Joe Medwick of the Cardinals slid hard into Tigers third baseman Marv Owen. Medwick knocked Owen over, and as he fell, Owen stepped on Medwick's shin. As both lay on the ground, Medwick kicked Owen in the chest. As they scrambled to their feet, the two squared off but were separated before any blows could be struck. When Medwick took his defensive position in left field, he was pelted with bottles and garbage by angry Detroit fans. The Tigers sold the bleachers on an unreserved general admission basis, and many fans arrived early in the morning to get the choice seats, bringing their lunches in picnic baskets and brown paper bags. With plenty of leftover food in their possession, in addition to apple cores, banana peels, chicken bones, and other assorted remnants of their midday meal, the fans seemed to have an inexhaustible supply of ammunition to throw at Medwick. Efforts to quell the crowd proved futile, and faced with the possibility of a riot, Commissioner Kenesaw Landis removed Medwick from the game. The delay lasted 17 minutes, and Chick Fullis took Medwick's place in left. Cardinals pitcher Dizzy Dean had to wait out the delay, and when play resumed, he retired Mickey Cochrane, Charlie Gehringer, and Goose Goslin, all future Hall-of-Famers, on only three pitches. The Cardinals went on to win 11–0 with Dean pitching the complete game to take the world championship.

Even the Browns and the Cubs

When Chicago sportswriter Warren Brown was asked about his pick for the 1945 World Series between the Cubs and the Tigers, he replied, "I don't think either one of them is capable of winning." With World War II raging in Europe, Asia, and the Pacific Islands, major league rosters were populated by fill-in players who were exempt from military service for one reason or another. This led to two unique World Series.

1. **ST. LOUIS BROWNS**

The St. Louis Browns were established in 1902 when the original Milwaukee Brewers moved to Missouri. The franchise existed until 1953, when the club left St. Louis for Baltimore, where they were renamed the Orioles. The Browns were almost always short of cash and near the bottom of the American League standings. The club reached the World Series only once, in 1944. Their opponent was the Cardinals, which created the only all–St. Louis World Series in history. Both teams played at Sportsman's Park, a ballpark owned by the Browns. It was the third time in which the World Series was played in just one facility. The other two were in 1921 and 1922 at the Polo Grounds in New York, when the Giants played the Yankees. The 1944 Series was the only one in which the tenants defeated the landlord, as the Cardinals took the championship in six games.

2. LUKE SEWELL

The only manager to lead the Browns into a World Series was Luke Sewell. He had a 20-year playing career in the majors as a catcher beginning in 1921 and appeared in the 1933 World Series with the Senators. His older brother Joe is in the Hall of Fame, based on a career as a shortstop between 1920 and 1933, and played in the Fall Classic with the Indians in 1920 and the Yankees in 1932. Luke's 1944 Browns set a dubious World Series record when eight consecutive pinch-hitters struck out. In Game Five, Floyd Baker, Milt Byrnes, Chet Laabs, and Mike Chartak all went down on strikes, the last three in the ninth inning with the Browns trailing 2–0. In the 3–1 sixth-game defeat, Al Zarilla, Baker, Byrnes, and Chartak all struck out in a pinch-hitter role. Chartak made the final out in both games and earned the honor of being the last St. Louis Brown to bat in a World Series.

3. GEORGE McQUINN

In the first game in 1944, Browns first baseman George McQuinn hit a two-run homer in the fourth inning that stood up for a 2–1 victory. It was the only Series home run by a Browns player in history. The Browns won two of the first three games before dropping three in a row.

4. KEN O'DEA

Ken O'Dea drove in the winning run with a pinch-hit single in the second game, which gave the Cardinals a 3–2 win. A backup catcher for most of his 12 years in the majors, O'Dea played in five World Series, with the Cubs in 1935 and 1938 and the Cardinals in 1942, 1943, and 1944. In Series play, he had six hits, including a homer, in 13 at-bats for a .462 batting average.

5. BLIX DONNELLY AND TED WILKS

Two rather elderly Cardinal rookies starred out of the bull pen in 1944. Blix Donnelly, who was 30, pitched six innings over two games allowing no runs and two hits while striking out nine batters. Ted Wilks, 28, retired all 11 batters he faced, four on strikeouts, in the championship-clinching sixth game. Wilks had a 17–4 record during the 1944 regular season.

6. TRAVEL RESTRICTIONS

There was no need for travel in the 1944 Series since all the games were played in St. Louis, but the 1945 Fall Classic posed a problem because train travel was restricted because of the war. Although World War II had ended nearly two months earlier, soldiers returning home to their families still had priority over ballplayers. As a result, the first three games of the 1945 Series were played in Detroit, and the last four were staged in Chicago. The same format was set up in 1943, with the Yankees hosting the first three games in 1943 and the final four scheduled for St. Louis, although only two were played because the Cardinals won the Series in five games.

7. GAME SEVEN

The 1945 Series went down to a seventh game, but it was no contest as the Tigers prevailed 9–3 at Wrigley Field. Hal Newhouser pitched a complete game and struck out 10 batters. Cubs starter Hank Borowy, who pitched five innings as a starter in Game Five and four innings of relief in the sixth game, failed to retire a single batter.

8. CLYDE McCULLOUGH

Cubs catcher Clyde McCullough is the only player to appear in a World Series game following a regular season in which he didn't play in a game. McCullough was discharged by the navy in time for the start of the Series. He pinch-hit in the seventh game and struck out in the ninth inning against Hal Newhouser. Detroit pitcher Virgil Trucks started two games during the 1945 Series after appearing in just one game during the regular season. Like McCullough, Trucks was discharged from the navy in September.

9. CHUCK HOSTETLER

Chuck Hostetler was an example of many of the players who appeared in big league games during World War II. He made his major league debut in 1944 at the age of 40. Hostetler kicked around the minors for years, but by the start of the war he was working at a Boeing plant in Wichita and playing semipro ball when he was discovered by Tigers scouts. Hostetler was 0 for three as a pinch-hitter in the 1945 Series, but he reached base on an error in Game Six. Trying to score from second on a single by Doc Cramer, Hostetler slipped and fell flat on his face between third and home and was thrown out.

10. DON JOHNSON

To date, the last Chicago Cubs player to bat in a World Series is second baseman Don Johnson, who ended the seventh game by grounding into a force play. The last Cubs hit is a double by Bill Nicholson. The last homer is by Phil Cavaretta. Hank Borowy is the last winning pitcher and the last losing pitcher.

Commanders in Chief

Many of the nation's presidents have had a role in the World Series.

1. WOODROW WILSON

The first president to attend a World Series was Woodrow Wilson, who went to the second game in 1915, played between the Red Sox and the Phillies in Philadelphia. He also threw out the first ball. Wilson was accompanied by his fiancée, Edith Bolling Galt. The couple met in March 1915, six months after the death of his first wife, and were married the following December.

2. WARREN HARDING

During the 1921 and 1922 World Series, a private telegraph was installed in Warren Harding's office at the White House that transmitted the results of every pitch. Each play was recorded and sent to the president, while another operator kept a scorecard. Harding's office evidently didn't have a radio. The 1921 World Series was the first to be broadcast, although only the first game was aired. In 1922, every game was on the radio.

3. CALVIN COOLIDGE

Calvin Coolidge attended more World Series games than any other president, although he had a slight advantage since more Series games were played in Washington during his term than that of any other chief executive. Coolidge went to Games One, Six, and Seven in Washington in 1924 between the Senators and the Giants, and the third and fifth contests between the Senators and the Pirates at Griffith Stadium in 1925. Coolidge also witnessed the city of Washington's only world championship, staying until the jubilant conclusion of the Senators' 4–3 win in 12 innings in the seventh game in 1924.

4. **HERBERT HOOVER**

Herbert Hoover attended the fifth game in 1929 between the Athletics and the Cubs in Philadelphia and was given a fond ovation. A few weeks later, the stock market crashed, sowing the seeds for the Great Depression. In 1930, Hoover went to Game One in Philadelphia as the Athletics faced the Cardinals and went back to Philadelphia for the third game in 1931 as the A's and the Cards played each other again.

5. **FRANKLIN ROOSEVELT**

While in office, Franklin Roosevelt attended the first game in 1933, played in Washington between the Senators and the Giants. He was also at the Polo Grounds for the second game in 1936, when the Yankees routed the Giants 18–4 in the most lopsided game in Series history. As the governor of New York and the Democratic nominee for president, Roosevelt also showed up at Game Three in 1932 between the Yankees and the Cubs in Chicago, the contest in which Babe Ruth "called his shot."

6. **DWIGHT EISENHOWER**

Dwight Eisenhower attended the opener of the 1956 Series at Ebbets Field. He was driven onto the field from a gate in left field to his box in the presidential limousine. Before the game, Ike shook hands with players from both the Dodgers and the Yankees and threw out the first ball. It was a month before the presidential election, and Eisenhower was facing the Democratic nominee, Adlai Stevenson, for the second time. Stevenson went to Game Two. So as not to offend any fans of either club, he wore a Dodgers cap and a Yankees cap simultaneously. It didn't help. As in 1952, Stevenson lost the 1956 election to Eisenhower.

7. JIMMY CARTER

Jimmy Carter attended the seventh game of the 1979 World Series between the Orioles and Pirates in Baltimore. As an ex-president, he threw out the first ball at the first game in 1992 in Atlanta as the Braves faced off against the Blue Jays. Carter's mother, Lillian, a great baseball fan, threw out the first ball at Game Four before the Dodgers played the Yankees in Los Angeles in 1977.

8. RICHARD NIXON

Richard Nixon didn't attend a World Series game during his presidency, but he started the tradition of phoning the manager of the winning team to offer congratulations. The first to receive the call was Gil Hodges, who led the Mets to the world championship in 1969. Nixon's wife, Pat, attended the first game in 1969 and Game Two in 1971, both in Baltimore. At the 1971 contest, she threw out the first ball. Nixon did attend the fifth game of the 1952 World Series, a month before he was elected vice-president.

9. RONALD REAGAN

Ronald Reagan went to the first game of the 1983 World Series between the Orioles and Phillies in Baltimore. Reagan also depicted a famous World Series moment on the silver screen, playing Grover Cleveland Alexander in Alexander's 1952 film biography *The Winning Team*. In the penultimate scene, Reagan/Alexander came in from the bull pen to save the seventh game of the 1926 World Series for the Cardinals against the Yankees. In a bit of irony, Reagan played an individual who was named after a president. Grover Cleveland

Alexander was born in 1887 during Grover Cleveland's first term as president.

10. **GEORGE W. BUSH**

George W. Bush shook off security concerns and threw out the first ball before the third game of the 2001 World Series at Yankee Stadium, just 50 days after the September 11 terrorist attacks. Bush stood on the pitcher's mound and threw a perfect strike to Yankees catcher Todd Greene.

As Seen on TV

The first televised game in major league history took place on August 26, 1939, between the Reds and the Dodgers in Brooklyn. World War II, which began in Europe six days after the telecast, slowed the development of the new medium, but in 1947, the World Series was televised for the first time.

1. **1947**
The first televised World Series took place between the Yankees and the Dodgers, but the microwave technology that transmitted the images from New York City was available to just four cities on the eastern seaboard. The only stations to telecast the Series were in New York, Philadelphia, Washington, and Schenectady, New York. Only a small handful of individuals had televisions sets in their homes in 1947, as there were only 160,000 televisions in operation nationwide. Most of those who watched the games on TV saw them in appliance stores selling the sets or in establishments such as bars and lunch counters. The rights to the 1947 Series were sold for $65,000 to the Gillette Safety Razor Company and the Ford Motor Company. Liebmann Breweries offered $100,000 for the rights, but it was turned down by Commissioner Happy Chandler on the grounds that it wouldn't be

good public relations for baseball to have the Series sponsored by the producer of an alcoholic beverage.

2. **1948**

Gillette paid $175,000 for the exclusive rights to the 1948 Series, played between the Cleveland Indians and the Boston Braves. No station in the country telecast the entire six games, however, because the technology linking the East Coast to the Midwest was not yet available. The games in Boston were telecast in the Northeast, while the contests played in Cleveland were shown only in the Midwest.

3. **1949**

Gillette paid $800,000 for the right to telecast the 1949 World Series between the Dodgers and Yankees. An estimated 10 million people watched the Series, which was shown only on stations in the Northeast and the Midwest. Gillette again paid $800,000 for the 1950 Series, in which the Yankees swept the Phillies in four straight games. The company sold the rights to any network or station willing to show the event. NBC, CBS, and ABC each paid $350,000 to telecast the Series. In New York City, the games were shown simultaneously on four stations. The 1950 Series was not available to any stations west of Omaha, Nebraska, or south of Jacksonville, Florida.

4. **1951**

For the first time, the World Series was shown on the West Coast. On September 6, it was announced that the Series would be the first sporting event ever telecast from coast to coast, but events proved otherwise. The Giants and the Dodgers finished the regular season in a tie for first place, and a best-of-three play-off was necessary to determine the National League champion. The play-off, which ended with Bobby Thomson's storybook home run, was televised by NBC to the Pacific coast with Chesterfield Cigarettes as a sponsor. Gillette paid $6 million to sponsor the World Series for a period of six years from 1951 through 1956. Beginning in 1951, rights to telecast the Series were sold to only one network. From 1951 through 1975, NBC had exclusive rights to the World Series. Although the 1951 Fall Classic was the first telecast in California, the event still wasn't available in the future major league cities of Denver, Seattle, Phoenix, Miami, and Tampa–St. Petersburg. The first truly national telecast of the World Series took place in 1952, between the Yankees and the Dodgers.

5. **1954**

Havana, Cuba, received live television coverage of the 1954 World Series, between the Giants and Indians, for the first time. A Cuban television network chartered a DC-3 to fly over the Gulf of Mexico to serve as a relay for the transmission from a station in Miami.

6. **1955**

The 1955 World Series was the first to be televised in color, although the transmission went to only a small fraction of the 180 stations in the United States and 20 in Canada that carried the games. Most stations had not yet acquired the equipment to transmit color images. It was probably just as well, as the process wasn't technologically sound in the mid-1950s. Jack Gould of *The New York Times* reported that the "tinted version was far from impressive, because the outdoor pick-ups are not yet electronic color's strong feature. [Yankees first baseman] Joe Collins appeared to be skipping around on an artist's palette."

7. **1971**

The fourth game of the 1971 World Series between the Pirates and Orioles was the first to be played at night. In 1972, all three weeknight games were telecast at night. The first weekend night game was in 1976, on a cold Sunday night in Cincinnati, with the Reds facing the Yankees. The first Series in which every contest was staged under the lights was in 1985.

8. **1975**

One of the most enduring television images in World Series history took place in the 12th inning of Game Six in 1975, when Carlton Fisk ended the contest with a home run to give the Red Sox a thrilling 7–6 victory over the Reds. Fisk stopped to watch the flight of the ball while he was positioned a few feet down the first base and waved his arms in an attempt to use body English to steer the ball into fair territory. After the ball struck the foul pole for a homer, Fisk leaped into the air and circled the bases amid jubilant fans who stormed the field. Television cameras may not have captured Fisk's gyrations if it hadn't been for a large rat inside the Fenway Park scoreboard. Cameraman Lou Gerard was stationed inside the scoreboard with his lens poked through a hole in the board, and his instructions were to follow the flight of the ball. When Fisk made contact with Pat Darcy's pitch, Gerard was distracted by the rat four feet away from him, and the sight of the rodent froze him long enough to allow him to stay with Fisk and get the famous reaction shot. Since then, reaction shots have been a staple of sports television coverage.

9. **1989**

Just minutes after ABC went on the air for Game Three of the 1989 World Series between the Athletics and the Giants at Candlestick Park in San Francisco, Tim McCarver was narrating highlights of the second game when his voice broke for a second as the press box swayed. Al Michaels quickly interjected, "I'll tell you what, we're having an earth . . ." The word *quake* never made it on the air as power at the ballpark was knocked out at 5:04 P.M. local time, 20 minutes before the scheduled start of the game. The network returned to air a few moments later with auxiliary power, and Michaels and McCarver described the almost festive air at the ballpark as fans and players were relieved at coming

Boston Red Sox

Carlton Fisk's big fly and body-language plea that it stay fair remains the foremost image of World Series history.

through unscathed by what appeared to be only a tremor. Commissioner Fay Vincent postponed the game because there was no indication when power to the ballpark would be restored. There was only about an hour of daylight left in the Bay Area, and Vincent and stadium security personnel wanted to ensure that fans could leave safely before nightfall. As fans calmly filed out of the stadium, the mood soon turned somber as it became known that the quake registered 7.1 on the Richter scale, a freeway in Oakland had collapsed trapping dozens of motorists, part of the Bay Bridge had also fallen, and the Marina neighborhood in San Francisco was in flames. The third game, originally scheduled for October 17, wasn't played until October 27. The quake took the lives of 67 people and caused billions of dollars in damage.

10. **1990**

Reds pitcher Tom Browning left Game Two of the 1990 World Series against the Athletics in Cincinnati in the seventh inning without club permission after learning that his wife, Debbie, had gone into labor. Browning didn't think he would be missed, since he was scheduled to start Game Three. But as the game headed toward extra innings, Reds manager Lou Piniella considered using Browning as a pinch-runner or relief pitcher. Piniella was told by a clubhouse employee that Browning had left and asked Reds radio broadcaster Marty Brennaman and CBS analyst Tim McCarver to issue an all points bulletin urging Browning to return to Riverfront Stadium. Browning didn't learn of the summons until McCarver reported it as the Reds came to bat in the 10th inning. He remained with his wife, however. Browning's teammates bailed him out by scoring in the 10th to win 5–4. Debbie Browning gave birth to a son 40 minutes after Game Two ended. Browning assisted with the birth while he was still wearing his uniform.

Other Sports

M any players and umpires who have appeared in the World Series have had success in other sports.

1. **JIM THORPE**

Jim Thorpe won both the pentathlon and the decathlon at the 1912 Olympics, held in Sweden but had to return his gold medals when it was discovered that he played minor league baseball. He played in the majors from 1913 through 1919 with the Giants, the Reds, and the Braves as an outfielder, with limited success, batting .252 with seven home runs. Thorpe was on the Giants World Series roster in both 1913 and 1917. He sat on the bench throughout the 1913 Series and was credited with playing in one contest in 1917 against the White Sox, even though he didn't participate in any game action. The unusual situation took place in the sixth game. Giants manager John McGraw penciled Thorpe's name onto the lineup card in right field and in the sixth spot in the order as an extra right-handed bat to face Chicago lefty Reb Russell. Russell faced only three batters, however, and was replaced by right-hander Eddie Cicotte. When it came time for Thorpe to bat in the top of the first, he was lifted for pinch-hitter Dave Robertson. Robertson had three hits in five at-bats (and 11 hits in 22 at-bats during the Series), but the Giants lost 8–5. Thorpe's best sport by far was football. He played professionally from 1915 through 1928 and was elected to the first class of the Pro Football Hall of Fame in 1963. In 1950, Thorpe was voted the greatest athlete of the first half of the 20th century in a nationwide poll of sportswriters.

2. **GREASY NEALE**

Greasy Neale is the only individual to play on a World Series winning team and coach an NFL champion. Neale was an outfielder on the 1919 Reds and collected 10 hits in 28 at-bats in the victory over the White Sox. He left the Reds in late August 1921 to take a position as the head football coach at Washington & Jefferson College in Pennsylvania. Neale was an immediate success as a coach and led his squad to the Rose Bowl, where they held heavily favored California to a 0–0 tie. Neale later coached the Philadelphia Eagles to NFL championships in 1948 and 1949. He was elected to the Pro Football Hall of Fame in 1969.

3. **HINKEY HAINES**

Hinkey Haines is the only athlete to play on world champion teams in both professional football and baseball. Haines played in two games in the 1923 World Series for the Yankees against the Giants as a pinch-hitter and defensive replacement in the outfield. In 1925, he played in the backfield of the NFL New York Giants. Darrin Erstad is the only athlete to play on a collegiate football champion and a World Series winner. Erstad was a punter on Nebraska's 1994 NCAA championship team and played center field for the 2002 Anaheim Angels.

4. **DEION SANDERS**

Deion Sanders is the only individual to play in both the World Series and the Super Bowl. He was in the World Series in 1992 with the Braves against the Blue Jays and collected eight hits, including two doubles, in 15 at-bats for a .533 average. Sanders also stole five bases. Atlanta's six-game loss to Toronto cost Sanders a chance to join Hinkey Haines as the only athlete to compete on major league baseball and professional football champs. Sanders was on the winning side in the Super Bowl with San Francisco following the 1994 season and with Dallas a year later. He is the only athlete to score a touchdown in the NFL and hit a home run in major league baseball in the same week, which he pulled off in September 1989 with the Falcons and the Yankees.

5. **GENE CONLEY**

Gene Conley is the only athlete to play on a world champion team in both baseball and basketball. He was a six-foot-eight pitcher on the 1957 Milwaukee Braves club that defeated the Yankees in seven games and was a backup center to Bill Russell on the Boston Celtics NBA champs in 1959, 1960, and 1961. During a major league career that lasted from 1952 through 1963, Conley was 91–96 with the Braves, the Phillies, and the Red Sox. In the NBA, he averaged 5.9 points per game. In the 1959 NBA finals, Conley's Celtics defeated the Minneapolis Lakers, which included Steve Hamilton, who pitched for the Yankees in the World Series in 1963 and 1964.

6. **DICK GROAT**

Dick Groat is the only individual to earn All-American honors in college basketball, play in the NBA, win a Most Valuable Player award in major league baseball, and play on a club that won the World Series. Groat was an All-American at Duke University on the hardwood in both 1950–51 and 1951–52. He began his major league baseball career as a shortstop with the Pirates in 1952 and during the 1952–53 NBA season played 26 games for the Fort Wayne Pistons, averaging 11.9 points per game. In 1960, Groat won the National League batting title, hitting .325, and won the MVP award. He acquired world championship rings, with the Pirates in 1960 and the Cardinals in 1964.

7. **RON REED**

Ron Reed didn't play in the NBA finals during his brief career with the Detroit Pistons, which began in 1965 and ended in 1967, but he did play in the World Series with the Phillies in 1980. Reed played 19 seasons in the majors, from 1966 through 1984, ending his career at the age of 42 with a 146–140 record.

8. **TIM STODDARD**

Tin Stoddard is the only individual to play on an NCAA champion team and in the World Series. Stoddard was the starting forward on North Carolina State's national championship team in 1974 and began a 12-year career as a relief pitcher in the major leagues in 1975. He played for the Orioles in the 1979 World Series against the Pirates and pitched in four games. In Game Four, Stoddard pitched three scoreless innings and was the winning pitcher in a 9–6 decision. Stoddard also had his first major league at-bat in the fourth game of the Series and hit a single to drive in a run during an eighth inning in which Baltimore scored six runs. It was the last hit by an American League pitcher in a World Series until Mike Moore of the Athletics doubled in the fourth game in 1989 against the Giants. In between, AL pitchers were hitless in 70 consecutive at-bats.

9. **RED ROLFE**

Red Rolfe is the only person to coach in the NBA and manage a club in major league baseball. He also played third base for the Yankees in six World Series from 1936 through 1942. Rolfe coached the Toronto Huskies of the NBA for part of the 1946 season to a 17–27 record. He managed the Detroit Tigers between 1949 and 1952. None of his Tigers clubs played in the Fall Classic, but his 1950 team finished second to the Yankees, only three games out.

10. **HANK SOAR**

Hank Soar is the only individual to play in the NFL, coach in the NBA, and umpire in major league baseball. Soar played for the NFL New York Giants from 1937 through 1946, coached in the NBA for the Providence Steamrollers in 1947–48 (to a 2–17 record), and umpired in the American League from 1950 through 1973. He played in four NFL championship games and umpired in three World Series. Several other World Series umpires have had connections to other professional sports. Cal Hubbard was an all-pro lineman in the NFL from 1927 through 1936, mostly with the Giants and the Packers. He was an American League umpire from 1936 through 1951 and was an arbiter in four World Series. Hubbard is the only individual to be inducted into both the Baseball Hall of Fame and the Pro Football Hall of Fame. Bill Stewart was an umpire in the National League from 1933 through 1954 and in four World Series. He was also a referee in the National Hockey League for nine years and a coach for two years. In 1937–38, he coached the Chicago Blackhawks to a 14–25–9 record during the regular season before pulling off a stunning upset to win the Stanley Cup.

Hi! I'm Felipe. This Is My Brother Matty. And This Is My Other Brother Jesus.

Many sets of brothers have played a prominent role in the World Series.

1. **THE JOHNSTONS**

Doc Johnston and his brother Jimmy were the first brothers to oppose each other in the World Series. In the 1920 Fall Classic, Doc was a first baseman for the Indians while Jimmy played third base for the Dodgers. The Indians won the best-of-nine Series in seven games. Jimmy played in all 155 regular-season games for Brooklyn in 1920 and appeared in the first four Series games before missing the final three with an injury. Replacing Johnston at third base was Jack Sheehan, who had played only three games during the regular season and had just two hits in five at-bats during his major league career before making his first postseason appearance. Sheehan was two for 11 in the three Series games he played. They were his final two hits in the majors. In 1921, Sheehan was hitless in 12 at-bats and went back to the minors. He's the only player in history to appear in fewer than 10 regular-season games but play in a World Series.

2. **THE MEUSELS**

Irish Meusel and his younger brother Bob played each other in the World Series three years in a row beginning in 1921. Both were outfielders. Bob played with the Yankees and Irish with the Giants. The Giants won the Series in 1921 and 1922, and the Yankees took the title in 1923. A Meusel was the leader in runs batted in in all three Series. Irish drove in seven runs in 1921 and seven more in 1922, while Bob had eight RBI in 1923. Bob was also in the World Series in 1926, 1927, and 1928.

3. **THE ALOUS**

The Alou family is the only one with three brothers to appear in the World Series. They all played on San Francisco Bay area teams. Felipe played for the Giants in 1962, Matty with the Giants in 1962 and the Athletics in 1972, and Jesus with the Athletics in 1973 and 1974. Although the Athletics defeated the Reds in seven games in 1972, Matty suffered through a horrid slump, collecting only one hit, a single, in 24 at-bats. Felipe's son Moises played in the 1997 World Series with the Marlins.

4. **THE DEANS**

During spring training in 1934, Dizzy Dean boasted that he and his brother Paul would win 50 games for the Cardinals. Dizzy was only one win shy of his prophecy. Dizzy won 30 games while Paul won 19. Dizzy put himself on the line again on the eve of the World Series, stating that "me and Paul'll win two games apiece" against the Tigers. This prediction was right on the mark. Each won twice in the Cardinals' seven-game victory. Combined, the Deans were 4–1 with a 1.43 ERA in 44 innings. "It ain't bragging," said Dizzy, "if you can do it."

5. **THE COOPERS**

Pitcher Mort Cooper and catcher Walker Cooper starred for the Cardinals in the World Series in 1942, 1943, and 1944.

They had to overcome personal tragedy in the second game of the 1943 Series against the Yankees. On the morning of the game, they learned that their father had died. With Walker calling the signals, Mort defeated the Yankees 4–3, surviving a two-run rally in the ninth. Walker was one for three with a sacrifice bunt.

6. THE BARNESES

The New York Giants won the National League pennant four straight seasons beginning in 1921, and a Barnes brother pitched in each of the four World Series. Jesse Barnes pitched against the Yankees in 1921 and 1922 but was traded to the Braves in midseason in 1923. Jesse's younger brother Virgil picked up the family tradition by pitching for the Giants against the Yankees in 1923 and the Senators in 1924. In Game Six in 1921, Jesse struck out 10 batters during an $8^{1}/_{3}$-inning relief stint and was the winning pitcher in an 8–5 decision.

7. THE WANERS

Paul and Lloyd Waner both made the Hall of Fame and played in the same outfield for the Pirates in the 1927 World Series against the Yankees. Combined, they had 11 hits in 30 at-bats for a .367 batting average, but the Pirates lost the Series in a four-game sweep.

8. THE ALOMARS

Sandy Alomar Jr. and his younger brother Roberto have both had their share of moments in the World Series. Roberto tied the record for the most hits in a six-game Series. Leading the Blue Jays to a six-game victory over the Phillies in 1993, he had 12 hits, including two doubles and a triple, in 25 at-bats for a .480 average. Sandy Jr. had 11 hits, including two homers and a double, in 30 at-bats and drove in 10 runs for the Indians against the Marlins in 1997. Their father, Sandy Sr., was on the roster of the Yankees during the 1976 Series but didn't appear in a game.

9. **THE HERNANDEZES**

Either Orlando or Livan Hernandez played in every World Series from 1997 through 2002. Orlando pitched for the Yankees in 1998, 1999, 2000, and 2001, while Livan was with the Marlins in 1997 and the Giants in 2002. Thus far, they have never pitched against each other in the World Series. Orlando, who is nine years older than Livan, has been far more successful. In the Fall Classic, Orlando is 2–1 with a 2.27 ERA in $27^2/_3$ innings. Livan is 2–2, but his earned run average is 8.37 in $19^1/_3$ innings.

10. **THE WORRELLS**

Todd and Tim Worrell have both given up runs that cost their clubs world titles. In 1985, the Cardinals led the Royals three games to two and held a 1–0 advantage entering the ninth inning of Game Six, but Todd allowed two runs to lose the game 2–1. The Royals won the championship in Game Seven. In 2002, the Giants won three of the first five games and led 5–3 when Tim gave up three runs in the eighth inning to hand the Angels a 6–5 win. The Angels beat the Giants 4–1 in the seventh game. On the positive side, Todd provided one of the most dominant relief performances in Series history in Game Five in 1985. In a two-inning stint, he struck out all six batters he faced, each of them on a swinging strike.

One and Only Hitters

Hitters who have accomplished something unique in the World Series include:

1. **JIM GILLIAM**

Jim Gilliam is the only player to appear in a perfect game both in the World Series and during the regular season. Gilliam played second base for the Brooklyn Dodgers in the only perfect game in World Series history when Don Larsen spun his magic for the Yankees in Game Five in 1956. Gilliam was at third base for the Los Angeles Dodgers on the winning side of a perfect game on September 9, 1965, as Sandy Koufax beat the Cubs 1–0 in Los Angeles.

2. **TOMMY HERR**

Tommy Herr of the Cardinals is the only player to hit a two-run sacrifice fly in the World Series. It happened in Game Four in 1982 against the Brewers in Milwaukee. In the second inning with Willie McGee on third base and Ozzie Smith on second with one out, Herr sent a deep fly that was caught by Gorman Thomas in center field. Thomas slipped on the warning track, however, and Smith raced around from second to score after McGee. The unusual play gave the Cardinals a 3–0 lead, but the Brewers rallied to win 7–5.

One and Only Hitters

3. IRV NOREN

Acting as a one-man rally-killer, Irv Noren is the only player to ground into five double plays in a single World Series. Playing for the Yankees in the 1955 Series against the Dodgers, Noren had just one single in 16 at-bats for an .063 batting average in addition to his five GIDPs.

4. WILLIE MAYS

Willie Mays is the only player to ground into three double plays in a single game. Batting seventh in the New York Giants batting order in the fourth game in 1951 against the Yankees, Mays hit into double plays in the second, fifth, and ninth innings. The Yankees won the game 6–2.

5. HANK BAUER

Yankees outfielder Hank Bauer is the only player with a consecutive-game World Series hitting streak as long as 17 games. Bauer's record streak included all seven games in both 1956 and 1957 and the first three games in 1958. He had 25 hits, including six homers, in 76 at-bats during the stretch. In the third game in 1958 against the Braves, Bauer became the only player to drive in all four runs scored in a Series game. He drove in two runs with a fifth-inning single and hit a two-run homer in the seventh to lead the Yankees to a 4–0 victory in New York. In the seven-game 1958 Fall Classic, Bauer had 10 hits, four homers, and eight runs batted in. He had another big moment in the sixth and final game versus the Giants in 1951. With a runner on second base, two outs in the ninth inning, and the score 4–3 in favor of the Yankees, Bauer made a running catch of a drive by pinch-hitter Sal Yvars to end the Series. Hank played in nine World Series with the Yankees, from 1949 through 1958. He was also the manager of the Orioles in 1966, when the club defeated the Dodgers in four straight games.

6. ROGER BRESNAHAN

Roger Bresnahan is the only catcher to bat leadoff in a World Series game. Playing for the Giants against the Athletics in

1905, Bresnahan reached base 11 times, on five hits, four walks, and was twice hit by a pitch in 22 plate appearances.

7. BENNIE TATE

Bennie Tate is the only pinch-hitter to draw three walks in a single World Series. They came in the only three World Series plate appearances of Tate's big league career. Playing for the Senators against the Giants in 1924, Tate walked with the bases loaded in the third game and loaded the bases with a pass in Game Seven, which Washington won 4–3 in 12 innings. At the time, he was a rookie who had drawn only one base on balls in 21 big league regular-season games. Tate went on to have a 10-year career as a backup catcher in which he had 29 hits in 81 pinch-hit at-bats for a .358 batting average.

8. FRANKIE FRISCH

Frankie Frisch is the only player to appear in at least 50 World Series games without a home run. Frisch played in more World Series games than any player who wasn't a member of the Yankees, and no one has played in more Series games without a home run. Despite his lack of power, Frisch hit well with the Giants in 1921, 1922, 1923, and 1924 and the Cardinals in 1928, 1930, 1931, and 1934. He batted .294 and holds the all-time record for the most career doubles with 10. Oddly, Frisch was a slugger in the All-Star Game. He hit the second and third home runs ever struck in the star-filled contest with round-trippers in both 1933 and 1934.

9. WILLIE WILSON

Left fielder and leadoff hitter Willie Wilson of the Royals is the only player to strike out as many as 12 times in a single World Series. Wilson was fanned a dozen times by Phillies pitchers in 1980. The Series ended with Wilson striking out with the bases loaded against Tug McGraw. Wilson had only four hits in 26 at-bats in the six games.

10. **GEORGE PIPGRAS**

Yankees pitcher George Pipgras is the only batter to strike out five times in a World Series game. He struck out five times in five plate appearances against three Cubs pitchers in the third game in 1932. On the bright side, Pipgras was the winning pitcher in a 7–5 decision made famous by Babe Ruth's "called shot."

One and Only Pitchers

Pitchers who have accomplished something unique in the World Series include:

1. **ORVAL OVERALL**

Cubs pitcher Orval Overall is the only pitcher to strike out four batters in an inning. He accomplished the one and only feat in the first inning of the fifth and final game of the 1908 World Series against the Tigers in Detroit. The four-strikeout inning was possible because Tigers first baseman Claude Rossman swung and missed at a pitch with two out but reached base safely when the ball sailed past catcher Johnny Kling. Overall also struck out Charley O'Leary, Ty Cobb, and Germany Schaefer. The Cubs won 2–0 as Overall pitched a three-hitter and struck out 10 batters. The crowd numbered only 6,210, the smallest in World Series history, and the game ended in one hour and 25 minutes, the fastest Series game ever played.

2. **JIM PALMER**

Jim Palmer is the only pitcher in World Series history to throw a shutout before his 21st birthday. Palmer provided the Orioles with a 6–0 victory in Game Two in 1966 in Los Angeles. He is the only player to draw two bases-loaded walks in a Series contest, when he coaxed bases on balls out of Pirates pitchers Bruce Kison and Bob Veale in the fourth and fifth innings in Game Two in 1971. The Orioles won 11–3 in Baltimore.

3. **ALLIE REYNOLDS**

Allie Reynolds is the only pitcher to win a World Series game five years in a row. Reynolds composed a 7–2 lifetime record in the Series, all with the Yankees. He was 1–0 in 1947, 1–0 in 1949, 1–0 in 1950, 1–1 in 1951, 2–1 in 1952, and 1–0 in 1953. Reynolds also recorded four saves in the Series, with one each in 1949, 1950, 1952, and 1953.

4. **LEFTY GOMEZ**

Yankees pitcher Lefty Gomez is the only pitcher with a 6–0 win-loss record in World Series play, holding the record for most victories without a loss. Gomez was 1–0 in 1932, 2–0 in 1936, 2–0 in 1937, and 1–0 in 1938. Jack Coombs and Hall-of-Famer Herb Pennock both had 5–0 records in the Fall Classic.

5. **WILMER "VINEGAR BEND" MIZELL**

Wilmer "Vinegar Bend" Mizell is the only individual to play in the World Series and serve in the United States Congress. Mizell was born in Leakesville, Mississippi, but took his nickname from the town of Vinegar Bend, Alabama, 15 miles away. He was 13–5 for the 1960 Pirates and pitched in two games, one of them a starting assignment, in the World Series that fall against the Yankees, although without much success. Mizell gave up four runs in $2^{2}/_{3}$ innings for an ERA of 15.43. He served in Congress representing a House district in North Carolina from 1969 through 1975. Mizell was also the assistant secretary of commerce in the Gerald Ford administration, and the assistant secretary of agriculture under Ronald Reagan.

6. **DAROLD KNOWLES**

Oakland's Darold Knowles is the only pitcher to appear in seven games in a single World Series. Knowles claimed the record for most games pitched in a Series when he was called upon to take the hill in all seven games in 1973 against the Mets. Knowles pitched 6⅓ innings of shutout baseball and earned two saves.

7. **MIKE STANTON**

Mike Stanton is the only pitcher to make at least 20 career relief appearances in the World Series. Stanton relieved for the Braves five times in 1991 and four in 1992 and with the Yankees on one occasion in both 1998 and 1999, four in 2000, and five in 2001. Through 2003, Stanton had a 3-0 record with one save and a 1.54 ERA in 23⅓ World Series innings.

8. **THREE FINGER BROWN**

Cubs Hall-of-Famer Three Finger Brown is the only pitcher to throw shutouts in the World Series three years in a row. Brown beat the White Sox 1-0 in Game Four in 1906, the Tigers 2-0 in Game Five in 1907, and the Tigers again 3-0 in the fourth game in 1908.

9. **OREL HERSHISER**

Orel Hershiser is the only individual to pitch a shutout and collect three hits in the same World Series game. He starred at the plate and on the mound in the second game in 1988 for the Dodgers against the Athletics in Los Angeles. In addition to pitching a three-hitter, Orel was three for three with the bat. Among his three hits were a pair of doubles. Hershiser put together one of the most dominating pitching performances in baseball history in 1988. He closed the regular season with a major league record 59 consecutive scoreless innings. In the NLCS against the Mets, Hershiser pitched 24⅔ innings with an ERA of 1.09, in which he made three starts and a relief appearance. In Game Seven, Hershiser beat the Mets 6-0. In the fifth and final game of the World Series, he downed the A's 5-2. In his final 101⅔ innings in 1988, including the postseason, Hershiser allowed only five earned runs. The only pitchers with shutouts in both the League Championship Series and the World Series in the same year are Hershiser in 1988 and Randy Johnson with the Diamondbacks in 2001.

10. **JOE BLACK**

Joe Black is the only pitcher to start a World Series game after only two career regular-season starting assignments. Black was a rookie with the Dodgers in 1952 and was a revelation as a reliever. He had a 15–4 record and 15 saves with a 2.15 ERA in 56 games and 142$^1/_3$ innings. Brooklyn manager Chuck Dressen gambled by starting Black in the World Series against the Yankees and gave him two starts during the final week of the regular season as a tune-up. Black started the opening game of the Series and pitched a complete game, winning 4–2. He also started the fourth and seventh games but lost 2–0 and 4–2.

The Case of the Three-Year-Old Batboy

Here is a collection of odd, peculiar, extraordinary, and inexplicable occurrences from the actual case files of the World Series.

1. **FLYOVERS**

Flyovers of military aircraft are commonplace before important outdoor sporting events such as the World Series. The first flyover at a World Series game took place in 1918 with the country involved in World War I. Prior to the Red Sox–Cubs matchup in Game One in 1918 in Chicago, 60 U.S. Army airplanes flew over the field in military formation. It was only 15 years after the Wright Brothers' first successful flight. Two incidents involving airplanes at the World Series had near tragic consequences. During the second game of the 1919 World Series between the White Sox and Reds in Cincinnati, a stuffed dummy was dropped out of a low-flying airplane and landed between second and third base. It was apparently a practical joke. No players were injured, nor was anyone arrested. During the eighth inning of Game One in 1943, a B-17 zoomed low over Yankee Stadium, startling the crowd of 68,676. It swung back two minutes later and, five minutes after the second pass, returned again. The third pass was frightening, as the huge four-engine bomber was no more than 200 feet off the ground and hedge-hopped over the roof, narrowly missing the flagpoles. The roar of the plane drowned out the nationwide radio broadcast and stopped play as the players stood and watched the plane. New York mayor Fiorello LaGuardia demanded that the Army Air Force discipline the pilot. The AAF admitted that it had no idea who piloted the plane. If the military ever learned his identity, it was never revealed to the public.

2. **1951 NEW YORK GIANTS OUTFIELD**

The first outfield in baseball history that included three African-Americans occurred in the World Series when the 1951 New York Giants had Monte Irvin in left field, Willie Mays in center, and Hank Thompson in right. The three had never played together in the same outfield before the Series and never again played in the same outfield afterward. Regular right fielder Don Mueller had fractured his ankle in the final play-off game against the Dodgers. Giants manager Leo Durocher put Thompson, normally a third baseman, in right field for the Series against the Yankees, even though he had played only 10 games in the outfield during his career and none at all during the 1951 season. Unfamiliar with the position, Thompson made two errors during the six-game loss to the Yankees. The next time three African-Americans played in the same outfield was in 1954, when the Braves had Hank Aaron, Bill Bruton, and Jim Pendleton. The next all-African-American outfield in the World Series was the Braves' 1958 combination of Aaron, Bruton, and Wes Covington.

3. **JOSH DEVORE**

Many left the third game of the 1912 Series, won by the Giants 2–1 at Fenway Park, believing that the Red Sox had won. Hick Cady batted for the Red Sox with the Giants leading 2–1 with two out in the ninth inning and runners on second and third. Cady sent a long drive to right center, and Giants right fielder Josh Devore made a spectacular running catch to end the game with a 2–1 Giants victory. Devore never broke stride while heading straight for the clubhouse with the ball still in his glove. Many in the ballpark were convinced that the ball had fallen safely and went home happily with the notion that both runners had scored and that the Red Sox had won a thrilling 3–2 decision.

4. VENDOME HOTEL

When the 1903 Pittsburgh Pirates played in the World Series in Boston, the club stayed at the Vendome Hotel. A century later, it still exists at the corner of Commonwealth and Dartmouth Avenues in Boston's Back Bay. Built in 1871, it was Boston's most fashionable hotel at the time of baseball's first World Series and once boasted Presidents Ulysses S. Grant and Grover Cleveland as its guests, in addition to Mark Twain, Oscar Wilde, and Sarah Bernhardt. The Vendome was renovated as a condominium complex during the 1970s, although with tragic consequences. A fire broke out during the renovation, and nine Boston firefighters lost their lives combating the blaze.

5. JOHN BRUSH

John Brush is the only owner to watch World Series games from an automobile parked on the playing field. Brush owned the New York Giants when his club was in the World Series in 1911 and 1912, after a long illness had left him a semi-invalid. An enclosure similar to a garage with two open ends was built in foul territory in deep right field, which allowed Brush to watch the games through the windshield. A huge board was placed in front of the large automobile to prevent balls from rolling under the wheels. Brush died in November 1912.

6. PEPPER MARTIN

During fielding practice before Game Six of the 1931 World Series, a man with a rifle rushed onto the field and headed toward Cardinals outfielder Pepper Martin. It turned out to be

The Case of the Three-Year-Old Batboy 301

a gun manufacturer, who presented the rifle to Martin, an avid hunter, as a gift.

7. BOSTON AND PHILADELPHIA

Boston and Philadelphia are the only two cities to participate in back-to-back World Series involving four teams. In 1914, the Boston Braves played the Philadelphia Athletics. In 1915, the Boston Red Sox faced the Philadelphia Phillies. Oddly, neither Boston club used its home ballpark in either Series. In 1914, the Braves used the Red Sox' home at Fenway Park because it had many more seats than their own South End Grounds. In 1915, the Braves moved into new Braves Field, and the Red Sox used the Braves' ballpark. In 1916, the Red Sox played at Braves Field once more. The only other club to use a ballpark other than its own was the Chicago Cubs in 1918. The Cubs played at Comiskey Park instead of Wrigley Field, which was then known as Weeghman Park.

8. SHIELA STODGILL

Shiela Stodgill, an 18-year-old from Rochester, New York, was arrested during the 1972 World Series on a charge of manslaughter. According to the police report, Shiela stabbed her 17-year-old brother Ronald to death during an argument over whether the family radio would be tuned to the World Series. Two hours after the stabbing, the game was postponed by rain.

9. LINDA THE SWEEPER

A popular attraction of Baltimore Orioles home games during the early 1970s was a blond-haired teenage girl named Linda Wareheim, who wore a pair of hot pants and swept off the bases at the end of the fifth inning. At the end of her routine, Wareheim playfully swept dirt in the direction of the opposing team's third base coach. During the 1971 World Series, Pirates third base coach Frank Oceak took exception to the routine and gave her a swift kick, which fortunately missed its target.

10. DARRIN BAKER

Darrin Baker, the three-year-old son of Giants manager Dusty Baker, got himself in harm's way during the fifth game of the 2002 World Series against the Angels. Darrin was acting as one of the Giants batboys when he went to retrieve Kenny Lofton's bat after Lofton's two-run triple. The problem was, J. T. Snow and David Bell were racing toward the plate as Darrin headed toward it. Snow grabbed Darrin and got the youngster out of the way to avoid a potential tragedy. Darrin's action led to a rule passed by major league owners in January 2003 that stipulated that batboys must be at least 14 years old. The next time Darrin will be able to serve as a batboy will be in 2013.

Cool Things That Didn't Fit in Any Other List

Here are more fascinating facts and odd and unusual tales of the World Series.

1. ATLANTA BRAVES

The Braves are the only franchise to compete in the World Series in three different cities. The Braves were in Boston in 1914 and 1948, in Milwaukee in 1957 and 1958, and in Atlanta in 1991, 1992, 1995, 1996, and 1999. The Braves are also the only franchise to host the World Series in five different ballparks. The club played at Fenway Park in 1914; Braves Field in 1948; County Stadium in 1957 and 1958; Atlanta-Fulton County Stadium in 1991, 1992, 1995, and 1996; and Turner Field in 1999.

2. CASEY STENGEL

Casey Stengel managed the Yankees in 10 World Series without a set lineup. Only in 1949, when Phil Rizzuto led off the Yankees batting order in all five games, did Stengel use the same leadoff hitters throughout the Series. Stengel used two leadoff hitters (Gene Woodling and Rizzuto) in 1950, four (Mickey Mantle, Woodling, Hank Bauer, and Rizzuto) in 1951, three (Bauer, Rizzuto, and Gil McDougald) in 1952, three (McDougald, Woodling, and Mantle) in 1953, five

(Bauer, Bob Cerv, Irv Noren, Elston Howard, and Rizzuto) in 1955, two (Bauer and McDougald) in 1956, two (Bauer and Tony Kubek) in 1957, three (Bauer, Norm Siebern, and Andy Carey) in 1958, and five (Kubek, Cerv, McDougald, Clete Boyer, and Bobby Richardson) in 1960.

3. SPARKY ANDERSON AND DICK WILLIAMS

Sparky Anderson and Dick Williams opposed each other as managers twice in the World Series, 12 years apart and with four different teams between them. Managing the Reds, Anderson lost to Williams and the Athletics in 1972 in seven games. Twelve years later, while managing the Padres, Williams lost to Anderson's Tigers in five games. Anderson and Williams were teammates with Fort Worth in the Texas League in 1955 and with Montreal in the International League in 1956 while in the Dodgers farm system.

4. SAMUEL LONG

Samuel Long was judged to be legally competent because he predicted that the St. Louis Cardinals would play in the World Series. Long was an 81-year-old president of a warehouse company in St. Louis who in October 1934 sought in probate court to have a guardianship imposed by his children removed so that he could run his own business. During the court proceedings, Long testified that with two weeks remaining in the season, he predicted that the Cards would play in the Series even though they were four games out of first place. Long cited baseball prophecy as proof of his mental alertness. The judge agreed, and Long was free to make his own decisions.

5. LOSING PROPOSITIONS

James Ridner had to push a baby carriage from Kentucky to Michigan because he lost a bet on the 1935 World Series. He wagered that the Cubs would defeat the Tigers, and as usual, the Cubs came out on the losing end. To settle the bet, Ridner pushed the carriage from his home in Harlan, Kentucky, to Detroit. Inside the carriage was Arson "Fireball" Stephens, the winner of the wager, along with provisions for the journey. The 550-mile trip took 30 days and ended at home plate at Tiger Stadium. Ridner wore out two baby carriages and three pairs of shoes. Pennsylvania senators Hugh Scott and Richard Schweiker rode an elephant past the U.S. Capitol after betting the Maryland senators that the Pirates would beat the Orioles in the 1971 World Series. J. Glenn Beall Jr. and Charles Mathias Jr., the two losing Maryland legislators, had to lead the elephant while carrying peanuts and shovels.

6. TOM WEIR

USA Today columnist Tom Weir had an eerie premonition about the earthquake that interrupted the 1989 World Series between the Giants and the Athletics. "The only real local flavor from the Bay Bridge World Series is an earthquake," wrote Weir on the eve of the first game, "and the Athletics and Giants just might be capable of rattling one up without Mother Earth's help." The last line of the column read, "So bring on that earthquake, Seriesly." The earthquake struck the Bay Area four days later, before Game Three.

7. GENE MAUCH

Gene Mauch is the only individual to manage in the majors for more than 25 seasons without managing a team in the World Series. Mauch managed in the majors for 26 seasons, with the Phillies (1960–67), the Expos (1969–75), the Twins (1976–80) and the Angels (1981–82 and 1985–87). In 1964, his Phillies had a 6½-game lead with two weeks left in the season but finished in second place. In 1982, the Angels had a two-games-to-none lead in the best-of-five ALCS over the Brewers but lost three in a row. In 1986, the Angels held a three-games-to-one advantage against the Red Sox in the ALCS but lost three in a row once more. Mauch won 1,932 games as a manager during the regular season, the most of any manager who didn't put a team in the Series. Others with at least 900 regular-season wins, through the 2003 season, who didn't manage a team in the Fall Classic include Jimmy Dykes (1,406), Bill Rigney (1,239), Art Howe (1,058), Bill Virdon (995), Paul Richards (923), and Don Zimmer (906). Dykes, Rigney, Virdon, Richards, and Zimmer each played in at least one World Series.

8. MEMORIAL COLISEUM

Memorial Coliseum in Los Angeles was the only World Series site that could hold crowds of more than 90,000. The Dodgers used the facility as their home grounds from 1958 through 1961. The Dodgers reached the World Series in 1959 against the White Sox, and the three games there drew 92,394, 92,650, and 92,706. It was also the first World Series played west of St. Louis. Built for football and track, Memorial Coliseum had little to recommend it for baseball. The left field foul line was only 251 feet long and was topped by a 40-foot-high wire screen. The Coliseum hosted the Olympics in 1932 and 1984 and is one of only two stadiums to be used for both the Olympics and the World Series. The other is Turner Field in Atlanta. Memorial Coliseum also hosted the first Super Bowl, in 1967. Other stadiums used for both a Super Bowl and a World Series include Qualcomm Stadium in San Diego, the Metrodome in Minneapolis, and Pro Player Stadium in Miami. The Metrodome is the only facility used for a World Series, a Super Bowl, and an NCAA basketball Final Four. The Metrodome hosted the three events in a six-month span from October 1991 through April 1992.

9. 1917

The 1917 World Series was played with the nation involved in World War I. The day after the Series ended with the White Sox polishing off the Giants in six games, the two teams played an exhibition game before a group of 6,000 soldiers who were about to be shipped off to France. The contest was played at Camp Mills in Mineola, New York.

10. **THE NATIONAL ANTHEM**

The 1918 World Series was the second to be played during World War I. During the 1918 Series, the National Anthem was played in the middle of the seventh inning. The tradition of playing the National Anthem before every major league baseball game began in 1942, when the United States was involved in World War II.

World Series Lasts

There have been many World Series occurrences that we'll probably never see again.

1. **FREDDIE PARENT**

Freddie Parent, who played shortstop for Boston in 1903, was the last surviving participant from baseball's first World Series. Parent died in 1972, three weeks before his 97th birthday. Parent and five other players from 1903, including Hall-of-Famers Cy Young and Fred Clarke, threw out the first ball before the six games of the 1953 World Series.

2. **THE TEAM WITH THE BEST RECORD**

The last World Series in which the two teams with the best win-loss records in their leagues automatically proceeded to the World Series was in 1968, when the Cardinals met the Tigers. Division play began in 1969 with the division leaders meeting in a best-of-five League Championship Series. The League Championship Series was expanded to a best-of-seven format in 1985. Baseball went to three divisions in 1994, with four play-off teams in the postseason, including the wild card, but there was no postseason that year due to the strike that ended the season in August. The current three-tiered play-off system to determine the world champion began in 1995.

3. **DESIGNATED HITTER**

The last World Series in which the designated hitter rule wasn't used was in 1985. The American League began using the DH during the regular season in 1973. The rule was used in the World Series for the first time in 1976. Lou Piniella of the Yankees was the first DH in World Series history, while Dan Driessen of the Reds was the first National League designated hitter. From 1976 through 1985, the DH was used in all games in even-numbered years and not at all in odd-numbered years. Since 1986, the designated hitter has been used only when the American League club is playing at home.

4. **TWO-HOUR GAMES**

With three-hour games the norm in major league baseball, especially during the World Series, it's difficult to believe that games played in less than two hours were once routine. The last Series game played in less than two hours was the fourth contest in 1966, when the Orioles defeated the Dodgers 1–0 in Baltimore. The time of the game was one hour 45 minutes.

5. **ALL-WHITE TEAM**

Before 1947, every team in the World Series was composed only of white players. The last all-white team in the World Series was the 1953 Yankees. The Yankees integrated their roster in 1955. The last all-white World Series was the one in 1950, played between the Yankees and the Phillies. The last major league team to integrate was the Red Sox in 1959. The last team to go through an entire year without a player of African descent was the Kansas City Athletics in 1960.

6. **NO TRAVEL DAYS**

The last World Series without a travel day was the one in 1956 between the New York Yankees and the Brooklyn Dodgers, which was played on seven consecutive days. Since 1957, there has been a scheduled travel day between the second and third games and the fifth and sixth games, even when the participants are from the same geographic area.

7. FOUR UMPIRES

The last World Series in which four umpires were on the field was in 1946. Beginning in 1947, two additional umpires were added on each foul line. There were only two umpires—one behind the plate and one on the bases—from 1903 through 1909. Four umpires were used beginning in 1910, with one behind home plate, one on the bases, one on the left field foul line, and one on the right field foul line. From 1917 through 1946, the four umpires were stationed at home plate, first base, second base, and third base.

8. NO STOLEN BASES

The only World Series without a stolen base was in 1944 between the St. Louis Cardinals and the St. Louis Browns. The only three teams since 1976 to go through an entire World Series without a stolen base are the 1979 Pirates, the 1986 Red Sox, and the 2000 Mets.

9. NO HOME RUNS

The last World Series without a home run was the one in 1918, played between the Red Sox and the Cubs. The only years in which there were no World Series homers were 1905, 1906, and 1907. The only team since 1940 without a World Series home run is the 1950 Phillies.

10. GAMES IN SEPTEMBER

The last time a World Series game was played in the month of September was in 1955, when the Dodgers and the Yankees opened the Fall Classic on September 28. That is also the earliest date for a World Series game with the exception of 1918, when the Series was played during World War I. That season the Series between the Red Sox and the Cubs began on September 5 because the federal government shut down the regular season on Labor Day, ordering major league players to either join the military or take a war-related job. Ironically, if the World Series had been played during its normal period in early October, it might have been canceled by a flu epidemic. From late September through November, a virulent form of influenza struck the nation. Public gatherings in many cities, including Boston and Chicago, were banned by health officials during October and November. Estimates are that 20 to 25 percent of the nation's population was struck by the flu. The epidemic caused between 400,000 and 500,000 deaths nationwide and 20 million worldwide.

Bibliography

Books

Cantor, George, *Inside Sports Magazine World Series Factbook*. Detroit, MI: Visible Ink Press, 1996.

Charlton, James, *The Baseball Chronology*. New York: Macmillan, 1991.

Cohen, Richard M., and David S. Neft, *The World Series*. New York: Collier Books, 1986.

Dewey, Donald, and Nicholas Acocella, *The Biographical History of Baseball*. New York: Carroll & Graf, 1995.

Dickey, Glenn, *The History of the World Series Since 1903*. New York: Stein and Day, 1984.

Hoppel, Joe, *The Series: An Illustrated History of Baseball's Postseason Showcase*. St. Louis, MO: The Sporting News, 1993.

Shatzkin, Michael, *The Ballplayers*. New York: Arbor House, 1990.

Solomon, Burt, *The Baseball Timeline*. New York: Avon Books, 1997.

Thorn, John, and Pete Palmer, *Total Baseball*. New York: Warner, 2002.

Periodicals

The Cincinnati Enquirer
The New York Times
The Sporting News
Sports Illustrated

Index

Aaron, Hank, 27, 58, 162, 299
Abstein, Bill, 60
Adams, Babe, 87, 127
Adcock, Joe, 27
Agee, Tommie, 139
Agnew, Sam, 63
Aguilera, Rick, 237
Aikens, Willie, 145, 167
Aldridge, Vic, 17
Alexander, Grover, 24, 159, 273–74
Alomar, Roberto, 171, 288
Alomar, Sandy, Jr., 160, 288
Alomar, Sandy, Sr., 288
Alou, Felipe, 27, 287
Alou, Jesus, 287
Alou, Matty, 27, 287
Alou, Moises, 22, 120, 287
Alston, Walter, 32, 236, 237, 238, 248
Altobelli, Joe, 238
Amoros, Sandy, 33
Anderson, Garret, 23
Anderson, Sparky, 238, 239, 304
Andrews, Mike, 42–43
Andujar, Joaquin, 19
Antonelli, Johnny, 139
Appier, Kevin, 120

Appling, Luke, 13
Armbrister, Ed, 51
Ashburn, Richie, 232, 258
Ashford, Emmett, 143
Attell, Abe, 39
Ayala, Benny, 132

Babb-Sprague, Kristin, 150,
Bagby, Jim, Sr., 121
Baker, Bill, 199
Baker, Darrin, 302
Baker, Dusty, 23, 302
Baker, Frank (Home Run), 264
Balboni, Steve, 19
Banks, Ernie, 11
Barber, Turner, 63
Barnes, Jesse, 16, 128, 288
Barnes, Virgil, 288
Barnett, Larry, 51
Barrett, Marty, 170–71
Barrow, Ed, 230–31
Bates, Billy, 134
Bathe, Bill, 128–29
Bauer, Hank, 139, 172, 291, 303
Baylor, Don, 209
Bearden, Gene, 215–16
Beaumont, Ginger, 2
Beazley, Johnny, 138, 215

Becker, Beals, 61
Belanger, Mark, 34
Bell, David, 120, 302
Bell, Hi, 159
Bell, Jay, 23
Belliard, Rafael, 183
Belushi, Jim, 7
Bench, Johnny, 70, 108, 165–66
Bender, Chief, 87, 88
Bentley, Jack, 16, 122, 159
Benton, Rube, 72
Berardino, Johnny, 207
Berg, Moe, 204–6
Berger, Wally, 182
Bernhardt, Sarah, 300
Berra, Yogi, 18, 29, 33, 53, 139, 147, 156, 161, 186, 194, 200, 203, 222, , 232
Bevacqua, Kurt, 129
Bevens, Bill, 32, 104–5
Bigbee, Carson, 17
Bishop, Max, 31, 72, 107
Bithorn, Hiram, 10
Black, Don, 191
Black, Joe, 143, 297
Blair, Paul, 62, 97, 139
Blake, Sheriff, 108
Blanchard, Johnny, 199–200

Index

Blass, Steve, 34
Boddicker, Mike, 218
Boehringer, Brian, 214
Bolton, Cliff, 206
Bonds, Barry, 8, 146, 159, 160, 235
Bonilla, Bobby, 22, 235
Borowy, Hank, 269, 270
Boswell, Ken, 128, 172
Boswell, Tom, 9
Bottomley, Jim, 72
Boudreau, Lou, 5, 7, 244
Boyd, Oil Can, 140
Boyer, Clete, 157, 200, 304
Boyer, Cloyd, 157
Boyer, Ken, 157, 160
Branca, Ralph, 147
Breadon, Sam, 243
Bream, Sid, 29
Brecheen, Harry, 26, 90
Brenly, Bob, 255
Brennaman, Marty, 280
Bresnahan, Roger, 291–92
Brett, George, 191, 213
Brett, Ken, 212–13
Brickell, Fred, 208
Bridges, Marshall, 155
Briles, Nelson, 80, 124
Brock, Lou, 28, 170, 172
Brossius, Scott, 110
Brouhard, Mark, 207–8
Brown, Bobby, 172–73
Brown, Jumbo, 206–7
Brown, Three Finger, 77, 296
Brown, Warren, 267
Browning, Debbie, 280
Browning, Tom, 280
Brush, John, 45, 300
Bruton, Bill, 123, 299
Buckner, Bill, 20, 70
Buford. Don, 128
Bunker, Wally, 97, 259
Burdette, Lew, 90, 123
Burkhardt, Ken, 50
Burton, Jim, 19
Busch, August, 232
Bush, Barbara, 59

Bush, Donie, 208
Bush, George W., 22, 274
Bush, Joe, 211
Byrne, Tommy, 49
Byrnes, Milt, 268

Cady, Hick, 299
Camnitz, Howie, 185, 226
Campanella, Roy, 83
Canseco, Jose, 129, 177–78
Caray, Harry, 253
Carbo, Bernie, 19, 50, 108, 148–49
Carew, Rod, 11–12
Carey, Andy, 304
Carey, Max, 17
Carlton, Steve, 248
Carrigan, Bill, 245
Carroll, Clay, 149
Carroll, Tom, 207
Carter, Gary, 20
Carter, Jimmy, 273
Carter, Joe, 107
Carter, Lillian, 273
Casey, Hugh, 106, 189
Cash, Norm, 28, 81
Castillo, Marty, 130
Cavaretta, Phil, 213, 270
Cepeda, Orlando, 8
Cerv, Bob, 151, 304
Chambliss, Chris, 159
Chance, Frank, 5, 184, 242–43
Chandler, Happy, 247, 276
Chaote, Randy, 262
Chapman, Ray, 191–92
Chartak, Mike, 268
Christenson, Larry, 167
Churn, Chuck, 165
Cicotte, Eddie, 37–41, 93, 282
Cimoli, Gino, 189
Clark, Jack, 19
Clarke, Fred, 185, 226, 243–44, 308
Clemens, Roger, 54–55
Clemente, Roberto, 160

Cleveland, Grover, 274, 300
Cleveland, Reggie, 161
Clifton, Flea, 182
Cline, Ty, 50
Coakley, Andy, 196
Coates, Jim, 18
Cobb, Ty, 40, 127, 185, 251, 294
Coble, Drew, 52
Cochrane, Mickey, 5, 107–8, 244, 266
Coffman, Dick, 69, 261
Coleman, Vince, 188, 201
Collins, Eddie, 38, 72–73, 94, 170, 185
Collins, Jimmy, 5
Collins, Joe, 25, 161, 277
Collins, Ripper, 26
Comiskey, Charley, 37–38, 41, 94, 198
Concepcion, Dave, 118
Conigliaro, Tony, 192
Conley, Gene, 283
Coolidge, Calvin, 85, 271–72
Coombs, Jack, 88, 295
Cooney, Terry, 55
Cooper, Mort, 85, 287–88
Cooper, Walker, 287–88
Counsell, Craig, 22, 135
Coveleski, Stan, 89–90
Covington, Wes, 299
Cox, Bobby, 245, 249
Craig, Roger, 156, 165, 248
Cramer, Doc, 31, 277
Crawford, Sam, 4, 127
Crawford, Shag, 50
Crawford, Willie, 213
Cronin, Joe, 5, 208, 239, 241
Crosetti, Frankie, 54, 222
Crystal, Billy, 151
Cuellar, Mike, 233
Culberson, Leon, 25
Cunningham, Bill, 200–201

Index

Curtis, Chad, 167–68
Cuyler, Kiki, 17, 208

Dahlen, Bill, 183
Darcy, Pat, 108–9, 278
Darling, Ron, 118
Davenport, Jim, 79
Davidson, Bob, 52
Davis, Eric, 189–90
Davis, George, 184, 197
Davis, Mike, 152
Davis, Ron, 151
Davis, Tommy, 194
Davis, Willie, 61–62, 170
Dayley, Ken, 156
Dean, Dizzy, 25, 193, 266, 287
Dean, Paul, 25, 287
Denkinger, Don, 19
Dent, Bucky, 200
Devlin, Art, 183
Devore, Josh, 299–300
Dickey, Bill, 106, 112, 203–4
DiMaggio, Dom, 25, 90
DiMaggio, Joe, 104, 106, 112, 160, 221, 222
DiMuro, Lou, 49–50
Dinneen, Bill, 5, 87
Dobson, Pat, 233
Doby, Larry, 143
Doerr, Bobby, 26
Doheny, Ed, 3
Dolan, Cozy, 42
Donahue, Jiggs, 77
Donatelli, Augie, 49
Donnelly, Blix, 269
Donovan, Wild Bill, 67, 84, 86, 184
Doolittle, Jimmy, 206
Dougherty, Patsy, 137, 184
Douthit, Taylor, 160, 177
Doyle, Brian, 200
Doyle, Denny, 64
Doyle, Larry, 264–265
Drabowsky, Moe, 86, 259
Drebinger, John, 111

Dressen, Charlie, 44, 156, 206, 297
Dreyfuss, Barney, 60, 67–68
Driessen, Dan, 309
Drysdale, Don, 102, 117, 144
Duren, Ryne, 27, 216–17
Durocher, Leo, 25, 148, 232, 247, 258
Dyer, Eddie, 239–240
Dykes, Jimmie, 31, 66–67, 72, 108, 305
Dykstra, Lenny, 140–41

Earnshaw, George, 78, 83, 181
Eastwick, Rawly, 149
Eckersley, Dennis, 134, 152
Ehmke, Howard, 83–84
Eisenhower, Dwight, 272–73
Eisenreich, Jim, 22
Eller, Hod, 94
Elliott, Bob, 164
Engle, Clyde, 15–16
English, Charlie, 51
Ennis, Del, 232
Epstein, Mike, 182–83
Erskine, Carl, 83
Erstad, Darrin, 23, 282
Essegian, Chuck, 148–49
Estes, Shawn, 55
Etchebarren, Andy, 62, 113
Evans, Dwight, 108–9, 118
Evers, Johnny, 195

Faber, Red, 72, 89
Feliciano, Jose, 46–47
Feller, Bob, 164
Felsch, Happy, 41, 72, 94, 164,
Fernandez, Tony, 22
Fewster, Chick, 127
Figueroa, Ed, 165–66
Fingers, Rollie, 28, 70, 196

Finley, Charlie, 42–43, 63, 254
Fisk, Carlton, 19, 51, 64, 108, 109, 149–50, 278–79
Fitzgerald, John, 57
Fitzsimmons, Freddie, 188–89
Flack, Max, 63
Flanagan, Mike, 233
Fletcher, Art, 67
Flood, Curt, 28
Flowers, Jake, 191
Flug, Phyllis Orjikoff, 55
Ford, Whitey, 33, 79, 91, 186, 199, 216, 295
Forsch, Bob, 156
Foster, George, 108
Fox, Pete, 25
Foxx, Jimmie, 70, 107
Foster, George, 64
Frazier, George, 112–13
Freehan, Bill, 28
French, Walter, 107
Frey, Jim, 233
Frey, Lonny, 182
Frisch, Frankie, 5, 43, 292
Fullis, Chick, 266
Fullmer, Brad, 187
Furillo, Carl, 104, 171, 186

Gabler, Frank, 261
Gainor, Del, 104
Galehouse, Denny, 85–86
Galt, Edith Bolling, 271
Gandil, Chick, 39–40, 94
Gant, Ron, 29, 52
Garagiola, Joe, 132–33
Garcia, Kiko, 132
Gardner, Larry, 16
Garland, Wayne, 233
Garrett, Wayne, 140
Garvey, Steve, 160
Gaspar, Rod, 50
Gaston, Cito, 143
Gedman, Rich, 118
Gehrig, Lou, 111, 116–

Index

17, 140, 160, 178, 195, 257
Gehringer, Charlie, 266
Gentry, Gary, 139
Gerard, Lou, 278
Geronimo, Cesar, 51, 108, 118
Giambi, Jason, 160
Gibson, Bob, 28, 81, 91, 121, 123-25
Gibson, Kirk, 152-53, 177, 199
Gilliam, Jim, 60, 167, 290
Gionfriddo, Al, 104-5
Gladden, Dan, 30, 156
Glaus, Troy, 23, 168
Glavine, Tom, 43
Gleason, Kid, 39
Gomez, Lefty, 295
Gonzalez, Alex, 109
Gonzalez, Luis, 23
Gonzalez, Mike, 204
Goodman, Ival, 222
Gordon, Joe, 106, 221
Goslin, Goose, 116, 266
Gould, Jack, 277
Gowdy, Hank, 16, 132, 185
Grace, Mark, 23
Granger, Wayne, 125
Grant, Mudcat, 123
Grant, Ulysses, 300
Gray, Jim, 58
Greenberg, Hank, 25, 194-95
Gregg, Hal, 32
Green, Dick, 177
Greenberg, Hank, 182
Griffey, Ken, Sr., 108
Griffith, Clark, 241
Grim, Bob, 49
Grimes, Burleigh, 31, 68, 78, 121
Grimm, Charlie, 51, 71, 253
Grissom, Marquis, 171, 172
Groat, Dick, 283
Groh, Heinie, 210-11
Grove, Lefty, 83
Gruber, Kelly, 53

Guerrero, Pedro, 118
Guidry, Ron, 118, 217-18
Gullett, Don, 213-14
Gumbert, Harry, 69, 261
Guthrie, Mark, 237
Gwynn, Tony, 120

Haas, Mule, 107-8, 178-79
Hafey, Chick, 67, 177
Haines, Hinkey, 282. 283
Haines, Jesse, 24, 122, 160
Hallahan, Wild Bill, 31
Hamilton, Jack, 192
Hamilton, Steve, 283
Hamner, Granny, 232
Haney, Fred, 90, 248-49
Harding, Warren, 278
Harper, Terry, 29
Harris, Bucky, 5, 16, 17, 32, 104, 238, 242
Harris, Joe, 116, 142
Hartnett, Gabby, 71, 253
Harwell, Ernie, 47
Hatcher, Billy, 174-75
Hatcher, Mickey, 199
Hawkins, Andy, 129
Heilmann, Harry, 14
Henderson, Dave, 20, 129
Henderson, Rickey, 107, 141, 170
Hendricks, Elrod, 34, 50, 139
Henrich, Tommy, 101, 106
Henriksen, Olaf, 131-32
Herman, Billy, 164
Hernandez, Livan, 289
Hernandez, Orlando, 289
Herr, Tommy, 290
Hershberger, Willard, 198
Hershiser, Orel, 118-20, 296-97

Herzog, Buck, 68
Herzog, Whitey, 156
Hildebrand, George, 48-49
Hiller, Chuck, 27, 154-55
Hodges, Gil, 49, 139, 181-82, 186, 273
Hoerner, Joe, 28
Holke, Walter, 73
Holtzmann, Ken, 125
Hooper, Harry, 15, 163-64
Hooton, Burt, 159
Hoover, Herbert, 272
Hornsby, Rogers, 5, 24, 40, 243, 253
Horton, Willie, 28, 81, 239
Hostetler, Chuck, 270
Hough, Charlie, 159
Houk, Ralph, 246, 253-54
Howard, Del, 85
Howard, Elston, 143, 200, 222-23, 304
Howe, Art, 305
Howser, Dick, 172
Hoyt, Waite, 77-78
Hrbek, Kent, 29-30, 52, 156
Hubbard, Cal, 285
Hubbell, Carl, 69, 114, 143, 206
Hudson, Charlie, 162
Huggins, Miller, 238
Hughes, Dick, 112, 263
Huizenga, Wayne, 22
Hunter, Brian, 61
Hunter, Catfish, 140
Hutchinson, Fred, 44, 123

Iorg, Dane, 19, 134
Iorg, Garth, 134
Irvin, Monte, 148, 173, 186, 299
Isbell, Frank, 173

Jackson, Joe, 38, 40-41, 94
Jackson, Reggie, 52,

Index

127, 140, 158–59, 193–94
Jackson, Travis, 177, 214
James, Bill, 93
Jansen, Larry, 263
Jaster, Larry, 155, 263
Javier, Julian, 75
Jenkins, Ferguson, 12
Jennings, Hughie, 238, 251–52, 253
Jensen, Jackie, 149
Jeter, Derek, 61, 110, 141, 160
John, Tommy, 113, 195
Johnson, Ban, 17, 42, 47
Johnson, Billy, 222
Johnson, Charles, 22, 120
Johnson, Darrell, 239
Johnson, Davey, 113
Johnson, Deron, 62
Johnson, Don, 270
Johnson, Lou, 34
Johnson, Randy, 91–92, 150, 219
Johnson, Walter, 2, 17, 85, 86, 122, 241, 242
Johnston, Doc, 286
Johnston, Jimmy, 286
Johnstone, Jay, 151
Jolson, Al, 164
Jones, Andruw, 145, 214
Jones, Bobby, 141
Jones, Cleon, 49
Jones, Davy, 127
Jones, Fielder, 5
Jones, Nippy, 49
Jones, Sad Sam, 100, 126
Jones, Willie, 232
Jorgens, Arndt, 203–4
Justice, David, 29, 43, 53

Kaat, Jim, 225–26
Kaline, Al, 28, 81, 238
Kauff, Benny, 164
Keane, Johnny, 157, 232–233

Keefe, Tim, 85
Keller, Charlie, 106, 112, 221–22
Kelly, George, 42
Kelly, Tom, 237
Kennedy, Brickyard, 114
Kennedy, John F., 57
Kennedy, Monte, 263
Kent, Jeff, 264
Kerr, Dickie, 93–94
Kilduff, Pete, 121
Killebrew, Harmon, 160
Killilea, Henry, 67–68
Kim, Byung Hyun, 109–10
Kison, Bruce, 113, 295
Klem, Bill, 48–49, 265
Klesko, Ryan, 61
Kling, Johnny, 294
Klinger, Bob, 25
Kluszewski, Ted, 164–65
Knabe, Otto, 57
Knight, Ray, 20
Knoblauch, Chuck, 30, 61
Knowles, Darold, 295–96
Koenig, Mark, 71
Koosman, Jerry, 125
Kopf, Larry, 95
Koufax, Sandy, 34, 62, 82–83, 91, 290
Kowalik, Fabian, 194
Kubek, Tony, 47, 189, 222–223, 304
Kucks, Johnny, 33, 96–97
Kuenn, Harvey, 254–55
Kuhn, Bowie, 43, 44
Kurowski, Whitey, 138
Kuzava, Bob, 26

Laabs, Chet, 268
Labine, Clem, 60, 96, 169, 172
Lackey, John, 218–19
LaGuardia, Fiorello, 299
Landis, Kenesaw, 41, 42, 48–49, 164, 252, 266

Landrum, Tito, 201
Lansford, Carney, 129
Lapp, Jack, 131, 185
Larkin, Gene, 30, 135
La Russa, Tony, 238
Larsen, Don, 33, 53, 74, 104, 109, 138, 155, 161
Lary, Lyn, 241
Lasorda, Tom, 51, 152, 236–37
Lavagetto, Cookie, 104–5
Lawless, Tom, 126–27
Lazzeri, Tony, 24, 69, 154
Leach, Tommy, 4, 222
Lee, Bill, 19, 161
Leever, Sam, 3–4, 137
Lefferts, Craig, 129
Ledee, Ricky, 202
Leibold, Nemo, 16
Leibrandt, Charlie, 105–6
Leifeld, Lefty, 226
Leiter, Al, 136
Leius, Scott, 135
Lemke, Mark, 135
Lemon, Bob, 113, 148, 172, 258
Lewis, Duffy, 16, 163
Leyland, Jim, 234–35
Leyritz, Jim, 150–51
Liddle, Don, 258
Lindeman, Jim, 201
Lindsay, John, 44
Lindstrom, Fred, 16, 173, 212
Lockman, Whitey, 186
Loes, Billy, 43–44
Lofton, Kenny, 168, 302
Lolich, Mickey, 28, 91, 124
Lollar, Sherm, 147
Lollar, Tim, 162
Lombardi, Ernie, 78, 198, 222
Long, Samuel, 304
Lonborg, Jim, 75, 123
Lopat, Eddie, 139
Lopes, Dave, 140, 166–67

Index

Lopez, Al, 259
Lopez, Albie, 110
Lopez, Hector, 199–200
Lord, Bris, 178
Luque, Dolph, 227
Lynn, Fred, 64, 108
Lyons, Ted, 13, 204

Maas, Duke, 123
Mack, Connie, 83–84, 88, 236, 238, 244, 247–56
Maharg, Billy, 39
Mails, Duster, 95, 105
Malone, Pat, 107
Mancuso, Gus, 69
Mangual, Angel, 172
Mantle, Mickey, 117, 151, 156–157, 160, 172, 194, 200, 214, 222, 223, 303
Manush, Heinie, 57–58
Maranville, Rabbit, 185
Marberry, Firpo, 88, 228, 242
Marichal, Juan, 8, 178
Maris, Roger, 27, 79, 117, 143–44, 151, 194, 200
Marquard, Rube, 68, 95, 264
Marquez, Gonzalo, 172–73
Marshall, Mike, 64
Martin, Billy, 26, 33, 171–72
Martin, J. C., 50
Martin, Pepper, 67, 220–21, 300–301
Martinez, Tino, 110
Mason, Jim, 129
Matchick, Tom, 239
Mathews, Eddie, 49
Mathewson, Christy, 15, 87–88, 90, 96, 131, 264
Mauch, Gene, 305
Maxvill, Dal, 176, 180
Mays, Carl, 63, 99, 192
Mays, Willie, 8, 27, 62, 79, 162, 167, 223, 258, 291, 299

Mazeroski, Bill, 18, 27, 107, 189, 262
McAuliffe, Dick, 28
McCarthy, Joe, 107, 231–32, 238
McCarver, Tim, 186–87, 204–205, 278, 280
McCovey, Willie, 8, 27, 169
McCullough, Clyde, 269–70
McDougald, Gil, 26–27, 33, 154, 186, 222, 303
McEnaney, Will, 19
McGee, Willie, 190, 223–24, 290
McGinnity, Jack, 87
McGowan, George, 67
McGraw, John, 45, 70, 198, 236, 238, 245, 251, 281
McGraw, Tug, 292
McKeon, Jack, 249
McInnis, Stuffy, 63
McKechnie, Bill, 172, 199, 254
McKeon, Jack, 230
McLain, Denny, 91, 170
McLean, Larry, 198
McMullin, Fred, 41
McNally, Dave, 49, 121, 124–25, 128, 233, 259
McNally, Mike, 185
McNamara, John, 234, 239
McNeely, Earl, 16, 66
McQuillan, George, 159
McQuinn, George, 268
McRae, Hal, 19
Medich, Doc, 263
Medwick, Joe, 160, 265–66
Merkle, Fred, 15, 114, 209–10, 264
Mesa, Jose, 22
Messersmith, Andy, 125
Meusel, Bob, 100, 185–86, 287
Meusel, Irish, 287

Meyer, Russ, 156
Meyers, Chief, 15–16, 61, 198
Michaels, Al, 278
Mikklesen, Pete, 187
Miller, Bing, 78, 107–8
Miller, Bob, 102
Miller, Otto, 121
Miljus, Johnny, 115
Mincher, Don, 173
Mitchell, Clarence, 121–22
Mitchell, Dale, 53, 138
Mitchell, Fred, 99
Mitchell, Kevin, 20
Mize, Johnny, 139, 147–48
Mizell, Vinegar Bend, 295
Mogridge, George, 242
Molitor, Paul, 107, 171, 174, 221, 224
Moore, Eddie, 17, 129–30
Moore, Jim, 72
Moore, Mike, 162, 284
Moore, Terry, 96
Moran, Charlie, 57
Moret, Roger, 19, 51
Morgan, Joe, 19, 51, 103, 108
Moriarty, George, 51, 58, 185
Morris, Jack, 29–30, 96, 103, 155, 210
Mueller, Don, 299
Mullin, George, 66
Munson, Thurman, 51–52, 166, 174
Murray, Eddie, 162
Murray, Red, 15, 181
Musial, Stan, 94, 96
Musmanno, Michael, 44
Myers, Hy, 105

Nagy, Charles, 22
Nallin, Dick, 72
Neal, Charlie, 139, 148–49
Neale, Greasy, 282
Nehf, Art, 78, 100, 108
Nen, Rob, 23

Index

Newcombe, Don, 101, 143, 147, 161
Newhouser, Hal, 269, 270
Newson, Bobo, 32
Nicholson, Bill, 270
Niekro, Joe, 228
Niekro, Phil, 13–14, 228
Nixon, Pat, 273
Nixon, Richard, 273
Nolan, Gary, 108, 144
Noles, Dickie, 167
Noren, Irv, 291, 304
Northrup, Jim, 28, 155, 239, 263

Oveak, Frank, 301
O'Connell, Jimmy, 42
O'Dea, Ken, 268
Odom, Blue Moon, 103
Ogden, Curly, 242
Oglivie, Ben, 207
Oliver, Joe, 134
O'Leary, Charley, 294
O'Malley. Walter, 33, 206, 248
O'Neill, Paul, 61
Ormsby, Red, 69
Orta, Jorge, 19
Otis, Amos, 145
Ott, Mel, 142–43, 227
Overall, Orval, 294
Owen, Marv, 176, 182, 265
Owen, Mickey, 106
Owens, Paul, 234, 248
Oyler, Ray, 239

Pagan, Jose, 79
Page, Joe, 32
Paige, Satchel, 143
Palmer, Jim, 50, 139, 219, 233, 259, 294–95
Parent, Freddie, 308
Passeau, Claude, 75–77
Payne, Freddie, 66
Pearson, Monte, 78
Peckinpaugh. Roger, 17, 78
Pena, Alejandro, 30, 152

Pena, Tony, 44
Pendleton, Jim, 299
Pendleton, Terry, 29, 52–53, 127
Pennock, Herb, 295
Pepitone, Joe, 157
Percival, Todd, 23
Perez, Timo, 67
Perez, Tony, 19, 161–62, 248
Perry, Gaylord, 8, 12
Perry, Jim, 12
Pesky, Johnny, 25
Petrocelli, Rico, 64, 112
Petry, Dan, 129
Pettitte, Andy, 103, 214, 262
Pfeister, Jack, 197
Phillippe, Deacon, 3, 5, 87
Phillips, Tony, 129
Piazza, Mike, 54–55
Pick, Charlie, 62–63
Pinelli, Babe, 53, 138
Piniella, Lou, 52, 134, 280, 309
Pipgras, George, 293
Pipp, Wally, 201
Plank, Eddie, 98
Podres, Johnny, 32–33, 138, 156
Polonia, Luis, 210
Poole, Jim, 43
Posada, Jorge, 110
Powell, Boog, 62
Puckett, Kirby, 29–30, 108
Pulli, Frank, 51–52
Purkey, Bob, 200

Quinn, Jack, 225

Randolph, Willie, 200
Rariden, Bill, 72–73
Raschi, Vic, 101, 139, 160
Reagan, Ronald, 273–74, 295
Reardon, Jeff, 36, 150
Reed, Howie, 123
Reed, Ron, 248, 284
Reese, Pee Wee, 33, 189

Reiser, Pete, 104
Remlinger, Mike, 168
Renteria, Edgar, 22, 138
Reynolds, Allie, 101, 139, 186, 295
Rhem, Flint, 159
Rhoden, Rick, 158
Rhodes, Dusty, 148, 172, 258
Rice, Sam, 227–28
Richards, Paul, 305
Richardson, Bobby, 27, 154, 200, 304
Richardson, Gordon, 157
Richert, Pete, 50
Rickey, Branch, 231
Ridner, James, 304–5
Righetti, Dave, 113
Rigler, Cy, 228
Rigney, Bill, 305
Ring, Jimmy, 94
Ripken, Cal, Jr., 178
Ripple, Jimmy, 32
Risberg, Swede, 41
Rivera, Mariano, 23
Rizzuto, Phil, 137–38, 139, 303–4
Roberts, Robin, 102, 232, 258
Robertson, Dave, 282
Robinson, Brooks, 117, 144
Robinson, Don, 141
Robinson, Frank, 97, 113, 117, 125, 160
Robinson, Jackie, 26, 60–61, 143, 160, 223
Robinson, Wilbert, 68
Rodriguez, Francisco, 219
Rodriguez, Frankie, 23
Roe, Preacher, 148
Rogell, Billy, 25, 193
Rohe, George, 197
Rolfe, Red, 284
Roosevelt, Franklin, 272
Roosevelt, Theodore, 6
Root, Charlie, 108, 111, 117
Rose, Pete, 19, 28, 58,

126, 140, 223, 229, 248
Roseboro, Johnny, 178
Rossman, Claude, 294
Roush, Edd, 38
Rowe, Schoolboy, 25
Rowland, Pants, 230
Rudi, Joe, 63
Ruel, Muddy, 16, 66
Ruether, Dutch, 122
Russell, Allan, 122
Russell, Bill, 52
Russell, Jack, 143, 227
Russell, Reb, 281
Russo, Maruis, 189
Ruth, Babe, 7, 24, 40, 63, 79, 99, 105, 111–112, 116–117, 126, 127, 140, 143, 159–60, 201, 204, 223, 231, 257, 272, 293
Ruthven, Dick, 191
Ryan, Nolan, 85, 139
Ryan, Rosy, 122
Ryba, Mike, 226–27

Saberhagen, Bret, 20
Sabo, Chris, 134, 162
Sain, Johnny, 101
Salkeld, Bill, 101
Salmon, Tim, 23
Sand, Heinie, 42
Sanders, Deion, 52–53, 282–83
Sanders, Reggie, 120
Sanford, Jack, 27
Santiago, Jose, 124
Sawyer, Eddie, 232
Sebring, Jimmy, 4
Selkirk, George, 143
Schacht, Al, 99
Schaefer, Germany, 294
Schalk, Ray, 39, 94
Schiraldi, Calvin, 20
Schmidt, Boss, 85
Schmidt, Butch, 185
Schmidt, Jason, 168
Schultz, Barney, 109, 157
Schumacher, Hal, 261
Scott, Everett, 63, 178
Scott, Jack, 95

Shea, Spec, 32
Schang, Wally, 63
Shields, Scot, 264
Schott, Marge, 58–59, 190
Schulte, Wildfire, 67
Seaver, Tom, 86, 128
Seminick, Andy, 232
Sergio, Michael, 55
Sewell, Luke, 227, 268
Shafer, Tilly, 61
Shannon, Mike, 178
Sheckard, Jimmy, 180
Sheehan, Jack, 286
Sherdel, Bill, 116–17, 159
Sherry, Larry, 217
Shotton, Burt, 32, 247
Show, Eric, 162
Sianis, Sam, 6
Sianis, William, 6
Siebern, Norm, 304
Sierra, Ruben, 109
Silvera, Charlie, 203
Simmons, Al, 31, 107–8
Simmons, Curt, 102, 117, 232
Sisler, Dick, 101
Sisler, George, 12
Sister Sledge, 34
Skowron, Bill, 156
Slagle, Jimmy, 66, 184
Slaughter, Enos, 25, 60, 96, 138, 229
Smith, Al (1954, 1959), 139
Smith, Al (1936), 263
Smith, Earl, 17, 211, 228
Smith, Elmer, 121, 154
Smith, Hal, 18
Smith, Lonnie, 29, 155, 209
Smith, Mayo, 91, 238
Smith, Ozzie, 290
Smith, Reggie, 112
Smith, Sherry, 105
Smoltz, John, 103
Snider, Duke, 26, 160
Snodgrass, Fred, 15–16, 114, 264
Snow, J. T., 302

Soar, Hank, 284–85
Sojo, Luis, 136
Soriano, Alfonso, 110
Sosa, Elias, 159
Spahn, Warren, 26, 50, 79, 90
Sparma, Joe, 124
Speaker, Tris, 5, 15–16, 61, 222, 248
Spencer, George, 263
Spezio, Scott, 23, 187
Sprague, Ed, Jr., 150
Sprague, Ed, Sr., 150
Springstead, Marty, 233
Stahl, Chick, 2–3, 56
Stahl, Jake, 5
Stainback, Tuck, 51
Stallings, George, 237, 256
Stanky, Eddie, 104
Stanley, Bob, 20
Stanley, Mickey, 28, 239
Stanton, Mike, 296
Stargell, Willie, 35
Steinbrenner, George, 172, 192, 248
Steinfeldt, Harry, 85
Stengel, Casey, 27, 74, 100, 138, 200, 222, 231, 242, 246–47, 303
Stephens, Arson (Fireball), 305
Stevenson, Adlai, 273
Stewart, Bill, 101, 285
Stewart, Dave, 190, 199
Stoddard, Tim, 284
Stodgill, Ronald, 301
Stodgill, Shiela, 301
Stone, Steve, 233
Strawberry, Darryl, 202
Street, Gabby, 31, 252–53
Stuper, John, 263
Sturdivant, Tom, 33
Sullivan, Bill, Jr., 181
Sullivan, Billy, Sr., 181
Sullivan, Sport, 39
Summers, Ed, 54, 114–15
Summers, Bill, 186

Index

Sutton, Don, 158, 263
Swift, Bob, 77

Tannehill, Lee, 197
Tapani, Kevin, 52
Tate, Benny, 16, 292
Tenace, Gene, 70, 143–44, 214
Terry, Bill, 69
Terry, Ralph, 18, 27, 200
Thomas, Fred, 63
Thomas, Gordon, 224
Thomas, Ira, 131
Thompson, Hank, 299
Thompson, Junior, 112
Thomson, Bobby, 101, 276
Thorpe, Jim, 281–282
Tidrow, Dick, 166
Tolan, Bobby, 28
Toney, Fred, 99
Topping, Dan, 246
Torre, Joe, 136, 248
Torrez, Mike, 233
Trail, Chet, 207
Tresh, Tom, 223
Trucks, Virgil, 270
Tudor, John, 19
Turley, Bob, 26–27, 33, 60
Twain, Mark, 300
Tyler, Lefty, 99

Uecker, Bob, 204
Urbina, Ugeth, 109

Valenzuela, Fernando, 218
Vance, Dazzy, 226
Vaughn, Greg, 120
Vaughn, Hippo, 99
Veale, Bob, 295
Veeck, Bill, 191, 207
Veil, Bucky, 137
Vincent, Fay, 59, 280
Viola, Frank, 36, 127

Virdon, Bill, 189, 305
Vizcaino, Jose, 135–36

Waddell, Rube, 196
Wagner, Heinie, 57
Walberg, Rube, 83
Walk, Bob, 167
Walker, Harry, 25
Walsh, Ed, 77, 84
Walters, Bucky, 122–23
Wambsganss, Bill, 52, 121–22
Waner, Lloyd, 208, 282
Waner, Paul, 208, 282
Wanninger, Pee Wee, 178
Ward, John Montgomery, 238
Wareheim, Linda, 301–2
Warwick, Carl, 172
Washburn, Jarrod, 146, 264
Washburn, Ray, 263
Washington, Claudell, 214
Washington, Herb, 63
Watson, Bob, 145
Weaver, Buck, 40, 72
Weaver, Earl, 233, 238
Weaver, Jeff, 109
Webb, Del, 246
Weber, Ben, 264
Weir, Tom, 305
Weis, Al, 128
Weiss, George, 138, 246
Wells, David, 120
Wertz, Vic, 258
West, David, 65
West, Dick, 199
White, Devon, 53
White, Ernie, 96
Whitehead, George, 63
Whitson, Ed, 162
Wiggins, Alan, 152
Wilde, Oscar, 300
Wilks, Ted, 269
Willard, Jerry, 135
Williams, Billy, 13
Williams, Dib, 31

Williams, Dick, 70, 129, 173, 239, 254, 304
Williams, Lefty, 37–40
Williams, Matt, 129, 210
Williams, Mitch, 106–7, 112
Williams, Ted, 8, 77
Willis, Ron, 263
Willis, Vic, 226
Wilson, Art, 61
Wilson, Hack, 108
Wilson, Jimmie, 71–72, 123
Wilson, Mookie, 20, 70
Wilson, Willie, 292
Wilson, Woodrow, 271
Wiltse, Hooks, 114
Winfield, Dave, 106
Winningham, Herm, 175
Wise, Rick, 118
Witasick, Jay, 262
Witt, George, 169
Wohlers, Mark, 43
Womack, Tony, 23
Wood, Smokey Joe, 15, 57, 88, 96
Woodling, Gene, 138–39, 303
Worrell, Tim, 22, 288
Worrell, Todd, 19, 288
Wyckoff, Weldon, 185

Yastrzemski, Carl, 64, 112, 165
Yde, Emil, 116
Yeager, Steve, 118
Yerkes, Steve, 15–16
York, Rudy, 26, 75
Young, Clara Kimble, 164
Young, Cy, 2, 4, 308
Youngs, Ross, 42

Zarilla, Al, 268
Zeile, Todd, 67
Zimmer, Don, 186
Zimmerman, Heinie, 72–73

About the Author

John Snyder has a master's degree in history from the University of Cincinnati and a passion for baseball. He has authored 12 books on baseball, soccer, football, hockey, tennis, and travel, including Brassey's, Inc.'s *Soccer's Most Wanted: The Top 10 Book of Clumsy Keepers, Clever Crosses, and Outlandish Oddities*. His *Redleg Journal: Year by Year and Day by Day with the Cincinnati Reds Since 1866* (Road West Publishing Company, 2000), with Greg Rhodes, won the 2001 Sporting News–SABR Baseball Research Award. He lives in Cincinnati.

About the Author

Floyd Conner is the author of more than a dozen books. His sports books include *Hockey's Most Wanted, Basketball's Most Wanted, Golf's Most Wanted, Baseball's Most Wanted, Day by Day in Cincinnati Bengals History*, and *This Date in Sports History*. He also co-authored *Day by Day in Cincinnati Reds History* and the best-selling *365 Sports Facts a Year Calendar*. He lives in Cincinnati with his wife, Susan, and son, Travis.

Index

Thurston, Sloppy, 73
Tidrow, Dick, 73
Tinker, Joe, 107, 146, 147
Tipton, Joe, 155
Torre, Joe, 61
Traficant, James, 62
Trammell, Alan, 69
Travis, Cecil, 103
Traynor, Pie, 111, 116
Tresh, Tom, 158
Trucks, Virgil, 86
Turley, Bob, 201
Turner, Ted, 66
Turner, Tina, 21

Uecker, Bob, 14, 27

Valo, Elmer, 55
Van Doren, Mamie, 85
Van Haltren, George, 99, 203
Vance, Dazzy, 234
Vander Meer, Johnny, 83
Veach, Bobby, 119
Veeck, Bill, 5, 50, 66, 241
Verban, Emil, 164
Versailles, Zoilo, 113
Voiselle, Bill, 67
Von der Ahe, Chris, 74
Vonderhorst, Harry, 203

Vukovich, John, 173

Waddell, Rube, 53, 68
Wagner, Honus, 9, 50, 53, 120, 130
Walk, Bob, 43, 206
Walker, Fleet, 237
Walker, Tilly, 95
Wallace, Bobby, 106, 179, 189
Walsh, Ed, 47, 136, 141
Walsh, Ed, Jr., 47
Waltz, John, 203
Waner, Paul, 60, 116
Ward, John Montgomery, 80
Warneke, Lon, 30, 198
Washington, Herb, 227
Watkins, George, 93
Weatherly, Roy, 221
Weaver, Buck, 23, 241
Weaver, Earl, 197
Welch, Bob, 245
Wendelstedt, Harry, 204
Werden, Percival, 82
Westrum, Wes, 112
White, Bill, 210
White, Deacon, 206
White, Fred, 212
White, Will, 96
Wickware, Cannonball, 49
Wilkinson, Bill, 70

Wilks, Ted, 94
Willard, Jerry, 212
Williams, Bernie, 146
Williams, Billy, 188
Williams, Charlie, 152
Williams, Cy, 121
Williams, Ken, 121
Williams, Lefty, 241
Williams, Ted, 33, 114, 115, 130, 131, 134, 187, 194, 240, 244
Williams, Walt, 219
Wilson, Hack, 58, 73, 95
Wilson, Willie, 118
Wilson, Woodrow, 16
Winfield, Dave, 114
Wise, Sam, 1
Witasick, Jay, 186
Wolf, Chicken, 181
Wood, Joe, 80, 87
Woodward, Woody, 164
Wrigley, Philip, 229
Wrona, Rick, 210
Wynn, Early, 42, 52, 102, 148

Young, Cy, 3, 68, 137, 179
Yount, Robin, 118

Zimmer, Don, 29, 203
Zimmerman, Jeff, 229

Index

Regan, Phil, 20
Repoz, Roger, 157
Rettan, Abe, 14
Reulbach, Ed, 121
Rhodes, Dusty, 148, 168
Rice, Jim, 171
Rice, Sam, 118
Richards, Paul, 165
Richmond, John Lee, 84
Rigler, Charles, 205
Ripken, Cal, 118, 224
Risberg, Swede, 241
Rivers, Mickey, 210
Rixey, Eppa, 105
Rizzuto, Phil, 109, 210
Roberts, Dave, 211
Roberts, Robin, 17, 183, 191
Robertson, Charlie, 84
Robinson, Brooks, 67, 145, 190
Robinson, Frank, 63, 120, 128, 145, 148
Robinson, Jackie, 49, 108, 114, 123, 150, 237, 240, 241
Robinson, Wilbert, 14
Robinson, Yank, 74
Robison, Matthew, 179
Rodgers, Buck, 85
Rodriguez, Alex, 25, 147
Rodriguez, Aurelio, 9
Rose, Pete, 45, 74, 89, 121, 132, 144, 150, 152, 153, 191
Rose, Pete, Jr., 45
Roush, Edd, 21
Rowan, Dave, 77
Ruffing, Red, 145, 152
Ruppert, Jacob, 27, 213
Rusie, Amos, 238
Russell, Bill, 165
Russell, Reb, 81
Ruth, Babe, 1, 3, 7, 18, 20, 33, 43, 50, 57, 62, 65, 79, 85, 119, 121, 126, 127, 133, 143, 144, 145, 149, 150, 182, 185, 190, 210, 228, 237, 239, 241, 244
Ryan, Jimmy, 99
Ryan, Johnny, 71
Ryan, Nolan, 104, 138, 139, 211
Ryan, Rosie, 39
Rye, Gene, 158

Sabathia, C.C., 225
Sabo, Chris, 208
Sakata, Lenn, 226
Sandberg, Ryne, 217
Santo, Ron, 102, 188
Sawyer, Eddie, 183
Schalk, Ray, 107
Schiraldi, Calvin, 185
Schmidt, Henry, 159
Schmidt, Mike, 128, 191
Schmit, Crazy, 180
Schmitz, Johnny, 32
Schulte, Frank, 113
Schuster, Bill, 207
Scioscia, Mike, 170
Score, Herb, 44, 212
Scully, Vin, 204
Seaver, Tom, 139, 154, 191
Sebring, Jimmy, 3
Selkirk, George, 145
Seybold, Socks, 233
Seymour, Cy, 15, 81
Shafer, Tillie, 39
Sheehan, Tom, 182
Shelton, Skeeter, 172
Shepherd, Jean, 165
Sherlock, Vince, 75
Shires, Art, 40
Shore, Ernie, 85
Silva, Jose, 224
Simmons, Al, 111, 120, 144, 150
Simmons, Ted, 104
Simpson, Wayne, 88
Sisler, Dick, 48, 78
Sisler, George, 48, 121, 129, 135
Sisti, Sibby, 111
Skaugstad, Dave, 76
Skizas, Lou, 201
Skopec, John, 2
Skowron, Moose, 37, 201
Smith, Charley, 154
Smith, Elmer, 81, 227
Smith, Germany, 227
Snider, Duke, 102, 114, 150, 240
Snodgrass, Fred, 151
Sosa, Sammy, 113, 116, 127, 133, 187
Spahn, Warren, 12, 137
Sparks, Steve, 226
Speaker, Tris, 116, 130, 240
Spooner, Karl, 87
Stallings, George, 202
Stargell, Willie, 120
Stearnes, Turkey, 51, 124
Stengel, Casey, 47, 59, 64, 146, 177, 181, 182, 199, 201, 210, 211, 220, 222
Stenzel, Jake, 227
Stephens, Vern, 104
Stevens, Connie, 85
Stillwell, Kurt, 23
Stone, Steve, 161, 163, 217, 218, 219
Stovey, Harry, 100
Stratton, Monty, 7
Straub, Joe, 55
Strawberry, Darryl, 124
Strike, John, 43
Stuart, Dick, 171
Suck, Tony, 37
Summa, Homer, 43
Sutcliffe, Rick, 92
Sutherland, Suds, 77
Suzuki, Ichiro, 54, 147
Swormstedt, Len, 76

Taft, William Howard, 19, 31
Terry, Bill, 106, 243
Tesreau, Jess, 151
Thevenow, Tommy, 162
Thompson, Fresco, 167
Thomson, Bobby, 56, 66
Thorpe, Jim, 207
Throneberry, Marv, 181

Index

McCarthy, Joe, 197
McCarthy, Tommy, 105
McCovey, Willie, 190
McCurdy, Harry, 154
McDonald, Ben, 61
McDonald, Darnell, 170
McDougal, John, 176
McDougald, Gil, 44
McDowell, Sam, 153
McGraw, Bob, 154
McGraw, John, 33, 50, 111, 117, 151, 238
McGriff, Fred, 32
McGwire, Mark, 5, 113, 127, 128, 133, 190
McLain, Denny, 244
McMahon, Sadie, 41
McMullin, Fred, 241
McNally, Dave, 145, 148
McPhee, Bid, 12
McRae, Hal, 204
Meadows, Rufe, 77
Medwick, Joe, 26, 133, 186
Mele, Sam, 94
Merkle, Fred, 33
Messersmith, Andy, 65
Meusel, Bob, 119, 143
Meyer, Billy, 183
Mientkiewicz, Doug, 208
Miller, Bing, 120, 144, 166
Miller, Roscoe, 93
Miller, Russ, 176
Mize, Johnny, 115
Molesworth, Carlton, 36
Molitor, Paul, 114
Moore, Mike, 212
Morales, Jose, 122
Moren, Lew, 26
Moreno, Omar, 67
Morgan, Joe, 121, 144, 150
Morgan, Ray, 85
Moyer, Jamie, 148
Mulcahy, Hugh, 33
Mullane, Tony, 99
Murphy, Rob, 70
Murray, Bill, 218
Murray, Eddie, 115

Murray, Jim, 234
Murray, Red, 184
Musial, Stan, 130, 135, 143
Myers, Elmer, 182

Nabors, Jack, 176, 182
Nash, Jim, 92
Necciai, Ron, 156
Nelson, Jeff, 8
Neville, Dan, 77
Newcombe, Don, 115
Newhouser, Hal, 148
Nicholson, Dave, 157
Nixon, Richard, 17, 20
Nixon, Russ, 169
Noles, Dickie, 59
Novikoff, Lou, 229
Nuxhall, Joe, 221

O'Day, Henry, 202
O'Doul, Lefty, 79, 183
O'Farrell, Bob, 113
O'Hara, Novella, 13
O'Leary, Charley, 112
O'Malley, Walter, 240
O'Neill, Paul, 145
O'Neill, Tip, 133
O'Toole, Patsy, 12
Oliva, Tony, 61
Olivares, Omar, 65
Oliver, Al, 120
Oliver, Tom, 163
Orr, Dave, 100
Orta, Jorge, 165
Ott, Mel, 113, 192, 193
Overall, Orval, 146
Owen, Marv, 186
Owens, Brick, 85

Paciorek, John, 75
Padgett, Don, 161
Pafko, Andy, 11
Paige, Satchel, 50, 51
Palmer, Jim, 61, 88, 136, 145, 224
Parrish, Lance, 21
Parrott, Tom, 206
Partenheimer, Stanwood, 36
Pascual, Camilo, 239
Patterson, Roy, 2

Peckinpaugh, Roger, 113
Peel, Homer, 154
Peitz, Heinie, 209
Pellagrini, Eddie, 66
Pendleton, Terry, 220
Pennock, Herb, 143
Perconte, Jack, 210
Perdue, Hub, 110
Perez, Tony, 121, 144, 150, 185
Perry, Gaylord, 153
Pettis, Gary, 10
Pettit, Paul, 156
Pfiester, Jack, 146
Piazza, Mike, 116
Pickering, Urbane, 38
Piersall, Jim, 19
Pike, Lipman, 71, 227
Pinelli, Babe, 220
Piniella, Lou, 37, 60, 222
Pinson, Vada, 120
Pipp, Wally, 1
Plank, Eddie, 23
Plunk, Eric, 42
Poffenberger, Boots, 64
Poles, Spotswood, 51
Poloni, John, 154
Pool, Harlin, 92
Popovich, Paul, 204
Portugal, Mark, 220
Powell, Boog, 145, 148
Powell, Sherman, 13
Power, Vic, 44
Pregenzer, John, 13

Quinn, Joe, 179, 180
Quirk, Jamie, 222
Quisenberry, Dan, 234

Radbourn, George, 46
Radbourn, Hoss, 46, 140
Ramos, Pedro, 239
Ramsey, Toad, 29, 181
Raymond, Bugs, 63
Reach, Al, 25
Reagan, Ronald, 17, 216
Reese, Pee Wee, 102, 108, 150, 169, 240

Hoover, Herbert, 18
Hornsby, Rogers, 129, 134, 194
Hough, Charlie, 168
Houk, Ralph, 199
Hoyt, LaMarr, 96
Hoyt, Waite, 22, 57, 62, 143, 213
Hubbs, Ken, 9
Hudson, Tim, 5
Hughey, Jim, 179
Hulbert, William, 230
Hunter, Jim, 30, 146
Hunter, Skinhead, 207
Hutchinson, Fred, 220

Incaviglia, Pete, 125, 167
Irwin, Art, 2

Jackson, Andrew, 217
Jackson, Joe, 5, 116, 129, 241
Jackson, Larry, 95
Jackson, Ransom, 217
Jackson, Reggie, 128, 146, 168, 191
Jacoby, Brook, 72
James, Bill, 159
Jenkins, Ferguson, 159
Jeter, Derek, 146, 203
John, Tommy, 103
Johnson, Davey, 160
Johnson, Judy, 41, 51
Johnson, Randy, 61, 224
Johnson, Walter, 8, 49, 88, 136, 140
Johnstone, Jay, 10
Jolley, Smead, 166
Jones, Bumpus, 83
Jones, Charley, 71, 181

Kaat, Jim, 104
Kafora, Jake, 63
Kaline, Al, 114
Kanehl, Rod, 32
Kapler, Gabe, 67
Kelly, Bob, 213
Kelly, King, 167
Kelly, Pat, 219
Kelly, Tom, 198

Kennedy, John, 19
Kerfeld, Charlie, 11, 61, 72
Kieschnick, Brooks, 217
Killebrew, Harmon, 102, 128, 192
Kilroy, Matches, 142
Kiner, Ralph, 126, 211
Kingman, Dave, 224
Kittle, Ron, 68, 226
Klein, Chuck, 183
Klutts, Mickey, 36
Knickerbocker, Austin, 36
Kolb, Eddie, 180
Konstanty, Jim, 113
Koosman, Jerry, 26
Koufax, Sandy, 87, 139, 240
Krock, Gus, 161
Kruk, John, 57, 65
Kubek, Tony, 224
Kuenn, Harvey, 160
Kuiper, Duane, 163
Kull, John, 75

Laabs, Chet, 22
Lajoie, Nap, 134, 189
Landis, Kenesaw, 241, 242
Lange, Bill, 231
Lanier, Hal, 112
Larkin, Barry, 23
Larsen, Don, 29, 86, 93
LaRussa, Tony, 199
Lasorda, Tom, 61, 170, 198
Latham, Arlie, 68
Lawless, Tom, 152
Lazzeri, Tony, 143, 145
Lee, Bill, 29, 203
Lee, Hal, 182
Lefler, Wade, 75
Leja, Frank, 157
Lemon, Bob, 60, 148
Lemon, Chet, 124
Leonard, Buck, 50, 237
Leonard, Dutch, 140
Levsen, Dutch, 243
Leyland, Jim, 198
Lloyd, John Henry, 50

Logan, Johnny, 210
Lombardi, Ernie, 169
Long, Herman, 101
Lopat, Ed, 146
Louise, Tina, 85
Lowenstein, John, 208
Luque, Dolf, 220
Lynch, Tom, 233
Lyons, Steve, 154, 208
Lyons, Ted, 188

Mack, Connie, 28, 51, 97, 136, 144, 182
MacPhail, Larry, 70
Maddux, Greg, 136
Madlock, Bill, 67, 211
Magrane, Joe, 223
Mails, Duster, 206
Mangual, Pepe, 165
Manning, Jack, 71
Mantle, Mickey, 6, 36, 57, 144, 146, 158
Manuel, Charlie, 212, 225
Maranville, Rabbit, 58, 106, 207
Marichal, Juan, 102
Maris, Roger, 126, 127, 144, 154, 158
Marquard, Rube, 151
Marshall, Mike, 216
Martin, Billy, 10, 59, 234
Martin, Pepper, 30, 73
Martinez, Carlos, 167
Martinez, Tino, 145
Mathews, Bobby, 2
Mathews, Eddie, 102, 114, 195
Mathewson, Christy, 46, 136, 137, 141, 151, 159, 204, 238
Mathewson, Henry, 46
Maxvill, Dal, 185
May, Carlos, 66, 219
May, Dave, 153
May, Lee, 121
Mays, Willie, 53, 115, 120, 127, 148, 152, 192
McAleer, Jimmy, 35
McBride, George, 166

Index 251

Drysdale, Don, 102, 240
Duffy, Frank, 153
Duffy, Hugh, 106, 135
Dugan, Joe, 57
Dunlap, Fred, 96
Dunn, Jack, 112
Dunston, Shawon, 224
Durocher, Leo, 33, 59, 168, 169, 194, 196, 203
Durst, Cedric, 152
Dykes, Jimmy, 165

Earnshaw, George, 144
Ebbets, Charles, 159
Eisenhower, Dwight, 17
Elia, Lee, 60
Ellsworth, Dick, 9
Engle, Joe, 227
Ens, Jewel, 111
Epps, Aubrey, 75
Estrada, Chuck, 88
Evers, Johnny, 107, 146, 147, 195
Ewing, Bob, 229
Ewing, John, 181

Fain, Ferris, 22
Faul, Bill, 62
Feller, Bob, 11, 27, 148, 156
Felsch, Oscar, 241
Felton, Terry, 176, 212
Fernandez, Sid, 65
Ferrell, Rick, 105
Ferrell, Wes, 105, 221
Fidrych, Mark, 89
Fielder, Cecil, 43, 171, 226
Fields, Bruce, 42
Fingers, Rollie, 146
Finlayson, Pembroke, 37
Finley, Charles, 30, 233
Fisher, Cherokee, 1
Fisher, Jack, 244
Flick, Elmer, 240
Foley, Will, 71
Force, Davy, 163
Ford, Gerald, 19

Ford, Whitey, 60, 136, 145, 146
Foster, Eddie, 162
Foster, George, 144, 153
Foster, Rube, 53
Foutz, Dave, 81
Fox, Nellie, 155
Foxx, Jimmie, 28, 120, 126, 144
Francona, Tito, 160
Frazee, Harry, 238
Fregosi, Jim, 57, 122
Frisch, Frankie, 117, 210, 220, 223
Funk, Liz, 39
Furillo, Carl, 150

Gaedel, Eddie, 66
Gallagher, Al, 72
Gandil, Chick, 21, 241
Garagiola, Joe, 169
Garner, John Nance, 166
Garvey, Steve, 104
Gastfield, Ed, 172
Gehrig, Lou, 5, 50, 65, 119, 135, 143, 144, 145, 149, 150, 157
Geishert, Vern, 153
Gettman, Jake, 55
Gibson, Bob, 141
Gibson, Josh, 26, 49, 237, 241
Gillenwater, Carden, 36
Gomez. Lefty, 27, 145
Gonzalez, Fernando, 211
Gonzalez, Luis, 5
Gooden, Dwight, 90
Gordon, Joe, 19, 103
Gossage, Goose, 224
Gould, Charlie, 71
Gowdy, Hank, 110
Graddock, Frank, 15
Graney, Jack, 3
Grant, Eddie, 110
Grant, Ulysses, 16
Grantham, George, 34
Gray, Dolly, 40
Greenberg, Hank, 106
Greengrass, Jim, 43

Greif, Bill, 37
Griffey, Ken, 45
Griffey, Ken, Jr., 45, 116, 126, 147, 187
Grim, Bob, 91
Grimes, Burleigh, 242
Groom, Bob, 85
Grove, Lefty, 137, 144, 150
Grove, Orval, 112
Grubb, Johnny, 211
Guillen, Ozzie, 206
Gullett, Don, 89
Gwynn, Tony, 132, 243, 244

Hahn, Ed, 162
Hall, Irv, 163
Hamric, Odbert, 36
Hanlon, Ned, 203
Harding, Warren, 20
Harper, Terry, 225
Harris, Gail, 40
Harris, Greg, 226
Harrison, Benjamin, 16
Harshman, Jack, 79
Hastings, Scott, 71
Hawley, Pink, 209
Heath, Jeff, 124
Hebner, Richie, 24
Hecker, Guy, 80, 183
Heilmann, Harry, 130, 189
Henriksen, Olaf, 56
Herman, Babe, 103, 167
Herman, Billy, 194
Hernandez, Roberto, 225
Herrera, Jose, 170
Herriage, Troy, 175
Herrmann, Garry, 62
Hershiser, Orel, 190
Herzog, Buck, 205
Hill, Bill, 180
Hodges, Gil, 102, 108, 150, 184, 240
Hogan, Shanty, 170
Holbert, Bill, 162
Hollingsworth, Bonnie, 41
Holloman, Bobo, 84

Index

Brenly, Bob, 218
Bresnahan, Roger, 195
Bressler, Rube, 82
Brett, George, 12, 214, 222, 244
Bridges, Rocky, 152, 213
Bridwell, Al, 34, 162
Brock, Lou, 117
Brookens, Tom, 123, 224
Brown, Eddie, 34
Brown, Mordecai, 121, 142, 146, 147, 195
Brown, Willard, 123
Browning, Pete, 98, 168
Buckner, Bill, 7, 61, 74, 185
Bunker, Wally, 88
Bunning, Jim, 17
Burdette, Lew, 10
Burkett, Jesse, 32, 117, 179
Bush, George H. W., 20
Bush, George W., 16
Bush, Guy, 244
Bush, Joe, 182
Butler, Brett, 225
Butler, John, 174

Cabell, Enos, 211
Cahill, George, 3
Caldwell, Mike, 211
Campanella, Roy, 115, 150, 240
Canseco, Jose, 167, 224
Cantwell, Ben, 176, 178
Caray, Harry, 17, 216, 217, 218, 219
Caray, Skip, 219
Cardenal, Jose, 225
Cardwell, Don, 86
Carew, Rod, 244
Carey, Max, 50
Carlton, Steve, 139, 245
Carman, Don, 172
Caruthers, Bob, 99
Cash, Norm, 97, 160
Castleman, Foster, 36
Castro, Fidel, 239
Cater, Danny, 35

Caudill, Bob, 60, 123
Caylor, O.P., 202
Cepeda, Orlando, 123
Cerv, Bob, 201
Cey, Ron, 30
Chance, Dean, 22, 87
Chance, Frank, 107, 146, 147
Charboneau, Joe, 91
Charleston, Oscar, 50
Chester, Hilda, 13
Chiles, Pearce, 35
Chrisley, Neil, 40
Christenson, Walter, 29
Christmas, Steve, 158
Churn, Chuck, 182
Cicotte, Eddie, 96, 241
Clarke, Fred, 120
Clarkson, John, 71, 141
Clay, Ken, 153
Clemens, Roger, 67, 139
Clemente, Roberto, 54, 120
Cleveland, Grover, 16, 17
Cobb, Ty, 6, 50, 51, 67, 73, 116, 119, 129, 130, 134, 146, 152, 187, 189, 191, 239
Cochrane, Mickey, 117, 120, 144
Coleman, Choo Choo, 181
Coleman, Jerry, 210, 211
Coleman, John, 175
Colliflower, Harry, 175, 180
Collins, Eddie, 116
Combs, Earle, 143
Comiskey, Charles, 83
Compton, Pete, 41
Cone, David, 146
Connor, Roger, 193
Consolo, Billy, 157
Coolidge, Calvin, 20
Corbett, Gene, 173
Corcoran, Larry, 100
Cottier, Chuck, 201
Cox, Bobby, 199
Craft, Molly, 39

Crandall, Del, 210
Cravath, Gavvy, 231, 234
Creeden, Pat, 35
Criger, Lou, 111
Crystal, Billy, 7
Cuellar, Mike, 145, 148
Culver, George, 83
Cummings, Candy, 71, 107

Dandridge, Ray, 51
Dark, Alvin, 193
Davidson, Billy Joe, 156
Davis, Daisy, 39
Davis, Pamela, 4
Davis, Peaches, 39
Davis, Willie, 184,
Dawson, Andre, 217
De Haas, Frank, 179
De Leon, Jose, 178
Dean, Daffy, 90, 223
Dean, Dizzy, 89, 223
Delahanty, Ed, 47, 117
Delahanty, Frank, 47
Delahanty, Jim, 47
Delahanty, Joe, 47
Delahanty, Tom, 47
Delgado, Carlos, 67
Dernier, Bob, 217
Deshaies, Jim, 111
Devlin, Art, 14
Devlin, Jim, 140
Dewald, Charlie, 77
Diaz, Bo, 170
Dibble, Rob, 220
Dickey, Bill, 106, 117, 145
DiMaggio, Dom, 47, 58
DiMaggio, Joe, 47, 58, 106, 145, 238
DiMaggio, Vince, 47, 58
Ditmar, Art, 186
Doby, Larry, 148
Donohue, Tom, 21
Donovan, Patsy, 39
Douglas, Whammy, 38
Douglass, Astyanax, 38
Drabowsky, Moe, 56
Drago, Dick, 245
Dressen, Chuck, 201
Dropo, Walt, 92

Index

Aaron, Hank, 10, 45, 126, 127, 153, 161, 245
Aaron, Tommie, 46
Adcock, Joe, 152
Adduci, Jim, 172
Aguirre, Hank, 172
Alexander, Grover Cleveland, 17, 83, 137, 142, 154
Alfonseca, Antonio, 29
Allen, Lee, 202
Alston, Walter, 198
Andersen, Larry, 213
Anderson, Brady, 160
Anderson, Harry, 161
Anderson, John, 55
Anderson, Sparky, 89, 143, 199
Ann-Margret, 85
Anson, Cap, 16
Appling, Luke, 193
Aragon, Angel, 173
Armbruster, Charlie, 173
Ashburn, Richie, 95
Ashford, Tucker, 211
Averill, Earl, 23, 48, 89
Averill, Earl, Jr., 48
Avila, Bobby, 148

Bagwell, Jeff, 213
Bailes, Scott, 226
Bailey, Sweetbreads, 61
Baker, Frank, 19
Baldwin, Lady, 39
Ball, Neal, 42
Bancroft, Dave, 106
Bankhead, Don, 3
Banks, Ernie, 104, 187, 188
Bannon, Jimmy, 97
Barfield, Jesse, 210
Barnes, Ross, 1
Barr, Scotty, 173
Bates, Frank, 180
Batts, Matt, 42
Baumgardner, George, 25
Beaumont, Ginger, 120
Beck, Boom Boom, 59
Beck, Erve, 2
Beck, Walter, 222
Beckwith, John, 49
Belinsky, Bo, 12, 14, 84
Bell, Buddy, 211
Bell, Cool Papa, 50, 237
Bell, George, 217
Belle, Albert, 221
Bench, Johnny, 69, 121, 144, 150, 158
Bender, Chief, 97
Berg, Moe, 245
Bergen, Bill, 173
Bergen, Marty, 110
Berger, Wally, 182, 186
Berra, Dale, 46
Berra, Yogi, 46, 70, 86, 122, 146, 199, 210, 211
Bertoia, Reno, 55
Bessent, Don, 29
Biggio, Craig, 72
Billings, Josh, 163
Biras, Steve, 76
Bisland, Rivington, 38
Blackburne, Lena, 40
Blass, Steve, 176
Blewett, Bob, 36
Blyleven, Bert, 102
Boggs, Wade, 115, 132
Bond, Tommy, 100
Bonds, Barry, 8, 45, 127, 133, 188
Bonds, Bobby, 45
Bonura, Zeke, 165
Booe, Everitt, 37
Boone, Bret, 148
Booth, Amos, 209
Boudreau, Lou, 244
Bouton, Jim, 97
Bowens, Sam, 91
Bradley, Alva, 221
Bradley, George, 92, 141, 142
Branca, Ralph, 56, 66
Bransfield, Kitty, 40
Branyan, Russell, 212
Breadon, Sam, 27

Nathan, David. *The McFarland Baseball Quotation Dictionary*. Jefferson, N.C.: McFarland and Company, 2000.

Nemec, David. *Great Baseball Feats, Facts, & Firsts*. New York: Plume Books, 1987.

Okrent, Daniel and Steve Wulf. *Baseball Anecdotes*. New York: Oxford University Press, 1989.

Peary, Danny. *Cult Baseball Players*. New York: Fireside Books, 1990.

Phillips, Louis and Burnham Holmes. *The Complete Books of Sports Nicknames*. Los Angeles: Renaissance Books, 1998.

Pietrusza, David, Matthew Silverman, and Michael Gershman. *Baseball: The Biographical Encyclopedia*. New York: Total Sports Publishing, 2000.

Rhodes, Greg and John Snyder. *Redleg Journal*. Cincinnati: Road West Publishing, 2000.

Shatzkin, Mike. *The Ballplayers*. New York: Arbor House, 1990.

Snyder, John. *Play Ball*. San Francisco: Chronicle Books, 1991.

Stone, Steve and Barry Rozner. *Where's Harry?* Dallas: Taylor Publishing, 1999.

Strang, Mark. *Cleveland Indians Illustrated*. Wilmington, Ohio: Orange Frazer Press, 2000.

Thorn, John and Pete Palmer. *Total Baseball*. New York: Warner Books, 1998.

Wheeler, Lonnie and John Baskin. *The Cincinnati Game*. Wilmington, Ohio: Orange Frazer Press, 1988.

Wolfe, Rich and George Castle. *I Remember Harry Caray*. Champaign, Ill.: Sports Publishing, 1998.

Zimmer, Don and Bill Madden. *Zim*. Kingston, N.Y.: Total Sports Publishing, 2001.

Bibliography

Blake, Mike. *Baseball's Bad Hops and Lucky Bounces*. Cincinnati: Betterway Books, 1995.

Boyd, Brendan and Fred Harris. *The Great American Baseball Card Flipping, Trading, and Bubble Gum Book*. Boston: Little, Brown and Company, 1973.

Dewey, Donald and Nicholas Acocella. *The Biographical History of Baseball*. New York: Carroll and Graf Publishers, 1995.

Dickson, Paul. *Baseball's Greatest Quotations*. New York: Edward Burlingame Books, 1991.

Fusselle, Warner. *Baseball . . . A Laughing Matter*. St. Louis: Sporting News Publishing, 1987.

James, Bill. *The New Bill James Historical Baseball Abstract*. New York: The Free Press, 2001.

Lyons, Jeffrey and Douglas Lyons. *Curveballs and Screwballs*. New York: Random House, 2001.

———. *Out of Left Field*. New York: Times Books, 1998.

Nash, Bruce and Allan Zullo. *Baseball Confidential*. New York: Pocket Books, 1988.

———. *The Baseball Hall of Shame*. New York: Pocket Books, 1985.

Tigers in 1968. The highest win total since McLain's incredible season was 27 by Philadelphia's Steve Carlton in 1972 and Oakland's Bob Welch in 1990.

9. **MOE BERG**

Moe Berg was a light-hitting catcher who played in the major leagues from 1923 to 1939. The brainy Berg was a magna cum laude graduate from Princeton, spoke a dozen languages, and was an atomic spy for the United States during World War II. Despite his vast intellectual interests, Berg's final thoughts were about baseball. Just before he died on May 29, 1972, Berg's last words were, "How did the Mets do today?"

10. **DICK DRAGO**

Hank Aaron hit his 755th home run on July 20, 1976. The home run king hit his final home run off of Dick Drago of the California Angels.

pitch were permitted to use it until their retirement. Grimes, who retired in 1934, was the last of the legal spitballers. The Hall of Famer won 236 of his 270 victories after the rule change.

4. GUY BUSH

Babe Ruth hit his 714th and final home run on May 25, 1935. It was Ruth's third home run of the game and the tape measure blast cleared the roof of Pittsburgh's Forbes Field. The pitcher who surrendered the historic homer was the Pirates' Guy Bush. Bush admitted, "I never saw a ball hit so hard."

5. TED WILLIAMS

Ted Williams was the last player to bat .400 in the major leagues. The Red Sox outfielder hit .406 in 1941. Since that time Rod Carew, George Brett, and Tony Gwynn all flirted with .400 only to fall a few points short.

6. LOU BOUDREAU

The last player–manager whose team won a world championship was Lou Boudreau. He played shortstop and managed the Cleveland Indians to a World Series victory in 1948. Boudreau batted .355 and was voted the American League's Most Valuable Player.

7. JACK FISHER

Ted Williams closed out his career in storybook fashion by hitting a home run in his last at-bat in 1960. The pitcher who served up Williams's last homer was Baltimore's Jack Fisher.

8. DENNY McLAIN

The last pitcher to win 30 games in a season was Denny McLain. McLain won 31 games for the Detroit

The Ninth Inning

Let's conclude the book with a list of notable baseball lasts.

1. DUTCH LEVSEN

The last pitcher to start and complete both games of a doubleheader was Cleveland righthander Dutch Levsen. On August 28, 1926, Levsen defeated the Boston Red Sox 6–1 and 5–1. Amazingly, Levsen did not strike out a batter in either game. Levsen retired in 1928 with a 21–26 record.

2. BILL TERRY

The last player to bat .400 in the National League was Bill Terry. The New York Giants' first baseman batted .401 in 1930. The closest anyone has come since is San Diego's Tony Gwynn's .394 mark in 1994.

3. BURLEIGH GRIMES

The last legal spitball pitcher in the major leagues was Burleigh Grimes. In 1920, the spitball and other pitches in which the ball was doctored were outlawed in major league baseball. Seventeen pitchers who relied on the

saw Landis banned the players from baseball for life. If the fix had not been uncovered, Shoeless Joe Jackson, a .356 lifetime hitter, would be in the Hall of Fame. Pitcher Eddie Cicotte, who won 208 games, might also have been enshrined in Cooperstown. The White Sox, who have not won a world championship since 1917, might have remained a contender instead of spending most of the next two decades in the second division. The job of the Baseball Commissioner, created to restore public confidence in the honesty of the game, might not have become the powerful position it is today. In all likelihood, there would have been more game fixing. In the film *Field of Dreams* some player other than Shoeless Joe Jackson would have emerged from the cornfield.

most of the 1952 and 1953 seasons to serve in Korea. Williams finished his career with 521 home runs but might have broken Babe Ruth's record of 714 had he not missed those seasons. Williams probably also would have been the career leader in runs, runs batted in, and walks.

9. BILL VEECK'S PHILLIES

Baseball's color barrier would have been broken in 1944 if Bill Veeck had had his way. In 1944, the maverick owner attempted to buy the Philadelphia Phillies. His plan was to stock the team with stars from the Negro Leagues. Major League baseball, headed by Commissioner Kenesaw Landis, was not yet ready to permit African Americans to compete. The Phillies were quickly sold to another owner. If Veeck had been allowed to buy the Phillies, the integration of baseball would have been expedited. Philadelphia, long a second division team, would have become an instant contender. Jackie Robinson, who broke the color barrier in 1947, would not have become a cultural icon, and the great Negro League catcher Josh Gibson would have had the opportunity to play in the major leagues.

10. THE BLACK SOX WERE NEVER BANNED

The Chicago White Sox threw the 1919 World Series to the Cincinnati Reds. Players involved in the fix were outfielders Shoeless Joe Jackson and Oscar Felsch; infielders Chick Gandil, Buck Weaver, Swede Risberg, and Fred McMullin; and pitchers Eddie Cicotte and Lefty Williams. Once the scandal was exposed, the eight players were tried in Chicago but were acquitted after their signed confessions mysteriously disappeared. However, new Baseball Commissioner Kene-

pered young outfielder Ty Cobb to Cleveland for the 1905 batting champion Elmer Flick. The Indians turned down the trade, a decision they would soon regret. Flick, bothered by a stomach ailment, played in only 99 games in his last three seasons and retired in 1910. Cobb starred with the Tigers until 1926, winning a dozen batting titles. If Ty Cobb had teamed with Tris Speaker in Cleveland, the Indians probably would have won more pennants.

7. THE BROOKLYN DODGERS

The Dodgers were the pride of Brooklyn from 1890 to 1957. During their last decade of existence, the Brooklyn Dodgers won six pennants. Their powerful lineup included Duke Snider, Jackie Robinson, Roy Campanella, Gil Hodges, and Pee Wee Reese. When owner Walter O'Malley moved the Dodgers to Los Angeles in 1958, he broke the hearts of the team's legions of devoted fans in the borough of Brooklyn. But in Los Angeles the Dodgers reached even greater heights, both on the diamond and financially. The move of the Brooklyn Dodgers and New York Giants to California signaled an exodus of teams to the west. Major league baseball finally became a bi-coastal game. If the Dodgers had remained in Brooklyn, the New York Mets may never have existed and Los Angeles would have never enjoyed the talents of Sandy Koufax and Don Drysdale.

8. TED WILLIAMS'S LOST YEARS

Ted Williams was one of the greatest hitters in baseball history, an amazing achievement considering that he missed five seasons in his prime to serve in the military. Williams missed three seasons during World War II and

because of concern about the injury. The New York Yankees signed DiMaggio, and the Yankee Clipper became one of the greatest players of his era. DiMaggio helped the Yankees maintain their excellence despite the loss of Babe Ruth. With DiMaggio in the lineup, the Yankees won ten pennants between 1936 and 1951. By contrast, the Chicago Cubs have not won a pennant since 1945 nor a world championship since 1908. If they had had DiMaggio, the Cubs probably would have won at least a few more championships and may have changed the direction of the franchise.

5. **IF FIDEL CASTRO BECAME A SENATOR**

In his youth, Fidel Castro was a talented pitcher in Cuba. He was so promising that he was given a tryout by the Washington Senators. In the 1950s, Washington signed Cuban pitchers Camilo Pascual and Pedro Ramos. Castro had good stuff but was not signed because of control problems. He gave up baseball and later became a revolutionary in Cuba. In 1959, Castro led a Communist revolt that overthrew the government. Since that time, Castro has been dictator. If he had been signed by Washington, we might have known Fidel Castro as a Senator. Cuba may not have become a Communist country and would still have diplomatic relations with the United States. There might have been no Bay of Pigs invasion or Cuban Missile Crisis. One thing might not have changed: the Washington Senators probably still would have finished last in the American League.

6. **COBB IN CLEVELAND**

The best trades are often the ones not made. In 1908, the Detroit Tigers considered trading their hot-tem-

1916, and 1918. In the worst decision in baseball history, Boston owner Harry Frazee sold his star to the New York Yankees for $125,000. Ruth became the greatest slugger in baseball history and played on seven pennant winners in New York between 1921 and 1932. The Yankees became the dominant team in baseball while the Red Sox have not won a world championship since the Babe's departure in 1919. If Ruth had not been sold to New York, perhaps Boston would have become baseball's most storied franchise. The Yankees, who had never won a pennant prior to acquiring Ruth, may have remained also-rans.

3. THE TRADING OF CHRISTY MATHEWSON

The Cincinnati Reds thought they made a good deal in 1900 when they traded 21-year-old pitcher Christy Mathewson to the New York Giants for 29-year-old Amos Rusie. Known as the Hoosier Thunderbolt, Rusie had already won 243 games, while Mathewson had not yet won a game. Mathewson won 372 games for the Giants between 1901 and 1916, while Rusie never won another game. The Giants won four pennants with Mathewson between 1905 and 1913 and became one of the National League's most successful teams. Cincinnati did not win its first pennant until 1919. If the trade had not been made, the Reds may have won several more pennants, and Giants' manager John McGraw may not have become a baseball legend.

4. THE CUB CLIPPER

Outfielder Joe DiMaggio was a hot prospect in the minor leagues until he tore cartilage in his knee getting out of a cab in 1934. The Chicago Cubs had the opportunity to purchase DiMaggio's contract but declined

What If?

Who knows what would have happened if Babe Ruth had stayed in this Red Sox jersey? Generations of Boston fans surely wish he had.

What If?

The source of baseball history might have been quite different if certain events had been altered.

1. **THE COLOR BARRIER**

In 1884, Fleet Walker became the first African American to play in the major leagues when he appeared in 42 games for the Toledo Blue Stockings of the American Association. Three years later, African Americans were prohibited from playing professional baseball. It would be 60 years before Jackie Robinson broke the color barrier with the Brooklyn Dodgers in 1947. If baseball had not excluded African Americans from the major leagues, it would have almost certainly expedited the elimination of segregation in the United States. Hundreds of black stars such as Josh Gibson, Cool Papa Bell, and Buck Leonard would have had the opportunity to display their skills in the major leagues.

2. **THE SELLING OF BABE RUTH**

Babe Ruth came up as a pitcher with the Boston Red Sox in 1914. The best lefthander in the American League, Ruth led the Red Sox to pennants in 1915,

was built in centerfield. Dubbed the Black Monster, it had none of the appeal of Fenway Park's Green Monster. The Reds were so enamored with the changes that they had a 27–54 record at home in 2001.

10. ENRON FIELD

Enron Field replaced the Astrodome as Houston's home field in 2000. The Enron Corporation signed a 30-year contract, paying 100 million dollars for the naming rights of the field. In 2001, Enron became the subject of a bankruptcy scandal. Embarrassed, the Astros bought back the rights to the name of the field. Once a new sponsor was found, it was renamed Minute Maid Park.

7. POLO GROUNDS

The New York Giants played in the Polo Grounds from 1891 to 1957. It was the home field of the New York Yankees from 1913 to 1922 and the New York Mets from 1962 to 1963. The Polo Grounds was built at the foot of Coogan's Bluff. In the early days, fans lined up on Coogan's Bluff to look down on the action. In the outfield, fans, some in carriages, encircled the field. When the field was enclosed, the field was shaped like a horse shoe. The leftfield line was 279 feet. The fence quickly deepened to 455 feet in left center and 483 feet to dead center. The rightfield foul pole was only 258 feet away from home plate.

8. AVENUE GROUNDS

From 1876 to 1879, the Cincinnati Reds played at the Avenue Grounds. On June 25, 1877, a storm nearly destroyed the grandstand. The roof was blown into a neighboring bean patch. There was a sign in rightfield that read "Betting, or offers to bet, are strictly prohibited. Umpires and players shall respect the public, and, in return, be respected." Late-arriving fans were herded into an area in foul territory known as the Bull Pen. The fans received a discounted ticket price of three for a quarter.

9. CINERGY FIELD

Cinergy Field, formerly known as Riverfront Stadium, was the home of the Cincinnati Reds from 1970 to 2002. In 2001, a huge section of outfield seats was removed to make room for the construction of the new Great American Park. The gap gave fans a breathtaking view of the construction site. A 40-foot-high wall

narrow lot bordered by Western, Findlay, McLean, and York Streets. The original design would have had a leftfield foul line extending 800 feet, The dimensions were shortened, but it was still 465 feet to left and 565 feet to center. In 1894, the groundskeeper used a herd of sheep to keep the grass short. On July 4, the sheep escaped, and it took two days to find them. That same year, a game was called at American Park because of the sun shining in the batters' eyes.

5. **BAKER BOWL**

The Baker Bowl was the home of the Philadelphia Phillies from 1887 to 1938. On August 6, 1903, twelve fans were killed when the leftfield stands collapsed into the street. The Baker Bowl was a notorious hitter's park because of its short dimensions. It was only 280 feet down the rightfield line. During the 1914 season, Phillies' outfielder Gavvy Cravath hit all 19 of his home runs at the Baker Bowl. Brooklyn ace Dazzy Vance refused to pitch at the Baker Bowl because it might "hurt my record."

6. **THE METRODOME**

The Metrodome has been the home field of the Minnesota Twins since 1982. The stadium has been a target of insults since its construction. Manager Billy Martin said, "It's a mockery of baseball. This place should go down as the biggest joke in baseball history." Kansas City reliever Dan Quisenberry quipped, "I don't think there are good uses for nuclear weapons, but this place might be one." The 23-foot canvas fence in right field has been deemed the Hefty Bag. Sportswriter Jim Murray described it as looking like a "bunch of trash bags on hangers."

In April 1901, League Field was flooded by Mill Creek. Groundskeeper Matty Schwab built dikes made of rye bread, brass fillings, cheese, sawdust, sour beer, and cement. Any ball hit into the lake in left centerfield was a ground-rule double.

League Park was replaced in 1902 by the Palace of the Fans.

2. NATIONAL PARK

The Washington Senators played in National Park from 1892 to 1899. An unusual feature of the park was a doghouse in centerfield, where the groundskeeper kept two huge mastiffs. In one 1899 game, Cincinnati outfielder Socks Seybold got his head stuck in the doghouse while trying to retrieve a ball. In 1896, the dogs got loose and attacked umpire Tom Lynch. He was saved when some players beat off the hounds with bats.

3. MUNICIPAL STADIUM

The Kansas City Athletics played in Municipal Stadium from 1955 to 1967. When Charles Finley bought the team in 1960, he made several changes at the ballpark in an attempt to attract more fans. Finley built a children's zoo in foul territory down the leftfield line. Sheep grazed on an embankment behind the rightfield fence. Finley installed a mechanical rabbit named Harvey that popped out of the ground to deliver balls to the umpire. Another device called Little Blowhard blew air to clear the dirt from home plate.

4. AMERICAN PARK

American Park was the home field of the Cincinnati Reds from 1884 to 1894. The park was built on a long,

Odd Ballparks

Over the years baseball has been played in some unusual parks. The Los Angeles Coliseum had a leftfield wall that was only 250 feet from home plate. Take a tour of some of baseball's most unusual venues.

1. **LEAGUE PARK**

The Cincinnati Reds played at League Park from 1894 to 1901. Fans attending games at the rickety ballpark risked their lives. On May 19, 1895, part of the rightfield stands, filled with 300 spectators, collapsed. Fortunately, no one was seriously injured. A barbed wire fence was built along the field-level Rooters Row to keep rowdy fans off the field. Players trying to catch pop flies risked being impaled on the barbed wire. League Park was a firetrap and caught fire on several occasions. On September 12, 1898, Reds players formed a bucket brigade to put out a fire. On May 28, 1900, the grandstand burned to the ground. The fire destroyed the Reds uniforms, so when they played their next game two days later, they wore Boston's road uniforms. A special ground rule was that any ball hit into the charred remains of the stand was in play.

9. GAVVY CRAVATH

Philadelphia outfielder Gavvy Cravath is virtually forgotten today, but he was one of baseball's first sluggers. Cravath led the National League in home runs six times between 1913 and 1919. In 1915, he hit 24 home runs, more than four other National League teams. Cravath hit more than 10 percent of the league's home runs that season.

10. BILL LANGE

Bill "Little Eva" Lange was one of the best hitters of the 1890s. The Chicago outfielder had a career .330 batting average. On September 6, 1898, Lange hit a long home run in a 9–8 loss to Cincinnati at League Park. The ball cleared the left centerfield fence and bounced into a saloon across the street. The ball shattered a mirror and came to rest at the feet of some men playing cards. Whether or not Lange had seven years' bad luck is open to debate. He retired the next season, ending a potential Hall of Fame career, to marry the daughter of a real estate tycoon. His father-in-law disapproved of baseball and convinced Lange to quit.

remarkable is that it took only two hours and 45 minutes to play. The average major league game today takes longer. The next day, Cincinnati scored 104 runs against a team from Dayton, Ohio.

6. 1939 BOSTON VS. CINCINNATI

On April 6, 1939, the Boston Red Sox and Cincinnati Reds played an exhibition game in Florence, South Carolina. The game was played in gale-force winds. The players' caps were blown off, and the infield was a virtual dust storm. The wind was so strong that ground balls actually took flight and flew over the outfield walls. The score was tied at 18–18 when the game was halted in the ninth inning. The reason for the stoppage was that the teams had run out of their supply of 54 baseballs.

7. 1884 INDIANAPOLIS

The American Association had a rule that prohibited baseball from being played on Sunday. On May 13, 1884, the Indianapolis team was arrested for violating the no-baseball-on-Sabbath rule. The team was jailed briefly. The rule was eventually changed.

8. THE 1880 CINCINNATI RED STOCKINGS

National League president William Hulbert passed a rule in October 1880 that prohibited alcohol being sold at the ballpark. The Cincinnati Red Stockings were expelled from the league when they refused to adhere to the new rule. Cincinnati was the home of more than two dozen breweries, and their fans liked to consume beer during the games. In 1882, Cincinnati joined the rival league, the American Association. Cincinnati rejoined the National League in 1890.

2. JEFF ZIMMERMAN

In 1994, Jeff Zimmerman was playing semi-pro baseball in France. Three years later, he was pitching for the Winnipeg Goldeneyes of the Northern League. The Texas Rangers bought his contract in exchange for two dozen baseballs. Zimmerman began the season with nine consecutive victories and posted an earned run average below 1.00.

3. BOB EWING

Bob Ewing hit the longest home run in baseball history. On July 28, 1908, the Cincinnati Reds defeated the Boston Braves 4–2 at Boston's South End Grounds. Ewing, a pitcher with Cincinnati, hit a ball that cleared the leftfield fence. It landed in an open car of a passing train and, by the time the train had stopped, was three miles away from the ballpark.

4. LOU NOVIKOFF

Outfielder Lou Novikoff played for the Chicago Cubs from 1941 to 1944. Cubs' owner Philip Wrigley decided that Novikoff was not aggressive enough at the plate. Wrigley offered Novikoff a five-dollar bonus for every time he struck out swinging. The strategy failed as Novikoff began swinging at pitches out of the strike zone. He hardly got rich anyway because he struck out only 71 times in his major league career.

5. 1870 CINCINNATI RED STOCKINGS

The Cincinnati Red Stockings, founded in 1869, were baseball's first all-professional team. For their first two seasons, they were virtually unbeatable. On May 25, 1870, Cincinnati routed the Urbana (Ohio) Unions by the score of 108–3. What made the game even more

Believe It or Not

Chattanooga Lookout's owner Joe Engle once traded a player for a turkey. Pinch runner Herb Washington played in 105 major league games and scored 33 runs without ever coming to bat. In 1877, Cincinnati's Lipman Pike led the National League in home runs with four. In baseball, sometimes truth is stranger than fiction.

1. **ELMER SMITH**

On July 20, 1894, in a game played at League Park, Cincinnati defeated Pittsburgh 7–6 on a 10th-inning home run by Germany Smith. Smith hit the ball into the bleachers. Under the rules of the day, the outfielder was allowed to go into the stands to retrieve the ball. Pittsburgh's leftfielder Elmer Smith tried to get the ball, but the Cincinnati fans held him down. When centerfielder Jake Stenzel tried to come to his aid, a fan pulled a revolver on him. While the Pittsburgh players were held at gunpoint, Germany Smith rounded the bases with the winning run.

7. RON KITTLE

Ron Kittle was a designated hitter for the New York Yankees. In 1987, he spent 15 days on the disabled list after a freak injury. Kittle pulled a muscle in his neck while carrying a stretcher for teammate Lenn Sakata.

8. GREG HARRIS

It's not unusual for a pitcher to hurt his arm, but Greg Harris hurt his elbow in a bizarre way. In 1987, the Texas Rangers' righthander injured his arm flicking sunflowers in the dugout. Harris's elbow swelled, forcing him to miss two starts.

9. STEVE SPARKS

Steve Sparks pitched for the Milwaukee Brewers in the early 1990s. Sparks dislocated his left shoulder attempting to tear a telephone book in half.

10. SCOTT BAILES

In 1991, California Angels' pitcher Scott Bailes injured his foot in a clubhouse accident. He sprained his right foot during a ping pong game.

He broke his nose during the team photo when Roberto Hernandez accidentally bumped heads with Ripken. The hard-nosed player calmly repositioned his nose and played in the All Star Game.

2. JOSE CARDENAL

Jose Cardenal played in 2,017 games from 1963 to 1980. The outfielder played for the Chicago Cubs from 1972 to 1977. Cardenal missed one opening day with the Cubs because his eyelid stuck shut.

3. BRETT BUTLER

Brett Butler was an outstanding leadoff hitter during the 1980s and 1990s. In 1991, the Dodgers' outfielder injured his left foot playing with his daughter. Pretending to be a shark, he chased his daughter and crashed into a wall.

4. C. C. SABATHIA

Cleveland Indians' pitcher C. C. Sabathia reported to the 2002 spring training weighing more than 300 pounds. Sabathia complained of a sore back. He claimed that he injured it sleeping on four pillows. When Cleveland manager Charlie Manuel was asked if he believed Sabathia's story, he replied, "I don't know. I didn't sleep with him."

5. TERRY HARPER

Terry Harper played outfield for the Atlanta Braves during the 1980s. He once dislocated his shoulder while waving a runner home.

6. CECIL FIELDER

Detroit's Cecil Fielder hit 51 home runs in 1990. In spring training the next year, the big first baseman strained ligaments when he slipped getting out of bed.

The Disabled List

Pittsburgh's Jose Silva injured his shoulder turning off an alarm clock. Baltimore pitcher Jim Palmer pinched a nerve in his neck looking over to first while holding on a runner. Detroit third baseman Tom Brookens pulled a hamstring during a home run trot. New York Yankees' shortstop Tony Kubek broke a bone in his neck while playing touch football. Shortstop Shawon Dunston injured his back lifting his baby out of a car seat. Jose Canseco jammed his middle finger in 1990 when he closed a refrigerator door on it. A's slugger Dave Kingman missed 11 games after injuring his knee when he turned to argue with the home plate umpire. Padres' reliever Goose Gossage missed five games after injuring his back sneezing. Cy Young winner Randy Johnson sprained his thumb in spring training while pulling up his socks. Here are ten more incredible injuries.

1. CAL RIPKEN

Baltimore's Cal Ripken was baseball's iron man. Ripken played in more than 2,600 consecutive games. At the 1996 All Star Game, Ripken suffered a freak injury.

an argument with an umpire, Piniella pulled out the first base bag and heaved it into right field.

9. **DIZZY DEAN**

In 1934, pitchers Dizzy and Paul Dean were fined by St. Louis Cardinals' manager Frankie Frisch for missing a train. Dizzy showed his displeasure by tearing up his uniform in front of Frisch. Always the performer, Dean reenacted the uniform-shredding tantrum for the press. He was fined $36 by the club for the cost of the uniforms.

10. **JOE MAGRANE**

St. Louis pitcher Joe Magrane once threw his bat into the Cardinals' dugout after making an out. The bat struck trainer Gene Gieselmann on the shoulder. Magrane said, "If it's going to hit anybody, it should hit Gene because he can treat himself."

George Brett checks his swing at a low pitch. Brett sometimes found it harder to check his temper.

Indians' outfielder hit 50 home runs and 52 doubles to become the first player in major league history to hit 50 doubles and home runs in the same season. When he was in the minor leagues, Belle was suspended several times as the result of his tantrums. In the majors, he threw a baseball at a heckler in the stands. Belle was ordered to attend anger-management courses by major league baseball. One Halloween, Belle reportedly chased trick-or-treaters who had egged his house.

6. **GEORGE BRETT**

Kansas City Royals' third baseman George Brett had 3,154 hits during his Hall of Fame career. Brett sometimes smashed things in the clubhouse when he lost his temper. Once, at Royals Stadium, Brett took out his frustration on a trash can. He beat on it with his bat, then threw himself into the can. Teammate Jamie Quirk found Brett in the can covered with garbage.

7. **WALTER BECK**

Walter "Boom Boom" Beck pitched from 1924 to 1945 and had a 38–69 career record. He frequently got shelled, giving him ample opportunities to lose his temper. One day in Philadelphia, he tossed a ball against the outfield wall after being removed from a game. Another time, Beck kicked over a bucket of ice water. Dodgers' manager Casey Stengel told him, "Stop that. If you break a toe, I won't be able to get anything for you."

8. **LOU PINIELLA**

Tampa Bay's manager Lou Piniella is known for his hot temper. His most famous temper tantrum occurred when he was manager of the Cincinnati Reds. During

Cincinnati Reds between 1952 and 1964. Hutch frequently smashed lights, water coolers, and anything else in his way after a tough loss. He would warn players to get out of the clubhouse before he came in, causing them to run for their lives. In Milwaukee, Reds pitcher Joe Nuxhall gave up a game-winning three-run home run in the ninth inning. After the game, Nuxhall, still dressed in his uniform, hailed a taxicab and locked himself in his hotel room until Hutchinson's rage subsided. On another occasion, Hutchinson punched a hole in the wall of his dining room. He told his wife to hang a picture over the hole and continued eating.

3. **WES FERRELL**

Pitcher Wes Ferrell won 193 games and lost only 128. The only thing more explosive than his fastball was his temper. Ferrell hated to lose. He ripped his glove to pieces, stomped on his watch, or took apart a water cooler. Once, he was so angered by being knocked out of the box that he refused to leave the mound.

4. **ROY WEATHERLY**

Outfielder Roy Weatherly played from 1936 to 1950. He was nicknamed Stormy because of his turbulent nature. Weatherly was frequently ejected from games because of arguments with umpires. In 1940, Cleveland Indians' owner Alva Bradley offered Weatherly $500 if he could play the entire season without being ejected. Everyone was surprised when Weatherly collected the bonus.

5. **ALBERT BELLE**

Albert Belle hit 381 home runs as one of the most feared sluggers of the 1990s. In 1995, the Cleveland

Temper Tantrums

Players show their anger in a variety of ways. Cincinnati reliever Rob Dibble threw Terry Pendleton's bat halfway up the backstop screen after he got a hit off him in 1989. Minnesota pitcher Mark Portugal fell on his back after he tried to kick a trash can and missed.

1. DOLF LUQUE

Dolf Luque won 193 games between 1918 and 1935. The Cuban-born righthander was notorious for his quick temper. When Cincinnati third baseman Babe Pinelli suggested how Luque should pitch to a batter, Luque tried to attack Pinelli with scissors. Luque threw an icepick during an altercation with a teammate. After Frankie Frisch of the New York Giants hit a homer off him, Luque followed him around the bases, screaming threats. The next time Frisch came to the plate, Luque dusted him. Once, when Luque was heckled by the Giants' bench, he stormed off the mound and punched Casey Stengel.

2. FRED HUTCHINSON

Nobody took a loss harder than Fred Hutchinson. He managed the Detroit Tigers, St. Louis Cardinals, and

she had passed away, he reminded Harry the next time Murray was a guest. Naturally, the first thing Caray asked was, "Bill, how's your mom doing?" Murray replied, "Well, she's dead, Harry. And don't ask me about my father, because he's dead too."

8. NO NECK

When Harry Caray was a broadcaster for the Chicago White Sox in the early 1970s, the team had an outfield consisting of Carlos May, Walt Williams, and Pat Kelly. May had lost part of his thumb in a grenade accident while he was in the Army reserves. Williams was nicknamed "No Neck" because it appeared that he did not have any. Kelly was known for having a weak throwing arm. Caray told his listeners, "Tonight, for the White Sox, we have no thumb in left, no neck in center, and no arm in right."

9. THE AGELESS WONDER

Harry Caray did not like to reveal his true age. He pretended to be six years younger than he really was. His son, Skip, a broadcaster with the Atlanta Braves, remarked in 1992, "How old is Dad? The last time I checked, he was 61. I'm 53 now. The way I've got it figured, in five years, I'll be older than he is."

10. IT MIGHT BE, IT COULD BE, IT IS

One of Caray's trademark sayings was, "It might be, it could be, it is." He said this every time a player hit a home run. In his last few years, Caray had trouble following the flight of a ball. Sometimes he would be in the middle of "It could be" when the outfielder was returning the ball to the infield.

admitted that after a game, "I have a couple of martinis, a couple of Budweisers, and a couple of Grand Marniers. By the time I get home, I'm feeling pretty good." Harry was constantly complaining after his doctor prohibited him from drinking. "Anyone who tells you that you can have as much fun sober as you can drinking is lying to you," Harry lamented. Until his dying day he said, "I wish I knew when I was going to die, because I'd like to have two martinis that day."

5. **THERE'S SOMETHING ABOUT HARRY**

Prior to a game at Wrigley Field, Caray went to the restroom. When he returned, Steve Stone noticed that Harry had forgot to zip his pants. Stone heard Caray let out a scream. In a situation similar to Ben Stiller's predicament in the movie "There's Something About Mary," Caray had got his penis caught in his zipper. After struggling for a few minutes in pain, Caray was able to free himself.

6. **THE GERBIL FAMILY**

Caray was known for reading notes from fans during the game. As a prank, someone passed him a note that the Gerbil family from San Francisco was in attendance. Caray told his audience, "A busload of Gerbils from downtown San Francisco are here to root for the Cubs today." His broadcasting partner Bob Brenly was in stitches, but Caray did not immediately get the joke.

7. **BILL MURRAY**

Comedian Bill Murray is a huge Chicago Cubs fan and was even a guest broadcaster when Harry Caray was recovering from a stroke. Murray was a frequent guest of Caray during Cub broadcasts. Caray always asked about Murray's mother. When Steve Stone heard that

rupted Reagan, "Excuse me, Mr. President, but Bobby Dernier just got a bunt single, and I got to get back to the baseball game." At that point, Caray hung up on the president.

2. SYNE RANDBERG

Late in his career, Harry had trouble correctly pronouncing many players' names. Steve Stone, his broadcast partner, spent an hour before the game going over the pronunciation of new players' names, but Harry still messed them up. Brooks Kieschnick became "Bryan Kleenex." Harry called slugger George Bell George Bush. Cubs' star outfielder Andre Dawson was confused with another president—Andrew Jackson. He sometimes called Steve Stone Ben Stein. Caray always seemed to have trouble with the name of All Star second baseman Ryne Sandberg. Some of the names he was called by Caray included, Syne Randberg, Scott Sanderson, Ryne Sanderson, and Ransom Jackson (a Cub player of the 1950s).

3. WATCH OUT BELOW

One of the reasons Caray stopped broadcasting on the road during his last few years was because he had a series of falls. During the 1983 season, Caray warned Steve Stone about a steel metal staircase leading to the broadcast booth in Cincinnati. During the game, Harry left the booth, and, when he returned, Stone heard him let out a yell. Stone turned to see Caray hanging upside down on the stairs. Stone quickly freed Caray, and Harry continued with the broadcast as if nothing had happened.

4. THIS BUD'S FOR YOU

It was estimated that Caray consumed 73,000 beers and 300,000 alcoholic drinks during his lifetime. Caray

Holy Cow!

Harry Caray was a broadcaster for more than fifty years. He spent the last two decades of his life in the booth for the Chicago Cubs. Caray died on February 19, 1998, but he continues to have legions of fans. Each year, on the anniversary of his death, Harry is toasted by an estimated 300,000 fans around the world. One fan toasted Caray while flying into a volcano, and another was in a tank in Yugoslavia. Caray's appeal had a lot to do with the incredible things he said on the air. When Dodgers' reliever Mike Marshall suffered an injury, Caray explained, "Mike Marshall went back to L.A. to get cocaine for his foot." He asked the bearded rockers ZZ Top if they were rabbis. Caray said, "If I can't watch baseball after I'm dead, it's going to kill me." Relive some of Harry Caray's greatest moments.

1. **RONALD REAGAN**

During the late 1930s, Ronald Reagan was an announcer on the Chicago Cubs radio network. Reagan remained a Cubs fan and, after he became president, called Harry Caray during a game. The two men chatted on the air for a few minutes. Suddenly Caray inter-

cheek. After managing an exhibition game against a Japanese team, Bridges quipped, "An hour after the game, you want to go out and play them again." When he managed a minor league team in Vancouver, he prohibited his players from eating sunflower seeds. "That's for birds to eat. I'm afraid my players might start molting or going to the bathroom on newspapers." Bridges described his own diet, "You mix two jiggers of scotch to one jigger of Metrecal. So far I've lost five pounds and my driver's license." Bridges joked, "It's a good thing I stayed in Cincinnati for four years—it took me that long to learn how to spell it."

7. BOB KELLY

Broadcaster Bob Kelly was responsible for a classic blooper. Kelly said, "That was a complicated play, fans, so we're going to run that down again for you sports fans scoring in bed."

8. JACOB RUPPERT

Jacob Ruppert owned the New York Yankees from 1915 to 1939. Ruppert was known for his malapropisms. He once chastised ace pitcher Waite Hoyt, "What's the matter with you? Other pitchers win their games 9-3, 10-2. You win yours, 2-1, 1-0. Why don't you win your games like the others?"

9. LARRY ANDERSEN

Relief pitcher Larry Andersen is best remembered as the player the Houston Astros traded to the Boston Red Sox for Jeff Bagwell. Andersen pondered the deep meanings of life. "I can't tell if I'm in a groove or a rut." "In the seventh inning, they all get up and sing 'Take Me Out to the Ballgame,' and they're already there." "What do you call a coffee break at the Lipton Tea Company?" "What do they ship Styrofoam in?" "Was Robin Hood's mother known as Mother Hood?" "I dropped spot remover on my dog and now he's gone." "Hey, you're only young once, but you can be immature forever."

10. ROCKY BRIDGES

Rocky Bridges was an infielder who played from 1951 to 1961. Bridges is remembered for always having a huge chaw of tobacco in his cheek. He claimed he could knock a bug out of the air by spitting. Some of his utterances could also be construed as tongue-in-

a base hit to centerfield as Santana can't get to it. But he gets there and makes the catch." "That's the great thing about baseball. You never know what's going on."

3. CHARLIE MANUEL

Cleveland Indians' manager Charlie Manuel is another with his own way for words. He summed up his philosophy by saying, "I'll tackle that bridge when I come to it." He observed, "Sometimes people don't see what they are seeing." His attention to detail carried over into the game, "When Russell [Branyan] is striking out, he's missing the ball a lot."

4. FRED WHITE

Announcer Fred White made a memorable on-the-air faux pas in 1982: "Well, I see in a game in Minnesota that Terry Felton has relieved himself on the mound in the second inning."

5. JERRY WILLARD

Jerry Willard was a catcher who played for the Cleveland Indians from 1984 to 1985. Told by the trainer that he should gargle with lukewarm water, Willard asked, "Where do you buy that stuff?" When he heard that the Minnesota Twins had won a doubleheader, he asked, "Who won the first game?"

6. HERB SCORE

Herb Score had a promising career as a pitcher ruined when he was struck by a line drive during a 1957 game. After he retired as a player, Score became an announcer in Cleveland. Occasionally, Score would mix his facts. A classic example: "Coming in to pitch is Mike Moore, who is 6 foot 1 and 212 years old."

language. Some Colemanisms: "I'm Johnny Grubb. No I'm not. This is Jerry Coleman." "There's someone warming up in the bullpen, but he's obscured by his number." "The ex-lefthander Dave Roberts will be going for Houston." "With one out in the first, Dave Roberts looks a lot better than the last time he pitched against the Padres." "The first pitch to Tucker Ashford is grounded in to left field. No, wait a minute. It's ball one, low and outside." "There's a hard shot to Le Master—and he throws Madlock into the dugout." "Next up is Fernando Gonzalez, who is not playing tonight." "Enos Cabell started out with the Astros. And before that he was with the Orioles." "Mike Caldwell, the Padres' righthanded southpaw, will pitch tonight." "That noise in my earphone knocked my nose off, and I had to pick it up." "Grubb goes back, back, he's under the warning track." "Kansas City leads in the eighth, four to four." "At the end of six innings of play, it's Montreal 5, Expos 3." "Over the course of a season, a miscue will cost you more games than a good play." "If you ask what the Achilles tendon of this team is, it would be pitching"; "Our hats are off to drug abusers everywhere."

2. **RALPH KINER**

New York Mets' announcer Ralph Kiner rivaled Jerry Coleman for memorable misstatements. Some Kiner beauties: "Nolan Ryan's fastball has been clocked at over 200 miles per hour." "We'll be right back after this message from Manufacturer's Hangover." "If Casey Stengel were alive today, he'd be spinning in his grave." "They will surpass the father–son tandem of Buddy Bell and Yogi Berra." "The Hall of Fame ceremonies are on the 31st and 32nd of July." "All his saves have come during relief appearances." "There's

Baseballese

Casey Stengel's unique brand of logic was known as Stengelese. Stengel and Yogi Berra were not the only people in baseball with their own way of speaking. When Chicago Cubs' catcher Rick Wrona hit his first homer in 1989, he exclaimed, "You don't get your first home run too often." Outfielder Mickey Rivers observed, "The wind was blowing about 100 degrees." New York Yankees' announcer Phil Rizzuto once introduced himself as his broadcasting partner, Bill White. When Toronto Blue Jays' outfielder Jesse Barfield was questioned about the chemistry on the team, he replied, "I don't know anything about chemistry. I flunked it in high school." Seattle manager Del Crandall said, "The only thing that has kept [second baseman Jack] Perconte from being a good major league player is performance." When asked who he thought was the greatest player of all time, shortstop Johnny Logan answered, "The immoral Babe Ruth." Sportscaster Frankie Frisch said, "It's a beautiful day for a night game."

1. **JERRY COLEMAN**

Jerry Coleman, the longtime announcer of the San Diego Padres, has delighted listeners with his skewered

body hair. He immediately began hitting. Mientkiewicz shaved his arms every week to avoid slumps.

9. **PINK HAWLEY**

Pink Hawley won 168 games from 1892 to 1901. He may have won more games if he hadn't suffered from an inferiority complex. Hawley had so little confidence that he consistently needed to be reassured during the game. He once called catcher Heinie Peitz to the mound and asked him, "Do you like to catch me?"

10. **AMOS BOOTH**

Amos "the Darling" Booth played from 1876 to 1882. Booth believed he got a hit for every hairpin he found at the ballpark. Apparently he did not find enough hairpins, as he finished his career with 98 hits.

5. STEVE LYONS

Steve Lyons was nicknamed Psycho. Lyons said, "If I get famous I might get some endorsements for chainsaws." While playing for the Chicago White Sox, Lyons got his pants dirty sliding into first base. In front of the crowd, Lyons dropped his pants to brush the dirt out.

6. JOHN LOWENSTEIN

John Lowenstein was an outfielder who played from 1970 to 1985. Lowenstein said, "I don't want to be a star, but I'd like to twinkle a little." When another player had a birthday, Lowenstein would destroy the cake with a bat. While sitting on the bench, he would exercise his wrists to keep them strong.

7. CHRIS SABO

Chris Sabo was the ultimate blue-collar ballplayer. In the minor leagues, Sabo worked at McDonalds to earn extra money. During his rookie season with the Cincinnati Reds in 1988, he earned $67,500. The frugal third baseman drove a five-year-old Ford Escort. "Some of these guys spend $70,000 on a car," Sabo said. "For $70,000, I could have a lifetime supply of Escorts." Sabo wore goggles when he played and had a flattop. On the "David Letterman Show," he described the flattop as a landing strip for paper airplanes. Sabo said he never understood why anyone wanted his autograph. "I mean, what's it worth, five cents?" Sabo asked.

8. DOUG MIENTKIEWICZ

Minnesota Twins' first baseman Doug Mientkiewicz has an unusual way to cure batting slumps. In the minor leagues, he was batting .052 when he shaved off all his

had a high opinion of his abilities. In spring training he had his own valet and personal trainer to carry his equipment. He once threatened to quit the Cincinnati Reds because the team refused to give his valet a ticket to the game. On May 10, 1894, Parrott gave up six home runs but still managed to defeat St. Louis 18–9. The versatile Parrott played every position except catcher. During the off-season he played the coronet in the Portland, Oregon, Symphony.

3. RABBIT MARANVILLE

A Hall of Fame shortstop, Rabbit Maranville was notorious for his flaky behavior. At a party in 1919 he and Jim Thorpe amused guests by swinging through the branches. On trains he would throw buckets of ice on strangers. He was known to dangle teammates from hotel windows. Maranville particularly liked to annoy umpires. He crawled through umpires' legs to get to the plate. After a bad call, he would place glasses on the umpire's face. After getting into a fight with an umpire, Maranville covered the umpire's face in iodine.

4. BILL SCHUSTER

Broadway Bill Schuster was an infielder who played for the Chicago Cubs from 1943 to 1945. Despite being a .234 lifetime hitter, Schuster was known for his showboat antics. On a sure groundout, Schuster sometimes ran down the third base line. Once, while playing in the minor leagues, he ran straight up the middle and slid between the pitcher's legs. The pitcher, Skinhead Hunter, tagged him so hard on his head that he knocked Schuster out. The players left him there on the mound.

Oddballs

Deacon White, the 1877 National League batting champion, believed the earth was flat. Infielder Ozzie Guillen put eye drops on his bat when he was in a slump. Pittsburgh pitcher Bob Walk once had a moth fly out of his mouth. All of these players were guilty of flaky behavior.

1. DUSTER MAILS

Duster Mails won 32 games during his career from 1915 to 1926. Although Mails had moderate talent as a pitcher, he was outstanding at self-promotion. On the days he pitched, he drove a car around Cleveland that had "The Great Mails" written on the side. He offered an autographed photo of himself to any woman who baked him a chocolate cake. Not surprisingly, after his pitching career was over, Mails worked in the public relations department for the San Francisco Seals' minor league team.

2. TOM PARROTT

Tom Parrott pitched from 1893 to 1896 and had a 39–48 record. Despite having a losing record, Parrott

usual idea about pitching. Prior to the 1918 season, he ordered several members of the Reds' pitching staff to have their tonsils removed. He believed inflamed tonsils had caused some of the pitchers to have arm trouble.

9. HAL McRAE

Hal McRae was known as an aggressive player, and he continued that approach as a manager. While managing the Kansas City Royals, he devised an unusual way of dealing with players on the disabled list. McRae dressed like a commando and hid in a trash can in the clubhouse. He would jump out and act as if he shot the injured player. It was his way of expressing that the player was dead to the team.

10. BUCK HERZOG

Buck Herzog managed the Cincinnati Reds from 1914 to 1916. On April 15, 1915, the opening day of the season, Herzog nearly choked to death on a piece of bubble gum while giving instructions to his players. On May 1, 1915, Herzog was suspended for five days after getting into a fight with umpire Charles Rigler over a disputed tag play. Herzog spiked Rigler's foot. The umpire retaliated by hitting Herzog across the face with his mask.

Leo Durocher shows perhaps why an umpire once called him "the lowest form of living matter."

and 1954. Durocher was described by umpire Harry Wendelstedt as "the lowest form of living matter." It was Durocher who said, "Nice guys finish last." In 1947, he was suspended for a year for "Conduct detrimental to baseball." Leo the Lip was never known for his gentle handling of his players. While managing the Chicago Cubs in 1966, he noticed that weak-hitting infielder Paul Popovich was going to the bat rack. "Sit down, Paul," Durocher yelled. "We ain't giving up yet." In 1976, Durocher agreed to manage in Japan. Dodger's broadcaster Vin Scully commented, "It took the United States 35 years to get revenge for Pearl Harbor."

8. **CHRISTY MATHEWSON**

Pitching great Christy Mathewson managed the Cincinnati Reds from 1916 to 1918. Mathewson had one un-

later became editor of the *New York Herald* and official scorer for the New York Giants.

5. DON ZIMMER

Don Zimmer has spent more than 50 years in baseball as a player, manager, and coach. In 1978, he nearly won the pennant as manager of the Boston Red Sox, blowing a big lead and losing a heartbreaking playoff game to the New York Yankees. Zimmer guided the 1989 Chicago Cubs to a divisional title. While in Boston, pitcher Bill Lee nicknamed Zimmer "the Gerbil." As a coach with the Cubs in 1986, he was knocked unconscious when he fell off an exercise bike. When he came to, he was asked who was the president. Zimmer replied, "Hell, I didn't know that before I hit my head." Zimmer gained more notoriety as a coach with the New York Yankees in the late 1990s. After being hit with a line drive while sitting in the dugout, Zimmer put on an Army helmet. Yankees' shortstop Derek Jeter frequently rubbed Zimmer's stubbled head for luck.

6. JOHN WALTZ

In 1892, Baltimore owner Harry Vonderhorst fired manager George Van Haltren after the team got off to a miserable 1–14 start. Vonderhorst, who had made his fortune as a brewer, hired beer salesman John Waltz as an interim replacement. With Waltz as manager, the Orioles were 0–2. Ned Hanlon was hired, and he led Baltimore to three consecutive pennants.

7. LEO DUROCHER

Leo Durocher won 2,010 games during his 24 seasons as manager. He won pennants with the Brooklyn Dodgers in 1941 and with the New York Giants in 1951

one that can throw and can't catch, and one that can catch but can't throw, and one who can't do either."

2. GEORGE STALLINGS

George Stallings is best known for managing the Miracle Braves to the National League pennant in 1914. Stallings had extremely bad breath. Once, a rookie in the dugout said, "It smells like a sewer in here." Stallings told the young player, "That's my breath. By this time tomorrow, you'll be too far away to smell anything."

3. HENRY O'DAY

Henry O'Day managed the Cincinnati Reds in 1912 and the Chicago Cubs in 1914. Both seasons his teams finished fourth. O'Day was nicknamed Silent Henry because he rarely spoke—even to friends or players. Writer Lee Allen described him as "Closed mouthed and mysterious as some strange mollusk one might find on a beach." His favorite pastime was sitting alone in the hotel lobby reading accounts of the baseball game.

4. O. P. CAYLOR

O. P. Caylor managed Cincinnati of the American Association in 1885 and 1886. Caylor was an ex-sportswriter with the *Cincinnati Enquirer*. That newspaper mercilessly made fun of Caylor in cartoons and articles. He was referred to as "Miss Management." On June 9, 1886, the *Enquirer* wrote of Caylor, "The present manager of the team wore dresses until he was twelve years of age, and, if he had his own way, would today be strutting around in a Mother Hubbard." Caylor

Colorful Managers

Brooklyn Dodgers' manager Chuck Dressen once tried to break a long losing streak by encouraging his players to go out and get loaded. In 1985, Seattle manager Chuck Cottier picked his starting lineup out of a hat and still lost. These managers didn't always go by the book.

1. CASEY STENGEL

Casey Stengel won ten pennants as manager of the New York Yankees. When Stengel won his first pennant in 1949, he said, "I never could have done it without my players." Stengel had first baseman Moose Skowron take dancing lessons at Arthur Murray's to improve his movement around the bag. He believed Lou Skizas hated the baseball because he was a good hitter and avoided it in the outfield. On pitcher Bob Turley, Casey said, "He don't smoke. He don't drink. He don't chase women, and he don't win." When outfielder Bob Cerv was traded, Stengel sat next to the player and said, "Nobody knows this, but one of us has just been traded to Kansas City." When Stengel managed the hapless New York Mets, he lamented his catching corps, "I got

for the Athletics, Braves, and Cubs. La Russa struggled at the plate and finished with a career .199 batting average. As Chicago White Sox manager in 1983, La Russa said, "The toughest thing for me as a young manager is that a lot of my players saw me play. They know how bad I was." In 1983, he led the White Sox to a divisional title. His greatest success came in Oakland, where he managed the Athletics to three consecutive pennants from 1988 to 1990.

1988, Lasorda's teams won four pennants and two world championships.

7. SPARKY ANDERSON

Sparky Anderson batted .218 in 1959, his only season as a major league player. The Philadelphia Phillies' second baseman was so bad that his daughter Shirlee booed him "so people wouldn't know he was my father." Sparky admitted, "I couldn't play when I played." Luckily, he was a much better manager than he was a player. He led the Big Red Machine teams in Cincinnati to four pennants and two world titles between 1970 and 1976. In 1984, Anderson managed the Detroit Tigers to a world championship.

8. RALPH HOUK

Ralph Houk was a back-up catcher to Yogi Berra on the New York Yankees from 1947 to 1954. He appeared in only 91 games during those eight seasons. In 1961, Houk replaced Casey Stengel as manager of the Yankees, and his team won three consecutive pennants and two world championships.

9. BOBBY COX

Bobby Cox played third base for the New York Yankees in 1968 and 1969. Cox averaged only .225 for those two seasons. As a manager, Cox's teams in Atlanta dominated the National League during the 1990s. The Braves, under Cox, won pennants in 1991, 1992, 1995, 1996, and 1999.

10. TONY La RUSSA

Second baseman Tony La Russa played six seasons in the major leagues. Between 1963 and 1973, he played

3. TOM KELLY

Tom Kelly played eleven seasons in the minor leagues but played only one season in the majors. The first baseman batted .181 in 49 games with the 1975 Minnesota Twins. Kelly took over the managerial reins of the Minnesota Twins in 1986 and was one of the best managers in baseball for more than a decade. His Twins won the World Championship in 1987 and 1991.

4. JIM LEYLAND

Jim Leyland never played in the major leagues, but he sure could manage. After many outstanding years as manager of the Pittsburgh Pirates, Leyland led the Florida Marlins to a World Series victory over the Cleveland Indians in 1997.

5. WALTER ALSTON

Walter Alston's major league career consisted of one at bat. On September 27, 1936, Alston, playing for the St. Louis Cardinals, struck out against Chicago's Lon Warneke. When Alston was hired to manage the Brooklyn Dodgers in 1954, a headline read, "Walter Who?" They soon found out. In 1955, he led the Brooklyn Dodgers to their only World Championship. Alston's Dodgers won seven pennants between 1955 and 1974.

6. TOMMY LASORDA

Tommy Lasorda's career as a major league pitcher was short but definitely not sweet. The lefthander pitched in 26 games for the Brooklyn Dodgers and Kansas City Athletics from 1954 to 1956. Lasorda had a 0–4 record with a 6.48 earned run average. He replaced the legendary Walter Alston as the Dodgers' manager and continued the winning tradition. Between 1977 and

Skilled Skippers

While great players often make mediocre managers, the reverse is also true. Everyone on this list had an undistinguished career as a player, followed by an outstanding career as a manager.

1. **JOE MCCARTHY**

Joe McCarthy never played in the major leagues. He managed for 24 seasons and never finished out of the first division. His teams won 2,126 games, and his .614 winning percentage is best among managers. Six times his teams won more than 100 games. McCarthy won eight pennants with the New York Yankees between 1932 and 1943 and one with the Chicago Cubs.

2. **EARL WEAVER**

Earl Weaver was another Hall of Fame manager who never played in the major leagues. The fiery Weaver managed the Baltimore Orioles from 1968 to 1986. He had five seasons in which his team won more than 100 games. Weaver's teams won pennants in 1969, 1970, 1971, and 1979.

twentieth century. The Hall of Fame second baseman played in four World Series as a player, but never as a manager. Evers managed three seasons with the Chicago Cubs and White Sox, compiling a 196–208 record.

seasons as manager, his teams never finished higher than sixth.

7. ROGER BRESNAHAN

Roger Bresnahan was a Hall of Fame catcher who played in the major leagues from 1897 to 1915. Bresnahan managed the St. Louis Cardinals from 1909 to 1912 and the Chicago Cubs in 1915. He had only one winning season, and his teams never finished higher than fourth. His career record was 328 wins and 432 losses.

8. EDDIE MATHEWS

Eddie Mathews hit 512 home runs and is considered one of the best third basemen in baseball history. Mathews played with the Braves from 1952 to 1966. Mathews starred on the pennant-winning teams of 1957 and 1958. He managed the Atlanta Braves from 1972 to 1974 but was unable to lead them to the playoffs. During those three seasons, the Braves won 149 and lost 161.

9. MORDECAI BROWN

Mordecai Brown won 239 and lost only 129 games during his career as a pitcher from 1903 to 1916. He had a streak of six consecutive 20-win seasons with the Chicago Cubs. While he was a winner on the mound, he was less successful as a manager. In 1914, he managed St. Louis of the Federal League to a 50–63 record.

10. JOHNNY EVERS

Johnny Evers was a teammate of Mordecai Brown on the great Chicago Cubs' teams of the first decade of the

1936. Ott was elected to the Hall of Fame in 1951. Ott managed the Giants from 1942 to 1948 but never duplicated his success as a player. The team's record during his tenure was 464–530. It was about Ott that Leo Durocher made his famous quote, "Nice guys finish last."

4. **TED WILLIAMS**

Ted Williams won six batting titles and led the American League in slugging percentage eight times. Williams was elected to the Hall of Fame in 1966. Williams became manager of the Washington Senators in 1969. His team had a winning record the first year, but the win total dropped from 86 to 70 to 63 to 54 in successive years. His four-year record as manager was 273 wins and 364 losses.

5. **BILLY HERMAN**

Hall of Fame second baseman Billy Herman played from 1931 to 1947. A .304 lifetime batter, he hit above the .300 mark eight times. Herman managed the Pittsburgh Pirates in 1947 and the Boston Red Sox from 1964 to 1966. His teams never finished higher than eighth. Herman's record as a manager was 189–274.

6. **ROGERS HORNSBY**

Second baseman Rogers Hornsby had a .358 career batting average. During his career from 1915 to 1937, he led the National League in virtually every offensive category. Hornsby managed 13 seasons and had a record of 680–798. In 1926, as player–manager of the St. Louis Cardinals, he led his team to the world championship. It would be his only pennant. In his final eight

Mismanaged

Great players don't usually make great managers. It has been said that superstar players can't understand why ordinary players cannot do the things they could do on the field.

1. ROGER CONNOR

Hall of Fame first baseman Roger Connor played from 1880 to 1897. Connor batted .318, and his 233 triples rank fifth all time. Connor's brief managing career was less successful. In 1896, he was fired after St. Louis lost 37 of the 46 games in which he managed.

2. LUKE APPLING

Luke Appling was a Hall of Fame shortstop who played for the Chicago White Sox from 1930 to 1950. Appling won the American League batting titles in 1936 and 1943. He managed Kansas City in 1967, but the Athletics had a 10–30 record after Appling replaced Alvin Dark late in the season.

3. MEL OTT

New York Giants' outfielder Mel Ott batted in 100 or more runs eight consecutive seasons from 1929 to

manager batted only .219, 84 points below his career average.

8. WILLIE MAYS

Another superstar who played a bit too long was Willie Mays. The 42-year-old outfielder batted .211 for the New York Mets in 1973. Mays hit the final six of his 660 home runs that season.

9. HARMON KILLEBREW

Six times Harmon Killebrew led the American League in home runs. He spent his greatest seasons with the Minnesota Twins. In 1975, Killebrew played his final season in Kansas City. The 39-year-old designated hitter batted .199 and hit only 14 home runs.

10. MEL OTT

Mel Ott hit 511 home runs and led the National League in homers six times. The Giants' outfielder batted .308 in 1945, but his production declined dramatically the next season. He batted .074 in 1946 with only one home run.

3. REGGIE JACKSON

California Angels' outfielder Reggie Jackson led the American League with 39 home runs in 1982. The next season, Jackson's homer total dropped to 14, and he hit only .194. Jackson struck out 140 times in just 397 at-bats.

4. MIKE SCHMIDT

Philadelphia third baseman Mike Schmidt hit 548 home runs. In 1973, his rookie season, Schmidt batted .196 with 18 home runs. After his disappointing rookie season, Schmidt led the National League in home runs three consecutive years.

5. ROBIN ROBERTS

Robin Roberts won 286 games and was elected to the Hall of Fame in 1976. He led the National League pitchers in victories for four consecutive years from 1952 to 1955. Roberts's last season with the Philadelphia Phillies was disastrous. In 1961, the righthander had a 1–10 record with a 5.85 earned run average.

6. TOM SEAVER

Tom Seaver won 311 games and struck out 3,640 batters. In 1981, Seaver led the National League in wins and winning percentage. The Cincinnati Reds' righthander struggled the next season. Seaver was 5–13 with an uncharacteristically high 5.50 earned run average.

7. PETE ROSE

In 1985, Pete Rose broke Ty Cobb's all-time hit record. The next season, it became apparent that his bat speed had dropped dramatically. The 45-year-old player–

Seasons They'd Rather Forget

Baltimore third baseman Brooks Robinson batted .149 in 1977, his final season. In 1980, San Francisco first baseman Willie McCovey batted .204 with only one home run. In 2000, Los Angeles pitcher Orel Hershiser, a former Cy Young winner, had a 1–5 record with a 13.14 earned run average. Even superstars have bad seasons.

1. BABE RUTH

Babe Ruth was offered a one-dollar contract by the New York Yankees after hitting 22 home runs in 1934. Ruth decided to end his career where it started, in Boston. He played 28 games with the Braves, but was only a shadow of his former greatness. The 40-year-old batted .181 and hit six home runs before calling it quits.

2. MARK MCGWIRE

In 1998, Mark McGwire became the first player to hit 70 home runs. By 2001, the St. Louis Cardinals' first baseman was hobbled by injuries. Big Mac retired after batting .187 with 29 home runs.

Sox have not won a World Series since 1917, and Lyons never played in the Fall Classic.

8. HARRY HEILMANN

Harry Heilmann played most of his 17-year career with the Detroit Tigers. The four-time batting champion had a .342 career batting average. Despite playing 13 seasons in the same outfield with Ty Cobb, Heilmann never had the opportunity to play in a World Series.

9. BOBBY WALLACE

Hall of Fame shortstop Bobby Wallace played 25 seasons in the major leagues. Wallace played for the Cleveland Spiders, St. Louis Cardinals, and St. Louis Browns from 1894 to 1918. Despite having one of the longest careers in baseball history, Wallace never played in a World Series.

10. NAP LAJOIE

Second baseman Nap Lajoie had 3,251 hits and was elected to the Hall of Fame in 1937. He played 21 seasons but was never in a World Series. In 1915, Lajoie was traded to the Philadelphia Athletics, a team that had won four pennants in the previous five years. Lajoie played two more years, but Philadelphia finished in last place both seasons.

ries with Detroit from 1907 to 1909, but the Tigers lost each time. Cobb was only 22 years old when Detroit lost to the Pittsburgh Pirates in the 1909 series and probably believed he would play in many more. Cobb played 19 more seasons but never appeared in another World Series.

4. BARRY BONDS

Barry Bonds set the single season home-run record in 2001. He has accomplished almost everything a player could achieve in baseball, except one thing. To date, Bonds has never played for a World Champion.

5. RON SANTO

Ron Santo played third base for the Chicago Cubs from 1960 to 1973. Santo hit 342 home runs and was a frequent All Star. Like teammate Ernie Banks, Santo never appeared in a World Series because he played for the Cubs.

6. BILLY WILLIAMS

Outfielder Billy Williams played 16 seasons with the Chicago Cubs. Williams hit 426 home runs and was elected to the Hall of Fame. It appeared Williams's luck might have changed when he was traded to the Oakland Athletics in 1975. The A's had won three consecutive world titles. Williams played his final two seasons in Oakland, but never reached the World Series.

7. TED LYONS

Ted Lyons pitched for the Chicago White Sox from 1923 to 1946. Lyons won 260 games and was elected to the Hall of Fame in 1955. Unfortunately, the White

They Never Won the World Series

Sammy Sosa and Ken Griffey, Jr., are two of baseball's greatest sluggers, but neither of them have played in the World Series. None of these superstars ever played on a World Championship team.

1. **ERNIE BANKS**

Ernie Banks played 19 seasons with the Chicago Cubs. He hit 512 home runs during his Hall of Fame career. Since the Cubs have not won a pennant since 1945, Banks did not have the opportunity to play in the Fall Classic.

2. **TED WILLIAMS**

Ted Williams was one of the greatest hitters in baseball history. He had a .344 batting average and hit 521 home runs during his 19-year career with the Boston Red Sox. Williams played in only one World Series. He batted .200 as Boston lost in seven games to the St. Louis Cardinals in the 1946 World Series.

3. **TY COBB**

Ty Cobb was a 12-time American League batting champion. Cobb played in three consecutive World Se-

drive in a run as Cincinnati lost in five games to the Baltimore Orioles.

7. **WALLY BERGER**

Wally Berger hit 242 home runs during his career, but he picked an inopportune time for a slump in the 1939 World Series. The Cincinnati outfielder went hitless in 15 at-bats as the Reds were swept in four games by the New York Yankees.

8. **JAY WITASICK**

In game six of the 2001 World Series, New York Yankees' reliever Jay Witasick set a record he'd rather be without. In one and one-third innings, Witasick gave up 10 hits and nine runs in a 15–2 loss to the Arizona Diamondbacks. Witasick established a new record for the most earned runs given up by a pitcher in the World Series. The Diamondbacks upset the Yankees in seven games.

9. **ART DITMAR**

Art Ditmar won 15 games for the New York Yankees in 1960. In the 1960 World Series against the Pittsburgh Pirates, Ditmar was shelled in both of his starts. Ditmar lost games one and five and had a 21.60 earned run average. Despite outscoring Pittsburgh 55 runs to 27, New York lost to the Pirates in seven games.

10. **MARV OWEN**

Detroit third baseman Marv Owen batted .317 in 1934. Owen had a miserable World Series, with only two hits in 29 at-bats, as the Tigers lost to the St. Louis Cardinals in seven games. In game seven, St. Louis outfielder Joe Medwick slid hard into Owen at third base, causing a near riot.

3. DAL MAXVILL

Dal Maxvill was a weak-hitting shortstop with the St. Louis Cardinals. He had his best season at the plate during the 1968 season. Maxvill set a record for hitting futility in the 1968 World Series by going 0 for 22 as the Cardinals were upset by the Detroit Tigers in seven games.

4. BABE RUTH

Babe Ruth batted .326 and hit 15 home runs in ten World Series. His performance in the 1922 World Series was the worst of his career. The Babe batted .118 and was homerless as his Yankees were swept by the New York Giants. Sportswriter Joe Vila dismissed Ruth as a fluke. Vila wrote that Ruth could not hit "brainy pitching." He concluded, "Ruth, therefore, is no longer a wonder." Ruth proved his critics wrong by batting .368 and slamming three home runs as the Yankees defeated the Giants in the 1923 series.

5. CALVIN SCHIRALDI

Everyone remembers Bill Buckner as the goat of the 1986 World Series, but relief pitcher Calvin Schiraldi certainly deserves a share of blame for Boston's loss to the New York Mets. Schiraldi had a 1.41 earned run average during the 1986 season. In the World Series, he was the losing pitcher in games six and seven and had a 13.50 earned run average.

6. TONY PEREZ

Cincinnati Reds' third baseman Tony Perez hit 40 home runs and batted in 129 runs during the 1970 season. In the 1970 World Series, Perez batted .056 and failed to

Worst World Series Performances

Los Angeles Dodgers' centerfielder Willie Davis had a terrible World Series in 1966 against the Baltimore Orioles. At the plate, he managed only one hit in 16 at-bats. In game two, Davis made three errors in the fifth inning. The Dodgers were swept in four games by the Orioles. Here are some more wretched World Series performances.

1. **RED MURRAY**

Outfielder Red Murray led the National League in home runs in 1909. He batted cleanup for the New York Giants in the 1911 World Series. Murray went hitless in 21 at-bats and was 0 for 12 with runners in scoring position. The Giants lost to the Philadelphia Athletics in six games.

2. **GIL HODGES**

First baseman Gil Hodges knocked in more than 100 runs for the Brooklyn Dodgers for seven consecutive seasons. Hodges was hitless in 21 at-bats in the 1952 World Series. With Hodges in a slump, the Dodgers lost to the New York Yankees in seven games.

Braves finished 61 1/2 games out of first place and with a 38–115 record.

7. 1961 PHILADELPHIA PHILLIES

The Philadelphia Phillies were so bad in the early 1960s that manager Eddie Sawyer quit after the first game of the 1960 season. He explained his sudden resignation, "I'm 49, and I want to live to be 50." While the 1960 Phillies were bad, the 1961 team was even worse. Philadelphia won 47 games and lost 107. The team set a modern record for futility by losing 23 consecutive games. Robin Roberts, who was a six-time 20-game winner with Philadelphia, had a 1–10 record.

8. 1890 PITTSBURGH

Pittsburgh finished 66 1/2 games out of first place in 1890. Managed by Guy Hecker, the team won 23 and lost 113. The pitching staff yielded 1,235 runs, and no pitcher won more than four games.

9. 1952 PITTSBURGH PIRATES

The Pittsburgh Pirates of the early 1950s were terrible, and none was worse than the 1952 team. The Pirates won 42 and lost 112. They were so bad that manager Billy Meyer told them, "You clowns can go on 'What's My Line?' in full uniforms and fool the panel."

10. 1930 PHILADELPHIA PHILLIES

The 1930 Philadelphia Phillies batted .315 as a team. Rightfielder Chuck Klein batted .386, and leftfielder Lefty O'Doul hit .383. Despite scoring more than six runs a game, the Phillies lost 102 games. The reason was that their pitchers gave up 1,199 runs. There was a huge Lifebuoy soap sign in right field at the Baker Bowl. One scribe wrote, "The Phillies use Lifebuoy, and they still stink."

Mets considering color-coding his fingers. Mets' pitchers were disconcerted because Coleman constantly moved behind the plate. When Mets' pitcher Chuck Churn was asked who was the toughest man in the league to pitch to, his answer was, "Choo Choo Coleman."

The Mets' pathetic play amazed even manager Casey Stengel. The Old Professor said, "Been in this game a hundred years, but I see new ways to lose them I never knew existed before." After watching a series of bad plays, Stengel asked, "Can't anyone here play this game?" Stengel explained, "The only thing worse than a Mets game is a Mets doubleheader."

5. **1916 PHILADELPHIA ATHLETICS**

From 1910 to 1914, Connie Mack's Philadelphia Athletics' dominated the American League. After the 1914 season, Mack began selling off his star players in a cost-cutting measure. The A's finished last in 1915 and were even worse in 1916. The team won 36 games and lost 117. Pitchers Joe Bush and Elmer Myers each lost 20 games. John Nabors and Tom Sheehan had a combined record of 2–36. The team was so bad that it finished 40 games behind the next worst team, the Washington Senators.

6. **1935 BOSTON BRAVES**

The 1935 Boston Braves are best remembered as Babe Ruth's last team. The Babe batted .181 in 28 games before retiring. His replacement, Hal Lee, did not hit a home run all season. While the Braves did have outfielder Wally Berger, the National League's home-run and runs-batted-in leader, they had little else. The

Pictured here from his days managing the Yankees, not even the "Ol' Perfesser" Casey Stengel could keep the expansion New York Mets from a 40–120 record in 1962. The only thing "Amazing" about that year's Mets was their finish, 60$^1/_2$ games out of first place.

cluding someone named Chicken Wolf. Pitcher John Ewing lost 30 games, and Toad Ramsey had a 1–16 record. On one road trip, Louisville lost all 21 games. On another road trip the team nearly lost more than a game. They were traveling by train when they were caught in the deadly Johnstown Flood in May that claimed more than 2,500 lives. For a time it was believed that the entire team had perished. When it was learned that the team had survived, there was almost a sense of disappointment in Louisville. The *Louisville Commercial* newspaper wrote, "If the entire team had been standing in front of the Johnstown reservoir when it broke last Friday evening, the majority of the people of Louisville would have viewed the calamity as just a visitation of providence."

3. **1876 CINCINNATI REDS**

The National League was formed in 1876. Cincinnati finished the season with a 9–56 record. The team scored 238 runs and allowed 579. Cincinnati made 469 errors, averaging more than 7 a game. The team hit only four home runs, all by outfielder Charley Jones.

4. **1962 NEW YORK METS**

The 1962 New York Mets were an expansion team managed by Casey Stengel. The Amazin' Mets finished the season with a 40–120 record, finishing 60 1/2 games out of first place. The team was a combination of washed-up veterans and fringe players. The player who most represented the Mets' ineptitude was first baseman Marvelous Marv Throneberry. He once hit a triple only to be called out because he failed to touch first and second base. Jimmy Breslin wrote, "Having Marv Throneberry play for your team is like having Willie Sutton work for your bank." Catcher Choo Choo Coleman had such trouble giving signals to pitchers that the

who won four games and led the National League with 30 losses. Hughey got nicknamed Coldwater not because of all the early showers he took, but because he was from Coldwater, Michigan. One can only guess how Crazy Schmit got his nickname, but he drove Cleveland fans crazy by losing 17 of his 19 decisions. Rounding out the starting rotation was Frank Bates (1–18), Harry Colliflower (1–11), and Still Bill Hill (3–6).

As the losses mounted, a Cleveland sportswriter, in a vain effort to lift the team's spirits, made a list of rules the Spiders could live by:

1. There is everything to hope for and nothing to fear.
2. Defeats do not disturb one's sleep.
3. An occasional victory is a surprise and a delight.
4. There is no danger of any club passing you.
5. You are not asked fifty times a day, "What is the score?" People take it for granted that you lost.

In spite of these inspiring words, team morale worsened. The Spiders were forced to play their last 35 games on the road, earning them various nicknames, including the "Forsaken" and the "Wanderers." Cleveland lost 40 of their last 41 games. For the season they lost a mind-boggling 101 games on the road. On the final day of the season, manager Joe Quinn allowed a cigar store clerk named Eddie Kolb to pitch the game in exchange for a box of cigars. The Spiders lost 19–3. When the season was over the team presented its traveling secretary a diamond locket for having to endure watching every game.

2. **1889 LOUISVILLE**

The 1889 Louisville team of the American Association won 27 and lost 111. The team had four managers, in-

Baseball's Worst Teams

For every great team there's usually a terrible team. The 1961 New York Yankees won 109 games, but that same year the Philadelphia Phillies lost 107 games.

In 1988, the Baltimore Orioles lost their first 21 games and finished the season with a dreadful 54–107 record.

1. **1899 CLEVELAND SPIDERS**

The 1899 Cleveland Spiders made the 1962 New York Mets look like the 1927 New York Yankees. Managed by an Australian undertaker named Joe Quinn, the Spiders won 20 games, lost 134, and finished a whopping 84 games out of first place. The 1898 team finished 13 games above .500 and had future Hall of Famers Cy Young, Jesse Burkett, and Bobby Wallace on the roster. Following the season, owners Frank De Haas and Matthew Robison transferred their best players to St. Louis, another team they owned. The defections left the Spiders with a motley crew of players.

The Cleveland pitching staff allowed 1,252 runs. The "ace" of the staff was "Coldwater" Jim Hughey

hander led the National League with 25 losses while winning only four games. Never a strikeout pitcher, Cantwell fanned only 34 batters in 210 innings.

10. JOSE DeLEON

Unlike Ben Cantwell, Pittsburgh's Jose DeLeon was a strikeout pitcher. As a rookie in 1983, DeLeon struck out 118 batters in 108 innings. Two years later, he had a 2–19 record and led the National League in losses.

4. TERRY FELTON

Terry Felton couldn't win, literally. His lifetime record was 0–16. In his final season, Felton had a 0–13 record with the 1982 Minnesota Twins.

5. RUSS MILLER

Righthanded pitcher Russ Miller won only one game in his career. His second and final season was with the 1928 Philadelphia Phillies. Miller lost all 12 decisions and struck out only 19 batters in 108 innings.

6. STEVE BLASS

For most of his career, Pittsburgh's Steve Blass was an outstanding pitcher. He won 18 games and led the National League in winning percentage. Blass won 19 games and had a 2.49 earned run average for the 1972 Pirates. Inexplicably, Blass completely lost his control the next season. He walked 84 in 88 innings, and his earned run average soared to 9.85. His record for the season was 3–9.

7. JOHN McDOUGAL

John McDougal was a rookie pitcher with St. Louis in 1895. McDougal was 4–10 with a high 8.32 earned run average. He gave up 187 hits in 114 innings and struck out only 23.

8. JACK NABORS

Jack Nabors had a 1–25 record with terrible Philadelphia Athletics teams. Nabors had a 1–20 record in 1916.

9. BEN CANTWELL

Ben Cantwell's name during the 1935 season should have been Ben Cantwin. The Boston Braves' right-

"Sigh" Young Awards

The Cy Young Award is presented each year to the best pitcher in each league. Until now, no award has been given to the worst pitcher. We are announcing winners for the Sigh Young Award.

1. **JOHN COLEMAN**

John Coleman was a rookie pitcher with Philadelphia in 1883. Coleman led the National League with 48 losses while winning only 12 games. He gave up an incredible 772 hits. The rest of his career wasn't any better, and he retired in 1890 with a 23–72 record.

2. **HARRY COLLIFLOWER**

Harry Colliflower pitched only one season in the major leagues, for good reason. He pitched for the 1899 Cleveland Spiders, probably the worst team in baseball history. Colliflower had a 1–11 record with a dreadful 8.17 earned run average. He struck out only eight batters in 98 innings while allowing 152 hits.

3. **TROY HERRIAGE**

Troy Herriage was another one-year blunder. Herriage was a rookie with the Kansas City Athletics in 1956. He had a 1–13 record with a 6.64 earned run average.

1970 to 1981. Vukovich hit above his 190 pound playing weight only two seasons.

10. **JOHN BUTLER**

John Butler was a catcher who played for Milwaukee, St. Louis, and Brooklyn from 1901 to 1907. Butler batted only .134 and never hit a home run.

4. SCOTTY BARR

Scotty Barr played six different positions and could not hit at any of them. Barr had 12 hits in 107 at-bats for the Philadelphia Athletics in 1908 and 1909. The 175 pounder had a .112 career batting average.

5. ANGEL ARAGON

Angel Aragon played third base, shortstop, and the outfield for the New York Yankees from 1914 to 1917. Aragon weighed 150 pounds and batted only .114. He had only one extra base hit and a career slugging percentage of .127.

6. GENE CORBETT

First baseman Gene Corbett played for the Philadelphia Phillies from 1936 to 1938. The 190-pounder batted only .080 in 1938 and finished his career with a .120 batting average.

7. BILL BERGEN

Catcher Bill Bergen hit above .200 in only one of his 11 seasons. Bergen hit two home runs in 3,028 at-bats. Bergen weighed 184 pounds but batted only .170 during his career.

8. CHARLIE ARMBRUSTER

Catcher Charlie Armbruster played from 1905 to 1907. Armbruster never hit a home run and batted only .149, far below his 180-pound weight.

9. JOHN VUKOVICH

Third baseman John Vukovich batted .161 while playing for Philadelphia, Milwaukee, and Cincinnati from

They Didn't Hit Their Weight

Pitcher Hank Aguirre, a lifetime .085 hitter, said, "I got one hit in three years, and I thought I was batting .333." Another pitcher, Don Carman, a .057 batter, said, "I'm seeing the ball real good, I just can't hit it." None of these players could even hit their own weight.

1. **SKEETER SHELTON**

Skeeter Shelton played briefly for the New York Yankees in 1915. The outfielder managed only one hit in 40 at-bats. His .025 batting average was far less than his 175-pound playing weight.

2. **JIM ADDUCI**

Jim Adduci was a 200-pound first baseman who played for St. Louis and Milwaukee. Adduci had only one hit in both 1983 and 1986, and his career batting average was .065.

3. **ED GASTFIELD**

Ed Gastfield was a catcher for Detroit in 1884 and 1885. In 88 at-bats, Gastfield had only six hits. His career batting average was a lowly .068.

six bases in 13 years. In his final six seasons, Hogan did not steal a base.

8. CECIL FIELDER

Cecil Fielder hit 250 home runs before he stole his first base. The huge first baseman joined the big leagues in 1985 but did not steal his first base until April 3, 1996.

9. DICK STUART

First baseman Dick Stuart could best be described as a good hit, no field, no run player. Stuart played from 1958 to 1969. During that time, he hit 228 home runs but stole only two bases in nine attempts.

10. JIM RICE

Boston Red Sox outfielder Jim Rice hit 382 homers, but he did not run the bases much faster than his home run trot. In 1984, Rice set a major league record when he grounded into 36 double plays. He led the American League in hitting into double plays four consecutive seasons.

3. MILT MAY

Catcher Milt May stole four bases in 15 seasons. In 1975 the Houston Astros' catcher stole his first base in his sixth major league season. "I thought they'd stop the game and give me second base," May remembered.

4. BO DIAZ

Bo Diaz was another slow-footed catcher who played in the major leagues from 1977 to 1989. Plagued by bad knees, Diaz's running resembled a slow-motion waddle.

5. DARNELL McDONALD

Zippy Chippy was one of the slowest thoroughbreds ever to race. The gelding never won in 90 starts. On August 17, 2000, Zippy Chippy was matched against Rochester Red Wings' centerfielder Jose Herrera in a 40-yard race. Herrera won by three horse lengths. On August 8, 2001, the 10-year-old gelding got a rematch against another Rochester player, outfielder Darnell McDonald at Frontier Field. This time the horse prevailed in the 50-yard race.

6. MIKE SCIOSCIA

Mike Scioscia played for the Los Angeles Dodgers during the 1980s. While he was an excellent defensive catcher and a decent hitter, Scioscia was a notoriously slow baserunner. His manager Tommy Lasorda said, "If he raced his pregnant wife, he'd finish third."

7. SHANTY HOGAN

Shanty Hogan was an overweight catcher who couldn't run a lick. He played from 1925 to 1937 and stole only

Slow Runners

Former catcher Joe Garagiola said, "The wind always seemed to be blowing against catchers when they are running." Not surprisingly, many catchers are on the list of baseball's slowest runners.

1. ERNIE LOMBARDI

Hall of Fame catcher Ernie Lombardi's lack of speed is legendary. Lombardi won two batting titles but undoubtedly would have won more had he not been one of the slowest runners in baseball history. The infielders played unusually deep because they could still throw out Lombardi from the outfield grass. "It took me four years to find out (Brooklyn shortstop) Pee Wee Reese was an infielder," Lombardi mused. Shortstop Leo Durocher said one of the reasons he retired was because Lombardi beat out a grounder to him.

2. RUSS NIXON

Catcher Russ Nixon played in the majors from 1957 to 1968. Opposing first basemen did not have to worry about holding him on base. In 12 seasons, Nixon did not steal a base.

was obvious that Incaviglia would never win a gold glove, but Rangers' pitcher Charlie Hough suggested he might have a glove made of another metal. Hough said, "He has a glove contract with U.S. Steel."

8. DUSTY RHODES

Dusty Rhodes is best remembered for hitting two home runs for the New York Giants against the Cleveland Indians. Rhodes spent much of his career as a pinch hitter because his outfield play was so poor. Every fly ball was an adventure. Giants' manager Leo Durocher said, "I've seen Rhodes pound his glove and the ball fall 20 feet behind him."

9. REGGIE JACKSON

Leo Durocher described Reggie Jackson as "a butcher in the outfield." Jackson agreed with the negative assessment of his fielding, "The only way I'm going to get a gold glove is with a can of spray paint."

10. PETE BROWNING

One of the best hitters of the nineteenth century, Pete Browning was also one of the worst fielders. He was nicknamed "the Gladiator" because he constantly battled fly balls. Once Browning refused to run through a mud puddle to catch a fly ball.

Defenseless

4. KING KELLY

Michael King Kelly was a two-time batting champion and was elected to the Baseball Hall of Fame in 1945, but he may have been the worst fielder of all time. He holds the lowest fielding percentage records at two different positions. His .820 fielding percentage is the lowest among outfielders and his .892 percentage ranks at the bottom for catchers.

5. BABE HERMAN

Another good hit, no field player was outfielder Babe Herman. A lifetime .324 hitter, he never quite mastered the art of fielding. Herman denied ever being hit on the head by a fly ball. "Once or twice on the shoulder, maybe, but never on the head," the Babe said. Herman once objected to having to share a locker with second baseman Fresco Thompson, who was batting around .250 at the time. "How do you think I feel dressing with a .250 hitter?" Herman asked, Thompson replied, "How do you think I feel dressing with a .250 fielder?"

6. JOSE CANSECO

Slugging outfielder Jose Canseco actually did have a fly ball bounce off his head. In a game against Cleveland on May 25, 1993, Canseco let a ball hit by Carlos Martinez hit off his head and bounce over the wall for a home run. Canseco admitted his play in the outfield was a major reason he later became a designated hitter. "If I played all my career in the outfield, I'd have 500 homers and 600 errors," he joked.

7. PETE INCAVIGLIA

Texas rookie Pete Incaviglia hit 30 home runs in 1986, but also led American League outfielders in errors. It

grounder. Unperturbed, he laughed, tossed his glove in the air, and waved to the crowd. Despite his fielding faults, the colorful Bonura had many devoted fans. One of the biggest Bonura supporters was Vice President John Nance Garner. When Bonura played for Washington in 1938 and 1940, Garner gave him a hug every time he hit a home run.

2. **SMEAD JOLLEY**

Outfielder Smead Jolley had a .305 batting average but played only four years in the major leagues because of his atrocious fielding. His most famous debacle, while he was playing for Boston, occurred in a game during the early 1930s against the Philadelphia Athletics. Bing Miller hit a liner that went through Jolley's legs. The ball hit the wall, and, as Jolley turned to play the carom, he let the ball go through his legs a second time. Because of Jolley's fielding and throwing errors, Miller was able to advance three bases, and Jolley was assessed three errors on the play.

3. **GEORGE McBRIDE**

George McBride was a weak-hitting infielder who played from 1901 to 1920. Early in the 1909 season, the Senators' shortstop had a fielding slump and made several errors. Between innings, a drunk came onto the field and put on McBride's glove. The tipsy fan then demonstrated to the stunned shortstop how to use the glove. The instruction must have worked because McBride finished the season leading American League shortstops in fielding.

Defenseless

In 1976, Chicago White Sox manager Paul Richards said of second baseman Jorge Orta, "He never met a ground ball he liked." That same year sportswriter Jack Lang said of New York Mets' outfielder Pepe Mangual, "He can drop anything he can get his hands on." After Los Angeles Dodgers' shortstop Bill Russell made several errors in a game, Mel Durslag wrote, "I've seen better hands on a clock." When these players were on the field, the defense rested.

1. ZEKE BONURA

"Banana Nose" Zeke Bonura batted .307 and knocked in more than 100 runs four times, but his career was cut short because of his terrible fielding. The lumbering first baseman actually led the American League in fielding percentage in 1936. The problem was that he let too many ground balls get by him. Humorist Jean Shepherd said Bonura had a range of "about six inches." Chicago White Sox manager Jimmy Dykes said, "This has to be the worst first baseman who ever lived. He doesn't wave at balls, he salutes them." On one memorable occasion, Bonura missed an easy

9. EMIL VERBAN

Emil Verban played second base for St. Louis, Philadelphia, Chicago, and Boston from 1944 to 1950. In 2,911 at-bats, Verban hit one home run.

10. WOODY WOODWARD

Shortstop Woody Woodward played eight seasons before hitting his first home run in 1970 while playing for the Cincinnati Reds. It proved to be Woodward's only homer in 2,187 at-bats.

4. DUANE KUIPER

Second baseman Duane Kuiper played for the Cleveland Indians and San Francisco Giants from 1974 to 1985. Kuiper had 3,379 at-bats and hit only one home run. It came off of Steve Stone of the Chicago White Sox on August 29, 1977. Kuiper said, "One is better than none, but any more people start expecting them." He joked that he intentionally did not hit home runs.

5. JOSH BILLINGS

Josh Billings played in the majors with the Cleveland Indians and St. Louis Browns from 1913 to 1923. In 11 seasons, the light-hitting catcher failed to connect for a home run.

6. TOM OLIVER

Outfielder Tom Oliver played for the Boston Red Sox from 1930 to 1933. As a rookie in 1930, Oliver led the American League with 646 at-bats but failed to hit a home run. In fact, Oliver did not hit a home run in his 1,931 major league at-bats.

7. IRV HALL

Irv Hall was an infielder with the Philadelphia Athletics from 1943 to 1946. Hall went homerless in 1,904 at-bats.

8. DAVY FORCE

Shortstop Davy Force was nicknamed Tom Thumb because he stood 5'4" tall and weighed only 130 pounds. Force played from 1876 to 1886. He hit a home run in 1882, his only round tripper in 2,950 at-bats.

Power Outage

Shortstop Al Bridwell hit only two home runs in 11 seasons. Outfielder Ed Hahn hit only one homer in 2,045 at-bats. When these batters came to the plate, you could expect a power outage.

1. **TOMMY THEVENOW**

Infielder Tommy Thevenow hit two home runs for the St. Louis Cardinals during the 1926 season. He played until 1938 but never hit another home run. He went homerless in his last 3,347 at-bats.

2. **BILL HOLBERT**

Catcher Bill Holbert played in the major leagues from 1876 to 1888 and never hit a home run. Holbert had 2,335 at-bats during that period.

3. **EDDIE FOSTER**

Third base is often a position played by power hitters, but not when Eddie Foster manned the hot corner. Foster hit six home runs in 13 seasons from 1910 to 1923. He did not hit a homer in his last seven seasons. Foster went 3,278 at-bats without a home run.

than 18 home runs in a season. With the Atlanta Braves in 1973, Johnson belted 43 home runs, three more than teammate Hank Aaron. In his final four seasons, Johnson hit a total of 27 home runs.

7. DON PADGETT

Catcher Don Padgett batted .399 with the St. Louis Cardinals in 1939. He had batted .271 the previous season and batted .242 the following year. His career batting average was 111 points below his best season.

8. STEVE STONE

Steve Stone averaged less than nine victories during his first nine seasons. In 1980, the Baltimore right-hander led the American League with 25 wins. After winning only four games the next season, Stone retired.

9. GUS KROCK

Lefthanded pitcher Gus Krock won 24 games as a rookie with Chicago in 1888. Krock's success was brief as he won only seven more games in his major league career.

10. HARRY ANDERSON

For one season, Philadelphia outfielder Harry Anderson was one of the best hitters in the National League. In 1958, his second season, Anderson hit .301 and batted in 97 runs. In the next two seasons, Anderson's batting average dropped to .240 and .214, and he was out of baseball by 1961.

James's only miraculous season. He won only five more games.

3. NORM CASH

First baseman Norm Cash batted .271 during his 17-year career. Only once did he hit above .300. In 1961, Cash batted .361 to win the American League batting title. Cash joked, "The only mistake I made in my whole baseball career was hitting .361 that one year, because ever since then people expected me to keep on doing it." Cash never hit more than .283 again.

4. TITO FRANCONA

Tito Francona was a journeyman player who batted .272 during his career from 1956 to 1970. In 1958, Francona batted .254 as a part-time outfielder. He did not become a starter in Cleveland until two months into the 1959 season. Francona was the hottest batter in the American League and was flirting with the .400 mark in early September. He finished the season with a .363 average, but did not have enough plate appearances to qualify for the batting title. Detroit's Harvey Kuenn won the batting crown with a .353 average. Francona never again challenged for a batting title.

5. BRADY ANDERSON

Outfielder Brady Anderson was a leadoff hitter with good power, but he went on a homer barrage in 1996. The Baltimore outfielder hit 50 home runs, twice as many as his previous best season. He also set a record with 12 leadoff homers.

6. DAVEY JOHNSON

Second baseman Davey Johnson played for the Baltimore Orioles from 1965 to 1972. He never hit more

One-Year Wonders

Some players have career years, in which their performance far exceeds anything they had previously done or would ever do again. They are known as one-year wonders.

1. **HENRY SCHMIDT**

Henry Schmidt won 21 games as a rookie with Brooklyn in 1903. In his first game he defeated the great Christy Mathewson of the New York Giants. The Texas-born pitcher shocked Brooklyn owner Charles Ebbets when he informed him, "I do not like living in the East and will not report." True to his word, Schmidt never played in the majors again.

2. **BILL JAMES**

As a rookie pitcher with Boston in 1913, Bill James had a 6–10 record. The next season, James won 26 games and led the National League in winning percentage. His earned run average was a sensational 1.90. James was a major reason for the unexpected pennant-winning season of the team known as the Miracle Braves. It was

but drew few comparisons to Roger Maris. Repoz batted .220 in his only full season in New York. He remained in the major leagues until 1972 but retired with a .224 batting average.

8. **TOM TRESH**

Early in his career, Tom Tresh was compared to another Yankee, Mickey Mantle. Both players began as shortstops and moved to the outfield. Tresh batted .286 and hit 20 home runs as a rookie in 1962, but his stats declined steadily. By 1968, Tresh batted only .195.

9. **GENE RYE**

Playing for Waco of the Texas League, Gene Rye hit three home runs in one inning in a game against Beaumont. The minor league slugger joined the Boston Red Sox in 1931. Rye batted .179 and went homerless in 39 at-bats.

10. **STEVE CHRISTMAS**

The Cincinnati Reds thought Steve Christmas might be the man to replace Johnny Bench. The catcher joined the Reds in 1983, Bench's last season. Unfortunately, Christmas batted only .059 and was traded to the Chicago White Sox. Christmas left the major leagues with a .162 batting average and one home run.

starts Rocket Ron fanned a total of 51 batters. The last place Pittsburgh Pirates rushed the hard-throwing righthander to the major leagues in 1952. Necciai had a 1–6 record with a 7.08 earned run average. Plagued by a sore arm and ulcer, Necciai never pitched in the majors again.

4. BILLY CONSOLO

Infielder Billy Consolo was 18 years old when he was signed by the Boston Red Sox in 1953. The Red Sox thought Consolo was going to be their next big star. Boy, were they wrong. Consolo played ten years as a utility infielder, batting only .221.

5. DAVE NICHOLSON

The Baltimore Orioles paid slugging outfielder Dave Nicholson a $200,000 bonus. Nicholson rewarded their confidence by hitting five home runs in 113 at-bats and striking out nearly 50 percent of the time. In two seasons in Baltimore, Nicholson batted .186 and .173. Nicholson set a dubious record by striking out every 2.48 at-bats during his seven-year career.

6. FRANK LEJA

The New York Yankees believed they had another Lou Gehrig when they signed first baseman Frank Leja to a big bonus. The Yankees soon discovered that Leja was not the second coming of the Iron Horse. Leja had only one major league hit in 23 at-bats for an anemic .043 batting average.

7. ROGER REPOZ

Another highly publicized Yankees' prospect was outfielder Roger Repoz. Repoz joined the Yankees in 1964

Major Disappointments

Some players come into the major leagues highly touted. Many live up to their promise and become stars. Others prove to be disappointments.

1. **BILLY JOE DAVIDSON**

Billy Joe Davidson was a celebrated bonus baby in the 1950s. The Cleveland Indians, convinced they had another Bob Feller, gave the young pitcher a $100,000 bonus. Davidson was no Feller and never pitched in the major leagues.

2. **PAUL PETTIT**

The Pittsburgh Pirates were certain they had a young pitching star when they signed lefthander Paul Pettit. The bonus baby had pitched six no-hitters in high school and was considered a can't miss prospect. He made his major league debut at age 19 in 1951. By 1953, Pettit's major league career was over. He won one game and had a 7.34 earned run average.

3. **RON NECCIAI**

On May 13, 1952, Ron Necciai struck out 27 batters in a minor league game against Welch. In consecutive

10. **JOE TIPTON**

Joe Tipton was a catcher who hit .236 during his seven-year career. In October 1949, the Chicago White Sox traded Tipton to the Philadelphia Athletics for second baseman Nellie Fox. Fox spent 14 seasons with the White Sox and led the American League in hits four times.

6. STEVE LYONS

On June 29, 1986, the Boston Red Sox traded Steve "Psycho" Lyons to the Chicago White Sox for pitching great Tom Seaver. Lyons was better known for his flaky behavior then for his play. Seaver, at the end of his fabulous career, won 33 games in two-plus seasons in Chicago.

7. BOB McGRAW

In December 1929, the Philadelphia Phillies traded outfielder Homer Peel and pitcher Bob McGraw to the St. Louis Cardinals for pitcher Grover Cleveland Alexander and catcher Harry McCurdy. McGraw, a pitcher with a 26–38 record, never won another game. Peel batted .164 in 26 games with St. Louis. Alexander, winner of 373 games, retired after going winless in nine games in Philadelphia.

8. JOHN POLONI

On December 14, 1977, the Texas Rangers traded pitcher John Poloni to the Boston Red Sox for pitcher Ferguson Jenkins. Poloni won only one game in the majors, while Jenkins won 18 games for Texas in 1978 and 16 the following season.

9. CHARLEY SMITH

Third baseman Charley Smith was traded seven times between 1961 and 1969. On December 8, 1966, the St. Louis Cardinals traded Smith to the New York Yankees for outfielder Roger Maris. Smith batted .225 in his two seasons in New York. Maris, who had played in five World Series with the Yankees, spent two seasons in St. Louis, and both years the Cardinals won the pennant.

Charlie Williams. Williams never won more than six games in a season. Mays played his final two seasons in New York and appeared in the 1973 World Series.

3. **DAVE MAY**

Like Pete Rose and Willie Mays, Hank Aaron played his final few seasons in the city where he began his career. In 1974, the Atlanta Braves traded Aaron to Milwaukee for outfielder Dave May. May hit 15 home runs in two seasons with Atlanta. Aaron also played two seasons with Milwaukee, hitting the final 22 homers of his record-breaking career.

4. **FRANK DUFFY**

Shortstop Frank Duffy had a .232 career batting average during his major league career that lasted from 1970 to 1979. Despite his mediocre stats, Duffy was involved in two major league trades. On May 29, 1971, the Reds traded Duffy and pitcher Vern Geishert to the San Francisco Giants for outfielder George Foster. In Cincinnati, Foster blossomed into a star and led the National League in runs batted in three consecutive years. Six months later the Giants traded Duffy and pitcher Gaylord Perry to the Cleveland Indians for pitcher Sam McDowell. While McDowell was a disappointment, Perry won 24 games and the Cy Young Award in Cleveland.

5. **KEN CLAY**

In August 1980, the New York Yankees traded pitcher Ken Clay to the Texas Rangers in exchange for pitcher Gaylord Perry. Clay won two games in Texas and had a career 10–24 record. Perry won 314 games during his Hall of Fame career.

Trading Places

Occasionally a great player will be traded for an obscure one.

In 1953 the Cincinnati Reds traded first baseman Joe Adcock to the Milwaukee Braves for infielder Rocky Bridges. Adcock hit 305 home runs while playing for the Braves, while Bridges hit two for the Reds. The New York Yankees traded outfielder Cedric Durst to Boston for pitcher Red Ruffing. Durst hit one home run in Boston and then retired. Ruffing won 231 games with the Yankees.

1. TOM LAWLESS

On August 16, 1984, the Cincinnati Reds traded second baseman Tom Lawless to the Montreal Expos for Pete Rose. Rose became the player-manager of the Reds and broke Ty Cobb's all-time hit record in Cincinnati. Lawless played only 11 games in Montreal, batting .176.

2. CHARLIE WILLIAMS

In May 1972, the San Francisco Giants traded aging superstar Willie Mays to the New York Mets for pitcher

9. **1912 NEW YORK GIANTS**

Managed by Joe McGraw, the 1912 New York Giants finished the season with a 103–48 record. Rube Marquard led the National League with 26 wins, and rookie Jeff Tesreau had the league's lowest earned run average. Christy Mathewson won 23 games. New York played Boston in the World Series. The Giants lost the eighth and deciding game of the series (one game ended in a tie) when outfielder Fred Snodgrass dropped a fly ball.

10. **1954 NEW YORK YANKEES**

After the New York Yankees won five consecutive world championships between 1949 and 1953, the 1954 team won 103 games, more than any of the championship teams, but they did not even win the pennant. The Yankees finished eight games behind the Cleveland Indians.

pected to win a third consecutive world title. Outfielder Al Simmons batted .390 to win the batting crown, and pitcher Lefty Grove won 31 games. The A's were beaten in seven games by the St. Louis Cardinals in the 1931 World Series.

6. **1953 BROOKLYN DODGERS**

The 1953 Brooklyn Dodgers won 105 games and had one of the most dangerous lineups in baseball history. Rightfielder Carl Furillo won the batting title with a .344 average and catcher Roy Campanella led the National League with 142 runs batted in. First baseman Gil Hodges batted in 122 runs. The lineup also included future Hall of Famers Pee Wee Reese, Duke Snider, and Jackie Robinson. In the World Series, the Dodgers lost to their nemesis, the New York Yankees, in six games.

7. **1931 NEW YORK YANKEES**

The 1931 New York Yankees scored 1,067 runs, a modern record for runs scored. First baseman Lou Gehrig set an American League record with 184 runs batted in, and rightfielder Babe Ruth knocked in 163 runs. Despite winning 94 games, the Yankees finished 13 $1/2$ games behind the pennant-winning Philadelphia A's.

8. **1973 CINCINNATI REDS**

The Cincinnati Reds were heavily favored in the 1973 National League Championship Series against the New York Mets. The Reds had won 99 games, while the Mets finished just three games above .500. Cincinnati's high-powered offense included Pete Rose, Johnny Bench, Joe Morgan, and Tony Perez. New York upset Cincinnati in five games.

Babe Ruth and Lou Gehrig relax before a ballgame. They combined to help the 1931 New York Yankees set a modern-day record for runs scored in a season, yet fell short of the World Series.

League Most Valuable Player. Second baseman Bret Boone led the league with 141 runs batted in. Left-handed pitcher Jamie Moyer won 20 games. The Mariners never reached the World Series, as they lost to the New York Yankees in the American League Championship Series.

3. **1954 CLEVELAND INDIANS**

The Cleveland Indians dominated the American League with 111 victories in 1954. Second baseman Bobby Avila hit .341 to win the batting title, and outfielder Larry Doby led the American League in homers and runs batted in. The Indians' pitching staff was one of the greatest in baseball history. The staff included four Hall of Famers: Early Wynn, Bob Lemon, Bob Feller, and Hal Newhouser. Wynn and Lemon both won 23 games. Stunned by Dusty Rhodes's clutch hitting and Willie Mays's miraculous over-the-shoulder catch in game one, the Indians were swept in four games by the New York Giants.

4. **1969 BALTIMORE ORIOLES**

The 1969 Baltimore Orioles won 109 games, finishing 19 games ahead of Detroit in the American League East Division. The offense was led by first baseman Boog Powell and rightfielder Frank Robinson, who each batted in at least 100 runs. Starters Mike Cuellar and Dave McNally both won 20 games. The Orioles were heavily favored to win the World Series, but fell to the Miracle Mets in five games.

5. **1931 PHILADELPHIA A'S**

The Philadelphia A's won the World Series in 1929 and 1930. The 1931 team won 107 games and was ex-

They Weren't World Champions

The 1942 Brooklyn Dodgers won 104 games and did not even win the pennant. The 1943 St. Louis Cardinals won the National League pennant by 18 games only to lose the World Series in five games to the New York Yankees. Not every great team won it all.

1. **THE 1906 CHICAGO CUBS**

The 1906 Chicago Cubs had the best record in major league baseball history, 116 wins and 36 losses. The team featured future Hall of Famers Mordecai Brown, Frank Chance, Johnny Evers, and Joe Tinker. The Cubs were overwhelming favorites to win the World Series but lost to the crosstown Chicago White Sox. Known as the Hitless Wonders, the White Sox had a .230 team batting average. The White Sox shocked the Cubs by winning the Series in six games.

2. **2001 SEATTLE MARINERS**

Despite losing stars Ken Griffey, Jr., and Alex Rodriguez in the previous two years, the Seattle Mariners tied the major league record by winning 116 games. Outfielder Ichiro Suzuki batted .350 and was the American

in more than 100 runs. Outfielder Bernie Williams batted .339, and shortstop Derek Jeter hit .324. Twenty-game winner David Cone led the pitching staff. The Yankees swept the San Diego Padres in four games to win the World Championship.

8. **1972 OAKLAND A'S**

The Oakland A's won three straight world championships from 1972 to 1974. The 1972 team defeated Cincinnati four games to three in the World Series. The colorful A's were led by slugging outfielder Reggie Jackson. The strong pitching staff featured 21-game winner Catfish Hunter and reliever Rollie Fingers.

9. **1907 CHICAGO CUBS**

The 1907 Chicago Cubs won 107 games and coasted to the National League pennant by 17 games. The Cubs swept Ty Cobb's Detroit Tigers in the World Series. The Cubs' solid infield included first baseman Frank Chance, second baseman Johnny Evers, and shortstop Joe Tinker. The sensational pitching staff posted an earned run average of 1.73. Orval Overall and Mordecai Brown both won 20 games, and Jack Pflester led the league with a 1.15 earned run average.

10. **1953 NEW YORK YANKEES**

Managed by Casey Stengel, the New York Yankees won a record five consecutive world championships between 1949 and 1953. The 1953 club was led by catcher Yogi Berra's 108 runs batted in. Twenty-one-year-old outfielder Mickey Mantle batted in 92 runs. Whitey Ford won 18 games, and 16-game winner Ed Lopat led the American League in earned run average.

Yankees hit 240 home runs. Maris broke Babe Ruth's record with 61 homers and led the league with 142 runs batted in. Mantle hit 54 home runs and batted in 128 runs. New York had six players who had more than 20 home runs. The pitching staff was led by Whitey Ford, who had a 25–4 record. New York defeated the Cincinnati Reds four games to one in the World Series.

5. **1936 NEW YORK YANKEES**

The 1936 New York Yankees won the American League pennant by 19 1/2 games. The team scored 1,065 runs, averaging seven a game. First baseman Lou Gehrig led the league with 49 home runs. Gehrig, Joe DiMaggio, Bill Dickey, Tony Lazzeri, and George Selkirk all batted in more than 100 runs. The pitching staff included Hall of Famers Red Ruffing and Lefty Gomez. The Yankees defeated the New York Giants in six games in the World Series.

6. **1970 BALTIMORE ORIOLES**

The 1970 Baltimore Orioles had a superb combination of hitting and pitching. The Orioles won 108 games and won the pennant by 15 games. The balanced offense was led by rightfielder Frank Robinson, third baseman Brooks Robinson, and first baseman Boog Powell. Pitchers Mike Cuellar and Dave McNally each won 24 games and Jim Palmer had 20 victories. Baltimore used timely hitting and sensational fielding to defeat Cincinnati four games to one in the World Series.

7. **1998 NEW YORK YANKEES**

The 1998 New York Yankees won 114 games to finish 22 games ahead of runner-up Boston. First baseman Tino Martinez and rightfielder Paul O'Neill each batted

144   Baseball's Most Wanted II

2. 1976 CINCINNATI REDS

The 1975 Cincinnati Reds won 108 games and defeated the Boston Red Sox in a memorable World Series. The 1976 Reds may have even been better. They won 102 games during the regular season, then swept the Philadelphia Phillies in the three-game National League Championship Series. Cincinnati capped their season by sweeping the New York Yankees in the World Series. The Big Red Machine was led by Hall of Famers Johnny Bench, Joe Morgan, and Tony Perez. Baseball's all-time hit leader Pete Rose batted .323, and leftfielder George Foster led the National League with 121 runs batted in. Cincinnati led National League teams in runs, doubles, triples, home runs, batting average, slugging percentage, stolen bases, and fielding percentage. The balanced pitching staff had seven pitchers who won 11 or more games.

3. 1929 PHILADELPHIA A'S

Managed by Connie Mack, the 1929 Philadelphia A's had a 104–46 record and finished 18 games ahead of a New York Yankees' team led by Babe Ruth and Lou Gehrig. Philadelphia leftfielder Al Simmons led the American League with 157 runs batted in. First baseman Jimmie Foxx batted .354 and knocked in 117 runs. Catcher Mickey Cochrane hit .331, and rightfielder Bing Miller batted .335. Pitcher George Earnshaw led the league with 24 wins, and Lefty Grove won 20. In the World Series, Philadelphia defeated the Chicago Cubs in five games.

4. 1961 NEW YORK YANKEES

The 1961 New York Yankees won 109 games. Led by the M and M boys, Roger Maris and Mickey Mantle, the

Terrific Teams

Led by Stan Musial, the 1944 St. Louis Cardinals won 105 games and won the National League pennant by 14 1/2 games. The 1984 Detroit Tigers, managed by Sparky Anderson, won 35 of their first 40 games and led the standings from the first day of the season to the last. Each of these great teams were world champions.

1. 1927 NEW YORK YANKEES

Of all the great New York Yankees teams, the 1927 club remains the most famous. The Bronx Bombers had a 110–44 record and won the American League pennant by 19 games. Rightfielder Babe Ruth hit 60 home runs and batted in 164. First baseman Lou Gehrig hit 47 homers and led the league with 175 runs batted in. Second baseman Tony Lazzeri and leftfielder Bob Meusel each had more than 100 runs batted in, and centerfielder Earl Combs batted .356. The pitching staff was led by two Hall of Famers, 22-game winner Waite Hoyt and lefthander Herb Pennock, who won 19. In the World Series, the Yankees swept the Pittsburgh Pirates in four games.

led his league in winning percentage, complete games, strikeouts, shutouts, and saves.

8. GROVER CLEVELAND ALEXANDER

Grover Cleveland Alexander won 33 games with the Philadelphia Phillies in 1916. Alexander led the National League in earned run average, complete games, and strikeouts. He pitched 16 shutouts, tying George Bradley's record.

9. MORDECAI BROWN

Mordecai Brown had a 26–6 record and pitched 10 shutouts for the Chicago Cubs in 1906. His 1.04 earned run average led the National League and is one of the lowest in baseball history. A childhood accident with a corn shredder injured his pitching hand. Part of his right index finger was severed, and, in another farm accident, two other fingers were gnarled. Brown's unusual grip allowed him to spin the ball in a manner that made it difficult to hit.

10. MATCHES KILROY

Matches Kilroy was a rookie with Baltimore of the American Association in 1886. The 20-year-old left-hander won 29 games and struck out a record 513 batters.

Johnson also led all American League pitchers with 243 strikeouts and 11 shutouts.

3. BOB GIBSON

1968 was the year of the pitcher, and the pitcher of the year was Bob Gibson. The St. Louis Cardinals' right-hander compiled a 22–9 record. He gave up only 198 hits in 304 innings and pitched 13 shutouts. Gibson led the National League with 268 strikeouts and a 1.12 earned run average.

4. GEORGE BRADLEY

George "Grin" Bradley was the best pitcher in 1876, the National League's inaugural season. He was the first pitcher to devise a signal system with his catcher to call the pitches. Bradley won 45 games and led the league with a 1.23 earned run average. He pitched 16 shutouts, a record that has never been surpassed.

5. JOHN CLARKSON

Hall of Famer John Clarkson won 53 games pitching for Chicago in 1885. Clarkson led all pitchers with 318 strikeouts and 10 shutouts. He had 68 complete games that season, more than most pitchers today would have in a career.

6. CHRISTY MATHEWSON

Christy Mathewson of the New York Giants had many great seasons, but his finest was 1908. Mathewson led the National League in wins (37), earned run average (1.43), complete games (34), strikeouts (259), and shutouts (12). He also led the league in saves.

7. ED WALSH

The best pitcher in the American League in 1908 was Chicago's Ed Walsh. Big Ed won 40 games and also

Sensational Seasons

In 1877, Louisville's Jim Devlin pitched every inning of his team's 61 games. Dutch Leonard had a 1.01 earned run average with Boston in 1914, the lowest earned run average in modern major league history. The pitchers in this list had seasons in which they were unhittable.

1. OLD HOSS RADBOURN

Old Hoss Radbourn was the ultimate workhorse with Providence during the 1884 season. Radbourn won 60 games, a record that will probably never be broken. He had 73 complete games and struck out 441 batters. His 1.38 earned run average also led the National League. Radbourn paid the price for his frequent trips to the mound. Sometimes his right arm was so sore he could not lift it to comb his hair.

2. WALTER JOHNSON

Walter Johnson's greatest season was 1913. The Washington Senators' ace had a 36–7 record and led the American League with a 1.09 earned run average.

The Greatest Pitchers of All Time

7. SANDY KOUFAX

Sandy Koufax was 19 years old when he won his first game with the Brooklyn Dodgers in 1955. It took the hard-throwing lefthander six years to find his control and become a winner. From 1962 to 1966, Koufax led the National League in earned run average five consecutive years. He pitched four no-hitters during his career.

8. NOLAN RYAN

Nolan Ryan was baseball's strikeout king. Blessed with a 100 mile-per-hour fastball and a tireless arm, Ryan struck out 5,714 batters, 1,578 more than runner-up Steve Carlton. Ryan won 324 games and threw a record seven no-hitters.

9. TOM SEAVER

Tom Seaver lived up to his nickname Tom Terrific. A five-time 20-game winner, Seaver won 311 games between 1967 and 1986. He struck out 3,640 batters, fifth on the all-time list.

10. ROGER CLEMENS

The only pitcher to win six Cy Young Awards, Roger Clemens is closing in on the 300 win mark. Third on the all-time strikeout list, the Rocket had two games in which he struck out 20 batters. In 2001, at age 39, Clemens posted a 20–3 record with the New York Yankees.

Nolan Ryan comes toward the plate during one of his record seven no-hitters, this one against the Baltimore Orioles in 1975.

had an earned run average of less than 2.00. The Big Train led the American League in strikeouts twelve seasons. His 110 shutouts is a major league record.

3. LEFTY GROVE

Lefty Grove pitched from 1925 to 1941. The Philadelphia Athletics' ace led the American League in strikeouts his first seven seasons. Nine times Grove led the league in earned run average. From 1927 to 1933, he had seven consecutive 20-win seasons. Grove retired in 1941 with a record of 300 wins and 141 losses.

4. CY YOUNG

Cy Young won a record 511 games. A pitcher could have 25 20-win seasons and still fall 11 victories short of Young's record. From 1891 to 1904, Young had 14 consecutive seasons with 20 or more wins. Young won more than 30 games five times.

5. GROVER CLEVELAND ALEXANDER

Grover Cleveland Alexander led the National League in victories six times between 1911 and 1920. Alexander had six consecutive seasons in which his earned run average was below two runs a game. His 90 shutouts ranks second all time. Alexander's 373 career wins tied him with Christy Mathewson.

6. WARREN SPAHN

Warren Spahn was 25 years old when he won his first major league game in 1946, but by the time he retired 19 years later, Spahn had 363 victories, a National League record for a lefthanded pitcher. The Braves' ace had an amazing 13 20-win seasons. At age 42 in 1963, Spahn had a 23–7 record.

The Greatest Pitchers of All Time

Chicago White Sox pitcher Ed Walsh had a record 1.82 career average. Nicknamed the Chairman of the Board, Whitey Ford had a lifetime record of 236 wins and only 106 losses. Baltimore righthander Jim Palmer had eight 20-win seasons. Atlanta's Greg Maddux has won four National League Cy Young Awards. These men are some of the best pitchers in baseball history.

1. CHRISTY MATHEWSON

Philadelphia A's manager Connie Mack said, "Christy Mathewson was the greatest pitcher who ever lived." Matty used his perfect control to win a National League record 373 games. Mathewson led the league in earned run average five times and had a 2.13 career ERA. He had four 30-win seasons and topped the 20-victory mark 13 times. Big Six threw 80 shutouts while pitching for the New York Giants from 1900 to 1916.

2. WALTER JOHNSON

Walter Johnson won 416 games with the Washington Senators from 1907 to 1927. Eleven times Johnson

7. LOU GEHRIG

In 1931, New York Yankees' first baseman Lou Gehrig set an American League record with 184 runs batted in. The Iron Horse led the league with 211 hits, 46 home runs, and 163 runs scored. Gehrig ranked fifth in the league in batting with a .341 average.

8. GEORGE SISLER

In 1920, St. Louis Browns' first baseman George Sisler batted .407 and set the major league record with 257 hits. Two years later, Sisler had even a better season, batting .420 and leading the American League in hits, triples, runs, and stolen bases.

9. HUGH DUFFY

Boston outfielder Hugh Duffy had an unbelievable season in 1894. Duffy batted .438, a major league record that will probably never be broken. He led the National League in hits, doubles, homers, runs batted in, and slugging percentage.

10. STAN MUSIAL

Stan Musial had his greatest season in 1948. The St. Louis Cardinals' outfielder batted .376 and led the National League in hits, doubles, triples, runs, runs batted in, and slugging percentage. Stan the Man also slammed 39 home runs.

even better. The Babe led the American League with 59 home runs, 177 runs scored, 171 batted in, and a .846 slugging percentage. Ruth batted .378 for the season to finish third in the batting race.

3. **ROGERS HORNSBY**

Rogers Hornsby had many great seasons, but none greater than 1922. The Rajah paced the senior circuit with 250 hits, 46 doubles, and 141 runs scored. He won the Triple Crown by batting .401 with 42 home runs and 152 runs batted in.

4. **TY COBB**

In 1911, Ty Cobb batted .420, the highest average of his career. Cobb led the American League with 248 hits, 47 doubles, 24 triples, 147 runs scored, 144 runs batted in, and 83 stolen bases.

5. **NAP LAJOIE**

In 1901, the American League's inaugural season, Philadelphia second baseman Nap Lajoie batted .422, still the highest mark in league history. Lajoie hit 14 home runs and batted in 125 runs to complete his Triple Crown. He also led the league in hits, doubles, runs, and slugging percentage.

6. **TED WILLIAMS**

Ted Williams had many great seasons, but none was more memorable than 1941. The 23-year-old Boston Red Sox outfielder batted .406, the last player to top the magical .400 mark. Williams also led the American League in home runs, runs scored, walks, and slugging percentage. His on-base percentage for the year was .551.

Monster Seasons

In 1887, St. Louis outfielder Tip O'Neill batted .435 and led the league in hits, doubles, triples, home runs, runs, batting average, and slugging percentage. Cardinals' outfielder Joe Medwick won the Triple Crown in 1937 and led the National League in hits, doubles, home runs, runs, runs batted in, batting average, and slugging percentage. Chicago Cubs' Sammy Sosa batted .328 in 2001 and hit 64 home runs, scored 146 runs, and batted in 160 runs. These players had seasons to remember.

1. **BARRY BONDS**

Barry Bonds made baseball history during the 2001 season, setting single-season records in three major offensive categories. His 73 home runs broke Mark McGwire's record. Bonds' .863 slugging percentage topped the record of .847 set by Babe Ruth in 1920. He also set the record for the most walks in a season with 177.

2. **BABE RUTH**

Everyone remembers Babe Ruth's 1927 season in which he hit 60 home runs, but his 1921 season was

seasons, Heilmann batted above .390. His best season was 1923 when he batted .403. Heilmann's career batting average was .342.

8. **PETE ROSE**

Pete Rose had 200 or more hits in a record ten seasons. Rose is baseball's all-time hit leader with 4,256. The Cincinnati Reds' star won batting crowns in 1968, 1969, and 1973.

9. **Tony Gwynn**

San Diego outfielder Tony Gwynn was an eight-time National League batting champion. Gwynn won his first batting title in 1984. He won four consecutive batting crowns from 1994 to 1997. Gwynn flirted with the .400 mark in 1994 when he batted .394.

10. **WADE BOGGS**

This Boston Red Sox third baseman won five batting titles between 1983 and 1988. Boggs batted above .350 each of those seasons. He retired with 3,010 hits and a .328 career batting average.

The Greatest Hitters Who Ever Lived

"All I ever wanted out of life is that when I walk down the street, folks will say, 'There goes the greatest hitter who ever lived.'"—Ted Williams.

3. **TED WILLIAMS**

Ted Williams said, "All I ever wanted out of life is that when I walk down the street, folks will say, 'There goes the greatest hitter who ever lived.'" The last man to hit .400 in a season, Williams won six American League batting titles between 1941 and 1958. In 1957, at age 39, the Boston Red Sox outfielder batted .388. Teddy Ballgame retired in 1960 with a .344 career batting average.

4. **STAN MUSIAL**

Stan Musial starred with the St. Louis Cardinals from 1941 to 1963. Stan the Man won batting titles in 1943, 1946, 1948, 1950, 1951, 1952, and 1957. Musial batted above .300 during his first 17 seasons. His career batting average was .331.

5. **HONUS WAGNER**

An eight-time National League batting champion, Pittsburgh shortstop Honus Wagner was a .329 lifetime hitter. From 1897 to 1913, Wagner batted above .300 every season. Wagner ranks in the top 10 in career hits, doubles, and triples.

6. **TRIS SPEAKER**

Despite a career .344 batting average, Tris Speaker won only one batting title. The reason was because much of his career overlapped with Ty Cobb. The Cleveland outfielder won his lone batting crown in 1916 when he batted .386. His 793 doubles is a major league record.

7. **HARRY HEILMANN**

Detroit Tigers' outfielder Harry Heilmann won batting titles in 1921, 1923, 1925, and 1927. Each of those

The Greatest Hitters Who Ever Lived

Shoeless Joe Jackson had a .356 career batting average. George Sisler twice hit above .400 in a season. These players hit for a high average, but they were anything but average hitters.

1. TY COBB

Ty Cobb's .366 career batting average is the highest in major league history. Cobb won nine consecutive batting titles from 1907 to 1915, and 12 overall. Eight times he led the American League in hits. Cobb hit above .400 in 1911, 1912, and 1922.

2. ROGERS HORNSBY

Rogers Hornsby's .358 career batting average is the highest for a right-handed hitter. Hornsby said, "I don't like to sound egotistical, but every time I stepped to the plate with a bat in my hands, I couldn't help but feel sorry for the pitcher." The slugging second baseman won seven batting titles between 1920 and 1928. He batted .424 in 1924 and averaged above .400 during a five-year stretch from 1921 to 1925.

1998 during his memorable home run duel with Mark McGwire. The Chicago Cubs' outfielder always leaps out of the batters' box when he hits a homer.

7. FRANK ROBINSON

Frank Robinson hit 586 home runs during his career from 1956 to 1976. Robinson had 11 seasons in which he hit 30 or more home runs. In 1966, the Baltimore Orioles' outfielder led the American League with 49 home runs.

8. HARMON KILLEBREW

Hall of Famer Harmon Killebrew had eight seasons in which he hit 40 or more home runs. He led the American League in homers six times between 1959 and 1969. For his career, Killebrew belted 573 home runs.

9. REGGIE JACKSON

Reggie Jackson led the American League in homers in 1973, 1975, 1980, and 1982. His career high was 47 home runs in 1969. Jackson retired in 1987 with 563 home runs.

10. MIKE SCHMIDT

Third baseman Mike Schmidt slugged 548 home runs with Philadelphia from 1972 to 1989. Eight times Schmidt led the National League in homers. In 1980, he hit 48 home runs and led the Phils to their only world championship.

2. HANK AARON

Despite never hitting 50 home runs in a season, Hank Aaron holds the career record with 755 home runs. The consistent Aaron hit 40 or more home runs eight times. The Braves' outfielder led the National League in homers in 1957, 1963, 1966, and 1967.

3. BARRY BONDS

San Francisco Giants' outfielder Barry Bonds set a single season record when he slammed an incredible 73 home runs in 2001. Through the 2002 season Bonds had 613 home runs. If he stays healthy, he may someday be the all-time home run king.

4. WILLIE MAYS

Willie Mays' 660 home runs ranks behind only Hank Aaron and Babe Ruth. The Giants' outfielder led the National League in home runs four times. Mays hit more than 50 home runs in both 1955 and 1965.

5. MARK McGWIRE

In 1998, St. Louis first baseman Mark McGwire became the first major leaguer to hit 70 home runs in a season. His 70 homers shattered the single season record of 61 set by Roger Maris in 1961. In 1987, McGwire set a rookie record by hitting 49 home runs with Oakland. Big Mac holds the major league record with a home run every ten at-bats. He retired after the 2001 season with 583 home runs.

6. SAMMY SOSA

Sammy Sosa hit 64 home runs in 2001, making him the only major leaguer ever to hit more than 60 home runs in three seasons. Sosa hit 66 round trippers in

Supreme Sluggers

The home run is probably the most exciting play in baseball. Many great power hitters have played the game over the years. Jimmie Foxx led the American League in home runs four times and slugged a personal high of 58 with the Philadelphia Athletics in 1932. Pittsburgh outfielder Ralph Kiner led the National League in home runs during his first seven seasons. One of today's most feared sluggers, Ken Griffey, Jr., has hit as many as 56 homers in a season.

1. BABE RUTH

His single-season and career home run marks may have been broken, but Babe Ruth still personifies the long ball hitter. The Sultan of Swat led the American League in home runs 12 times between 1918 and 1931. Many of his blasts were tape measure shots. In one season, the Bambino hit more home runs than any other American League team. In 1927, Ruth set a single-season record with 60 home runs. The record lasted 34 years until broken by another New York Yankee outfielder, Roger Maris. His record of 714 career homers stood for 39 years until broken by Hank Aaron.

10. PETE INCAVIGLIA

Pete Incaviglia hit 30 home runs as a rookie with the Texas Rangers in 1986. The free-swinging outfielder also set a rookie record by striking out 185 times that season. Incaviglia hit the ball so hard when he did make contact that he once broke 114 bats in a season.

played outfield for the St. Louis Browns. One day, he picked up a bat discarded by outfielder Jeff Heath. The knob had broken off, but Brown liked the feel of the bat. He taped on the knob and went to the plate, but the umpire refused to let him use the taped bat. Brown removed the knob and hit a home run, the first by an African American in the American League and the only one of his career. Displeased that Brown had used his bat, Heath shattered it.

7. **CHET LEMON**

Chet Lemon was a hard-hitting outfielder who played for the Chicago White Sox and Detroit Tigers during the 1970s and 1980s. His best season was 1979 when he batted .318 for Chicago and led the American League with 44 doubles. Lemon took good care of his bats. When he was with Detroit, he put his bat in a stretch sock and took it back to the hotel with him after the game.

8. **DARRYL STRAWBERRY**

Power hitter Darryl Strawberry led the National League in home runs in 1988. The tall outfielder loved his bat so much that he once slept with it during a rain delay.

9. **TURKEY STEARNES**

Turkey Stearnes was a lifetime .352 batter in the Negro Leagues. Stearnes talked to his bats, giving them instructions on where he wanted to hit the ball. He had bats of different lengths, depending on how far he planned on hitting the ball. One bat was used for hitting the ball against the wall. Another was for hitting home runs. Stearnes had special cases for each bat.

tice his swing. Morales liked his bat so much, he would sometimes kiss it.

3. **TOM BROOKENS**

Tom Brookens was a third baseman with the Detroit Tigers during the 1980s. The light-hitting infielder batted only .214 in 1983. He joked that he scuffed his bats to make it look like he hit the ball.

4. **BILL CAUDILL**

Bill Caudill was an outstanding relief pitcher who won 12 games and saved 26 for Seattle in 1982. While his job was to keep batters from hitting, he proposed a unique way to end a team batting slump that had resulted in a long losing streak. Caudill burned his teammates' bats in a bonfire. The team responded by winning the very next game.

5. **ORLANDO CEPEDA**

The Hall of Fame first baseman collected 2,351 base hits during his major league career from 1958 to 1974. Many hitters believed they get more hits with certain bats and will use them as long as possible. Cepeda, on the other hand, was convinced that each bat had only one hit in it and would always change bats after getting a hit.

6. **WILLARD BROWN**

Willard Brown was one of the first African Americans to play major league baseball. In 1947, the same year Jackie Robinson broke baseball's color barrier, Brown

Going Batty

Yogi Berra frequently changed his bats during slumps. "I never blame myself when I'm not hitting. I blame the bat," Yogi reasoned. Some players go batty for their bats.

1. **JIM FREGOSI**

Infielder Jim Fregosi had 1,726 hits during his career from 1961 to 1978. During a batting slump, Fregosi asked team physician Robert Kerlan to give his ailing bat a shot of cortisone. It seemed to give the bat new life as Fregosi hit for the cycle, getting a single, double, triple, and home run in a single game.

2. **JOSE MORALES**

One of baseball's best pinch-hitters during the 1970s, Jose Morales led the league four times in pinch hits. In 1976, while playing for the Montreal Expos, he set a major league record with 25 pinch hits in a season. While with the Minnesota Twins in the late 1970s, Morales insisted on taking his bat with him everywhere. At his hotel, he would stand in front of a mirror and prac-

7. KEN WILLIAMS

Outfielder Ken Williams played from 1915 to 1929 and was a .319 career hitter. In 1922, he led the American League in home runs with 39 and runs batted in with 155. As great a player as he was, Williams was never as good a hitter as teammate George Sisler.

8. LEE MAY

First baseman Lee May slugged 354 home runs from 1965 to 1982. He played on the Cincinnati Reds from 1965 to 1971. May was the Reds' hitting star in the 1970 World Series and averaged 37 home runs from 1969 to 1971. Despite his clutch hitting, he was overshadowed by teammates Pete Rose, Johnny Bench, and Tony Perez. To make matters worse, he was traded to Houston in the Joe Morgan trade and missed being on the great Big Red Machine teams of the mid-1970s.

9. ED REULBACH

Ed Reulbach was a star pitcher on the Chicago Cubs teams that won four pennants between 1906 and 1910. Reulbach led the National League pitchers in winning percentage in 1906, 1907, and 1908. He had a career record of 181–105 with a 2.28 earned run average. Reulbach was never the ace of the staff because he pitched on the same team as Mordecai "Three Finger" Brown.

10. CY WILLIAMS

Cy Williams led the National League in home runs in 1916, 1920, 1923, and 1927. The Philadelphia Phillies' outfielder is little remembered today because he was overshadowed by the American League home run king Babe Ruth.

3. BING MILLER

Outfielder Bing Miller played from 1921 to 1936. The .312 lifetime hitter was a key member of the great Philadelphia A's teams from 1929 to 1931. Miller's contribution was overlooked because he was overshadowed by his Hall of Fame teammates Jimmie Foxx, Al Simmons, and Mickey Cochrane.

4. AL OLIVER

One of the most underrated players of his time, outfielder Al Oliver had 2,743 hits during his career from 1968 to 1985. The .303 lifetime hitter won the National League batting title in 1982. Oliver played ten seasons with the Pittsburgh Pirates and did not receive the same attention as teammates Roberto Clemente and Willie Stargell.

5. GINGER BEAUMONT

Ginger Beaumont was one of the best outfielders in the National League during the first decades of the 1900s. Beaumont led the National League in hits four times and was the batting champion in 1902. The Pittsburgh outfielder, a .311 career hitter, was overshadowed by teammates Honus Wagner and Fred Clarke.

6. VADA PINSON

Speedy Vada Pinson had 2,757 career hits, including four 200-hit seasons, between 1959 and 1965. The Cincinnati Reds' centerfielder twice led the National League in hits, doubles, and triples. Pinson remained in the shadow of teammate Frank Robinson and also had the bad luck of playing centerfield the same time as Willie Mays.

Shadow Players

In baseball history there have been many players who have been overshadowed by more accomplished teammates. None of these shadow players is in the Baseball Hall of Fame, but all had outstanding careers.

1. BOB MEUSEL

Bob Meusel played outfield for the New York Yankees from 1920 to 1929. A .309 lifetime hitter, in 1925 Meusel led the American League in home runs and runs batted in. An important slugger in the Yankees' Murderers' Row, Meusel was overshadowed by teammates Babe Ruth and Lou Gehrig.

2. BOBBY VEACH

An outfielder with the Detroit Tigers from 1912 to 1923, Bobby Veach had a .310 lifetime batting average. Three times Veach led the American League in runs batted in, and twice he led the league in doubles. Veach played 12 seasons in the same outfield as Ty Cobb and never received the recognition he deserved.

3,023 hits during his career. He batted above .300 for eight seasons but never won a batting title.

8. CAL RIPKEN

Baseball's iron man Cal Ripken had 3,184 hits during his career as a shortstop and third baseman for the Baltimore Orioles. Although Ripken is thirteenth on the all-time hit list, he never won a batting title. In 1983, he finished fifth in the batting race with a .318 average.

9. ROBIN YOUNT

Like Cal Ripken, Robin Yount was a shortstop who had more than 3,000 base hits. His 3,142 hits are the sixteenth most in baseball history. In 1982, the Milwaukee infielder led the American League in hits and batted .331. That year Yount lost the batting title to Willie Wilson by one point.

10. SAM RICE

Washington outfielder Sam Rice had six 200-hit seasons and fell just 13 hits shy of the 3,000 career hit mark. A .322 hitter, Rice had 15 seasons in which he topped the .300 mark. He hit as high as .350, but he never finished in the top five in a batting race.

3. MICKEY COCHRANE

Hall of Fame catcher Mickey Cochrane had a .320 career batting average, the highest among catchers who have completed their careers. Cochrane batted .357, finishing fifth in the American League batting race, for the 1930 world champion Philadelphia A's. He finished fourth in the 1931 batting race.

4. FRANKIE FRISCH

Second baseman Frankie Frisch played for the New York Giants and St. Louis Cardinals from 1919 to 1937. A .316 lifetime batter, Frisch had eleven consecutive seasons in which he batted above .300. Frisch never won a batting crown, although he did finish fifth in the 1923 batting race.

5. JOHN McGRAW

Best remembered for his long career as manager of the New York Giants, John McGraw batted .334 as a third baseman from 1891 to 1906. In 1899, McGraw batted .391 for Baltimore. He finished third in the batting race behind Ed Delahanty and Jesse Burkett.

6. BILL DICKEY

Bill Dickey was the catcher for the New York Yankees from 1928 to 1946. A .313 hitter, Dickey topped the .300 mark eleven times. Dickey finished third in the 1936 American League batting race when he batted .362.

7. LOU BROCK

Outfielder Lou Brock played for the Chicago Cubs and St. Louis Cardinals from 1961 to 1979. Brock had

They Never Won a Batting Title

Mike Piazza, Sammy Sosa, and Ken Griffey, Jr., are among the current stars who have never won a batting championship so it is hardly surprising that many superstars in baseball history never won a batting crown.

1. **EDDIE COLLINS**

Second baseman Eddie Collins played 25 seasons and had a career batting average of .333. Collins had ten seasons in which he batted above .340. He had the misfortune of playing during the same time as Ty Cobb, Tris Speaker, and Joe Jackson. Collins finished second in the batting race to Ty Cobb in 1914 and 1915, but he never won a batting title.

2. **PIE TRAYNOR**

Pie Traynor batted .320 while playing third base for the Pittsburgh Pirates from 1920 to 1937. His best season was 1930 when he batted .366. Traynor finished fifth in the 1927 batting race, behind Paul Waner.

son, Roy Campanella, and Don Newcombe each won MVP awards, Snider never received the honor.

8. **EDDIE MURRAY**

Eddie Murray is the only switch hitter ever to reach both 3,000 hits and 500 home runs. His 1,917 runs batted in ranks seventh on the all-time list, ahead of such greats as Willie Mays and Ted Williams. Despite having many great seasons, the first baseman never won the MVP award.

9. **WADE BOGGS**

Third baseman Wade Boggs won five American League batting titles and had seven 200-hit seasons. The .328 career batter collected 3,010 hits. Despite being one of the best hitters in the 1980s and 1990s, Boggs was never voted Most Valuable Player.

10. **JOHNNY MIZE**

First baseman Johnny Mize batted .312 and hit 359 home runs during his career from 1936 to 1953. Four times the Big Cat led the National League in home runs and he was the RBI leader three times. Mize finished second in the MVP vote in 1940.

Most Valuable Player award. His best finish was fourth in 1938.

3. EDDIE MATHEWS

Eddie Mathews hit 512 homers between 1952 and 1968. The Braves' third baseman led the National League in home runs in 1953 and 1959. Although never an MVP, Mathews did finish second in the voting in 1953 and 1959.

4. AL KALINE

One of the greatest players in Tigers' history, outfielder Al Kaline had 3,007 hits and 1,583 runs batted in during his years in Detroit from 1953 to 1974. Kaline finished second in the MVP voting in 1955 and 1963.

5. DAVE WINFIELD

Outfielder Dave Winfield compiled amazing stats in his long career, which ended in 1995. Winfield had 3,110 hits, 465 home runs, and 1,833 runs batted in. The 12-time All Star never won a Most Valuable Player award.

6. PAUL MOLITOR

Ted Williams said that Paul Molitor had one of the best batting strokes he had ever seen. Molitor is eighth in the all-time hit list with 3,319 and tenth in doubles with 605. Molitor was a World Series MVP, but never won the regular season award.

7. DUKE SNIDER

Brooklyn Dodgers' outfielder Duke Snider had five consecutive 40–home run seasons from 1953 to 1957. Snider led the National League in runs scored three seasons in a row. Although teammates Jackie Robin-

Least Appreciated Players

The Most Valuable Player Award is presented each year to the best player in each league. Over the years many less-than-great players have received the award, including Frank Schulte, Bob O'Farrell, Roger Peckinpaugh, Jim Konstanty, and Zoilo Versalles. Surprisingly, many of the game's best players never received an MVP award.

1. **MARK McGWIRE**

Mark McGwire hit 583 home runs during his career. In 1998 the St. Louis first baseman became the first player to hit 70 home runs in a season. Despite his record-breaking year, McGwire finished second in the Most Valuable Player voting to Chicago outfielder Sammy Sosa.

2. **MEL OTT**

Mel Ott was the National League's first great slugger. The New York Giants' outfielder led the National League in home runs six times and hit 511 in his career from 1926 to 1947. The Hall of Famer never won the

earned run average. During the 1940s, Dunn received three Hall of Fame votes.

7. **WES WESTRUM**

Wes Westrum caught for the New York Giants from 1947 to 1957. A .217 hitter, he batted below .250 every full season that he played. In 1964, he received two votes for the Hall of Fame.

8. **HAL LANIER**

Hal Lanier was a weak-hitting shortstop who played for the San Francisco Giants and New York Yankees between 1964 and 1973. The .228 hitter only once hit above .233 in a season. One sportswriter overlooked his hitting limitations when he voted for Lanier in 1979.

9. **CHARLEY O'LEARY**

Shortstop Charley O'Leary played from 1904 to 1913. O'Leary also played one game at age 51 in 1934. A .226 hitter, O'Leary did not hit a home run in his final eight seasons and had only four in his career. For some reason, O'Leary received three votes for the Hall of Fame.

10. **ORVAL GROVE**

Orval Grove pitched for the Chicago White Sox from 1940 to 1949. His career record was 63–73, hardly qualifying him for Hall of Fame consideration. Amazingly, Grove received 12 votes for the Hall of Fame.

run average. When he became eligible for the Hall of Fame, Deshaies conducted a tongue-in-cheek Internet campaign for his election. Deshaies received one vote from Houston Chronicle sportswriter John Lopez. Although Deshaies fell 386 votes short of election, he felt vindicated by the vote.

3. LOU CRIGER

Lou Criger was a catcher who played from 1896 to 1912. Criger had a .221 career batting average and had seven seasons in which he batted less than .200. So why did Criger outpoll more than 30 future Hall of Famers, including John McGraw, Al Simmons, and Pie Traynor? The reason was because Criger had turned down a $12,000 bribe to throw the 1903 World Series.

4. JEWEL ENS

An infielder for the Pittsburgh Pirates from 1922 to 1925, Jewel Ens had only 54 hits and one home run during his brief major league career. This did not stop one sportswriter from voting for him in the 1950 Hall of Fame election.

5. SIBBY SISTI

Sibby Sisti played for the Braves from 1939 to 1954. The utility infielder averaged less than 60 hits and 20 RBIs per season. Inexplicably, he received one Hall of Fame vote in 1960.

6. JACK DUNN

Jack Dunn played third base, shortstop, second base, and the outfield between 1897 and 1904. A .245 lifetime batter, he hit only one home run in eight seasons. As a pitcher Dunn compiled a 64–59 record with a 4.11

What Were They Thinking?

The Hall of Fame was created in 1936 to recognize the greatest players in baseball history. Over the years many players not of Hall of Fame caliber have received votes. Eddie Grant, a third baseman with a .249 career batting average, received nine votes for the Hall of Fame, primarily because he was killed in action during World War I. Catcher Hank Gowdy, who never had more than 89 hits in a season, received a total of 436 votes. Pitcher Hub Perdue, who had a 51–64 record, received votes in 1938 and 1939.

1. **MARTY BERGEN**

Despite only playing four seasons, catcher Marty Bergen received votes for the Hall of Fame in 1937, 1938, and 1939. Bergen had a .265 average and only once had more than 100 hits in a season. But there is a much more disturbing reason why Bergen should not have received Hall of Fame consideration. On January 19, 1900, Bergen took an ax and razor and murdered his wife and two young children before taking his own life.

2. **JIM DESHAIES**

Jim Deshaies was a lefthanded pitcher for the Houston Astros who had an 84–95 record with a 4.14 earned

mings was one of the first to perfect the pitch, several other pitchers laid claim to being the first curveballer.

10. **PHIL RIZZUTO**

Before his election to Baseball's Hall of Fame in 1994, New York Yankees' shortstop Phil Rizzuto said, "I'll take any way to get into the Hall of Fame. If they want a bat boy, I'll go in as a bat boy." Rizzuto had one outstanding year as a hitter when he batted .324 in 1950 and was voted the American League Most Valuable Player. During his thirteen years with the Yankees, Rizzuto batted .273 and averaged less than three home runs per season.

6. JOHNNY EVERS

Shortstop Joe Tinker, second baseman Johnny Evers, and first baseman Frank Chance were the double play combination of the great Chicago Cubs teams of the first decade of the twentieth century. A famous poem, "Tinker to Evers to Chance" immortalized the threesome. In 1946, Tinker, Evers, and Chance were all inducted into the Baseball Hall of Fame. Chance, the team leader, was a solid choice, but Evers's selection had less merit. In 18 seasons, Evers hit only 12 home runs and batted .270.

7. JOE TINKER

Joe Tinker's Hall of Fame selection was as questionable as teammate Johnny Evers'. Tinker batted only .263 and hit 31 home runs in fifteen seasons.

8. RAY SCHALK

Catcher Ray Schalk's .253 lifetime batting average is the lowest of anyone in the Hall of Fame, other than pitchers. In 17 seasons with the Chicago White Sox, Schalk had only 1,345 hits and 12 home runs. His 1955 election to the Baseball Hall of Fame was primarily recognition for his defensive skills and ability to handle pitchers. Schalk was also one of the White Sox players not involved in throwing the 1919 World Series.

9. CANDY CUMMINGS

Candy Cummings pitched only two seasons in the National League. His lifetime record was 21–22, and he was 5–14 with Cincinnati in 1877, his final season. Yet Cummings was inducted into the Baseball Hall of Fame in 1939. The main reason for his selection was the belief that he had invented the curveball. While Cum-

thy's election had more to do with being one of Boston's "Heavenly Twins" with teammate Hugh Duffy. Duffy, who set a single season record when he batted .438 in 1894, had been selected to the Hall of Fame in 1945, a year before McCarthy's selection. McCarthy was a good player, but his 1,496 hits and .292 batting average were well below the norm for Hall of Fame outfielders. McCarthy also had a 0–7 record as a pitcher.

3. **DAVE BANCROFT**

When shortstop Dave Bancroft was selected to the Hall of Fame by the Veterans' Committee in 1971, he admitted, "I was more surprised by my election than anything that ever happened to me." Bancroft batted .279 during his 16-season career. He averaged only two home runs and less than 40 runs batted in per season.

4. **BOBBY WALLACE**

Bobby Wallace never received more than seven votes in Hall of Fame balloting. Regardless, Wallace was selected by the Veterans' Committee in 1953. Wallace batted .267 and hit only 35 home runs during his 25-year career.

5. **RABBIT MARANVILLE**

Rabbit Maranville was a shortstop who was even a weaker hitter than Dave Bancroft and Bobby Wallace. Maranville batted .258 and hit 28 home runs in 23 seasons. Rabbit never batted .300 during a full season. Despite his offensive limitations, Maranville was elected to the Hall of Fame in 1954. Incredibly, some of the players he finished ahead of in the balloting included Joe DiMaggio, Bill Dickey, Bill Terry, and Hank Greenberg.

Cooperstown Question Marks

In 1963, upon learning that he had been elected to the Baseball Hall of Fame, pitcher Eppa Rixey said, "They're really scraping the bottom of the barrel, aren't they?' There are no bad players in the Hall of Fame, but some of those enshrined have been questionable selections.

1. RICK FERRELL

When catcher Rick Ferrell was selected by the Hall of Fame Veterans' Committee in 1984, many shook their heads. Ferrell had never received more than one vote in the annual Hall of Fame balloting conducted by sportswriters. Some thought that Rick's brother, Wes, would have been a better choice. Wes was a pitcher who had six 20-win seasons. Wes was actually a better hitter than Rick. Wes had 38 home runs, ten more than his brother, who had nearly 5,000 more at-bats.

2. TOMMY McCARTHY

Prior to his selection by the Veterans' Committee to the Hall of Fame in 1946, Tommy McCarthy had received only one vote in the balloting. It was said that McCar-

game winner with the Los Angeles Dodgers in 1977 and twice won 20 games with the New York Yankees. Only Nolan Ryan pitched in the majors longer than John.

7. JIM KAAT

Lefty Jim Kaat won 283 games during his 25-year career. In 1966, Kaat, pitching for the Minnesota Twins, led the American League with 25 wins. Perhaps the best fielding pitcher in baseball history, Kaat won a record 16 Gold Gloves.

8. TED SIMMONS

Ted Simmons had 2,472 hits, the most for any catcher. Simmons hit 483 doubles, 248 home runs, and batted in 1,389 runs. His best season was 1975 when the Cardinals' catcher batted .332 and batted in 100 runs.

9. STEVE GARVEY

Steve Garvey set a National League record by playing in 1,207 consecutive games. Garvey had 2,599 hits, including six 200-hit seasons. Five times the Dodgers' first baseman batted in more than 100 runs.

10. VERN STEPHENS

Prior to the emergence of Ernie Banks, Vern Stephens was the best power-hitting shortstop in baseball history. Stephens led the American League in home runs in 1945 and in runs batted in in 1944, 1949, and 1950. In his first three seasons with the Boston Red Sox, Stephens drove in 440 runs. His greatest season was 1949 when he hit 39 home runs and batted in 159.

370 home runs during his career and had seven consecutive 100-RBI seasons from 1949 to 1955. In 1969, Hodges managed the New York Mets to an unexpected World Championship.

3. **BABE HERMAN**

One of baseball's most colorful players, Babe Herman batted .324 during his thirteen-year career. In 1930, the Brooklyn outfielder batted .393, had 241 hits, scored 143 runs, hit 35 homers, and batted in 130 runs. While his batting ability was unquestioned, he was known for an occasional baserunning blunder or misplay in the outfield.

4. **CECIL TRAVIS**

Washington shortstop Cecil Travis averaged .327 from 1933 to 1941. Travis batted .359 in 1941 and led the American League in hits with 218. He missed nearly four seasons while in the armed services during World War II. Travis suffered frostbitten feet during the Battle of the Bulge. When he returned to baseball, he never hit above .252. He still finished his career with an outstanding .314 batting average.

5. **JOE GORDON**

Second baseman Joe Gordon hit 253 home runs during his 11 years in the majors. The 1942 American League Most Valuable Player, Gordon played on five pennant winners with the New York Yankees and one with the Cleveland Indians. Gordon had four seasons in which he batted in more than 100 runs.

6. **TOMMY JOHN**

Tommy John pitched in the major leagues for 26 seasons and won 288 games. The lefthander was a 20-

On the Outside Looking In 103

Gil Hodges crosses the plate to congratulations from Jackie Robinson (42) and Pee Wee Reese (1) after hitting a home run, one of 370 in his career.

On the Outside Looking In

Fewer than 300 players have been enshrined in the Baseball Hall of Fame. Many worthy candidates have been overlooked. For example, Bert Blyleven won 287 games and pitched 60 shutouts, and his 3,701 strikeouts place him fifth on the all-time list. Despite these achievements, Blyleven is still awaiting his call to Cooperstown.

1. RON SANTO

Ron Santo played third base for the Chicago Cubs from 1960 to 1973. Despite being diabetic, Santo hit 342 home runs and batted in 1,331 runs. A superb fielder, he won five Gold Gloves.

2. GIL HODGES

Brooklyn Dodgers' first baseman Gil Hodges received the most votes for any player who has not yet been elected to the Hall of Fame. Hodges reached as high as third in the balloting. Hall of Famers who finished behind him in various years included Early Wynn, Pee Wee Reese, Eddie Mathews, Don Drysdale, Harmon Killebrew, Juan Marichal, and Duke Snider. Hodges hit

10. **HERMAN LONG**

Shortstop Herman Long was considered one of the best shortstops of the nineteenth century. Long played from 1889 to 1904. He led the National League in runs scored in 1893 and in home runs in 1900. He scored 1,460 runs and had 2,145 hits.

6. HARRY STOVEY

Harry Stovey was one of baseball's first great sluggers. Stovey played the outfield and first base during his major league career from 1880 to 1893. He led the league in home runs five times, triples four times, and runs scored four times.

7. DAVE ORR

Dave Orr played only eight seasons, but the first baseman never hit below .300. His .342 career batting average is one of the highest marks in baseball history. In 1890, his final season, Orr batted .373 for Brooklyn of the Players' League. Orr retired at age 31 after suffering a stroke.

8. LARRY CORCORAN

Larry Corcoran was one of the best pitchers of the 1880s. The Chicago righthander won 43 games as a rookie in 1880 and averaged 34 wins during his first five seasons. For his career, Corcoran had a 177–90 record and a 2.36 earned run average. Corcoran pitched no-hitters in 1880, 1882, and 1884.

9. TOMMY BOND

Irishman Tommy Bond was the only pitcher in baseball history to win 40 or more games in three consecutive seasons. Known for his curveball, Bond led the National League in wins in 1877 and 1878. His best season was 1879 when he won 43 games for Boston and pitched 12 shutouts.

2. GEORGE VAN HALTREN

Nearly forgotten today, George Van Haltren was one of the most talented players of his time. Van Haltren had a 40–31 record as a pitcher but spent most of his career as an outfielder. During his major league career from 1887 to 1903, he had 2,536 hits, scored 1,639 runs, stole 583 bases, and had a .316 batting average.

3. BOB CARUTHERS

Bob Caruthers won 40 games in 1885 and 1889. Caruthers's lifetime record was 218 wins and 97 losses, and his .692 winning percentage is one of the best in baseball history. Caruthers also played the outfield and had a .282 career batting average.

4. JIMMY RYAN

Chicago outfielder Jimmy Ryan played from 1885 to 1903. A .309 lifetime hitter, Ryan had 2,529 hits and scored 1.643 runs. Twelve seasons Ryan hit above .300.

5. TONY MULLANE

Born in Cork, Ireland, pitcher Tony Mullane was nicknamed The Apollo of the Box because of his good looks. He was so handsome that female fans jammed the ballpark on Mondays when he pitched, and the Cincinnati Red Stockings created the tradition of Ladies' Day, in which women were given reduced admission. Mullane had five 30-win seasons and won 285 games during his career from 1881 to 1894. Mullane had the ability to pitch with either hand, making him baseball's first ambidextrous pitcher.

Forgotten Stars

Many nineteenth-century stars are virtually forgotten today. Passed over by the Hall of Fame, these players have not received the recognition they deserved.

1. PETE BROWNING

Outfielder Pete "the Gladiator" Browning was one of major league baseball's first great hitters. Browning won batting titles in 1882, 1885, and 1890 and compiled a .343 career batting average. Browning was so obsessed with hitting that he kept his current batting average written on his sleeve. He was the player responsible for starting the customized bat industry. In 1884, Browning ordered a bat be made to his specifications at the J. F. Hillerich wood shop in Louisville, Kentucky. Eventually, Browning owned more than 700 bats, each of which he named. Other players also ordered customized bats and the woodshop became Hillerich and Bradsby, maker of the famous Louisville Slugger bat.

The next season White led the circuit with 42 losses while his win total dropped to 18.

7. CHIEF BENDER

Chief Bender was the ace of Connie Mack's outstanding Philadelphia Athletics' teams of the 1910s. Bender had his last great season in Philadelphia in 1914 when he went 17–3 and led the American League in winning percentage. Bender jumped to the newly formed Federal League the next season and had his worst year in the majors. Bender won only four and lost 16 while pitching for Baltimore.

8. NORM CASH

Detroit first baseman Norm Cash won the American League batting title in 1961 when he batted .361. Cash slugged 41 home runs and batted in 132 runs. In 1962, Cash's average fell 118 points, and he batted in 43 less runs.

9. JIM BOUTON

Jim Bouton was the New York Yankees' pitcher who wrote the tell-all best-seller, *Ball Four*. Bouton, a 21-game winner in 1963, had an 18–13 record in 1964. It would be Bouton's last good year. He suffered through his worst season in 1965 with a record of 4–15.

10. JIMMY BANNON

Jimmy "Foxy Grandpa" Bannon batted .350 for Boston in 1895. Bannon's stats fell off dramatically the next season. A .320 career hitter, he batted .251 and did not hit a home run.

and batted in 99 runs. The following year Walker hit only two home runs and knocked in 16 runs.

3. FRED DUNLAP

St. Louis second baseman Fred Dunlap had a career year in 1884. Dunlap led the league in batting average, hits, home runs, and slugging percentage. In 1885, Dunlap's batting average fell from .412 to .270, and he hit only two home runs.

4. EDDIE CICOTTE

Eddie Cicotte is remembered for being one of the Black Sox banned from baseball for conspiring to throw the 1919 World Series. Prior to the scandal, Cicotte was one of the best pitchers in the American League. In 1917, the White Sox righthander led the league with 28 wins and a 1.53 earned run average. The following season Cicotte led American League pitchers with 19 losses. Cicotte rebounded in 1919 to again lead the league with 29 victories.

5. LaMARR HOYT

LaMarr Hoyt was another White Sox hurler who experienced his ups and downs. Hoyt led the American League in wins with 19 in 1982. Hoyt was even better in 1983 when he led the league with 24 victories. In 1984, Hoyt had his worst season, leading the American League with 18 losses.

6. WILL WHITE

Will "Whoop-La" White had three 40-win seasons during his career. White won 43 games for Cincinnati in 1879 and pitched an outstanding 75 complete games.

You're Only As Good As Your Last Season

Rookies are not the only baseball players who experience off seasons following an outstanding year. Veteran players sometimes have an off year. Chicago Cubs' pitcher Larry Jackson had his best season in 1964 when he led the National League with 24 wins. The next season Jackson lost 21 games. In 1958 Philadelphia outfielder Richie Ashburn won the National League batting title with a .350 average and led the league in hits, triples, and walks. Ashburn had one of his worst seasons the next year when he slumped to .266.

1. HACK WILSON

Cubs' outfielder Hack Wilson had an incredible year in 1930, setting a National League record (since broken) with 56 home runs. His 191 runs batted in is a record that may never be topped. Wilson had nowhere to go but down. In 1931, his homer total dropped from 56 to 13 and his runs batted in fell from 191 to 61.

2. TILLY WALKER

Philadelphia Athletics' outfielder Tilly Walker had his best season in 1922. Walker slammed 37 home runs

7. ROSCOE MILLER

Roscoe "Rubberlegs" Miller won 23 games as a rookie with Detroit. Rubberlegs lived up to his nickname the following year when he had a 7–20 record.

8. GEORGE WATKINS

St. Louis Cardinals' outfielder George Watkins had a sensational rookie season in 1930. Watkins batted .373 and knocked in 87 runs in 119 games. The following season, Watkins's batting average dropped 85 points and he batted in 36 fewer runs.

9. SAM MELE

Sam Mele batted .302 as a rookie outfielder with the Boston Red Sox in 1947. The next year Mele's batting average dropped 69 points. He hit only two home runs and batted in 25 runs, 48 less than the previous year.

10. TED WILKS

Ted Wilks led the National League in winning percentage in 1944 when he won 17 games and lost only four. The St. Louis Cardinals' righthander slumped to a 4–7 record in 1945. After suffering the sophomore jinx, Wilks rebounded to 8–0 in 1946.

2. WALT DROPO

Walt "Moose" Dropo had one of the best rookie seasons in baseball history in 1950. The big Red Sox first baseman batted .322, hit 34 home runs, and batted in a league-leading 144 runs. The next season Dropo slumped to .239 with 11 home runs.

3. RICK SUTCLIFFE

Rick Sutcliffe was voted the National League Rookie of the Year in 1979 when he won 17 games for the Los Angeles Dodgers. In 1980, Sutcliffe had a 3–9 record and inflated 5.56 earned run average.

4. JIM NASH

Kansas City pitcher Jim Nash had a 12–1 record as a rookie in 1966. Jumbo Jim also won 12 games the next season. Unfortunately, the big righthander lost 17 games.

5. GEORGE BRADLEY

George "Grin" Bradley won 45 games for St. Louis in 1876, the National League's inaugural season. He led the league with a 1.23 earned run average and pitched a record 16 shutouts. The next season Bradley's grin turned to a frown when his record slipped to 18–23 with only two shutouts.

6. HARLIN POOL

Harlin "Samson" Pool batted .327 as a rookie outfielder with Cincinnati in 1934. Someone must have cut Samson's hair because he batted .176 the next season, his last in the majors.

Sophomore Jinx

In baseball history, many players have been affected by the sophomore jinx. Baltimore outfielder Sam Bowens hit 22 home runs as a rookie in 1964. The next season he batted .163. New York Yankees' pitcher Bob Grim won twenty games during his rookie season in 1954. Grim's victory total dropped to seven the next season.

1. **JOE CHARBONEAU**

Joe Charboneau was one of baseball's biggest characters. He opened a beer bottle with his eye socket and ate cigarettes. Super Joe once cut off a tattoo with a razor blade and pulled out one of his teeth with a pair of pliers. In 1980, Charboneau was voted Rookie of the Year after the Cleveland Indians' outfielder hit 23 home runs and batted in 87 runs. Charboneau said that he had heard of the sophomore jinx but planned to go straight to his junior year. As it turned out, Charboneau was unable to avoid the sophomore jinx. Bothered by a back injury, he hit only .210 in 1981. His junior year turned out not to be very good either as he batted .214 with two home runs.

soon and injured his pitching arm. Dizzy never won more than seven games in a season after the injury.

9. DAFFY DEAN

Dizzy Dean's brother, Paul, won 19 games as a rookie with the St. Louis Cardinals in 1934. Nicknamed Daffy, he was again a 19-game winner in 1935. The following season, he held out for more money. When he returned, Dean hurt his arm and never again won more than five games in a season.

10. DWIGHT GOODEN

Nineteen-year-old Dwight Gooden led the National League with 276 strikeouts as a rookie with the New York Mets in 1984. The next season Gooden won the Cy Young Award with a 24–4 record and a remarkable 1.53 earned run average. On June 19, 1989, the 24-year-old Gooden became the third youngest pitcher to reach 100 wins. The same year, he injured his shoulder. Gooden pitched for another decade but never duplicated the brilliance of his early years.

All Star Game. During the season, Simpson hurt his shoulder and won only one more game. Simpson won four games the next season, and the Reds traded him to Kansas City in 1973.

6. **DON GULLETT**

Pete Rose said of Don Gullett, "Gullett's the only guy who could throw a baseball through a car wash and not get the ball wet." Cincinnati Reds' manager Sparky Anderson predicted Gullett would end up in the Hall of Fame. In 1971, the 20-year-old lefthander led the National League in winning percentage. He had winning records in eight of his nine major league seasons. By the time he was 27 years old, Gullett's arm problems forced him to retire. His .686 winning percentage is one of the highest in baseball history.

7. **MARK FIDRYCH**

Mark "The Bird" Fidrych took baseball by storm in 1976. The Detroit Tigers' rookie won 19 games and led the American League with a 2.34 earned run average. Fidrych talked to the baseball and occasionally flapped his arms like a bird when he got a batter out. The 21-year-old with the long blonde curls injured his arm the next season. He won only ten more games the rest of his career.

8. **DIZZY DEAN**

Dizzy Dean won 30 games with the St. Louis Cardinals in 1934. The next season he again led the National League with 28 wins. At the 1937 All Star Game Dean was hit by a line drive off the bat of Earl Averill and broke his toe. Dean tried to return from the injury too

Johnson. Wood said, "I threw so hard, I thought my arm would fly right off my body." In 1913, Wood broke the thumb on his pitching hand and his victory total fell to 11. By 1916, the 26-year-old fireballer had hurt his shoulder so badly that he was unable to pitch.

3. WALLY BUNKER

The Baltimore Orioles had a number of great pitching prospects in the 1960s. Jim Palmer overcame arm problems early in his career to go on to a Hall of Fame career. Others were not so lucky. Nineteen-year-old Wally Bunker pitched two one-hitters during his rookie season in 1964. That year Bunker had a 19–5 record and led the American League in winning percentage. Bunker developed tendonitis and never approached the effectiveness of his rookie season. In 1970, Bunker was 2–11 with the Kansas City Athletics. His career was finished at age 26.

4. CHUCK ESTRADA

Chuck Estrada was another Oriole phenom whose career was shortened by arm miseries. In 1960, the 22-year-old rookie righthander led the American League in wins with 18. The next season, Estrada was 15–9. A sore elbow caused the victory total to plummet. In 1962, he led the American League in losses with 17. By the next season Estrada won only three games. In his final season, he was 1–2 with a 9.41 earned run average with the 1967 New York Mets.

5. WAYNE SIMPSON

Wayne Simpson was a 21-year-old rookie with the Cincinnati Reds in 1970. The hard-throwing righthander won 13 of his first 14 decisions and was selected to the

Arm Problems

Dean Chance, a two-time 20-game winner, said, "One day you can throw tomatoes through brick walls. The next day you can't dent a pane of glass with a rock." Many great pitching careers have been derailed by arm injuries.

1. KARL SPOONER

No pitcher had a more sensational beginning to a career than Karl Spooner. On September 22, 1954, the Brooklyn lefthander struck out fifteen in a major league debut, a three-hit shutout of the New York Giants. In his next start, he pitched a four-hit shutout against Pittsburgh. In his first two major league games, he had struck out 27 batters. Unfortunately, Spooner injured his arm the next season. Struggling with arm problems, he finished the season with an 8–6 record. Spooner was replaced by another hard-throwing young southpaw named Sandy Koufax.

2. JOE WOOD

Smoky Joe Wood had a 34–5 record for the 1912 Boston Red Sox. It was said that he threw as hard as Walter

9. **DON LARSEN**

In 1954, Don Larsen had a 3–21 record with the Baltimore Orioles. Traded to the New York Yankees, he was shelled in game four of the 1955 World Series, losing to Brooklyn 8–5. The following season, Larsen started game two of the World Series against the Dodgers and was knocked out of the box in the second inning of a 13–8 loss. Despite his lack of success against Brooklyn, Larsen was selected to start game five on October 8. Larsen pitched a perfect game as the Yankees defeated the Dodgers 2–0. Sportswriter Shirley Povich called Larsen's perfect game a "million-to-one shot." Catcher Yogi Berra told Larsen, "That might have been the best game you ever pitched." In 1960, Larsen was traded to Kansas City and had a 1–10 record that year. He retired in 1967 with an 81–91 record.

10. **DON CARDWELL**

Chicago Cubs' pitcher Don Cardwell pitched a no-hitter against the St. Louis Cardinals on May 15, 1960. Chicago won the game 4–0. Cardwell finished 1960 with a 9–16 record, his fourth consecutive losing season. He finished his career with a 102–138 record.

gan was thrown out trying to steal second. Shore then retired the next 26 batters to complete an unusual no-hitter. The Red Sox won the game 4–0.

8. **VIRGIL TRUCKS**

Detroit's Virgil Trucks had his worst season in 1952 when he had a 5–19 record. Two of those victories were no-hitters. On May 15, Trucks no-hit the Washington Senators in a 1–0 victory. His second no-hitter occurred on August 25 when he defeated the New York Yankees 1–0.

Lightning can strike anywhere and anytime in baseball, as proven by Don Larsen, a career 81–91 pitcher—shown here in mid-pitch during the only perfect game in World Series history in 1956.

pitcher dated several actresses including Mamie Van Doren, Ann-Margret, Connie Stevens, and Tina Louise. On May 5, 1962, the rookie lefthander pitched a no-hitter against Baltimore, a 2–0 victory. The night before his no-hitter, Belinsky had stayed out until 4 A.M. with an attractive blonde. Before the final out, Belinsky called his catcher Buck Rodgers to the mound to point out a well-endowed woman in the stands. After the game Belinsky told reporters, "If I'd known I was going to pitch a no-hitter today, I would have gotten a haircut." Belinsky lamented that he actually lost money because of the no-hitter because he had to buy everyone drinks after the game. He retired in 1970 with a 28–51 record. Belinsky summed up his career when he said, "I think I have gotten more publicity for doing less than any player who ever lived."

6. **BOB GROOM**

As a rookie with Washington in 1909, Bob Groom had a record of 7–26 and led the American League in losses. On May 6, 1917, Groom, playing for the St. Louis Browns, pitched two hitless innings in the first game of a doubleheader against Chicago. Groom started the second game and pitched a no-hitter in a 3–0 victory. That season Groom had a 8–19 record and led the league in losses for the third time. He retired the next season with a 120–150 record.

7. **ERNIE SHORE**

Ernie Shore is the only relief pitcher to throw a no-hitter. On June 23, 1917, Boston Red Sox pitcher Babe Ruth was ejected after punching umpire Brick Owens after a disputed ball-four call to Washington's leadoff batter Ray Morgan. Shore came in to relieve Ruth. Mor-

1893 season with a 1–4 record and an astronomic 10.19 earned run average.

2. BOBO HOLLOMAN

Bobo Holloman of the St. Louis Browns made his first major league start against the Philadelphia Athletics on May 6, 1953. Holloman pitched a no-hitter, but he never rediscovered the magic of that night. Six days later he was knocked out of the box in the second inning by the same club he no-hit. Holloman had a 3–7 record with a 5.23 earned run average in 1953, his only major league season.

3. CHARLIE ROBERTSON

Charlie Robertson played eight seasons in the major leagues and had a losing record each season. His lifetime record was a dismal 49–80. However, for one day in his career, Robertson was unhittable. On April 30, 1922, the Chicago White Sox hurler pitched a perfect game against the Detroit Tigers. His stuff was so good that day that Tiger batters repeatedly asked the umpire to check if Robertson was doctoring the ball.

4. JOHN LEE RICHMOND

John Lee Richmond was a 23-year-old rookie pitcher with Worcester (then a National League team) in 1880. On June 12, Richmond pitched a perfect game against Cleveland in a 1–0 victory. Two years later Richmond led the National League with 33 losses. He retired in 1886 with a 75–100 record.

5. BO BELINSKY

Bo Belinsky was better known for his off-the-field activities than for his pitching. The Los Angeles Angels

Nobody's Perfect

Grover Alexander won 373 games and had 90 shutouts, but he never pitched a no-hitter. On the other hand, many pitchers with mediocre careers have thrown no-hitters. Cincinnati pitcher George Culver had an 11–16 record in 1968. On July 29, 1968, Culver, despite having an upset stomach and an ingrown toenail, pitched a no-hitter against Philadelphia. Johnny Vander Meer, the only player in major league baseball history to pitch consecutive no-hitters, had a losing career record.

1. BUMPUS JONES

On the final day of the 1892 season, Bumpus Jones entered the Cincinnati Reds clubhouse and told manager Charles Comiskey that he wanted to be a major league pitcher. Comiskey decided to let the brash Ohio farmboy pitch that afternoon game against the Pittsburgh Pirates. Jones astonished everyone by pitching a no-hitter as Cincinnati defeated Pittsburgh 7–1. Jones was not even paid for the game. Signed to a contract the next season, Jones injured his shoulder in his first start and was never effective again. Jones finished the

As an outfielder with the 1922 Pittsburgh Pirates, Russell batted .368 and knocked in 75 runs in 60 games.

9. **PERCIVAL WERDEN**

In his only year as a major league pitcher, Percival Werden had a 12–1 record with St. Louis of the Union Association. Werden spent the rest of his seven-year career as a first baseman. In 1893, Werden, playing for St. Louis, led the National League in triples with 33.

10. **RUBE BRESSLER**

Rube Bressler was 10–4 with a 1.77 earned run average as a rookie pitcher with the Philadelphia Athletics in 1914. Bressler spent most of his 19-year career as an outfielder. From 1924 to 1926, the Cincinnati outfielder batted .347, .348, and .357.

5. CY SEYMOUR

Cy Seymour won 20 games for the New York Giants in 1897 and 25 games the next year. Both seasons he led the National League in strikeouts. Problems with his control caused Seymour to give up pitching and become an outfielder. Playing for Cincinnati in 1905, Seymour won the National League batting crown with a .377 average. He also led the league in hits, doubles, triples, runs batted in, and slugging percentage. Seymour retired in 1913 with 1,723 hits and a .303 batting average.

6. ELMER SMITH

Elmer Smith won 33 games for Cincinnati of the American Association in 1887. The following season he won 22 games and led the league in earned run average. Smith converted himself to becoming an outfielder when an arm injury ended his pitching career. He batted .356 for Pittsburgh in 1894 and .362 two years later. Smith had a career .311 batting average.

7. DAVE FOUTZ

Dave Foutz won 41 games while pitching for St. Louis of the American Association in 1886. His career record was 147–66, and his .690 winning percentage was the second best in baseball history. Foutz also played first base and the outfield. In 1887 he batted .357 in 102 games.

8. REB RUSSELL

Reb Russell won 22 games with a 1.91 earned run average for the Chicago White Sox in 1913. In 1917, Russell won the American League in winning percentage.

2. JOHN MONTGOMERY WARD

John Montgomery Ward won 22 games and led the National League with a 1.51 earned run average as an 18-year-old rookie in 1878. The following season, Ward led the league with 47 victories. He won 161 games in seven seasons before injuring his arm. An excellent hitter, Ward played shortstop, second baseman, and the outfield after he was unable to pitch. By the time he retired in 1894, Ward had 2,123 hits.

3. JOE WOOD

Smoky Joe Wood was a hard-throwing righthander who pitched for the Boston Red Sox from 1908 to 1915. In 1912, Wood had a 34–5 record and pitched a league-leading 10 shutouts. Three years later, he led the American League with a 1.49 earned run average. An arm injury derailed a potential Hall of Fame career. Wood's lifetime record was 116–57 and his 2.03 earned run average is one of the lowest in baseball history. Wood played outfield for the Cleveland Indians from 1918 to 1922. His best season as a hitter was 1921 when he batted .366. In 1922, his final season, Wood batted in 92 runs.

4. GUY HECKER

Guy Hecker won 177 games during his major league career. In 1884, Hecker won 52 games for Louisville of the American Association and led the league with 385 strikeouts. Two years later, he became the only pitcher in major league history to win a batting title when he hit .342. On August 15, 1886, Hecker scored seven runs, had six hits, hit three home runs, and pitched a four-hitter. Not bad for a day's work.

Double Threats

A few players have excelled at both pitching and hitting in the major leagues.

Jack Harshman said, "If you don't succeed at first, try pitching." Harshman came up with the New York Giants in 1948 as a first baseman but made a successful transition to pitching and won 69 games in the major leagues. On July 7, 1923, Boston Red Sox pitcher Lefty O'Doul gave up 13 runs in a game. He converted himself into an outfielder and won a National League batting title in 1929 when he batted .398 for the Philadelphia Phillies.

1. **BABE RUTH**

Babe Ruth had a 94–46 record as a pitcher with a 2.28 earned run average. He won 23 games for Boston in 1916 and 24 for the Red Sox the following year. Although he was one of the best pitchers in the American League, Ruth became a full-time outfielder in 1920 because he was such an incredible hitter. Ruth led the American League in home runs twelve times.

game experience. At the time, the team seemed out of contention. But Cincinnati went on a nine-game winning streak while the first place Philadelphia Phillies lost 10 in a row. Manager Dick Sisler, suddenly in the midst of a pennant race, decided not to try the untested rookie. The Reds finished one game behind the pennant-winning St. Louis Cardinals. It was assumed that Neville would pitch in the majors for many years to come, but he never had another opportunity and retired a few years later.

6. DAVE ROWAN

First baseman Dave Rowan played 18 games with the St. Louis Browns in 1911. Rowan batted .385 in 65 at-bats but never again played in the big leagues.

7. SUDS SUTHERLAND

Harvey Suds Sutherland had a 6–2 record in 13 games with the 1921 Detroit Tigers. Sutherland was also a pretty good hitter, batting .407 in 27 at-bats. It was Sutherland's only year in the majors.

8. CHARLIE DEWALD

Another double threat on the mound and at the plate was Charlie Dewald. In 1890, he pitched two games for Cleveland of the Players' League. Dewald won both decisions and gave up only one earned run in 14 innings. He also batted .375, with three hits in eight at-bats. It was the only year for the Players' League, and Dewald's only year in the major leagues.

9. RUFE MEADOWS

Rufe Meadows had one of the shortest careers in major league history. On April 18, 1926, Meadows pitched to one batter for the Cincinnati Reds in an 18–1 loss to Chicago. The 18-year-old hurler retired the only batter he faced.

10. DAN NEVILLE

Dan Neville was a top pitching prospect in the Cincinnati Reds organization in the early 1960s. In September 1964, the Reds brought up Neville after he won 14 games with San Diego of the Pacific Coast League. The Reds intended to give the young pitcher some valuable

his only fielding play. Kull is the only player in baseball history to have a perfect 1.000 winning percentage as a pitcher, 1.000 hitting average, and 1.000 fielding percentage.

3. **DAVE SKAUGSTAD**

Seventeen-year-old pitcher Dave Skaugstad made his major league debut on September 25, 1957. He pitched four shutout innings for the Cincinnati Reds in a 7–5 loss to the Chicago Cubs. He pitched in one more game that season, ending the year with an excellent 1.59 earned run average. The next season Skaugstad had a 3–11 record and 6.77 earned run average in the minors. Despite his promising start, he never returned to the major leagues.

4. **STEVE BIRAS**

Second baseman Steve Biras played in two games for the Cleveland Indians in 1944. Biras made the most of his opportunity, collecting two hits in his only two at-bats.

5. **LEN SWORMSTEDT**

Len Swormstedt had three cups of coffee in his brief major league career. As a rookie pitcher with Cincinnati in 1901, Swormstedt was 2–1 with a 1.73 earned run average in his three game tryout. The next season he pitched two games with the Reds. Four years later, Swormstedt had an outstanding 1.29 earned run average in three games with Boston. Despite having a terrific 2.22 career earned run average, Swormstedt never pitched again in the majors.

Cups of Coffee

When a player has a short career in baseball, it's referred to as a cup of coffee. In 1935, Pittsburgh catcher Aubrey Epps had three hits in his only four major league at-bats. Outfielder Wade Lefler had a .556 batting average during his six-game career in 1924. Second baseman Vince Sherlock batted .462 in eight games for the Brooklyn Dodgers in 1935.

1. JOHN PACIOREK

The ultimate one game-wonder was Houston outfielder John Paciorek. On September 29, 1963, the 18-year-old Paciorek had a perfect three-for-three day at the plate. He scored four runs and batted in three. The next season Paciorek injured his back and batted just .135 while playing Class A ball. He never played again in the major leagues.

2. JOHN KULL

Pitcher John Kull only played one game in the major leagues. On October 2, 1909, Kull pitched three innings of relief for the Philadelphia A's. Kull won the game, got a hit in his only at-bat, and had an assist in

led the National League in stolen bases three times, dirtied his uniform with his famed Comanche slide.

8. PETE ROSE

The front of Pete Rose's uniform was usually dirty because of his trademark head-first slides. Rose said, "I don't get my uniforms any less dirty than when I was nine years old. The only difference is that my mother used to wash it."

9. BILL BUCKNER

Bill Buckner won his only batting crown in 1980 when he batted .324 for the Chicago Cubs. During a 15-game hitting streak that season, Buckner refused to change his underwear.

10. YANK ROBINSON

Second baseman Yank Robinson was nearly blacklisted because of his dirty pants. On May 2, 1889, St. Louis Browns' owner Chris Von der Ahe ordered Robinson to change his dirty trousers. Robinson sent the clubhouse boy back to the hotel for a pair of clean pants, but when he did not return in time Von der Ahe fined Robinson $25. Angered, Robinson left the team. Von der Ahe said he would blacklist Robinson if he did not return and backed down only when the Browns' players threatened to go on strike. The next season Robinson decided to sign with Pittsburgh of the Players' League.

clean his uniform during a 22-game hitting streak at Santa Clara.

3. **DICK TIDROW**

Dick Tidrow won 100 games during his major league career from 1972 to 1984. He was nicknamed Dirty Dick because his uniform was always filthy. Before the game Tidrow liked to play a game called flip. He dove in the dirt to tip the ball back to the other player with his glove.

4. **TY COBB**

Ty Cobb was considered the dirtiest player in the game in more ways than one. The Tigers' outfielder was superstitious and believed a dirty uniform was good luck. He refused to wash his uniform for weeks at a time.

5. **HACK WILSON**

Slugger Hack Wilson prided himself on wearing the dirtiest uniform. While standing in the batters' box, Wilson reached down and scooped dirt on his uniform and arms.

6. **SLOPPY THURSTON**

Hollis Thurston won 89 games during his career from 1923 to 1933. Thurston won 20 games for the Chicago White Sox in 1924. He was nicknamed Sloppy because he often spilled food and drink on his uniform.

7. **PEPPER MARTIN**

Pepper Martin was one of the rowdiest members of the St. Louis Cardinals' Gas House Gang teams that won world championships in 1931 and 1934. Martin, who

Dirty Players

Houston Astros' second baseman Craig Biggio has worn the same filthy, beat-up batting helmet for years. Cleveland third baseman Brook Jacoby, who hit 32 home runs in 1987, never washed his t-shirt because he believed it gave him strength. Some players refuse to clean up their act.

1. **CHARLIE KERFELD**

Reliever Charlie Kerfeld had an 11–2 record with the Houston Astros in 1986. Kerfeld tried to keep his uniform as filthy as possible in order to make the batters overconfident. He chewed tobacco and spit juice on his jersey. Kerfeld once threw up on his shoes and did not bother to clean them off.

2. **AL GALLAGHER**

His full name was Alan Mitchell Edward George Patrick Henry Gallagher, but everyone called him Dirty Al. The third baseman played in the major leagues from 1970 to 1973. Gallagher got his nickname because his uniform was always covered in dirt. His obsession with dirty uniforms began in college when he refused to

run average. Murphy swore that he never pitched without wearing his lucky black silk underwear.

9. JOHN CLARKSON

John Clarkson won 326 games and lost only 177 during his brilliant career from 1882 to 1894. His 53 victories for Chicago in 1885 are the second most ever recorded in a season. Clarkson wore a large shiny silver belt buckle when he pitched because he believed the glare off it would blind the hitter.

10. 1877 CINCINNATI REDS

The 1877 Cincinnati Reds wore different color caps to identify the positions they played. The Cincinnati roster featured pitcher Candy Cummings (red cap), first baseman Charlie Gould (yellow and black), shortstop Jack Manning (blue), third baseman Will Foley (red with white stripe), right fielder Johnny Ryan (green), center fielder Lipman Pike (blue and white), and left fielder Charley Jones (white with red stripes). Catcher Scott Hastings also wore a red hat, the same as the pitchers.

durable player, he did suffer one unusual injury. At a Halloween party, Trammell dressed in a Frankenstein costume. Not used to wearing the elevated boots, he tripped and injured his knee so badly that he required surgery.

6. **YOGI BERRA**

Yogi Berra was a sought-after catching prospect in the mid-1940s. The New York Giants offered the New York Yankees $50,000 for the young catcher, but the offer was refused. Yankees' general manager Larry MacPhail had second thoughts after meeting Berra for the first time: "The instant I saw him my heart sank and I wondered why I had been so foolish as to refuse to sell him. In bustled a stocky little guy in a sailor suit. He had no neck and his muscles were virtually busting the buttons on his uniform. He was one of the most unprepossessing fellows I ever set eyes on in my life." Fortunately, Berra's questionable taste in clothing was no reflection on his baseball ability, and he quickly became a star.

7. **BILL WILKINSON**

Bill Wilkinson was a left-handed relief pitcher with Seattle in the late 1980s. During the 1987 season, he threw away his baseball shoes every time he had a bad outing. Wilkinson pitched in 56 games that year and had a 3–4 record. He disposed of his unlucky shoes at least five times.

8. **ROB MURPHY**

Rob Murphy was a hard-throwing left-handed reliever with the Cincinnati Reds in the late 1980s. He was nearly unhittable during the 1986 season when he posted a 6–0 record with a microscopic 0.72 earned

hand me fifteen bucks or I'll punch you in the eye!" Rube screamed at the driver, "You aren't going to ruin my clothes and get away with it."

3. ARLIE LATHAM

Third baseman Arlie Latham played in the major leagues from 1880 to 1899. In 1909, at age 49, he played in a four-game comeback with the New York Giants. Nicknamed the Freshest Man on Earth, Latham was a chatterbox on the field. One fan, sick of hearing his constant chatter, offered him a box of silk socks and underwear if he could remain quiet for one game. Latham accepted the offer but was unable to keep his mouth shut.

4. JOHNNY BENCH

In the early 1970s the Atlanta Braves hired an attractive young woman named Susie the Sweeper. Dressed in hot pants, she would come out between innings and sweep the bases and home plate. Once she was finished, she would kiss the umpire. On August 14, 1972, Cincinnati Reds' All Star catcher Johnny Bench did his impression of Susie the Sweeper during the Braves' Husbands and Wives game. Wearing his Reds jersey and shorts, Bench swept the bases and planted a kiss on the cheek of Jerry Quarry, the heavyweight boxing contender who was acting as the celebrity umpire. In the Reds–Braves game that followed, Bench hit a home run and knocked in five runs as Cincinnati clobbered Atlanta 12–2.

5. ALAN TRAMMELL

Alan Trammell debuted with Detroit in 1977, and for two decades he starred at shortstop for the Tigers. A

Clothes Encounters

During the 1911 season a haberdasher in Cincinnati named Golde gave Reds players a silk shirt each time they made a great play. Ron Kittle, a slugging designated hitter for the New York Yankees in the late 1980s, kept bras and garters in his locker that had been given to him by female fans. These players had less than uniform behavior.

1. CY YOUNG

Cy Young's 511 victories is a record that will probably never be approached. At the beginning of his career, he was not considered such a great prospect. In 1890, the minor league team Canton sold Young's contract to Cleveland in exchange for $300 and a suit of clothes.

2. RUBE WADDELL

Rube Waddell was known for his outrageous behavior. The Philadelphia A's pitcher led the league in strikeouts six consecutive seasons from 1902 to 1907, but he is best remembered for the bizarre stories about his life. Once Rube was struck by a hit-and-run driver. Incredibly, Waddell got up and chased down the car, "You

May 17, 1948. With his name and number, the back of his uniform said "May 17."

7. BILL VOISELLE

Bill Voiselle won 21 games for the New York Giants in 1944. When Voiselle joined the Boston Braves in 1947, he asked to wear number 96. The reason was that he lived in Ninety-Six, South Carolina.

8. GABE KAPLER

On September 27, 1999, the Detroit Tigers played their last game in Tiger Stadium. The Detroit players wore vintage uniforms, and each starter wore the number that had been worn by a Tiger great. Outfielder Gabe Kapler did not have a number on his uniform, a tribute to Ty Cobb. Cobb did not wear a number during his major league career.

9. BILL MADLOCK

When the third baseman joined the Pittsburgh Pirates in 1979, he offered outfielder Omar Moreno $5,000 for the number 18. Madlock had worn the number 18 for other teams. Moreno refused to give up his number. Madlock decided to wear number 5 as a tribute to his hero, Baltimore third baseman, Brooks Robinson.

10. ROGER CLEMENS

Roger Clemens is the only pitcher in baseball history to win six Cy Young awards. When Clemens became a member of the Toronto Blue Jays, he gave Carlos Delgado a $15,000 Rolex watch for the number 21.

channel of the superstation operated by Braves' owner Ted Turner.

3. EDDIE GAEDEL

On August 19, 1951, St. Louis Browns' owner Bill Veeck sent midget Eddie Gaedel to the plate in a game against the Detroit Tigers. It was one of Veeck's outrageous promotional stunts. The three-foot seven-inch Gaedel wore the number 1/8 on his tiny uniform.

4. RALPH BRANCA

Unlike many players, Brooklyn Dodgers' pitcher Ralph Branca was not superstitious about wearing the number 13. On April 13, 1951, Friday the 13th, Branca posed for a publicity shot wearing his uniform number 13 with a black cat sitting on his shoulder. Branca won 13 games in 1951. In the deciding game of the 1951 National League playoffs, Branca's luck ran out when he gave up the ninth-inning game-winning home run to the Giants' Bobby Thomson.

5. EDDIE PELLAGRINI

Infielder Eddie Pellagrini wore number 13 because he considered it his lucky number. Pellagrini was born on March 13, 1918. His wife was also born on the 13th of the month. When he retired in 1954, Pellagrini had 13 career triples, 13 stolen bases, and had been hit by a pitch 13 times.

6. CARLOS MAY

Carlos May played for the Chicago White Sox from 1968 to 1976. May is the only player in baseball history to wear his birthday on his uniform. He was born on

The numbers Game

Omar Olivares wore the number 00 while playing for the Philadelphia Phillies in 1995. Pitcher Sid Fernandez wore number 50 because he was born in Hawaii, the 50th state admitted to the Union. Babe Ruth and Lou Gehrig wore numbers 3 and 4 because it represented their position in the Yankees batting order.

1. **MITCH WILLIAMS**

When reliever Mitch Williams was traded to Philadelphia in 1993 he asked John Kruk if he could have the number 29. Kruk agreed to give Williams his number in exchange for two cases of beer. Williams said, "I knew it would be beer or Ding Dongs." Williams also wore the number 99 because he said it inspired him to throw every pitch 99 miles per hour.

2. **ANDY MESSERSMITH**

Andy Messersmith won 20 games with the California Angels in 1971 and the Los Angeles Dodgers in 1974. When Messersmith joined the Atlanta Braves in 1976, he wore "Channel 17" on his back to promote the

it more difficult to keep his weight down, he went on a grapefruit diet. Robinson lost 20 pounds but wondered if it was worth the suffering. "After four days you're hallucinating," Robinson recalled, "And after a week you want to find a grapefruit farmer and blow his head off."

9. **BOOTS POFFENBERGER**

Boots Poffenberger won 16 games while pitching for the Detroit Tigers in the late 1930s. As a rookie in 1937, Poffenberger ordered room service at a hotel. "I'll have the breakfast of champions," he said. When asked if he wanted cereal, Poffenberger exclaimed, "Hell, no. Two fried eggs and a bottle of beer."

10. **CASEY STENGEL**

Casey Stengel was known for his outrageous comments. When asked what he would be willing to autograph, Casey replied, "I'll sign anything but veal cutlets. My ball point pen slips on cutlets."

touched the asparagus in his salad. "Mr. Ruth, don't you care for the salad?" she asked. "Oh no, it's not that," the Babe replied, "It's just that asparagus makes my urine smell." Not that Babe hated all vegetables. In 1934, he claimed that eating scallions was the best cure ever invented for a batting slump.

6. JAKE KAFORA

Jake Kafora was a catcher who played for the Pittsburgh Pirates in 1913 and 1914. He was nicknamed Tomatoes because he ate them at every meal. Kafora claimed that the tomatoes increased his strength and speed. It must not have worked since Kafora never hit a home run or stole a base in the majors. His lifetime batting average was an anemic .125.

7. BUGS RAYMOND

Pitcher Bugs Raymond was known more for his heavy drinking than for his diet. Raymond's best season was 1909 when he won 18 games for the New York Giants. On July 4, 1907, Raymond pitched and won both games of a doubleheader. Between games Raymond got loaded, believing he pitched better when intoxicated. He also ate a bunch of bananas. He took one of the banana peels to the mound and rubbed the ball. The unusual substance made the ball move and his pitches even more effective. Raymond's banana ball was nearly impossible to hit.

8. FRANK ROBINSON

Frank Robinson belted 586 home runs during his Hall of Fame career. In 1966, Robinson won the Triple Crown while playing for Baltimore. After his playing days were over, Robinson became a manager. Finding

2. GARRY HERRMANN

Garry Herrmann was the eccentric owner of the Cincinnati Reds team that won the 1919 World Series. Herrmann liked to introduce himself as the champion sausage eater and beer drinker. He carried his own specially made sausages with him wherever he went. Herrmann ate enormous meals. One of his favorite treats was Thuringian blood pudding.

3. JAMES TRAFICANT

In 1994, a dispute between major league baseball and the players' union resulted in the season being shortened. James Traficant, an outspoken congressman from Ohio, offered a unique quick solution to the stalemate. Traficant suggested that the negotiators be locked in a room with no windows or air conditioning. They were to be fed baked beans, fries, cheese, hard-boiled eggs, and chocolate kisses. No one was to be let out of the room until the dispute was settled.

4. BILL FAUL

Bill Faul was a flaky pitcher who pitched in the major leagues from 1962 to 1970 and compiled a 12–16 record. Faul said that he bit the heads off parakeets and swallowed live toads. He claimed the toads gave him a little extra hop on his fastball.

5. BABE RUTH

Teammate Waite Hoyt said of Babe Ruth, "If you cut that big slob in half, most of the concessions of Yankee Stadium would come pouring out." Normally Ruth gorged himself with ordinary food such as hot dogs and ice cream. Once the Babe was invited to a formal dinner party, and the hostess noticed that he had not

Food for Thought

Houston Astros' reliever Charlie Kerfeld was fined $250 for eating a slab of barbecue ribs during a game at Shea Stadium. At the end of the 1987 season, Boston first baseman Bill Buckner shaved his moustache because he thought there were a lot of food particles and bad luck in it. Pitcher Sweetbreads Bailey got his nickname because he ate the delicacy before each start. Baltimore pitcher Ben McDonald insisted on eating sardines before he pitched. Both Jim Palmer and Randy Johnson loved to eat pancakes. Minnesota outfielder Tony Oliva ate mangoes because he believed they were good luck and gave him strength. Let's see what else is on the menu.

1. TOM LASORDA

Joe Torre said, "Tommy Lasorda will eat anything as long as you pay for it." The former Los Angeles Dodgers' manager was known for his prodigious appetite. In 1991, Lasorda won a bet when he ate 100 watermelons in a day.

said of Caudill, "He's not a high ball pitcher. He's a highball drinker."

10. **PAUL WANER**

Despite a serious drinking problem, Paul Waner had 3,152 hits during his Hall of Fame career. One of the ways he would sober up was to do backflips before the game. Waner explained his secret to hitting, "I see three baseballs, but I only swing at the middle one."

5. LEO DUROCHER

Most managers discourage their players from drinking, but not Leo Durocher. He not only liked alcohol, but he encouraged his players to drink. "If any of my players don't take a drink now and then, they're gone," Leo said.

6. BILLY MARTIN

Billy Martin was a fiery player and manager whose frequent rages were often fueled by alcohol. Martin said, "I made a vow in church when I was a kid that I would not drink until I was 18. I've made up for it ever since." Sportswriter Dick Young said, "It's not that Billy drinks a lot. It's just that he fights a lot when he drinks a little." Teammate Whitey Ford said of his friend, "He's got a good heart, but I can't say much for his liver."

7. BOB LEMON

Bob Lemon won 207 games during his Hall of Fame career and later managed the New York Yankees. Lemon said that if he had a bad game, he never took it home with him—he left it in the bar on the way home. He said, "I drink after wins. I drink after losses. I drink after rain outs."

8. LOU PINIELLA

Lou Piniella played 18 seasons before embarking on his successful managerial career. Piniella said he knew it was time to retire when he "couldn't have those eight drinks of Jack Daniels and play the next day."

9. BILL CAUDILL

Bill Caudill had a 6–18 record during his three seasons pitching for the Chicago Cubs. Cubs' manager Lee Elia

2. RABBIT MARANVILLE

Shortstop Rabbit Maranville played 23 seasons in the major leagues and was elected to the Baseball Hall of Fame in 1953. One of baseball's biggest characters, Maranville was a heavy drinker early in his career. Rabbit joked, "There's much less drinking now than before 1927. That's because I quit drinking on May 24, 1927."

3. HACK WILSON

In 1930, the Chicago Cubs' outfielder set a major league record when he batted in 191 runs. Wilson led the National League in homers four times. Wilson was known almost as much for his drinking as his slugging. Sportswriter Shirley Povich described Wilson, "He was built along the lines of a beer keg and not unfamiliar with its contents." Wilson said of himself, "I never played drunk—hungover, yes, but never drunk." In a game played on July 4, 1934, Brooklyn pitcher Boom Boom Beck, angry because he was being removed from a game by manager Casey Stengel, threw the ball off the outfield field fence. Wilson, hungover in center field, heard the ball ricochet off the fence and retrieved the ball. Thinking the ball had been hit, he fired a perfect strike to second base.

4. DICKIE NOLES

Dickie Noles's best season as a pitcher was when he won 10 games with the Chicago Cubs in 1982. Late in his career Noles realized that he was slowing down, "I used to be able to put away three cases of beer a night. Now I can't handle that much. If I have only 15 beers, I'm totally gone."

Cheers

Many baseball players have been known to have a taste for alcohol.

Jim Fregosi, an infielder who played 18 seasons in the majors, said if he ever wrote a book it would be titled *The Bases Were Loaded and So Was I*. Mickey Mantle sometimes played with a hangover and once hit a home run against the Baltimore Orioles while drunk. Outfielder John Kruk called a bar he owned in West Virginia Third Base because it was the last place you stopped at before you went home.

1. BABE RUTH

Babe Ruth had an almost inhuman ability to consume alcohol. When Ruth learned that his former teammate, pitcher Waite Hoyt, had a case of amnesia, he thought it was a new brand of beer. Ruth's funeral took place on a hot August day in 1948. Joe Dugan, the third baseman on the great 1927 Yankee team, told Waite Hoyt, "I'd give a hundred dollars for a cold beer." Hoyt replied, "So would the Babe."

seasons in which he batted above .300. In 1955, Valo batted .364 in 112 games for the Kansas City Athletics.

8. MOE DRABOWSKY

Moe Drabowsky pitched for 17 seasons in the big leagues. The native of Ozanna, Poland, was an excellent reliever. In both 1967 and 1968 Drabowsky had earned run averages below 2.00 while pitching for the Baltimore Orioles. He is best remembered for winning game one of the 1966 World Series. In that game, Drabowski pitched six-and-two-thirds innings of shutout relief. He permitted the Los Angeles Dodgers only one hit and fanned 11.

9. OLAF HENRIKSEN

Olaf Henriksen played seven seasons for the Boston Red Sox. The outfielder played in three World Series for Boston between 1912 and 1916. Despite being born in Denmark, his nickname was Swede.

10. BOBBY THOMSON

Born in Glasgow, Scotland, Bobby Thomson was nicknamed the Staten Island Scot. Thomson had eight seasons with 20 or more home runs and hit .264 during his 15-year career. While playing for the New York Giants, the hard-hitting outfielder had four 100-RBI seasons. In game three of the 1951 National League playoffs, Thomson hit the home run off Ralph Branca of the Brooklyn Dodgers that propelled the Giants into the World Series. The blast, known as the "Shot Heard Round the World," is generally considered the most famous home run in baseball history.

crash while attempting to deliver supplies to victims of an earthquake in Managua, Nicaragua. He was elected to the Baseball Hall of Fame in 1973.

3. JOE STRAUB

Catcher Joe Straub played parts of three seasons in the major leagues between 1880 and 1883. Born in Germany, Straub's career was probably hindered by the fact that he could not speak English.

4. JAKE GETTMAN

Jake Gettman was one of the few major leaguers born in Russia. Gettman, an outfielder, played with Washington from 1897 to 1899. After batting .315 as a rookie, he saw his batting average steadily decline in his final two seasons.

5. RENO BERTOIA

Reno Bertoia was born in St. Vito Udine, Italy. When Detroit brought up the 18-year-old infielder in 1953 they thought he was a real prospect. Plagued by nerves, Bertoia averaged .186 during his first four seasons in Detroit. A major disappointment, Bertoia had a .244 career batting average during his 10-year career.

6. JOHN ANDERSON

Outfielder John Anderson was born in Sasbourg, Norway, in 1873. Anderson played 14 seasons in the major leagues. His best season was 1898 when he led the National League in triples and slugging percentage.

7. ELMER VALO

Born in Ribnik, Czechoslovakia, Elmer Valo played 20 seasons in the major leagues. The outfielder had seven

The International Pastime

Baseball may be the national pastime, but it has always had players from around the world. Many of today's superstars were born in Latin America.

1. ICHIRO SUZUKI

There have been Japanese players in the major leagues, but none had the impact of outfielder Ichiro Suzuki. A seven-time batting champion in Japan, Suzuki helped the Seattle Mariners win 116 games in 2001, his first season in the major leagues. Ichiro won the American League batting crown with a .350 average. He also led the league with 242 hits and 56 stolen bases. Suzuki was voted the American League Most Valuable Player and Rookie of the Year.

2. ROBERTO CLEMENTE

The first great Latin player in the major leagues was Roberto Clemente. Born in Puerto Rico in 1934, Clemente starred for the Pittsburgh Pirates from 1955 to 1972. The outfielder won four National League batting titles and finished his career with 3,000 base hits. Clemente died on December 31, 1972, in an airplane

spite his success, Dandridge was never promoted to the major leagues. While at Minneapolis, he helped instruct a promising young outfielder by the name of Willie Mays. Dandridge was elected to the Baseball Hall of Fame in 1987.

10. **RUBE FOSTER**

Rube Foster has been called the Father of Negro Baseball. Honus Wagner called Foster one of the greatest pitchers he had faced. Foster competed against some of the top major league pitchers in exhibition games and defeated Rube Waddell in a memorable 1902 duel. Besides being a dominant pitcher, Foster was an outstanding manager. He was recognized for his many achievements when he was elected to the Baseball Hall of Fame in 1981.

often among the league leaders in home runs. Once the color barrier was broken, Bill Veeck offered to sign Leonard to a major league contract, but the first baseman, who was by this time over 40, reluctantly declined.

6. JUDY JOHNSON

Often called the best third baseman in the Negro League, Judy Johnson was elected to the Baseball Hall of Fame in 1975. Philadelphia A's manager Connie Mack told Johnson that if he were white he could name his price to play in the major leagues. In 1929, Johnson batted .401 with Hilldale.

7. TURKEY STEARNES

Satchel Paige said Turkey Stearnes was one of the greatest hitters of all time. The slugging outfielder had a .352 career batting average. Stearnes led the league in home runs seven times.

8. SPOTSWOOD POLES

Outfielder Spotswood Poles was sometimes referred to as the black Ty Cobb. One of the greatest players in the Negro League, Poles batted an incredible .487 in 1914. Poles batted .610 in ten exhibition games against major league competition.

9. RAY DANDRIDGE

Ray Dandridge was a slick fielding third baseman who starred in the Negro and Mexican Leagues. In 1949, the 35-year-old Dandridge was signed to a minor league contract by the New York Giants. Assigned to the Giants' AAA farm club at Minneapolis, Dandridge won the league's Most Valuable Player award in 1950. De-

2. OSCAR CHARLESTON

Outfielder Oscar Charleston was regarded by John McGraw as the best player in the Negro Leagues. He was known for his outstanding hitting and base-stealing skills, which rivaled those of white major leaguers Ty Cobb and Max Carey. It was said that his defensive skills in center field were unsurpassed. Charleston was finally recognized with his Hall of Fame induction in 1976.

3. COOL PAPA BELL

Satchel Paige said that Cool Papa Bell was so fast that he could turn off the light and be in bed before the room got dark! Bell was so fast that he once scored from first on a bunt. He was such a good hitter that he batted .430 in the Mexican League when he was 43 years old. In 1951, the 48-year-old Bell was offered a chance to play with the St. Louis Browns, but he declined because he was past his prime. Bell was elected to the Baseball Hall of Fame in 1972.

4. JOHN HENRY LLOYD

Babe Ruth said that John Henry Lloyd was the best player he ever saw play. Lloyd was shortstop who was often favorably compared to Honus Wagner. The 44-year-old Lloyd batted .564 in 37 games while playing for the New York Lincoln Giants in 1928. Lloyd was a 1977 Hall of Fame selection.

5. BUCK LEONARD

Buck Leonard was the best first baseman in the Negro League. A 1972 Hall of Fame inductee, Leonard was a line drive hitter frequently compared to Lou Gehrig. Leonard had a .341 career batting average and was

Blackballed

Jackie Robinson broke the color barrier with the Brooklyn Dodgers in 1947. Prior to Robinson, many great Negro League stars were denied an opportunity to play in the major leagues. Cannonball Wickware, a pitcher for the Mohawk Giants, once defeated Walter Johnson's All Stars, striking out 17. John "The Black Bomber" Beckwith was known for his tape measure home runs.

1. JOSH GIBSON

Josh Gibson was the best hitter in Negro League history and one of baseball's greatest catchers. His career .384 batting average was a Negro League record. Gibson led the league in home runs nine times. He hit a number of home runs that were measured at nearly 600 feet. Gibson said, "I don't break bats, I wear them out." The 35-year-old slugger died of a stroke on January 20, 1947, a few months before Jackie Robinson became the first African American to play in the National League. Gibson was elected to the baseball Hall of Fame in 1972.

8. TOM DELAHANTY

There were five Delahanty brothers who played in the major leagues. By far the most talented was Ed, an outfielder who three times batted .400 and had a .346 career batting average. Jim Delahanty, a second baseman, played 13 seasons in the majors and finished with a respectable .283 batting average. Outfielder Frank Delahanty played six seasons, although he batted only .226. Another outfielder, Joe Delahanty, played two seasons as a starter with St. Louis in 1908 and 1909. The least accomplished of the Delahanty brothers was Tom, an infielder, who played only 19 games in the majors.

9. EARL AVERILL, JR.

Earl Averill batted .318 during his big league career from 1929 to 1941. The Hall of Fame outfielder scored more than 100 runs in nine different seasons with Cleveland. His son, Earl, was a catcher who was brought up by the Indians in 1956. Earl Averill, Jr., batted .242 during his seven-year career.

10. DICK SISLER

St. Louis Browns' first baseman George Sisler set a major league record when he had 257 hits during the 1920 season. Sisler batted .407 that year and two years later won a second batting crown with a .420 batting average. His son, Dick, also a first baseman, was a decent player, although he never approached the success of his father. Dick played eight seasons and batted .276. His sole claim to fame was hitting a home run on the last day of the 1950 season to clinch the pennant for the Philadelphia Phillies.

Vince, Joe, and Dom DiMaggio (left to right) pose at a San Francisco Seals reunion in the early 1950s.

ting average. Younger brother Dom twice led the American League in runs scored while playing for Boston. Older brother Vince is best remembered for striking out. Vince led the National League in striking out six times. Casey Stengel said of him, "Vince is the only player I ever saw who could strike out three times in a game and not be embarrassed."

7. **ED WALSH, JR.**

Hall of Fame pitcher Ed Walsh won 40 games with the Chicago White Sox in 1908. His 1.82 career earned run average is the lowest in major league history. Walsh's son, Ed, also pitched for the White Sox. In four seasons with the Sox, Ed Walsh, Jr., won 11, lost 24, and had a high 5.57 earned run average.

joined him on the Braves in 1962 and played seven seasons. Tommie was not nearly the player his brother was and hit only 13 home runs during his career.

3. HENRY MATHEWSON

Christy Mathewson was one of baseball's greatest pitchers. Matty won 373 and lost only 188 during his Hall of Fame career. His 2.13 career earned run average is fifth all time, and he is third on the career shutout list with 80. Christy's younger brother, Henry, joined him on the Giants in 1906. Henry appeared in three games for New York, losing his only decision and walking 14 batters in 11 innings.

4. GEORGE RADBOURN

Hoss Radbourn won 308 games during his Hall of Fame career. In 1884 the Providence pitcher set a record that will never be broken when he won 60 games. His younger brother, George, pitched three games for Detroit in 1883. George gave up 38 hits and struck out only two batters in 22 innings. He finished with a 6.55 career earned run average, nearly four runs a game higher than his brother.

5. DALE BERRA

Dale Berra said of himself and his father, "Our similarities are different." His father, Yogi, is considered by many to be the best catcher in baseball history. The three-time American League Most Valuable Player appeared in a record 14 World Series with the New York Yankees. Dale Berra, an infielder, batted .236 in a undistinguished career that lasted from 1977 to 1987.

6. VINCE DIMAGGIO

Joe DiMaggio was considered the greatest all-around player of all time. The Yankee Clipper won two batting titles, two home run crowns, and had a career .325 bat-

Family Affairs

Ken Griffey, Jr., was an even better player than his father, Ken Griffey, Sr. Bobby Bonds was a terrific player who hit 332 career home runs, but his son, Barry, will probably double that total before he retires. However, there have been many players who never approached the success of relatives who played baseball.

1. **PETE ROSE, JR.**

Pete Rose holds the all-time major league record with 4,256 base hits. Ten times Rose had 200 or more hits in a season, and he won three batting titles. His son, Pete, Jr., spent many years in the minor leagues before making his major league debut with the Cincinnati Reds on September 1, 1997. Rose got two hits that season and struck out nine times in 14 at-bats. The next season he returned to the minors. Unless he makes it back to the major leagues, he will fall 4,254 hits short of his father.

2. **TOMMIE AARON**

Hank Aaron is major league baseball's home run king with 755. Aaron also holds the record for the most runs batted in with 2,297. Hank's younger brother, Tommie,

on a summer day. Jim Greengrass had a couple of good seasons playing the outfield in Cincinnati's Crosley Field. His best year was 1953 when he batted in 100 runs for the Reds.

9. **VIC POWER**

Vic Power was an excellent first baseman who played in the American League from 1954 to 1965. A three-time .300 hitter, he had enough power to hit 126 home runs during his career. His best power season was 1955 when he belted 19 homers for the Kansas City A's. The slick-fielding first baseman also won seven Gold Gloves for his defense.

10. **HERB SCORE**

The first question anybody would ask about a baseball game is, "What's the score?" When Herb Score was on the mound, his Cleveland Indians were usually ahead. In his first two seasons, Score led the American League in strikeouts, and he had a 36–19 record. His brilliant career was derailed on May 7, 1957, when he was struck in the face by a line drive off the bat of New York's Gil McDougald. Score missed the remainder of the 1957 season, and an arm injury the next season slowed his once blazing fastball. Score won only 19 more games after his injury.

first major league game with the Washington Senators. He was 21 when he won his first game in 1941. In 1963, he recorded his 300th and final win. Wynn was elected to the Hall of Fame in 1972.

4. HOMER SUMMA

Homer Summa was an outfielder whose best years were with the Cleveland Indians from 1922 to 1928. A good hitter, he had a .302 lifetime batting average. Despite his name, he possessed only moderate power. Summa hit 18 homers during his career.

5. JOHN STRIKE

The strike is a pitcher's best friend. John Strike pitched in two games for Philadelphia in 1886. He threw enough strikes to strike out 11 batters in 15 innings.

6. BOB WALK

The walk is the bane of pitchers. Bob Walk pitched for Philadelphia, Atlanta, and Pittsburgh during the 1980s. During his rookie season, he walked 71 batters in 152 innings.

7. CECIL FIELDER

A better name for Cecil Fielder might have been Cecil Slugger. The big Detroit first baseman led the American League with 51 home runs in 1990. Two years later, Fielder became the first player since Babe Ruth to lead the American League in runs batted in three years in a row.

8. JIM GREENGRASS

Nothing is more beautiful to a baseball fan than the green grass of the outfield of his or her favorite ballpark

Born to Be Baseball Players

Hall-of-Fame pitcher Early Wynn debuted at the "Early" age of 19 and hurled his way to 300 "Wynns" before retiring in 1963.

Born to Be Baseball Players

Some players were born with ideal names to play the game. Bruce Fields was an outfielder who played with the Detroit Tigers in 1986. Eric Plunk had an intimidating name for a hard-throwing relief pitcher.

1. NEAL BALL

What could be a better baseball name than Ball? Neal Ball was a middle infielder who played in the major leagues from 1907 to 1913. On July 19, 1909, Ball, playing for Cleveland, completed the first unassisted triple play in major league baseball history in a game against Boston. Ball was not known for his defensive prowess, however. In 1908, he was charged with 81 errors while playing for New York.

2. MATT BATTS

Matt Batts was a catcher who played ten seasons in the majors. His best season with the bat was 1948 when he hit .314 for the Boston Red Sox.

3. EARLY WYNN

Pitcher Early Wynn certainly lived up to his name. Early Wynn was only 19 years old when he pitched his

games despite a respectable 2.63 earned run average. In 1911, Gray's final season, he lost 13 of 15 decisions and posted a dreadful 5.06 earned run average. His career record was 15 wins and 51 losses.

7. **ANNA COMPTON**

Outfielder Pete Compton's real first name was Anna. Compton played for St. Louis, Boston, Pittsburgh, and New York between 1911 and 1918. He hit only five home runs in his career and twice batted below .200.

8. **JUDY JOHNSON**

Judy Johnson was considered the best third baseman in the Negro Leagues during the 1920s and 1930s. Johnson played for the Homestead Grays, Darby Daisies, and Pittsburgh Crawfords. His best season was 1929 when he batted above .400. Johnson was elected to the Baseball Hall of Fame in 1975.

9. **BONNIE HOLLINGSWORTH**

Bonnie Hollingsworth played four seasons in the major leagues and was on the roster of a different team every year. Hollingsworth had brief stays with Pittsburgh, Washington, Brooklyn, and Boston. In four seasons, Hollingsworth compiled a 4–9 record.

10. **SADIE McMAHON**

Sadie McMahon was a workhorse pitcher during the 1890s. He started 60 games and had 55 complete games in 1890. McMahon twice led the American Association, then considered a major league, in wins with 36 in 1890 and 34 in 1891. He had three consecutive 20-win seasons for Baltimore of the National League from 1893 to 1894.

2. LENA BLACKBURNE

Lena Blackburne was a weak-hitting infielder who played in the major leagues from 1910 to 1919. Blackburne's career batting average was only .214. He compiled a 99–133 record as manager of the Chicago White Sox from 1928 to 1929. During his tenure as manager, he came out on the short of several fights with one of his players, Art Shires.

3. KITTY BRANSFIELD

William Bransfield was nicknamed Kiddy as a youth. When he got to the major leagues, a reporter misheard the nickname and began calling him Kitty. Bransfield, a first baseman, played in the first World Series in 1903 as a member of the Pittsburgh Pirates.

4. BARBRA CHRISLEY

Outfielder Neil Chrisley's first name was Barbra. A part-time player, Chrisley played five seasons and had a .210 career batting average. The low part of his career occurred in 1959 when he batted .132 for the Detroit Tigers.

5. GAIL HARRIS

One of Neil Chrisley's teammates on the 1959 Tigers was first baseman Gail Harris. Harris's middle name was Gail. He spent six seasons in the majors. His best year was 1958 when he hit 20 home runs.

6. DOLLY GRAY

As a rookie pitcher with Washington in 1909, Dolly Gray had a 5–19 record. On August 28, 1909, he set a major league record by walking seven consecutive hitters. The next season Gray managed to lose 19

A Ballplayer named Sadie

A woman has never played in the major leagues, but you could never tell that from some players' names and nicknames. Tillie Shafer played infield for the New York Giants from 1910 to 1913. Pitcher Rosie Ryan won 52 games during his 10-year major league career. Daisy Davis pitched for Boston in 1884 and 1885. Cincinnati pitcher Peaches Davis won 27 games between 1936 and 1939. Molly Craft pitched four seasons with Washington without winning a game. Outfielder Patsy Donovan had 2,249 hits during his career, which lasted from 1890 to 1907. Liz Funk was an outfielder who played for the Detroit Tigers and Chicago White Sox from 1930 to 1933.

1. LADY BALDWIN

Charles Baldwin was nicknamed Lady because, unlike most players of his day, he did not drink, smoke, or curse. The pitcher used a hop, skip, and jump delivery similar to a cricket bowler. In 1886 Baldwin led the National League with 42 victories while pitching for Detroit.

Brooklyn in 1908. Finlayson pitched one more game for Brooklyn in 1909 before he was sent to the minors. His career earned run average was 11.05.

7. **RIVINGTON BISLAND**

Shortstop Rivington Bisland was one of the worst hitters in major league history. From 1912 to 1914 he played for the Pittsburgh Pirates, St. Louis Browns, and Cleveland Indians. His best season was 1913 when he batted an anemic .136 for St. Louis. Bisland had only one extra base hit in three seasons, and his career batting average was an abysmal .118.

8. **ASTYANAX DOUGLASS**

Catcher Astyanax Douglass batted .143 in four games with the Cincinnati Reds in 1921. Four years later Douglass returned to Cincinnati and batted .176 in seven games. Douglass's lifetime batting average was .167, and he never had an extra base hit in the majors.

9. **WHAMMY DOUGLAS**

Charles "Whammy" Douglas played his rookie season with the Pittsburgh Pirates in 1957. Despite control problems, Douglas had a 3–3 record with a respectable 3.26 earned run average. Perhaps Douglas could not overcome his nickname "Whammy" as he never pitched in the major leagues again.

10. **URBANE PICKERING**

Third baseman Urbane Pickering played for the Boston Red Sox for two seasons. A mediocre hitter, he posted a career .257 batting average. After leading American League third basemen in errors in 1932, Pickering exited the majors for good.

with an earlier Yankee superstar. Unfortunately, he did not share Mickey Mantle's ability. Klutts averaged less than two home runs per season during his eight-year career.

3. **TONY SUCK**

If ever a player had a name that summed up his career, it was Tony Suck. He played catcher, shortstop, outfield, and third base during his brief major league career, which lasted from 1883 to 1884. While he may have been versatile on the field, his hitting sucked. He batted only .151 in 205 at-bats.

4. **EVERITT BOOE**

When Lou Piniella came to bat, the fans yelled "Lou." When Moose Skowron stepped up to the plate, his fans yelled, "Moose." One can only imagine what the fans yelled when Everitt Booe came to bat. Booe, an outfielder who played for the Pittsburgh Pirates in 1913, batted .200 with 0 home runs in his only season in the National League.

5. **BILL GREIF**

Fans probably exclaimed "Good Grief!" when Bill Greif took the mound, but not to describe his pitching. Greif was a righthander who pitched from 1971 to 1976 and never had a winning season in the major leagues. His worst season was 1972 when his record was 5–16 with a 5.60 earned run average for the San Diego Padres. His career record was a dismal 31–67.

6. **PEMBROKE FINLAYSON**

Pembroke Finlayson had an astronomical 135.00 earned run average during his rookie season with

No-Chance Names

Mickey Mantle had the perfect baseball name. It's masculine, simple, easy to remember, all American. It was no surprise that Mickey Mantle became a baseball icon. Some players are not so lucky. Can you imagine Stanwood Partenheimer, a pitcher during World War II, becoming a star? You can't and he wasn't. Other players with a similar handicap were second baseman Foster Castleman, pitcher Carlton Molesworth, pinch-hitter Odbert Hamric, outfielder Austin Knickerbocker, and outfielder Carden Gillenwater. These players were doomed from the start by their names.

1. BOB BLEWETT

A player with an unfortunate name was pitcher Bob Blewett. He pitched five games for New York during the 1902 season. Blewett lost both of his decisions and gave up 39 hits in only 28 innings.

2. MICKEY KLUTTS

Mickey Klutts was a utility infielder who came up with the New York Yankees in 1976. He shared his first name

the National League in hits with 201 in 1926. Brown was nicknamed Glass Arm because of his weak throws from the outfield.

7. WHAT'S THE USE?

Outfielder Pearce Chiles played for Philadelphia from 1899 to 1900. Chiles got the nickname What's the Use? because he used the phrase about opposing players. He should have said it about himself as he slumped to .216 in 1900 and was shipped to the minors for good.

8. WHY ME?

Danny Cater was an excellent hitter who finished second in the American League in batting in 1968. Cater believed that he was robbed of more than his share of hits by great defensive plays. Whenever someone made a great play to cost him a hit, Cater exclaimed, "Why me?"

9. WHOOPS

Second baseman Pat Creeden played in five games for the Boston Red Sox in 1931. Creeden was hitless in eight at-bats during his brief stay in the majors. Apparently he wasn't that good in the field either as his nickname, Whoops, attests.

10. THE LOAFER

Jimmy McAleer was an outfielder who played in the major leagues from 1889 to 1907. McAleer's nickname, The Loafer, was misleading. He did not receive the nickname because of a lack of effort. He was called the Loafer because of the effortless way he ran down fly balls.

nickname Bonehead because of one mistake he made. In a game against the Chicago Cubs on September 23, 1908, Merkle, then a 19-year-old rookie, was on first base when Al Bridwell hit what appeared to be a game-winning hit. Merkle ran off the field without touching second base. The Cubs retrieved the ball and forced out Merkle at second. The teams finished the season in a tie, and the disputed game was replayed to determine the pennant winner. Chicago won the replayed game and Merkle was branded a bonehead for costing the Giants the pennant.

4. **WILD THING**

Mitch Williams was a top reliever of the late 1980s and early 1990s. He would have been even more effective if he had had better control. Sportswriter Frank Luksa wrote, "Mitch has walked more people than a seeing-eye dog." Williams said of himself, "I pitch like my hair's on fire." There was never a dull moment when Wild Thing was on the mound. Asked if he had a trick pitch, Williams answered, "Yeah, if I throw a strike more than once in a while." Williams took the nickname in stride, "It's better than being called 'Bum.'"

5. **BOOTS**

George Grantham was one of the best-hitting second basemen of the 1920s. He batted above .300 for eight consecutive seasons from 1924 to 1931. His fielding was another story. He was nicknamed Boots because he booted so many ground balls. During the 1923 season Grantham made 55 errors.

6. **GLASS ARM**

Another good hit, no field player was outfielder Eddie Brown. He had a .303 career batting average and led

Why Me?

Babe Ruth was the Sultan of Swat. One of Ted Williams's nicknames was Teddy Ballgame. Not every player can be a star or have a flattering nickname.

1. **THE ALL-AMERICAN OUT**

Leo Durocher is best remembered as a Hall of Fame manager. Despite a .247 career batting average, Durocher played shortstop in the major leagues from 1925 to 1945. Durocher was such a weak hitter that he was nicknamed the All-American Out by Babe Ruth.

2. **LOSING PITCHER**

Philadelphia Phillies' pitcher Hugh Mulcahy led the National League in losses with 20 in 1938 and 22 in 1940. His 45–89 lifetime record gave him the worst winning percentage of a pitcher in the twentieth century with more than 100 decisions. Mulcahy's losing ways earned him the nickname Losing Pitcher.

3. **BONEHEAD**

New York Giants' John McGraw thought that first baseman Fred Merkle was one of the smartest players he ever managed. It is ironic that Merkle was given the

received his nickname because his running resembled the waddle of a penguin.

7. THE CRAB

Jesse Burkett had a .341 career batting average. Burkett, an outfielder, batted above .400 in 1895, 1896, and 1899. He was nicknamed the Crab because of his irritable disposition.

8. THE MOLE

Rod Kanehl was a utility player on the atrocious New York Mets teams from 1962 to 1964. The Mets finished in the cellar all three seasons. Kanehl was named the Mole because of his fascination with subways.

9. BEAR TRACKS

Johnny Schmitz pitched in the major leagues from 1941 to 1956. His career record was 93 wins and 114 losses. Schmitz was nicknamed Bear Tracks because of his enormous feet.

10. THE CRIME DOG

First baseman Fred McGriff was one of the most prolific home run hitters of the 1990s. His nickname, the Crime Dog, derived from his last name's similarity to McGruff, the Crime Dog. McGruff was an animated dog that wore a trench coat and offered suggestions on how to fight crime.

Because of the extra finger, Alfonseca was nicknamed the Octopus. Alfonseca recorded 45 saves for the Florida Marlins during the 2000 season.

3. CATFISH

Jim Hunter won 20 games for five consecutive seasons from 1971 to 1975. In 1964 Kansas City Athletics' owner Charles Finley signed Hunter to a $50,000 bonus. Finley liked to give his players colorful nicknames. He made up a story that Hunter was nicknamed Catfish because he had caught a catfish when he was a child. Although the story was completely fabricated, the nickname stuck.

4. THE VULTURE

Reliever Phil Regan was nicknamed the Vulture. He received the nickname because he finished off the game for the starting pitcher. Twice, Regan led the National League in saves. In 1966, Regan had a 14–1 record with the Los Angeles Dodgers.

5. THE ARKANSAS HUMMINGBIRD

Pitcher Lon Warneke was born in Mt. Ida, Arkansas, in 1909. Warneke, a three-time 20-game winner, had a 193–121 record during his career from 1930 to 1945. He was nicknamed the Arkansas Hummingbird because he sometimes hummed on the mound. Warneke also played the ukulele in Cardinals' teammate Pepper Martins' band.

6. THE PENGUIN

Third baseman Ron Cey slammed 316 home runs during his major league career from 1971 to 1987. Cey

They're Animals

Over the years many baseball players have had animal nicknames. Cincinnati outfielder Walter Christenson was nicknamed Cuckoo. Brooklyn Dodgers' pitcher Dan Bessent was known as the Weasel. Detroit infielder Joe Sargent is remembered for his nickname, Horse Belly. Knuckleballer Thomas "Toad" Ramsey struck out 499 batters for Louisville in 1886. Don Larsen, who pitched a perfect game for the New York Yankees against the Brooklyn Dodgers in 1956, was called "Gooneybird."

1. **THE GERBIL**

Don Zimmer was an infielder who played in the majors from 1954 to 1965. Zimmer managed the Boston Red Sox from 1976 to 1980. One of the players in Boston who did not care for Zimmer was pitcher Bill "Spaceman" Lee. Noting Zimmer's chubby-cheeked appearance, Lee gave him the unwanted nickname of the Gerbil.

2. **THE OCTOPUS**

One of the best relief pitchers in baseball today, Antonio Alfonseca was born with six fingers on each hand.

10. **JIMMIE FOXX**

Slugging first baseman Jimmie Foxx won the American League Triple Crown in 1933 when he batted .356 and hit 48 home runs and batted in 163 runs. Philadelphia A's owner Connie Mack, claiming the team was cash strapped because of the Depression, suggested that Foxx's salary be cut from $16,333 to $12,000. Mack pointed out that Foxx's homer total had dropped from 58 to 48. Foxx eventually agreed to sign for $16,000, a $333 cut.

League in doubles and runs batted in. Medwick was shocked when Cardinals' owner Sam Breadon threatened to substantially cut his contract. Medwick reluctantly agreed to a $2,000 cut. Breadon, known for being tight with his money, told Medwick, "I am not giving you the $2,000, I'd rather throw it out the window." Medwick replied, "If you threw $2,000 out the window, you would still be holding on to it."

7. BOB UECKER

Catcher Bob Uecker signed with the Milwaukee Braves for a $3,000 bonus. Uecker joked, "That kind of money bothered my dad at the time, because he did not have that kind of money to pay out." Uecker justified his small bonus by hitting only .200 during his six-year big league career.

8. BOB FELLER

One of the hardest throwers in major league history, Bob Feller won 266 games between 1936 and 1956. Rapid Robert led the American League in wins six times and led the league in strikeouts seven seasons. In 1936, the teenager accepted a one-dollar bonus to sign with the Cleveland Indians.

9. LEFTY GOMEZ

Lefty Gomez was 26–5 and led the American League in earned run average, strikeouts, and shutouts while pitching for the New York Yankees in 1934. The next season Gomez slumped to a 12–15 record. Yankees' owner Jacob Ruppert wanted to cut Gomez's salary from $20,000 to $7,500. Gomez told Ruppert, "You keep the salary and I'll take the cut."

3. **LEW MOREN**

Lew Moren was known as the Million Dollar Kid. Moren pitched for Pittsburgh and Philadelphia between 1903 and 1910. He received his nickname because his father, a wealthy steamboat and coal barge operator, gave his son $100 every time he won a game. In his major league career, Moren won 48 games, earning him a total of $4,800 in bonuses. To live up to his nickname, Moren would have had to win 10,000 games.

4. **JOSH GIBSON**

Negro League star Josh Gibson swatted more than 800 home runs during his career. If he were playing in the major leagues today he would probably earn at least 15 million dollars a year. In 1933, the catcher hit 35 home runs and batted in 239 runs. During that time, Gibson earned between $250 and $400 a month.

5. **JERRY KOOSMAN**

Southpaw Jerry Koosman won 222 games during his 19-year major league career. Koosman won 17 games for the 1969 Miracle Mets team and added two more victories in the World Series against Baltimore. The New York Mets originally offered Koosman a $1,600 bonus. When he refused the initial offer, the club dropped the bonus offer to $1,200. Koosman accepted the lower offer. He reasoned, "I'd figured I'd better sign before I owed them money."

6. **JOE MEDWICK**

In 1937, Joe Medwick, star outfielder for the St. Louis Cardinals, won the Triple Crown when he batted .374 and had 31 homers and 154 runs batted in. The next season Medwick batted .322 and led the National

Contract Players

Today, the average major league baseball player's salary exceeds two million dollars a year. Texas shortstop Alex Rodriguez earns more than 25 million dollars per year. High salaries weren't always the norm in baseball.

1. GEORGE BAUMGARDNER

George Baumgardner pitched for the St. Louis Browns from 1912 to 1916. His best season was 1914 when he won 14 games. Baumgardner was a farm boy from West Virginia. The Browns paid his salary in dollar bills to make it seem more substantial.

2. AL REACH

Al Reach was baseball's first professional player. He received a small salary while playing for the Brooklyn Eckfords in the early 1860s. In 1865, Reach was paid $25 a week in expenses to play for a team in Philadelphia. Years later, Reach made a fortune as a sporting goods manufacturer and was part owner of the Philadelphia Phillies from 1883 to 1902.

10. **RICHIE HEBNER**

Richie Hebner played third base in the major leagues from 1968 to 1985. He hit 25 home runs for the Pirates in 1973. During his youth in Massachusetts, Hebner worked as a gravedigger.

ment, Chance has had a number of jobs. For a time he managed a heavyweight boxing contender named Ernie Shavers, who once fought Muhammad Ali. Chance also worked in the carnival business for several years.

6. **BUCK WEAVER**

Chicago White Sox third baseman Buck Weaver was banned from baseball in 1920 for his involvement in the throwing of the 1919 World Series. Although Weaver claimed he did not participate in the fix, he was never reinstated. One of Weaver's post-baseball jobs was as a parimutuel clerk at a thoroughbred racetrack.

7. **KURT STILLWELL**

Kurt Stillwell was a rookie shortstop with the Cincinnati Reds in 1986. In 1987, he lost his starting job to Barry Larkin. Stillwell later opened his own taxidermy shop.

8. **EARL AVERILL**

Outfielder Earl Averill batted .318 during his Hall of Fame career that lasted from 1929 to 1941. In 1936, while playing for Cleveland, he batted .378 and led the American League with 232 hits. Averill's most unusual job was as a fireworks tester.

9. **EDDIE PLANK**

Lefthander Eddie Plank won 327 games during his 17-year major league career. Eight times Plank won 20 or more games. He was known as Gettysburg Eddie because he was born and lived in Gettysburg, Pennsylvania. Plank served as a tour guide at the historic Gettysburg battlefield, where a decisive battle of the Civil War was fought in 1863.

2. WAITE HOYT

Pitcher Waite Hoyt won 237 games during his Hall of Fame career. His best season was 1927 when he led the American League with 22 wins while pitching for the New York Yankees. Hoyt's father-in-law was a funeral home director, and early in his baseball career Hoyt considered becoming a mortician. Once, Hoyt picked up a corpse from a hospital and put it in his car trunk. He drove to Yankee Stadium, where he calmly pitched a shutout. After the game, Hoyt delivered the body to his father-in-law's funeral home.

3. FERRIS FAIN

Philadelphia A's first baseman Ferris Fain won American League batting crowns in 1951 and 1952. Following his retirement, Fain became a farmer in California. In March 1988, Fain's farm was raided, and more than a million dollars of marijuana was confiscated. Fain swore that he never used the stuff and that he grew the crop purely for profit.

4. CHET LAABS

St. Louis Browns' outfielder Chet Laabs worked part-time in a defense plant during the 1944 season. That season, the Browns won their only American League pennant. Laabs inspected pipe lengths that were shipped to Tennessee and used in building the first atomic bomb.

5. DEAN CHANCE

In 1964, Los Angeles Angels' pitcher Dean Chance led the American League in wins (20), shutouts (11), and earned run average (1.65). Chance retired from baseball in 1971 with 128 career victories. Since his retire-

Keeping the Day Job

Major league baseball players have worked all kinds of jobs off the field.

Hall of Fame outfielder Edd Roush worked as a cemetery manager in Indiana following his retirement from baseball. Powerhitting catcher Lance Parrish once was employed as a bodyguard for rock star Tina Turner. First baseman Chick Gandil, banned from baseball for his involvement in the Black Sox scandal, worked as a plumber in California after his playing days were over.

1. TOM DONOHUE

Tom Donohue was a catcher who played for the California Angels in 1979 and 1980. While playing baseball, Donohue was studying to be a mortician. On team flights, Donohue would read his mortician books. During one particularly turbulent flight, Donohue unnerved his teammates by reading aloud passages of how to prepare the remains of charred crash victims. Donohue then reached into his briefcase and passed out toe tags to his speechless teammates.

ambition was to become a professional baseball player, but that no one would sign him. Ford became president when Richard Nixon resigned because of the Watergate scandal in 1974. Ford once said, "I watch a lot of baseball on radio."

9. **GEORGE H. W. BUSH**

George H. W. Bush served as president from 1989 to 1993. Bush remembered that his first love as a child was baseball. He played first base for his college team at Yale. In 1948 Bush met his hero, Babe Ruth, when he visited Yale.

10. **CALVIN COOLIDGE**

Calvin Coolidge became president when Warren Harding died in 1923. Although Coolidge's knowledge of baseball was limited, he did frequently attend games in Washington. Coolidge threw out the first ball at Opening Day in 1924 and the first pitch at the 1924 World Series between Washington and the New York Giants. Coolidge once said that he believed Babe Ruth made a big mistake when he gave up pitching.

6. **WILLIAM HOWARD TAFT**

In 1882, William Howard Taft vowed never to play baseball again after he was shelled while pitching a semi-pro game. Although his career as a player was over, Taft never lost his love of the game. On April 14, 1910, Taft began the tradition of the president throwing out the first pitch on opening day. The occasion was marred when Vice President James Sherman was knocked unconscious by a foul ball, hit by Philadelphia third baseman Frank "Home Run" Baker. A few weeks later, on May 4, 1910, President Taft attended a game between the Reds and the Cardinals in St. Louis. That same day, Taft walked two blocks to Sportsman's Park to watch an American League game between the St. Louis Browns and Cleveland Indians. During the dead ball era, Taft suggested to major league baseball officials that they bring more hitting into the game. "I love the game when there's plenty of slugging," Taft remarked.

7. **JOHN KENNEDY**

John Kennedy developed a friendship with outfielder Jim Piersall. During the 1960 presidential campaign, Kennedy asked Piersall, who was playing for the Cleveland Indians, if he had any suggestions that would help him win the Ohio Democratic primary. Piersall replied, "I have big problems with Cleveland manager, Joe Gordon. Don't bother me with your little ones." Kennedy went on to win the presidential election in November.

8. **GERALD FORD**

Gerald Ford was an outstanding football player at the University of Michigan. Ford admitted that his lifelong

Presidents and Baseball

A former semi-pro pitcher who left the sport after a shelling, President William Howard Taft was the first president to throw out a first pitch, on April 14, 1910.

coming the attorney for the Major League Players Association. Nixon, a big baseball fan, expressed interest in the position. However, the deal fell through when the executive director of the Players' Association, Marvin Miller, refused to work with Nixon. In 1968 Nixon defeated Hubert Humphrey to become president of the United States. Nixon prided himself on being a baseball expert and picked his own All Time team while president. Occasionally, Nixon would send notes to players with suggestions on how to improve their play. In 1985, the former president served as an arbiter during a salary dispute between major league umpires and management. Nixon, who had instituted wage and price controls during his administration to reduce inflation, rewarded the umps with a 40 percent salary increase.

5. **HERBERT HOOVER**

Herbert Hoover, president from 1929 to 1933, once said, "Next to religion, baseball has furnished a greater impact on American life than any other institution." Despite his appreciation of baseball, as president Hoover had a number of embarrassing moments related to the game. During the 1928 presidential election, Babe Ruth refused to have his photo taken with Hoover because he supported his Democratic rival, Al Smith. When Ruth signed a Yankees' contract for $80,000 in 1930, reporters pointed out that the Babe was earning more than President Hoover, who was struggling to lead the country through the Great Depression. Ruth replied, "I had a better year." Hoover attended game three at the 1931 World Series between the Philadelphia A's and the St. Louis Cardinals. As Hoover left his box, Philadelphia fans, tired of Prohibition, began chanting, "We want beer!"

2. RONALD REAGAN

Before he became an actor, Ronald Reagan was an announcer for the Chicago Cubs. In 1937, Reagan accompanied the team to California for spring training. Reagan was discovered by an agent and launched a successful acting career. In 1952, Reagan portrayed Hall of Fame pitcher Grover Cleveland Alexander in the film, *The Winning Team*. Alexander had been named for another president, Grover Cleveland. Reagan was elected president of the United States in 1980. On September 30, 1988, Reagan joined Harry Caray in the announcing booth at Wrigley Field in Chicago during a Cubs game.

3. DWIGHT EISENHOWER

As a child Dwight Eisenhower told a friend that he wanted to be a major league baseball player when he grew up. His friend said his ambition was to be elected president of the United States. As Eisenhower mused, "Neither of us got his wish." Eisenhower said, "Not making the baseball team at West Point was one of the greatest disappointments of my life, maybe the greatest." Eisenhower displayed his baseball ability when he batted .355 for Junction City of the Class D Central Kansas League. Eisenhower served as president of the United States from 1953 to 1961. On April 15, 1957, President Eisenhower threw out the ten-millionth Spalding baseball used in the major leagues at a game played at Washington's Griffith Stadium.

4. RICHARD NIXON

During the 1960s, Richard Nixon was approached by player reps Jim Bunning and Robin Roberts about be-

Presidents and Baseball

Many U.S. presidents have been fans of the national pastime. On June 26, 1869, Ulysses S. Grant welcomed the undefeated Cincinnati Red Stockings, baseball's first professional team, to the White House. In 1886 Chicago's star first baseman Cap Anson asked President Grover Cleveland to attend a baseball game. Cleveland replied, "What do you imagine the American people would think of me if I wasted my time going to the ballgame?" On June 2, 1892, Benjamin Harrison became the first president to attend a major league game, a 7–4 victory for Cincinnati against Washington. In 1915, Woodrow Wilson became the first president to throw out a pitch at a World Series game, at game two of the Boston Red Sox–Philadelphia Phillies series.

1. GEORGE W. BUSH

George W. Bush was an owner of the Texas Rangers before he was elected president in 2000. Bush was the first president to play Little League baseball as a child. In 2001, President Bush organized T-Ball games on the White House lawn. Children aged five to eight participated in the games.

9. FRANK GRADDOCK

On July 8, 1969, Frank Graddock murdered his wife, Margaret, at their home in Queens, New York. Graddock had become enraged when his wife insisted on watching the Gothic soap opera, *Dark Shadows*, instead of the New York Mets game.

10. CY SEYMOUR

In the early days of baseball, fans frequently lavished gifts on their diamond heroes. In April 1904, Cincinnati Reds' outfielder Cy Seymour hit a home run. In those days a home run was a rarity. Appreciative fans gave him a suit, a pair of shoes, a gross of pencils, 60 cigarette coupons, and a dozen Easter eggs.

bets Field. For 25 years Chester used her voice to heckle opposing players and umpires. To drum up Dodger rallies she would ring a cowbell or hit a frying pan with an iron ladle. She frequently led the snake dance of Brooklyn fans through the aisles.

6. ABE RETTAN

Unlike Hilda Chester, Abe Rettan was a fan the Brooklyn Dodgers could do without. Rettan sat in the stands behind third base and cheered loudly for the opposing team. It got to be so annoying that Dodgers' manager Wilbert Robinson offered to give Rettan a free season pass if he cheered for Brooklyn. Rettan accepted the offer, but after a few games changed his mind and returned to hooting the home team.

7. ART DEVLIN

Art Devlin played third base for the New York Giants from 1904 to 1911. Devlin was bothered by a cross-eyed woman who sat in the stands behind third base. The woman was obsessed with Devlin and attended every game at the Polo Grounds. Devlin became so self-conscious of her that he slumped badly. Only after she stopped coming to the games did his batting eye return.

8. PHILADELPHIA FANS

Philadelphia fans have always had the reputation of being the toughest in baseball. Pitcher Bo Belinsky said, "Philadelphia fans would boo funerals, an Easter Egg hunt, a parade of armless vets, and the Liberty Bell." Bob Uecker agreed, "They even boo the National Anthem."

they hit a home run. By the time the player rounded the bases and arrived back at the dugout, the florist had delivered him a bouquet of roses.

3. NOVELLA O'HARA

Every fan has his or her favorite player. For San Francisco Giants' fan Novella O'Hara, her favorite player was pitcher John Pregenzer. Although Pregenzer won only two games during his brief stay in the major leagues from 1963 to 1964, O'Hara was obsessed with the young pitcher. When the Giants purchased his contract from a minor league team for $100, O'Hara offered them $110 for Pregenzer. She founded the John Pregenzer Fan Club and somehow talked 3,000 others to join it. Not even Pregenzer's demotion to the minor leagues halted O'Hara's efforts on his behalf. She tried to organize a Bring Back John Pregenzer Day.

4. REVEREND SHERMAN POWELL

During the late nineteenth century, baseball was banned on Sunday in many cities. Anyone playing on Sunday could face going to jail. On July 10, 1899, Reverend Sherman Powell attended a Sunday game in Fort Wayne, Indiana. The Reverend Powell was there for the purpose of writing down the names of the players who ignored the Sunday ban. When fans realized what he was doing, they took away his pen and paper. Powell required a police escort to leave the ballpark unscathed.

5. HOWLING HILDA CHESTER

The Brooklyn Dodgers had their share of colorful fans. Perhaps the most famous was Howling Hilda Chester. She was known as the Queen of the Bleachers at Eb-

Baseball Fanatics

Colorful pitcher Bo Belinsky said, "Someday I would like to go into the stands and boo some fans." In 1989 a young autograph hunter told 68-year-old Hall of Fame pitcher Warren Spahn that he wanted his autograph because "You're getting old and you're going to die soon and it's going to be valuable." A fan once asked Kansas City Royals' third baseman George Brett for his autograph, then tore it up in front of him. A Detroit fan named Patsy O'Toole yelled so loud that she was known as the "All American Ear-ache."

1. **1890s BALTIMORE FANS**

The fans of the Baltimore Orioles in the 1890s were among the rowdiest in baseball history. Cincinnati second baseman Bid McPhee said that the opposing team was taken to the ballpark in a horsecart. The players had to lie on the floor because kids threw rocks and tomatoes at them. McPhee recalled that if you won the game, your life would be in danger.

2. **THE FLORIST**

During the 1920s a mysterious fan in Cincinnati nicknamed "the Florist" rewarded Reds' players whenever

but he is best remembered for his stormy stints as manager of the New York Yankees. He was managing the Detroit Tigers when he posed for his 1982 Topps card. Martin is standing next to the batting cage leaning on a bat. A closer look reveals that he is extending his left middle finger in an obscene gesture.

8. ANDY PAFKO

Outfielder Andy Pafko hit 36 home runs while playing for the Chicago Cubs in 1950. Twice he batted in more than 100 runs. Although Pafko was never a superstar, his 1952 Topps card recently sold at auction for $83,870. The reason is because Pafko's card was number one in the set. Many collectors rubber banded their cards and Pafko's card was often creased because it was on the outside. His cards in mint condition are extremely rare.

9. BOB FELLER

The 1938 Goudey "Heads Up" baseball card set is one of the most unusual. The cards feature photos of the players' oversized heads superimposed on comic drawn bodies. One of the most amusing cards is of Cleveland Indians' ace Bob Feller. Rapid Robert has a snickering expression as he winds up to pitch.

10. CHARLIE KERFELD

Charlie Kerfeld was a relief pitcher for the Houston Astros. He had his best season in 1986 when he posted an 11–2 record. On the back of his 1986 Fleer card his height was listed as 5'11" and his weight reported as 175 pounds. In fact, Kerfeld was 6'6" and 250 pounds.

card unusual is that the photo is not of Rodriguez. The young man on the card is actually a 16-year-old bat boy named Leonard Garcia. Rodriguez had switched places with Garcia as a joke.

3. GARY PETTIS

California Angels' outfielder Gary Pettis also pulled a fast one on Topps. His 1985 card features a photo of his younger brother.

4. HANK AARON

Any baseball card of home run king Hank Aaron is desirable, but his 1957 Topps card is also a curiosity. Topps accidentally reversed the negative. As a result the right-handed hitting Aaron is shown in a left-handed stance.

5. LEW BURDETTE

Right-handed Lew Burdette was a teammate of Hank Aaron's on the Milwaukee Braves from 1954 to 1963. A two-time 20-game winner, Burdette won 203 games during his 18-year major league career. As a prank, Burdette posed for his photo for his 1959 Topps card in a southpaw pose.

6. JAY JOHNSTONE

Outfielder Jay Johnstone played in the major leagues from 1966 to 1985. Johnstone was known as one of baseball's greatest practical jokers. He displayed his sense of humor on his 1984 Fleer card, on which he appeared wearing a Budweiser umbrella hat.

7. BILLY MARTIN

Billy Martin was known for his fiery temper. Martin played second base in the majors from 1950 to 1961,

It's in the Cards

Baseball cards are collected by everyone ranging from small children to professional-sports memorabilia dealers. The value of a card can range from a few cents to thousands of dollars. The most valuable card, the 1909 T-206 card of Pittsburgh shortstop Honus Wagner, sold for $640,500 at a 1996 auction. See if you remember these unusual cards.

1. DICK ELLSWORTH

Left-handed pitcher Dick Ellsworth won 22 games for the Chicago Cubs in 1963. His 1966 Topps card represents one of the most embarrassing mistakes in baseball card history. The photo is actually of Cubs' second baseman Ken Hubbs. What makes the error even more painful is that Hubbs had been killed in an airplane accident two years earlier. In 1966, Ellsworth led the National League with 22 losses.

2. AURELIO RODRIGUEZ

Third baseman Aurelio Rodriguez played 17 seasons in the major leagues. The 1969 Topps baseball card of Rodriguez is a favorite of collectors. What makes the

Years later, Stratton's artificial leg was offered at auction at Christie's. The artificial leg failed to sell.

8. **WALTER JOHNSON**

Walter Johnson was one of baseball's greatest pitchers. On February 22, 1936, Johnson tossed a silver dollar across the Rappahannock River. The liberty head silver dollar later sold for $25,875.

9. **JEFF NELSON**

In 2002, pitcher Jeff Nelson tried to auction his bone chips following elbow surgery. Bids reached $23,600 before eBay pulled the item.

10. **BARRY BONDS**

On October 7, 2001, Barry Bonds hit his 73rd home run. The historic home run ball was thought to be worth more than a million dollars. A fan named Alex Popov claimed to have caught the ball but had it taken away in the ensuing scuffle. A court trial was necessary to determine the rightful owner of the ball.

Comedian Billy Crystal paid $239,000 for a glove worn by Mantle during the 1960 season. A fan paid $6,900 for a lock of Mantle's hair. One of his credit cards sold for $7,175. Thirty-three items were withdrawn from the auction because they were deemed too personal. These included prescription medicine bottles, a bathing suit, a green terrycloth robe, socks, a pair of reading glasses, and a neck brace. Another piece of Mantle memorabilia not for sale was a pair of physicians' gloves used to examine Mantle's hemorrhoids.

5. BABE RUTH

A brass spittoon owned by Babe Ruth was auctioned for $8,625. Ruth's silver whiskey flask sold for $24,150. Two of the Babe's undershirts received a high bid of $1,840. A collector paid $8,625 for Ruth's alligator wallet. In 1934, Ruth paid only $20 to a fan for his 700th home run ball.

6. BILL BUCKNER

Despite an outstanding career, Bill Buckner is best remembered for letting the ball go through his legs, permitting the winning run to score in game six of the 1986 World Series between the New York Mets and the Boston Red Sox. The glove Buckner wore in that game and his high top shoes sold at auction for $51,750.

7. MONTY STRATTON

Monty Stratton won 15 games as a pitcher for the Chicago White Sox in 1938. In November 1938 Stratton shot himself in the right leg in a hunting accident. The bullet pierced the femoral artery, and it was necessary for the leg to be amputated. Stratton died in 1982.

$10,000 was made for the discarded gum. By contrast, a baseball signed by Gonzalez after his Arizona Diamondbacks won the 2001 World Series sold for only $350. The story became even more absurd when the authenticity of the gum was questioned. To end the controversy, Gonzalez agreed to chew another piece of gum.

2. HAGERSTOWN SUNS

The Hagerstown Suns are the Class A minor league affiliate of the San Francisco Giants. Like all professional baseball teams, Hagerstown has giveaways to attract fans. In 2002, the team proposed an Osama bin Laden bobble-head doll promotion. The idea was to give fans the dolls of the suspected terrorist to smash. The idea was scrapped when an Internet poll indicated that 72 percent of the respondents found the promotion distasteful.

3. TY COBB

A 1928 Philadelphia A's jersey worn by Hall of Fame outfielder Ty Cobb sold for $332,500. By contrast, Karen Shemonsky paid $7,475 in 1999 for Cobb's dentures. Shemonsky explained that her father had been a dentist for 55 years, and she had to have Cobb's false choppers.

4. MICKEY MANTLE

Anything associated with former New York Yankees' slugger Mickey Mantle is highly collectible. Mantle joked that he had a dream that after he died he went to heaven, but God denied him entrance because of the life he lived. His parting words for Mantle were, "Before you go, would you sign six dozen baseballs?"

Babe Ruth's Underwear

For baseball memorabilia collectors, almost anything related to their heroes is collectible. A fan paid $50 for dirt from the cleats of Tim Hudson. The Oakland A's pitcher also auctioned whiskers from his trimmed goatee for $75. An 1847 baseball was auctioned for more than $100,000 even though it was falling apart and had spool showing. Owner Bill Veeck's wooden leg sold for $10,000. A fishing rod used by Lou Gehrig was auctioned for $10,500, and an anonymous bidder paid $389,500 for the Iron Horse's first baseman's mitt. The Black Betsy model bat used by Shoeless Joe Jackson, one of the 1919 Chicago Black Sox banned from baseball for throwing the 1919 World Series, sold for $577,610. Mark McGwire's 70th home run ball from his record-breaking 1998 season sold for more than three million dollars.

1. LUIS GONZALEZ

Arizona Diamondbacks' outfielder Luis Gonzalez slugged 57 home runs during the 2001 season. A piece of gum chewed by Gonzalez during the 2002 spring training was put up for auction. Incredibly, a bid of

pitcher gave up 10 hits in three and one-third innings in his debut on August 26, 1947. Bankhead had a 9–5 record during his three year career, with a high 6.52 earned run average.

10. **PAMELA DAVIS**

The first woman to pitch for a minor league baseball team was Pamela Davis. On June 4, 1996, the 21-year-old righthander pitched one inning of scoreless relief for the Double A Jacksonville Suns in a game against the Australian Olympic team.

2 to register his first win. Patterson won 20 games that season.

6. JIMMY SEBRING

Pittsburgh outfielder Jimmy Sebring hit the first home run in World Series history. He homered off Boston's Cy Young in game one of the 1903 World Series. Pittsburgh won the game by the score of 7–3. Sebring hit only six home runs in his career.

7. GEORGE CAHILL

The first night game in major league history took place in Cincinnati's Crosley Field in 1935. However, 26 years earlier, on June 18, 1909, a night baseball game was played between two amateur teams at Cincinnati's Palace of the Fans. The lighting system, which consisted of five portable light towers, was designed by George Cahill. He traveled the country to demonstrate the feasibility of night baseball.

8. JACK GRANEY

Jack Graney's career included a number of baseball firsts. In 1914 the Cleveland outfielder was the first batter to face Boston pitcher Babe Ruth. In 1916, the Cleveland Indians became the first team in the twentieth century to wear numbers on their uniforms. On June 26, 1916, Graney was the first player to step to the plate with a number on his uniform. In 1932, he became the first former major league baseball player to become a broadcaster. Graney was a broadcaster for the Cleveland Indians for 32 years.

9. DAN BANKHEAD

The first African-American pitcher to play in the major leagues was Dan Bankhead. The Brooklyn Dodgers'

2. BOBBY MATHEWS

The pitcher credited (or discredited) with throwing the first spitball was Bobby Mathews. A three-time 30-game winner, Matthews won 166 games during his career from 1876 to 1887. In those days the spitter was legal. What makes the pitch so effective is that it drops suddenly as it reaches the plate. The baseballs were rarely replaced and became blackened during the game. Mathews used his saliva to create a white spot on the ball. The revolving white spot created an optical illusion, which befuddled the batters.

3. ART IRWIN

During the 1885 season, Providence Grays' shortstop Art Irwin broke two of his fingers. To protect his injured fingers, he wore a padded buckskin glove. The primitive glove was baseball's first. The advantages of using a glove to improve fielding was not immediately apparent, and it would be more than a decade before all players wore gloves.

4. ERVE BECK

On April 24, 1901, Cleveland second baseman Erve Beck doubled in a game against Chicago. It was the first extra base hit in American League history. The next day, Beck hit the first home run in league history. The blow came off Chicago's John Skopec. Beck hit only nine home runs in his major league career.

5. ROY PATTERSON

Roy "Boy Wonder" Patterson was the first pitcher to win a game in the American League. On April 24, 1901, the Chicago White Sox rookie defeated Cleveland 8 to

The First Inning

What came first, the San Diego chicken or the goose egg? The first batter to strike out more than 100 times in a season was Boston shortstop Sam Wise, who fanned 104 times in 114 games in 1884. Babe Ruth was not the first New York Yankee to lead the American League in home runs. That distinction belonged to first baseman Wally Pipp, who hit a league-leading 12 home runs in 1916. Here are 10 more notable baseball firsts.

1. ROSS BARNES

The first major league home run was hit by Chicago second baseman Ross Barnes on May 2, 1876. The historic blast came off Cincinnati pitcher Cherokee Fisher. Barnes, the National League's first superstar, led the National League in hits, doubles, triples, runs, walks, and slugging percentage. He was also major league baseball's first .400 hitter, with a .429 batting average. Ironically, Barnes hit only that one home run during the 1876 season and only two more in his major league career.

There are players who never see the error of their ways. It was said of second baseman Jorge Orta that "he never met a ground ball he liked." Pete Browning was nicknamed The Gladiator because he battled every fly ball. King Kelly was such a poor fielder that he had the lowest fielding percentage at two positions, catcher and outfielder. Reggie Jackson admitted that the only way he would have a gold glove was to spray paint it.

Baseball players occasionally suffer freak injuries. Iron man Cal Ripken broke his nose when he was accidentally headbutted by Roberto Hernandez while posing for a team photo at the All Star Game. Cy Young winner Randy Johnson sprained his thumb pulling up his socks. Chicago Cubs' outfielder Jose Cardenal once missed opening day because his eyelid stuck shut. Pitcher Greg Harris injured his elbow flicking sunflower seeds. New York Yankees' designated hitter Ron Kittle pulled a muscle in his neck carrying a stretcher for an injured teammate.

This book introduces you to nearly 700 more of baseball's most wanted players whose offenses range from inept play to outrageous behavior. Be on the lookout for them.

so loud that she earned the nickname "the All American Ear-ache." Brooklyn Dodgers' superfan Howling Hilda Chester was known as the Queen of the Bleachers. By contrast, Abe Rettan attended Brooklyn games just to boo the Dodgers.

Collecting baseball memorabilia has reached the level of absurdity. Someone paid $10,000 for a piece of bubble gum chewed by Arizona Diamondbacks' slugger Luis Gonzalez. A spittoon used by Babe Ruth sold for $8,625. Ty Cobb's dentures brought $7,475 at an auction. Owner Bill Veeck's wooden leg was auctioned for $10,000. A lock of Mickey Mantle's hair went for $6,900. There was a bid of $23,600 on eBay for bone chips removed from the pitching elbow of Jeff Nelson.

Many baseball players have had eccentricities. Cleveland Indians' pitcher Duster Mails gave an autographed photo of himself to any female fan who would bake him a chocolate cake. Amos "the Darling" Booth believed that he would get a hit for every hairpin he found at the ballpark. Pitcher Tom Parrott insisted on bringing his valet with him to the clubhouse. Minnesota's Doug Mientkiewicz prevents batting slumps by shaving his body hair.

Some players go batty for their bats. During a slump, Jim Fregosi gave his bat a cortisone shot to make it well. Ozzie Guillen tried solving his batting problems by putting eyedrops on his bat. Turkey Stearnes had different bats for how hard he wanted to hit the ball. Seattle pitcher Bill Caudill started a bonfire of his teammates' bats because they weren't hitting. Detroit third baseman Tom Brookens said he put scuff marks on his bats to make it appear as though he made contact more often.

Introduction

Like *Baseball's Most Wanted I, Baseball's Most Wanted II* honors more of the game's most outrageous offenders. The book contains top ten lists of the worst hitters, losingest pitchers, slowest runners, and poorest fielders ever to play the game. The lists feature the biggest flakes, most colorful managers, rabid fans, bizarre memorabilia, worst teams, and the strangest things ever to occur on the diamond.

Presidents of the United States have had ties to the national pastime. In 1910, William Howard Taft started the tradition of presidents throwing out the first pitch on Opening Day. Dwight Eisenhower batted .355 while playing in the minor leagues. Before he was an actor or politician, Ronald Reagan was an announcer on the Chicago Cubs radio network. After his presidency, Richard Nixon served as arbiter in a salary dispute between umpires and management. President George W. Bush was an owner of the Texas Rangers.

Baseball has had its share of memorable fans. A mysterious Cincinnati fan known as "the Florist" delivered a bouquet of roses to the dugout whenever one of the Reds hit a home run. Detroit fan Patsy O'Toole was

Photographs

William Howard Taft	19
Early Wynn	43
Vince, Joe, and Dom DiMaggio	48
Don Larsen	86
Gil Hodges	103
Ted Williams	131
Nolan Ryan	138
Babe Ruth and Lou Gehrig	149
Casey Stengel	181
Leo Durocher	204
George Brett	222
Babe Ruth	237

What If?	**236**
What might have been	
The Ninth Inning	**243**
Notable baseball lasts	
Bibliography	**247**
Index	**249**
About the Author	**256**

Contents

Baseball's Worst Teams — 178
Spiders and Mets

Worst World Series Performances — 184
Goats and disappointments

They Never Won the World Series — 187
Players who were never world champions

Seasons They'd Rather Forget — 190
Superstars with subpar seasons

Mismanaged — 193
Great players who were bad managers

Skilled Skippers — 197
Bad players who were great managers

Colorful Managers — 201
The Lip and the Gerbil

Oddballs — 206
Flakes, Clowns, and Showboats

Baseballese — 210
Baseball speak

Holy Cow! — 215
The best of Harry Caray

Temper Tantrums — 219
When players and managers lose their cool

The Disabled List — 224
Unusual injuries

Believe It or Not — 227
Strange baseball happenings

Odd Ballparks — 231
Not your average playing fields

The Greatest Hitters Who Ever Lived From Ty Cobb to Pete Rose	129
Monster Seasons The greatest offensive seasons	133
The Greatest Pitchers of All Time Big Six and the Big Train	136
Sensational Seasons The greatest seasons by pitchers	140
Terrific Teams Baseball's best teams	143
They Weren't World Champions Great teams that didn't win the World Series	147
Trading Places Stars traded for bench warmers	152
Major Disappointments Bonus busts	156
One-Year Wonders Short seasons in the sun	159
Power Outage They rarely went deep	162
Defenseless Lead glove winners	165
Slow Runners They can hide, but they can't run	169
They Didn't Hit Their Weight Hitters below the Mendoza line	172
"Sigh" Young Awards The worst pitching seasons on record	175

Contents

Double Threats They could pitch and hit	79
Nobody's Perfect Unlikely no-hitters	83
Arm Problems Promising pitching careers shortened by injury	88
Sophomore Jinx Second-year flops	92
You're Only As Good As Your Last Season Big production drop offs	95
Forgotten Stars Overlooked nineteenth-century greats	98
On the Outside Looking In Worthy Hall of Fame candidates	102
Cooperstown Question Marks Questionable Hall of Famers	106
What Were They Thinking? The worst players to receive Hall of Fame votes	110
Least Appreciated Players Superstars who never won MVP Awards	113
They Never Won a Batting Title Great hitters who never won a batting crown	116
Shadow Players Stars overshadowed by others	119
Going Batty Players who carried a big stick	122
Supreme Sluggers Long ball hitters	126

Why Me? 33
Baseball's most unflattering nicknames

No-Chance Names 36
Players with unfortunate names

A Ballplayer Named Sadie 39
Players with feminine names

Born to Be Baseball Players 42
Perfect baseball names

Family Affairs 46
They did not live up to the family name

Blackballed 50
African American stars who never played in the majors

The International Pastime 54
Foreign-born ballplayers

Cheers 57
Drinking men

Food for Thought 61
What baseball players eat

The Numbers Game 65
The stories behind the numbers

Clothes Encounters 68
They were what they wore

Dirty Players 72
Their uniforms never stayed clean

Cups of Coffee 75
Careers that were short but sweet

Contents

List of Photographs	xi
Introduction	xiii
The First Inning	1
Notable baseball firsts	
Babe Ruth's Underwear	5
Unusual baseball collectibles	
It's in the Cards	9
One-of-a-kind baseball cards	
Baseball Fanatics	12
Howling Hilda and Megaphone Lolly	
Presidents and Baseball	16
Baseball's number one fans	
Keeping the Day Job	22
Players with odd jobs	
Contract Players	26
Underpaid players	
They're Animals	30
A baseball menagerie	

Copyright © 2003 by Brassey's, Inc.

Published in the United States by Brassey's, Inc. All rights reserved. No part of this book may be reproduced in any manner whatsoever without written permission from the publisher, except in the case of brief quotations embodied in critical articles and reviews.

Library of Congress Cataloging-in-Publication Data

Connery, Floyd, 1951–
  Baseball's most wanted II : the top 10 book of more bad hops, screwball players, and other oddities / Floyd Conner.
    p. cm.
  Includes bibliographical references and index.
  ISBN 1-57488-362-3 (pbk.)
  1. Baseball players—Biography. 2. Baseball players—Miscellanea. I. Title.
GV865.A1C64 2003
796.357'092'273—dc21
                                           2002156002

Printed in the United States of America on acid-free paper that meets the American National Standards Institute Z39-48 Standard.

Brassey's, Inc.
22841 Quicksilver Drive
Dulles, Virginia 20166

First Edition

10 9 8 7 6 5 4 3 2 1

Baseball's Most Wanted II

The Top 10 Book of
More Bad Hops, Screwball
Players, and Other Oddities

Floyd Conner

Brassey's, Inc.
WASHINGTON, D.C.

Also by Floyd Conner

Hockey's Most Wanted: The Top 10 Book of Wicked Slapshots, Bruising Goons, and Ice Oddities

Hollywood's Most Wanted: The Top 10 Book of Lucky Breaks, Prima Donnas, Box Office Bombs, and Other Oddities

Tennis's Most Wanted: The Top 10 Book of Baseline Blunders, Clay Court Wonders, and Lucky Lobs

The Olympics' Most Wanted: The Top 10 Book of Gold Medal Gaffes, Improbable Triumphs, and Other Oddities

Basketball's Most Wanted: The Top 10 Book of Hoops' Outrageous Dunkers, Incredible Buzzer-Beaters, and Other Oddities

Golf's Most Wanted: The Top 10 Book of Outrageous Duffers, Deadly Divots, and Other Oddities

Wrestling's Most Wanted: The Top 10 Book of Pro Wrestling's Outrageous Performers, Punishing Piledrivers, and Other Oddities

Football's Most Wanted: The Top 10 Book of the Great Game's Outrageous Characters, Fortunate Fumbles, and Other Oddities

Baseball's Most Wanted: The Top 10 Book of the National Pastime's Outrageous Offenders, Lucky Bounces, and Other Oddities

Baseball's Most Wanted II